The Prehistory of Germanic Europe

THE PREHISTORY
OF GERMANIC EUROPE

Herbert Schutz

Yale University Press
New Haven and London
1983

Designed by Caroline Williamson and set in Monophoto Baskerville.
Printed in Great Britain by Butler & Tanner Ltd, Frome and
London.

Library of Congress Cataloging in Publication Data

Schutz, Herbert, 1937–
    The prehistory of Germanic Europe.
    Bibliography: p.
    Includes index.
    1. Man, Prehistoric—Central Europe.   2. Central
        Europe—Antiquities.
    3. Germanic antiquities.
I. Title.
GN803.S33   1983   936.3   83-40000
ISBN 0-300-02863-6

Contents

Foreword

This book attempts to present a systematic survey of central European cultural history from earliest times to the beginning of the historic period. For our purposes the term 'central Europe' includes Bohemia and Denmark though the emphasis is placed on German-speaking central Europe and its fringes.

It is the intention of this book to make accessible to students, scholars and other interested readers wherever English is read, a summary of the insights gained concerning this area during the past twenty years. At the moment the reader of English is not well served when it comes to research results pertaining to central Europe since these have been published mainly in German. Of course no claim to completeness can be made, as new and even spectacular finds continue to turn up. Nevertheless the basic pattern appears to have been established.

A review of the archeological evidence, especially when coupled with the new dating technique, shows that very early dynamic societies came into being in this area, capable of significant cultural achievement. That same evidence indicates that cultural change was only seldom caused by foreign, 'eastern' invaders and was more often the result of development within a cultural continuum brought about by inner migration and colonization. Already in earliest times central Europe maintained farflung connections, was open to outside stimuli, converted foreign influences with great skill and placed its characteristic stamp on imported objects, practices and ideas.

The extensive record of central European man's activities collected in the museums allows conclusions about the manner in which man guaranteed his survival and made his vessels and utensils, while the remnants of villages and fortified sites point to his social organization and the quality of his life. Occasionally spectacular, the finds yield valuable information about daily life, about primary and secondary industries, about their control and the manufacture and distribution of artefacts. Regardless of their medium, these early Europeans display a rich imagination. It found expression in the variety of forms, but especially in the wealth of ornamental motifs.

In treating these early efforts in European civilization the attempt is made to point to that interplay between continuity and change, without emphasis on ethnic identity. Only in the late phases is it possible to identify peoples as being Celtic or Germanic. Seldom homogeneous in the composition of its population, prehistoric central Europe was a pulsating multicultural unit.

To prepare this book it was necessary to visit the many museums and to prepare a photographic record of the pertinent objects in their care. This was only possible because I could count on the hospitality of my European relatives, to whom I express my thanks. Very special thanks are due to Mr. G. Kahlert, of Korneuburg, Austria, for preparing the computerized picture index which facilitated my work. I would like to take this opportunity to thank my university for its support and encouragement and to thank Mrs. Joyce Lucey for typing most of the manuscript. I am indebted to my colleague Prof. Claude R. Owen for taking the time to read the manuscript in its early stages and for his many constructive criticisms. I am especially indebted to Prof. F. R. Skilton of the Computer Center at Brock University, for guiding me through the preparation of the subject index. I would also like to express my appreciation to the Österreichische Nationalbibliothek in Vienna for granting me special privileges while doing most of my research there.

A book such as this could not come to completion without the interest and support of the museums. I would like to thank the directors and curators of the many museums and institutes which supplied the photographs or which granted me permission to photograph. For volunteering their help in locating objects and photographs, for offering helpful comments and corrections and for drawing my attention to and providing me with relevant publications I owe very special thanks to Dr. K. D. Adam, Staatliches Museum für Naturkunde Stuttgart; Dr. O. Höckmann, Römisch-Germanisches Zentralmuseum Mainz; Prof. em. W. Kimmig, Institut für Vor-und Frühgeschichte der Universität Tübingen; Herrn G. Dangel-Reese, Museum für Ur- und Frühgeschichte der Stadt Freiburg; Dr. H. Melichar, Naturhistorisches Museum Wien; as well as to Dr. R. Dehn, Landesdenkmalamt Baden-Württemberg, Außenstelle Freiburg; Frau Gisela Fischer, Institut für Ur-und Frühgeschichte der Universität Köln; Dr. D. Kaufmann, Landesmuseum für Vorgeschichte Halle/Saale; Herrn D. Kramer, Landesmuseum Joanneum Graz; Dr. F. Laux, Helms-Museum Hamburg-Harburg; Dr. H. Schirnig, Niedersächsiches Landesmuseum Hannover; and Dr. H. P. Uenze, Prähistorische Staatssammlung München.

I gratefully acknowledge the interest which Mr. John Nicoll, Editor, has shown in this project from the start. I should also like to thank Caroline Williamson for the understanding and meticulous attention to detail with which she has prepared this book for publication.

A statement of thanks, however formulated, is quite inadequate when expressing my appreciation to the members of my immediate family. For many years they have had to muster extraordinary patience, understanding and support, while putting up with considerable personal sacrifice in terms of time, consideration and funds. With my most sincere gratitude I dedicate this book to Alice, Andrea and Christopher.

Brock University,
St. Catharines, Ontario,
Canada
1983

1. The Paleolithic: Of Ice, Men, Stones and Things

During the last 2,000,000 years, great ice fields spread over large parts of the world on several occasions. This geological period, which ended about 8000 B.C., is called the Pleistocene period. The spread of the Pleistocene continental ice sheets must have been the consequence of a fundamental change in climatic conditions which in turn brought about extremely long and cold periods of weather—the Ice Ages. In Europe the ice spread from three centers: Scandinavia, the British Isles and the Alps. From the other mountain ranges smaller glaciers pushed into the valleys and adjoining lowlands. The ice from Scandinavia and Britain sometimes formed a continuous sheet across the depression now occupied by the North Sea. While the ice which covered Britain was largely confined to the British Isles—the south of England remaining ice-free—the Scandinavian ice pushed through the Baltic basin and continued for more than 2000 km into central and eastern Europe. At the center the ice reached thicknesses of approximately 3000 m.[1] Evidence from the vicinity of the North Sea points to six Pleistocene glaciations. It is now agreed that it was a decrease in temperature and not an increase in precipitation which brought about these glacial periods. The advance of the glaciers is attributed to the advent of a cold and damp climate: a cold and dry climate then developed over the expanse of the ice sheets.[2] While the Scandinavian and British ice fields pushed generally south, covering a total of some 6,000,000 km², the Alpine glaciers advanced northward, covering some 38,000 km².[3] Periodically, temperatures would rise to temperate or even near-tropical conditions, causing the ice to retreat. Evidence of these interglacial periods of warm weather is provided by finds of certain flora and fauna. Thus the area around Weimar enjoyed a mean temperature during the warmest month which must have reached at least 19°C with low summer rainfall.[4] Further south it was probably warmer still. Animals such as hippopotami, normally associated with the tropics, roamed southern England.

Although generally contemporary, the exact synchronization of glacial and interglacial periods as evident in the Alps and in northern Europe cannot readily be correlated, so that Alpine and northern glacial periods are identified with local names.[5] Thus in the south the ice ages have been named chronologically after the head waters of alpine glacial rivers, the last four being called the Günz, the Mindel, the Riss and the Würm periods. Evidence of an earlier period, the Danube glaciation, is only meager, while the Günz period is also only indicated in the Alps. Fragmentary evidence, however, points to considerable climatic changes in the early Pleistocene. Approximate dates cannot even be suggested. In the north the ice ages are named chronologically after the rivers

	Geological Division	Climatological Division	Lithic Cultures		Fossil Finds	Central European Cultural Features	
						Settlement	Tools
35,000 B.C.							
			Middle Paleolithic	Mousterian	Neanderthal Man	occupation of north central Europe	
	Upper Pleistocene	Würm Glaciation			200,000 B.C.– 35,000 B.C.	Rheindahlen open air station *c.* 200,000 B.C.	
100,000 B.C.					*homo sapiens*		
		Riss-Würm Interglacial *c.* 180,000 B.C.				Balve, cave occupation	
180,000 B.C.				Levalloisian			
200,000 B.C.		Riss Glaciation			Steinheim Man	open air stations	
240,000 B.C.				Clactonian	Bilzingsleben Man	extensive occupation	
300,000 B.C.							flake tools
				Acheulean	350,000 B.C.		
350,000 B.C.		Mindel-Riss Interglacial *c.* 430,000 B.C.				some evidence of occupation around Hamburg and in Hungary	fist axes
400,000 B.C.	Middle Pleistocene				Heidelberg Man		
					Vertesszöllös Man		acquaintance with fire
500,000 B.C.					400,000 B.C.– 300,000 B.C.		
600,000 B.C.		Mindel Glaciation	Lower Paleolithic				crude core tools
				Abbevillean	*Homo erectus*	largely uninhabitable	
700,000 B.C.							
							pebble tools
800,000 B.C.	Lower Pleistocene	Günz-Mindel Interglacial					
900,000 B.C.							
						uninhabitable	
1,000,000 B.C.							
		Günz Glaciation					
2,000,000 B.C.							

Chart 1. The Paleolithic in Central Europe, Lower-Middle Paleolithic, before 35,000 B.C.

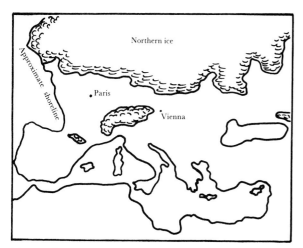

Map 1. Greatest expansion of the northern ice during the Pleistocene.

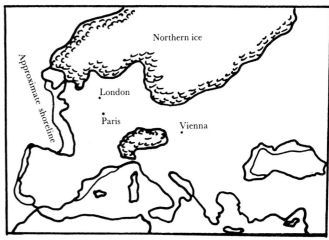

Map 2. Extent of the northern ice during the Würm glacial period (Aurignacian).

to which the ice advanced, the last four being the Weybourne (in England), the Elster, the Saale and the Vistula.[6] For purposes of simplification the Alpine terminology will be used. During the Mindel period the ice pushed from Scandinavia into central Europe and England and although it is not known when it reached either area, it appears to have ended approximately 220,000 years ago. The Riss period reached a line between Dortmund and Dresden and lasted some 60,000 years from approximately 240,000 to 180,000 B.C. The Würm period extended south as far as Schleswig-Holstein, Mecklenburg, and Pomerania and lasted approximately from 90,000 B.C. to 10,000 B.C.,[7] reaching a peak between 20,000 and 16,000 B.C.[8] The end of the Würm glaciation marks the end of the Pleistocene.

At no time, even when glaciation was most extensive, did the glaciers advancing from the north and the south join to form a solid cover of snow and ice over Europe. Corridors remained clear of ice throughout, but were no doubt also subject to prolonged cold spells. One such corridor crossed through central Germany linking parts of Spain, France, southern England and Ireland with the valley of the Danube, the Balkans and southern Russia.

The Ice Age climate of central Europe was that of northern Siberia with temperatures not rising significantly above 0°C. Thus, for instance, in Germany mean temperatures for July hovered around 5°C, for January around −22°C.[9] The Riss Ice Age had an annual mean temperature of approximately 8°C, while during the Würm period the drop in temperature in the northern hemisphere was 8°–13°C, and perhaps as much as 15°–16°C.[10] Even at the end of the Würm—10,000–9000 B.C.—July temperatures in central Europe were 4°C lower than they are now.

During the Riss period, for example, the thickness of the ice in Scandinavia reached some 2000 m,[11] creating a crushing downward pressure, forcing the ice to expand laterally, thereby pushing vast amounts of gravel and stone debris in front of it, filling up valleys, and levelling off hills. In all, Scandinavia lost 500 to 600 m off the top of its mountains, the debris being deposited in Germany to the amount of approximately 500,000 to 700,000 km³, the deposits of debris averaging between 50 and 80 m with maximum depths of 500 m, thereby creating the North German Plain.[12] The ice advanced at approximately 50 to 100 m per year so that the advance from Scandinavia into Germany took 10,000 years or more. During the Riss period all mountain ranges in Germany formed local centers from which the ice spread into the lowlands. In general

3

the ice advanced from two directions: from the north it reached a line stretching from Dortmund, to Leipzig and Dresden and beyond, while in the south it extended over the Black Forest into the plain around Munich and eastward to the Vienna Woods.[13] In the center, the ice was between 1 and 3 km deep, spread over an area of approximately 6,000,000 km².[14] To produce the many million cubic kilometers of ice the oceans had to give up their water which led to a lowering of the sea level by about 90 m during the last glaciation and an increase in the land mass. For instance, almost the entire North Sea was dry during the Würm period.

The interglacial periods, on the other hand, released vast amounts of water bringing about a rise in the sea level. Studies of shore line shelves indicate that the oceans rose above the mean sea level by 90-100 m during the Danube-Günz, 55-60 m during the Günz-Mindel, 28-32 m in the Mindel-Riss, and 18-20 m during the Riss-Würm interglacial periods.[15] This information by itself would indicate that the Würm glaciation was not the most severe, yet an ice shield covered Scandinavia and northern Germany while glaciers again pushed down from the Black Forest and the Vosges Mountains into the lowlands.[16] Even the ground of the ice-free parts of central Europe was permanently frozen. For northern and eastern France and the ice-free corridors of western and southern Germany, the presence of perma-frost required mean annual temperatures below $-2°C$, i.e. July temperatures were about 8°C cooler and January temperatures about 12°C cooler than they are today,[17] while for the west of France, enjoying more moderate climatic conditions because of its proximity to the ocean, temperatures decreased to 7°C in summer and 0°C to $-3°C$ in winter.[18] These climatic conditions are of importance when considering man and the preservation of his killed game.

That the last Ice Age was not brought about by large amounts of precipitation is indicated by the fact that there was only a very small drop in the snowline in the mountains.[19] Under the climatic conditions of today a drop in temperature of only 0·5°C would result in the lowering of the snow-line by 100 m, and a drop of 10°C should have produced a depression of the snow-line by 2000 m, which did not take place. The Würm Ice Age was shorter and weaker and came to a halt when the Scandinavian ice came somewhat south of a line from Flensburg via Kiel, Hamburg, Berlin and Kaliningrad approximately 20,000 years ago. The Elbe River was ice-free at the time.[20] Yet the climate was still very inhospitable, with its Arctic winters and summers that were only three months long.[21] The ice in its advance levelled everything, creating end moraines where the ice came to a halt before it retreated again. Thus Schleswig-Holstein received its present appearance during the Würm glacial period which deposited there a layer of gravel, sand and clay up to 500 m high.[22] The ice-free corridors[23] were conducive to the production of wind-tunnel effects, while the poor vegetation cover allowed the winds to blow away the top soil. It accumulated in dunes of dust of a yellow-brownish colour which in some areas reached a thickness of up to 9 m. This type of soil is called loess. Two separate levels are extant, the lower and older level having been deposited during the Riss glaciation, the upper and more recent level during the Würm. Soil analysis indicates that the separating layers were produced by forests during the interglacial periods. Later, these loess areas were to become favorite regions of settlement. It is a characteristic of loess that it is very low in calcium and therefore offers no possibilities for the preservation of organic substances containing calcium such as bones or antlers.[24] The area around Cologne was not under the ice like the rest of northern Germany. But it too was a cold, unfriendly and inhospitable region—treeless, like Arctic tundra, and not conducive to prolonged settlement. In the lowlands the prehistoric Rhine produced an array of swamps, dead arms and oxbows. During the interglacial periods the melting alpine glaciers turned the Rhine into a raging torrent which either swept everything away or buried it under thick layers of sand or gravel, while the winds swept together dunes of sand and dust.[25]

Gradually forest trees moved into the tundra-like landscapes, replacing the plants which favor the cold such as the glacier willow and the dryas (whence the term Dryasic period). First appeared the birch tree, then the pine. Following a return of the cold accompanied by a regression of the forests and a renewed dominance of polar tundra vegetation, the final forestation set in. In addition to birch and pine, other types of tree favouring warmer climates appeared, such as the hazel and the elm. The end of the last glacial period, the Würm, was also marked by a change of fauna—the disappearance of animals which preferred low temperatures such as the mammoth and the wolly rhino, which died out, the reindeer, musk-ox and polar fox, which followed the ice as it retreated north, and the ibex, chamoix and marmot which withdrew to higher ground. This change was also reflected among the small mammals and conchiferous animals. In some instances the glaciation could isolate certain areas as the living space of certain strains of animal, thereby promoting the development of certain types of species.[26] In other words, climatic changes contributed to changes in living conditions and affected the process of natural selection. Man, who had at most only a very small part in it, can not be blamed for this change.

Man-like creatures first appear some two, three or more million years ago, as indicated by finds in the Olduvai Gorge in Tanzania.[27] In larger concentrations they appear only some 500,000 years ago dispersed from England to China and south-east Asia and from Germany to South Africa. It must be assumed that during the Middle Pleistocene diverse forms of early man must have existed more or less side by side—the earlier *anthropus* types as well as those closer to the later *sapiens* types.[28] These first men differ so significantly in their bone structure, especially in the shape of their skulls, from any living race today that they are referred to as hominids rather than as *Homo sapiens*. Although there is evidence of many types, anthropologists group these hominids into three categories using bone structure as the organizing criteria: first, the Arch-*anthropinae* or *Homo erectus*, second, the Paleo-*anthropinae* or *Homo sapiens* and third, the Neo-*anthropinae* or *Homo sapiens sapiens*.

By about 500,000 years ago the hominids had achieved the modern level of bodily development. The evidence from the caves at Choukoutien near Peking shows that while the face, teeth and brain were still moderately primitive, taken as a whole the skeleton of Peking Man is almost indistinguishable from that of *Homo sapiens* of today. His biological adaptations had been completed. From now on man's further development was concentrated on the head; gradually the size of the brain, his cranial capacity, increased.[29]

It would appear that the first signs of a human occupancy of Germany coincides with an inter-glacial period, probably the Mindel-Riss period, some 350,000 to 400,000 years ago. Evidence is the jaw of Heidelberg Man (Fig. 1), found in 1907 at a depth of 24 m in a sandpit at Mauer, near Heidelberg.[30] Although the jaw of Heidelberg Man allows no conjectures about his intelligence such as could be derived from determining his cranial capacity—intelligence being a function of brain size—the great number of skeletal remains of his African and Asian contemporaries indicate an average cranial capacity of over 1000 cc. Heidelberg Man may have possessed a similar brain capacity. What is known is that the jaw is very massive, chinless and ape-like. Ape-like facial

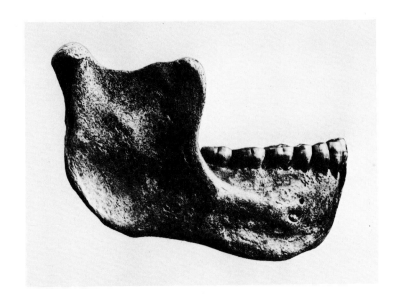

1. Jaw of Heidelberg Man from Mauer, perhaps as early as 500,000 B.C.

features may perhaps also be assumed—that is to say, heavy brows and the receding forehead. Yet his teeth are more similar in size and character to those of *Homo sapiens* than to other specimens of *Homo erectus*. But in the absence of other supporting evidence it has not been possible to determine whether he is some form of European *Homo erectus* or whether he and his kind had evolved to *Homo sapiens* during the Mindel glaciation or during the Günz–Mindel interglacial period. Flora and fauna found in association with the Heidelberg jaw point to these two periods.[31] Crude tools of quartzite and sandstone have also been dated to the Günz–Mindel interglacial period. However, no conclusive evidence supports the existence of a 'Heidelberg Culture' or an 'Altona Industry', although stone tools found at Altona, today a part of Hamburg, can also be placed in the Günz–Mindel and certainly point to the possibility of early man's at least temporary presence in northern Germany during that interglacial period.[32] Other sites in northern Europe may have been covered over by later advances of the ice. In spite of the assault-like research into European prehistory, no other evidence of Heidelberg Man has been found.

In April 1974 at Bilzingsleben, near Halle, a piece of human occipital bone as well as a piece of forehead were found, causing a stir in archeological circles, since the examination of other finds on the same site allowed the skull fragments to be dated as being up to 350,000 years old, i.e. from the Mid-Pleistocene.[33] The piece of forehead bone revealed that the man of Bilzingsleben had heavy brow-ridges and a receding forehead. This made him not unlike his cousin and 'near' contemporary, the woman from Steinheim an der Murr (found 1933) some 30 km north of Stuttgart. Dating of these few skull fragments has to be done with great caution. There is evidence of widely scattered settlement in central Europe during the very long and warm Mindel–Riss interglacial period which lasted from about 430,000 B.C. to about 240,000 B.C.: for instance, the unique find at Vértesszöllös in northern Hungary, datable at approximately 400,000–300,000 B.C.,[34] where fragments of occipital bone suggest hominid affinities with the later Steinheim skull while teeth are similar to Asiatic forms of *Homo erectus*. No sites were found in our area which were as spectacular as the remains of a settlement consisting of twenty-one locations of 17 m long gabled houses found at Nice in 1965.[35] Indications point to several groups of early *Homo sapiens* roaming over central Europe,

6

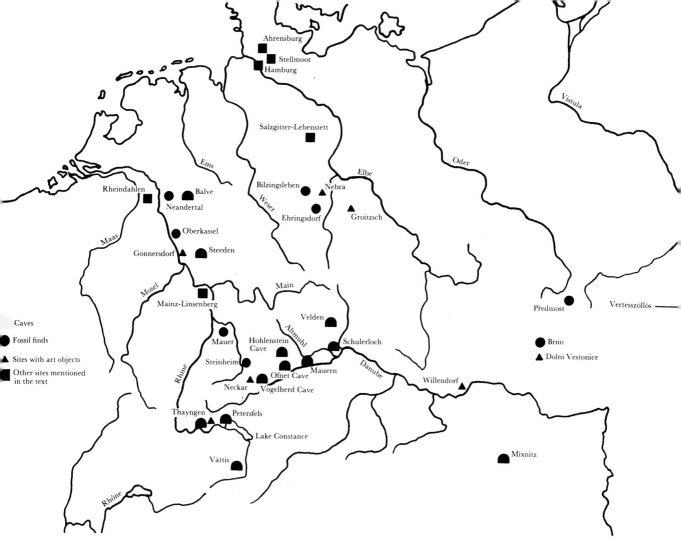

Map 3. Paleolithic sites in central Europe before 8000 B.C.

where the high temperatures and lush vegetation attracted great herds of animals which, in turn, attracted hunters to the rich hunting-grounds. The site at Bilzingsleben proved to be very productive in debris—one cubic meter yielded an average of 500 stone tools and up to 20 kg of bones. From these deposits it is evident that the man of Bilzingsleben hunted big game—mammoth, woolly rhino, bison, elk, wild horses, wild pigs as well as the cave bear, which at an upright height of 2·5 m and a weight of approximately 1250 kg was a most formidable foe.[36] It is probable that early man got the better of his prey by driving it into bogs and swamps to deprive it of its physical advantages. No doubt he bludgeoned it to death with boulders and then cut it up with sharpened stones. Since implements of wood have not survived it is not known whether he was equipped with fire-hardened and fire-sharpened spears in bringing down his kill. Definite evidence of fire-hardened spear points is not available till about 100,000 B.C.,[37] although the absence of evidence cannot be taken as proof.

When the skull fragments of Steinheim Man were found in 1933, datable to about 350,000 B.C. (Fig. 2), the Mindel–Riss interglacial period, they caused a stir in anthropological circles, for these skull fragments point to a shape of the head, the cranial vault that is, which could be called modern and therefore no longer representative of *Homo erectus*. A cranial capacity of 1150 cc places it at the lower end of the range for modern man. However, the Steinheim skull also has a face, and it is not modern. Although it

7

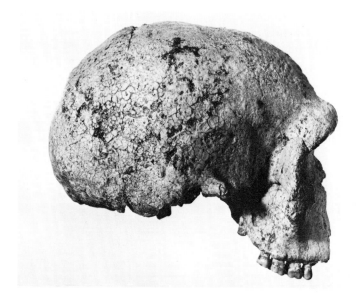

2. Steinheim skull,
c. 400,000–240,000 B.C.
from Steinheim an der
Murr.

has heavy brow ridges, the forehead shows moderate vaulting and the teeth are human, which suggests that the Steinheim skull did not belong to *Homo erectus*, but rather represents a transition toward *Homo sapiens* of the Neanderthal type.[38] Other variants of Steinheim Man are the skull of the woman from Swanscombe (1325 cc)[39] as well as the two skulls from Fontéchevade (1460–1470 cc) in south-eastern France.[40] The fragment of forehead belonging to the Bilzingsleben skull offers further support to the view that some 300,000 years ago an early type of Neanderthal Man appeared on the scene.

The Riss Ice Age (c. 240,000–180,000 B.C.) saw settlement during two interstadial periods when warmer short-term periods of 10,000 years or more favoured occupation of central Europe for relatively short periods. Finds from Lower Saxony also point to settlements in northern central Europe during the Riss–Würm interglacial period.[41] Until about 30,000 B.C. the face with the heavy brow ridges, yet with a noticeably vaulted forehead, will be one characteristic of the Middle Paleolithic, while a wider range of more sophisticated stone tools will be the other.

The beginning of human civilization has been described as being that point in time when a thinking being first produced a labor-facilitating device.[42] With the very earliest tools neither material, shape, function nor the method of manufacturing them was predetermined.[43] Paleolithic Man's universal tool was the hand-chopper—a coarse stone of either flint or quartzite intended for indiscriminate use.[44] The earliest such choppers belonged to the Olduvan industry, named after the Olduvai Gorge in Tanzania. These choppers were fashioned from roundish stones from which several chips had been knocked off one end, while the other remained round so as not to hurt the user's palm. This industry lasted one or two million years. In Europe this industry of the Lower Paleolithic is represented by the find at Vertesszöllös in Hungary.[45] At about the same time a new technique of stone tool manufacture was appearing in the debris at former settlement sites. The stones were still clumsy, but assumed a roughly pear-shaped form about 25 cm long and probably were intended to be used while clenched in the fist. The various techniques used to prepare the stone to be a functional tool make it possible to differentiate the many cultures of the Paleolithic. In the course of tool development two techniques of stone preparation become important: the preparation of core tools, whereby small fragments were chipped off the stone to produce first a cutting edge and only later a wedge or pear-shaped stone with two symmetrical, evenly worked cutting edges; the other and much later technique saw the stone treated in such a way that when struck at a certain spot a blade-like strip would flake off. Through additional chipping little stone scallops could be produced on these flaked blades which could then be used for a variety of increasingly specialized functions.[46]

The museums are crammed with varieties of stone tool types, but if each Paleolithic Man used only five such stones per day, then over a period of 300,000 years the total number of these early stone tools would be vast indeed. Until about 75,000 B.C. the prepared core stone is early man's multi-purpose tool for chopping, cleaning furs, cutting, drilling, rounding and scraping. The limitations of these tools lay in that their effectiveness depended very much on the skill and strength with which they were used, either as tools or as weapons. The earliest of these are identified as belonging to the Abbevillean industry,[47] the characteristics of which are fist axes, with heavy butts and rounded, pointed tips. The later types belong to the Acheulean category,[48] characterized by being smaller, or almond-shaped, trimmed to a thin edge all around the perimeter. Both types are the result of a technique which chipped flakes off each side of the flint nodule. The transition from Abbevillean to Acheulean covers a period of some 500,000 years,[49] an unbelievably slow rate of technical growth.

It was perhaps Steinheim Man who brought with him the Acheulean hand axe industry, that is, the knowledge of hand axe and flake-tool techniques, as he followed the retreating ice during the Mindel-Riss interglacial period. That this may indeed be the first phase of the hand axe culture is supported by the find of an early Acheulean hand axe in association with the Steinheim skull.[50] The suggestion has been made that central Germany and north-western Europe was on the extreme northern limit reached by early man during Middle Pleistocene times.[51]

The basis for the search into the cultural development of prehistoric man is provided by archeological finds of all those things created and used by Paleolithic Man. In view of the perishable character of organic materials it is only natural that stone and quartz artefacts should be dominant in quantity. In central Europe most of the early Paleolithic artefacts found east of the Rhine came from single finds, lost or discarded by their users.[52] The evidence concerning the life style of Middle Pleistocene Man is meager: it is assumed that he led a nomadic clan life gathering his food—roots, berries and wild fruit of many more varied species than have survived till today—as he followed the migration patterns of the animals he hunted: bear, woolly rhino, mammoth, bison, horse and reindeer. He travelled in small groups, probably staying for only short periods of one to two weeks at any one site, as the finds at Rheindahlen have indicated.[53] The manner of sustenance—gathering and hunting—exhausted the food supply of an area relatively quickly. It has been estimated that the space needed to sustain a community required 3 to 4 km² per person.[54] The people were thus forced to move on since there were limits to the distance that a hunter-gatherer could travel per day. It would also follow that the shores of rivers and lakes must have been preferred locations at least for temporary settlement. There the presence of game birds and animals, who would be drawn to the water as well as the constant availability of fish, would make the securing of the necessary food supply more certain.

Considering man's increasing ability to plan tools he must have been able to develop the idea of erecting at least rudimentary shelters against the weather, even in the very early periods. For the Middle Pleistocene free-land stations, that is open air camp sites

9

are indicated, such as the one at Vertesszöllös. A similar, though later site, quite without parallels was found at Rheindahlen near Düsseldorf, where 105 m² of terrain yielded over 10,000 artefacts. These were left there some 200,000 years ago, probably by a migrating band of hunters, who brought their raw flint nodules with them and then proceeded to work them at Rheindahlen. Over a hundred thousand years later the site was still in use.[55] Evidence from other sites suggests that the shelters would have been such that they could be erected easily—covered tents or huts made of branches and foliage weighted with stones and large pieces of bone such as the shoulder blades of mammoth. It is interesting to note that overhangs of rock, the entrances to caves and the caves themselves were not the immediately obvious choice as camp sites. Not until post-Acheulean times does man seek them out to shelter himself. One such cave is located near Balve in Nordrhein-Westfalen.[56] Systematically examined in 1925–26, it revealed itself to be one of the richest in central Europe, yielding 700 stone tools, 2000 flakes and 6400 pieces of rejects from stratified layers, the earliest being late Acheulean, as well as 1500 artefacts and some 30,000 pieces of rejects from deposits that could not be stratified. It is of course readily apparent that a homogeneous layer of deposit belongs to a specific period of occupation, while the presence of an unproductive, i.e. sterile layer separating deposit layers would demonstrate that occupation of the site was not continuous but recurrent. Similarly the varying thickness of the different strata would say something either of the length of occupancy or vacancy of a site.[57]

The earliest indications that *Homo erectus* knew how to control fire and how to use fire as a tool comes from the cave at Choukoutien as well as from Vertesszöllös where it is associated with Acheulean artefacts.[58] Man's first acquaintance with fire was most certainly accidental—fires started by lightning, volcanic eruptions and perhaps spontaneous combustion. But that must have been the extent of his experience for several hundred thousand years, for the step towards the taming and controlling of fire must have depended on man first developing the mental capacity to appreciate its advantages. And even then he would at first not have been a fire-maker, but only the keeper of the flame.

Although the cave at Balve provides an almost complete sequence of stratification, it continues to be true that only by typological comparison with finds from type stations in western Europe, i.e. France, can finds in Germany be dated into the Paleolithic. Attempts by German archeologists to establish a consistent system of type stations based on mutually associated types of artefacts named after German locations, such as the Altmühl cultural groups, have not been totally successful.[59] By 1966 a total of at least 68 sites had been identified in Germany (55), Austria (6) and Switzerland (7).[60] Since then a number of additional locations have been discovered in free-land as well as cave stations. This is partly because central Europe during the glacial periods was hostile to human occupation, so that the process of 'colonization' does not really get under way until the late Paleolithic with artefacts of the late Paleolithic cultures as evidence, and partly because research into the Paleolithic, and even the Neolithic for that matter, in Germany and in the rest of Europe did not acquire the significance in the whole context of early and prehistoric research that it had in France. In fact, only recently has the term 'archeology' become a legitimate term in Germany when not applying it to Classical Antiquity. As a result largely French terminology, derived almost exclusively from type stations in France, continues to be used.

Four main phases of stone tool preparation are associated with the longest period of the Lower Paleolithic.[61] The Abbevillean industry, although usually found in the lowest

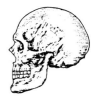

Heidelberg Man   Steinheim Man   Neanderthal   Oberkassel

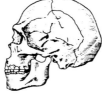

Ehringsdorf   Předmost   Cro-Magnon

3. Paleolithic skulls from central Europe (Müller-Karpe, *Handbuch der Vorgeschichte.* 1, Tafel 271).

strata, is not restricted to that oldest layer. The tools from this industry still appear among later levels of deposit, thereby providing serious obstacles to the dating of associated materials. While the Abbevillean technique uses stone exlusively with which to chip stone, the Acheulean technique which succeeds it uses stone as well as wood and probably even bone to work the stone nodule. In other words it introduces a technological refinement making possible greater formal accomplishment. The third main technique of the Lower Paleolithic is named Clactonian after the type station at Clacton-on-Sea in England. It is a pronounced flake-technique in that it first knocks off the cap of a stone in order to prepare a platform before pushing or striking off elongated flakes by pressing the stone against another serving as an anvil.

A related economical technique which already points to the transition towards the Middle Paleolithic is named after the type station Levallois. Levalloisian is a flaking technique which was characterized by the preparation of the stone surface through retouching so that the facetted surface received the appearance of a turtle shell, before a well-planned stroke severed the 'turtle shell' flake from the core.[62]

If it can be said that the evidence concerning Middle Pleistocene Man is meager, then by comparison for the Middle Paleolithic we face a veritable information explosion. While only fragmentary evidence exists about *Homo erectus*, his successors are much better documented, allowing conclusions to be drawn about man's appearance, his life styles, habitations, his social conditions, his care of the dead, even making cautious speculation possible about his cults, ritual practices and his relationship to the world around him.

While it appears that *Homo erectus* prepared his tools more or less as specific needs arose, his successor designed and planned his artefacts, at the same time adding new materials to his tool making inventory. The new culture bears the name of the type station Le Moustier, hence the term Mousterian.[63] From about 100,000 to 35,000 B.C. it is the dominant culture of the Middle Paleolithic, carried by *Homo sapiens neandertalensis*—the Neanderthal Man. The new type of man had established himself by 100,000 B.C. In view of the established association of the new Mousterian tool industry with Neanderthal Man it must therefore be assumed that wherever the Mousterian is

	Geological Division	Climatological Division	Lithic Cultures	Fossil Finds	Central European Cultural Features
Present					
	Holocene				
8,000 B.C.					
10,000 B.C.			Magdalenian		Gönnersdorf Ofnet Cave
			Solutrean	Cro-Magnon Man	
20,000 B.C.		Upper Paleolithic	Gravettian	*Homo sapiens sapiens*	bone tools flake tools retouching
			Aurignacian		Venus figures
30,000 B.C.			Châtelperronian	Předmost Man	not indicated in central Europe
				Brno Man	Vogelherd Cave
40,000 B.C.				Ehringsdorf Man	
50,000 B.C.	Upper Pleistocene	Würm Glaciation		Oberkassel Man	cave bear cult in Alpine caves
60,000 B.C.					
70,000 B.C.		Middle Paleolithic			open air stations at Mönchen-Gladbach and Salzgitter-Lebenstett
80,000 B.C.					
90,000 B.C.				Neanderthal Man	some flaking and retouching of tools
100,000 B.C.				*Homo sapiens*	
200,000 B.C.					

Chart 2. The Paleolithic in Central Europe, Middle-Upper Paleolithic, before 8000 B.C.

evident, the former presence of Neanderthal Man may also be deduced.[64] As such the former presence of Neanderthal Man is well documented through fossil finds—remnants of burials, skulls, jaws, bones and even footprints—from Europe (except England),[65] Asia, the Near East and North Africa. Some 45 sites and 200 individuals have been located.

The Mousterian is marked by a general shift away from hand axes, those pear-shaped stone tools, to a greater emphasis on flakes, producing tools which were long and slim, or wide and short, or pointed oval and flat, made from one flake and worked on only one side. These tools have been identified (1) as scrapers—those long curved or straight blades, sometimes pointed, or with rounded corners or with cutting edges around the perimeter, or (2) as choppers, the link with the typical forms and techniques of the Lower Paleolithic, which are to be found throughout the Mousterian.[66] While in typical Mousterian layers the hand axes virtually disappear, points become common. If one goes so far as to identify these as spear-points then the Neanderthal's ability to combine sticks and stones into workable tools with handles must also be accepted. The assumption that they were exclusively handheld is questionable. There is extensive evidence of the use of bones for tools so that it is probable that bone found a much more extensive use than is usually supposed. More than we might at first imagine it is probable that the Paleolithic economy must have used very efficiently all materials available to it, including bones, for the manufacture of scoops, spades, knives; hollow bones as containers, tubes, pipes, perhaps even whistles; flat ones as work surfaces. The suggestion has been made that the half jaws of carnivores with the projecting canines still in place would make ideal ripping tools.[67] Pieces of wood, bone and even antler were definitely used in the retouching, i.e. the sharpening of cutting edges and the finishing of surfaces, by striking or by applying pressure at a specific point.[68] At the same time it must be remembered that many designations for prehistoric tools are modern interpretations applied with hindsight.

The name of Neanderthal Man is the best known of the prehistoric Europeans (Fig. 3). In popular opinion he is the very embodiment of the cave man. This is quite incorrect. How did he come to bear this name? In about 1674 Joachim Neander, a writer of hymns and rector of the Latin School in Düsseldorf, would on occasion leave his school and retreat to an idyllic valley not too far away. In time the locals came to call the valley the Neanderthal (Tal = dale, valley). The idyllic valley has long since become an industrial site. In 1856 workmen blasting in the limestone cliffs of the valley discovered bones. Suggestions advanced that the bones belonged to a species of prehistoric man were no more acceptable in 1856 than in 1849 when the first skeletal remains of the species had been found in Gibraltar.[69] This rejection is not too surprising when one considers the controversial reception of Darwin's *Origin of Species* in 1859. In the end it was the Neanderthal which gave the species its name. The controversy surrounding the find was great.[70] The bones were held to be those of a Cossack, who died during his pursuit of Napoleon, and who had been suffering from rickets and crippling arthritis, the curvature of his leg and thigh bones obviously pointing to a life on horseback. English opinion considered him to have been a criminal, as his appearance was taken to indicate. It was not until 1886 that two partial skeletons found at Spy in Belgium and associated with Mid-Paleolithic artefacts established that prehistoric man had produced some of the Paleolithic cultures. Neanderthal Man first appeared during the Riss–Würm interglacial period some 200,000 years ago. The evidence of his former presence is so voluminous that from the middle Würm onwards, the inhabitable regions must have undergone a population explosion. Opinions are still divided on whether the representatives of *Homo erectus*, such as the fragments found at Bilzingsleben or Steinheim, can be considered to be prototypes of Neanderthaloid Man.[71] These fossils do not represent clearly a specifically Neanderthal morphology.[72] In spite of his popular cave man image, *the* Neanderthal Man did not exist. Nor can the customary representation of a bow-legged shuffling flatfoot with bent knees, drooping head, torso hunched forward, receding forehead and bent spine be accepted as universally applicable. An almost upright posture is just not physically possible.[73]

During the last fifty years the evidence has accumulated demonstrating that two groups of Neanderthal Man existed: an Early Group, more 'modern' in its anatomical appearance, which extended eastward from central Europe, and the so-called 'classic' Neanderthal, concentrated towards the West.[74] The basis for the differentiation between the 'classic' west-European Neanderthal and his more 'progressive' contemporary is that while the latter had a well-rounded, shorter, narrower and more finely structured skull with a more highly arched cranial vault and a small facial skeleton, the 'classic' Neanderthal is characterized by a coarser structure of the skull with lower vaulting, heavier brow-ridges and a protruding occiput.[75] Earlier opinions concerning Neanderthal Man were based exlusively on the fossil finds from Western Europe. The explanations advanced point out that the 'classic' type had evolved in isolation, largely cut off by the extensive glaciation of the Würm which contributed to the concentration of genetic features. 'Classic' Neanderthal came to have a highly curved thighbone, short legs in proportion to the thighs, bowed shafts, small heels, low arches with the weight carried on the outer edge of the foot and the big toes set somewhat apart (footprints have been found). His forearm was short compared to his upper arm. He had a retreating forehead and a large face marked by heavy fused brow-ridges.[76] However, with a cranial capacity of 1300 to 1600 cc his brain size can be called modern. Long and prominent processes at the back of the cervical vertebrae point to heavy neck muscles, which, it was long believed, held the head upright, yet the cranial base is oriented upward. The head was properly placed on a short and massive spinal column.[77]

It was also held that his physique caused him to be rather slow, which, however, induced him to make use of his inventiveness to produce better tools and weapons, well planned, designed and made. It is now held that early man's physiology should not be seen as constituting too great a handicap for his survival. He was not significantly inferior in physical fitness.[78] His cranial capacity had reached that of modern man. He was obviously able to adapt his life style for tens of thousands of years in the face of an often harsh and even hostile environment. Earlier opinion held that while Mousterian Man was producing his culture, somewhere in the wings, off to the East, in Asia Minor, or in North Africa a modern species evolved and developed the bases for the cultures of the Upper Paleolithic, whose descendants then pushed into Europe during the middle of the Würm, exterminating the Neanderthal as they encountered him. For a while it was even held that cannibalistic orgies played a role.[79] It was also held that the racial traits of Neanderthals and the new race were so different that interbreeding was made impossible.[80] This was to account for the absence of Neanderthal survivors among the skeletal finds of the Upper Paleolithic. Furthermore, the specialization of the hunt for particular species, for instance, a lifestyle determined by the pursuit of the reindeer as a source of clothing and food—was seen to have forced conservatism on Neanderthal Man making it difficult for him to break out of long-established patterns and to adjust to changed environmental conditions.[81] During the last twenty years accumulating evidence has demonstrated that the two supposedly incompatible racial types belonged to the same species.[82] Neanderthal finds associated with Mousterian deposits were discovered in Palestine and in Iraq alongside genuine skeletons of *Homo sapiens sapiens* and others with mixed Neanderthal and *Homo sapiens sapiens* traits, that is to say, transitions towards modernized Neanderthals.[83] More recently, finds in central and eastern Europe have confirmed the conclusions reached in the Near East. Although the 'classic' Neanderthal was a distinct variety of *Homo sapiens*, he was not an independent species,[84] nor did he 'suddenly' die out. Indeed the evidence points to a wide range of variability in the features of skull and spine of Neanderthals of the Middle Paleolithic, so that the traits of 'classic' Neanderthal Man appear in association with *Homo sapiens sapiens*, both in individual fossils and within fossil populations fron single sites.[85] Over-lapping in time and space make for great variability. Unlike the Western Neanderthals, the Eastern group, unconfined in its wanderings, interbred with other populations thereby not succumbing to the concentrating effects of inbreeding. As they moved West they continued their interbreeding practices, and the 'classic' Neanderthal population was absorbed during the next few thousand years.[86]

In 1914 at Ehringsdorf near Weimar, skull fragments had been discovered.[87] Without the more recent insights it had not been possible to place this Ehringsdorf Man into his proper place, for morphologically he was more similar to *Homo sapiens sapiens* than to Neanderthal Man.[88]

The use of the cave as a shelter comes very readily to mind when dealing with prehistoric man, yet early man did not in fact begin as a 'cave man', not even Nean-derthal Man. The evidence—growth stages of antlers—from the earliest occupied caves, those of Choukoutien, suggests that Peking Man inhabited them in winter only.[89] Neanderthal Man seems to have camped in the open air rather than in caves. Some open air stations indicate that the sites saw both summer hunting camps and winter quarters. This erroneous view concerning cave habitation is natural if one considers that the caves do offer much more favorable conditions for the preservation of artefacts than would camp sites on what was then largely tundra. Recently the open air stations in the loess area of the Lower Rhine, at Mönchengladbach for instance,[90] have proven to be most productive sites formerly occupied during the Middle Paleolithic, or the site at Salzgitter-Lebenstedt in Lower Saxony, where radio-carbon dating points to the pres-ence some 50,000 years ago of a small group of hunters probably in search of mammoth and reindeer. Indications are that the latter site was near the then most northerly tree line allowing short-term expeditions and seasonal occupancy.[91] The conclusions which open-air campsites allow about the relationship between man and his environment suggest a nomadic life. However, it is not probable that man coordinated his own wanderings with the migrating herds of reindeer. Since the reindeer travels at a trot, far too rapidly for man to follow over any great distance,[92] man must have known where to intercept the herds, and lie there in ambush, preparing his weapons for the hunt and the tools for cutting up the kill. Camp sites found in Russia datable to the Middle Paleolithic and attributable to hunters of the mammoth give some indication of a portable type of shelter probably constructed of poles, furs and skins, perhaps similar to the teepee of the North American Indian. The tent-like structures, measuring up to 8 m × 5 m, appear to have had their edges weighted down by stones and heavy bones as protection against strong winds.[93] As man ventured out into the tundra he must have dragged at least the poles with him as part of his supplies. The site at Salzgitter-Lebenstedt allows similar though cautious conclusions, frost and repeated flooding having seriously disturbed the site. It also appears probable that natural hollows in the ground were roofed over. In all likelihood man of the Middle Paleolithic had not yet developed sufficient distance between himself and the world in which he lived to do anything but adapt himself to whatever conditions nature had in store for him. The realization that he had other options open to him may very well have been reflected in his choice of the cave as an alternative to the open air camp site (Fig. 4).

That the caves were originally avoided by man is indicated by the absence of hominid fossil fragments in the earliest layers of the Lower Paleolithic.[94] In the caves the remains of big cats using the caves as lairs are frequent. It therefore seems plausible that man's fear must have made the caves rather unattractive until he had developed not only psychologically to contest the caves with cave lions, sabre-tooth tigers, bears, and so on, but also until he had the necessary arsenal of weapons to make the contest come out in his own favor. In the open, using snares and pit traps, he could best them, but on the animal's own ground man's chances were slim. At best the caves provided only temporary shelters, they were not used for making tools, cutting up the kill or making fires. The actual occupation of the cave at the end of the Lower Paleolithic, and the necessity of fighting predators for it must reflect a psychological turning point, in that it shows man converting a part of his world to his own use and utilizing it for his own benefit. The occupation was at first hesitant; one cautiously nestled under rock overhangs, in the mouths of caves or in shallow caves.[95] That man of the Middle Paleolithic restricted himself to the mouth of the caves is evidenced, in the earlier layers, by the location of fireplaces and flat stones, which probably served as anvils for stone tool manufacture, at the entrance to caves, such as the Vogelherd cave, where late Acheulean tools were found outside of the cave, while all the Mousterian tools were found just under the entrance to the cave. Not until the Aurignacian culture of the Upper Paleolithic are Aurignacian artefacts distributed throughout the cave.[96] It is to the question of dating that archeological research first devoted itself. The preserved stratifications of soil and artefact deposits in the caves made it possible to gain important information in questions of chronology, as for instance, in the case of the cave at Balve in Westphalia, which proved especially valuable since its undisturbed layers made possible a system of dating the Middle Paleolithic in Western Europe.[87] Although there are next to no traces left, it must be assumed that the caves underwent modest adaptations by Paleolithic interior decorators, to increase the rather limited possibilities for comfort—perhaps a screen of poles and skins to keep out the winter storms[98] and thereby increase the effect of man's fires. From the Middle Paleolithic on, fire making must have been known—sulphur nodules have been found at Mousterian levels which at least point to man's knowledge of how to produce a flame. It is also possible that man knew how to make fire by drilling. Both wood and bones were used for fuel.[99] It has been suggested that since Paleolithic Man made such extensive use of bones for fuel, the large accumulations should attract no more attention than a similar pile of wood, so that a cultic significance need not be attached to the deposits.[100] It is reasonable to assume that the cave entrances were used for cultic activities. In general the caves must be considered to have been seasonal residential alternatives. A purely sedentary cave-dweller society is not indicated, nor would it have been logical.[101]

Recent American research has tried to demonstrate that Neanderthal Man could not articulate anything but grunts and groans. On reconstructed models it was shown that the larynx was situated right under the oral cavity, as it is in chimpanzees and newly-born children. This anatomical feature would remove the vowels a, i, u from his

4. Vogelherd cave near Stetten ob Lontal, as it appeared in the spring of 1982.

inventory of sounds.[102]. However that may be, for organizational purposes, during the
hunt for instance, he must have had the ability to express his intentions and give
instructions.[103] The proven presence of long-houses during the Lower Paleolithic would
indicate the existence of family units, perhaps clans, with twenty to a hundred members,
and since there is evidence that these houses contained spaced fireplaces it would also
suggest that these large family units may have been subdivided into family associations.
The mixture of finds on certain sites would argue that the Neanderthals were not
isolated and encapsulated groups but probably travelled and camped together at least
on occasion.[104] Did they meet to plan and carry out organized hunts? Indications are
that in spite of the so-called 'population explosion' during the Würm glaciation, the
Neanderthals roaming over ice-free Europe would still be very few in number, so that
the chance meeting of even unrelated groups must have been a welcome relief from
tedium. It is difficult to imagine that even for the Neanderthals only biological urges
and hungers needed satisfying. That these encounters were not always peaceful is
indicated by the scars which some of the skulls show. They must have been capable of
emotional associations. Perhaps the male was polygamous, more probably the female
was polyandrous. The Neanderthals must have been able to transmit some sense of
group membership to one another, some concern for the care and protection of the
members of the group. That this need for community, the personal concern for the

17

individual must have existed is indicated by the burial practices in which they engaged. These customs make it clear that Neanderthal society was indeed a human society with its own very specific character. At the same time the burial customs of the Middle Paleolithic are the first to allow insight into the social relations of prehistoric man. Though the evidence is fragmentary, it seems definite that interment of the deceased was the established practice of the Mousterians. The attention which was paid to the deceased may even have assumed ritualistic forms. Thus the corpses of men, women and even children received special treatment during the burial ceremonies: the deceased were bedded in shallow graves, often accompanied by carefully worked flint implements and occasionally by bones, which at the time of burial may have had meat attached.[105] A special feature which is first introduced during Mousterian times is the use of red ochre as part of the interment ceremony. It was strewn very liberally onto the floor of the graves as well as on the corpses. Thus the double grave at Oberkassel, to name only one, dating from the very late Würm period, had the skeletons reddened. The accompanying bone carvings also bore traces of red and must have been intended as burial gifts.[106] That the graves also tended to have a covering of flat rocks, or even mammoth shoulder blades, perhaps to protect the corpse, points not only to some ritualistic treatment but also to concern for the dead. The same conclusions can be derived from the positioning of corpses in relation to one another. Thus a find of two adult skeletons more or less side by side, with the skeletons of infants or young children placed at their feet, might point to familial concerns, perhaps even loving care for all.[107] The double grave at Oberkassel contained the skeletons of a sixty-year-old man and of a young woman of twenty to twenty-five years of age. The man had been suffering from arthritis and had sustained fractures as well as injuries to his skull (Fig. 5). The woman lay alongside the man but not facing in the same direction (Fig. 6). Although there is no indication of a ritual sacrifice of the woman, this burial would point to the special relationships which must have existed between people.[108] In other parts of Europe, at Grimaldi and at La Ferrassie, and at several other sites, multiple burials can be regarded as evidence for the existence of human relationships which were not limited to the needs of daily living but were extended to include the care of the deceased. It has frequently been suggested that the red ochre was used as a surrogate for blood and an attempt has been made to explain its use as early man's attempt to reverse death, by restoring color to the pallid skin of the deceased.[109] The same sort of explanation has been advanced that early man buried his dead near the fire places in order to return warmth and thereby life to the body. Objections, however, have been raised to both the ochre and the fireplace theories,[110] in view of the very persistence in both practices—surely, in 30,000 to 60,000 years it would have become evident to even the simplest human mentality that to persist in the practice was futile. Whatever else it might mean, owing to the very liberal use of ochre in the daily life of early man it would have been difficult not to get red ochre stains on almost everything. Recent research among modern primitives has shown that if they are limited in their identification of color, such as the mere identification of colours in terms of light and dark, so that 'light as the sky' is the equivalent of blue, and 'dark as the grass' a synonym for green, then red will be the next color which they will identify.[111] These findings may be relevant in the context of the Middle Paleolithic. Objections have also been expressed about the location of corpses in ashes: in the course of the many centuries during which caves and other campsites were used, albeit intermittently, it was only too natural that the entire floor of a cave, for instance, would be covered by a layer or even layers of ash. Consequently, the

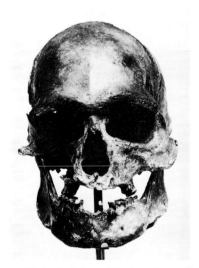
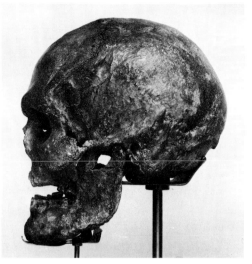

5. Male skull from Oberkassel near Bonn, c. 50,000 B.C.

6. Female skull from Oberkassel near Bonn, c. 50,000 B.C.

association of red ochre and ash with skeletal remains need not at all point to specific burial customs. Further clarification may yet be produced.

There is strong evidence that Neanderthal Man did engage in some ritual with severed heads. The idea has been put forward that the very predominance of skulls or skull fragments among the finds of *Homo erectus* and early *Homo sapiens* may be attributable to special attention which may have been paid to the head from earliest times on.[112] The possibility that early man opened the back of the skulls of the deceased in order to extract the brain or break long bones for their marrow and eat it attracted a great deal of a somewhat morbid fascination in the earlier literature. It has even been held that cannibalistic orgies played a role in the disappearance of Neanderthal Man.[113] In the publications of recent years this aspect does not receive the same degree of emphasis. It is even stated that although perhaps probable, cannibalism cannot be demonstrated on the basis of the extant evidence. Cutting marks and teeth marks on skeletons need not point to cannibalism; the cave-hyena can be blamed for at least some of the evidence.[114] Since bones were used for fuel, the presence of partly charred human bones does not necessarily mean that a given part of the body had been roasted.[115] To establish why interment as well as some indication of burning coexist is not possible. Though there is some evidence that bones of all sorts may have been of non-materialistic interest, such as decorated bones and expecially bored teeth of such diverse animals as bear, lion, wolf, lynx, wild horse, stag and wild pig, and even fossilized shark's teeth as yielded by the Petersfels cave near Konstanz in Baden-Württemberg,[116] their use need not necessarily have been cultic. On the other hand, vast accumulations of cave bear bones have been found all over Europe. In many instances chance and many generations of cave bear occupancy would account for the vast accumulations of bear bones in many caves suitable for hibernation,[117] for instance the Repolust cave near Mixnitz in Styria/ Austria, which yielded remains of some 50,000 bears which had died there in the course of tens of thousands of years.[118] However, puzzling deposits of cave bear bones have been discovered in German, Austrian and Swiss alpine caves which cannot be explained satisfactorily without considering some intentional arrangements by man. These arrangements offer considerable support to the theory that Neanderthal Man practiced a bear cult which paid special attention to the skulls. The best known site is the

19

Drachenloch (Dragon's hole) near Vättis in Switzerland,[119] located at an altitude of 2445 m above sea level. In the central and rear portions of a 70 m long cave remains were found of some 500 to 1000 cave bears ranging in age from two to eight years. In the middle of the cave, in addition to a fireplace, a box-like structure of stacked stone slabs (0·4 m × 0·35 m) held a thick layer of charcoal with ashes and partly burned bear bones. The box was covered by a heavy stone slab. Very close nearby another larger stone box (0·95 m × 0·9 m × 1·00 m) contained the well preserved skulls of seven cave bears as well as some long bones. The skulls all faced east, that is towards the entrance of the cave. For two of the skulls the two upper vertebrae were also found in the box. This is of some significance, since it means that at least these two bears were beheaded while skin and flesh still covered the heads, in other words they were deposited as heads and not as skulls. Whatever it may mean, it points to a variation in the practice. An area had been separated from the cave by running a 5·5 m long wall, 0·8 m high, at a distance of 0·4 to 0·6 m from the left rock face of the cave. In that space some bear bones had been piled, sorted into skulls, pelvic bones and long bones. On that same wall six or seven skulls had been placed into niche-like recesses each resting on a stone slab, encased on all sides and covered by stone slabs. The base of one skull was surrounded by tightly packed stones, while another, and this is most interesting because it is such an unusual arrangement, had a complete thigh bone placed through an eye socket, the two pieces resting on two well preserved long bones, the four bones coming from four different bears. At the rear of the middle portion of the cave a gallery of nine skulls was found, lined up against the rock face, each skull protected by an inclined stone slab. Two of these skulls rested on slabs, while a third, resting on two long bones, was surrounded by snail shells. Carbon-14 analysis of the charcoal from one of the fireplaces shows it to have been burned over 50,000 years ago. The Wildenmannlisloch in Switzerland yielded five skulls arranged with long bones, while the Wildkirchli,[120] also in Switzerland, contained the remains of some 500 to 1000 bears. The Petershöhle, near Velden in Bavaria,[121] contained two fireplaces which yielded the charred bones of cave bear, in addition to skulls placed unusually and probably quite intentionally in recesses in the walls. One skull lay between stones, imbedded in and covered by charcoal. In several instances up to ten skulls were arranged in piles and surrounded by stones. At Reyersdorf in Lower Silesia[122] earlier excavation is said to have revealed a row of bear skulls covered with clay, a niche expanded to form a stone box contained the skull of a young female, its lower jaw and two vertebrae still in place, again pointing to a head and not a skull deposition. Other sites in Russia, in the Carpathian Mountains, in Slovenia and in Yugoslavia offer variations on the practice. Quite obviously the cave bear was hunted to provide the hunters with meat and fur, but why did early man pursue the bear to such inaccessible elevations as the Drachenloch at 2445 m, the Salzofenhöhle at 2005 m, the Wildenmannlisloch at 1628 m above sea level, when other game, even cave bears could be hunted much less strenuously in the low lands, especially since man was not vying for the occupancy of the cave with the bear, these altitudes being far too inhospitable? Not till the later Magdalenians, who followed the last retreat of the great glaciers, is any evidence of a prolonged stay indicated. It has been suggested that poorly armed Neanderthal Man attacked the bear while it hibernated (Figs. 7, 8), rather than seeking an equal confrontation with an animal the size and weight of the Alaskan Kodiak bear, a vegetarian though it was, as the teeth indicate. The idea must have been attractive even to Neanderthal Man expecially if one considers the possibilities which such a larder offered to a band using a cave as winter quarters.[123] But a wintertime

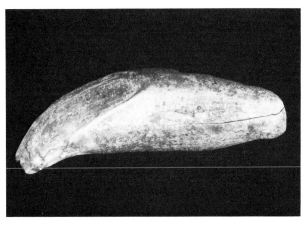

7. Stone artefacts from the Repolust cave near Mixnitz in Styria, Austria.

8. Bone artefact from the Repolust cave near Mixnitz in Styria, Austria.

occupation of the caves in the high Alps is unrealistic even under the climatic conditions of today. The evidence from the sites mentioned above makes a different type of search appear probable, one not linked to food and clothing. It is reasonable to assume that the ritualistic deposition of bear skulls is the first concrete evidence of cultural and perhaps even religious ideas. If the bears were sacrificed, which the small number of decapitated heads could suggest, then this sacrifice is probably man's first recorded cultural ceremony. Was it performed by representatives of a cultural elite, under ritualistic, cultic or magic considerations in anticipation of a kill or as thanks for the successful completion of the hunt? It is too hazardous to speculate on a purpose. To draw on modern-day anthropological evidence, to refer to the bear-hunting rituals in contemporary Siberia, as is done so often, does not help answer the questions left open.[124] However, it must have been a significant realization, an intellectual revolution, when man came to terms with the cave bear, perhaps venerating its might, eating its meat, and perhaps partaking of its brain as the source of its strength in the hope of adding to his own. It is of course not known whether the conception that the source of its power was located in the head was familiar to the Neanderthal hunters, or whether it was this conception which led to the special treatment of the skulls. Nor is it known whether it was a totemistic rationale which saw the veneration of the bear as a veneration of an ancestral animal, as has been suggested.[125] One can only speculate about the possibility that the cult around the bear skull was an extension of a possible cult around the human skull by earliest man. Some evidence from Italy points to Neanderthal Man treating his own kind with rituals similar to that given the bear.[126] Whatever the reasons, the bear cult persists into the Upper Paleolithic, over a period of 40,000 years, into the time of the Magdalenians. The theory has even been advanced that it was the later Magdalenians who ascribed cultic values to the bear skulls and that it was they who arranged them.[127] In France recent analysis of Magdalenian cave paintings and their relationship to the respective location in the caves has tried to show that besides being realistic representations of the wild life, these animals are masculine and feminine sexual symbols, often representing sexual acts.[128] In this analysis it was shown that 91 per cent of the representations are female symbols and were to be found in the central parts of the caves. It is left open whether the cave itself was suggestive as a feminine symbol. However, the layout and topography of the cave strongly suggested the vision of the cave as an organized world. Such an analysis of caves has not been

21

	Geological Division	Climatological Division	Lithic Cultures		Fossil Finds	Central European Cultural Features: Settlement types and sites	Central European Cultural Features: Arts and Crafts
5,000 B.C.	Holocene		Mesolithic (Naglemose in the north)				
						Ahrensburg	Lyngby axes
8,000 B.C.							
							reindeer economy
9,000 B.C.							
				Magdalenian		Stellmoor	
10,000 B.C.							
						Gönnessdorf 'Ofnet' cave	tools of organic materials
						open air stations	
13,500 B.C.							
						Hamburg	
15,000 B.C.							
				Solutrean		cave occupation	
18,000 B.C.							
20,000 B.C.				Gravettian			bone tools flake tools retouching
22,000 B.C.			Upper Paleolithic				
		Würm Glaciation					
	Upper Pleistocene			Aurignacian			
					Cro-Magnon Man		Venus figures
28,500 B.C.							Vogelherd Cave
				Châtelperronian		not indicated in central Europe	
35,000 B.C							
					Homo sapiens sapiens		
40,000 B.C.							

Chart 3. The Paleolithic in Central Europe, Upper Paleolithic, before 8000 B.C.

undertaken in central Europe. The Austrian, Swiss and German caves are devoid of paintings, nor do the reports specify the relationship of the finds to the respective location in the caves other than differentiating between the entrance to the cave or the inner parts of the cave. The Drachenloch is different in this respect, in that the cultic activity is specified to have taken place in the central portions of the cave.[129] Some cautious analogies between the deposits of bear skulls and the cave paintings could perhaps be hazarded, especially if the bones and skulls were indeed arranged by the Magdalenians. Whatever the evidence may mean, a religious attitude cannot be denied to Neanderthal Man.

In central Europe the dividing line between the Middle and Upper Paleolithic can be clearly drawn since transition periods such as Châtelperronian have not yet been indicated, so that Mousterian is followed immediately by Aurignacian,[130] the first major culture after the interval. The 'classical' Neanderthal type, generally associated with Mousterian, ceases to be the sole carrier of cultural forms in western Europe at the end of the Middle Paleolithic. One used to interpret the introduction of this entire spectrum of cultural innovations as the effect of the appearance of a new race.[131] First identified in France,[132] the new man was named after the type station Cro-Magnon. He was seen to have moved into central Europe from the east[133] and on his way west, to have exterminated the indigenous Neanderthal population. Not only has the theory of the Neanderthal's catastrophic end become less convincing, but the Cro-Magnon anatomy is cruder in appearance when compared to the earlier but more refined skeleton of Brno in Czechoslovakia or the Châtelperronian skeleton from Combe-Capelle.[134] The conclusion that the cultural innovations can be attributed to the arrival of a new race, cannot be demonstrated.[135] While the transitional Châtelperronian is found very frequently in association with Aurignacian, it is also often missing in Aurignacian levels, only to reappear related to Gravettian, as though Aurignacian and Gravettian were later derivatives.[136] That Aurignacian was introduced by foreigners cannot be maintained on the basis of the evidence. To link the beginning of the Upper Paleolithic with Aurignacian is therefore more useful for purposes of classification than as proof of a population change-over. Satisfactory explanations for the coincidence of modern skeletons and new tool-making cultures are not available. The two phenomena need not even be related. What can be said is that from the end of the Middle Paleolithic on, Neanderthal Man's more modern cousins from the east gradually assert their dominance and establish themselves throughout Eurasia. The Châtelperronian skeletons would support this. It is likely that rather than being an assault-like onslaught, the settlement pattern was more of a gradual infiltration of migrating groups. In the course of this transition 'classical' Neanderthal Man was either eliminated or assimilated or forced into isolated retreats. The genetic concentrations of his anatomy, the specialization of his lifestyle, of his hunt, of his entire economy in fact, all adapted to life under colder conditions probably presented obstacles to his adjustment to the changes which followed the retreat of the glaciers. Changes in climate,[137] in flora and fauna must have affected the structure of his economy, making his position very vulnerable. The cultures of the Upper Paleolithic show themselves to be less dependent on a specialized economy, more versatile in their tools and weapons, with new approaches to the world around them, to life and to death.

The Upper Paleolithic has four major representative techniques of tool manufacture: the Aurignacian, Gravettian, Solutrean and Magdalenian cultures. The specialists have of course identified additional, more or less important manufacturing techniques.

9. Aurignacian fist axes, *c.* 30,000–20,000 B.C., from the Speckberg near Meilnhofen, Administrative District Eichstätt

10. Pre-Solutrean retouched scrapers, *c.* 20,000 B.C., from the Weinberg caves near Mauern.

Henceforth all younger cultures of the Upper Paleolithic are European and Near Eastern and no longer exclusively French, although most of the finds are not equal to those found in France.[138] While it has been possible to establish a separate terminology for Northern Germany—Hamburger-, Federmesser-, Ahrensburgerkultur—the attempt to develop an independent terminology named after type stations in Southern Germany, such as the Schulerlochkultur after the Schulerloch in the valley of the Altmühl, or to speak of an Altmühl Group, has not been successful for the Paleolithic.[139] As a result, for purposes of classification the terminology applied in Germany leans on the one developed for Western Europe. At the same time it is useful to remember that the various cultures which mark the Upper Paleolithic must not be seen as a rigid sequence of stages but as a flexible yet progressive co-existence of various traditions with extensive interconnections brought about by migrations which in turn promoted inventive syntheses. For central Europe the cultures belonging to Aurignacian, Gravettian, Solutrean and Magdalenian are ascertained, though not necessarily all on the same site. Thus, while Austria contributes the most famous Aurignacian—the so-called Venus of Willendorf—it has yielded no Solutrean and only little Magdalenian.[140] In Belgium, Germany, Switzerland, the Alps and the Jura Mountains, the later Magdalenians are in evidence as they followed the last retreat of the great glaciers.[141]

The first culture of the Upper Paleolithic with a characteristic technique of tool manufacture is the Aurignacian, named after the type station Aurignac in France (Fig. 9). Initially the term Aurignacian was applied collectively to Châtelperronian, Aurignacian and Gravettian as Lower, Middle and Upper Aurignacian, respectively, to account for the diversity and continuance of earlier traditions of artefact manufacture. At the same time it is not certain to what extent these divisions represent a chronological sequence, since the productive strata are not always separated by sterile layers.

While the Mousterian technique was generally characterized by core tool hand axes, the post-Châtelperronian techniques are characterized by flake tool blades to the extent that one can speak of 'blade cultures',[142] blades often so small that they can have been used only when fastened to a shaft of wood, horn or hollow bone. This shift from core to flake tool also marks a shift from all purpose tools to specialized tools as represented by

24

a wealth of forms and diverse purposes. Bearing in mind that functional designations are applied with hindsight, Aurignacian layers yield saws, burins pointed at both ends, awl-like drills, stylus-like scratchers, scrapers, blades with peripheral retouching on both sides (Fig. 10), as well as notched blades. Aurignacian man adds bone and antler to his source of tool making materials: reindeer antlers and ivory yield spearpoints and daggers. Though harder to work than wood, bones and antler offer superior elasticity. The long ivory tipped spear becomes his main weapon. Besides tools of stone, bone or ivory, ornaments of bone or ivory such as hair rings and beads, as well as 'art' objects appear in Aurignacian layers. In France Châtelperronian finds, or as some term it Lower Aurignacian finds, are associated for the first time with skeletons of the Neo-*anthropinae*— *Homo sapiens sapiens*, who in turn are associated with the first representation of a horse's head scratched on a stone, and a burial for which the deceased had been decorated with shells, perhaps from a necklace or the trim of some type of headwear.[143] Both of these elements represent important cultural innovations, pointing to the development of art and the use of ornamental objects.

Gravettian is the last cultural level to be found in the loess deposits of central Europe,[144] so that it coincides with the climatic transition which witnessed the retreat of the continental and alpine glaciers, and the increase of vegetation which put an end to the drifting dust. In Austria the loess station at Willendorf revealed five levels of Gravettian in its upper layers. Characteristic Gravettian complexes have been found at Mauern in the Weinberghölen overlooking an interglacial valley of the Danube, at Mainz-Linsenberg and in the Wildscheuerhöhle at Steeden on the river Lahn.[145] Most characteristic among the great diversification of forms of tool manufacture are the so-called Gravettian points—small and very pointed flaked stonetips, which, it has been concluded, must be arrow heads, so that the invention of bow and arrow can be placed at around 30,000 B.C.[146] Bows and arrows themselves have been preserved only from about 12,000 B.C. on, largely because of the perishable nature of their material. The stone flaking produced during this period had attained such a high level of precision that retouching became largely superfluous.

A total innovation were the statuettes of stone or ivory, mainly female representations, which now appeared as a typical cultural expression of the Gravettian levels. Over one hundred sculptures and reliefs of these female and male figurines have been found from France to Siberia.[147] The representative arts underwent development and enrichment.

The Solutrean culture,[148] besides experiencing a flowering of surface-retouched symmetrical and asymmetrical stone tips, developed a lance-blade of antler with a barb-like retention hook—the ancestor for the harpoons of the Magdalenians, while bone-tool techniques produced needles with eyes.

It is quite apparent from this brief outline that since the beginning of the Upper Paleolithic man distinguished himself by carrying out innovative modifications of his tool inventory and an ever increasing number of cultural refinements. Who were the inhabitants of the Upper Paleolithic? Traditionally one called them Cro-Magnon Men, so modern in appearance that it was easy to identify them with modern men. It has since become apparent that though perhaps the most prominent type, Cro-Magnon Man was neither the only one nor the most refined.[149] Fossil finds from Grimaldi in Italy, Combe-Capelle and Chancelade in France, and Brno and Předmost in Czechoslovakia suggest many other divergent regional types in Europe alone. He reveals himself to have been a robust individual, nearly 1.80 m tall, with a large and vaulted head, high forehead, moderate brows, prominent cheekbones and a strong chin. His cranial capacity is modern—up to 1600 cc.[150] Man of the Upper Paleolithic then has the same mental capacity to create culture as has modern man. A modern intelligence implies a similar reaction towards the world, so that it is possible to expect the same ability to transform appearances into cultural symbols.

The last of the Upper Paleolithic cultures, the Magdalenian, is represented in all parts of central Europe. Again it is fair to assume that the presence of Magdalenian artefacts also attests to the former presence of the Magdalenians. Often the Magdalenian is the only cultural level on the site. This would mean that entirely new areas had become accessible to man, perhaps the still inhospitable wastes of tundra skirting the retreating icefields.[151] Altogether some thousand Magdalenian sites have been identified in western Europe.[152] The spread of artefacts and ideas reflects the extent of travel and the probable interrelation of the various groups of people. A more or less close contact between neighbouring migrating groups must be assumed as normal, for the hunt for instance, leading to a rapid spread of techniques, customs, concepts and perhaps even cults. It is not likely that the individual groups could have survived if totally encapsulated. In spite of the nomadic life-style, limited 'tribal' territories are probable in which the groups lived, wandered, hunted and developed culturally.[153] If modern nomads can serve as examples than these territories were likely to have been selected and loosely defined by tradition.

To facilitate the hunt it seems logical that man would have kept approaches and carrying distances to a minimum, a factor which would let him roam in only relatively small territorial limits. As pointed out earlier, the romantic view is not realistic of reindeer hunters tracking their prey for great distances into the treeless tundra as with the advent of summer the game moved north to escape the heat and the swarms of insects. Carrying his tentpoles as part of his baggage he could not keep up the pace over the marshy terrain for which the reindeer with its splayed toes and dew-claws is so well equipped. Instead the Magdalenians too had to reach their hunting grounds earlier in order to lie in wait at their open air campsites and thereby maximize their kill. Some of these campsites were dug out pit-huts, 3–5 m in diameter and about 2 m deep, with paved or stamped floors, walls dressed with stone or wood. Evidence points to fireplaces in the huts. It is possible that the huts were actually larger than the size of the pit would suggest. That there must have been a superstructure is indicated by stone slabs, tusks, large hollow bones and shoulder blades of mammoth found in circular arrangements, probably used to weigh down the edges of skin tents. In various places the evidence points to upright, pole-supported tents made of reindeer skins, not unlike the North American Indian teepee, as at Stellmoor, to be discussed more fully later on, located at the edge of the ice and occupied during the last glacial period.[154] The occupation of these campsites must have been influenced by seasonal factors. Thus the Stellmoor site was occupied only during the summer months, as indicated by the growth stages of the reindeer antlers found there. The winter quarters of these reindeer hunters must have been further to the south,[155] probably in caves and heat reflecting overhangs,[156] still favorite dwellings as they had been in Mousterian times, but also in tent shelters, as for instance at Gönnersdorf on the Middle Rhine north of Koblenz.[157] The foundations of two circular shelters, providing room for some fifty to sixty people, have been excavated. Considering all the intervening changes a cautious reconstruction would suggest that one of the shelters was of the teepee variety, while the other had vertically supported walls and a roof sloping towards the center. By determining the age of the hunted game it has been possible to establish that the shelters were occupied during the winter from

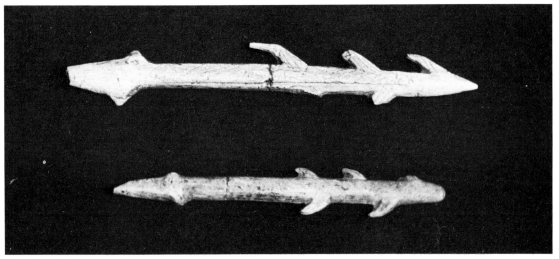

11. Harpoons of reindeer antler, *c.* 10,000 B.C. from the Petersfels near Bittelbrunn, north of Singen.

12. Pierced 'baton' of antler with engravings of reindeer, from the Petersfels near Bittelbrunn, north of Singen. It has been claimed that the reindeer bull on the right is in rut.

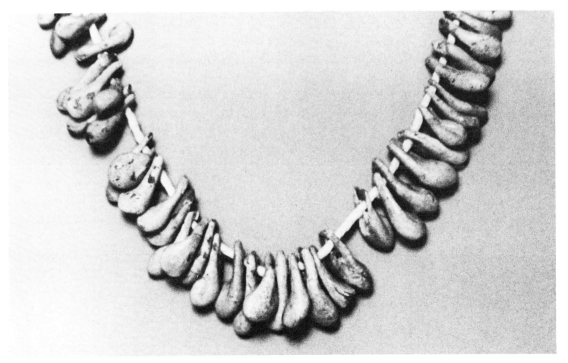

13. Necklace of elk's teeth, *c.* 10,000 B.C. from the Ofnet cave near Nördlingen.

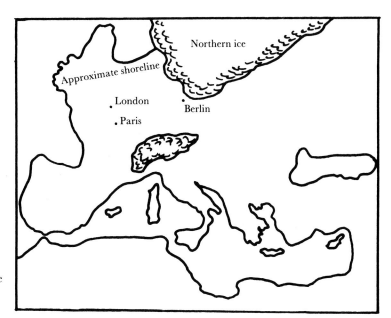

Map 4. Extent of the northern ice during the late Würm glaciation (Magdalenian).

September to March. Here too the floors had been paved. Slate had been brought from half a kilometer away. Large stones from the Rhine valley were used to hold down the sides of the tents. The traces of reindeer hunters have been found in the Swiss Jura, the hunters living in transportable skin tents and hunting in the area around the Moossee as long as reindeer were in the area, and then moving into other regions. The choice of settlement was then influenced by two factors—seasonal conditions, and the proximity to the game—each to guarantee the necessary food supply.

The Magdalenian culture offers the most accomplished tradition of Paleolithic tool manufacture. Contrary to previous periods Magdalenian type forms are not based on stone artefacts but on organic materials, such as bone, ivory and reindeer antler (Fig. 11). Harpoons of antler are now fully developed from having one or two rows of barbs in the early period, to big barbs in the middle period, to having two rows of big barbs in the late period. Contemporary with the harpoons are spear throwers, propulsors, designed to extend the length of the arm and thereby increase not only leverage, but velocity, range and accuracy of the projectile as well. Also characteristic for the Upper Paleolithic is the appearance of an artefact often beautifully engraved, but with no known purpose. Made from the lower portion of antler, the first tine is removed and a fairly large hole is drilled through the side at or near the former juncture point (Fig. 12). These holes present the first evidence of Paleolithic man's knowledge of drilling techniques. There has been an attempt to identify these perforated antler-staves as insignia of rank, such as command batons analogous to the batons carried by field-marshals.[158] The German term 'Lochstab'—literally a stick with a hole—is perhaps the most apt term since it identifies the artefact without burdening it with a function. The suggestion has been put forward that it was the inhabitants of the tundra regions especially who during the last glacial period came to master effective techniques of working bone and antler to compensate for the lack of usable wood in those glacial regions. The scarcity of wood is also invoked to argue that the spearheads and harpoons must have been detachable since stone, bone and antler warheads were easier to replace than wooden spearshafts.

That man was busy expanding his cultural inventory is indicated by the discovery

28

that the bones of water fowl and other birds could be used as or transformed into flutes and pipes, and if there was music, then dance could not be far behind. An extensive inventory exists of body ornaments—jewellery in the form of bored teeth (Fig. 13) and shells, carved discs of bone and antler, pendants, pearls, engravings on bone, ivory, stone and red and black amber, as well as carvings of these materials.

By comparison the stone tool inventory is harder to typify since there is no significant deviation from Gravettian or Solutrean techniques. Generally they are a response to specific needs.[159]

The disappearance of the Magdalenians is usually linked with the disappearance of certain game from western and central Europe.[160] Thus the reindeer moved north, the alpine fauna occupied higher regions, the mammoth and woolly rhino died out. The end of the Magdalenian culture can be quite clearly linked with the end of the last glacial period around 10,000 to 8000 B.C.

At what point in his cultural development did man begin to suspect that he was not only body, that the possibility existed of being at least a duality, that existence might not be limited to a physical life in time and space, but that for both body and life there might be a 'more'? At what point did man differentiate between body and person? And if he was conscious of being more than a body moving in space and time then how did he indicate it? It is generally accepted that it is in the care of the dead that man's concerns about identity, life and death find expression.

The Lower Paleolithic provides no evidence which would reflect early man's attitude towards death. However, some significance has been assigned to the fact that skulls and jaws are found rather than other skeletal parts and that this circumstance just could point to some specific funerary rituals involving the preservation of the skull.[161] The evidence from Choukoutien and Steinheim shows that the skull did receive special attention, in that the spinal base was enlarged. Whether Peking Man and Steinheim Man artificially enlarged the base of the skull to insert his hand to extract the brain in order to eat it is not certain.

With the tool inventories of the Middle Paleolithic, Neanderthal Man has also left some evidence of his care for the dead. Although the evidence is far too fragmentary to allow specific conclusions about final purposes, it does suggest that funerary ritual was involved in the treatment of the deceased. The likelihood that the deceased were buried near the hearth in the pathetic hope of restoring warmth to the body and thereby life, or that ochre was used as a surrogate of blood, or used to restore the color of life has already been discounted.[162] It remains probable that none of these practices had any magical intentions at all, but may have been simply associated with festive rites. The camp at Gönnersdorf reveals, Magdalenian though it is, that red ochre covered all interior surfaces of the shelters for no obvious reasons.[163] It has been demonstrated that the abundant use of ochre was traditional, so that its presence at a burial as well should not be surprising. The dead were placed into natural or specially prepared hollows, sometimes on a carpet-like layer of red or reddened earth, as at Oberkassel, the head and torso covered with a stone slab or a mammoth shoulder blade. Two possible reasons might account for this precaution—protection against predators or probably less likely, fear of a return of the deceased. Sometimes the corpses were wedged into cracks in the rocks. Some evidence indicates the graves of Neanderthal Man to have been directioned NW–SE.[164] Multiple burials, perhaps members of the same social unit, tend to be grouped together. If early man can be termed human, then he can also be credited with some capacity for emotion so that burial arrangements can be taken to suggest social motives and probably religious ones as well. In some burials grave equipment appears during this period. From La Ferrasie comes an instance where a child's grave had been equipped with tools.[165] Were these farewell gifts or was it a case of provisioning the deceased for life in some other reality if tools cannot really be considered as belonging to children?

In central Europe a number of skulls show that death came violently, by blows to the head.[166] Could the cause be sought in some form of cultic sacrifice? If so, then for what purpose? Again the spinal hole had been enlarged and the possibility continues to exist that the brain was extracted. Even though the evidence points only to the severing of heads which then received special treatment before being preserved, some form of ritualistic cannibalism may have taken place.[167] A rationale for such a practice, however, can only be arrived at by analogy with recent practices among head-hunters. It involves notions of the ritual transfer of a respected victim's special qualities, his strength and virtues thought to have their source in the brain, which could be absorbed by eating the brain. On the evidence available no definite conclusions can be put forward concerning the use to which the brain was put. Mixed with grease it could be an ingredient in the preparation of skins. Since a number of skulls have been found in association with the two uppermost vertebrae it is apparent that the heads themselves were interred. It is therefore apparent that the evidence does not support the existence of a uniform skull-cult during the Middle Paleolithic. As yet no conclusive relationship has been advanced linking the skull-cult of the cave bear with a cult centered around human heads or skulls.

The burial rites of the Upper Paleolithic are elaborations of customs which first appear during the Mousterian culture of the Middle Paleolithic. Both prone and fetal positions occur.[168] If stretched out then the arms are frequently pulled up with the hands held at the height of the neck, or one arm rests alongside the body while the other lies angled across the lower chest. In the fetal position the hands are often tied while the legs are laced tightly to the body in a crouching position. The reasons given for the latter practice link it with fear of a possible return of the dead, especially if the deceased had also been covered with heavy stones. The funerary practices of the Upper Paleolithic are in marked contrast to those of the Middle Paleolithic in that they now see the regular inclusion of body ornaments accompanying the deceased, such as perforated animal teeth and a predominance of shells. Although the shells found in Germany are mainly local species,[169] mussels and snail shells from the Mediterranean and Italy as well as from the area around Bordeaux also occur with some frequency. The Kesslerloch in Switzerland even yielded shells which are known only in the Red Sea.[170] Their distant origins clearly point to them as an important trade commodity. These shells were found around the skulls, necks, hips, upper arms, elbows, wrists, knees and ankles. The question about the possible purpose behind this practice has led the interpreters to concentrate especially on the various types of *Cypraea* or cowrie shell which, because of its vaginal shape, is seen as a symbol of the gate into the world. Because it is so closely linked to the feminine it allows an interpretation as fertility symbol.[171] Its association with burials encourages interpretations in terms of death in this world, rebirth in some other realm. It is of course equally possible that man of the Upper Paleolithic completely missed the symbolic connection and saw in these shells only the element of rare value and prosperity which was to accompany the deceased in the manner of a burial gift. These farewell gifts took other forms as well, such as stone artefacts without signs of having been used previously. The presence of animal bones points to provisioning the grave, again as farewell gifts and therefore of cultic significance. The ideas of a journey into the afterlife need not necessarily follow. Burials of men, women and children observed these common forms.

The Upper Paleolithic continues the practice of head burial, indicated by the presence of neck vertebrae which means that the flesh was still attached at the time of the deposition. From the Aurignacian to the end of the Paleolithic the evidence from such caves as the Vogelherd, Lautsch, Kaufertsberg, Hohlerstein and Ofnet suggests that ritual must have played a role.[172] At the Hohlerstein one male, one female and one infant skull—perhaps a family—lower jaw and vertebrae still in place, were deposited together, and probably at the same time, in a hollow or a layer of red earth. Only the woman's head had been decorated with fish teeth. The late Magdalenian levels of the Ofnet cave near Nördlingen revealed two 'nests' of skulls, i.e. heads, which had been deposited in two hollows and arranged in concentric circles from the center. The two hollows, one meter apart, contained twenty-seven skulls in one and six skulls—with jaws and vertebrae—in the other, bedded on ochre and ashes. Altogether the heads of four men, nine women and twenty children had been deposited here perhaps over a short period of time. All the skulls faced west, i.e. towards the cave entrance. The idea that the heads were arranged to face the sunset is attractive but cannot be proven. Only the skulls of the women and children were decorated, with two hundred eye teeth of deer as well as four thousand perforated snail shells, some of them originating in the Mediterranean. Ritual death is the most probable explanation, for all the skulls show fatal head injuries. In general the indications are that for the Magdalenians the dead were an object of attention and care even beyond death. The deceased was not just dragged to the back of the cave or allowed to lie wherever he fell. Judging by the evidence of burials, positioning, orienting, provisioning with ornamentation and even food, a cult around the dead may be inferred. Even the red ochre may have played a role to ease the tension of passage from this world. By engaging in a ritual of concern and affection, those who remained could seek to appease the spirits, indicate their respect of the dead and control their fear of the unknown.

The frequent finds, far inland, of ornamental snails originating from the Atlantic, the Mediterranean, the Red Sea and even the Indian Ocean document the far-reaching connections which man of the Upper Paleolithic maintained. Quite obviously a modest form of trade must have existed to obtain these luxuries. Yet it is difficult to guess what these central Europeans could possibly have given in return. Obviously the culture attached great significance to these shells from far away and must have gone to great pains to obtain them. These finds would indicate that the economy of the Upper Paleolithic was not exclusively a savage economy of hunting, fishing and gathering. Of course the basis of securing the food supply was the hunt and the gathering of fruit, berries, nuts, roots, mushrooms, seeds and herbs. No doubt man had some need of elementary curative knowledge. Owing to the differences in regional and climatic conditions great variations in the vegetation and the animal life must have made for anything but a uniform diet for Paleolithic Man during the various periods. In the vicinity of the ice fields and especially during the very cold periods the food supply may have consisted purely of meat. The hunt for big game would have required a special measure of courage, skill and foresight. An individual equipped with only a fire-hardened or at best a stone tipped spear is not likely to have attacked a mammoth single-handed. Therefore a considerable amount of planning by a group of hunters based on the habits of the prey and maximizing on its deficiencies and handicaps must have been required. In 1954 a unique find was made in a former interglacial lake at Lehringen in Lower Saxony.[173] The almost complete skeleton of a 45-year-old forest elephant—about two inches taller than its modern descendant—was found with a fire-hardened spear between its ribs, stuck in through its chest. A death-defying hunter must have rushed in under its head and lodged the spear in its chest. The thrust was not immediately fatal. In escaping the elephant probably pushed the prodding spear ever deeper into its chest, finally collapsing at the edge of the lake, where it bled to death, gradually sinking into the soft ground. The hunters probably only cut off a small portion of the kill, perhaps those parts which could be reached most conveniently, hence the missing bones. The chase must have taken them a great distance from their campsite so that the distance which the meat had to be carried must have been considered when the kill was cut up. Bone finds at various campsites and where the kill was first cut up show that one chose those parts of the carcass which yielded the most meat. Of interest is the location of hastily prepared—throw-away—stone tools which were found strewn in the vicinity of the skeleton. Quite evidently Paleolithic Man was practical and did not weigh himself down with unnecessary ballast but made at least some of his cutting tools as he needed them. Apparently the spear was not used as a throwing weapon but rather for thrusting and jabbing. It is most unlikely that the hand axe was used in this context. The risks to the user would have been far too great.[174]

There are indications that during the Upper Paleolithic, perhaps occasioned by regional characteristics, specialized hunts for certain animals took place, for the Saiga antelope, the cave bear, and so forth. Thus in Czechoslovakia the preferred game was mammoth—at Dolni Vestonice 90 per cent of bones found belong to mammoth, while at Předmost skeletal remains of over a thousand mammoths were found. Bone quantities at some sites point to mass hunts for some animals, for instance remnants of an estimated 100,000 horses killed in the course of time have been found at one site.[175] Specialization of the hunt of course need not mean an exclusive concentration, nor is there any need to speak of the mammoth or cave bear hunters as having formed a homogeneous culture because of this preference, as one might speak of a Reindeer Culture among the late Magdalenians in northern Germany. Obvious hunting sites would be the watering places, probably because the game attracted to them provided the possibility of a variety in the diet. In the mountains man would face the challenge of searching the difficult terrain for mountain goat, moufflon, chamoix and ibex. In the lowlands mammoth, woolly rhino, bison, horse, wild ass, antelope and stag would be the focus of his attention. Judging by the popularity which the representation of wild bovines such

Map 5. Settlement sites of the Hamburgians, c. 14,000 B.C.– c. 12,000 B.C.

Map 6. Settlement sites of the Ahrensburgians, c. 9000 B.C.

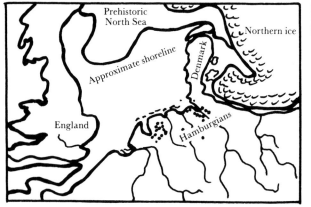

as steers and buffalo enjoy in cave art, they must have played an important role in the real or perhaps even cultic hunt for game animals. The mass hunts are likely to have used fire as a means to compensate for insufficient numbers of hunters, grass or bush fires helping to stampede the herds over cliffs, into chasms and swamps. No doubt man was guilty already then of practicing a waste economy of over-kill. In themselves, however, these mass hunts are not responsible for the disappearance from western and central Europe of mammoth and the woolly rhino during Magdalenian times. Changes in the climatic conditions, although increasingly more favorable to man, made Europe unbearable for these Ice Age creatures and they died out.[176]

The rather contentious suggestion has been made that the cultural preoccupation with the reindeer far exceeds its material and economic value as game.[177] This conclusion is derived from the fact that compared to other animals the reindeer is only rarely represented in the cave art of south-western Europe, either engraved or painted. It is also based on the questionable assumption that the killing of game and the artistic representation of game animals reflects a magical relationship. This is all the more surprising as during the Ice Age two types of reindeer—the smaller tundra reindeer and the larger forest reindeer—are known in Spain, the south of France, the Swiss Alps and the rest of central Europe. On the other hand representations of the reindeer are very frequent as part of *Kleinkunst*—portable art, engravings on articles. There also is some evidence from representations at La Piletta, Spain, that fencing of the reindeer may have been practised.[178] If this was so, then a shift from hunting to butchering may have been emerging. The advantages of 'domestication', of having a ready meat supply, over a laborious search followed by random killing would have been gratifying.

In the north man is so dependent on the reindeer, precisely because of its material value, that one can speak at least of a 'reindeer economy' and perpaps of a 'reindeer culture', since its inventory of artefacts depends almost entirely on the reindeer as a source of raw materials, with only a little emphasis on stone.[179] As such the reindeer economy was a very efficient economy in that almost the entire carcass could be utilized.[180] The origin of the people of this 'reindeer Economy' is uncertain. The culture is represented by two levels, an earlier one, 14,000-12,000 B.C., first identified at Hamburg and therefore termed the Hamburg Group[181] which is relieved by a later Ahrensburg Group around 9000 B.C., more frequently referred to as Ahrensburg Level. Other groups seem to have visited the area around 10,000 B.C.

It is held that some 15,000 years ago various cultural groups, bearers of the Magdalenian, left south-western Europe and in a wide front stretching from England to central Germany moved into the northern lowlands probably following the herds of game to new grazing lands.[182] The retreating ice-fields of the late Würm glaciation made at least a seasonal occupation of the area from southern Holstein to Hannover possible. Apparently, for about 1000 years it was possible for these hunters of the Hamburg Group to winter in the regions east of the Elbe River, all the more convenient since this area also offered winter grazing for reindeer. The mild spell was only a short interstadial followed by a relapse into a colder climate[183] during which the area saw a general return of the reindeer hunter culture—the Ahrensburg Level. Now only the summer hunt was possible in East-Elbian regions.[184] Indications are that the Ahrensburgians no longer sought their winter quarters in the south, south-west or south-east, but on the lowlands now occupied by the southern North Sea—from Holstein to the Netherlands and sometimes even south-east England—where the vicinity of the sea made life more bearable.[185] Some fifty sites have been found on the southern edge of this area.

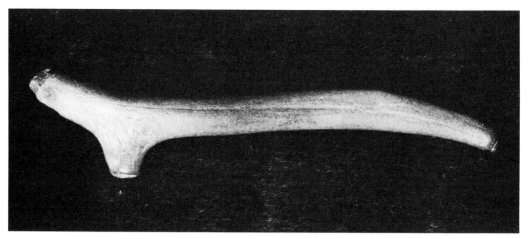

14. Axe of reindeer antler, so-called Lyngby axe, *c.* 10,000–8,000 B.C. from northern Jylland.

The attempt has also been made to trace certain ornamental motifs found on some implements to Czechoslavakia (Předmost) and to the Ukraine thus claiming eastern origins for the Hamburgians[186] and/or the Ahrensburgians, even going so far as to see in them the vanguard of the later north Europeans.[187] However, these eastern origins are not conclusive; on the contrary, the find of a harpoon and of an engraved horse head at the key site of the Hamburgian argues against eastern origins while it favours links with the contemporary south-western Magdalenians.[188] During the late Würm glaciation the lowlands made long-term settlement possible and attractive, thereby facilitating contacts and the transmission of influences by 'neighbouring' older cultural groups, especially from south of the Maas area. Tools of the Magdalenian type, the so-called 'Federmesser', from the west have been located in the north.[189]

It seems conclusive that the two cultural levels are intricately linked to the special economic form provided by the reindeer. The sites of the Hamburgian at Meiendorf,[190] Stellmoor, Borneck and Poggenwisch dating from about 13,500 B.C. demonstrate an almost total, at least seasonal, dependence on the reindeer as a source of survival. Bones and antlers provide the raw material for scrapers, whistles, and skinners. Bone awls and needles are used with sinews for sewing skins for tents, and fat and marrow for softening the skins used for clothing. While the Hamburgians knew how to cut elastic strips from antlers softened by soaking, the Ahrensburgians are characterized by the special type of antler axe, on which the shortened yet sharpened bottom tine serves as cutting blade—the so-called Lyngby Axe (Fig. 14). Part of their arsenal consists of detachable antler harpoon heads as well as harpoon-like arrow heads which separate from the shaft once the head is lodged in the kill.[191] The shaft was thus available for re-use. According to the growth of the antlers the animals were hunted during the arctic summer months, from June to September. Both cultural groups decorated their implements with fishbone patterns, meanders and geometric figures, but as 'art' the inventory of designs exhausts itself in V-patterns and strokes.[192] This area of externals alone must suffice to mark the decline of the Ahrensburg Level.

Around 8000 B.C. the Würm glaciation ceases to be an ecological factor. The change in climate brings about new vegetation and with the coming of new animals the last Paleolithic culture also comes to an end.[193] The tundra changes to forest—the first stone axes are in evidence, the familiar food animals have migrated to colder climates or died out and the new game—red deer and stag—is harder to hunt since it is more easily scared off. This change may have begun as early as the Gravettian when the use of bow and arrows takes precedence over the spear. The nomadic culture based on the reindeer disappears from central Europe.

Had the Magdalenians really specialized to such an extent in their hunt of the reindeer that their dependence on it was not only seasonal but total, that they had become so tied to it for survival that they depended on its movements?[194] That, free to hunt the reindeer they had become unfree to do anything else? That the rhythms of its life had become their rhythms, with no other choice but to follow it or perish? No doubt an extreme view, yet the Magdalenians and the reindeer disappear together from central Europe.

As has become apparent so far, culture at this first stage of hunting, fishing and gathering was static. Contrary to the dynamism of modern cultures, culture based on a savage economy can continue to exist at the same economic level for tens of thousands of years. Thus the innovative refinements which made the Magdalenian period the most significant period of tool manufacture were produced over thousands of years by minds trapped in a Paleolithic framework. Even though artefacts were being produced with foresight, they were only extensions of older basic technical principles. They represent a realization that the strength and the reach of the arm can be augmented by mechanical devices.

However, coincident with the high degree of refinement and sophistication in the preparation of his stock of tools and weapons man of the Upper Paleolithic appears to have crossed a threshold of a different order. It is evident that he has turned his intellectual capacity and the power of his imagination to aspects complementary to the purely functional—his tools are being ornamented. One can take this to mean that he is beginning to prize his tools. From our perspective he is giving them an esthetic value as well. That the ornamentation, consisting of animal engravings for instance, may have had magical connotations has also been suggested, making the so-called command-batons possibly part of a religious magical inventory. However, the whole question of Paleolithic Man's cultic practices is very much a matter of inference and conjecture making for much dispute. Yet if man of the Upper Paleolithic had a 'modern' intelligence, does that not suggest the same power of reflection? In general one has chosen to discuss Paleolithic Man's sense of the aesthetic almost exclusively in terms of his religion, his magic or a combination of both. The reasons for this approach are not difficult to find. With the exception of the cave bear skull ritual or Paleolithic burial practices, Paleolithic Man's artistic expression though not necessarily intended to be considered as art, offers some evidence that the other creatures with which he shared the world were perceived in a new way. Magdalenian sites whether in caves or in the open air point to the presence of cults, of rituals, of symbols, of cultural ceremonies, all indicating an awareness most probably religious in character. It is in this realm of psychic activity that the cultures of the Paleolithic, certainly of the Middle and Upper Paleolithic, do demonstrate development, even though the development took tens of thousands of years.

What fundamental motives, concepts and intentions lie at the basis of this new awareness? The evidence is so fragmentary and so often isolated as to allow only inconclusive explanations and speculations based on possibly deceptive appearances. The responsibility born by each extant piece of evidence is far in excess of the role it may actually have played in its own context, though a mystical intention should not be excluded. The analogy is valid of a modern tourist briefly passing by the highlights of an unfamiliar culture and then being tempted to render a systematic analysis of it with no other frame of reference than his own culture. The only access he would have had was to tangibles, to superficial, observable representations. But what of the cultural context provided by words, acts, gestures, observances, relationships or social attitudes? In trying to systematize the accumulated evidence, twentieth-century thought has been used to provide cohesive rationales,[195] constructing Paleolithic Man's range of psychological activity out of a mist of conjecture. Being aware of the speculative elements in any interpretation of Paleolithic Man's intentions, it is not entirely unlikely that he had the same power of reflection as has modern man. His 'modern' intelligence implies reactions *vis-à-vis* the unknown, *vis-à-vis* the great questions, to be at least similar to the reactions with which modern primitives face the unknown. Anthropological observations of Eskimos, Indians, African, Australian and Asian aborigines still leading a Stone Age existence have been applied to Paleolithic Man in an attempt to shed some light on his rituals, attitudes and beliefs. The conclusions, by no means undisputed, point to a religious content and/or magical practices. In general the interpretations see man of the Upper Paleolithic trying to cope with questions of his survival: how to deal with the uncertainties of life—the weather, shelter, hunt, birth and death, and perhaps most important, how to guarantee the availability of his food supply. These uncertainties must have been a constant burden, imposing sustained pressures on man to seek relief.

It is generally assumed that man of the Upper Paleolithic was capable of projecting mentally and spiritually a metaphysical, transcendental order, abstracted from his experience of the world. Maintaining salutary and profitable relationships with that transcendental order, man at a very early stage will have produced symbols and devised rituals to help him extend bridges from his physical world to his projected metaphysical world, to help him bear his existential crises with a degree of confidence. Through ritual problems can be sublimated, the fear of the inexplicable can be overcome, burdens can be relieved in the knowledge that the appeal to supra-natural powers has been made and that nothing has been left undone which might jeopardize the mystical relationship between man and the source of life. The purpose of the cult then is sustenance. Ritual and magic are to influence nature, to make the forces favorably inclined to those practising the cult, to guarantee abundance. The magical emphasis appears to be on the continuance of and the success in maintaining the food supply. If such interpretations are indeed correct then the primary concern is with the success of the hunt, with the kill, and not so much with the fertility, procreation and multiplication of the prey. In this case a significant intellectual step has been taken, reflected in the assumption that man can influence the world around him.

It would appear that the cave bear cult with its assumed sacrificial elements and other rituals was the first cultural ceremony on record. As a ritualistic exercise its meaning may be sought in terms of a mystical relationship between Mousterian Man and the animals of his environment, in which religious awareness is focused on nature in a spiritual manner—the cult as a means of appeasing such spirits as may be perceived behind things. With modern hindsight, again by analogy with the practices and beliefs of modern primitives as well as through the application of philosophical concepts elaborated in detail since classical times, the behavior of man of the Middle and Upper Paleolithic is interpreted to have been based on beliefs stemming from a view of his world in which at least the animal world was animated, that is to say that a spirit was believed to dwell in the animal. Using this hypothesis it would then follow that if this spirit could be 'captured' as through artistic representation, then the spirit in the beast could also be controlled and the hunt end successfully. It is probably only a short step from these ideas, to notions of always trying to be on the best terms with the Bear Spirit, or the Reindeer Spirit, and others, of dealing with the moods and dispositions of the spirit, of placating its displeasures and angers in order to maintain the salutary relationships. Attempts at appeasing the spirit would then have led man to deposit offerings and make sacrifice—thanksgivings to a benevolent spirit in times of plenty to assure the continuance of abundance, placating sacrifices and offerings to angered spirits in times of scarcity, famine or other natural disasters, to solicit a return to more favorable conditions. One sacrificed bears to the Bear Spirit, reindeers to the Reindeer Spirit, to assuage and console them over the losses necessitated by the need for survival. Admittedly the logic is not compelling. However, the sacrifice then assumes a restitutional function—it is paying homage to life-generating principles. On the slim basis of analogy, Paleolithic Man is credited with having conceived of a transcendental order, of having had recourse to metaphysical suppositions in order to try to solve problems encountered in the physical world, to gain favor with and perhaps even power over supernatural forces which must have had both physical and metaphysical characteristics of being. The evidence to justify the analogy is provided by the cave bear cult and by cave art. The suggestion has even been advanced that the composite drawing consisting of parts of reindeer, wolf, lion, horse and man—the so-called sorcerer from Trois-Frères—is *the* god, being not only a composite drawing but also a representation of the total conceptual composition of the spirit world as a personified divinity. The fundamental question whether man could project a meta-reality beyond himself and his world can only be answered in terms of the above. Unfortunately, it is a circular argument: man engaged in sacrifice and other ritual because he wanted to pay homage to a world of spirits and he had conceived of an animated world because he had engaged in practices which appear to have been cultic in motivation.

As stated previously, it is held that the cultural preoccupation with the reindeer far exceeded its material and economic value as game. Although known from Spain to central Europe it is only a late branch of the Magdalenian culture in northern Germany—the Hamburgian and Ahrensburgian levels—which appear to have developed an economic dependence on it. There was no Paleolithic 'reindeer period' as such. Compared to other hunted animals the reindeer is only seldom represented on the walls of the caves, yet it is a favourite motif on partable objects,[196] which when if passed from hand to hand, as perforated batons could be, probably made them much more of an accessible 'everyman' type of art, somewhat more dynamic even, than the stationary paintings located in the more inaccessible recesses of the caves, associated with restricted rituals engaged in by the initiated and the priest-magicians. However, the preoccupation with the reindeer increases in significance when seen in the wider context of the attention paid to cervides, such as elk and stag, and their prominence during the Upper Paleolithic. An analysis of 300 teeth[197] originating from Spain to Russia and prepared for stringing showed a surprising 25 per cent to be stag, which is all the more significant since the stag was rare. Even more importance can be attached in view of the fact that stag teeth were also imitated in ivory, bone and stone. It is agreed that the stag and elk always were and still are symbols of virility and fertility, treated as surrogates of the male principle and its symbols.[193] Even today there is a flourishing business in antler as the basis for an elixir which promises a restoration of vitality. Across Eurasia many

15. Horsehead, engraved on amber, after *c*. 28,000 B.C.

Paleolithic deposits of stag skulls have been located arranged in such a fashion as to suggest cultic motifs, such as the find of stacked and specially treated stag skulls at Achenheim, just west of Strasbourg.[199]

Of interest in this context are the finds from the Stellmoor near Ahrensburg, where during the late Magdalenian, Hamburgian hunters who skirted the ice fields killed two-year-old female reindeer, placed heavy stones into the chest cavity and then sank them in a pond.[200] While the Hamburgians used each of a number of ponds on only one occasion, their successors, the Ahrensburgians returned to one pond as a settlement site on numerous occasions so that some 20,000 fragments and 1200 antlers have been retrieved as well as evidence of thirty females. As though a continuation of the Hamburgians, the Ahrensburgians engage in the depositing of two-year-old female reindeer.[201] In addition a pole had been erected in the water surmounted by the skull complete with antlers of the oldest reindeer, a sixteen-year-old female. All the fragments of the approximately 1000 others were of younger reindeer. What do these finds indicate? Were the ponds believed to offer access to some other world? Eternal hunting grounds? Were the reindeer being sacrificed to some notion of spirit or divine being? Was it indeed a sacrificial ritual?[202] Is the ritual to be understood in terms of maintenance and a plea for regeneration of the economic basis of the society? Was it fertility magic? Can one even speak of a reindeer cult? Since reindeer society is matriarchal and since the bulls do not travel with the females, is it surprising to find only females? But why only two-year-olds? Were the carcasses immersed in the water to preserve the meat and to protect it from predators, since in the treeless tundra the kills could not be hung? The permafrost made preservation in water unnecessary. In view of the absence of trees, how can the pole be accounted for on which the female skull had been impaled through the mouth? It would have had to be dragged along from the tree line, just like the tent poles. The exact motives of the practice may never be known. Yet there is something intentional about the exercise which allows an interpretation in terms of cult and sacrifice.

From the Gravettian layer in the Weinberghöhlen at Mauern comes evidence of a curious event. On a thick layer of red earth the complete skeleton of an approximately ten-year-old mammoth was found, both its tusks still lodged in the skull.[203] Finding a complete mammoth skeleton in a cave is curious enough if one envisages the tremendous effort it must have required to drag the carcass into it. The mystery thickens though in view of the numerous ivory beads and well worked silex artefacts, dyed red, found scattered about the skeleton and with which the carcass must once have been covered. Many fragments of mammoth skeleton, ivory pendants and bored animal teeth surrounded the central find. The whole arrangement has similarities with the human burial practices of the Upper Paleolithic and it is fair to assume that it was a sacrificial site used by the mammoth hunters at Mauern. The mammoth was becoming ever less numerous during the Upper Paleolithic. Were these Gravettians trying to reverse a natural process, trying to shore up their conditions for life, through the attention to specific ritual? Was it magic or was it religion?

Although Neanderthal Man knew colour and was able to appreciate form (Plate 1a), as indicated by the well-shaped tools found in Mousterian levels, and although the Mousterians carved bone and horn and decorated it with regularly spaced incisions, to date there is really no evidence of representational art produced by them.[204] So far the oldest example comes from a Châtelperronian level[205], that period of transition from Middle to Upper Paleolithic—a representation of a horse's head scratched on a stone (Fig. 15). However, the absence of art objects from any stratum cannot be taken as proof for their non-existence, all the more so since when art appears, it does so suddenly and fully developed, in all categories—painting, drawing, engraving, relief and in the round. The idea that art was introduced only after the fading of Neanderthal Man and with the appearance of his successors is perhaps only a hypothesis. As mentioned earlier, evidence of a new awareness towards his surroundings suggests itself in the practices of man of the Upper Paleolithic. Not only does he seem to grapple with the unknown, but his living environment suddenly appears to be perceived in a new way, as though an adjustment to his optics had suddenly moved the world in which he lived into new focus.[206] It will of course never be known what confluence of factors struck upon the human consciousness, compelling man to represent pictorially a selection of subjects which he had experienced.[207] It is interesting that vegetation, such as trees, or geographic formations do not appear to have interested the artists of the Paleolithic.

Why did Magdalenian Man concentrate on depicting the animals he hunted in his paintings, his engravings and carvings? Was it magic, designed to give him strength and courage to pit himself against the animal world, to gain dominion over nature, to gain the support of the supernatural powers, to predetermine a successful outcome in the encounter of man and beasts?[208] No doubt his artistic activities reflect a purpose, it being pretty well agreed that it was not an exercise in art for art's sake,[209] but it remains inconclusive whether through the representation the food animals gain in sacred significance, thereby reflecting man's efforts to guarantee his survival through the maintenace of favorable ritualistic and magical relationships. If in the imagination the kill can be foreseen one can also grasp it and represent it artistically—that is possible. But is it also probable that one would expect to gain control over it physically? If this latter assumption is acceptable then magic must have played an important role.[210] It would point to the great importance which the artist-magicians would have assumed in dealing with questions of survival. Do the magicians then come into being at this time? Does it reflect the emergence of a group of initiates which wields psychological and spiritual powers, of specialists supported out of the communal food supply to the obtaining of which they have made only an indirect contribution? Is the Magdalenian culture affluent enough to be able to exempt some members of a group from the hunt? Is the culture so rationalized and diversified in its functions as to be able to afford priest-magicians who concentrate on bringing down the game with their mystical-magical powers, who wound it or at least incapacitate it through ritualistic procedures? Can it be generally assumed that a craftsman culture of specialists had evolved, of tool making artists and magician-priests, all more or less exempted from the hunt? Is social stratification emerging? With our hindsight we can certainly see advantages in the more economic and efficient use of raw materials and manpower. The existence of tool specialists can, however, not be readily assumed. The manufacture of artefacts in excess of personal needs implies the possibility of a barter system. The popular idea of magician-priests, of shamans,[211] cannot be supported unequivocally either, although quite naturally some individuals would emerge as leader personalities by virtue of their superior insights and abilities. Similarly the idea of the 'resident' artist-magician can only be upheld if mediocre and poor efforts are ignored. On the other hand, was 'art' something in which everyone was engaged?

The answers to these questions are pertinent to a discussion of Magdalenian spiritual concerns as they appear in Europe as a whole and in the Franco-Spanish area in particular, where the analysis of cave art is intricately linked to magic and religion. In central Europe circumstances are significantly different in that cave paintings are not a factor, since none exist. Whether the artistic 'capture' is intended to guarantee a successful outcome of the hunt is a question which can therefore not even be raised in the German context. To see the representation of animals on portable objects as related to hunting magic seems more problematic than to see it solely in terms of ornamentation. That is not to say, however, that hunting-magic does not play a role.

A latent system of cave art has been worked out drawn mainly from the Franco-Spanish area, a brief summary of which is offered here to provide a framework for the incomplete evidence from central Europe.[212] In the course of 40,000 years and identifiable as five distinct periods, Paleolithic art begins in the abstract and tends towards ever more realistic forms of representation. A pre-figurative period, Mousterian at about 50,000 B.C., knows ochre but no figural representations, while Châtelperronian, c. 35,000 B.C., introduces decorative forms—bones and stones bear regularly spaced incisions, and one sketch of a horse head scratched on a stone has been found. Ochre is used in great abundance. With the Aurignacian, c. 30,000 B.C., a primitive period begins. From now on styles can be identified. Style I, c. 30,000 B.C. yields painted and engraved figures, both abstract and awkward in representation, along with the heads or foreparts of unidentifiable animals, mixed with representations of genitalia. Style II, c. 25,000–20,000 B.C., emerging slowly from Style I during the Gravettian and Solutrean cultures, produced rather uniformly constructed animals to which characterizing details were added identifying the animals as bison, horse, mammoth, and so forth. Human representations were subjected to similar stylizations showing an exaggerated central portion with no relation to the size of the head or arms and legs—the so-called Venus figures. An archaic period, *c.* 20,000–15,000 B.C., witnesses the ripening of Style III, demonstrating a mastery of technique. Painting, sculpture and engraving are of extraordinary quality. Human forms are still large, while heads and extremities are still not in proportion. The Magdalenian culture, *c.* 15,000–10,000 B.C., represents a classical period, identified as early Style IV and characterized by a realism of forms with great attention to accurate detail. It is the climax of cave wall painting. Humans now appear with more modest midriffs, but have neither chest nor head, and no arms. The caves witness an invasion of their depths often only by means of very hazardous access. An advanced Style IV marks a late period, *c.* 10,000 B.C., during which caves are no longer being painted, and art becomes portable, perhaps reflecting a population which has become mainly mobile. Figures become striking in their realism of form and movement. By 9,000 B.C. art of the Upper Paleolithic undergoes a sudden decline. Rare finds show awkwardness and schematization. Style IV ceases while portable art continues for another two to three thousand years.

The same analysis reveals a total cave art 'population' of almost 1800 examples.[213] A breakdown by percentages is interesting: horse 24 per cent, signs 15 per cent, bison 15 per cent, ibex 7 per cent, reindeer 6·5 per cent, stag 4·5 per cent, man 4 per cent, bear 3 per cent, fish 3 per cent, woman 2·5 per cent, cat 2 per cent, bird, mammoth and rhino 1 per cent each, while chamoix, musk ox, wolf, hyena, snake and 'monsters' are represented by less than 1 per cent. These many examples are generally executed with a richness of expression. But even though new examples, especially of portable art, are continually being discovered, yet there is a limitation of themes in that Paleolithic art shows a preoccupation with only three types of subject: animals 78·5 per cent, man 6·5 per cent and signs 15 per cent.[214] Especially the animals are often portrayed with a sort of shorthand, concentrated and even stylized, with a view to producing a striking impression. Even the representation of a group was mastered by the artists, who like the Impressionists had discovered that the flow of movement can be given to a group by dissembling the form, by compressing it through representational treatment, as for instance the depiction of a stampeding herd of reindeer.[215] Here the effect is achieved by the complete representation of the first and last reindeer only, while the rest of the herd is intimated by a *pars pro toto* blur of antlers. It is difficult to believe that a purely aesthetic and creative satisfaction did not also play a role, especially on portable art objects, in addition to possible magic and religious motives.[216] During its peak Paleolithic art is naturalistic art which can stress the minutest details if such are necessary for the characteristics of an animal, at the same time demonstrating the keen powers of observation of the Ice Age artists.[217] In connection with possible concerns about fertility, reindeer bulls are represented in rut, cows and mares are shown pregnant. There is a sense of composition, even of perspective. Although there are some frontal views most of the animal representations, whether on the walls of the caves or on portable objects, are done in profile, showing the animals grazing, running, leaping and even mating. One does not need to read complex motives into Paleolithic art to see that the statements are intelligible, intelligent and elegantly expressed. It is of course probable that the artist is the creator of a message, a synopsis of the dominant feeling for life and its purposes, an essential symbolical summary of the myths of its time by means of which man assures himself of both his physical and psychical presence in the appearance of the form and movement which surround him.[218] On the basis of the evidence it can be concluded that by the time the Magdalenians painted the walls of the caves, engraved their portable objects with animals and produced animal sculptures in the round, they

16. Miniature of a mammoth carved from ivory, found in the Aurignacian layer in the Vogelherd cave near Stetten ob Lontal.

had also developed the power to translate into symbols the physical world in which they lived.[219] It is in this context that there is agreement that the various art forms belong into the religious sphere. Whether at the same time it also pretends to serve a magic function is a matter of dispute. What his art definitely reflects is an extremely complex system very rich in variation pointing to the existence of a mythology. To the extent that Paleolithic art also portrays the merging of human and animal forms, such as the 'sorcerer' from Trois Frères, or the combining of anthropomorphic or zoomorphic forms with signs, it may indeed provide a clue to understanding: in the association of the human form with the sheer physical force of the animal, the human derives superhuman powers which give him access to the supra-natural.[220] Myths originating in the Neolithic Near East bear out this process, and as late as during the nineteenth century the Rivermen, the boat- and raftsmen along the Mississippi, attributed their strength to being half horse, half alligator. It is possible that totemistic ideas are relevant here. The animal is animated and seen to be similar to man. The animal's body can be entered mystically, and although totemistic relationships are complicated systems of spiritual communication they do imply relatedness of being, possibly ancestral relationships with the animal world which can be mobilized to intervene on behalf of man.

Cave paintings are restricted to south-western Europe. In Germany only one cave—the Schulerloch near Essing in the valley of the Altmühl—is known to contain a rock relief.[221] This has created the impression that the south-west is the cradle of art, yet, the small feminine sculptures notwithstanding, the Franco-Spanish area has no animal sculptures comparable in age or quality to those found in central Europe.[222] Sculptures

17. Miniature of a wild horse carved from ivory, found in the Aurignacian layer in the Vogelherd cave near Stetten ob Lontal.

18. Miniature of a big cat, probably a cave lion rather than a panther, carved from ivory, found in the Aurignacian layer in the Vogelherd cave near Stetten ob Lontal.

in the round are rather more frequent outside of south-western Europe, where they can be found all the way to Siberia. In Germany the Vogelherd cave yielded a beautiful series of animal statues, most excellent examples of Paleolithic workmanship, all the more significant since they come from the Aurignacian layer, the oldest archeological stage from which art objects are known.[223] Especially significant are small animal figurines, carved of ivory, such as a mammoth (Fig. 16), a wild horse, a cave lion, and the fragments of a cave bear's or cave lion's head. Originally the mammoth's trunk, now broken off, must have touched the animal's toes. As no tusks are indicated the carving represents a young animal. While the sculpture as a whole is polished, head, shoulders, flanks and belly bear crisscross markings, a definite attempt by the Aurignacian carver to give texture to his sculpture. A particularly graceful object is the wild horse (Fig. 17). Although its legs have broken off, it does not fail to create a very pleasing effect with its combination of gently molded curves, indentations and a boldly and elegantly arched neck. It resembles more a pure-bred Arabian tossing its head than a stocky wild horse. Notches crisscross its body. The Paleolithic sculptor made the attempt to portray the mammoth with legs individually worked out, by perforating the space between the forelegs. Since the hindlegs are broken off one can only speculate that they too were treated individually. On the cave lion (Fig. 18) there is no doubt that the four legs were carved out individually, while the elongated muscular body of the cave lion is also marked with spotlike rows of indentations as well as a few crisscrossing slashes. Other pieces could be retrieved only in fragments. It is remarkable that already in this earliest layer the carvings are so accomplished, all the more interesting since there is no evidence from the lower levels of preliminary, more hesitant beginnings. From a later Aurignacian level comes an additional set of figurines, which by contrast are less rounded, but more relief like and flat, among them a bison of mammoth tusk

19. Miniature of a bison carved from ivory, from the Aurignacian layer in the Vogelherd cave near Stetten ob Lontal.

20. Miniature probably of a woolly rhino rather than of a cave lion, carved from ivory and found in the upper strata of the Aurignacian layer in the Vogelherd cave near Stetten ob Lontal.

21. Grazing reindeer bull, engraving on an antler 'baton', from the Swiss Magdalenian layer in the Kesslerloch near Thayngen, north-east of Schaffhausen.

(Fig. 19), a woolly rhino of ivory, a mammoth made of the kneebone of a horse, and an ivory figure difficult to identify but anthropomorphic in appearance although neither face nor arms nor any other details are indicated. The rows of indentations remove any doubt that this object too has been completed. A very good piece is the woolly rhino (Fig. 20). It too has clear rows of indentations across its back, its shoulders and haunches, while a grid-like pattern of strokes marks its flank. Its ears and mouth are clearly worked out, yet it has no eyes. Its legs have also broken off. Although these animal representations then do not differ in style from those of the earlier Aurignacian level, they do differ in form.

22. Horsehead engraved on stone, c. 12,000 B.C., from Gönnersdorf.

44

Thus while the earlier ones are ivory sculptures in the round, the more recent ones are relief figures with flat undersides made of ivory as well as of the knee bones of wild horses. This difference in the form is all the more interesting since the inventory of stone artefacts associated with both sets of figurines shows no significant differences between the earlier and later Aurignacian. It is probable that none of these statuettes had a purely decorative function, although each piece seems to have its own, self-contained meaning, reflecting at least the presence of esthetic concerns. That the figurines were oriented towards the performance of some task, determined by social and environmental conditions, is therefore likely.[224] By the time of the Magdalenians the trend had fully developed towards the almost unrestrained decoration of portable objects—his tools and weapons. Superb examples of Magdalenian artistic skill are the many reindeer which populate man's tools, such as the 'Grazing Reindeer Bull' (Fig. 21) on the Lochstab from the Kesslerloch at Thayngen in Switzerland,[225] or the many horse heads, jumping ibexes and birds which decorate the spearthrowers of the period, or the beautiful engraving of the head of a wild horse scratched into a flat stone (Fig. 22), found at Gönnersdorf near Koblenz. Through artistic representation the animal world— at least symbolically and perhaps even magically—becomes an integral part of his immediate surroundings.

That figural art probably belongs in the religious sphere is generally accepted, but just what purpose it served has not been established with certainty. Most popular is the view that it is a part of man's arsenal of devices used for the hunt.[226] As hunting magic the pictures and carvings become a type of medium through which the hunters gain control over their prey. This argument is usually based on evidence from cave art where in a few instances 'wounds' seem to have been inflicted upon the painted animal as though in a ritualistic pre-hunt ceremony. In central Germany, at Groitzsch near Leipzig, the outlines of three horses, carved on slate, were found which had deep punctures in the throat area.[227] Again it is attractive to attribute this practice to the probable belief that to 'kill' the model would guarantee the positive outcome of the hunt. The possibility of course remains that it is only the representation of an idea, which need not be interpreted as a means to coerce future events. The evidence is insufficient to assume pre-hunt to hunt relationships. The realism of the representations speaks highly enough of man's powers of observation and artistic skill.

Compared to the thousands of animal representations produced by the Upper Paleolithic, the human representations are few indeed, only several hundred in all. At the same time the human representations are not at all comparable in quality to the animal representations. This discrepancy has encouraged speculations that the reluctance to depict human beings was the result of certain taboos, which saw in all forms of representation an expression of magic and in all artistic form the same processes at work as in reality, so that the depiction of a being or an object anticipated its destruction in the real world.[228] This view would see in artistic representation an act of ritual killing, and in a wider sense hold magic to be the source of art. The fact that the human forms tend to be headless, or faceless or wearing masks could lend some validity to the taboo-theory.[229] Stories of modern primitives refusing to allow themselves to be photographed, the Second Commandment, the belief in the 'reality' of religious figurines or in the power of icons, Oscar Wilde's story *The Picture of Dorian Grey*, or the practice of Voodoo and witchcraft in which the possession of a replica reputedly gives the owner power over the individual represented, all of these would then be derivative of tabuistic ideas originating during the Paleolithic.

The best known human representations are female figurines, the so-called Venus figures, a particularly unfortunate designation since the term, derived from later cultural concepts, suggests that the figurines represent the Stone Age ideal of woman, as well as being earth-, mother-, fertility goddesses. These inferences are all the more risky since one knows nothing definite about the significance which Paleolithic man gave them.[230] So far over a hundred of these female figurines have been found, spread across the entire Ice Age area from the Atlantic to Siberia and datable to the Upper Paleolithic from Aurignacian to Magdalenian.[231] Made of ivory, bone, limestone, black amber, red ochre or clay, most of these statuettes belong to the portable inventory. They have been found in graves, probably intended as burial gifts, and on campsites especially near the inside walls of huts and shelters in niches or hollows, or near fireplaces—the figurine from Dolni Vestonice was actually found in a fireplace. These feminine representations are also known from rock relief.

One of the best known figurines is the 'Venus' of Willendorf (Fig. 23), found in 1908 in the loess deposits of the Danube valley. Carbon-14 dating has the sculpture made about 32,000 years ago.[232] A typical characteristic of many of these figurines are their exaggerated proportions which one interprets almost immediately as portraying advanced stages of pregnancy. From there it is only a short step to see in them representations of fertility, or even fertility goddesses.[233] Before jumping to any such conclusions, even to the casual observer the Willendorf 'Venus' reveals herself to be extraordinarily obese. This little limestone figurine, 11 cm tall and still bearing the traces of red ochre all over, is so fat that her thighs form rings over the knees, the fat deposits circle her ample midriff from buttock to buttock in a wide flabby welt, while her oversized breasts reach down to the level of the navel. Each of her spindly, understated arms is folded across a breast. The fingers of each hand though are worked out individually. Seen from above the head is covered by six rows of a concentric braid-like arrangement, usually interpreted to be hair, which reaches down to a receding chin thus obliterating her face. That this could be the sort of head-dress richly ornamented with the shells often found around heads and skulls has not been considered. The attention to detail—the full calves, dimpled knees, fat thighs, vaginal detail, body folds on front and back, explicitly worked out shoulders, elbows and hands, and especially the intricate treatment given to the head, makes the omission of facial features a deliberate exclusion. That the legs taper downward is of course a realistic observation, but because of other, more stylized treatments, as well as the general—perhaps accidental—absence of feet, it is suggested that these figurines may have been pushed into the ground, or were to be held in the hand.

Figurines have been found at Mauern, the Vogelherdhöhle and at Nebra, near Halle. In the Petersfelshöhle were found stylized headless figurines with holes drilled into the upper end as though intended for stringing (Fig. 24), to be worn as pendants.[234] At Dolni Vestonice similar pendants were found, only this time consisting only of torsos with pronounced breasts. It is not known if these pendants were worn by men or women or both, or why, or if at all. Of interest is a comparison of the figurines from Nebra found in 1962,[235] with equally stylized carvings from Gönnersdorf on the Rhine. In profile they show a slender torso with protruding breast while from the waist to the knee the body is a triangular stylization of the buttocks. The figurines from Nebra are a bit more curvaceous. The real surprise at Gönnersdorf, in 1968, were the engravings in the slate floor tiles of gracefully drawn women shown singly, or behind one another or in pairs, facing one another as though swaying in a supple dance (Fig. 26), and dating

23. Female statuette of limestone, so-called Venus of Willendorf, *c.* 30,000 B.C., from Willendorf, Lower Austria.

from about 10,000 B.C.[236] In appearance they are completely unlike the familiar voluptuous 'Venus' figures. Without heads or feet, they are shapely, straight backed, big bosomed, wasp-waisted representations of femininity, whose hips and buttocks are still pronounced, partly because the figures are shown doing a partial dip at the knee. Again thighs and calves are tapered to form a point. In all, individual examples of the Gönnersdorf type have been found on nineteen sites between the Pyrenees and the Ukraine (Fig. 25). It is interesting that although some 20,000 years separate the Willendorf Venus and her Aurignacian contemporaries from France, Czechoslovakia and elsewhere, from these female Magdalenians, heads and feet are still missing.

It is a common impression that it was the Upper Paleolithic male who preferred his ideal woman to be corpulent. In fact, all types have been found—girlish, slim, graceful, mature, obese, pregnant and even giving birth. Because many of the figurines had been reddened, a link was sought with the festive use of red in connection with burials, and the attempt was made to establish a death–rebirth–fertility cycle in which the 'pregnant' statuettes, as well as the cowrie-shells played a significant role. Whether these figurines were objects used in fertility rites, or represented some archetypal mother-cult or whether they themselves were objects of veneration, as an externalization of fertility or as household divinities, has not been established. The great variety of female figures found in cave art and especially the great scarcity of male figurines, has led to the assumption that the female principle was dominant in the realms of experience and religion, so much so that these old societies are supposed to have been subject to a

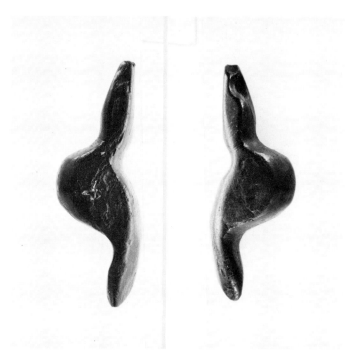

24. Anthropomorphic figurine made of black amber, from the Petersfels.

25. Anthropomorphic engraving on limestone from the Hohlenstein near Ederheim. Three such outlines can be found on other parts of this slab of stone. 'Correct' view is problematic.

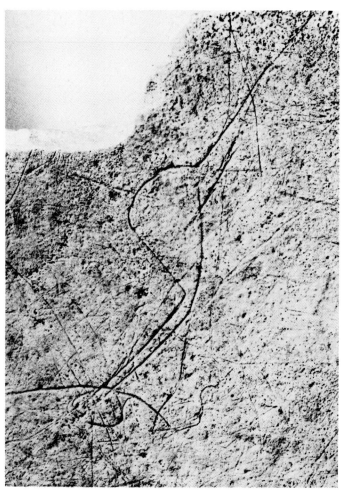

26 (facing page). 'Dancing' women, engraved on stone, c. 10,000 B.C., from Gönnersdorf.

27. Anthropomorphic statuette of ivory sometimes thought to be male, from the Hohlenstein near Ederheim.

matriarchal order where women enjoyed greater rights and bore the responsibilities for cultic acts.[237]

A set of basic questions remains: may these human representations be considered as individuals—the possibility exists that these figurines are portraits or self-portraits—or are they supra-natural beings, are they abstractions, concrete embodiments of ideas and motifs such as fertility, motherhood and sexual principles? Were there also male figurines to be associated with the feminine figures? Did they form couples?

In 1939 fragments of ivory—of mammoth tusk—were found near Nördlingen in the Hohlensteinhöhle in the valley of the Lone (Fig. 27). Only thirty years later were the splinters pieced together. This painstaking effort produced a statuette, 28 cm tall, the largest figurine yet found belonging to the Upper Paleolithic. Dated as 32,000 years old, the sculpture is contemporary to the Willendorf 'Venus'. The reconstruction of the statuette is not complete; too many pieces had disintegrated, thus the head is faceless, the right arm is missing, as is a section of the back, while the genital area is partially broken. The stocky figure is not entirely proportional: seen frontally, the legs and the one arm are shorter than the length of the body would demand. A navel is indicated. Seen in profile the upper arm is powerful and marked with seven horizontal notches, crossed vertically. Slightly angled at the elbow the forearm is short, the hand appears to be clenched. The lower portions of the body are solidly set, hips are wide, thighs are strong, the calves are developed, knees are slightly bent, and the figurine has feet, pointing slightly downward. The figure also has ears, though set too high on the head to be human. When seen frontally the head creates a feline effect, while in profile the nape of the neck is covered as though with a neck-guard, or a mane. The suggestion has been made that the head was covered by a mask, and perhaps by analogy with the 'Sorcerer' from Trois-Frères, this statuette has been dubbed 'The Magician', perhaps in jest, since there is no such evidence.[238] Did he represent a being of higher nature? What do the crossed notches signify? Do they provide a link with the animal statuettes from the Vogelherdhöhle? Are they decorative or cultic? So far they are unexplained.

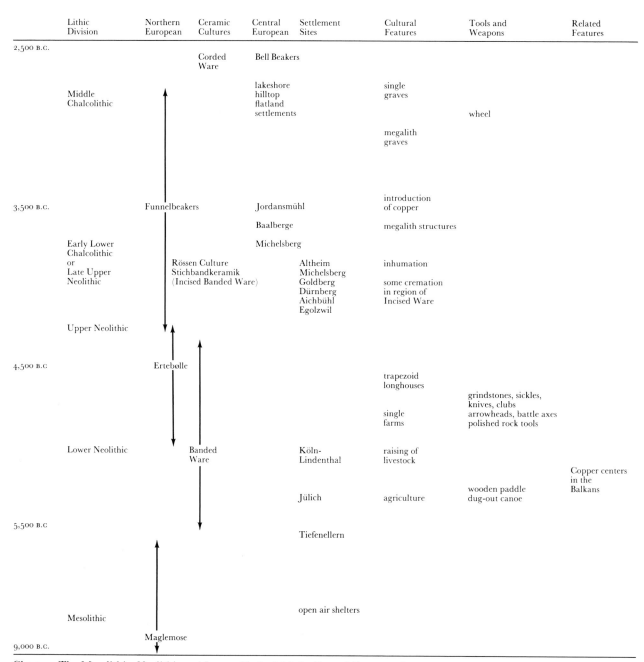

	Lithic Division	Northern European	Ceramic Cultures	Central European	Settlement Sites	Cultural Features	Tools and Weapons	Related Features
2,500 B.C.			Corded Ware	Bell Beakers				
	Middle Chalcolithic				lakeshore hilltop flatland settlements	single graves	wheel	
						megalith graves		
3,500 B.C.		Funnelbeakers		Jordansmühl		introduction of copper		
				Baalberge		megalith structures		
	Early Lower Chalcolithic or Late Upper Neolithic		Rössen Culture Stichbandkeramik (Incised Banded Ware)	Michelsberg	Altheim Michelsberg Goldberg Dürnberg Aichbühl Egolzwil	inhumation some cremation in region of Incised Ware		
	Upper Neolithic							
4,500 B.C		Ertebølle				trapezoid longhouses		
						single farms	grindstones, sickles, knives, clubs arrowheads, battle axes polished rock tools	
	Lower Neolithic		Banded Ware	Köln-Lindenthal		raising of livestock		Copper centers in the Balkans
				Jülich		agriculture	wooden paddle dug-out canoe	
5,500 B.C				Tiefenellern				
				open air shelters				
	Mesolithic	Maglemose						
9,000 B.C.								

Chart 4. The Mesolithic, Neolithic and Lower Chalcolithic in Central Europe, *c*.8500–*c*.2800 B.C.

2. The Ceramic Age: Immigration from Within

The Upper Paleolithic lasted nearly 30,000 years. In Germany the last 3600 years of this period were marked by a brief intensification of the glacial conditions of the late Würm period. This glacial period lasted from about 11,600 B.C. to about 8000 B.C. The geological period after 8000 B.C. to the present day is called the Holocene period. While today the mean temperature for July is about 18°C and the mean temperature for January about −1°C,[1] the late Upper Paleolithic Ahrensburg group of hunters experienced a drop in temperature to an average of about 14°C for July between 10,000 and 9000 B.C., and a drop to a mean July temperature of about 10°C between 9000 B.C. and 8000 B.C.[2]

During that period a fairly small population moved along the rim of the ice-fields, hunting those animals which fed on cold climate vegetation such as mosses and lichens. Their austere lifestyle, industry and economy were entirely adapted to prevailing conditions. Although man had become a highly specialized hunter of game that migrated in herds, using a sophisticated arsenal of weapons, his food supply was almost certainly not secured. His cultic life was probably designed to help him meet such basic crises in his life. Population growth must have been slow, birth rates exceeding death rates only slightly. In general the population of the Upper Paleolithic was stable, not given to wandering far or hurriedly.

After 8000 B.C. Europe witnessed a general improvement in the climate. Mean July temperatures rose to 14°C.[3] For the specialized Ice Age nomad-hunters this 'improvement' had catastrophic consequences. By c. 4500 B.C., the coming of a warmer climate caused the sea and ground water levels to rise; the North and Baltic Sea basins, partly inhabitable, were now inundated; the British Isles only now came to be separated from the mainland; previously dry land now turned into moors and bogs.[4] Pioneer vegetation—shrubs and birch trees—invaded the tundra, only to be replaced in turn by mountain pine. By about 7000 B.C. the forests won out over the tundra. The combination of warmer climate and increasing forestation forced the disappearance of the migratory cold-loving animals, while it favored the establishment of such non-migratory animals as red deer, moose and wild pig. As the warming trend continued, reaching modern mean July temperatures of about 19°C, the pine in turn was displaced by deciduous trees—oak, elm, linden and especially hazel—which now determined the appearance of the forests.[5]

For central Europe the beginning of these post-glacial conditions also marked the beginning of the Mesolithic Period, the so-called Middle Stone Age, an intermediary

28. Amber pendants with non-figurative engravings, after *c.* 7500 B.C., from Ejsing, western Jylland.

29. Club of aurochs bone with engraving of a 'family', after *c.* 7500 B.C., from Rykmaksgård on Sjaelland.

stage during which the old ways of life continued, though modified to suit new environmental conditions of climate, geography, vegetation and wild-life.[6] In Switzerland, for instance, Mesolithic Man continued to occupy small caves and *abri* (rock overhangs). As such the Mesolithic Period was part of a chronological continuum, since the people carried on with the Paleolithic way of life far into post-glacial Mesolithic times, so that it is most difficult to trace a dividing line separating the fading Upper Paleolithic from the Mesolithic. If anything, the transition was marked by cultural retrogression and impoverishment indicated by the deterioration of artistic and flint working techniques.[7] In spite of the much greater availability of wood there was no apparent increase in its utilization. On the other hand the switch was made from the use of reindeer horn to stag antlers.[8] The only significant innovation in the stone industries was the development of microliths, i.e. the preparation of small stone points and blades, either triangular or trapezoid in shape, used for the tipping and/or barbing of hunting and other weapons which thereby become capable of inflicting more severe injuries on prey or enemy.[9] A refinement was the fitting of stone or antler tips or stone blades to wooden shafts or handles by means of wood, bone or antler adapters and couplings. A sleeve or elbow fitting of antler could be easily worked to hold spear points or axe blades inserted at one end while spear shafts or axe handles were fitted into the other end. Binding by means of leather thongs would secure the parts, adding to the efficiency of tools and weapons. In general, however, the bone, antler and stone inventories inherited from the Upper Paleolithic saw no significant additions.

Owing to the perishable nature of the materials used, little is known about the manner in which early post-Paleolithic man sheltered himself against the weather. There is no evidence to suggest that in central Europe he did not continue his Paleolithic ways and erect portable tents or wigwam-like dwellings[10] and roof-over pits and hollows.

Items of curiosity are humming devices of unknown intention—thin flaked stone blades which when spun about on thongs or sinews produce a sonorous drone.[11]

30. Animal of amber, after *c.* 7500 B.C., from central Jylland.

Even in artistic expression the cultural impoverishment is evident. Art was restricted to simple ornamentation by means of notches and engraved designs on such items as amber pendants (Fig. 28), pieces of bone (Fig. 29), antler and ivory, and wood. Only a few animal figurines of amber (Fig. 30) are reminiscent of the great carving skill displayed by man during the Upper Paleolithic.[12] This is all the more surprising when one considers that it is common today to see the advent of Paleolithic figural art as an expression of the step-by-step development of human consciousness, of the unfolding of man's independence *vis-à-vis* his environment, a milestone in his psychological evolution.

It should be noted here that the terms Mesolithic and Neolithic are retained largely as a matter of traditional convenience. The term 'lithic' is actually inappropriate when describing these two periods, if not misleading and outdated. The lithic industries no longer assume that almost exclusive role as cultural indicators which was assigned to them by necessity when attempting to bring order into the evidence left by Pleistocene Man. The evidence left by early Holocene Man is so much more extensive that even the Neolithic flowering of the lithic industries, conspicuous by great refinements, when it comes several thousand years later, is overshadowed by man's alimentary self-sufficiency, social organization,[13] settlement and housing, not to say urbanization, all reflected in his invention and development of pottery. Until the advent of the Bronze Age, ceramic styles and techniques are the cultural indicators, in Europe as well as in the Near East.[14]

The chain reaction which set in during the post-glacial period—increase in temperature, gradual increase of forestation with accompanying decrease in tundra areas, the establishment of a stationary forest fauna replacing the migrating steppe and tundra animals—brought about a reduction in nomadism and an increase in a limited sedentariness. For the Mesolithic hunters the terrain became ever less penetrable until their hunting grounds were restricted to the less fertile sandy soils. The food supply was still dependent upon hunting, fishing and gathering. The new game, however, had to be sought out, stalked and hunted down. Lying in wait for red deer does not guarantee results even if their customary trails are known. In underbrush the throwing spear, harpoon or bow and arrows would be of only limited effectiveness, while the game itself is too easily startled to allow the hunter to come close enough to use his lance. It is not known if dogs were used in the hunt.[15] Only along the shores of the North and Baltic

55

31. Dugout canoes, after *c*. 4000 B.C., found in the Weser river near Bremen-Farge.

Seas did a few groups adjust better to life in post-glacial conditions, establishing shoreline settlements along lakefronts, on ponds and river banks, using peninsulas, islands and elbow bends in rivers for added protection.[16] Along the water's edge man had made a most significant innovation; by splitting a log, burning it out with red-hot stones and embers and then working it with a stone axe, a hollowed-out watergoing craft could be constructed (Fig. 31). The oldest such dug-out was found in Holland, datable to about 8000 B.C.[17] A paddle from about 7000 B.C. has also been found in northern Germany.[18] Great heaps of mussels indicate that certain seafoods were a staple in his diet,[19] while large accumulations of hazelnut shells would point to man's continuing activities as a gatherer. It is apparent that man enjoyed varied foods, very high in protein. No doubt, edible roots and greens provided at least some vegetables, but only berries would have offered a welcome relief from a somewhat monotonous diet.[20]

At Dyrholm in Denmark split human bones have been found.[21] The splitting of bones is usually associated with the extraction of marrow. This find would then suggest that a form of cannibalism, perhaps with ritualistic intent, was practised during the Maglemose period, as the Mesolithic is called in Denmark.

While central Europe persisted in this static economic and intellectual framework of cultural development till about 5000 B.C., significant changes were taking place in the Ancient Near East,[22] especially in that region referred to as the Fertile Crescent, an area arching from the shores of the eastern Mediterranean to the southern reaches of Anatolia, into Mesopotamia—the Land between the Rivers Tigris and Euphrates.[23] There the coincidence of good climatic, geological and botanical conditions favored the emergence of those dynamic cultures which first made the transition to agriculture and the herding of livestock.[24] Thus Anatolia knew the dog and the domestication of sheep and goats—up to 60 per cent of the bones found stem from sheep and goat kids, which suggests the butchering of males for meat and the raising of females to supply milk and cheese.[25] In Egypt, cattle and the donkey had been domesticated in predynastic times, while in Mesopotamia the dog, several types of sheep and goat, cattle, the pig and the donkey are in evidence from as early as 8000 B.C.[26] These same cultures first refined polishing techniques for stone implements, developed ceramic industries and moved towards social organizations in urbanized societies. All of these innovations are the characteristic indicators of the Neolithic period, a term applied to that stage in human civilization which precedes the introduction of metal industries.[27]

Probably the most important factor promoting the Neolithic developments in the

Near East is provided by the natural conditions of growth for certain cereal grains. In the Fertile Crescent, barley and early forms of wheat, as well as flax, grew as wild grasses and were at first harvested by gatherers.[28] Only with the identification of irrigation ditches can one safely assume deliberate cultivation of foodstuffs. It is of significance that even in historic times the annals of Mesopotamian kings register with pride their efforts to extend and improve the system of irrigation. It is an interesting question whether the cultivation of the land and the keeping of livestock led to sedentary settlements in village communities, or whether innovative building techniques using durable, weather-resistant materials such as stamped clay and air-dried brick as well as timber contributed to more stationary settlements, which in turn brought about regional overhunting and excessive exploitation of available resources, thereby making the deliberate development of supplementary sources of food a necessity. The latter appears to be the case. Ancient Near Eastern archeology has shown that it was at first a village population of hunter-farmers who shifted from a gathering to a producing economy, thereby introducing the Neolithic to the Fertile Crescent by 9000 B.C.[29] Harvesting and the problems of storage associated with it would eventually make forms of urbanization necessary.[30] Large and unwieldy carved vessels of highly polished stone as well as heavy grinding blocks which have been found indicate a reluctance to move too frequently. In fact the Tell (Arabic word for hill) cultures of the Near East indicate that favorable sites were not abandoned. Instead, new buildings were erected where old ones had collapsed or had been torn down, until, in the course of many centuries, the settlement rose on its own hill to dominate the surrounding plain. Vertical incisions into these artificial hills have provided the archeologist with virtual calendars and diaries of human occupation, as the stratifications can be 'read' chronologically by proceeding upward from the lowest to the uppermost levels. As everywhere, refuse provides inventories which show the development of Neolithic cultures and their use of artifacts, plants and animals. As early as 8000 B.C. the site at Jericho was such an urban center.[31] The indications in the Near East suggest that the need to satisfy the demand for food and to escape from the uncertainty of circumstances induced man to take measures which would secure his food supply through planning and active personal intervention in nature, by resorting to agriculture and the raising of livestock to supplement his activities as a hunter and gatherer. It is apparent then that the cultural changes and innovations which mark this Neolithic period as being different from the Paleolithic and Mesolithic are based on an assessment of given circumstances, an exploration of possibilities, resulting in conscious judgement. These superior insights were developed by a population living in a somewhat restricted part of the world, from which the cultural influences radiated as far as north-western Europe.[32] However, when a pebble is thrown into a pool the ripples it sends out are not all in the same phase, nor is the activity as intense on the periphery as at the point of origin. Similarly not all parts of the world which experienced the Neolithic were at the same stage of development at any given point in time.[33] Of course, the coexistence of phases persisted for thousands of years. Yet in spite of its many aspects, its regional and chronological diversity, the Neolithic does represent a cohesive stage in the development of civilization.[34] This fundamental transformation of man's whole life-style was not based entirely on economic motives and considerations but was also rooted in the realm of his maturing critical attitude and the ensuing increased awareness of himself and his world. One can detect a desire for self-sufficiency and a reduced dependence on chance and circumstance, a need to be able to expand the framework of his intellectual, religious, cultural, economic, social and technological existence in a stage before philosophy.

It took about four thousand years, to the second half of the sixth millennium before our era, for the Neolithic to come into reliable evidence in central and northern Europe.[35] In fact the fully developed Neolithic cultures did not come about until central Europe came under the influence of the moist Atlantic climate.[36] In accordance with the diffusionist theories, it used to be held that the Neolithic evidence spread from Anatolia to the Balkans and the Danube region[37] and from there in a continuous sweep towards north-western Europe. The calibrated Carbon-14 dates obtained in this region, however, demonstrate that the Neolithic cultures of the Balkans and of the middle and lower Danube were not derivative cultures dependent on the cultural achievements of the Aegean, of Anatolia and the eastern Mediterranean; the Balkan and Danubian Neolithic and early copper-using cultures predate those of Greece and the Aegean, as well as those of the eastern Mediterranean.[38] The 'cradle' of European civilization is located instead in the plains of the Danube and the river valleys of its tributaries.

Of the several early Neolithic peasant cultures which dotted south-eastern Europe, two have to be singled out: the Starčevo culture, with early uncalibrated dates of about 5200 b.c.,[39] ranging between approximately 6000 and 5200 B.C. in calendar years,[40] and the Vinča culture with early uncalibrated dates of about 4290 b.c.,[41] 4426 ± 60 b.c.,[42]

Map 7. Direction of the Neolithic influence, c. 8000 B.C.–c. 4000 B.C.

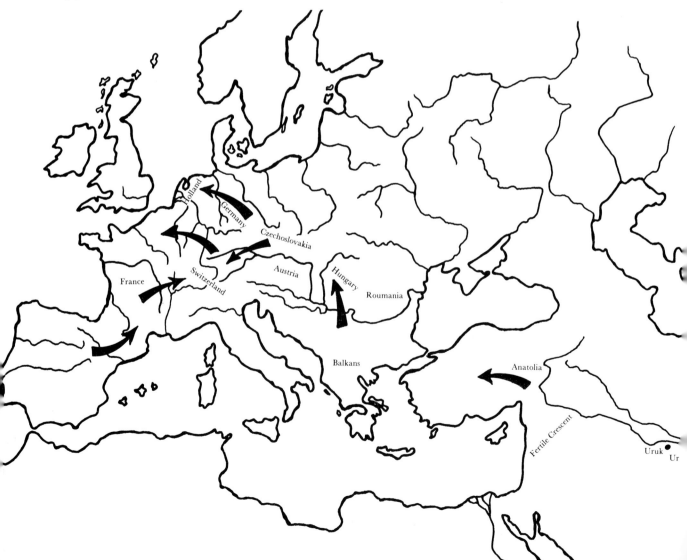

32. Human head, fragment of a figurine, Banded Ware period, after *c.* 4400 B.C., found near Meindling in Bavaria. Human representations are rare west of Bohemia.

33. Lug beaker with white paste incrustation from Ludanice, Moravia, after *c.* 4000 B.C.

calendar dates ranging from approximately 4000 B.C. to 5300 B.C.[43] Both of these sites were located north of the Danube in the Banat in Yugoslavia, part of the great, fertile plain drained by the rivers Danube, Tisza and Sava. The Vinča culture is seen to be a development from the Starčevo culture. The sites of this Danubian region are characterized by tells, those artificial elevations created by centuries of settlement debris.[44] The cultural evidence includes a distinct pottery of monochrome hemispheric forms, such as bulging bowls[45] decorated with angular (Fig. 33), or more frequently, curvilinear 'spiral meander' patterns[46] which will be the distinguishing feature of the central European Banded Ware Culture; polished stone shoe-last 'axes', which might also be hoes or plow-shares;[47] and flint sickle-blades and implements for grinding grain.[48] Grain bins and bread ovens have been located at Starčevo.[49] Whether the shoe-last was a hoe or a plow-share, the implement will have induced the farmers to use it on the soft loess and chernozem—black earth—soils and obliged them to seek out such soils as the cultures expanded.[50] Agriculture was complemented by the raising of livestock. The evidence indicates that this area accomplished the synthesis of a livestock–cereal economy which allowed the settlement and cultivation of the dry loess soil and the penetration of the mixed oak, pine, hazel, elm, lime and birch forests.[51]

Additional extraordinary accomplishments fall into the period of the Vinča culture: possibly the independent development of copper metallurgical techniques, several centuries earlier than in the Aegean and more or less simultaneous with such developments in the Near East; as early as the Starčevo culture, the production of small zoomorphic and anthropomorphic figurines of clay; and thirdly, the use of incised markings on pottery and other clay objects.[52] Thus awls and other small objects of native copper belonging to the Vinča culture were made before 4700 B.C., while cast

59

shaft-hole axes were being produced by 4000 B.C.[53] Of those some have been found throughout the Carpathian Basin and in Bohemia.[54] As will be pointed out below, figurines did not generally get transmitted into central Europe west of Bohemia.[55] The incised markings have been interpreted as signs and as a form of proto-writing,[56] an expression of local needs originating in a religious context. As signs or as seals they may have been made in the course of religious ceremonies, to be destroyed at their conclusion.[57] They were probably not part of a generally understood code.

From the Balkans and the Danube region the Danubians expanded north-west through Hungary into Lower Austria, Moravia and Bohemia, following the plains into southern Germany, Switzerland—also subjected to influences from the south-west—into Alsace and the Paris Basin, while a northern prong crossed the mountains into central Germany and the Netherlands.[58] Denmark, Sweden and Great Britain were not settled by peasant populations until after 5000 B.C.[59] In the early phases cultural innovations were probably not borne by migrating tribal groups but by expeditions in search of raw materials and the exchange of goods. By acculturation, Neolithic attitudes, cultic practices, ideas and the effects of technological innovations would be adopted by Mesolithic populations, while they retained their roving life as hunters and gatherers.[60] It would follow that younger generations in search of their own land would in time migrate into those areas[61] opened up by a vanguard, and that there would be war. The colonization of America could serve to illustrate the methods used even in Neolithic times.

The settlement of central Europe proceeded relatively rapidly.[62] By avoiding areas not favorable to human occupation, the early Neolithic cultures spread in far-reaching sweeps from one base area to another.[63] That the cultivation of cereals was introduced to Europe from the east is certain. What is not known is the manner in which these cereals were introduced. Pollen analysis has demonstrated that grain pollen differs in size from that of wild cereal grasses. It has also been shown that Europe lacked those cereal grasses in post-glacial times from which food could be derived. It is therefore of interest that the Federsee Moor in southern Germany has yielded grain pollen from the earliest period of mixed oak-hazel forestation.[64] This means that long before there is any evidence at all of a Neolithic cultural presence there is this botanical evidence of cultivation in the area. Similar pollen finds have been made in central Germany. Though natural climatic factors may have played a role in depositing such pollen, man's involvement cannot be discounted. In a moor near Satrup, south-east of Flensburg in Schleswig-Holstein, spade-like tools of wood have been found from which agricultural activities can be assumed.[65] After c. 6000 B.C. the first flat stone hoes appeared.[66] This fragmentary evidence would, however, suggest that the Neolithic movement to the north-west did not command the entire cultural inventory. With successive waves of new people came the knowledge of agriculture and the raising of livestock, the cultivation of legumes, cereals, flax, of weaving, ceramic skills and refined techniques for the working, and especially the polishing and drilling, of stone. These innovations, as well as the forms which they gave to their houses and settlements, their graves and their burial rites, their ornaments, would appear to have come into being sequentially rather than simultaneously, no doubt the result of assimilated populations and the synthesis of their ideas. One can speak of a pre-ceramic Neolithic, since pottery as an indicator appears late on the scene, not until the Upper Neolithic. Thus the oldest and first uniform style of Neolithic pottery in central Europe, the Banded Ware, can not be dated back to the time of the first colonization. It can be identified only at a stage when most cultural characteristics of the Neolithic were already fully developed.[67] The uniformity of pottery styles would suggest strongly that a number of cultural syntheses had taken place justifying the concept of a Banded Ware culture, borne by a dominant part of the population, which in all probability treated the Mesolithic natives with anything but compassion. There is evidence that, as with Near Eastern practices, human sacrifice was sometimes included among the votive offerings as part of the burial ritual.[68]

The extent to which the hunt had been displaced by the butchering of livestock is indicated by the finds from sites of the Banded Ware culture, which show that more than 90 per cent of the demand for meat was met through the butchering of cattle, sheep, goats and pigs, of which cattle provided 60 per cent of the bone finds, belonging to animals between the ages of three and seven years.[69] This suggests that they were raised primarily for their meat rather than as a source of dairy products. Sheep and goats were probably raised for that purpose. Since the animals were butchered soon after they had reached adulthood, one can conclude that the selection depended on whether they were likely to survive the winter.[70] Here too it appears that domestic animals were imported during the colonization, since wild forms of the species were not native to those areas of central Europe settled by the Banded Ware culture.[71] The cattle were much smaller—cows stood 140 cm high, steers 160 cm—than the native bovines.[72] However, because the variety of sizes remained constant over thousands of years, that is to say, since there is no natural deterioration of the stock, no natural reduction of size through excessive inbreeding, crossing with wild stock must have been taking place, although more by accident than by man's design. There is then no breeding in the sense of aiming for superior strains but merely haphazard encounters between straying domestic cows and curious aurochs bulls. Of domesticated animals, dogs, cattle, pigs, sheep and goats are in evidence. The castration of bulls was practised, which raises the question whether oxen were employed as draught animals or beasts of burden, perhaps to ride, since oxen have really very little other use. Did they then also know the wheel and use it on vehicles? It seems to have appeared only shortly before 3000 b.c.; till then sled-like devices were used for hauling.

There is no proof that the sheep was kept for its supply of wool. It stood about 60 cm high, while goats were about 65 cm high. The domestic pig was smaller than the wild pig,[73] and all of the domestic species were smaller than they are today. The horse was still wild and was hunted as game, not being domesticated until post-Neolithic times. That the dog enjoyed a special status is indicated by frequent evidence of specific burials. Although there is no evidence of the stabling of animals, the traces of sheep and goat droppings on settlement sites allow the conclusion that the animals were perhaps kept inside the settlements during the night for reasons of security. This might explain why villages were fenced.[74] The animals which Neolithic Man would encounter in their wild state were beaver, badger, fox, wolf, bear, hamster, hare, deer, elk, moose, aurochs, bison, wild horse and wild pig. No doubt they all contributed to his supply of meat, as did wild ducks and geese and a type of heron, as well as swamp turtle, carp and sturgeon. Mussels and sea snails appear to have been in demand more for their decorative value than as an enrichment of man's diet. That the hunt plays a subordinate role is evident from the distribution of bones to be found in the refuse pits—only about 6 per cent belong to wild animals, reptiles, fish and fowl.[75] It can of course not be determined what proportion the supply of meat constituted in the over all diet.

Beside the keeping of domesticated animals, agriculture is Neolithic Man's main

34. Scratch plow, after *c.* 4000 B.C., found near the Weser and Lesum rivers near Bremen.

activity in central Europe. The people of the Banded Ware culture engaged in a mixed peasant economy. It is from them that the European peasant cultures of the Upper Neolithic developed after 4000 B.C. Preferred areas of settlement were the end moraines and loess areas deposited during the glacial periods, regions of maximum fertility, with a soil structure which made the use of the scratch plow—at first only a sturdy branch (Fig. 34)—a practical device with which the soil surface could be ripped open.[76] However, the hoe of polished stone or flint was the actual agricultural tool.[77] Its significance as an implement is demonstrated in that it figured prominently in the grave equipment.[78] That not all regions were in the same phase is shown in the area drained by the river Ems in northern Germany, where hoes are absent, but where arrowheads were part of the grave inventories (the bows and arrows not having survived owing to their organic nature).[79] Evidently not all Neolithic groups considered farming a priority. Some may also have subscribed to the limited nomadism of herdsmen.

Of interest are some votive statuettes and discs, which have been found in a settlement of the Upper Neolithic in Transylvania. These clay objects bear figural representations and signs modelled after the style of the Uruk period in Mesopotamia dating from about 4500 b.c. However, while the Mesopotamian originals were clearly inscribed, the Transylvanian designs were no longer understood as writing, but at most as pictorial or symbolic representations and most probably only as ornamentation.[80] This example demonstrates a rather universal process: whether borne by migrating splinter groups or transmitted through contacts, the further a cultural impulse or set of impulses moves away from the point of origin, the more it is diluted and weakened; it loses its creative thrust, its original wealth and complexity are dissipated, it is estranged from its original intention and meaning until it becomes a rigid and empty tradition. The surrounding cultural context is alien, new situations demand new solutions, but the impulse has lost its ability to respond, the aims of its carrier have become different and old forms and designs yield to new necessities and in general revert to earlier functional forms. What remains are more or less isolated regional characteristics. It is by means of such a gradation that distinct stages of successive colonizing movements can be determined. Colonizing outposts make do with essential attitudes and functional implements designed to guarantee subsistence, while secondary waves can be and are less restrained in their inventories. While the primary colonizers are content to attain rudimentary forms of existence aimed primarily at survival, later settlement stages proceed with a further, more extensive occupation of the land, for instance, and the development of an appropriate culture which has its own forms and motifs.

It is attractive to place into the Neolithic the beginning of the rivalry between those who have and those who have not, those who are culturally more advanced and those less so. While the Paleolithic reflected man's preparedness to accept the environment and to adjust to it using adaptive techniques to secure the food supply, at the same time promoting non-aggressive inter-group contacts, recommending cooperation rather than hostilities, Neolithic attitudes suggest a complete transformation of human behaviour. Neolithic Man's deliberate intervention in his environment appears to be paralleled by social aggression, by war. The new relationship to his surroundings seems to have brought about new concepts of value and awakened thoughts of property ownership. This more keenly felt self-awareness, referred to earlier, apparently included the intentional appropriation by force of the belongings of others. Thus the history of ancient Mesopotamia is marked by recurrent invasions of tribes who left their austere lives and descended as conquerors from the mountains to the north and east into the fertile and luxuriant plains, formed a new high culture, were assimilated with the indigenous population, and suffered a decline, only to be overcome in their turn by a new wave of invaders. For several thousand years each new wave of conquerors was first attracted to and then conquered by the lush Neolithic cultures and the possibilities of life which they offered.

That aggressive interaction among groups as a component of the Neolithic way of life is demonstrated by rock paintings of eastern Spain and northern Africa which depict battle scenes among archers and executions. It is certain that the process of acculturation did not always proceed by peaceful means. As new areas were caught up in the sphere of the Neolithic cultural upsurge, aggressive thinking appears to have been adopted as an accompanying phenomenon. The indicators of such belligerent attitudes are held to be the geometric microliths, those triangular and trapezoid stone flakes which had already appeared during the late Upper Paleolithic and which were used to tip and barb spears and arrows designed to inflict serious injury. It is held that they were reserved for weapons to be used in combat.[81] It is also held, with regret, that while the other positive accomplishments of the Neolithic spread only slowly and with great effort, belligerence—a negative side effect of this progress—spread easily and rapidly, being adopted even by those populations still roaming about as hunter-gatherers who had no immediate intention of adopting the remainder of the Neolithic life-style. Other indications of man's war-like activities came about during the Upper Neolithic from which period defendable positions and fortified settlements have been discovered.[82] But more important is the presence of weapons as part of the grave inventory, demonstrating the evolution of specific types of weapons, such as battle axes, clubs and daggers. In fact the graves best equipped with funerary gifts belong to warriors severely wounded or killed in battle, who were obviously singled out and specially honored for their valor in combat.[83]

Can the modern suggestion that war is an outbreak of dammed-up, repressed, aggressive tendencies be reconciled with human behavior during the Neolithic? It is probably easier to apply to the Neolithic the idea that war is an expression of some awareness of a 'territorial imperative', based on language. The new economic forms and ensuing lifestyles would lead to increases in populations, to the crystallization of regional tribal groups, to the solidification of given social orders, forming strong links to certain regions, leading to the eventual emergence of regional dialects and languages. The effect would resemble that of the Biblical Tower of Babel—a general cultural experience giving way to the diversification of regional particularism. While the individual or the small loosely-knit group of individuals, when left to pursue a free and unimpeded existence, tends not to be a killer, the large group, especially when regionalized, urbanized and organized, develops a group mentality that differs markedly in its behavior patterns and rules of conduct. Having no identity of its own other than what it is not, it relishes its otherness, assuming it readily to be manifest superiority. Having no will of its own it falls easy prey to incitement and flights of fancy, and is vulnerable to inflammatory language, being only too easily convinced that the enforced acculturation of others is really in everyone's best interests. Not self-satisfied, nor bent on the preservation and administration of what it has, the 'civilized' group has a latent urge to expand and to acquire. It is not content with cultural transfer through contact, but rather seeks colonization, domination and acculturation.

It would seem that when the building of the great Ziggurat, the Tower of Babel, that first government-inspired make-work-project, came to naught, the energies harnessed to challenge the heavens were set free to seek a more modest target, each in his own confused way. Man became the victim of his own aggressiveness. Perhaps for the first time he invested a critically active consciousness, an alertness which questioned events, intervened in nature and reshaped it to his needs. He justified his actions by means of intellectual attitudes which divided the world of appearances into a personal 'I'—those appearances with which he could cope—and a religious 'thou'—those natural phenomena which he admitted to be subject to forces larger than himself.[84] This intellectual upheaval was the real 'Neolithic revolution'. It set man on his errant way to discover his own inner autonomy.

The inventive spark which induced man to dry clay and then to bake it in fire—the latter probably by accident—had ignited man's imagination already during the Upper Paleolithic when he molded his terracotta figurines. It took over 20,000 years, however, before he applied that knowledge to the manufacture of functional vessels and containers. During those 20,000 years man in central Europe seems to have forgotten these skills so that when they reappear in Europe they are part of an imported inventory. The earliest known pottery is Japanese, from the eighth millennium B.C. South-east Asia and the Near East know it from a slightly later period. What the proportions of accidental discovery and human inventiveness were, or what the sequential process was that led to the invention of pottery, can only be surmised. There is only occasional evidence to suggest that man first of all lined baskets in clay.[85] There is little existing pottery with such tell-tale patterns. It is significant only that man had the insight to realize the potential which working with clay offered him, to use this technology to his advantage. The most commonly held belief is that man made this invention when the need arose to store his harvest and to cook his food. As long as he ate his roots and greens raw and roasted his meat on a stick over an open fire, or preserved it by hanging it up to dry, storage in waterproof containers was not necessary. Only when it became essential that his grain harvest be kept dry and protected from rodents, and that his produce be made edible and halfway palatable by grinding and cooking, did the need for receptacles recommend itself. Such is the logic of hindsight.[86] Most certainly man did not stumble across the usefulness of clay in his search for a material more durable than wood, leather, bone or stone.

From an archeological standpoint, clay has the singular advantage that once burned it never degenerates into dust by itself, unlike other materials available to prehistoric man. Furthermore, though it may have been copied or imitated by neighboring groups, pottery was hardly ever traded, so that it is found in regionally compact areas.[87] It is this fact which justifies the designation of cultures on the basis of the ceramic evidence and its inventory of shapes and ornamentation. Areas within the sphere of that culture's influence will reflect that influence by means of adaptations; for instance, the basic form may be the same, while the ornamentation varies surprisingly. Important for questions of dating, deviations from established forms and designs may indicate a sequence of phases.

For central Europe the Banded Ware culture was the first consistently Neolithic culture. From about 5400 B.C. onwards it dominated central Europe for the next

Map 8. Core area of the Banded Ware culture, *c.* 5400 B.C.–*c.* 4400 B.C.

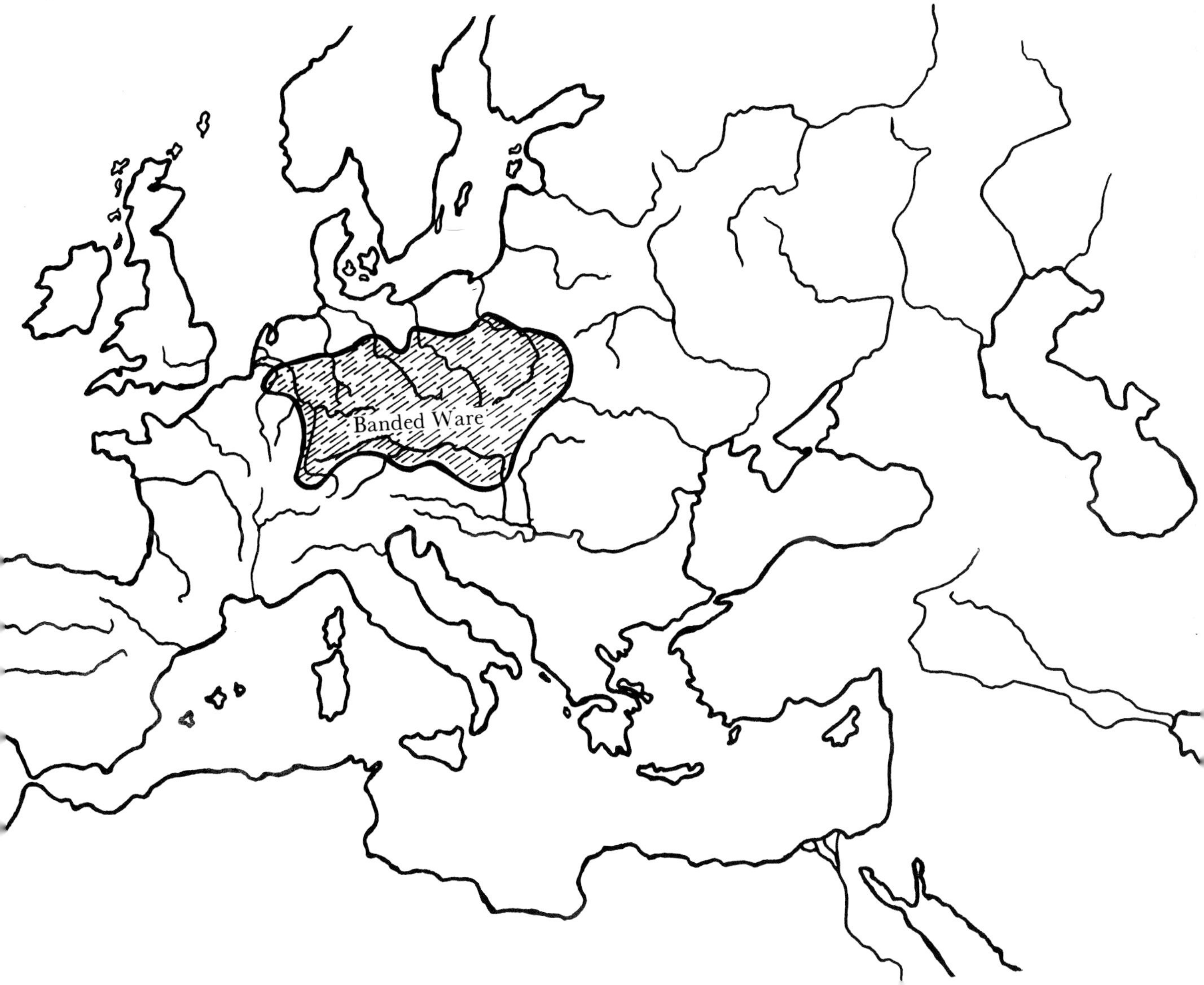

thousand years.[88] Within the Neolithic framework it was characterized by typical funerary practices, stone tools, manner of settlement, shapes of houses and above all by that particularly characteristic ornamentation of pottery from which the name of the entire culture derives: scratches, grooves and relief patterns arranged in bands of waves, spirals, meanders and curves (Plate 1b). Two elements of style differentiate between a main characteristic and a later derivative technique. While the earlier designs represent linear bands—*Linienbandkeramik* (Banded Ware)—the later technique arrives at the suggestion of bands through rows of incisions, impressions, notches and punctures—*Stichbandkeramik* (Incised Banded Ware). This later technique was already a prolongation of the banded style dating from a period when the Banded Ware culture was in the process of being fragmented into regional cultures, which after centuries of internal modification become identifiable as the Rössen and Michelsberg cultures, to name only two.[89]

The earliest forms of Banded Ware came from the core area of the culture located in Moravia, western Hungary, Lower Austria, Bohemia, central Germany, the upper Danube region, the area of the upper Rhine, the area drained by the Neckar, and in Hesse. The pottery inventory displays a great variety of forms: jugs, deep bowls, flasks and large storage jugs (Fig. 35). Most of the bowls have a definitely flattened base to facilitate standing, others are equipped with pierced lugs for hanging, or with knobs or curved handles for safer handling. The range of forms includes unusual shapes: bowls standing on several human legs, thin-waisted double conical bowls, flat-bottomed steep-walled vessels, twin vessels, occasionally with spouts, even two- and three-necked flasks. All of the pottery is characterized by good workmanship. It is the ornamentation which gives the pottery its name—engraved bands of spirals, waves, meanders and zigzag row patterns, diverse spandril patterns, rows of interlinked triangles, chevrons, double axes, wing motifs and comb patterns, arranged in single, double or even triple rows.[90] The decorative techniques include representation of human and animal figures depicted on the walls of vessels either in relief or engraved, but these play a subordinate role. An additional, perhaps transitional type of ornamentation shows the application of red or white color paste, sometimes arranged in alternating red-white-red designs (Fig. 36). Considering that the central European contribution to Neolithic pottery is a black gloss finish, typical for Banded Ware, the use of vivid red and white would contrast sharply and effectively against the dark background.

The evolution of techniques and styles is so imperceptible that stages can not be differentiated except through the later expansion into new settlement areas.[91] In general crude vessels were not ornamented, while for the finer ware a better quality clay was used and finished with a high gloss slip to reduce porousness.[92] The ornamentation is evidence of an aesthetic sense, not as highly developed, incidentally, as was that of the Magdalenians. During the late phase the engravings gave way to decoration solely by means of painted lines and designs. The last stage once again resorted to the design of bands by means of stylus-like impressions showing rows of triangular fields filled with strokes, rows of incisions, comb pattern imprints, furrows and more complicated geometrics—Incised Banded Ware (Fig. 37).

The people are often referred to as Danubians. The evidence of their occupation of central Europe comes from thousands of sites. With a slash-and-burn method of claiming, occupying, clearing and then cultivating the land,[93] they first shifted their settlements westward along the Danube, then across the Rhine to the Seine, north to the Baltic Sea, then to the lower Oder River, along the Vistula and finally south-east into

35. Banded Ware pot, raised ornamentation, *c.* 5400–4400 B.C. from the Jungfernhöhle at Tiefenellern near Bamberg.

36. Banded Ware flask with incised ornamentation and white paste incrustation and with raised knobs, *c.* 5400– *c.* 4400 B.C. from the Jungfernhöhle at Tiefenellern, near Bamberg.

37. Vessel of the Hinkelstein group from Worms-Rheingewann, *c.* 4500 B.C. During the late period similarities with incised lineband ware beginning to appear.

the Ukraine to the Dniester River. The archeological evidence shows the core area to have been located between the river Maas in the west and Lower Austria and Moravia in the east, the most extensively colonized region being that south of the Baltic—eastern France and the area north-east of the Carpathians not having come under the influence of the Banded Ware culture until its latest stage. The evidence also shows that in spite of its derivative dependence on the Lower Neolithic culture of south-eastern Europe, the Banded Ware culture of central Europe was successful in gaining individuality, cultural uniformity and stability.

That a warrior attitude was an essential mark of the Neolithic cultures is demonstrated by the Banded Ware people, who were not groups of peaceful farmers but people with rather belligerent dispositions, if their grave equipment is being correctly interpreted. From the earliest phases weapons figure prominently in the male burials of the Banded Ware culture—battle axes, clubs and arrowheads of stone (Fig. 38). It is especially noteworthy that battle axes, sometimes so small as not to be useable, are also found in children's graves. This practice would suggest that these axes must also have had a use as status symbols, perhaps of a dominant group, beyond that of being mere ritualistic grave equipment.[94] It is apparent that these stone clubs and axes enjoyed particular significance in that they were the very first stone implements through which a hole had been drilled,[95] probably to receive a handle (Fig. 39). For weapons to be the first tools to be singled out for this refinement would indicate that a way of life in which they assumed such a priority must have been central to the Banded Ware people. Although some tools were bored during the Banded Ware period, most bored tools belong to the Upper Neolithic.

38. Pierced stone axe of polished rock, associated with Incised Ware, c. 4500 B.C., from Königsfeld near Bamberg.

39. Pierced stone-disc club, associated with Incised Ware, c. 4500 B.C., from Konradshofen near Augsburg.

40. 'Battle'-axe of polished rock, after c. 4000 B.C., from Dillingen-Pachten.

69

41. Flint harvest knives and cutting edges for setting in a blade of organic material, *c.* 4000 B.C., from Barkaer, Jylland, Denmark.

Beginning with the Banded Ware period, polished rock tools came into use. While axes of flint were unknown, hard rock came to be employed, especially basalt and granite (Fig. 40). Wedge-like stones were roughed out by chipping and flaking using the familiar lithic techniques, ground against a wet stone base until smooth, and then rubbed until shiny.[96] Many variations of large wedge-shaped tools were manufactured, up to 25 cm long and 10 cm wide at the blade. That they were used as hoes or plows or plowshares is hypothetical. Their use as wood-working tools or as weapons is more likely. However, it is not easy to imagine wooden handles attached to them since no holes had been drilled through them. It has been suggested that they were used as cross-cut axes, hoe-like, perhaps as hand-held choppers. A very high quality of flint is exported from around Maastricht to wide areas of central Europe to be used for scrapers and knives with which to work wood or bone. The blade preparation resembles that employed on core tools during the Upper Paleolithic.[97] Some of the smaller stone blades show a high gloss such as can be produced only by the cutting of straw or other plants containing silicium. Finds suggest that two or three such blades when fastened to wood or antler would form sickles or harvesting knives (Fig. 41). The grain was usually cut just under the ear. Using a smaller stone the kernels were crushed rather than ground to flour on a millstone. This flour must have contained a quantity of sand. It is significant that the Banded Ware people, though peasants, never included such sickles among the grave inventories, although grindstones were a common funerary gift, both for the grinding of grain and for the pulverization of ferrous oxides yielding red color, such as limonite and hematite, the latter producing a blood-red color. These millstones sometimes provided headrests for the deceased. Occasionally the graves were reddened, reminiscent of Paleolithic customs. While the men were accompanied by weapons, the graves of women yielded ornamental shells.[98] In general men and women received the same funerary ritual treatment. The provisioning of the graves with food raises the customary questions about the belief in another life. The evidence from central Europe, however, is so fragmentary that any discussion of religion during the Banded Ware period would have to rely almost exclusively on information obtained in the Near East and the Balkans. Some of the graves in Germany and Czechoslovakia contained stretched-out corpses which had their arms extended over their heads. Since that position resembles that of some figurines the gesture must have cultic significance. Some burials placed the corpse face down, probably as an indication of the deceased's rejection. Puzzling is the burial of partly dismembered skeletons, such as some separate head burials. Thus a child's head was found in a Banded Ware vessel. There is evidence that the corpses were clothed or wrapped up, perhaps even tightly wound, judging by the position of the legs. Here too the fear of the deceased's return may have been a factor. Already during the period of the Banded Ware culture there is some evidence that cremation was practised, a ritual which was to become the predominant form of interment of later cultures.[99]

In spite of evidence to the contrary it has been claimed that the Banded Ware farmers were peace-loving vegetarians, who did not possess any distinctly war-like weapons, and who practised peaceful coexistence with the indigenous population of hunter-gatherers among whom they settled. From Tiefenellern, near Bamberg, comes a different example of the social interaction between one group of Banded Ware people and Mesolithic natives.[100] A 'treasure hunter' digging in the Jungfernhöhle, near Tiefenellern, found nothing but shards, stone tools and a large number of bones both human and animal. A lengthy investigation could find no evidence that this cave had ever been inhabited, or used as a burial site. The pottery shards dated the depository use of the cave to the period of the Banded Ware people. One of their settlements was found in the vicinity. The finds of the Jungfernhöhle expand the area of Banded Ware settlement into a region where they would not normally be expected to have lived. In view of their usual selection of fertile, soft alluvial, loess and chernozem soils for settlement—owing to the fragility of their agricultural tools—this site on the stony, poor agricultural soil of the Franconian Jura is unusual, especially since the regions not immediately suitable for tillage were still occupied by the Mesolithic hunter-gatherers.[101] The deposits in the cave suggest that at least for a short period the relationship between the conquerors and the conquered was one of sacrificers and sacrificed. Altogether the remains of forty human skeletons were identified: 11 adults over eighteen years of age, 5 juveniles over twelve, 10 children between five and seven, 8 between three and four, 6 infants under one. Among all the skeletal remains the extant bones were all well preserved, but there were only 20 skulls. This would suggest that at least some of the skulls received a different treatment, perhaps separate burial. The long bones of the adults and juveniles and all the skulls show intentional openings, with the usual implications. The interference of animals must be excluded since they would not have avoided the children's bones. Some of the bones show burns. Another sinister detail is that all the jaws are without incisors and canines, all of them apparently removed by force. In all some 500 teeth are missing. Since the jaw bones show no tendency to reclose following the extraction, the teeth must have been broken out either just before or shortly after death. There is some evidence that death was violent—the skulls were broken. Analysis has shown that the skulls were related to those of the Ofnet cave.[102] These inhabitants of the Jura were delicate, older Cromagnids, who had come to form pockets in the Mesolithic population. No doubt the older population continued in the same area for some time, since new superimposed populations do not necessarily change or exterminate the older established groups. The probability is that the older inhabitants fell victim to cultic rituals, including processes related to cannibalism. It is possible that the move to poorer soil by these Banded Ware people was not voluntary and was induced by rival groups.

The manner of settlement belongs to the most significant characteristics of the Banded Ware culture. It clearly marks the difference between these people and their neighbors, while at the same time clearly contrasting this period with the preceding and succeeding periods. From Moravia to Holland the Banded Ware people erected dwellings of such a uniform design that one can suspect a standardized 'building code'.[103] These houses were large rectangular structures 5–8 m wide and 20–36 m long, built of five rows of posts, of which the three inner rows bore the roof, while the two outer rows supported the walls of interwoven rods, branches and switches of hazel, birch and poplar, packed with clay. The surfaces were smoothened and whitewashed on the interior side (Fig. 42). These longhouses were usually positioned in a NW–SE or N–S direction, with the northerly end being much more solidly constructed—the posts were sunk in a ditch and placed much more closely together. All posts were secured through rocks wedged in at the base. The posts themselves were of oak placed 1·5–3·5 m apart. Since there were more posts than would be needed to support the roof it is probable that some of them were used to support a storage level under the roof. It appears that the southerly part of the house was used for storage, while the northerly part served as a stabling area for the animals, leaving the central section for human occupation. The logic is compelling:

Map 9. Core area of the Banded Ware culture, c. 5400 B.C.–c. 4400 B.C.

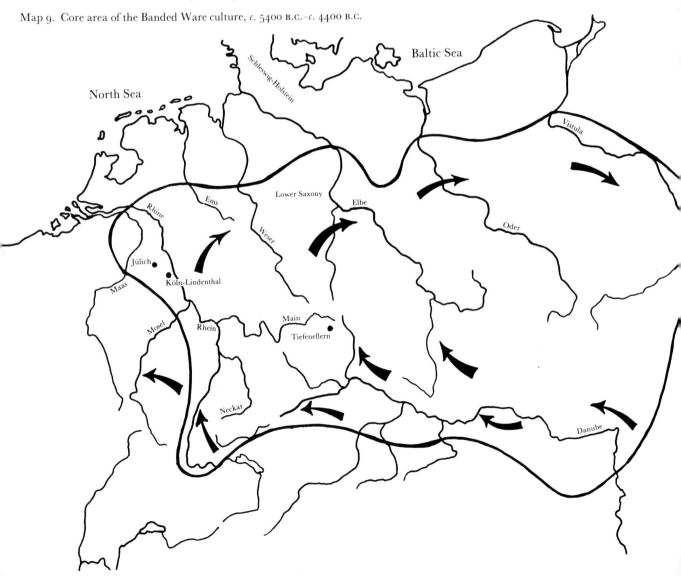

42. Model of a Banded Ware village after *c.* 5000 B.C., reconstruction based on excavations at Köln-Lindenthal.

man placed the warmth-generating stable area between himself and the direction of the prevailing winds. Farmhouses along the North Sea from Holland to Denmark have retained this building arrangement to this day. Some ovens and hearths of the baking-oven type have been located. It is probable that the length of these houses was arrived at through the gradual joining of modules which originally had their individual purposes. Some smaller units have been found having the same width but only 8–10 m long, and having only three or four rows of supporting posts. It is held that the larger structures allowed an occupancy by extensive social units, such as clan-like families, numbering from thirty to sixty members including children. The structures suggest an efficient use of available living space and resources. It would follow that all activities were of a communal nature.

The reason behind this design is probably to be found in the isolated locations in which these longhouses were built.[104] Even though the sites reveal clusters of longhouses, investigation has shown that the foundations were laid sequentially over many years, rather than simultaneously, since many of the outlines made by the post-hole markings overlap. Since the ground was razed preceding each new reconstruction, no house floors with tell-tale indications have been preserved. However, the refuse deposited in the ditches created when the clay was dug to form the walls yielded ample evidence of pottery shards. Considering that untreated wood can be expected to last some twenty-five years, the occupation of a site over a period of 400 years would produce only about sixteen outlines, so that the 160 longhouses located on a loess area of 240,000 m² near

73

Jülich in the Rhenish brown-coal district would have no more than a dozen buildings occupied in the course of a generation.[105] This circumstance has led to the conclusion that instead of living in villages, the Banded Ware people were generally scattered across the land in settlements of one or two longhouses located in a circular 'yard' up to 100 m in diameter contained by a ditch.

The brown-coal surface mining operations on the Aldenhovener Platte, a slanting plateau 10 km south-west of Jülich, revealed unique cross-cut profiles, providing insight into the cultural stratifications stretching over an entire landscape.[106] Originally it was a loess landscape deposited during the Würm period. The advent of the Atlantic climate and of forestation allowed humus levels to accumulate. Since erosion and relocation of the alluvial deposits began only with the Neolithic, the soil stratification indicates that the first agricultural settlers did not establish themselves until after c. 5000 B.C. At Langweiler 2, one of the open pit mines, a Banded Ware settlement, established over an area of 35,500 m², has been excavated revealing the remains of twenty-one houses, fences and many pits.[107] Of these pits, 123 contained shards of Banded Ware pottery. A great number of the house plans overlapped, pointing to a period of occupation of that site from earliest Banded Ware times. Four types of houses had been laid out without any regular plan of location. Six of the houses revealed a slightly trapezoid form,[108] a characteristic of the succeeding 'architectural' style. The largest of the houses, 30 m × 6·4 m, and the only undisturbed house plan, was attributed to the earliest period of settlement. The pits of various depths, shapes and sizes served as cellars, for storage, as ovens and as work areas.[109]

The ceramic evidence displayed the extremely rich imagination of the Banded Ware potters. Six main forms consisted of flasks, jugs, bowls and a category of individualistic shapes, including bowls with feet. There were ten types of lugs and handles and seven types of barbotines. The vessels were decorated on the neck with up to five circular lines, patterns of dots and/or strokes between the lines, or on single or double lines; dotted patterns of large or small dots or semi-circles, running around the necks of the vessels, or crowded together to form whole fields of dots, thirty-two types in all. The bellies of the vessels bore variations of spaced or crowded oblique lines, ladder patterns, with irregular stroke or sieve patterns between emphasized borders, wavy line patterns, or a wide range of 'domino' designs. In all, the potters used twenty-two types of ornamentation to decorate the walls. In addition they used another forty-two types of complete and forty-two types of incomplete motifs. As though that were not enough, the potters knew thirty-three different interruptions and nineteen different terminations of the line bands.[110] The lithic inventory is also very extensive in its variation.[111]

Botanical analysis shows the food source to have been obtained from such plants as einkorn, emmer, millet, lentils, linseed, and setose poppy, as well as hazelnuts and wild fruit and berries, in all fifteen wild plants and 'weeds'. The food supply was secured by the annual cultivation of large-kerneled grains, such as einkorn and emmer. None of the Banded Ware settlements along the Rhine grew barley.[112] Einkorn and emmer were always found together, suggesting that they were sown together. Brome grass, a type of oats, made up 37·9 per cent of the combined grain samples, hence it was not cultivated deliberately, nor was millet grown intentionally—not till the Iron Age. Lentils were rare. Pea seeds, lentils and poppy have been identified, but their deliberate cultivation could not be confirmed.[113]

The most frequently used woods were ash, oak, and maple, but elm, hazel and spruce were also present, hazel sticks being used to form the core of the wattle walls. No doubt such wild fruit as the apple, pear and plum, as well as the berries of hawthorn, mountain ash and sloe and many others, were enjoyed when in season.[114]

In this settlement too, the largest house was contained by a ditch. In the beginning the Banded Ware settlements were not fortified, which points to a peaceful period. Only towards the end of the Banded Ware period did more resistant enclosures, earthworks, moats and palisades come into being.[115] When the site at Köln-Lindenthal revealed that a moat ran through the outline of a foundation it became clear that the moat dated from a later period.[116] Why the defensive encapsulation? Was there an increase in belligerence? Were the hostile attitudes a result of a scarcity of supplies or of an overabundance which had led to an increase in population? Were the population pressures the result of internal expansion and inner colonization? Was the indigenous population striving to reclaim its former position? No doubt they must have watched the behavior of these people with some bewilderment. Or were new waves of colonizers searching for land to settle? Was it perhaps the invasion of a whole new people that spread hostile tensions through the land? As yet there is no trace of new immigrants.[117] It is not known why the population would see fit to fortify its settlements.

With the end of the Banded Ware culture the single farms are gradually abandoned in favor of villages, perhaps evidence of an increased need for protection or as an early indication of a new type of community life—single family units coordinated within a larger social framework. The earliest of the villages already belong to the later Rössen culture.

At the time of its greatest expansion, the Banded Ware culture reached from the Black Sea in the east to the Netherlands in the west. The cultural evidence suggests it to have been a rather uniform culture throughout, in a way never again known in Europe, spread by small groups of immigrants whose technological advances must have been readily apparent to the indigenous population. The superiority of a producing economy over a savage economy practised by hunter-gatherers must have recommended itself, leading to the adoption not only of this economic innovation but of the modes of settlement as well. Compared to the previous rate of development, this cultural change in the course of only a few hundred years is rapid change indeed. It is probable that the adoption of the economic form was followed by the adoption of tools, pottery, techniques of ornamentation, manner of settlement and perhaps even religion. Of the latter, however, there is no direct evidence.

There is some disagreement as to the extent of involvement by the native populations in the settlement of the good soil of the elevated mixed-oak forest regions, especially of the fertile loess areas of the Bavarian and Austrian Danube plains, the Neckar region, the Main valley, the Rhine-Main area, the Lahn-Mosel district, southern Lower Saxony and the area between Cologne and Aachen. It has been suggested that the native population was not involved, but that the Banded Ware people, who during the sixth and fifth millennium B.C. settled almost exclusively in the heavily forested alluvial and black earth—chermozem—areas, moved in around the hunter-gatherers settled on the lighter soils.[118] Why the latter should voluntarily have been content with poorer soil is not clear. According to the evidence, around 5000 B.C. the native hunter-gatherers of northern Germany appear to have adopted the new economy based on agriculture and the raising of cattle. The new lifestyle associated with it is reflected in cultural innovations. A certain enrichment indicates that the northern population was more readily adaptable than those further south.[119] However, by 5000 B.C. only very few groups continued to cling to the savage economy south of the German central highlands. After

5000 B.C. special developments soon became apparent in various areas of Banded Ware settlement on the basis of which the gradual evolution of regional groups can be observed. Thus the so-called Rössen culture began to assert itself in Germany not only in those areas formerly occupied by the Banded Ware culture in the German central highlands between Rhine and Elbe, the Rhine-Main area, the Neckar region and along the Upper and Lower Rhine, but also in areas previously not occupied, even in such uninviting regions as the Eifel. There is no evidence that the Rösseners were a new group of peoples. The impulses, therefore, which induced the populations to occupy the poorer soils, as at Tiefenellern in the Franconian Jura, must have been strong indeed, and must have entailed confrontations. No doubt this move must have affected a change in economy and in lifestyle, perhaps signaling a turn to increased cattle breeding.[120] However, from styles of pottery markings alone, it is impossible to say if such stylistic differences also represent economic and social changes, perhaps indicating no more than differing adjustments to various environments. Unfortunately the evidence in the form of tools, food remnants, burial rites, house construction, or the form and location of settlements, is too scarce to allow conclusions about socio-cultural changes. The transition appears to have been of only short duration—perhaps of a few decades only—at the beginning of the fifth millennium B.C.

The Rössen culture owes its name to a village near Merseburg, in central Germany. It used to be put forward that the Rössen culture was native to central Germany.[121] It is most probable though that, especially in south-west Germany, the Rössen culture is linked to late phases of the Banded Ware culture, while *Stichbandkeramik* appears in the

Map 10. Rössen culture, *c.* 4500 B.C.–after *c.* 3500 B.C.

INCISED WARE

Rössen

RÖSSEN WARE

Goldberg

Aichbühl

43. Model of a longhouse erected by the Rössen Culture after *c.* 4800 B.C., based on excavations at Bochum-Hiltrop, Hillerberg.

eastern regions of the Rössen culture.[122] Both the Großgartach culture near Heilbronn in the south-west[123] and the Stichband Ware of east central Germany and Bohemia provide links with the previous era. On the other hand, stone tools and house construction of this transitional period already point to the Rössen culture.

As noted above, with the end of the Banded Ware culture the isolated large family dwellings come to be complemented by closer settlements. At the same time the pattern of settlement shifts: villages come to be located on higher ground, thus the Goldberg settlement near Aalen, a Rössen village located on a hill and fortified by a ditch and a palisade, is typical for many such villages located on protective elevations.[124] Shards found on the peaks around Salzburg are evidence of defensible settlements in that area, while ceramic evidence on the Dürnberg near Hallein, famous for its salt, points to salt mining there already during Upper Neolithic times.[125] The fortification of sites becomes a characteristic during this period.[126]

Another departure from the customary settlements of the Upper Neolithic are the numerous sites, some fortified, located along lake shores, especially along the smaller lakes of Upper Swabia, such as the Federsee at Bad Buchau, where the settlements on the southern shore near Aichbühl yielded the most information,[127] or at Egolzwil on the Wauwilersee in Switzerland.[128]

Although it would be stretching the point to speak of 'architecture' during the Upper Neolithic in central Europe, one can speak of the building arts—wall building, timber work, thatching, and so forth—especially in view of the evidence of an esthetic sense. Thus the villages of the Rössen culture indicate that the exterior clay surfaces of the walls were not only white-washed, but also decorated with the zigzag, spiral, arch and complicated meander designs akin to those applied to Rössen pottery.[129] In general Rössen building types are closely related to the isolated, large trapezoid longhouses, up to 85 m long, slightly convex, the narrower end facing north-west, descended from the Banded Ware period (Fig. 43). These familiar forms remained in use by other

77

contemporary ceramic groups, such as the Stichband Ware people of east central Germany, Bohemia and along the Vistula in Poland.[130] In west central Germany, at Bochum-Hiltrop, there is ceramic evidence pointing to the continued occupation of the site by both Banded Ware and Rössen Ware people.

Quite different is the type of building used in the fortified Goldberg settlement in the south-west of Germany, where the houses were small, of more or less rectangular construction, resting on three rows of posts, 5–11 m in length and 3·5–7 m in width, with the walls of split logs or beams and packed clay set in foundation trenches.[131] The houses were positioned either NW–SE or NE–SW. Each of a total of seven houses consisted of two rooms, the fore-room being smaller, with the entrance located either on a corner or in the middle of the south side of the building. The stone tools used by the inhabitants were the same as those used by other groups, while their pottery was Rössen Ware as well as a type akin to that found at Aichbühl[132] and Egolzwil further to the south-west.

The lakeshore settlements at Aichbühl and Egolzwil have yielded extensive information about building techniques.[133] In all about fifty foundations have been uncovered in the two areas and although they are not all necessarily contemporary, they did form cohesive village units. The village at Aichbühl yielded remnants of twenty-two buildings which must have housed some 180 people.[134] The peat of the moor having preserved the logs and timbers, complete floor plans came to light. The houses at Aichbühl had not been erected on pilings. Early photographs show that the floors of poles and split logs rested on ties placed directly onto the peat.[135] This floor was then covered with sheets of birchbark which in turn was covered with a layer of clay. The houses averaged 5 m × 8 m in size, were divided by a separating wall—perhaps of straw—into a smaller fore-room and larger back-room,[136] their entrance always facing the lake, with an unroofed 'porch' of similar construction as the floors, providing a solid footing in front of the house.[137] 'Bridges' linked these platforms. It was on this site that the preservative function of peat was first appreciated by the excavators, since organic matter dating to the Mesolithic period was found here, evidence of man's repeated, if not continuous, occupation of the site from as early as c. 8000 B.C. Neighboring villages were erected on pilings (Fig. 44), not in the water as used to be believed, but on the marshy shores of the lake.[138] One corner post was found to be 6 m long of which 2.65 m had been driven into the soggy ground. It has been estimated that one house at Aichbühl required 150 to 190 tree trunks, while the entire village would have required the felling of about 3500 trees.[139] Some of the houses yielded baking ovens and/or hearths, as well as millstones. Along the sides of the back-rooms were found 'benches' of clay, which have been interpreted as beds. Analysis of the site points to a continuity of occupation as well as established principles of ownership of the parcelled village lands.

Some time between c. 3550 b.c. and c. 3150 b.c.,[140] i.e. between c. 4400 B.C. and c. 3900 B.C., there existed at Ehrenstein near Ulm a Neolithic village of about 30 houses located on an oval site, some 120 m long and 85 m wide.[141] Dendrochronology showed that the settlement had existed for a maximum of about 100 years. During this time it had burned down completely four times. Following the last fire the site appears to have been abandoned. The village had flanked a stream, the Blau, which ran through a stand of willows and alders. In laying out the village, the settlers appear to have taken the trees into consideration, so that the houses were placed among the trees, for protection and shade perhaps.[142] Since the ground was not firm, branches were thrown down to increase its firmness. Positioned N–S, the houses rested on longitudinal ties, 75–115 cm apart, covered with lateral logs, mostly 10–15 cm thick. Such a 'raft' was then

44. Model of a lakeshore settlement as built on Lake Constance in southern Germany during the Neolithic, *c.* 3700 B.C.

covered with a layer of lime-clay, also used to fill in cracks, then with a layer of birch bark and finally another layer of 8–10 cm of clay.[143] In the earlier phase the walls were of wicker, later of split oak planks. Upright logs have also been observed.[144] Once covered with clay, the wattle walls were agout 9 cm thick. The presence of post holes, up to 1 m deep, would suggest that the houses had a saddle roof, the gables facing south and north respectively. House plans resemble those at Aichbühl in size, arrangement and furnishings.[145] A porch of timbers and stamped clay on the southern exposure extended the house into the 'street'. Trees often prevented the laying out of a regular plan; consequently the space between houses was not consistent. The 'streets' were solidified by means of sticks, ashes and especially fired clay and kitchen remains. To keep the clay floor indoors clean, the soiled surface was scraped off and tossed into the street.[146] As the floors were removed, the street level rose. That circumstance, as well as the weight of the superstructure and its inhabitants and furnishings, caused the house to sink gradually and unevenly, a fact demonstrated by the compensating thicknesses of the clay floor applied to maintain the living surface level.[147] To escape the moisture seeping up, new floor 'rafts' had to be laid out with birch bark insulation against the wet, causing the whole village to rise, until the last habitation level was 2 m higher than the first,[148] leaving a stratification not unlike those found in the tells of the Balkans and in the Near East.[149]

The pottery made here is evidence of high quality workmanship. Though still built up by hand without benefit of rotation, the potters achieved wall thicknesses of 3–4 mm on vessels 30 cm in diameter.[150] The presence of Tulip Beakers points to an association with the later Michelsberg culture.[151] The lack of any stylistic development would support the archeological evidence that the settlement had only a short lease on life.

The settlement at Aichbühl yielded another element of interest pertaining to the development of the village community—it had a village square on which there was a central building similar in construction to the other houses and standing markedly apart from them. Its individual position warrants the conclusion that it must have served some special communal function. At the same time the presence of this building

79

suggests that the village structure was not merely an accumulation of buildings, but rather formed a unit of particular significance in which one central building was assigned a common social and/or cultural function.[152] This development of a new form of settlement during the Upper Neolithic marks the end of a development which began as an isolated communal structure during the period of the Banded Ware culture.

It would appear then that the era during which Rössen Ware was the dominant style of pottery was not at the same time dominated by one coherently co-ordinated culture with consistent cultural indicators. Rather it was a loose association of cultural groups which spread the cultures of the Upper Neolithic.

While the Banded Ware culture had penetrated only to the northern edge of the German central highlands, the Rössen culture colonized the regions to the north taking the fully developed lifestyle of the Upper Neolithic-to Schleswig-Holstein and Denmark (Fig. 45).[153] In the west, although several sub-groups existed, eastern France and the Rhenish area along with its tributaries produced pottery collectively known as Rössen Ware. In the east, comparison with the late *Stichbandkeramik* of Bohemia and east central Germany shows that Rössen Ware has some similarities to the Stichband Ware. Although stone tools and ornaments point to connections with this culture, it has been established that Rössen Ware did not evolve from Stichband Ware.[154] It suggests rather the adaptation of certain stylistic techniques as a new cultural group encountered an older group, already firmly established. Northern Switzerland yields pottery contemporary with Rössen Ware from south-western Germany, especially of the type found on elevated sites. However, the Egolzwil, and to some extent the Aichbühl lakeshore cultures manufactured pottery which was much more limited in range—generally unornamented and bulbous in shape—and this is interesting, much more akin to the ceramics produced in south-eastern France and Liguria, especially related to a western and upper Italian group.[155]

Rössen Ware is characterized by footed bases, achieved either by preparing a flattened base or by having the bowl terminate in a molded stand (Fig. 46). The squat vase-like bowls and ball-shaped beakers either bulge out from the base, then narrow slightly above the shoulders into a gently curved neck, to end in a gentle flange above the neck, or they sweep out in straight lines from a flattened base to assume shapes similar to those described above, or resemble the inverted base of a decapitated cone. If the vessels

45. Model of longhouses of the Rössen type, after *c.* 4000 B.C., as erected in Denmark at Barkaer on Jylland.

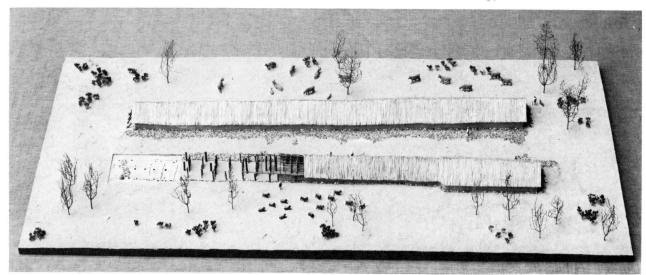

46. Pottery of the early Rössen culture from Oppau near Ludwigshafen, *c.* 4400 B.C.

47. Fragment of Rössen Ware, after *c.* 4400 B.C., from Westhausen.

are ornamented then the designs are deeply embedded, double rows of horizontal, oblique or vertical indentations, similar to those made by a goat's foot, set closely together, occasionally interrupted by inverted V patterns or linear designs in the area of the neck, with contrasting bands of impressions to emphasize the shoulders, occasionally enriched by a zigzag pattern around the underside of the bowl. These designs usually cover the entire surface (Fig. 47). Remains of incrustation in the indentations indicate that the sense of embellishment went beyond that of creating an aesthetic effect through varied textures but also through the use of color which covered the closely knit indentations. Contrary to the incrustations found in individual lines or rows of dots on Banded or Stichband Ware, here the large connected surfaces were painted, on which the patterns of indentation created a negative effect. In some instances the surface had been roughened up to facilitate the bonding of colored paste and surface.

The end of the Rössen culture after 3700 B.C. points to the development of regional groups. Transitional forms in all aspects point to a continuity of development, the evidence for which extends to Switzerland, France and the northern lowlands of Germany. In the end it was influential in the development of the Funnel Beaker culture in northern Germany.[157]

One would expect that the new attitudes with which man of the Upper Neolithic approached the world would be reflected in the attitudes with which the human ego approached questions of life and death, that is to say, one would expect man's psychological evolution to be reflected in his religion. However, while the Neolithic Near East offers extensive information about man's religious concepts, for central Europe the evidence for Upper Neolithic religion is even more elusive and fragmentary than was the case for the Paleolithic. Yet it is reasonable to assume that an increasing independence in assuring the food supply should have been associated with greater self-assertion, greater self-reliance and greater independence *vis-à-vis* spiritual representations of the universe—the bite from the apple off the Tree of Knowledge, so to speak. In view of the absence of indicators by which to decipher man's spiritual life, it would be futile to speculate about the metaphysical background to this significant change in attitude—from dependence to independence.

Burial practices, from which one might hope to deduce some insights, offer next to no information. Inhumation in single graves is the dominant form of burial.[158] These graves must have been marked externally, since there is no overlapping of graves even under crowded conditions. The dead were not buried in coffins. During the Banded Ware period the deceased was generally placed in a fetal position on his left side, with his head placed in the E or NE, facing S or SE. During the later phases of this culture the corpse was placed more frequently facing upward, the head placed in the W or NW. In central Germany the Rösseners were placed in a right-sided fetal position, the head always turned to the right, even when the corpse was in a left-sided fetal position, as was the case once. Since S–N positioning dominates, the deceased would be facing east. Some significance was evidently attached to this direction. Among the Rösseners in south-west Germany, however, a stretched out oriented position was preferred, the head placed in the W or NW. Rössen practices mark a significant departure from those of the Banded Ware culture.

Interesting to note is the gradual transition indicated in late Banded Ware burials, which in matters of positioning—the facing of corpses—and in their non-ceramic grave inventories are closer to Rössen usage than to the customary Banded Ware practices. It is significant that the change in burials was not paralleled in the development of pottery.

A totally new feature to appear in association with the Stichband culture is cremation. The ashes were either scattered across the base of the grave or placed in a little pile which was then covered by a vessel. Stone axes and other tools, as well as pottery, show traces of fire, which indicates that these implements accompanied the deceased onto the funeral pyre.[159] It is doubtful whether as early as at this stage cremation implies a belief in the duality of body and soul, whereby the soul is freed to continue its spiritual existence. Such analogies with later cultures are attractive. That a concern for continuance beyond death may have been common is indicated by the grave inventories which have yielded as many as fourteen vessels and which probably contained food—beans, linseeds and hazelnuts. Vessels have sometimes been found turned upside down and it is probable that they once contained fluids.[160] Of interest is the presence of red dyes, especially in the area of the head, pointing to the continued use of the color red during festive occasions.[161]

From finds on the housing sites certain cultic practices can be deduced dealing with socio-cultural processes. Thus skeletal remains and vessels containing animal remains have been found buried deep under the floor of buildings, while stone tools were recovered from post-holes. In Hungary sites even yielded human clay figurines.[162] Sacrificial pits have been excavated showing clear demarcations of levels, suggesting that regular—perhaps annual—deposits were made. Caves, such as the Jungfernhöhle at Tiefenellern in the Jura discussed above, a site near a Banded Ware settlement, were used as depositories throughout Europe. It is not clear whether they were used as burial or sacrificial sites, though some sinister evidence would support the latter.[163] Concentrated deposits of artefacts, such as stone tools and pottery, depot finds in other words, present something of an interpretive problem to the archeologist, not just for the Neolithic period but right up to Germanic times, in that it can not be clearly established whether at any time these depots came into being as a result of having been hidden, only to be forgotten, perhaps because the owner(s) had been killed, or whether such depots had been deliberately established. If the latter is the case, then an explanation in terms of sacrifice becomes attractive, but beyond that no generally acceptable explanations have come forth. To which cosmic concept were they made, if any at all? Why were these 'sacrifices' made? Were they supplicatory, intercessional or indications of gratitude? Again, the presence of red ochre may point to deliberate offertory practices.

It is probable that the human dwelling itself was considered to be enveloped by a religious sphere arising out of a need for protection based on feelings of interdependence with superior forces. There is some evidence that the gables of houses were decorated, probably by means of representations of a sacrificial animal—the crossed horseheads still traditional in areas along the North Sea are perhaps just one indication of a continuation of such a prehistoric practice—intended as a means of mediation with the cosmic forces. It is also held that the hearth was the focus of some domestic cult(s). It is possible therefore that the community which occupied a longhouse also formed a cultic community. To date no cult buildings dating to this period have been found. Whether that special 'assembly' building identified in the lakeshore village of Aichbühl qualifies for such a designation has yet to be determined.[164]

It is a curious phenomenon that the number of human representations in clay, whether in the form of figurines or as facial features on pottery, decreases markedly towards the NW of Europe. Thus while the Balkan countries, Romania, Hungary, Czechoslovakia, Poland and Russia, yield a considerable number of male and female figurines, only a few such fragments have been documented west of Czechoslovakia and

48. Zoomorphic vessel with lineband designs, from Heinheim, south-west of Kelheim, c. 4600 B.C.

Poland. Technically, typologically and even stylistically, these figurines are derived from the Near East.[165] With the exception of a few Mesolithic examples of engraved stylized human representations on bone found in Denmark, there appears to be no continuity into the Neolithic period of that highly accomplished Paleolithic figural art in central Europe. Nor can the suggestion be supported that the extant figurines are representations of divinities, as can be claimed in the Near East. The human figurines of the European Neolithic are most probably votive figurines to be linked with ritual practices. Not unusual are vessels with either anthropomorphic or zoomorphic bases, that is to say, bowls with feet (Fig. 48). Again probably ritualistic in intent, they are often molded into animal shapes, perhaps suggested by sacrificial animals.

Clay was also put to use in the manufacture of spindle whirls and loom weights, pointing to a domestic textile industry. Clay beads shaped into cylinders or cones and strung together to make long neck chains served for personal ornamentation. The rims of large shells were fashioned into arm rings, bracelets, discs and chain links. In some instances shell ornaments were imitated in clay. Chains of animal teeth are rarely found.

At this point in the Upper Neolithic several transitional cultures co-exist in central Europe, each consisting of diverse components, subject to various influences, yet capable of integrating these influences to form regional sub-cultures. Only the major groupings have been dealt with, since the derivations named after more contained local type stations are far too numerous. These, however, make it clear that the potters of the Upper Neolithic knew how to apply a vivid imagination to their products when it came to their ornamentation.

It is conceivable that a Neolithic stone-tool maker in his search for workable flint nodules came upon a 'rock', heavier than others, of a different color, which when struck did not fracture or flake, but rather changed its shape and shone brightly when ground and polished. The archeological evidence points to copper rather than gold as the primary metal. The oldest objects of beaten copper have been found in the highlands of southern Iran, near the Persian Gulf, and in south-western Turkey, dating from the eighth and seventh millennia B.C.—much older than any known European finds. Gold is first in evidence at levels of the early fourth millennium B.C. on a site in northern Mesopotamia.[166] The manner of its treatment, however, is already so well-developed that an earlier knowledge may be assumed. For the working of copper both casting and beating were known. The first copper mine, from after 5500 B.C., has also been located in central Iran.[167] From about 5000 B.C. onward, the knowledge of working copper is in evidence in south-eastern Europe as well.[168]

For western, northern and central Europe it is customary to include this 'Copper Age' in the discussion of the Upper Neolithic. The term Chalcolithic—Copper Stone Age—has been adopted to identify this transitional phase of the Stone Age. Again, for the convenience of classification the period is suitably divided into Lower, Middle and Upper Chalcolithic, their respective cultures still named after ceramic type stations, the ceramic designations being more precise in establishing a workable chronology.

In general, pottery and stone artefacts belonging to the Lower Chalcolithic groups inhabiting central Europe show continuity with the Neolithic as regards ornaments, weapons, and types of houses as well as settlement patterns and economic peculiarities. Certain questions do remain open. To what extent does the Chalcolithic continue the Neolithic process of colonization? Does the direction of the movement still originate in south-eastern Europe and the Balkans and Asia Minor? Technological and economical innovations seem to indicate this; evidently the old chronology is no longer acceptable. In what manner do the various cultural groups come into being? What of the indigenous population? Studies done in the 1930s suggest that 30 per cent of skeletons belonging to this period still show Cro-Magnon characteristics, though the types are not uniform.[169] Anthropological analysis showed the Banded Ware people and their successors to have been short Mediterraneans,[170] i.e. immigrants in search of good agricultural land.

One outstanding characteristic of the Chalcolithic period is the monumental evidence of stone constructions using large rocks, some weighing up to thirty tons—the megaliths

Map 11. The Chalcolithic, Megaliths and Early Copper, after c. 5000 B.C.

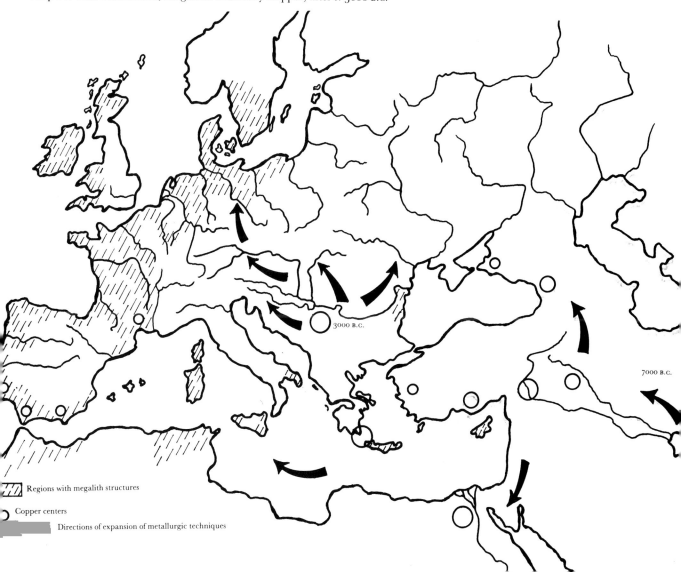

3000 B.C.

7000 B.C.

Regions with megalith structures

Copper centers

Directions of expansion of metallurgic techniques

	Lithic Division	Ceramic Cultures	Settlement Sites	Cultural Features	Tools and Weapons	Related Features
1,800 B.C.					fishtail daggers	
	Upper Chalcolithic	Bell Beakers		raising of livestock	horse-drawn chariots	copper mining in open pits
2,000 B.C.				peasant culture		shaft mining
				agriculture	metal tools	
				scratch plow		
		Corded Ware		stone cists		introduction of bronze to the north
				trepanation	battle axes	
3,300 B.C.		Federsee	fortified settlements			
		Mondsee				
		Attersee				
		Horgen	lakeshore settlements	single graves		
		Goldberg				
		Michelsberg				
	Middle Chalcolithic	Dürnberg	hilltop settlements			
		Baden		megalith graves		
		Cham				
		Walternienburg	flatland settlements			
		Bernburg				
		Salzmünde				
3,700 B.C.						
		Altheim				
	Early Lower Chalcolithic or Late Upper Neolithic	Michelsberg				
		Baalberge				
		Jordansmühl				
4,000 B.C.				menhirs		
		Funnel Beakers				introduction of copper

Chart 5. The Chalcolithic in Central Europe, Lower-Middle-Upper Chalcolithic, *c.*4000–*c.*1800 B.C.

49. Megaliths near Visbeck, south of Oldenburg, after *c.* 3000 b.c. (uncalibrated date, cf. note 16).

(Fig. 49), erected in southern, western and northern Europe from *c.* 5000 B.C.[171] to 1000 B.C. While the cultural force which led to the megalithic constructions in Greece, Malta, Sardinia and Spain used to be considered to be derivative of Near Eastern cultures, the dispute over the relationship with west and north European megaliths from Mediterranean origins is being resolved.[172] New techniques, such as radiocarbon dating and dendrochronology—tree-ring dating—are causing a reassessment of the traditionally accepted interlink of Mediterranean and ancient Near Eastern cultures and their 'parental' relationships with Europe. There is now an increasing reluctance to accept the Near East as the 'cradle of civilization', which necessitated the acceptance of theories of cultural diffusion towards the European north-west coupled with the notion of a 'downhill' effect of cultural sophistication. The information obtained through the use of these new techniques suggests that man in Europe had developed a level of civilization, including metallurgical skills, quite independently and that his architectural achievements in stone predate those of the inhabitants of the rim of the eastern Mediterranean; in other words, that the builders of Stonehenge were not supervised by architects from Mycenae.[173] Conclusions must remain fragmentary, however, for both dating techniques depend on the availability of organic materials[174] since stone alone cannot provide the necessary information. What is indicated is that the assumptions concerning European dependence on influences from areas around the eastern Mediterranean have to be revised significantly, as some Near Eastern civilizations are no longer a reliable frame of reference.[175] Claims based on carbon dating, that the West European 'Megalithicum' is of independent origin,[176] do now justify a fundamental reassessment of the phenomenon. The offending notion is that of a 'Megalith culture' spread by a 'Megalith people' originating in the Mediterranean, who colonized Sicily,

87

Malta, southern Italy, southern and northern Spain, Portugal, all of France, Ireland, parts of Britain, northern Germany, Denmark and southern Sweden.[177] It can be said that the idea of using large stones for building purposes existed but the methods of executing this idea varied with each locale.[178]

Although the various groups of monuments in France, the British Isles, northern Germany and Scandinavia have a basic 'Megalithic' character, they are also sufficiently different in design, purpose and age, that a common origin must not necessarily be assumed. At the same time the 'Megalithic' concept involves not only the obvious monumental stone structures used as grave chambers, but generally includes aligned avenues of menhirs—free-standing upright stones—and the construction of barrows and tumuli, sepulchral structures, and monumental cult sites, which may have been of stone such as Stonehenge, or of wood, as at Woodhenge and elsewhere in Britain.[179] This lack of uniformity in 'Megalithic' expression makes the idea of 'Megalithic colonizers' questionable, especially since for some areas the 'Megalithic' presence predates the migration and colonization. Apparently the megalithic mode is a spontaneous phenomenon, adapted to local conditions, serving regional needs. It is interesting that copper implements are occasionally associated with the megaliths in northern Europe. More important is the association of Funnel Beakers with megalithic funerary practices.

It has been stated above that transitional ceramic forms of the Rössen culture were influential in the development of the Funnel Beaker culture in northern Germany,[180] a Neolithic peasant culture which evolved under diverse influences. As such it is the result of acculturation of a local indigenous population, probably still Mesolithic, by the Danubian Banded Ware people.[181] For northern Germany, Denmark, southern Sweden and southern Norway there are no Neolithic cultures engaged in agriculture and the

Map 12. Ceramic cultures of the Lower Chalcolithic, Northern Funnelbeakers, *c.* 4200–after 2800 B.C.

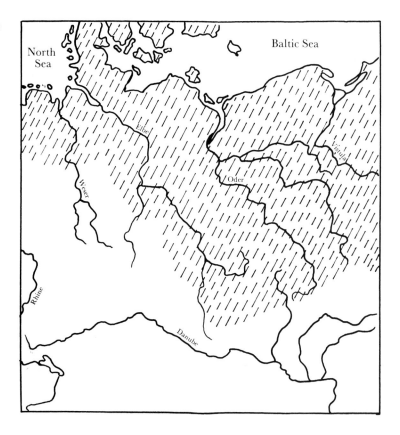

raising of livestock that are identifiable by means of their own particular style of pottery development until the very end of the period.[182] It is the Funnel Beaker culture which marks the beginning of this development. Owing to this shortcoming the inhabitants of these northern regions were identified as belonging to a 'Megalith Grave' culture which extended from central Poland in the east to Holland in the west, where it linked up with the western 'Megalith' culture. By contrast, a 'Single Grave' culture was seen to have replaced the builders of megalithic monuments.

In the north generally, the sequence of cultural periods is not in phase with the rest of central Europe: while the northern terminology identifies the Maglemose period as Paleolithic, it is contemporary with the more southerly Mesolithic; the Funnel Beaker and Single Grave cultures are considered to be Lower and Middle Neolithic periods in the north, while in southern terminology they are contemporary with late Upper Neolithic, i.e. Chalcolithic pottery cultures. As mentioned above, it is more precise to use ceramic terminology than such terms as 'Megalithic' period, since the practice of erecting megalithic structures was not confined to a specific pottery culture and thus blurs the transition to the next period.

Ceramic terminology allows for the establishment of a differentiating terminology for central Europe, especially since during the Chalcolithic central Europe witnesses a veritable explosion of ceramic styles, comparatively speaking. Between the fortieth and twenty-first centuries B.C. at least twelve major type stations and one significant new category of pottery, as well as a characteristic technique of ornamentation, have been identified, some of them of course being contemporaries of one another.

Map 13. Ceramic cultures of the Early Lower and Lower Chalcolithic, c. 4200 B.C.–3300 B.C.

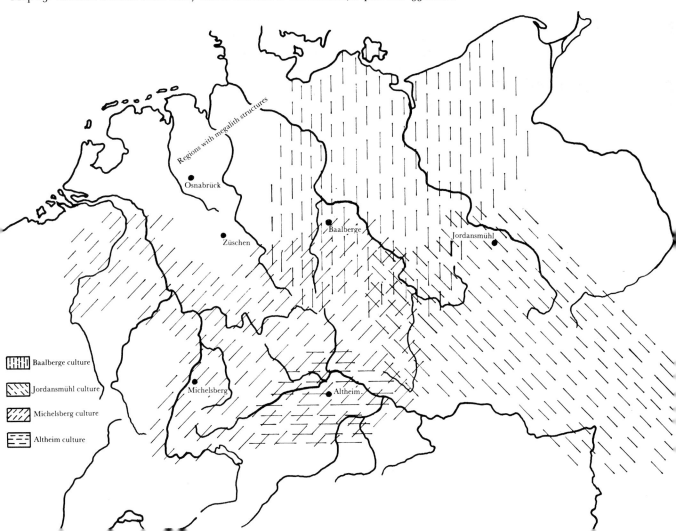

Owing to the continuous occupation of certain sites, the settlement strata facilitate the determining of stylistic chronologies. Corroborating cross-referencing with stratifications at other sites aids in establishing the sequence.[183] Thus a Lower Chalcolithic, before *c.* 4000 B.C., is represented by two type stations—Jordansmühl, representative for east central Europe, and Baalberge, concentrated in central and north-east Germany;[184] a Lower Chalcolithic is also indicated at the type station Michelsberg in south-west Germany,[185] which extended from Belgium to Salzburg, and at the type station Altheim representative of a style found from the Upper Danube across Bavaria to Salzburg. The Middle Chalcolithic, *c.* 3500–2000 B.C., is in evidence at eight major sites from Hungary to Switzerland—the Lakeshore cultures in the Alps—to the Upper Danube, to northern Bavaria, to Hesse and to north central Germany.[186] The Corded Ware culture of the twenty-sixth and twentieth centuries B.C. brings the Middle Chalcolithic to a close serving at the same time as transition to the Upper Chalcolithic.[187] That these divisions are an artificial convenience is indicated by the extensive contemporaneity of Corded Ware and Bell Beaker cultures,[188] the transition from stone to metal industries thereby being advanced. First bronze and then iron became the cultural indicators.

As the names of these cultures suggest—Baalberge, Michelsberg, Goldberg, Federsee, Mondsee, Attersee—mountains or locations protected by water were generally preferred sites of settlement. Thus throughout the Chalcolithic period, people occupied plateaus, table-top mountains, peninsulae partially protected by moors, rivers and lakeshore swamps, or islands in lakes. The proximity to water obviously held an economic attraction, in that it supplied ready access to food. However, flatland settlements were also quite common, especially in fertile areas.[189] Exceptional settlements are known from the area around Salzburg in such difficult terrain that they only appear sensible if associated with copper mining. The size of the settlements seems to vary with the locations; thus Egolzwil, a lakeshore village in Switzerland, was rather small, 45 m × 15 m, while one plateau settlement measured 600 m × 150 m, which probably was not all occupied at once. By comparison one flatland community covered a site of 1275 m × 840 m.[190] Again it is improbable that all of the area was inhabited at any one time. It is therefore difficult to determine the population density of these settlements.

The evidence concerning housing is fragmentary. While a great deal of information is available about the cultural areas of the eastern Mediterranean—Tyrins, Knossos— only the Lower and Middle Chalcolithic provide any archeological evidence for the north, mainly from the Swiss, Austrian and south-west German lakeshore dwellings and north-west German moor settlements. Beams and boards of oak, matting of willow or hazelnut branches, and clay were the building materials. Floor logs, held in place by short pilings, covered with boards and/or clay, would support open hearths or domed ovens, sometimes of stone, resting on layers of stone or bark. The walls were not necessarily joined to the floor but fastened along the side. In central Europe rectangular, probably gabled houses, showing regional variations in size from 4 m × 4 m to 8 m × 20 m, with a veranda-type landing in front, have been uncovered. Storage sheds and pits are a part of each village. Larger villages might consist of about thirty houses, although many sites were occupied by no more than eight or ten. There is evidence of rebuilding following fires. One village had a layer of logs covering its 'main street'.[191] The layout of these villages adhered to no general plan, except that lakeshore villages would follow the water line. The land side of these villages was enclosed by frail palisades of posts, split logs and willow and hazel matting, probably designed as protection against wild animals and for the corralling of livestock, rather than as a means of defense. Completely debunked is the rather romantic interpretation, very popular with tourists, proposed since the turn of the century when these lake dwellings were first evaluated, that the pilings discovered below the surface of the lakes had formerly supported platforms high above the water, ideal for fishing, large enough to carry houses and livestock, interconnected by foot bridges and protected from attack by means of drawbridges. Reality has been shown to be more pedestrian. These lakeshore settlements had been placed on firm ground. Since then, however, either the water level has risen, or the lakes have filled up with silt.[192] In the former instance especially, unusual preservative conditions were created which allowed for very rich finds in artefacts, notably those of organic materials.

The need for protection may of course not be entirely discounted. The choice of sites so favorable for defense as well as the evidence of fortifications in some locations do indicate aggressive pressures. The rapidity with which the various cultures replace one another, the extent to which they are found to overlap in some regions, the manner in which some ceramic styles maintained themselves in isolated pockets would suggest that at times in certain places favorable terrain was in dispute. No stone wall fortifications are known north of the Alps. Instead earthworks, palisades and ditches sometimes up to 10 m wide, sometimes carved into solid rock, sometimes laid out in formidable, multiple systems of defense, exploiting the advantages offered by the site, have been located, as on the Michelsberg, the Goldberg and many other locations.

There is definite evidence in Europe that either in or near settlements cultic practices took place at special sites. The Michelsberg itself is possibly such a site. The mountain, the highest elevation in the area, derives its name from the chapel dedicated to St. Michael. It is of interest that churches and chapels dedicated to St. Michael were founded during the Christianization of Germany, usually on established pagan cultic sites—thereby preserving some of the old sacredness of the spot. How far back these sites go cannot always be determined since later occupation usually obliterated the evidence, though usually dark recollections continued in people's minds, so that for central Europe a few locations can be identified as having served as cult sites where sacrificial acts were performed.

For reasons about which one can only speculate, Chalcolithic Man felt the need to erect large stones called menhirs, singly, encircled by smaller stones, in long avenues, as at Carnac in Britanny, or in monumental rotundas as at Stonehenge. They have been a source of wonder and misinterpretation ever since. In contrast with western Europe there is no evidence that avenues or rotundas on the western model had ever been set up in Germany. The situation is confused in that large stones were set up not only during the late phases of the Neolithic, but also during the Bronze and Iron Ages, in Roman times, during the Middle Ages and in modern times. Thus a monolith was set up in the German Democratic Republic in 1953 and baptized *Aktivistenstein*.[193] As border markers, landmarks or milestones they have a long tradition. Attributed to the Middle Ages, but now long gone, was a circle of stones reputedly between 90 and 150 m in circumference circling a sandstone 3–4 m in height. This stone circle near Quedlinburg in Saxony was held to be a medieval place of justice.[194] In 1841 menhirs encircled by stones were still documented near Osnabrück in Westphalia. Tradition has it that blue stones or 'bleeding stones' characterize old court or execution sites. In eastern Germany some of these stones are called *Specksteine*. Etymologically the world 'speck'— normally meaning bacon—could be related to English 'speak', in which case these

50. Menhir with pinetwig patterns from
Ellenberg, *c.* 2700 b.c.

stones too could refer to medieval sites of justice or assembly, in keeping with a medieval
tradition of erecting stones in areas subject to Lower Saxon Law during the Middle
Ages. An examination of thirty-six such stones revealed that only nine were authentic
menhirs of the late Neolithic and Bronze Age periods. However, new regional surveys
are constantly bringing new stones to light.

Over the centuries legends have come to be associated with many of these stones,
usually trying to relate the presence of such a stone to some historical event or personage,
often to Charlemagne, or to St. Boniface in areas of early Christianization. Quite
popular are legends of the petrification of giants or men as punishment for abuses such
as cursing, mistreating food, disobedience—a girl who preferred to be turned to stone
rather than marry the man chosen by her father—and other similar misdemeanors. A
tradition, pre-Christian in tone, explains the presence of such isolated boulders by
suggesting that they had been lost by giants or used as projectiles in their fighting.
Christian versions of such stones frequently attribute the presence of these stones to the
Devil. According to folklore it was the Devil who had thrown these stones at churches,
chapels and monasteries, always missing his intended target, of course. What is most
likely is that during the period of Christianization the new religion intentionally selected
pagan cult sites, partly to demonstrate the impotence of the old cult, partly to supplant
the old cult more effectively, partly to preserve and absorb the old sacredness associated
with a certain site, especially since so much of the 'conversion' was really a case of
refunctioning and re-orienting. Folklore also links these old sites with will-o'-the-wisps,
those deceptive lights which lead people to their destruction. Notions of buried treasure
near these stones are more modern.

This very fragmentary evidence allows the conclusion that Germany is already on the distant fringe of the menhir idea. Though menhirs and the like are to be found in central Germany, they do not relate to west European models. No menhirs have been found in Bavaria, Württemberg and Austria, or in the Netherlands, where it is surmised though, that they might have been made of wood as a possible first stage. In western Europe, human features have been detected on these elongated, upright stones, and although no artistic value can be attached to them, they do allow for the intention to produce plastic representations. In northern Europe such anthropomorphic representations are not known. On the other hand, can one consider an elongated stone deliberately carved and circled in the middle as though with a belt, to be an anthropomorphic analogy (Fig. 50)? Geometrics—angles, chevrons and pine-twig patterns, that decorative arsenal of north and central European ornamentation utilized on pottery during the Neolithic—also ornament some of these stones. In south-western Europe the Bell Beakers bear some of the same designs as these menhirs, which suggests that the idea may be foreign to central Europe. Some motifs again show a close link with those used by the Corded Ware people. Both of these considerations would make these stones a very late element of the Chalcolithic period. However, a secondary use of the stones by later populations is not excluded, as was also the practice with other megalithic structures, so that an earlier dating is possible. Whether the Bell Beaker people introduced the practice into Germany has not yet been decided.[195]

There are several reasons why the evidence concerning not only menhirs and stone circles but also megalith tombs is so inconclusive in Germany. Their obvious presence in an area that is so poor in natural building materials as the northern German plain made these glacial left-overs, conveniently gathered together, prime targets for demolition. In Napoleonic times farmers had to provide stipulated amounts of stone for road construction. The expansion of agriculture and the improvement of agricultural tools, machinery and methods since the eighteenth century, such as the introduction of the steam plow to the plains of northern Saxony, contributed much to the reduction of their numbers since the presence of these stones on good land was wasteful and an obstacle to efficient land use. A map of 1829 of the Isle of Rügen in the Baltic Sea showed 236 megalithic graves. In other parts still as many as 219 tombs were documented some 150 years ago. One hundred years later only 14 were left. Although many of these grave sites came under government protection, as in the Kingdom of Hannover in 1840, of the 219 graves still recorded in 1846 only 15 are preserved today, many no longer complete.[196] Superstitions of the type mentioned above may have played a role in their removal.

The megalithic tombs are the first surviving evidence of northern man's architectural skills.[197] Considering that house construction for his own use was of perishable materials, it is significant that he erected such massive and durable structures to house the dead. As was stated above, there is no real evidence to link the north European megaliths with those of the rest of Europe,[198] for the superficial similarity in the rather simple use of large stones does not support any notions of cultural or even chronological unity.[199] Only the megalithic form of construction reaches northern Europe, so that it is quite unlikely that these tombs are the result of enterprising Neolithic undertakers merchandizing a new style of funeral. Since the megaliths are a coastal phenomenon, as though washed ashore, somewhat fanciful theories attribute them to the arrival of the 'star gazers', oceanic 'sea peoples' who originated in lands to the north and north-west, which have long since disappeared through cataclysms and upheavals, and who erected the structures in order to search for that cosmic knowledge so indispensable to human

51. Megalith tomb, popularly termed a 'Pagan Sacrificial Altar', near Visbeck, south of Oldenburg, *c.* 2500 b.c.

survival. The magical properties of stone being such as to enable it to receive and emit tellurgical and cosmic currents and to induce man to use stone towards protective and fecund ends, caused the megalith graves to be located in such places where tellurgical currents intersected subterranean streams, thereby bestowing beneficial and curative powers upon the magnetized waters.[200] In the face of such a theory the notion that giants were entombed in these 'giant's beds', according to folklore, has a naive appeal (Fig. 51).

The fact that the megalith tombs were used repeatedly, following a removal from the burial chamber of the previous funerary inventory, causes some confusion about the identity of their builders and their subsequent occupants. While Funnel Beakers, probably an indigenous development, have been associated with the early megaliths, Bell Beakers—their name derived from the shape of an inverted bell—are most commonly found in the later megalith tombs from Holland to Scandinavia. This Bell Beaker culture appears to have had its origins in south-western and in east central Europe,[201] yet its southern and central European groups did not know the use of megalithic graves.[202]

The arrival of a new population is not indicated, although something did cause a break in the continuity. The introduction of the Bell Beakers (Fig. 52), probably by lateral transfer, and the displacement of the northern Funnel Beakers points to a cultural rupture. Still plausible is the notion that the megalith idea was spread by coastal carriers in search of metals, while the Bell Beaker culture expanded overland, the two coming together in northern and north-western Europe. It is curious that the builders of one of the earliest of the tombs in northern Germany did not recognize an

52. Bell and Tulip Beakers from Butsbach and Gross Umstadt, east of Darmstadt.

53. Megalith tomb of quarried stone slabs, *c.* 2500 b.c., the so-called 'Karlsteine', at Osnabrück-Haste.

axe of native, pre-Chalcolithic production and simply built it into the dry-wall masonry of the tomb.[203] This could imply that they were strangers to the area, though their origin must remain obscure. In northern Germany the 'coastal' character of the 'Megalith' culture is demonstrated by its avoidance of loess areas and its location on the post-glacial plains, especially in old moraines or end-moraines where the receding ice had deposited an abundance of huge boulders, the essential building material for the monumental structures. One celebrated exception is the 'Karlsteine', on the northern outskirts of Osnabrück, and quite erroneously linked with Charlemagne.[204] This megalith tomb is distinct in that its builders did not or could not utilize glacial debris, the glacial ice not having reached this area, and instead chose to break the stone out of a nearby mountain, with the effect that all of the stones are flat and rectangular (Fig. 53). In view of the immense effort required, considering Neolithic technology, this accomplishment hints at the tremendous compulsion to which the builders must have responded, all the more curious since the location of Osnabrück is not 'coastal'. What of the northern population? What type of economy made them seek out the Pleistocene plains? Did another population retain control of the loess areas? It is indicated that the culture which made use of the megaliths overlaps only marginally with the neighboring and contemporary cultures of the Middle Chalcolithic in north central Germany.

While in other parts of Europe the megalith style includes dolmens, passage graves, rock-cut tombs, shaft graves, barrows and unchambered tombs, in northern Germany there are variations mainly of the dolmen and passage graves. Since the last century it has been held that the variation was actually an expression of a structural development from proto-dolmens, to dolmens, to passage graves, culminating in stone cists—large chest-like coffins of flat stones—with the proto-dolmens originating from c. 3000 B.C. onward and the passage graves developing after c. 2500 B.C.[205] It was held that the proto-dolmen was at first reserved for the burial of an exceptional personality[206] and that when the custom was extended to include other members of the distinguished family the grave chamber of the proto-dolmen had to be expanded to make multiple burials possible. New research, however, suggests that instead of such a development the various grave types may have been contemporaneous.[207] It is apparent that even when considering the megaliths in a limited area in Europe, the question of their origin is complex. Until recently it was also not known that the megalith tombs were accompanied by small earth graves, sometimes with a pavement-like stone covering. It is not yet clear whether these belonged to the same population or whether they reflect the burial customs of later descendants or the new styles of the 'Single Grave' (Hill Grave) culture. There is general agreement that the stone cists of central Germany are to be dated after 1800 B.C. and belong to the earliest stages of the Bronze Age.

The construction of these megalith graves presented no basic difficulties. With sleds and rollers, utilizing principles of leverage and the inclined plane, the stones weighing up to thirty tons would be moved into the desired positions. These may have been 'winter works projects' taking advantage of wintery conditions. In general the dolmen consisted of four to fourteen supporting vertical stones which were selected for their flat sides which would then provide inside walls of the grave chamber. Field stones, usually assembled into dry-stone wall, would be wedged in between the verticals for support. There is some uncertainty about the sequence of the construction. It is possible that the covering stones were moved into place on top of a wooden frame or a mound of earth and the supporting stones would then be fitted underneath, whereupon the earth or the wooden frame would be removed.[208] This technique recommends itself if the finished chamber was not to cave in while the cap stones were being fitted. Perhaps the chamber was filled with earth after the verticals had been placed, so that a cave-in was prevented in that fashion. Once the chamber was completed the floor received a stone pavement covered with a layer of clay or gravel of broken fired flint.

Evidence from Denmark even points to wood paneling having been used to line the rock-face.[209] Some time after the burial the tomb was probably covered with an earthen mound, a tumulus. The earth seems to have eroded since. This, however, is not conclusive for northern Germany, although tumuli are usual for Denmark and Schleswig-Holstein. In later times a low entrance, usually on the south side, allowed subsequent access to the tomb.

If the various types of megalith tombs are contemporaneous then it is appropriate to speak of styles rather than of stages. That the small (proto-) dolmens—called *dysser* in Denmark—are an independent development in northern Europe is generally accepted,[210] though a corroborating chronological priority cannot be demonstrated on the dolmen of France, for instance. Again, the obvious similarity is deceiving, while the details differ significantly.

The smaller northern (proto-) dolmens found mainly in Denmark, Schleswig-Holstein and Mecklenburg are stone boxes with dimensions of no more than 2 m × 1 m × 1 m providing just enough room for one corpse, placed on a layer of fired flint 5–30 cm thick. The walls consist of four stones of equal height, two long stones each to the left and right and a narrow stone at head and foot ends respectively. Only one large boulder was needed as a cover. It is characteristic of these tombs that they were made of clumsy and unwieldy stones.[211] Intended as single graves they were, however, used repeatedly. Since these tombs were closed off completely, the cap stone had to be moved each time entrance was sought. It is reasonable to assume that such an awkward approach would soon encourage the emergence of a new form, at least as a complement to the traditional structure. The larger tombs are adapted dolmens, consisting of two cap stones and five or six vertical wall stones with one stone at the southern side being smaller than the supporting stones, having the function of a 'sill' and providing for a movable 'door' stone allowing entrance and making it easier to introduce additional corpses into the chamber. This type is up to 1 m longer, wider and higher. This larger dolmen type is to be found mainly in Schleswig-Holstein and Mecklenburg. Another, perhaps individual development under western influences are polygonal dolmens, perhaps the result of the adaptation to multiple burials. However, they do not undergo any change in size, since the widening is accompanied by a shortening.[212]

The burials were by inhumation and only in the eastern reaches of the megalith style is there cremation. The corpse was stretched out or bent slightly at the knees. There is no evidence of fetal positioning.[213] The religious ideas behind the megalith graves will probably remain unknown. There is no indication of cultic, religious or even social uniformity in northern Germany at this time.[214] Their impressive monumentality can not have been their chief purpose, though perhaps there is a link between the human fear of being forgotten and the construction of a grave not subject to impermanence. Such considerations have led the the term 'pyramids of the north' to be applied to these tombs.[215] They did offer a solid residence for the dead with an airtight compartment in which the deceased could live on, securely sealed off from evil outside influences by one or sometimes two stone circles drawing a magical perimeter around the tomb and its tumulus. Or was it the magical intent of these circles to prevent the return of the dead? Do the airtight grave chambers suggest mummification and a possible belief in a

54. Fishtail daggers of flint,
c. 2000 B.C. Note the 'casting
seam' on the dagger top left.

physical resurrection? The grave inventories would suggest that the deceased was provisioned either for a journey to the beyond or for a continued life in the House of the Dead. The inventories, fragmentary though they are, consist of pottery, tools, weapons and ornaments. The pottery of this 'dolmen period' consists of Funnel Beakers, richly decorated with dots, lines and ribs, of pots and round-bellied flasks.[216] They may have contained perishable materials. The equipment in tools and weapons was made up of well-finished pointed stone axes with thick pointed necks, a style derived from Mesolithic flint cores, of flint core daggers 12–25 cm in length, of lance and spear heads, and of stone clubs.[217] Considering that secondary burials took place, it is not certain whether all of these implements belong to the 'dolmen period'. It is suspected that the narrow 25 cm long daggers of flint core are imitations of metal daggers (Fig. 54), and were prepared especially for cultic and/or funerary rites. Because of the fragile nature of stone of such a length, these daggers cannot have been functional, but only ceremonial.[218]

Equally curious and puzzling are designs and bowl-like indentations ground into the cap stones on some of these dolmen (Fig. 55). Usually attributed to cultic intentions of the subsequent Bronze Age populations, who also buried their dead in these tombs, these bowls imply that erosion had bared the cap stones by the middle of the second millennium before our era. More recently, however, it has been suggested that by association these 'bowl stones' are of Chalcolithic origin, related to the funerary ceremonies and that the stone surface was not immediately covered with earth.[219]

In dealing with the passage graves—also called walk-in graves—one again encounters the claim that the passage grave builders were Atlantic voyagers who arrived from western Europe and who introduced a new religion, or at least new mortuary cults, and that this conversion was all the more easily effected in an area where a tradition of building small megalith tombs—dolmens or *dysser*—already existed.[220] It is suggested that besides the skill in tomb building they also brought religious and military power and prestige with which they compelled the native population to perform the great labors of moving stones and earth.[221] It is a popular simplification which one encounters in writings about early times that the building of great edifices such as the pyramids of Egypt or the ziggurats of Mesopotamia could only be achieved with slave labor, oppression and brutality. Yet when dealing with Greek temples or medieval cathedrals they are the manifestation of nothing less than acts of faith and effort freely given. That the motivation may have been largely spiritual is a minor consideration. However, as in Egypt, it is likely that access to the afterlife was the exclusive preserve for outstanding individuals such as kings and priests. Only because they were thought to be divine could the pharaohs pass into the afterlife. Others, family, officials, lesser nobility, the common man, could participate in the glory only in a descending order of association with that distinguished personage. Building the tomb was perhaps such an act of faith and the extent to which the common man could hope to share in the post-terrestrial joys. The pyramid precincts indicate this hierarchical approach to the afterlife. This may also have been true for the 'pyramids of the north'.

While the continued presence of Funnel Beakers and collared flasks does not really contradict it, the theory of the Atlantic voyagers does not account for the presence of passage graves in Holland and northern Germany as early as 3500 B.C.,[222] nor for the presence of a new type of pottery, the Corded Ware of the Single Grave–Battle Axe culture.[223] This culture was known to have come from the east and in gradually asserting its cultural dominance it forced the megalith builders to retreat northward into the Danish peninsula, onto the islands and into the Elbe-Weser and Weser-Ems areas,

55. Dolmen with designs and 'bowls', *c.* 2000 B.C. at Bunsoh near Heide in Schleswig-Holstein.

99

56. Passage grave near Flögeln, north-east of Bremerhaven, *c.* 3000 B.C.

57. Walk-in grave chamber, with dry wall between the upright stones, long barrow, *c.* 3000 B.C. at Oldendorf, Lüneburger Heide.

58. Restored barrow at Kleinenkneten, east of Visbeck.

where the western group is known to have developed a secondary branch of the megalith style without links to Denmark.[224] While the Danish passage graves have long entrance passages leading into short chambers, for the north German graves the passage is unimportant in relation to the chamber (Fig. 56), in that they retain short passages of seldom more than two pairs of verticals but frequently with grave chambers over 20 m long.[225]

While a proto-dolmen and a polygonal dolmen show a basic conceptual development, the oldest passage grave and the longest chamber differ in no respect other than length. These larger chambers retain their entrance on the south side. The cap stones continue to be supported by large vertical stones with rock packing, dry-wall or clay filling the gaps, with packed clay, some plate paving or broken fired flint making up the floor of the chamber to increase dryness (Fig. 57). Since the principle of using boulders to cover the chamber transversely is retained, these chambers could not exceed a certain width— about 2 m. There is no indication that the stones were split artificially in order to produce the flat surfaces. At best there is some crude tailoring of the stone for fitting purposes. It is interesting that graves assessed as being older show more careful workmanship while in newer tombs the joints were not finished so carefully.[226]

The most striking feature of these walk-in graves is their immense size. The north German passage grave builders seem to have been motivated by an urge to raise over the tombs exceedingly long, though narrow barrows, rectangular or trapezoid in shape, surrounded by a retaining wall of upright megaliths. As extensions of the long sides, individual menhirs 3–4 m high had been placed at two diagonally opposite corners. Referred to as 'guardian' stones their presence suggests that the corners were given some special emphasis.[227] The reconstruction near Kleinenkneten, south of Oldenburg, of one such passage grave to its Neolithic appearance required 1200 m³ of earth and 85 vertical stones (340 tons) for the retaining wall (Fig. 58). Such were the requirements for a relatively medium-sized barrow 50 m in length.[228] The longest barrow—130 m long— is located at Wienberg in Schleswig. It is the length of these graves which induced folklore to associate these 'beds' with giants. Typical for this long style are two graves near Visbeck, today outlined only by their retaining stones. In one instance the dolmen chamber, 10 m long, is located near the western end of the enclosure—115 m long. In the other instance, some distance away, a shorter enclosure—80 m long—the dolmen chamber is located 15 m from the western end (Fig. 59). These two graves are known respectively as the 'Visbecker Bräutigam' and the 'Visbecker Braut', bridegroom and bride. Barrows such as these measured 6–10 m in width.[229] Noticeable is the disproportionate location of the grave chamber in relation to the barrow. A number of variations were used. Recent research shows that occasionally unchambered as well as chambered graves were dug into the barrows so that they provided for multiple burials. This practice may represent a late stage of the entire idea, when resources in manpower and organization no longer sufficed to carry out the immense task, for secondary burials in the long barrows are rare. One interesting exception is the other grave at Kleinenkneten which shows three dolmen chambers aligned with the axis, evenly spaced and probably built at the same time within the retaining enclosure of stones, the earth having eroded (Fig. 60). Another variation are four self-contained barrow graves at Grundoldendorf near Stade, expanded dolmen chambers at right angles to the axis, completely aligned and placed very close together. Radio-carbon tests date the construction to c. 3580 B.C. but analysis of structure and pottery shows that these graves were used and modified repeatedly up to the very end of the Neolithic.[230] Perhaps the three-chambered grave at

59. Eroded barrow at Engelmansbäke near Visbeck, so-called 'Visbecker Braut', 80m long.

60. Three-chambered walk-in grave at Kleinenkneten, east of Visbeck. The graves at Kleinenkneten yielded Funnel Beakers and Incised Ware.

Kleinenkneten was occupied by members of the same family. Some of these megalith graves are chamberless, in which case timbered chambers may have been used. The barrows are positioned in a general E–W direction, though not precisely or orderly. The E–W positioning might be explained in relation to ideas about the rising and setting sun. Did the deceased face east into the rising sun? When in groups, some graves are arranged parallel to one another, while others don't follow any particular plan, yet they have been dated to the same period.[231]

The funerary inventories of those passage graves have yielded daggers, axes, spear and arrow heads of flint, bones and animal teeth for ornaments such as necklaces and bracelets and even armrings. Metal ornaments of copper and bronze are also known from this period. Of some interest are necklaces of amber where the amber had been worked into the shape of double axes. These finds have been attributed to the influence of the eastern Single Grave–Battle Axe culture, which also knew gold, none of which has been found in the passage graves, however.[232] An early source of gold at this time was Ireland, which would suggest that there was some exchange of goods with the British Isles.

Following the examination of a group of barrow and tumulus graves near Oldendorf near the eastern fringe of Lüneburg Heath, it has been concluded that the graves in Lüneburg Heath were not hereditary or family burial grounds, but were erected for one individual during his life-time. The ceramic evidence points to successive generations. From the positioning of the corpses in the chambers and the arrangement of the funerary gifts around the deceased it was deduced that women and servants accompanied the deceased lord into the beyond, analogous, perhaps, to early Near Eastern practices which saw the retinue being buried with the master. The ceramic inventory contained loop-handled cups, imitations of vessels worked in precious metals, the style confirmed as having originated in the eastern Mediterranean. These finds would indicate that around 2400 B.C. northern Germany had tangible international connections and that the graves at Oldendorf served members of a high aristocracy.[233]

Most of the Neolithic–Chalcolithic burial sites yield evidence that the tombs were used not only by several generations but by successive cultures, including those of the Bronze Age.[234] Some of the megalith barrows came to be even higher when the cap stones served as bases for new graves.

In the central and north-eastern German cultural areas, single burials in monumental graves are known dating from c. 4500–3600 B.C., the Baalberge period of the Early Lower Chalcolithic.[235] By the time of the Walternienburg culture during the Middle Chalcolithic, c. 3500–2000 B.C., collective burials had become usual.[236] The logic of such a custom recommends itself not only for sociological (family ties) or religious (salvation by participation) reasons, the latter of course being difficult to determine, but also for practical economic reasons, in that such monumental edifices could not be erected for everyone. It is possible that the grave chambers may have been submitted to ritual purification by fire. There is some evidence which points to fire having been used in the chambers prior to the funeral, or before the final raising of the covering mound.[237] One chamber contained the remains of some 240 dead. Here it appears possible that these remains underwent a secondary burial in a grave treated as an ossuary. While in the east the grave hills were trapezoid in shape, towards the west there was an increasing tendency to raise oval mounds, surrounded by double rings of stones. It has been proposed with hesitation that the round grave hills with their circular stone settings are analogous to circular cultic sites related to the sun-cult and the realm of religious ideas, such as the henge rotundas in Britain, while the rectangular and even trapezoid earth mounds just might reflect the shape of houses.[238]

As has been stated above, the north saw not only the construction of the spectacular megalith graves but also more ordinary earth graves in the same vicinity. Two possibilities for such a coexistence of customs have been put forward: an older population may be seen clinging tenaciously to its traditions, or a foreign influence thrust itself into the area occupied by the builders of megalith tombs. For the area contained by the lower Weser and the lower Elbe the presence of the Single Grave culture during the time when the passage graves were being built is considered to have been confirmed.[239] Owing to its rather sudden appearance in the north, the Single Grave culture, the northern branch of the Corded Ware culture, was considered to reflect the appearance of conquerors.[340] Since the discovery of the arrival of the Indo-Europeans was fervently awaited by the academic establishment, historians and philologians alike, it was popular to equate the Single Grave 'people' with the Indo-Europeans. That both came from the east only reinforced these notions. The term 'Battle Axe culture' was therefore a favorite alternative designation, with just the appropriate ring of ferocity about it to be associated with conquerors. There is now general agreement that the Indo-Europeans did not arrive in northern Europe at this time. A cultural influence, of course, need not be carried by people. Yet the effect of a cultural influence is definitely apparent. Everywhere, not just in central Europe, funerary monuments and the cult of the dead take on new forms, in that sepulchral monuments are used not just to mark a site above ground but also as a site of veneration after the burial. It is, however, improbable that conquerors would take over the burial sites of the conquered. For instance, it is unthinkable that the white man in North America could even have considered taking over Indian burial grounds, let alone the Indian practice of exposing the deceased to the elements. On the other hand it is more likely that the established population adopted and adapted new influences, introduced new funerary rituals with the associated grave inventories, without discontinuing burial in the ancestral graves. The form of burial has great tenacity since it represents a main component of the religion. It has been accepted that the Single Grave culture made use of the megalith for secondary burial, indicated by the displacement of the Funnel Beakers by pottery akin to Corded Ware, the general ceramic indicator which brought the Middle Chalcolithic to a close at the end of the twenty-first century B.C. A characteristic item in the grave inventory is an early type of axe which resembles the shape of a modern claw hammer. It has been found in association with rock-axes of disc-like design, and chipped out of roughly ground thick-necked flint axes over the entire area occupied by the central European Corded Ware culture, and east of it.[241]

Burial during this period took the form of inhumation in stretched or fetal positions, the latter coming ever more into use as the period progressed, and cremation in the areas towards the east. The remains were deposited either in Single Graves or in collective chambers.[242] A high or low tumulus would be piled up over the grave. Such tumuli are known for the Mediterranean cultures, all of France, the British Isles, for central Europe up to the time of the Corded Ware culture at the end of the Middle Chalcolithic, for the north European Funnel Beaker and Single Grave cultures, as well as for the eastern cultures of Romania and southern Russia to the Caucasus. A diameter of 10–20 m with a height of 1 m is the most usual size in western Europe, though diameters of 85–90 m with an elevation of 10 m occur. These tumuli were often surrounded by dry-wall or a wreath of stones. In one such tumulus at Unterjettingen in Württemberg, south-west Germany, the wall consists of alternating white limestone and red sandstone, no doubt to brighten the visual effect of the monument. These tumuli were probably topped off with a menhir.[243] From the Middle Chalcolithic on, beam or tree coffins are in use, positioned E–W, resting on a packing of clay or stone.[244] From the Corded Ware period on, a curious practice comes into use. While the first grave is subterranean, the tumulus rising above it, a second grave would be placed into the angle formed by the slope and the level surface, the third grave was then situated on top of the first tumulus where the slope of the second grave joined with it, while a fourth grave might be tucked into the junction of the second and third graves. Only the first of these would have originated during the Corded Ware period.[245] Multiple burials appear with a certain frequency, so that one must assume simultaneous deaths. Widow burials are also probable.[246]

The positioning of the dead must have been connected with certain notions and intentions. The deliberate positioning of the face must have been of considerable importance in several cultures. Thus the Corded Ware culture placed men in a right-sided fetal position, the head placed in the west, while women were in a left-sided fetal position, their heads placed in the east, so that both sexes faced south. In areas occupied by the Bell Beaker cultures the deceased all faced east.[247] Perhaps this practice was also determined by a sun-cult unknown to us. While votive figurines are a definite part of the grave equipment in other parts of Europe, they are virtually absent in central Europe. Otherwise the deceased was provisioned with the customary funerary gifts—personal possessions, body and garment ornaments, artefacts, as well as farewell gifts such as food, cultic objects of symbolic character or insignia of rank, some or all of which may already have been in his possession during his lifetime. Tools and weapons accompanied the men, a battle axe placed at face or shoulder level, axes, chisels and knives usually hip high, i.e. worn in a belt, the ends of which are indicated by two amber discs at thigh level. A beaker was located either at the head or foot end. Women were equipped with a knife, pottery and amber beads, sometimes in the hundreds, at the head, neck or wrists. However, only a few graves had all these things.[248]

Among the funerary vessels of the Middle Chalcolithic, so-called drums are typical Fig. 61) for the Salzmünde, Walternienburg–Bernburg cultures, as well as the bulbous amphorae (Fig. 62).[249] Too fragile to fill the role of drums, these cylindrical

61. So-called drum, *c.* 3500–2000 B.C. from Pevestorf, west of Wittenberge. Found in an inhumation grave of the Bernburg culture.

62. Bernburg funerary ware, *c.* 3500–2000 B.C., from Pevestorf.

vessels have no known function, unless with a sieve-like cloth fastened over its mouth, libations were poured onto the ground during the funeral ceremonies. Curiously it is frequently observed that in the grave inventories all vessels remained intact, only the 'drums' being broken.[250] In the same context, is there any religious significance to animal funeral gifts? Evidence ranges from pieces of meat attached to bones, to larger pieces of beef, sheep, goat, pig and game, to the presence of entire animals represented by complete skeletons. Perhaps the portions reflect an expression of the individual's social status. Why would cattle be positioned similarly to humans and be accompanied by pottery? Sometimes the animals are even buried separately. In one pit an adult and a child were accompanied by two mares and a foal, one cow and a calf, one goat and kid, and one ewe and lamb, quite probably as funerary gifts for the deceased. Yet at the same time it appears to be a deliberate sacrifice, an act of symbolic and mythical significance for the relationship between the living and the dead.[251] Can one deduce an explicit belief in life after death from these funerary gifts? The absence of such gifts can certainly not be used to negate such a belief. Or were the deceased seen to be messengers charged with the task of interceding with the spirit world on behalf of the living? Nothing is known of the expectations of the living.

Contemporary with the construction of the late northern megalith graves and extending into the Bronze Age is the practice of building rectangular box-shaped stone coffins, called cists (kists).[252] Most common is a small cist, too small to contain a corpse other than in a fetal position, though cists of up to 30 m in length are known. Block cists and slab cists, both single graves, are the two main types of cists to have been identified. The block cists greatly resemble the dolmen. For Denmark a clear development progressing from dolmen to passage grave to stone cist is claimed. The same cannot be demonstrated for Germany, and although some links exist in northern

Germany, neither numbers, contents nor spread of the custom allow definite conclusions. It is held that the cultures of the Middle Chalcolithic—Bernburg and Corded Ware—were instrumental in spreading the custom from west to east. Spain, southern and central France and Brittany are considered to be its origin. This suggestion is based on the presence of patterns and designs on western menhirs and cist graves in central Germany. The path of the influence has not yet been determined. Greater numbers of stone cists have been found between Belgium and Lower Saxony, with a concentration in Westphalia. Menhirs and stone cists are known in Hesse and in south-western Germany and Switzerland. These general areas are considered to mark the end stages of the western entrance routes into central Europe.[253] There is, however, no even distribution of the types of cists over the entire cultural area, nor are the characteristic details to be found everywhere. The difference between stone blocks and slabs is of itself seen to be a development. Perhaps originally only 2 m long and 60–80 cm wide and so low as to be unsuitable for entry, they come to be large boxes set into the ground, 15–20 m long, 1–2 m wide and high enough to permit walking upright. They are commonly set into the ground, positioned N–S, with carefully laid stone floors and limestone walls and deck plates, and with only a low tumulus for a cover. The entrance, generally at one of the narrow sides, could be closed with a rolling stone. It led into an ante-chamber where a circular hole in the partition gave access to the main burial chamber. Only occasionally was the grave accessible from the side. Such a hole is a frequent feature in eastern and central parts of Germany, but at Courgenay in Canton Bern in Switzerland a cist with this feature has also been located.[254] In some instances this hole is too small to permit passage from the ante-chamber, so that a deck plate would have had to be removed, in which case the round hole must have played a purely symbolic role. It is assumed that certain cultic acts were performed in the ante-chamber. A popular designation for the hole is *Seelenloch*—a hole through which the soul of the deceased would be permitted to pass unhindered from burial chamber into the cultic ante-chamber.[255]

Cremation appears to have been the common practice prior to deposition in the cist. The remains as well as the ashes from the funeral pyre were spread evenly over the floor of the stone cist. The funerary gifts were then placed on the ashes. Where double graves have been found, ritual murder/suicide of the widow is a possibility. Skeleton graves also exist, frequently containing numerous weapons.[256] The deceased are generally classified as members of the Battle Axe culture, equipped with the battle axes associated with the Single Graves, that northern branch of the Corded Ware culture. Since this period coincided with the first stages of the Bronze Age, the stone work rises to a last flourish of excellence. Probably in competition with the new metal tools, or as an indication of a sacred reserve, the lithic industry produced daggers, so-called fish-tail daggers, and lance tips of the finest flint.[257] Amber-bead necklaces are similar to those found in the Single Graves of the north. Sickles and saws, bent knives with inserted flint blades and other cutting tools complete the inventories. It was not yet customary that the gifts accompany the deceased onto the funeral pyre.

To the extent that the small number of finds from the stone cists permits conclusions, the construction of the graves as well as the quality of the inventory suggests that the people buried in these cists belonged to a socially prominent group. For some graves up to 200 burials have been distinguished. The tombs may be the hereditary burial sites of a noble class.[258]

One of the stone cists, located at Züschen near Fritzlar in Hesse, bears engravings on the interior of pine-twig patterns, geometrics and figures produced by a pick technique

63. The stone cist grave at Züschen showing the partition slab with 'Seelenloch' and pinetwig engravings, c. 3500–2000 B.C.

64. Menhir-like stone from the stone cist at Züschen showing a bird's eye view of a team of oxen yoked to a cart, after c. 3000 B.C. It was not a wall slab.

(Fig. 63). Most interesting and unique for central Europe is a bird's-eye view of two bovines linked by a yoke, hitched to a cart (Fig. 64). It is these engravings which are related to the western menhir decorations and which suggest the west European origin of the stone cist burials.[259]

Funnel Beakers form the characteristic pottery inventory of the megalith graves. These beakers belong to a northern style developed in Denmark from early ceramic forms, generally contemporary with late Rössen Ware.[260] The concept 'funnel beaker' is first applied to ceramics found in western and central Poland, tall broad bulbous beakers, with or without lugs at the shoulders for stringing and hanging. From the shoulders the walls of the neck flare out widely. While in Denmark the older Funnel Beaker culture is coexistent with the older, still Mesolithic, Ertebolle culture,[261] isolated in pockets, the finds in Poland show the Funnel Beakers to be below the horizon of the bulbous amphorae[262] and at the horizon equivalent with that of the Baalberge style of pottery of the Early Lower Chalcolithic, c. 4500–3600 B.C. The Funnel Beaker is the most important type of vessel, though other typical forms include collared flasks, juglike vessels with handles, diverse bulbous bowls and footed bowls (Plate 1c). Remarkable is the wealth of decorative ideas with which an almost unlimited imagination ornamented its vessels.[263] By means of cords wound around the pots, pieces of string fastened to the tip of a stick and then rolled over the surface in a twirling motion, shells, stylus-like bones and combs of bone, rich combinations of decorative patterns were pressed into the clay vessels to produce designs of boxed angles, triangles, wedges, vertical lines, waves, cut lines, grooves, horizontal zigzags, fringe patterns, fish-bone and ladder patterns. Though these motifs are simple in themselves, their combined use makes for great diversity of appearance (Fig. 65). In general the pottery reflects the change from a pulling to an indenting and incising technique. The pottery is therefore often referred to as *Tiefstichkeramik*—a deeply incised pottery. An embellishing feature was added

65. Conical beaker with a wealth of incised ornamentation, from Skarpsalling, Denmark, *c.* 3500–2000 B.C. This beaker is one of the most beautiful of its kind.

when these indentations came to be filled with white paste emphasizing the designs even more.[264]

During the later period equivalent to the Middle and Upper Chalcolithic, Schleswig-Holstein represents a fringe area for the Danish sphere. In the area from Holland to the Elbe there is a predominance of collared flasks, the collar being a wedge-shaped ring circling the mid-section of the long neck.[265] Along the southern shore of the Baltic Sea a younger phase of Funnel Beaker pottery is represented by amphorae, Funnel Beakers and deep funnel bowls, especially attractive with designs of grooves and ladders.

The fragmentary evidence surrounding the Funnel Beakers does not allow a finely differentiated chronology. It is curious though, that before Funnel Beaker pottery disappears from the megalith graves, it first undergoes an impoverishment in that it gives up its characteristic forms and ornamentation before being displaced by Corded Ware.

As was pointed out above, there was contact between the megalith builders of northern Germany and areas further south. This is supported in that in central Germany collared flasks are most frequently associated with Jordansmühl and Baalberg, i.e. Early Lower Chalcolithic pottery. Further south they appear in the Middle Chalcolithic stone cists of Hesse.[266]

Very little is known about housing of this period, though the remains of two 85 m long houses have been located. That carts were in use is indicated by wagon wheels made of wooden discs, found in Danish and north German moors.[267]

There is some evidence of contact with other parts of Europe either in the form of influences or direct imports; thus flat copper axes are typologically close to those of the Altheim group in southern Germany, one dagger resembles Spanish work, arm spirals are related to others from central Germany, and discs resemble work found in Poland, all of which points to cultural contacts with central European developments.[268]

Typical implements of the Funnel Beaker culture are double axes, which were probably not only used as weapons, as they were often imitated in amber and formed part of the grave inventories. Flint axes were particularly numerous. Prepared with great care, these core tools had been worked and polished to a high finish. Modern tests have shown that with such an axe a birch tree 30 cm in diameter could be felled in twenty minutes.[269] Rock, however, was also used to make thin pointed axes or battle axes and clubs. It has been suggested that the elegantly shaped double-bladed axes with narrow necks and flaring rounded blades up to 40 cm long (Fig. 66) are stone imitations of copper axe models.[270]

The advent of the Chalcolithic in central Europe is marked by two type stations representative of an Early Lower Chalcolithic, *c.* 4500–3600 B.C., Jordansmühl in Silesia, and Baalberge near Bernburg, north-west of Halle. These two east central European cultures develop parallel to one another, but while the Jordansmühl group seems to stem from the Hungarian plain, spreading over Bohemia and Moravia, Silesia and Saxony, the Baalberge culture is concentrated further to the north-west from the middle Elbe and Saale rivers to Bohemia, stretching northward into Mecklenburg and Pomerania.[271] A wealth of copper articles is associated with the Jordansmühl culture, especially ornaments such as spirals, metal pendants with curled ends and spiral arm rings. Jordansmühl Ware is characterized by a new style of beaker with two looped handles, especially on cups. Also present are footed bowls, double cone beakers, Funnel Beakers, some zoomorphic vessels and collared flasks, all frequently ornamented with bands of chevrons, triangles and horizontal lines. The Jordansmühl group engaged in Single Grave burials, the corpses placed in fetal positions, the grave sometimes protected by stone settings. Some evidence of cremation comes from the Hungarian plain. The type station itself yielded no graves. For the Baalberge culture[272] undecorated pottery, showing some links with Rössen ware,[273] is the leading identifying element, where two, three or four

66. Double axe, *c.* 2500 B.C., so-called battle axe.

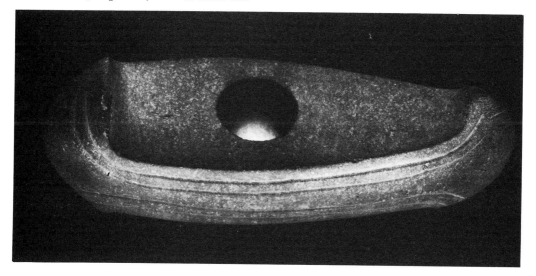

109

handled amphorae are typical, along with jugs, cups, Funnel Beakers and large funnel flanged vessels, bowls and pots, as well as lugged beakers and collared flasks, with standing bases. This pottery group dissolves towards the east and south-east. The Baalberge culture is still committed to the use of flint for scrapers, arrow heads and axes, and bone and antler implements. In that respect this group is still quite Neolithic, copper being evident only in one child's grave. The presence of Funnel Beakers links these two cultures with other contemporary cultures of the Upper Neolithic–Chalcolithic period. The Baalbergers were the first to use tumulus and stone cist burials, contrary to the preceding Neolithic cultures which used flat graves without monumental superstructures. They were also the first to have pottery grave inventories, though usually only one piece. The grave mounds are usually round, sometimes enclosed in stone circles. Stone cists, described above, are numerous. They are essentially E–W in position, the head placed in the east, facing north.

The Lower Chalcolithic culture which relieves the Neolithic Banded Ware cultures of south-western central Europe, such as the lake cultures, is dominated by a ceramic culture with characteristic tulip beakers (Fig. 67). Named after the type station Michelsberg[274] in south-western Germany, its presence is evident at over 200 sites, in eastern France from Alsace to Belgium, in the Ruhr area, in Hesse, in central Germany, in Bohemia and in south-eastern Bavaria to Salzburg. The settlements on flat land show extensive systems of fortifications, with moats up to 3 m deep and 10 m across, palisades and ditches and fortified gateways.[275] The graves, however, offer only fragmentary information about the people. The typical tulip beaker is unornamented except for a distinctive arcade pattern just under the rim made by finger impressions (Fig. 68). The surface is finger-smoothed. The vessels have generally been provided with loops or knobs for hanging and only occasionally do they have a flattened base for standing.

The stone tools associated with Michelsberg ware tend to be made of a stone found

67. Tulip beaker, Michelsberg Ware, *c.* 3900 B.C., from Appolding, Bavaria.

68. Typical ware with characteristic arcade impressions under the rim, *c.* 3600 B.C., from Altheim near Landshut in Bavaria.

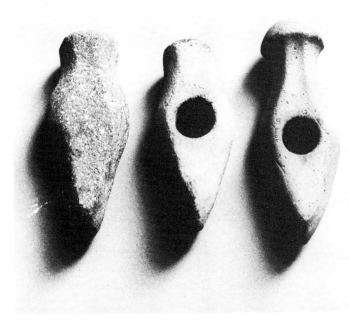

69. Axes, roughed in and finished of Michelsberg and Altheim styles, *c.* 3600 B.C., from Winkl, Hausen and Palsweis.

frequently in Belgium.[276] Blades are of silex and long points not normally known during the Neolithic first appear in association with this culture. Its rock axes have pointed necks and are either oval or rectangular in shape on the crosscut (Fig. 69). Wooden tools have been found in great numbers. Towards the fringes of the influence some special regional derivations come about in Switzerland and in south-western Germany in the lake area around Lake Constance, while type stations in the general vicinity of Munich show links with the south-western groups in Switzerland as well as with Jordansmühl ware towards the north-east. In these transitional cultural areas are interspersed pockets of original Michelsberg ware.[277]

What appears to have been an early and mainly central European network of ceramic influences during the Lower Chalcolithic is succeeded by a more complex system of cultural links during the Middle Chalcolithic, *c.* 3500–2000 B.C., contained in a frame extending from Asia Minor to Poland in the east, to the Swiss lakes and Westphalia in the west (Fig. 70). Thus the ceramic evidence and especially the knowledge of metallic implements, such as axes and daggers, from the type station at Baden in Lower Austria representing over 550 sites, explored mainly in Hungary, point to links with the Banat and Balkan cultural areas, where at Vinča Baden pottery follows directly upon Vinča ceramics.[278] The Baden group stands out particularly because of its custom of burying cattle and using them as grave gifts. It engages in the ritualistic, probably sacrificial depositing of vessels (Fig. 71). Though human corpses were placed in fetal positions, no specific attention was paid to direction. Cremation and the deposition of the ashes in urns was also practised, even in the same cemeteries, and since the graves did not overlap they must have been marked.[279]

Further north between the Elbe and Saale rivers, the Salzmünde group, named after a type station near Halle, is seen to descend from the Baalberge culture on the basis of the ceramic evidence.[280] The pottery, especially jugs with high cylindrical necks, equipped with one or two handles, the shoulders decorated with vertical grooves, is linked with that of the earlier Baalbergers, but also with that of the Baden styles, which

70. Depot find of polished rock wedges/axes, associated with one copper axe (left), after *c.* 3800 B.C., from Grossheubach near Miltenberg.

71. Gold discs from a depot at Stollhof, Lower Austria, *c.* 3000 B.C.

in turn were linked with Balkan and Danubian styles. Towards the east links with the southern Polish Funnel Beaker culture could also be established. Only very little metal can be associated with the Salzmünde group. Settled mainly on elevated sites, this group used the tumulus over a sunk grave box of thin stone plates bonded with clay, paved with shards, a characteristic of the culture. Usually the corpse was placed in a right-sided fetal position, either N-S or W-E.

Further towards the north the Salzmünde culture made contact with the Walternienburg group located in the area of the confluence of Saale and Elbe.[281] This type station

Map 14. Ceramic cultures of the Middle Chalcolithic, *c.* 3500 B.C.–after *c.* 2000 B.C.

Walternienburg

Bernburg
Salzmünde

Cham

Goldberg
Altheim

Corded Ware

Direction of cultural influence

Federsee
Dürnberg Attersee
Mondsee
Baden

Horgen

is a flat grave cemetery linked with a later gravefield at Bernburg, north of Halle. Most characteristic for this group are those so-called 'drums' mentioned above, often bearing symbolic signs, but also cylindrical beakers and amphorae with sharply profiled shoulders and two, four or eight handles. Though the pottery is not uniform it shows a consistent transition in the variation of forms. Bernburg pottery is characterized by rounded ware with simpler and generally poorer decoration even if carefully applied. 'Drums' and storage vessels also occur. The stone inventory consists of battle axes, arrowheads and arrow blades. Ornaments are of amber shaped into pearls or axeheads, bone fashioned into beads, and copper coils and finger spirals.[282] Bone was still used to make needles of various types. Both groups used single graves, with or without stone protection, stone cists as well as chambers of stone blocks or dry-wall. The Walternienburg–Bernburg groups are the most southerly to use megalith graves of the northern type, covered either with tumuli or barrows. No other group during the Chalcolithic in central Europe shows as much variation in pottery or in burial practices as do these two cultural groups, probably an effect of the confluence of the north German and central German influences. While this group tends towards north-western Germany, the more southerly Salzmünde group exerts itself towards the south-east, to Poland and Bohemia. The strata in this region show Bernburg ware to be superseded either by Corded Ware, bulbous amphorae or Únĕtician (Bronze Age) ware.[283]

In the south the area around Salzburg reflects influences from the lakeshore cultures of Upper Austria—Attersee, Mondsee—which show ceramic links with south-eastern Slovenian and north-eastern Moravian styles,[284] as well as some links with styles from Cham in northern Bavaria and the Goldberg Level III in south-western Germany. The joint appearance of ceramic and lithic elements of all these groups points to the importance of the Salzburg area in relation to the early mining of copper[285] and perhaps even of salt. The Goldberg in turn yields ceramics from Cham and Altheim above Michelsberg as well as shards of the later Corded Ware and bulbous amphorae, while some of the characteristics link Goldberg III with the Horgen culture, named after the type station on Lake Zürich, a lakeshore culture which extended from Lake Geneva to the Federsee and which is attested to on 70 sites. Though Horgen ware is very coarse and simple, it surprises with symbolic figural motifs. Horgen ware is also superseded by Corded Ware.[286]

It is curious that in southern Westfalia and northern Hesse grave forms are considered to be derivative of the *galeries couvertes* of the Paris Basin, similar to the stone cists, made of local lime- and sandstone, while the ceramic criteria for the Neolithic and Chalcolithic are not. Instead the pottery influences of all the cultural areas of the Middle Chalcolithic, even distant Badener ware, are in evidence. The graves contain next to no burial gifts, however. Ornaments consist of amber pearls, bone beads, small copper coils and very many bored animal teeth. The numerous finds of lower jaws of fox would suggest that some cultural significance was associated with them. Further eastward smaller but related graves, sometimes with wooden chambers, contained ceramic inventories related to the Walternienburg–Bernburg groups.[287]

The most dominant pottery culture of the Middle Chalcolithic and the one with which that period concludes is the Corded Ware culture (Plate 1d).[288] A localized northern term is that of Single Grave culture, to differentiate this group from the megalith builders who engaged in multiple burials.[289] Often the term Battle Axe culture is used to designate this late cultural phase of the Chalcolithic, owing to the presence of axes among the funerary equipment of the deceased (Fig. 72). By means of its rope-

72. Battle axe from a Corded Ware warrior grave, found in the Brunnleitenforst near Grafrath, south-west of Fürstenfeldbruck, Bavaria.

design ceramics, its characteristic single grave burial practices and its axes,[290] this Corded Ware culture has been located from Alsace and eastern Switzerland to the rivers Moskva and Dniestr in Russia and from the Alps and northern Hungary to central Sweden and southern Finland. In central Germany numerous secondary Corded Ware depositions supersede Baalberge, Salzmünde and Walternienburg–Bernburg burial inventories. Little information is available about this culture's settlements and construction practices, since their sites, with the exception of Switzerland, are largely unknown. Evidence comes mainly from graves, single finds and depots. But even so skeletal remains of Corded Ware users are rare.[291]

Considering the vast area in which the Corded Ware cultural presence has been identified, it cannot have been homogeneous in its expression. Instead there are regional variations in ceramic form and ornamentation. Although the battle axes are representative of a universal type from Switzerland to Moscow, there are numerous regional sub-types, not only because of different local rock, but also because of cultural differences,[292] and while burials adhere to a general practice—tumulus, single grave, E-W positioning—there are again regional differentiations.

Various manifestations of these characteristics have of course been observed during earlier cultural periods. Thus axes were used and worn before the appearance of Corded Ware, Single Graves were associated with Jordansmühl and megalith graves, tumuli were introduced by the Baalberge group and cord designs were used on Funnel Beakers. It is not, then, as though the Corded Ware culture had appeared suddenly and raced across Europe to occupy vast areas, as had been concluded hastily in order to accommodate the arrival of the Indo-Europeans in this general period.[293] Since a culture cannot usually be grasped archeologically until it has attained a stage where its identifiable and distinct component elements have become consolidated, it would appear instead that the Corded Ware culture is a central European synthesis. It has been suggested that central Germany, the Saale-Elbe region, formed the core area.[294]

What is acceptable is that towards the end of the Neolithic-Chalcolithic period, cultural groups were present in Europe whose chief characteristic was an ability to adapt, who used tamed horses, and whose economy was still based on agriculture. They seem to have known the plow, and to have placed a special emphasis on the raising of livestock; a cattle corral has been located in Holland,[295] and they kept sheep. They used wheeled vehicles (but not drawn by horses) and river craft. Did they look upon water as a means of communication and transport rather than as an obstacle? Did they build roads? Were they more mobile? Were they inclined towards nomadism? Were they a new people? Does the presence of axes testify to a warlike attitude? Are the bearers of these axes logical candidates for that idea of conquest and domination of an indigenous Neolithic-Chalcolithic population? It has been suggested that the megalith builders were a sedentary farming population, conservative in outlook, which clung to its ancestral burial grounds, but that the Single Grave 'people' was a migrant strain.[296] Armed with battle axes they maintained their volatile nature, transmitting this restlessness to their Germanic descendants as a happy *Wanderlust*. Since there is no marked break in the continuity with earlier cultures, an invasion of Battle Axe people who cleared their way from the Urals and the Black Sea into central Europe is not probable. The pottery styles are not totally unrelated to previous styles; instead innovations are adopted and adapted.[297] The idea has been advanced that the original peasant culture was transformed by the transmission of concepts, perhaps of an economic or a religious nature, such as a new burial cult, or by the infiltration of small groups, a sort of immigration from within. Research seems to indicate that small migrant groups can be expected to have been involved, as carriers, who adopted from and assimilated with the native populations. This would account for the continuity in certain localities, as well as for the degree of uniformity, a 'uniformity horizon' so to speak, which gave to the various Corded Ware groups that consistent genetic connection, that common denominator of form and ornamentation.[298] However, it is generally accepted today that the Corded Ware culture was not borne by a Corded Ware 'people'.

Corded Ware is characterized by short-necked, round-bellied amphorae, cups, bowls and beakers, often with handles or ears attached at the most bulbous part, and designs sometimes scratched but usually rolled on to neck and shoulders. The manufacture is very coarse in all details. The many subgroups and the great variation in detail within any group allow for chronological arrangements. Triangles both filled and outlined, arranged as rows of teeth—gaping jaw effect—bands of zigzag and ladder designs are complemented by fields of white-paste-encrusted rope impressions.[299]

The development of graves from subterranean, to surface, to above-surface levels, as well as the stone cist burials have already been described. Characteristic for the burial rites is deliberate fetal positioning of the deceased: resting on the right side, the head placed in the west for men, resting on the left side, the head placed in the east for women, so that both sexes face south. Female graves were furnished with ornaments of amber, bored shells worn as brooches or sewn onto garments, canine teeth to be worn as pendants or as chains, as well as spiral rolls and copper beads, copper arm rings, neck rings, arm and leg coils. Traces of textiles such as linen and wool have been identified.[300] Typical for the Corded Ware culture is the performance of an interesting medical operation. For unknown reasons some men, but never women, were subjected to trepanation, that neurosurgical procedure by means of which a circular disc of bone about 2 cm in diameter was removed from the skull. Usually this operation is designed to relieve pressure on the brain, but also to release evil spirits. The rounded edges on the cranial bone indicate that healing and bone regrowth had taken place and that the patient had not died of the operation (Fig. 73). Some men had even survived it twice.[301] Male graves were furnished with axes, and sometimes with clubs and silex knives, but only rarely with silex arrowheads, bone needles, boars' teeth or copper arm rings. It is

73. Trephined skulls, *c.* 2500 B.C., double trephine (left) from Døjringe bog on central Sjaelland, single trephine (right) from Naes on the island of Falster, Denmark.

74. Fishtail daggers and flint swords, *c.* 2500 B.C., with visible 'casting seams' on the daggers.

75. Flint weapons and their metallic models. Daggers and 'scimitars' from Barkaer on Jylland, Denmark.

the presence of these axes, so-called battle axes, which led to the identification of these populations as Battle Axe people. It has been proposed that these stone axes represent a regression from metallic to lithic skills brought about by the migration of metal-working groups into metal-poor areas, i.e. cultural impoverishment as a result of a lost technology. That stone axes and flint daggers attain highly elegant forms is frequently attributed to the competition between craftsmen working in stone and those of the new technology (Fig. 74).[302] The especially splendid workmanship of the stone implements suggests a ritual quality, and their intention to have been ceremonial rather than functional, equivalent in their prestige value to the status derived from the ownership of a copper dagger or axe (Fig. 75). Some copper axes have been found which, contrary to stone axes, do not come from grave inventories, but rather from moors or lakes, ponds and rivers, suggesting their use as sacrificial offerings.[303] In all probability these copper axes stimulated the manufacture of the various types of lithic axes used by the Corded Ware culture during the late Middle Chalcolithic. For the lithic industry these implements mark the peak of the stone tool culture, destined to disappear shortly afterwards.[304]

Contemporary with the Corded Ware culture, but only as a short-term phenomenon, *Kugelamphoren*, bulbous amphorae, appear to be the dominant ceramic style from Lüneburg in the west to southern Russia in the east.[305] Probably originating in the east, the pottery shows such uniformity across the entire area that no regional or developmental differences are apparent. The main forms are generally squat bulbous amphorae with slightly conical, sloped or cylindrical necks, round-bellied bodies, rounded bottoms, with two strong, ear-like handles spanning shoulder and neck. Consisting largely of triangular or diamond-shaped rope impressions, but also of fields of coiled rope impressions, ornamentation is reserved for the neck and shoulder areas. The link with Corded Ware is apparent, though chisel, scale, arc, chevron, dot, and circle impressions, as well as furrows and simple lines, are equally in evidence. The uniformity of the imprinted patterns suggests that stamps were used. The single flat graves contain corpses in left- or right-sided fetal positions, in an E-W direction and facing north or south. The inventories are rich, consisting of three or four vessels as a rule, but up to a dozen vessels are not unusual. The majority are bulbous amphorae, usually in pairs, associated with other styles. Silex axes, knives and arrow blades complete the inventory of implements. A typical element in the provisioning of these graves are bones of pig, in particular lower jaws and teeth. Especially noteworthy are entire carcasses of cattle deposited as funerary gifts.[306] In central and northern Germany the Bulbous Amphorae horizons appear as secondary burials in the tumuli of the Baalberge and Salzmünde groups and in the northern megaliths.[307] Associations with the Bernburgers and with the south-west German Goldberg III are also indicated.

As the Middle Chalcolithic draws to a close, the Corded Ware culture in central Europe shows links with the succeeding Bell Beaker cultures.[308] In southern Bavaria the Corded Ware culture is represented by battle axes and by beakers generally ornamented not with cord impressions but with circular or crescent-shaped imprints. Burial practices, however, correspond to the established pattern. For south-west Germany the evidence comes from hill graves, some equipped with wooden structures linked with encircling ditches. Amphorae and beakers bear cord imprints. From the Upper Neckar the last phase of the Corded Ware culture enters into Switzerland. Only above-surface-level graves are in evidence. Ceramics already betray some relationship with the Bell Beaker culture (Fig. 76), as well as links with northern Italy and southern

76. Bell Beaker from Praunheim, *c.* 2500 B.C.

Map 15. Ceramic cultures of the Upper Chalcolithic and Early
Bronze Age Bell Beakers, after *c.* 3500 B.C. (after Harrison, 1974).

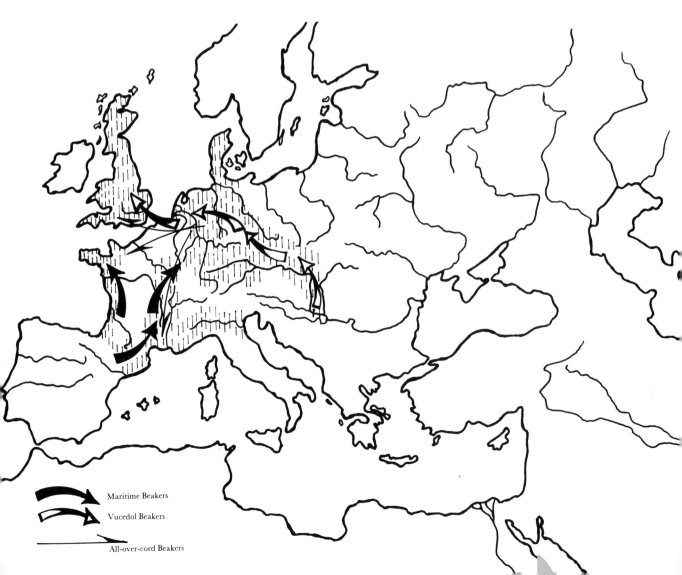

Maritime Beakers

Vucedol Beakers

All-over-cord Beakers

France. In their ornamentation some of the designs are already related to the early Bronze Age designs in Switzerland, so that in Switzerland one must speak of a relative contemporaneity of Corded Ware, Bell Beakers and the early Bronze Age. The coexistence of Bronze Age innovations and late Corded Ware styles is indicated in that the influences are reciprocal.[309]

Switzerland stands apart from the other Corded Ware provinces in that, contrary to the rest of central Europe, Corded Ware settlements are known. Along the lakeshores the users of Corded Ware adapted to their new environment and reoccupied older lakeshore villages.[310] Architectural details have not been preserved. The presence of the Corded Ware culture is indicated by pottery and tools of stone, wood and bone, as well as the presence of copper. A second departure from the norm is that the Corded Ware population of Switzerland cremated its dead and included spindle weights among the funerary gifts. Otherwise burial practices conform to northern usage.

The relationship to the Bell Beaker culture allows for the identification of a later phase of the Single Grave culture for northern Europe, as indicated especially in the surface and above-surface graves. This transitional phase constitutes the Upper Chalcolithic. The evidence indicates that some Bell Beakers came north as far as Jutland and Mecklenburg.[311] The new graves are more carefully laid out and especially in the secondary use of tumuli the hill graves now come to have stone paving for protection. Contrary to the previous E–W direction of the corpses the deceased, though still in fetal pose, are now positioned in a N–S direction. New now is the appearance of tree coffins. Inhumation is the dominant funerary practice, except that the corpse is now stretched and supine. Women's graves contain only a few amber beads, a flint knife and only one vessel. While men are still equipped with an axe or club, these are so fragile and of such inferior quality as to be completely unfunctional.[312] Instead this phase of the Upper Chalcolithic is marked by the use of splendidly worked flint daggers, quite probably copied in competition with copper models. One such dagger was found complete with wooden hilt, leather sheath and thongs for fastening to the belt.[313] Lancet-shaped daggers appear to be the characteristic weapon, so much so that following the period of the Single Graves a span of 100 years is called the Dagger Age.[314] Except for the location of some sites, nothing is known about settlements.

The origin of the Bell Beaker culture is not clear. In the end it was located from Ireland to Hungary and from Italy and Spain to Denmark. The last of the Chalcolithic cultures, it was seen[315] to have been carried rapidly by cattle breeders and hunters who originated in the area of the western Mediterranean around 2000 B.C. and moved up the Atlantic coast so that in a relatively short space of time their cultural presence was felt in western France, the British Isles, the Rhine valley, the Danube Basin into Hungary, north into Thuringia and on to Denmark. Their economic basis was ranching—cattle, horses, sheep and pigs—and hunting. The subordinate economic role played by agriculture has been attributed to the rapid mobility with which this culture is seen to have taken possession of Europe.[316]

The chronology of this cultural spread is not clear. Some evidence points to the contemporaneity and coexistence of Bell Beakers and Corded Ware in some locations. Generally Bell Beaker horizons supersede those of Corded Ware.[317] In gravefields there are some secondary Bell Beaker burials in Corded Ware tumuli, but side by side burials without overlap point to coexistence and/or continuity of the population at least in the use of the cemeteries. However, there have also been found typical Corded Ware burials containing a single Bell Beaker as ceramic inventory.[318] This would point at least to some association between the two cultures, either as an indication of two coexistent peoples or as a transitional phase of a cultural continuum, that did not necessarily involve the invasion of foreigners and the subjugation of a native population. From the battle axes as chief evidence one has deduced unsettled times for central Europe.[319] The new economic possibilities, new sources of prosperity, and new mobile life style (raiding parties?) are assumed to have brought groups into conflict with one another. Was it one of those periods of migration which Europe experienced periodically? Perhaps the Bell Beakers are the evidence of prehistoric trading parties who dealt in the export of cultural goods. This time though, the cultural and economic change to a way of life that depended on mixed farming and hunting as sources of sustenance is seen to have been connected with the dislocation of populations.[320]

Burial practices point to a radical break in continuity and the advent of a separate culture.[321] Several hundred sites show the graves to have been single flat graves, rectangular in shape, in stone cists where available, sometimes only with a covering. The deceased are placed in fetal positions, N–S or S–N in direction. Men rest on their left side, their heads placed north, and women on their right side, their heads placed south, so that both sexes face uniformly east. This is a characteristic feature of the culture and marks a complete departure from Corded Ware practice where both sexes faced south. A later phase sees cremation with the ashes deposited in urns—Bell Beakers—or with the urns inverted over the pile of ashes. Most Bell Beaker graves contain only one vessel, but towards the east up to eight vessels were placed in the grave. Contrary to previous cultures which set the vessel in front of the corpse usually at face level, the Bell Beaker culture placed it behind the deceased. The Bell Beaker was funerary ware, since very rarely have shards been found in those settlements that could be located. Conversely ordinary settlement ware is almost never found in graves.[322] Bell Beaker profiles vary from curvaceous, elongated ʃ-shapes to the angular. The clay-working techniques are good, the vessels are thin-walled and smooth. Frequent use is made of the color red, itself a significant departure from the light brown and white Corded Ware. The ornamentation covers the entire surface, contained in grooved or impressed horizontal zones. In east central Europe, handles may have been attached. From rim to base comb patterns, notches, incisions, and cut or wound cord patterns gird the vessel in zigzag bands, grill or ladder patterns, sometimes changing direction, giving the entire design a fishbone effect (Plate 2a).

Although it is the Bell Beaker culture which introduced the use of metal articles— weapons and vessels—into central and northern Europe, the emphasis continued to be on stone artefacts. Even so, copper daggers established themselves, at first with blade and hilt worked in one piece, then in a later phase fastened together by means of rivets. Copper, silver and gold ornaments, especially earrings, were worn, as were decorative platelets. Typical ornaments for Bell Beaker people were round conical antler buttons (Fig. 77). This fashion was restricted to this culture. The locations of these buttons in the graves indicate that they must have been decorations sewn on to garments, in a line from neck to waist, but also on neckbands and on the head-dress. From Spain, Portugal, Sardinia, Sicily, Italy, France, Holland, England, across Europe to the Caucasus Mountains and Iran, these buttons were the fashion. Amber buttons from northern Germany, Denmark, Sweden and the eastern Baltic coast did not play as significant a role.[323] Contrary to the customs of other Chalcolithic cultures, decorations of canine teeth were not popular. In addition it appears that men of the Bell Beaker culture wore rectangular stone platelets, with two or four holes for fastening, on their left arms at

Plate 1a. Magdalenian stone tools from the Petersfels cave.

Plate 1b. Banded Ware, Lineband type, *c.* 5400–4400 B.C., from Wettingen near Schweinfurt.

Plate 1c. Funeral Beaker from a megalith grave, Helvesiek, near Rotenburg in Lower Saxony.

Plate 1d. Corded Ware pierced lug beaker with lid from Kötschen, *c.* 2600–2000 B.C.

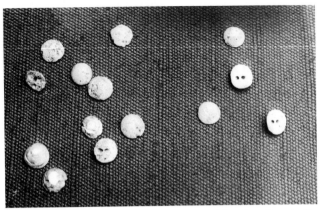

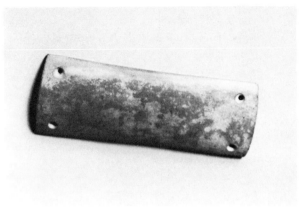

77. Conical antler buttons from a grave at München-Zamdorf, *c.* 2500 B.C.

78. Stone platelet from a grave at München-Sendling, *c.* 2500 B.C.

waist level. Well-made and decorated, these plates must have been more than an ornament and were probably a symbol of social rank (Fig. 78).

For the historical development of central Europe the Bell Beaker culture was significant owing to its contribution to the emergence of some of the native cultures into the early Bronze Age. Still a Neolithic–Chalcolithic culture, it introduced to Europe north of the Alps knowledge of the metal technology.[324]

Although agriculture and the raising of livestock provided the economic basis for the Neolithic–Chalcolithic, in northern Europe Mesolithic and Neolithic economies co-existed even during the Chalcolithic. In Denmark, for instance, along the coastlines peasants of the Funnel Beaker culture shared areas with the Mesolithic Ertebolle culture, which continued as mussel gatherers, fishers and hunters. Further south, the Baalbergers settled on chernozem, the Bulbous Amphorae on clay and sandy soils. In general mixed farming was the pattern. The earlier view that the Corded Ware or Bell Beaker cultures were borne exclusively by nomadic herdsmen could not be maintained after cereal grains had been found in their pottery. The grain was harvested with sickles or knives; threshing was done by means of flails. Experiments have shown that two hours of grinding grain on a stone could produce 3 kg of flour.[325] Prepared as a mush it would then be baked into flat pizza-like bread, perhaps on those puzzling circular clay plates. Pollen analysis shows a decrease in elm pollen accompanied by an increase in grass pollens, which may mark the increased clearing of the land to allow grazing.[326] This deforestation may also account for the increase in the number of flint and stone axes and wedges among the archeological evidence.

With the advent of the Funnel Beaker culture at the beginning of the Chalcolithic period, the hunt receded as the chief means of satisfying the demand for meat, although the presence in graves of bones of game and fowl indicates at least the occasional hunt for stag, deer, wild boar, hare, squirrel, duck, swan, goose, grouse, even seal and whale near the coast. Examination of the refuse pits shows that for the Baalbergers 80 per cent of all bones are cattle bones, for the Michelsbergers 54 per cent are cattle bones, while game, such as aurochs, stag, bear and deer constitute only 2·5 per cent of all bones. At Altheim 27 per cent are cattle bones, while 25 per cent are of game—stag and deer equally represented. In the Alpine foot-hills game is emphasized as a supply of meat; thus at Polling only 11 per cent are cattle bones, while 42 per cent are of stag alone, complemented by boar, deer, bear and beaver. For the Horgen and other cultures of the western Alps, up to 90 per cent of bone finds are of game, such as wild pigs, the latter related to wild species; i.e. pigs were allowed to roam freely. Sheep and goats appear to have been kept mainly for their milk, wool and fibers.[327] Domesticated horses first appear in central Europe during the period of the Corded Ware culture, not for riding but as draught animals. The moors of Oldenburg have yielded wheels datable to shortly before 3000 B.C.

It is not known to what extent the various industries rested in the hands of specialized craftsmen, or whether the various settlements met their respective needs by annual expeditions to acquire the necessary flint, copper ores and clay. Stones for tools sometimes came from some distance away, flint having to be mined in shafts and pits. Pottery clay is not available everywhere, and not all copper ores are equally suited for the manufacture of implements. In contrast to the Mediterranean area, in central Europe pottery appears to have been manufactured privately,[328] except that at the time of the Bell Beaker culture itinerant potters may have helped to spread the pottery style. While flint working shows signs of specialization, it cannot be concluded that it is the work of only a few specialized craftsmen. Domestic industries are indicated in wood carving, leather working and weaving—tools for the combing of hemp, spindles and clay spindle whorls, remnants of looms, loom weights and vegetable fibres, and even pieces of woven fabric have been found in the settlements. No doubt some articles were obtained through trade.

At the turn of the fourth to the third millennium B.C. there are no indications that metals were appreciated as anything but valued raw materials. In northern Germany gold must have been known in the form of nuggets washed along in rivers and streams, but otherwise there are no natural metallic resources there, so that they would all have to be imported.[329] Central Europe drew its copper from Transylvania, Slovakia, the eastern and western Alps, central Germany and northern Hesse. In the realm of the Baden culture in eastern Austria implements for casting metals have been found in great numbers. Very important as a source of copper was the valley of the river Salzach, where copper had been mined ever since the Mondsee settlements of the Middle Chalcolithic. Crucibles and smelting pots as well as molds for two types of axes have been found on the Rainberg in Salzburg.[331] The relatively high density of settlement in this area must be related to the mining of copper.

It would appear that by the time of the Middle Chalcolithic a value system had developed which recognized copper as a valuable, desirable and negotiable commodity. It is probable that the lithic industries involved a value system and one can assume that similar though less esteemed associations were made during earlier stages in regard to the mining, preparation, distribution and ownership of fine flint, or shells, ivory and perhaps even pottery. Such associations came to be made with metals. Once copper was generally accepted as a means of payment and exchange, the accumulation of copper hoards became a practical pursuit, giving those who supplied it, its miners, smiths, its distributors and those who owned and controlled it, a basis for wielding economic and probably political power.[332]

The settlements of the Chalcolithic give no evidence of the social stratification which would set segments of their populations apart from one another, nor is anything known about the administrative models which prevailed there. Was the ownership of a larger house also an indication of administrative predominance?[333] Was ownership hereditary? Do multiple burials—up to 200 over four to eight generations—in the grave chambers of the megalith tombs point to the existence of clans? Was the family the basic social unit? The form of the houses and the presence of a central hearth would support the

123

view of single family units. But what was the role of the family unit in the community? The equal treatment accorded men and women in the funerary practices would suggest equality of the sexes at least within the family unit.[334]

There are indications that in some locations at least society was arranged on estate lines during the Chalcolithic. The grave equipment points to the existence of socially distinct groups, which in turn indicates a degree of social stability. Some of the grave inventories contain weapons and ornaments for body and clothing which were probably intended to convey an abstract idea. Copper daggers and axes were evidently something exceptional in themselves and would have singled out distinguished individuals, perhaps underlined their social worth and princely, even royal station. That, however, cannot be deduced with certainty from the evidence. The unmarred condition of the battle axes contained in the Corded Ware burials would suggest that these axes were restricted to funerary use. That they had a symbolic function, perhaps as indicators of privilege and social status, of the existence of an armsbearing caste, is supported by the use of miniature axes in the graves of boys, and by the size, ornamentation and cast handles of some copper axes. Other distinguishing indicators are platelets of bone carefully carved and ornamented, and worn either as pendants or tied to the body, as well as 'armguards'—rectangular platelets of stone with little holes drilled into each corner to facilitate fastening. It is attractive to think of these items as indicators of leadership or as the attributes of ruling groups with hereditary rights, sacred functions and distinguishing occupations favored with possessions. Whether the absence of such differentiating features implies the existence of an estate of dispossessed workers, serfs and slaves cannot be deduced with certainty either. It is difficult to assess the extent to which the available evidence represents a fragmentary selection of largely accidental finds. Evidently the culture carriers—that group which had things to leave behind—are mainly represented in the finds. This group would be small and not representative of the total population of culture supporters. The possibility exists of course that the dependent population is represented by the more impoverished forms of the ceramic and lithic industries.[335] It must be assumed that the fortifications with their rings of mighty earthworks, as well as the lakeshore settlements, do reflect the existence of structured societies.

The existence of elevated fortifications in central Europe, often in the vicinity of copper ore deposits, suggests that these fortified sites exercised at least some control over the ownership, exploitation, working and distribution of these resources. No doubt these fortresses derived real political power and spheres of influence from the domination of this industry. It is also conceivable that this econo-political basis allowed the establishment of 'states' in central Europe.

3. The Bronze Age
The Inner Colonization

The coming of a new age was less of a cultural break than the term 'Bronze Age' suggests. The Neolithic way of life, based on the raising of livestock as a basis for providing sustenance, and on agriculture as a condition demanding a greater degree of sedentariness, of course, continued for very many centuries to come. The advent of the Chalcolithic period, which witnessed the gradual development of man's ability to transform ores into metal implements, served to familiarize man gradually with one additional option in preparing his tools, artefacts and ornaments. During the early Bronze Age, metal tools were only an occasional supplement to the predominant use of stone. Deeply reaching cultural changes are not noticeable in the transition from the Neolithic to the Bronze Age. The use of metals, that essential difference, had its origins far back in the Neolithic. It was during the Chalcolithic that the exploitation of ores, the control of the metal technology and the distribution of its products contributed to the consolidation of settlements and accompanied the evolution of social differences. This confluence forces the view of the evolution of culture without sudden ruptures. It is apparent that man was accumulating his cultural adjustments. He realized also that by engaging in the exchange of raw materials and of the products of his 'industrialization', he could increase the number of his benefits. There is now evidence that from the Chalcolithic onward, trade became an essential mechanism.[1] Already during the Chalcolithic some objects of pure copper, especially axes and beads, had been imported into Switzerland, for instance. Since copper and tin are not native to Switzerland, they had to be brought in, mainly from the mining areas of the eastern Alps.[2] At the same time the trade in raw materials increased the frequency of cultural contacts which allowed man to elaborate his way of life. A new yardstick of cultural development was introduced at the end of the Neolithic, when an extensive restructuring of the social order was accompanied by economic changes. It probably produced the social preconditions for the flowering of the Bronze Age.

Characteristic for the early Bronze Age is the pronounced regionalism of the finds; areas rich in finds are separated by corridors with no or only a few finds.[4] In searching for graves of the early Bronze Age, the archeologist's task is complicated in that it is not possible to determine externally whether a tumulus is of Upper Neolithic, Bronze or Iron Age origin, so that generally speaking the period of the early Bronze Age is poorly explored. Instead modern agricultural methods, new settlements and urban expansion, and industrialization have eliminated entire landscapes of evidence, such as grave fields, which were still extant in the early part of the nineteenth century. Only in forested areas

79. Vessel of the Urnfield period, *c.* 1250 B.C., from Grossheubach.

80. Cup of sheet gold, *c.* 2500 B.C., from Fritzdorf near Bonn.

or those unsuitable for cultivation has the evidence survived.[5] Unfortunately the manner of research in the early phases of archaeology had much in common with treasure hunts and obliterated much of the evidence. Unsightly settlement finds and unspectacular artefacts aroused little interest.

The development of the metal industries was accompanied by a gradual decline in pottery (Fig. 79). The evidence points to simple and functional receptacles, as well as clay devices used in metallurgy such as clay jets for bellows, crucibles, smelting pots, funnels and molds. While pottery and its styles and ornamentations are indigenous to certain areas and populations, thereby making possible the identification and migrations of such populations, metal objects are trade-borne, so that, although metal wares can suggest the range of cultural influences, their presence alone tells very little about historical events, such as invasions or conquests by new peoples. It is therefore all the more fortunate that the early use of bronze coincided with the appearance of the Bell Beaker culture during the twenty-seventh century B.C.

One would expect the effects of aggression, conquest and subjugation to show quite differently from peaceful adaptation. Central Europe enters the Bronze Age through gradual evolution and the adaptation of technical influences, perhaps brought about by a peaceful mingling of peoples. The introduction of metals did not bring about an abrupt change in the cultural profile. The secondary occupation of the Neolithic and Chalcolithic burial sites such as the megalith tombs and the tumuli of the Single Grave culture by the carriers of the Bronze Age, the presence of Bell Beakers among Corded Ware inventories, and the association of copper tools with Bell Beakers as far away as

Denmark, would speak for a degree of continuity of the Corded Ware population gradually accepting the influence of the Bell Beaker culture. The contact of these two mobile cultures – the Corded Ware culture from east central Europe, identifiable between *c.* 3400 B.C. and *c.* 1900 B.C.,[6] and the Bell Beaker Culture from southern Europe, identifiable between 2600 B.C. and 2100 B.C.[7] – brought various transitional groups into being, indicating the change to the coming Bronze Age.[8] Although the Corded Ware cultures came to be completely absorbed in the process, the spread of the Tumulus culture during the period of the Middle Bronze Age a thousand years later closely corresponds with the former extent of the Corded Ware culture.[9]

The carriers of the Bell Beaker culture knew the techniques of prospecting, washing, smelting and working copper as well as gold (Fig. 80). By the time they brought the knowledge of working bronze to the north, copper was already known in Denmark, where it was used for making axes and daggers.[10]

The conversion to bronze recommended itself, in that bronze proved to be more effective for the manufacture of implements, thereby allowing for new possibilities. In order to remain competitive with the new products the Neolithic stone industries produced their most accomplished work, such as the magnificently worked flint fishtail daggers, which do not reflect the traditional treatment of flint, and in some cases do not even suit the natural properties of flint. They are assumed to be delicately worked imitations of bronze designs, quite as effective as the metal originals.[11] The stone craftsmen even tried to make stone swords as though motivated by some pathetic hope of dissuading their deserting customers from acquiring the new-fashioned products. It is probable that these stone daggers and swords were reserved for ritualistic functions since the brittle nature of elongated stone blades made them predictable failures when subjected to vigorous use. The metal innovations, of course, had revolutionary consequences in that they displaced a craft which for many thousands of years had provided the very basis for culture and life.

The use of copper as a working metal had first been introduced in the Orient.[12] From about 5000 B.C. onward the knowledge of working copper was known in the Balkans as well.[13] In the Near East the working of copper was known some 9000 years ago.[14] By 3000 B.C. the skills associated with the working of bronze were known in south-eastern Europe,[15] and in central and northern Europe by 2200 B.C.[16] There the working of copper had been known from about 3500 B.C. on.[17] As one might expect the interval decreased between the introduction of copper and that of bronze as the metallic industries penetrated into the heart of Europe. It has been speculated that the spread of bronze metallurgy was promoted by the ore seekers themselves, who at first may have come as traders into regions where the largely Neolithic population was not yet familiar with the usefulness of various ores.[18] No doubt the knowledge of working metal ores was not shared gladly since profit and power were derived from that knowledge. This in itself would account for the rather slow spread of the metallurgical technology north of the Alps. The finds of metallic objects, such as copper and bronze spirals and ornamental discs, and especially axes of various types, in Neolithic, non-metal-working areas, point to an export-import industry, no doubt encouraged by the uneven distribution of ores. The exchange of metal artefacts for amber and other northern products would foster trade and other cultural relations.[19]

Copper ore was mined by driving a shaft into a slope. By dousing the fire-heated rock face with water, it was easier to loosen and break the stone.[20] Networks of shored-up shafts were then driven into the slope to a depth of 100 m. Problems of ventilation and drainage would impose such a limit. It has been estimated that the ore-mining area at the Mitterberg near Salzburg was worked by about 1000 miners at any one time. That the ore was a very valuable commodity is evident when one considers that it required one man-day to produce 50 g of copper. It follows that organization would be required and social differentiation and power would derive from the exploitation of the resource.[21]

Tin, the other ingredient required for the manufacture of bronze, was much less easily available and not readily discernible. Its discovery was certainly accidental.[22] Pure tin articles are known from Crete and Egypt, dating from *c.* 2000 B.C. and *c.* 1400 B.C. respectively.[23] There is no evidence from the west European sites in Spain, France and England that the tin deposits there were exploited at such an early stage.[24] The earliest Greek records—the historian Hecataeus of Miletus, *c.* 500 B.C.—indicate that tin was imported from beyond the Pillars of Hercules, that is from beyond the Straits of Gilbraltar.[25] It is assumed that the Trojans imported their tin from the Erzgebirge, the Ore Mountains in central Europe.[26]

What led to the discovery of 'real' bronze, the best quality of which consists of one part tin to nine parts copper?[27] In fact it could be argued that the term 'Bronze Age' is something of a misnomer: spectral analysis has shown that the early 'bronzes' consisted of copper-arsenic, or copper-antimony, as well as copper-antimony-lead alloys, because

Map 16. The Bronze Age, *c.* 2300 B.C.–*c.* 750 B.C. Resources and trade patterns.

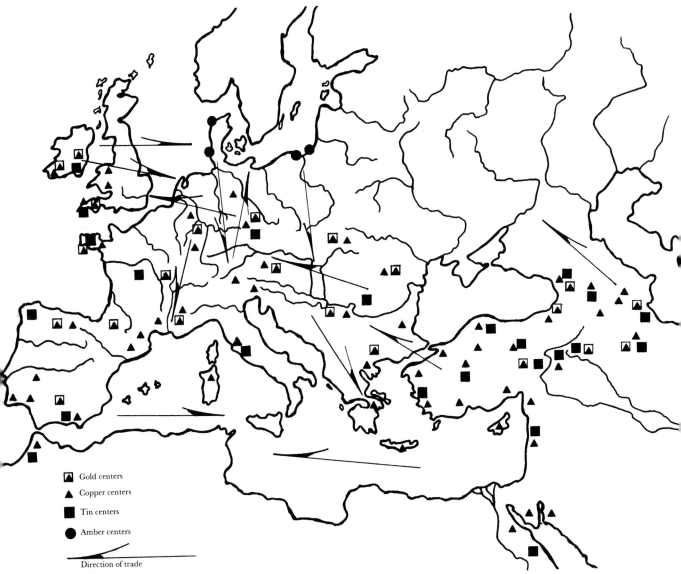

◨ Gold centers

▲ Copper centers

■ Tin centers

● Amber centers

◥ Direction of trade

most copper ores naturally contain such and other metals in varying proportions, depending on the area where these ores were mined.[28] This implies that the hardening and strengthening of copper through the addition of other metals was accidental at first. Only if more than 4 per cent of the alloy is present can one consider it to have been added deliberately.[29] Spectroscopic analysis has also shown that the tin content increased only gradually until it constituted 10 per cent of the proportions. No doubt experience showed that tin-bronze in these proportions flows thin and bubble-free and has the hardness of steel when solidified and hammered, the degree of hardness increasing with the increasing proportion of tin. The technology and end product are the best of which man was capable at that time. Considering that the melting point of copper is 1083°C and that the casting temperature was another 100°C to 300°C higher, and that molten copper absorbs air, which when the metal solidifies collects in blisters allowing for brittle fractures in the casting, it is self-evident that skilled craftsmen must have been involved. One must assume the building of furnaces and the construction of bellows to produce such high temperatures to have been the work of specialists. The addition of tin introduced a boon, in that the presence of 13 per cent tin reduces the melting point of copper to 830°C.[30] Providentially the firing of pottery had provided experience in the use and control of high temperatures.[31] In fact the manufacture of metal artefacts has a greater affinity with ceramics than with the lithic industries.

The Bronze Age smith had three casting techniques available to him: open (ingot) mold casting in which the liquid metal was poured into a ceramic open form negative; coquille mold casting in which the molten metal is gravity-poured into two matching shell-like ceramic negatives; lost form casting, for which a master mold of wax complete with scratched-in ornamentations and designs is tightly packed in a clay investment mold. Upon firing the mold the wax master mold melts out, whereupon the molten bronze is poured into the mold. The clay investment mold has to be broken to free the casting. Bronze tools were of differing consistencies, the smiths having taken function and elasticity into account; thus a sword blade is harder than the hilt, which in turn differs from the rivets, evidently deliberately. Keen cutting edges were produced by hammering.[32] As a consequence of his expert techniques the smith and especially the weapons-smith must have enjoyed great social prestige.[33] It follows that the production centres must have played leading cultural roles, influencing their neighbors and generally exercizing considerable control over those not yet sharing in the bronze technology. Having developed its own middle-men, itinerant traders complete with sample cases—one such sample case having indeed been found in Mecklenburg[34]—the Bronze Age made metal artefacts available on a broad basis. No doubt, a bronze dagger must still have been a rare luxury, yet in the north stone implements suddenly disappeared from the grave inventories.[35] The greater availability of bronze tools and weapons, thanks to mass-production and distribution, would in itself have had an equalizing effect for certain groups of the population.

The reciprocal interdependence of the bronze industry and long-distance trade is the actual revolutionary phenomenon of this period. In its wake it brought social differentiation through specialization, luxuries, fashions, and in the field of communications better vehicles and roads. Probably linking up with traditional flint routes, trade routes originated in the copper areas of central Europe and those of the Caucasus and the Urals to the east, in the amber regions of the south-eastern Baltic and on the Jutland peninsula, in the gold centres of Ireland, Bohemia and Transylvania, criss-crossing central Europe, moving up river, across the Alpine passes, bringing many cultures into mutual contact.[36] Important payments were made in amber, which found its way even into the eastern Mediterranean. Slaves and furs were other possible export commodities.[37] Evidence of the British-Irish connection is found in the North German plain, in Schleswig-Holstein and Jutland and southern Scandinavia.[38] The entire area is totally barren of natural metal resources. Only on its southern fringe did Saxo-Thuringia, especially the Erzgebirge, yield the greatest tin deposits in central Europe. Though it has not been proven yet, in central Europe the step to tin-bronze was probably taken in this very area, in the Ore Mountains which separate Saxony from Bohemia.[39] The region is rich in finds of artefacts made of arsenic-bronze.[40] The best quality work ultimately came out of east central Europe during the twenty-fourth to twenty-first centuries B.C., when the Únětician culture, named after the type-station Únětice, Aunjetitz, in Bohemia, famed for its fine axes, sickles, daggers and stave-daggers, engaged in an active trade of bronze wares and ores with the North Sea and Baltic regions.[41] In these regions none of the necessary ores was available, which makes the coming of the Northern Bronze—a purely secondary industry—all the more remarkable, being totally dependent on the import of bronze either as ingots or as semi-finished products, perhaps as a direct result of the amber trade.[42]

The overseas trade between the British Isles and central Europe fell into two distinct patterns: from northern Ireland and northern Britain across the North Sea to Jutland, Schleswig-Holstein and the Baltic; from southern Ireland and southern Britain to the Netherlands, Westphalia and the North German plain.[43] From the Netherlands a route went up the Rhine and the Mosel, overland to the Rhône and then to the Mediterranean.[44] The amber trade connection with the eastern Mediterranean accounts in part for the Mycenean influence during the Urnfield period of the Late Bronze Age, discernible in techniques, ornamental motifs and styles, such as the use of the (string?) compass to achieve circular designs, the spiral as a decorative detail, and the use of fibulae, razors and especially of swords, helmets, shields and greaves.[45] It is significant for future developments that tangents came to connect the spirals into undulating series of spirals, to be dissolved into wave patterns with the free ends developing into animal heads; in short, by c. 500 B.C. the spirals had been transformed into living forms, providing the basis for the intertwine of organic forms of both animal and vegetable interlace motifs.

During the Bronze Age, central Europe played the formative role.[46] From among a vast amount of still largely uncorrelated material three main phases have been identified, the Early, Middle and Late Periods of the Bronze Age. Reflecting the mobility and gradual expansion of populations and cultures the designations Upper, Middle and Lower which had been applicable to the Paleolithic and Neolithic are no longer useful, as for this period stratifications are either nonexistent or unreliable. Consequently no fixed and undisputable chronologies have been developed which are valid for all of central Europe, by means of which the various manifestations and phases of the Bronze Age could be categorized as a correlated classification.[47] For some regions only incomplete chronologies have been established.

In general the three phases of the central European Bronze Age have been identified as a progression from an Early Period, to a Tumulus culture, developing into the Urnfield culture.[48] This late phase affected all the cultures situated on the rim of the northern and eastern Mediterranean. By the twelfth century B.C. the people of the Urnfield culture had expanded into Italy, into the Balkan peninsula[49] and perhaps onto Crete where they may have brought an end to the Mycenean and Minoan cultures,

	Central Europe	Northern Europe	Sites and Type Stations	Trade	Cultural Features Society and Industry	Funerary Sites and Practices
		450 B.C.				
	Early Iron Age					
			Hallstatt			
	Hallstatt Culture					
				increasing penetration of iron		
750 B.C.						
				introduction of iron		'royal' grave of Seddin
			Seddin		fortified settlements	
	Late Bronze Age				hoards and depots	
			Bad Buchau			cremation urns
	Urnfield Culture					flat graves
			Acholshausen			
		The Northern Bronze Age				
					emphasis on weapons, body armor	
					socket axes	
				cultural synthesis in central Europe		
					horse-drawn chariots	
1550 B.C.						
				beginning of the great migrations	fibulae	inhumation in tree coffins under a tumulus
	Middle Bronze Age		Lüneburg	trade relations with the Minoans and Myceneans	shaft mining	
					hoards and depots	
	Tumulus Culture		Hilversum	expansion phase	flange axes	
1750 B.C.			Munich			
			Unterwölbling	trade in gold, tin and amber		'royal' graves of Leubingen and Helmsdorf
			Gemeinlebarn			
	Early Bronze Age		Sögel	introduction of bronze to the north	riding horses	
	Únětician Culture		Adlerberg		copper mining in open pits	inhumation in flat graves
			Helmsdorf		hoards and depots	continuing influences of Bell Beaker and Corded Ware Cultures
			Leubingen	trade networks		
			Únětice	introduction of swords from the Aegean	metal tools	
					fishtail daggers	
2300 B.C.						

Chart 6. The Bronze Age, *c.*2300 B.C.–*c.*750 B.C.

and to the coast of Asia Minor where they contributed to the fall of the Hittite empire.[50] In Egyptian records they were identified as the 'Sea People'[51], the Biblical Philistines, who gave their name to Palestine. Only the eastern parts of European Russia and northern Europe did not come directly under the Urnfield influence.[52]

Centered in the Danish islands and radiating south into the North German Plain and north into Scandinavia, the Northern Bronze Age developed as a relatively independent culture. As systematized by Oscar Montelius (1843–1921) it extended from 1700 B.C. to 450 B.C. Montelius arranged the Northern Bronze in six phases, of which the last two (900–450 B.C.) are already contemporary with the early phases of the Hallstatt culture of the south central European Iron Age.[53] It has been suggested that the Northern Bronze was the ancestral culture of the Germanic peoples.

Surrounded by numerous regional Bronze Age cultures, a chronologically systematic cultural sequence developed, flourished and expanded in east central Europe, in immediate succession to the Corded Ware and Bell Beaker cultures. This sequence has been identified as the Únětician-Tumulus-Urnfield cultural continuity,[54] entirely representative of the general classification into Early (2300–1700 B.C.), Middle (1800–1500 B.C.) and Late (1500–800 B.C.) cultural stages extending over about 1500 years.[55] It is the Únětician culture which marks the beginning of the real metal cultures in central Europe. As such the sequence represents an efficient cross-section of the age. The funerary practices offer the transitional cultural demarcations—from flat grave inhumation[56] to inhumation in hill graves, to the deposition of the cremated remains in urns.

Map 17. The Early Bronze Age, c. 2300 B.C.–c. 1750 B.C. The Únětician culture.

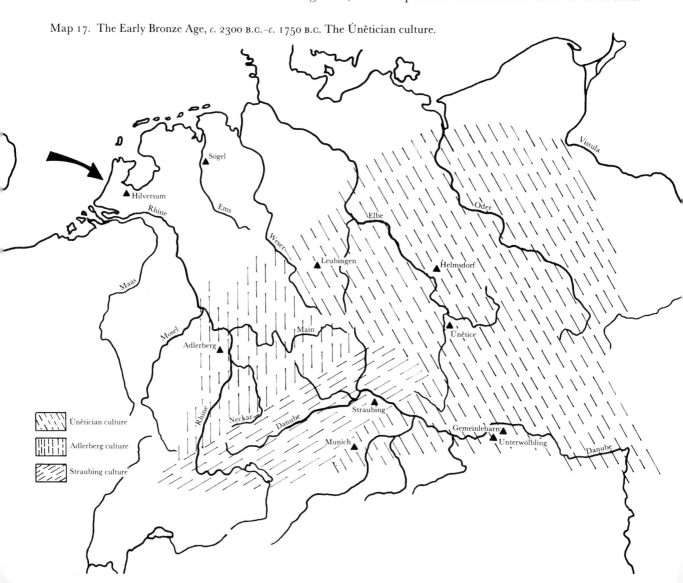

Participation in these practices delineates the expansion of the main culture and of its influence.

Each of the three phases has been subdivided.[57] Thus in the Únětician culture, an Early Period (*c.* 2230–1900 B.C.), a Classical Period (*c.* 2035–1900 B.C.) and a Late Period (*c.* 1900–1770 B.C.) have been differentiated.[58] The expansive phases of the culture, when it spread into east central Europe, was marked by the presence of hill graves and identified as the Tumulus culture. An Early Tumulus Period (*c.* 1770–1675/50 B.C.), a short Middle Tumulus Period (mid-seventeenth century B.C.) and a Late Tumulus Period (end of seventeenth century B.C.—*c.* 1550 B.C.) are indicated.[59] The Urnfield culture has been divided into five phases: an Early Urnfield Period (*c.* 1550 to the beginning of the fifteenth century B.C.), marked by expansion—to the east, south and south-east—during Phase I; Phase II, dated from the beginning of the fifteenth century B.C. to the end of the century; and a Late Urnfield Period which sees Phase III ending *c.* 1250 B.C., Phase IV ending *c.* 1030 B.C. and Phase V coming to a close at the beginning of the ninth century before our era.[60]

The exploitation of copper caused a strong cultural nucleus, the Únětician culture, to form in central Europe during the Early Bronze Age.[61] Though the Bell Beaker and Corded Ware cultures disappeared from east central Europe, they continued to exert an influence on the Early Period of the Únětician culture.[62] Other cultural influences on this culture came from the Danube Basin to the south and from beyond.[63] In accounting for the emergence of this culture during the Early Bronze Age it has been considered that by 3500–3400 B.C. an eastern people may have arrived in east and north-east central Europe, the Kurgan—pit grave—people from the eastern steppes.[64] It may have been their arrival which was responsible for the crystallization of new cultural groups formed by the integration of the older Chalcolithic cultures, especially those groups of the Corded Ware culture, which occupied southern and western Poland, eastern Germany, Bohemia and Moravia, Lower Austria, north-west Hungary and the north-west corner of the Ukraine. As stated above, the Únětician culture occupied areas previously occupied by the Corded Ware culture. The survival of pockets of the Corded Ware culture, and the perseverance of a cultural substratum as well as environmental differences, would lead to regional variations.[65]

It was during the Corded Ware period that domesticated horses had first appeared, not for riding, but as draught animals. Now bridles are in evidence, which suggest nomadic horsemen sweeping into central Europe from the plains of Russia. The increase in the slaughtering of domesticated animals—cattle, sheep, goats—as a means of stabilizing the food supply and the presence of animal bones in the graves has already been observed during the Chalcolithic. The Úněticians shared this economic form, perhaps having brought it from the east. They were breeders of livestock—sheep, pigs, cattle, especially oxen, and horses, and their staples were meat and milk products.[66] The engraving on the stone cist at Züschen, belonging to the late Chalcolithic/Early Bronze Age, probably to be associated with the Corded Ware culture, indicated that wagons were drawn by oxen, which of course does not indicate that horses were used for riding only.[67] The Úněticians cultivated wheat grains, using a stone hoe for working the fields. Grave inventories indicate that a stone-reinforced scratch-plow, perhaps drawn by oxen, was also in use.[68]

The Úněticians are known mainly from their graves; over a thousand have been excavated. However, too little is known about their settlements.[69] Their graves are rich in gold ornaments, similar in form to the decorative needles with ornamental discs, often paddle shaped, for the fastening of clothing, arm spirals, spiral tubes and curled rings of bronze, and even faience from the south.[70] In general the culture preferred massive, cast bronze tools. Depot finds add an enriching selection of metal artefacts to the grave inventories: flat and rectangular flanged axes—flanges to facilitate the fastening of handles—neck rings, neck ring ingots, neck rings with pointed ends, protective arm plates, arm spirals, ribbed cuffs, ribbed ornamented shields, halberd blades to be fastened adze-like to a shaft, dagger blades, triangular daggers, fullgrip daggers, lance points and axe heads.[71] This wealth of forms demonstrates both independent and creative craftsmanship among the Úněticians who were equally capable of inventing their own forms and of adopting products and influences from southern Germany and the area of the middle Danube which served as a pool for cultural, economic and technological impulses from the Aegean.[73] It is from the Danube lands that early Únětician metal workers of the twenty-second and twenty-first centuries B.C. imported ornaments to be imitated in a rich variety of forms.[74] In all likelihood the Danube lands passed the Baltic amber on to the Myceneans.[75] The most important innovation to come north from the Aegean was the sword, hitherto unknown and now the source of superiority for its bearer.[76] Its versatility as a weapon for striking and stabbing surpassed the functions of axe, lance and dagger, very quickly displacing that adze-like, halberd shaped, shafted dagger. By c. 1800 B.C., foundries producing swords had been established as far north as southern Scandinavia.[77]

As during previous periods, the funerary practices of the Úněticians shed light on that society. Inhumation in flat graves was the dominant practice. These graves are located in compact cemeteries which, it must be assumed, were in the vicinity of their settlements. In central Germany the deceased were occasionally placed in hill graves, but as secondary burials, an indication that cultural links with the previous cultures continued to exist and that one can assume some continuity in the population, at least as a substratum. Occasionally the flat graves were surrounded by a protective stone setting. Sometimes the corpse was placed in a cist of stone slabs, very rarely in dry-wall cists; the use of cists pointing to a continuing heritage.[78] Pottery tends to be linked typologically to Bell Beaker ware. Adding to the complexity of Únětician origins is the continuation of the Bell Beaker N–S, right-sided fetal positioning of the corpse for men and women alike, both sexes facing east. This though was a departure from Bell Beaker practice, where men lay on their left side and women on their right, both facing east,[79] and quite different from the practice of the Corded Ware Culture, which placed men on their left side and women on their right, both facing south. Almost as though it were a lingering on of earlier practices of collective burials, multiple burials, up to nine placed side by side or on top of one another, were characteristic for this culture.[80]

A special group of Únětician tumulus graves are the 'royal' tumuli of the Leubingen group in Saxony, some 40 km NNW of Weimar.[81] These are something totally new and without parallel in central Europe.[82] In the case of one of these a roof-like burial chamber, N–S in direction, about 1·70 m high, supported at the head end by a post and steadied by diagonal struts, contained two skeletons and a rich inventory of bronze and stone tools. A ridge piece was attached to the timber post and supported by rafters, their bottom ends placed in a foundation ditch, subsequently filled with stones, with planks fastened to the rafters by wooden nails and covered with a layer of reeds. The entire floor of the chamber had then been raised and covered with a floor of wooden planks. The tomb was covered with a stone mound, to form a tumulus of considerable size.[83] The princely skeleton lay stretched out in the middle of the mortuary house with

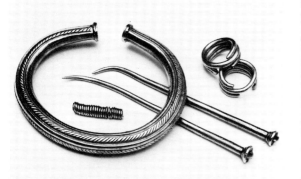

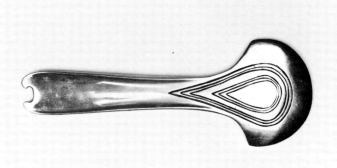

81. Gold ornaments from the 'royal' grave at Leubingen in Saxony, *c.* 1800 B.C.

82. Gold axe from Merseburg in Saxony.

the skeleton of a teenage girl across his torso. By his right leg were found a large stone hoe, perhaps a plough-share, stone chisel, bronze flanged axes, dagger blades, a halberd blade and chisels. At the right shoulder a gold bracelet, two pins, two hair rings and a spiral had been deposited (Fig. 81). A large vase stood in the corner by his left leg. Quite apparently the burial customs reflect the existence of an elevated (ruling?) class, who gave their deceased elaborate funerals. Height and size of the tumulus would in itself indicate the relative importance of the role which the deceased played in his society. The funerary inventories support this.[84] Whether the young woman was the widow, or his servant and/or companion who followed him into some other realm can of course not be determined.[85]

It was not unusual to face the interior of grave chambers with timber. Tree coffins were also used. Some graves yielded textiles, woollen cloth fragments woven together with linen threads. The remains of a vertical loom with over a hundred loom weights have been found.[86]

The lands of the Úněticians straddled the resource areas in central Europe, necessary for the making of bronze. It can be assumed that their industry produced a surplus of bronze wares which helped create a rather brilliant culture in central Europe, which was in a position to trade bronze, amber and gold (Fig. 82) across Europe from Britain to the Baltic and the Aegean. Tin bronzes appear during the classical and the Later Únětician Periods. Prior to that oxidic or carbonic copper ores were used. By the sixteenth century B.C. these resources had been exhausted and sulphuric ores were adopted. These had to be mined and a whole new technology had to be developed to process these ores. However, the copper from sulphuric ores contains a quantity of nickel, an ingredient which is characteristic of Late Únětician bronzes,[87] which facilitates determining the distances which trade carried them.

Other parts of central Europe participated in the Bronze Age to varying degrees. The north and north-west belonged to a group called the Sögeler Kreis, represented in Schleswig-Holstein, Lower Saxony, Oldenburg and Westphalia. These sources in turn point to the Úněticians towards the south-east. An earlier horizon points to influences from southern Germany. A northern influence was not significant. Somewhat later the area came under the influence of west European metal cultures.[88]

The Rhine-Weser area was not conducive to supporting a large population at that time. Neither agriculture nor herding predominated. Only a few stone sickles have been found. Instead the many finds of flint arrowheads suggest a continuing reliance on hunting as a means of sustenance. As pointed out above, the entire northern area is devoid of ores, a very unfavorable condition for economic development since all metals had to be imported both as raw materials and as finished goods. Since the area was not at all wealthy, however, even the number of imports was not extensive. In general, conditions were not favourable for the development of regional bronze production let alone of a many-faceted culture based on the bronze technology. Information is scarce, based only on a few isolated finds, some graves and a few depots. Again grave finds bear the major responsibility, there being few other indications about living conditions or settlement sites.[89] What is apparent is that the area absorbed a great variety of influences. For what little production there was, the imports served as models, so that all the evidence is reminiscent of the styles produced in neighbouring areas. Very slender double axe heads have been found with shaftholes far too small, however, to have been useful. Analysis has shown the alloys to have originated in Spain, so that it is most likely that the 'axes' were ingots strung together to facilitate handling. Already with the earliest metal evidence a north-west European influence is discernable. Thus wares from the British Isles have been identified. Some contacts with Switzerland must also have existed. Other bronze finds link the area with the northern Sögeler Kreis. These metal pieces have been found in culture levels still Neolithic, probably a persistent undercurrent in this area.[90]

In the area of the Middle Rhine, an Adlerberg group has been identified near Worms, extending over the Rhenish Palatinate, Rhenish Hesse, Hesse and northern Baden. This group is characterized by flat graves with fetal positioning of the corpse, preferably placed in E–W, or NE–SW direction, with some but not consistent differentiation by sex in the positioning and the facial direction. The Adlerberg group made only modest use of metals, when compared to other cultures. The pieces are usually small and ornamental in nature, such as spiral rings, little rolls of wire, and beads. Some of their pottery, as well as the use of horn buttons and protective arm plates, are reminiscent of the Bell Beaker culture. An exception to the graves described above is to be found in the Rhine-Main area where the deceased was placed in a stretched position, sometimes under a tumulus.[91]

Typologically related are graves in Alsace and Switzerland, in which daggers have been found up to 29 cm in length, which could be designated as short swords. For the Adlerberg group as well as the Alsace–Switzerland group, snails from the Mediterranean have been present among the finds. In fact among the Swiss finds some axe forms suggest links with older Italian styles.[92] In spite of other evidence of foreign influences, cultural development in Switzerland throughout the Bronze Age proceeded without major disturbances. Even stone cist graves continued to be characteristic for some regions. Contrary to other regions, even the Urnfield culture of the Late Bronze Age brought no upheavals. The Bronze Age Swiss set to occupying the valleys of the Jura and of the Alps, probably a result of an expansion of sheep and goat herding. The lakeshore settlements of Switzerland are remarkably similar to the settlements of the Neolithic.[93]

In southern Germany the so-called Straubing group is of the same horizon as the more eastern groups of the Úněticians in Bohemia and of Unterwölbling in Lower Austria. The Straubing cemeteries are characterized by flat graves, typical for southern Bavaria, NE–SW in direction, the men in left-sided fetal positions, their heads placed in the NE, the women in right-sided fetal positions, their heads placed in the SW, both men and women facing SE. The grave inventories contain little pottery but a great many bronze ornaments for body and clothing (Fig. 83).[94] Depot finds from all parts of southern

83. Women's ornaments of copper of the early Bronze Age, reconstructed from finds in a woman's grave of the Straubing culture, after *c.* 1800 B.C.

84. Depot of copper ingots, after *c.* 1800 B.C., from the Luitpold Park in Munich.

Bavaria yield flange axes, daggers, needles and many copper ingots—the Luitpold park in Munich held a depot of 500 bronze ingots weighing a total of 85 kg. The ingots were buried in their crude, unworked state, semicircular in shape (Fig. 84).[95]

The lakeshore settlements in the Austrian Alps—the Mondsee and Attersee—also show continued occupation since the Neolithic.[96] Spectroscopic analysis of the metal objects found there shows that they were made of Alpine copper, mined in the eastern Alps,[97] a mining area since the late Neolithic. But Únětician bronzes were also found, as well as articles from as far away as Transylvania.[98] It is not clear whether these were trade goods or a sign of migration. Some articles originating in the eastern Alps came into the Alps east of Salzburg by being transported up the rivers Enns and Traun. Spectroscopic analysis has shown that western Austria bought eastern Alpine copper only to sell it back to eastern regions such as Lower Austria, Bohemia and Moravia. In the lakeshore dwellings both crude ingots and finished ware have been found. Finished articles were probably brought in by people from the mining areas, who through systematic management had made mining and manufacture economically important. The presence of copper tools, such as axes and daggers, points to an existing mining industry prior to the introduction of tin for the manufacture of high quality bronzes.[99]

Along the Danube of Lower Austria the Unterwölbling settlement is a transition group. The weapons and ornaments of these people show that they were closely linked to the Únětician groups in Moravia, south-western Slovakia and western Hungary. The group is especially represented by the grave field at Gemeinlebarn of which over 200 graves have been examined (Fig. 85). Ceramics and other objects show that the group was related to the Bell Beaker culture. Its burial practices were also those of the Bell Beaker culture: N-S positioning, men in left-sided and women in right-sided fetal position, both facing east.[100]

137

85. Vessel with bovine heads, *c.* 1600–1300 B.C., from Gemeinlebarn in Lower Austria, found in a tumulus.

Map 18. The Middle Bronze Age, *c.* 1750 B.C.–*c.* 1550 B.C. Extent of the Tumulus culture.

Influences

Expansion

It is of course apparent when dealing with any of the prehistoric cultures that archeology can recognize a new 'culture' only when the archeological evidence— material remains—of a distinctly identifiable style or of transitions of styles can be recognized. Consequently the gradual reactions to cultural changes and the subtle adaptations to change which a stable population undergoes will not result in archeologically identifiable evidence. Easiest to grasp is the enforced passing of an old culture brought about by the intrusion of a new one.[101] The co-existence of continuing Bell Beaker characteristics and Únětician influences in Lower Austria serves well to illustrate the coming together of two cultural identities. This synthesizing process had been taking place throughout central Europe, as though in preparation for the Middle Bronze Age and the 'Tumulus cultures'—c. 1800–1500 B.C.[102]

Essential for the cultural relations of the Middle Broze Age were an economic network and a system of mutual dependencies founded on the supply and demand of metals, perhaps most skillfully developed in the Alpine regions but in evidence on a more rudimentary level throughout central Europe.[103] Depot and settlement finds of bronze ingots and wares mark the trade routes, while spectroscopic analysis indicates the farflung trading network.

There are indications that the transition from the Early to the Middle Bronze Age was also marked by a change in mining methods. While the Early Bronze Age gained its metals through open pit mining, the Middle Bronze Age turned to shaft mining to meet the greater demand. Greater availability of raw materials in turn led to an increase in trade goods and the opening up of new markets for raw materials and semi-finished and finished articles.[104] Since either production or finishing would be carried out at the point of destination by local craftsmen, it is understandable why one given object might reflect two different styles—the style particular to its distant point of origin in which the semi-finished article had first been cast and the regional style in which the article was finished. It is a truism that the form in which an article is cast is not determined primarily by the potential customers but by the producers, at least initially, who may be guided only secondarily by the increasing demands of their clientele.

The question concerning the origins of the Tumulus cultures is problematic. It is answered differently from region to region, all depending on the impact which the Early Bronze Age made on the various parts of central Europe.[105] Simplified, it can be stated that in those areas which had come under the influence of the Únětician cultural groups the evolution of styles proceeded without radical changes. The use of hill graves as the dominant funerary style is a consistent outgrowth of some Únětician practices as represented by the 'royal' tombs in Saxony. In the old Únětician areas immigration can be excluded, since the evidence there demonstrates the persistence of the Únětician culture. Here the terms Lower, Middle and Upper Bronze Age would be justified, since stratified habitation sites with continuous habitation levels are in evidence.[106] Constant elements in the social structures are indicated through the consistency of the burial practices.[107] Most of all, metallic and ceramic forms demonstrate an inherent endurance. In other parts, such as the North German Plain a significant difference has been noted between the Early and Middle Bronze Age, in that finds belonging to the Middle Bronze Age have been made on sites not previously occupied by the carriers of the Early Bronze Age.[108] Although it is difficult to determine whether the Middle Bronze was really carried by a new population, that suggestion has been found attractive,[109] in part at least by those looking for the arrival of the Indo-Europeans,[110] especially since the 'Tumulus people' had the sword as part of their armament, which, not unlike the earlier

86. Bronze ankle bands with reversing spirals, Tumulus period, *c.* 1750-1550 B.C., from Mutterstadt near Ludwigshafen.

87. Bracelets of the Middle Bronze Age, *c.* 1800-1500 B.C.

battle axes, would have given them a tremendous tactical advantage. On the other hand, the appearance of the Tumulus culture could argue for the revitalization of the Corded Ware–Single Grave Culture which had utilized the tumulus for its burials.

It is generally accepted, that the Tumulus Period does constitute the expansionist phase of the Únětician–Tumulus–Urnfield cultural sequence.[111] Near the end of the nineteenth century B.C. the Únětician culture had expanded east and south into the Carpathian Basin and beyond—Hungary, Transylvania and the southern Ukraine— and crossed the Danube into Yugoslavia. It came to exert a strong influence over eastern France, southern Germany, southern Scandinavia, the regions of the eastern Baltic, the lower Danube and the northern Adriatic, affecting the cultural patterns and population groupings in central Europe.[112] Heirs of the Únětician culture, the carriers of the Tumulus culture appear in control of the richest parts of central Europe with its fertile lands and ore deposits.[113] There was no other power in Europe at that time between the Rhine in the west and the Dnieper in the east. The expansion brought assimilations and new syntheses, and horizons showing a new uniformity of forms come into being as new dagger and sword forms appeared in the Tumulus cultural area, along with bronze arrow heads. Progress in metallurgy is reflected in greater specialization of tools and weapons and greater variation in the manufacture of spears, axes and especially of swords, which through a secondary casting now had blade and hilt fused.[114] It was also a time of increasing luxury, as indicated by such personal toilet articles as tweezers and varieties of bronze razors—the first of their kind—of bronze pins and needles, bracelets (Figs. 86 and 87), collars and necklaces, decorated with such minute ornamentations as the incisions of spirals, semicircles, triangles and other geometric designs. Spectroscopic analysis of typical bronzes of the time has shown that they were made of east Alpine copper and other ores from the western Carpathians.[115] The occupation of the ore-rich Carpathians facilitated the increase in the production of metal objects, while the assimilation of new peoples into the culture enriched the inventory of forms and designs, at the same time bringing the culture into direct contact with new influences on its periphery. These assimilations and new contacts account for the differences between the various cultural provinces of the Middle Bronze Age.

Trade relations with the Mycenaeans and Minoans brought eastern Mediterranean

140

influences to central Europe.[116] Objects and styles of the Aegean cultures such as Mycenaean cups, Minoan helmets and spiral-boss-decorated metal wares and pottery, but also inter-connected spiral and pulley motifs used in the eastern Mediterranean during and after the fourteenth century B.C. came to be imitated by the Tumulus culture of central Europe.[117] While in the main areas of this culture the remnants of the sub-cultures of Switzerland, western and southern Germany, Austria and Czechoslovakia ceased to be archeologically identifiable, a regional variation evolved in Holland. Known as the Hilversum culture it appears to have been introduced from England c. 1700-1500 B.C., in itself noteworthy, since it represents a reversal of the usual E-W flow of cultural influences.[118] In eastern Germany and western Poland a proto-Lusatian group began to form, closely related to the Tumulus cultural groups towards the south, destined to rise to its peak during the early period of the Urnfield culture.[119] At the same time northern Germany and southern Scandinavia entered the earliest phases of what came to be identified as the Northern Bronze Age.

For this period too, housing sites and settlements have not yet been submitted to adequate investigation, so that the assessment must continue to be based on finds made in moors, ponds, rivers and streams, where they had probably been deposited as votive offerings to a spirit world, and on the finds from graves.

From Bavaria to southern Scandinavia a uniform burial practice predominates—tree coffins surmounted by a tumulus, sometimes surrounded by a circle of stones. During the Tumulus Period, Chalcolithic hill graves were frequently re-occupied; in the south new graves were lowered into the tumulus, while in the north the grave was heightened when the new mound was raised over the new grave. Even new tumuli expanded through additional burials, up to thirty burials occupying one tumulus on some north Frisian islands, raising the grave mound up to 7-8 m.[120] Such a tumulus would consist either of sand and sod, or entirely of sod, in which case 1-1·5 hectares of sod would be required.[121] At the entry of the grave the tree coffin stood in a paved hollow, often packed with a layer of round stones.[122] Of the graves examined only one grave in four or five would contain funerary gifts. Male graves contained swords and/or daggers as standard equipment, though richer graves also contained a lance or a dagger. The south German graves suggest that men were armed with lances and bows and arrows rather than swords.[123]

In Württemberg and Bavaria individual graves were surrounded by a stone circle, sometimes of patterned stones. Here regular cemeteries of hill graves exist, many containing numerous burials. In Württemberg one exception has been noted where inhumation in flat graves continued to be the practice, though positioning and orientation no longer play a role. The great tumuli reflect a tendency to place the corpses in radial or tangential arrangements. Bell Beaker or Corded Ware customs of orientation are no longer in evidence.[124] In Bavaria the tumuli yield a wealth of pottery, bowls and urns, characterized by white paste encrustations.

Aside from tools, receptacles and weapons, the grave equipment consists of personal items which were deemed necessary to the deceased in the realm of the dead. Gold jewellery in the form of arm and finger rings appears to have been reserved for men. In hill graves south of Lüneburg women appear to have preferred spoked-wheel pins and fibulae with hanging spiral ends, and rings to be worn around the ankles.[125] The trade in razors and tweezers for men, blue glass beads and amber, as well as the wealth of jewellery worn by both sexes[126] imply that fashions must have exerted a significant force in society. If more recent trends in fashion can be applied to the Bronze

88. Vessel with stamped
pattern of the Tumulus
period, *c.* 1750–1550 B.C.,
from Bischoffingen near
Freiburg.

Age then the attention which men paid to their appearance—razors, tweezers, rich
jewellery and probably also fine garments—might be a reflection of the high degree of
women's emancipation. Men probably had to compete with others in attracting a
woman's attention. The extremely rich decoration of women's costumes, their metallic
finery of bracelets, spirals and pendulous neck hangings, their flowing garments, all
designed to emphasize body movement, was equalled only by the Myceneans. It is
reasonable to assume that in their interactions with men it was the woman who made
the final choice.

It follows that during the expansion phase and the post-expansion phase of consolidation the culture stands out for its creativity, its openness to influences and its ability
to adapt to innovations and to transform what it borrowed. An accomplishment for this
period was the introduction of a decorating technique by means of which bronze plates
were embossed, that is, reliefs were raised on the surface from the inside or underside.
The technique was applied equally to pottery which at this time came to be molded in
new and sophisticated forms, with bosses raised on the surface to be surrounded with
several concentric circles of dotted lines.[127] A certain ornateness, not to say baroqueness,
is a characteristic feature of this central European style.

From *c.* 1600 B.C. onward, a gradual decline set in for the Tumulus culture in central
Europe. It appears to have begun wandering off in a southerly direction. In some
pockets of southern and south-western Germany parts of the Tumulus culture continued
in an arrested state throughout the Bronze Age, remaining generally unaffected by the
ensuing changes, until it appeared in new archeological garb as part of the Early Iron
Age. The remainder of the Tumulus area generated the Urnfield culture which signaled
the advent of the Late Bronze Age in central Europe.

Shortly after 1600 B.C. extensive unrest appears to have set in. The events themselves are problematic: though names are known exact identifications of involved peoples are not yet possible, and though effects are known their causes remain doubtful.[128] In all probability Italy provided a cultural vacuum at the time and a new people occupied Italy.[129] In Greece the Mycenaean Empire had ceased to exist by *c.* 1200 B.C.,[130] probably as a result of overextension offering no resistance to occupation from the north.[131] The inner turmoil created by roving bands occurred within the vacuum left by Mycenaean disintegration.[132] A new impetus carried some groups to Minoan Crete. Others helped destroy the Hittite Empire in Asia Minor, while a group identified collectively as Achaeans were involved in the destruction of Troy. Splinter groups entered Egyptian records as 'Sea Peoples' when they made their presence felt in the eastern Mediterranean.[133]

The Tumulus period had been one of great wealth and prosperity marked by more rapidly developing rhythms of culture particularly for a recognizable elevated social group. In the Danubian lands especially valuable gold hoards have been unearthed while bronze hoards revealed increasing trends towards differentiation, variation and individualization of forms. Jewellery, clothing, implements, weapons and pottery submit to more frequent changes of fashion. During the seventeenth and the first half of the sixteenth century B.C., the uniformity of the early Tumulus period gave way to the

Map 19. The Late Bronze Age, *c.* 1550 B.C.–*c.* 750 B.C. Extent of the Urnfield culture. The great migrations.

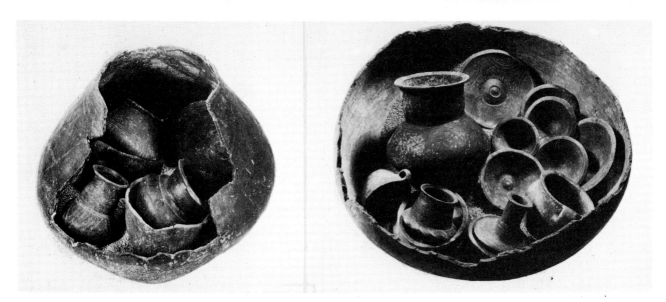

89. Urns with accompanying vessels from graves 1 and 4 of an Urnfield cemetery at Königschaffhausen near Freiburg. The assortment of vessels had been placed over the ashes.

development of distinct local styles, making it possible to distinguish five main configurations,[134] a Rhenish group centered in south-west Germany extending into Switzerland, eastern France and north to the Middle Rhine, a Saxo-Thuringian-Bohemian group, a northern Alpine group in Upper Bavaria and Upper Austria, Moravia, western Slovakia, western Hungary and north-western Yugoslavia with outposts around the northern Adriatic, and a Lusatian group in eastern Germany and western Poland, poor in metal but with distinct pottery styles. Though all of these groups shared a common cultural level, the richest finds continue to be made in the heartland of the culture, in Bohemia, southern Thuringia, Bavaria and Austria. The Rhenish and Lusatian areas were peripheral.

From *c.* 1700 B.C. onward, a significant change in the funerary practice becomes evident: inhumation was displaced by cremation as the almost universal style of burial for all social groups. Cremation had been practiced regionally since the Neolithic, so that its appearance as the dominant practice need not be seen as a radical revolution but rather as a gradual assertion.[135] Already during the Tumulus period tree coffins had been placed in funerary houses which had then been burned down and surmounted by a tumulus.[136] A change is to be registered in the transitional northern practice of strewing ashes into a tree coffin,[137] until the funerary ashes came to be gathered in urns to be deposited in extensive cemeteries—urnfields—giving rise to the term Urnfield culture. With only a few isolated, regional exceptions, cremation and the deposition of the ashes in urns buried under low mounds or in flat graves was the dominant practice till the middle of the eighth century B.C. (Fig. 89). The flat graves were perhaps marked externally with poles or steles.[138]

In spite of evidence to the contrary, great confusion has been created by assertions that the Tumulus culture has not continued into the Urnfield culture, that the carriers of the Tumulus culture had indeed been a foreign group of herders which had driven a cultural wedge into the continuous development from the Únětician ancestral culture to the descendant Urnfield culture.[139] Instead, the evidence reveals about 500 years of undisturbed development towards a respectable increase in cultural standards, as reflected in the inventories, which lent to central Europe a specific cultural aspect. The evolution of an Urnfield super-stratum out of a Tumulus sub-stratum is shown as a new impetus in the development of forms and expression, blending all of the participating groups and areas into a uniform domain.[140] The extent of the Urnfield culture can be fixed geographically by the presence of cremation graves from Spain to the Balkans. The designation, however, is an archeological concept which probably cannot be attributed to one single identifiable group of people.[141] It is rather a phenomenon of the period. Nevertheless, conflicting evidence has not yet been resolved. There appears to be no abrupt change in habitat, in the economy, the social structure, equipment and attire, with only a gradual modification in the funerary practices. Extended contacts over such great distances may have brought in their wake raids, unrest and upheaval, social changes and may have promoted migrations; however, the studies of this period express considered caution on that score. There is greater inclination, though not undisputed, to see new religious currents, new concepts about the beyond, as the motivation behind the adoption of cremation.[142] These were probably spread through economic contacts. Some support for the religious ideas may be derived from the appearance of a waterbird symbolism in the Later and Northern Bronze Age, probably introduced from the south-east. Mentioned in the same context are the embossed ceramics of the Lusatians which are deemed to have been of eastern and south-eastern origin. Turning to cremation and a bird symbolism could represent an incisive spiritual revolution;[143] the material evidence, on the other hand, does not reflect such an innovation, other than by becoming more ornate and somewhat baroque.

Recent theories suggest that the origins of the Urnfield culture are to be sought in the east, either in the metal-poor areas of Lusatia, or in metal-producing Transylvania, both regions quite within the borders of the Únětician and Tumulus cultures. In Transylvania cremation had been customary since the Neolithic. From there, it is maintained, the Urnfield culture expanded into Slovakia, to the northern valleys of the Alps and to the upper Danube, north to the Main river, south to the Rhône river and on to north-eastern Spain, and finally by way of the lower Rhine to south-eastern England.[144] Everywhere it superimposed itself over the Tumulus culture of the Middle Bronze Age. Fortifications and buried hoards which have been dated into this period are taken as evidence of hostilities and conflicts.[145] It is also assumed that this cultural expansion— perhaps agricultural in motivation—also involved great dislocations of people. That the migratory thrust into the south-east was paralleled by a similar thrust to the west and south-west, need not necessarily follow.[146]

The Late Bronze Age is marked by a further increase in the use of bronze and gold, without, however, being accompanied by a revolution in metallurgical techniques. Methods developed centuries earlier had to accommodate the increased demand. The limits to this growth are discernible. The depositing of bronzes as votive offerings and as funerary gifts for nearly a thousand years removed great quantities from circulation. Many tons of bronze ware and ingots were lost in depots; single hoards of over 1000 kg have been located.[147] That Bronze Age settlements have been identified only rarely and researched even less frequently rests on the circumstance that broken pieces of bronze were not left lying about or thrown into the refuse pits, but were recycled, which no doubt reflects an awareness that the metal was precious and its availability limited. To meet the greater need for gold and bronze objects, further demands must have been made on the ingenuity of the smiths, who now displayed great skill in turning out vessels of beaten gold and bronze (Fig. 90), shields and such body armour as helmets, breast-plates and greaves.[148] Beginning with the late Middle Bronze Age the metal-working

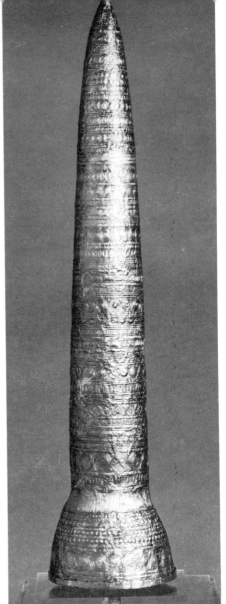

90. So-called Golden Hat from Schifferstadt near Ludwigshafen, *c.* 1200 B.C., probably a cultic vessel.

91 (right). Cone of embossed sheet gold, *c.* 1550–1000 B.C., from Ezelsdorf near Nürnberg.

92. Bronze Age swords and daggers, tang-, plate-, fullgrip- and antenna swords and daggers with and without guards, as well as socket-, shoulder ridge- and flange axes.

93. Bronze wing and socket axes, *c.* 1250 B.C., from Styria, Austria.

industry reached its apogee in the manufacture of sheets of gold and bronze, paper thin, embossed and engraved with great sophistication (Fig. 91).[149] In fact, as though in a last flourish, the Late Bronze Age is characterized by a great show of bronze without actually using that much of it. An insufficiency appears to have been turned into an artistic virtue.

The earlier periods had cast sword blades and hilts separately, fastening a full grip hilt to the blade with rivets, leaving the sword rather too weak for striking and usable only for thrusting and stabbing. A later development had allowed a strengthening of the sword by means of a technique described above, by means of which blade and hilt were cast together in a secondary process. The weapons smiths of the Late Bronze Age developed a sword whose blade continued as a tang into the grip, to be enclosed in wood, bone or some other organic material (Fig. 92). This new sword, reinforced at the hilt, its blade weighted towards the tip, was a cleaving sword. Its user did not need to fear that the force of the impact would sever the rivets which joined hilt to blade.[150] The inventory of axes was enriched through the development of a socket axe, designed to receive a knee-bent shaft from above, held in place by thongs (Fig. 93), and of an elongated axehead with pronounced wing flanges to receive a split knee-bent shaft from above, the flanges serving as vice grips once hammered into place to fit tightly.[151]

As was indicated above, the Urnfield culture allows classification into five chronological phases, the first two phases gathered into an Early Urnfield Period—*c.* 1550 B.C.–*c.* 1400 B.C.—and the last three grouped into a Late Urnfield Period—*c.* 1400 B.C.–*c.* 900 B.C.[152] Phase I of the Early Urnfield Period witnessed the great and swift cultural expansion described above which lent Europe cultural homogeneity. It was marked by a predominance of weapons over ornaments—spearheads, daggers, swords, armour, helmets (Plate 2b), shields and bronze horse trappings.[153] If this expansion was caused by emigrations from the original settlement areas, then it must be the result of over-population, for the areas do not reflect a decrease in the number of finds.[154]

There is no evidence that the north was subjected to invasion. Instead it appears to have been receptive to numerous cultural influences from the Urnfield groups to the south. Cremation was adopted while ornamental motifs and symbols on the northern bronzes reflect something of the cultural and spiritual dynamics which affected the south.[155]

94. Vessel with incised pattern, *c.* 1500 B.C., from Deutenhausen near Weilheim-Schongau in Upper Bavaria.

In general the urns were set into the slopes of the tumuli, usually protected by a box-like stone slab packing. A principal urn was frequently accompanied by smaller vessels and urns which may have contained food and drink (Fig. 94). The pottery itself was excellent, thin and evenly rounded, even though the potter's wheel was still not in use north of the Alps. At the same time there was a general decrease in the number of funerary gifts, restricted to things like razors and tweezers for men and jewellery and utensils for women. Urns could not usually receive the long swords, which meant that they were either not included among the gifts, or were laid beside the urn, or, frequently, were broken or bent to fit the urn.[156] Since they were obviously not meant to be worn by the deceased, what do they signify in the grave inventories? A gift to the gods? A bribe? Payment for the passage? Or very subtle views about the beyond?

Phase II of the Early Urnfield Period was already a post-expansion period marked by a return to normal conditions and increased prosperity. Metal production increased, if the gigantic hoards of sickles, axes, spearheads, and socketed celts—chisels—but also of bracelets, pins, belts and bronze vessels, are any indication. Fibulae—clasps—are an innovation in the list of ornaments.[157]

The Late Urnfield Period was a period of consolidation during which local characteristics amplified largely uniform styles,[158] and intensive trade linked the various groups with the metal centres of the Carpathians, the Alps and the Ore Mountains between Germany and Bohemia, leaving largely identical objects spread between eastern France and the Carpathians, and Scandinavia and the Adriatic.[159] Bavarian and Rhenish arm rings are related in form, though while the Bavarian rings show great variation in decoration, the Rhenish ones always show the same pattern. Some deletions in the ornamental inventory have been registered, thus arm spirals which had been an important part of the normal body decor during the Middle Bronze constitute only a small portion of the finds during the Late Bronze.

One significant aspect of the Late Bronze Age is the coincidence of a large part of it with the very early Iron Age, providing a trellis, so to speak, for the evolution of the latter to constitute the Middle Metal cultures of Europe. Though a discussion of the Iron Age follows, it should be kept in mind that iron was already present in all of the cultures described, at first as a precious metal, but nowhere yet did it possess any culture-changing significance. Only after *c.* 750 B.C. did iron penetrate any of the cultural groups in central Europe. Late bronzes have indeed been found in association with sufficient iron to allow the setting up of corresponding chronologies between the phases of the Urnfield culture and the Early Hallstatt culture, the first completely categorized culture of the Early Iron Age.[160]

During the Later Bronze Age influences from the south stimulated a counter-movement from the north, marked by an expansion along the eastern Baltic and in the North German Plain. Between the river Ems in the west and the Oder in the east, new production centres were established by the Northern Bronze which in turn staked out their own markets and entered into competition with one another along the southern fringe.[161]

As stated above, local groups show a gradual increase in differentiation, making for clearer divisions between the various Urnfield groups (Fig. 95). Dialect-like differentiations in pottery and bronze exist simultaneously from the Rhine to the Vistula, within the basic framework of the Urnfield culture.

In the northern moors of Oldenburg, interconnected but regionally limited networks of paths and roads had been laid out from which systems of communication can be inferred.[162] Evidence of firm settlements along the coastal strips can first be dated into Phase II of the Early Urnfield Period. Triple-naved hall-houses are indicated, subdivided into living quarters and cattle stalls,[163] perhaps derivatives of houses of the earlier Banded Ware and Rössen cultures. Active contacts must have existed with the southern Urnfield culture. The numerous impulses which affected artistic designs and techniques show a distinct dependence on the south. An important observation is the coincidence of the fading Bronze Age and a progressing deterioration of the climate. An increase in precipitation required a wintertime stabling of animals, which necessitated the gathering of fodder, of supplies, the storage of which in turn required alteration to buildings.

95. Tumulus ringed with engraved stones from the Mark Forst near Erlangen, Bavaria, *c.* 900–750 B.C.

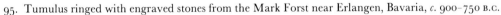

By the first century B.C. large areas of land had turned into salt-grass marshes unsuitable for anything but grazing, the people having been forced to raise the foundations of their houses into hillocks accumulated out of manure, twigs and clay.[164]

Extensive trade rather than immigration could account for the presence of Urnfield wares in Westphalia.[165] Nevertheless, c. 1250 B.C. Westphalia is the meeting ground of the southern Urnfield culture and the Northern Bronze. North of the river Sieg typical urnfields become increasingly rare, so that it would seem that the north-west of Germany was an outlying province of the Urnfield culture, which took on forms, customs and artefacts in an adapted form. The two cultures co-existed. In the end the northern influence remained the stronger, proving to be an obstacle to the full expansion of the Urnfield culture into Westphalia.[166] Thus, while the Urnfield culture burned the deceased *and* his burial gifts on the funeral pyre, depositing ashes and bronzes in the urns, the northern practice laid only the deceased on the pyre, placing the bronzes on top of the ashes in the urns, or beside the urns. Only with the advent of the Iron Age did the region adopt the Urnfield practice, which is all the more curious since during the Iron Age there was a reversion to inhumation in gravehills. It is an interesting feature that all cemeteries in the region were located on sandy soil rather than on the customary alluvial soil.[167] Further down the Rhine the number of bronzes in the graves decreases. Contrary to other areas the Late Bronze is not represented by depots.

To the south, the left Rhenish and the Saar-Mosel areas as well as eastern France tended to adopt south German and western forms, showing less disposition towards eastern and northern influences. This region differs from others in that it had not been a part of the core area of the Tumulus culture, in fact even prior to that, from the Paleolithic on, only sparse and insignificant finds can be made.[168] Only with the Late Bronze did bronze begin to figure prominently among the finds, as though colonized only recently by carriers of the bronze cultures. Here the use of urns, deposited in urnfields, did not exclude the continued use of hill graves which sometimes contained cremation urns, but also body graves. Of the bodies only a 'shadow', a discoloration of the soil remains. Owing to calcification of the bones, cremation ashes hardly ever disappear totally. Unlike the tumuli, flat graves always yield cremation urns. Here too they had often been placed into stone boxes, which accounts for the preservation of great numbers of urns.[169] It is held that the region of Saar and Mosel produced an indigenous Bronze Age culture, the arrival of a strange ethnic group not being indicated by the development of a new economic form, bronze implements, jewellery or weapons. As in other parts of central Europe the cultural modifications may be the result of an 'inner colonization'. The Saar-Mosel area yields an Urnfield culture curiosity—in two locations, at Altheim and Mendelsheim, barrow graves up to 112 m long were used, each a burial site for an entire settlement, deliberate expressions of a communal sense. The barrows are probably the largest gravehills of the Urnfield culture.[170]

In south central Europe the Urnfield culture penetrated into districts that had not previously been interesting to settlers. In southern Germany the population must have reached a considerable density, for here large urnfields, numbering up to a hundred graves each, have been found in close proximity of one another.[171] The south German Urnfield culture embraced an area from the Tirol to the Rhineland and eastern France. It is this group which provides the corresponding chronology with the Early Iron Age. It is here that Urnfield Phases II–V coincide with Hallstatt Phases A_1, A_2, B_1, B_2. Here the final phase of the Urnfield Culture, or Hallstatt B_2, appears to have been a period of extensive cultural unrest.[172]

The north-eastern variant of the Urnfield culture has been associated with the Lusatians, a cultural group evolved out of an older, perhaps native, Middle Bronze tradition, transformed by the grave and burial customs of the Late Bronze Age.[173] Though bronzes are scarce it is characterized by highly developed forms of pottery. Great numbers of pieces were preferred funerary equipment. This group has town-like, fortified settlements. It was once attempted to demonstrate that according to etymological evidence—place and water names—the Lusatians were Illyrians. Such attempts do not receive the same attention any more, though in some of the literature Lusatians and Illyrians are equated without reservations.[174] When at the end of the Late Urnfield Period the eastern regions of the culture no longer functioned as suppliers of the west Alpine Urnfield group, the trade pattern shifted to proceed diagonally through central Europe from the sw to the NE. Within that context it may be noteworthy that the Urnfield island village in the Federsee near Bad Buchau in south-west Germany showed similarities with a fortified island settlement of the Lusatians during the Early Iron Age.[175]

Significant for central Europe was the cultural link with late Mycenean Greece, when an exchange between the two areas brought central European bronzes into Greece— swords and daggers, socketed flame-shaped spearheads, axes, arm rings with spiral plates, their ends coiled in opposite directions, and simple violin-bow fibulae.[176] In return it is fairly certain that a cultic influence made its way into central Europe from the Balkans. In 1970 a stone-chambered tomb was unearthed at Acholshausen,[177] west of Ochsenfurt, containing the ashes of a man forty to fifty years of age. More important were two cymbal-like bronze discs among the grave gifts, measuring 20·6 cm in diameter. Though smaller discs have been found, for central Europe discs this size are unique; only in Greece are parallels to be found. Most important, however, was the find of a miniature four-wheeled vehicle surmounted by an urn-shaped kettle (Plate 2c). This kettle-wagon, 17·6 cm long and 12 cm high, has been dated to c. 1250 B.C., the Late Urnfield Period. This is not a unique find; others are known from Bohemia, Sweden, Denmark and northern Germany, Italy and Hungary, as well as from the Balkans, suggesting that area to be the source, at least of the idea.[178] From an aesthetic point of view, though, this vehicle is cast in the most pleasing form. Clay wheels which have been found at other sites may also point to similar vessel-vehicles made of organic matter. The chassis of this wagon was cast in double form, the curved-up ends terminating in elegantly profiled heads of aquatic birds. From c. 1500 B.C. on this bird motif, executed in sweeping ∫-curves, established itself as a most characteristic ornament. It has been suggested that the bird is a part of a sun symbolism common to the whole of central Europe and usually associated with circles, rings, wheels or wheeled vehicles (Fig. 96) and with sun discs.[179] Represented especially in connection with vehicles that must have had a cultic connotation, they often pull the wagon or have been made a part of it. A large number of bird castings has been found in the shape of ornamental buttons, about 2 cm tall, where a one-legged bird stands on a conical base, sometimes with two heads facing in opposite directions (Fig. 97). The floating water bird is a favorite ornament either engraved in similar fashion or in bossed lines on bronze urns and other vessels (Fig. 98).[180] When shown flanking a circle, the representation is reminiscent of the Ancient Near Eastern winged sun discs, the very important motif of the definitely Indo-European Hurrian-Mitannian kingdoms of the Fertile Crescent[181] and the variation of the motif in Egyptian Art of the Eighteenth Dynasty.[182]

The water bird has also been interpreted to be a symbol of fertility, some dynamic

96. Three-wheeled vehicle, *c.* 1250 B.C., with waterbirds and bovine heads from Burg-Cottbus (replica, original has been lost).

97 (below left). Ornamental buttons with birds, *c.* 1250 B.C., from a depot near Landsberg on the Warthe, now Poland.

98 (below right). Bronze amphora, *c.* 1250 B.C., Urnfield period, with sun disc and waterbird motifs, from Unterglauheim-Dillingen on the Danube, north-west of Augsburg.

mediator between the earthly and heavenly spheres.[183] A Greek coin of 400–344 B.C., of the Thessalian city of Crannon, shows a vehicle quite like the miniature vehicle from Acholshausen. The city of Crannon is said to have had a sacred wagon and two holy ravens.[184] During periods of drought the cauldron was set to vibrating in an attempt to move the god to intercede on the city's behalf and bring rain. The vibrating noise, perhaps amplified by striking of cymbals, may have been intended to simulate thunder. An additional though later piece of supporting evidence centers around Zeus, originally a northern sky-god, whose attributes are birds, including the swan. The sounding of discs was also associated with the altar of Zeus at Olympia. Ornamented discs attached to metallic circles with no conceivable function have been found in several of the Urnfield regions (Fig. 99). They may indeed be articles belonging to a Bronze Age cult, of which the cultic practices associated with Zeus are a late manifestation.[186] It is not clear whether the miniature vehicle from Acholshausen was imported as part of a cultic ritual or whether it was a local product reserved solely for the funerary rites.

While the grave inventories usually contain weapons, thereby representing a certain worldliness, the absence of weapons and the presence of such a cultic vehicle and the cymbals possibly point to priestly functions. If these considerations are correct then a division between priestly and princely function may have been crystallizing during the late phases of the Urnfield culture. It is known that the priesthood was not the first to develop, since the head of the family, clan, or larger socio-political unit performed the sacrificial functions. The evidence from the grave at Acholshausen could represent this transitional stage.[187] Up to Phase II of the Urnfield culture the graves reflect a fairly equal society. From that period on, however, richer jewellery, and even gold, shows the emergence of a wealthier social stratum in Bronze Age Europe. Towards the end of the Urnfield Period great social contrasts appeared; while an aristocracy is reflected in the funerary equipment, a poorer segment of the population reverted to stone implements.[188]

99. Clanging discs, *c.* 1000 B.C., from Wallerfangen near Saarlouis.

Numerous caches of bronze artefacts from the very late Urnfield Period suggest that it was a period of considerable unrest. Although it is not known what caused this, it is fairly certain that the source must have lain in the regions east of central Europe. It is held that during the late eighth century B.C. a steppe people appeared in eastern central Europe which introduced changes in the ethnic configurations.[189] While the Europeans of the Bronze Age knew two-wheeled horse-drawn chariots and four-wheeled carriages and wagons, horses now came to be ridden. Other demarcations have been determined: white encrusted, and especially graphite ornamented pottery is considered to indicate one dividing line separating Bronze from Iron Age (Plate 3a); new burial customs came into use in that cremation graves were replaced by body-graves under grave-hills, incidentally allowing for the deposition of richer inventories.[190]

The waning of the Bronze Age and the emergence of the Iron Age serve well to illustrate and document the principle that the advent of a culture does not constitute a sudden upheaval and rupture, but proceeds gradually, and that the new culture can only be grasped fully when it presents itself complete in all aspects. For the Iron Age, Hallstatt C represents that point in time. Over the preceding 400 years the central Europeans learned ever more about the new material before they could use it effectively. Technologically the very late Urnfield Period witnessed the co-existence of both metals.

Between c. 1700 B.C. and c. 450 B.C., northern Europe developed its own bronze culture, generally referred to as the Northern Bronze Age.[191] This culture appears to have been centred in the Danish islands and Jutland; it extended into Schleswig-Holstein, west along the North Sea coast to the Weser river, south into Lüneburg, east into Mecklenburg, Pomerania and northern Brandenburg, and north into Sweden as far as Stockholm. In this area a brilliant system unfolded of cohesive, mutually supportive,

Map 20. Area of the Northern Bronze Age, c. 1700 B.C.–c. 450 B.C.

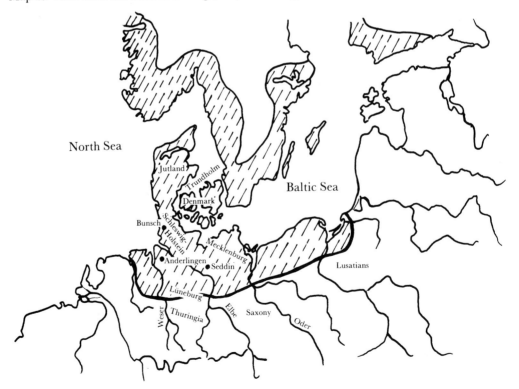

100. Bronze chariot wheel from Hassloch, west of Speyer, c. 700 B.C. Several such wheels, with four or five spokes, have been found between the Pyrenees and the North Sea. They may have been part of cultic vehicles.

cultural components, which gave to the Northern Bronze Age its own characteristic forms and implements, its own syntheses and its own techniques and motifs. Through southern influences it was a part of the Bronze Age in the wider sense (Fig. 100), yet the signs of cultural self-sufficiency and self-reliance gave to the Northern Bronze an unmistakable individuality. Being totally dependent on imports for its supply of raw materials, the Northern Bronze is an excellent example of a prehistoric culture overcoming a deficiency which should have arrested it in a cultural backwater.[192] Instead it reveals itself to have undergone an unhindered development from Neolithic beginnings to its encounter with the Iron Age, 1400 years later. The northern finds widen the spectrum of information available from the south, adding complementary details about trade links and influences, funerary practices, 'religious art' (i.e. symbols and other representations and implements of an artistic nature that must have belonged to cults and probably reflect religious ideas), and about artistic styles and ornamentation, as well as fabrics and clothing.

The population which produced this culture arose from an intermingling of groups of people, a northern Neolithic people of hunters, fishermen and megalith builders, and the Corded Ware–Single Grave–Battle Axe people, who had arrived in the area during the Chalcolithic, and whose area of settlement eventually included most of the lands around the Baltic Sea.[193] No further movements of people into this area are indicated, so that the development of the cultural profile remained unaffected by later immigrants.[194] This in itself of course suggests that the spread of the Bronze Age cultures into the north must have been a process by which styles, techniques and traditions were transferred from group to group, and that the expansion of the bronze technologies need not have involved the migration of peoples and conquests by carriers of a new culture at all. If this is valid for the north, it may also be a valid consideration when accounting for the spread of the Tumulus and Urnfield cultures across central Europe.

In all prehistoric periods the north was affected by streams of cultural influence originating in the south.[195] The Bronze Age was no exception. On the way to northern Europe the areas to the south of the North and Baltic Seas would be the first to have come under the new influences. It follows, therefore, that each region which came under the new influence would respond to it in its own particular way, so that it can not be suggested that the Northern Bronze presented a uniformity of styles for all its regions.[196] Areas offering convenient means of communication, such as the river valleys, especially

Plate 2a. Bell Beakers from Kollenbey and Neehausen, after *c.* 2500 B.C.

Plate 2b (right). Bronze helmet typical for the Urnfield period, *c.* 1200 B.C., reflecting southern influence, dredged from the river Lesum, near Bremen.

Plate 2c. Kettle vehicle from Acholshausen, *c.* 1250 B.C.

Plate 3a. White encrusted pottery, *c.* 750–500 B.C., from the necropolis at Schirndorf/ Kallmünz, north of Regensburg. White ornamentation has been renewed.

Plate 3b. Amphora with sun disc and water bird motifs, *c.* 1100 B.C., from Gevelinghausen, east of Meschede. The amphora is of the same type as the one found at Seddin.

101. Embossed gold bowls, *c.* 1500–1400 B.C., found in Denmark, imported from the south.

102. Bronze razor with cresting wave pattern, *c.* 1200 B.C., from Nindorf-Rendsburg.

103. Gold vessels, after *c.* 1500 B.C., from Unterglauheim-Dillingen.

104. Arm rings of bronze, *c.* 1200 B.C., from Hollingstedt, northern Dithmarschen.

those of the Weser, Elbe and Oder rivers, would reflect greater response to trends, since they provided the natural routes for the amber and bronze trade with the cultures to the south. As a result those areas of the North German Plain which engaged in the transit trade enjoyed a flowering, as bronze helmets, shields, embossed kettles and bowls made their way north (Fig. 101): daggers and axes from the Únětician areas in central Europe, swords, axes and lances from Hungary and Transylvania, tree coffin burials during the Tumulus Period, and gold vessels from Bavaria during the Late Urnfield Period were subjected to northern stylistic modifications. The north was able to absorb and transform these cultural influences and by exerting itself in the fringe areas of its own spheres of influence, affected first the outlying areas, for instance in Westphalia, and ultimately the Urnfield culture itself. The extent of the interchange of influences can be read from the spread of embossed and engraved bronzes. Thus while the north used an engraving technique exclusively (Fig. 102), the embossing technique is of southern or south-eastern origin and not known in the north (Fig. 103). Consequently the presence of either style in the area of the other points to imports, or at best imitations, i.e. to influences.

In 1885 Oscar Montelius, a Swedish archeologist, developed a system of classifying the northern bronzes still considered valid today. Based on typology, stratification and closed finds—pointing to contemporary deposition—the Montelius system arranged the northern materials in six chronological groups, of which the first three groups occupied the period c. 1700–c. 1100 B.C. and witnessed the development of the unique northern style.[197] During the last three phases, c. 1100–c. 450 B.C. the last 450 years of the Northern Bronze Age corresponded almost entirely to the first four cultural levels of the Hallstatt Culture, the Early Iron Age in the south.[198] During this time the individuality developed in the north gave way to the impetus developed by the introduction of the new metal, which caused a departure from the northern stylistic tradition in favor of varied motifs introduced from central Europe. It must be kept in mind that throughout this period of 1000 years, the north depended on the import of bronze, having none of the raw materials in its own area.

As during previous periods an absolute chronology for the northern and central European Bronze Age Periods is not possible, since the Montelius system of dating northern bronzes is not applicable to the southern bronze cultures. The Northern Bronze began nearly 600 years later and lasted 300 years longer. Thus while a Chalcolithic period was virtually non-existent in the heartland of the Northern Bronze,[199] the Hallstatt culture found no reverberations in the north either, which clung to the Late Bronze Age instead. It is therefore all the more amazing that in somewhat over 200 years the Northern Bronze not only made good the time lag but excelled in comparison with other bronze areas. By c. 1700 B.C.—the time of the Tumulus Period—northern swords, lances, axes, razors, tweezers, gorgets (curved collar discs), arm rings and ornamental belt discs had acquired great variety of form, individuality of ornamentation and elegance of style (Fig. 104), and were more than comparable with bronzes from the south.[200]

The last period of the Neolithic in the north ending c. 1800 B.C. is called the 'Dagger Period', because during this time the stone battle-axes were replaced by elegantly worked daggers as the most dignified weapon for their bearers.[201] It was during this 'Dagger Period' that the flint smiths attained the highest level of accomplishment in trying to compete with the bronze implements—daggers, spear- and arrowheads—just as had happened in the south several centuries earlier. The switch from stone to bronze was a technological process which came about gradually, first along the established trade routes, the river valleys and the coast lines, and correspondingly more slowly in the more remote areas of the interior. It has been suggested that the early supply of bronze came north from Spain, perhaps via Holland. Metal objects were copied in stone. Thus the fishtail daggers mentioned before would have been unthinkable without metal models, to the extent that the casting seams of bronze articles were copied in stone and treated as a decorative detail—a valiant attempt on the part of a 'developing country' to keep abreast of new developments. A few coexistent finds of bronze and gold in the graves speak of the high regard for bronze. This 'Dagger Period' came to an end *c.* 1400 B.C. as Phase I of the Northern Bronze Age according to the Montelius system.

During Phase II, *c.* 1400–*c.* 1200 B.C., a delight in the new possibilities of metal finds expression in new forms, new weapons and tools, in the manufacture of which an aesthetic appreciation also played a role (Fig. 105). Some implements are so highly ornamented that they could only have had a non-functional, ceremonial use. The innovations appear to have had an effect also on battle tactics. For fighting a short sword had been developed. Although it was still a full grip sword—blade and hilt fastened by rivets—the blade had been weighted towards the tip, indicating it to have been intended for striking and cleaving and not just for stabbing and jabbing.

Phase II of the Northern Bronze was also marked by the expansion of the culture along the south shore of the Baltic.[202] It has been claimed, perhaps unnecessarily, that this expansion was carried by a migration which, however, encountered the resistance of the Bronze Age cultures to the south and south-east, hence the existence of fortifications. Assuming that such a migration took place, it is reasonable that only the portable components of the culture would be present in an area of expansion, while immovable aspects such as house and settlement styles would remain behind in the area to which their styles were native. Considering that these shifts of entire populations proceeded at a very moderate pace, it is reasonable to assume that more permanent shelters would have been erected in the familiar styles, certainly at first, pointing out the direction of the migratory thrust. No evidence of such shelters has, however, been located.[203] To assume that local housing styles and settlement patterns were adopted immediately and totally is not probable. It is much less complicated to accept an indigenous population functioning as middle-men. The portable trade goods reflecting the culture could still be passed from hand to hand, while the absence of immovables need not be accounted for.

The gleaming new metal must have been very much in demand for use as body ornaments. At first thick and heavy bronze was worked into gorgets and pointed belt buckle discs (Fig. 107), all bearing finely engraved ornamentation of circular lines and spirals.[204] Of northern origin are the spoked-wheel pins, supposedly an abbreviated symbol of the sun, which enjoyed exceptional veneration in the north, also a constant find in the contemporary Tumulus culture of central Europe. The fibula too appears during this period, at first as a simple violin bow fibula, to become in time an ornately varying and exotically embellished cloak pin (Fig. 106). The stylistic transitions which the fibula underwent made it a useful chronological aid, especially in view of the impoverishment of pottery styles and ornamentation which ceased to make ceramics a useful aid to the dating of finds.[205]

The great number of combs among the inventories points to great attention being paid to physical appearance, more so than during any other prehistorical period. Razor-shaped knives were probably used for shaving. A decrease in the number of tweezers among the inventories has been observed.[206]

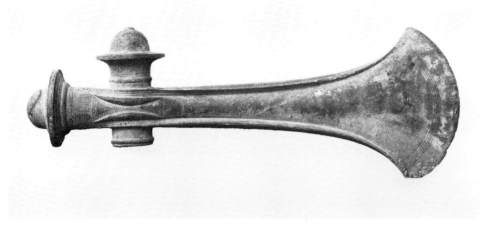

105. Ceremonial axe from Viby, Denmark, *c.* 1400–1200 B.C.

106. Fibula, *c.* 1200 B.C., from a depot find in Schleswig.

107 (below left). Beltplate from Langstrup, Denmark, *c.* 1300 B.C.

108 (below right). House urn dated to the very late Bronze Age, from Königsaue.

Until the end of the period, interment in tree-coffins or stone cists under a tumulus had been practised. Towards the end of Phase II, *c.* 1250 B.C., burial in tree coffins came to be displaced by cremation, probably in response to the same change in ideas about life and death that the south had experienced.[207] With the adoption of cremation the Northern Bronze had entered into the same time plane as the Urnfield culture to the south, at least for a time. The ashes of the deceased were placed in regular urns, or in house-shaped urns (Fig. 108), which have been found as far south as Lüneburg Heath.

Phase III, *c.* 1200–*c.* 1100 B.C., offered only minor innovations. The fibulae appeared in more ornate designs, allowing variations on the ends of the bow to twist into elaborate spirals, the ends rotating in opposite directions (Fig. 109). Gold came to be used in greater quantities, pointing to links with Ireland.[208] Swords and axes did not undergo any radical changes. Significant imports into the area were the miniature kettle-vehicles from the Danubian lands.[209] It was during this phase that the 'lurer' were cast by means of the lost-wax method. Lurer, to be discussed below, are long curved tubular horns on which a limited number of tones can be created, in quality not unlike the mellow sound of a euphonium.[210] Elsewhere the end of this period came to know iron, and although iron articles appeared occasionally in the north, northern Europe did not espouse the cause of iron, a traditional view prevailing instead. The north retained bronze as a working metal.[211] This is ironic when one considers Scandinavia's wealth in iron ores.

Phase IV, *c.* 1100–*c.* 900 B.C., appears to have been more confined to the southern coastlines of the Baltic Sea. The unrest which accompanied the period of expansion of the early Urnfield culture may very well have been the cause for this restriction of the geographic spread. Phase IV is marked by the beginning of a change in ornamentation: spirals recede in favor of derivatives of the spiral, such as the running pattern of craning-neck waterbird spirals, concentric circles or semicircles, forming arcades— perhaps descendant of the southern palmette—line patterns of cresting waves, or patterns in which the wave terminates in the elegantly swept waterbird motif. A greater tendency towards plastic ornamentation found expression in the representation of animal heads added to imported golden bowls.[212] Thus while the embossed patterns on the bowls point to their southern origins, their new owners embellished the vessels through the addition of artfully swept ladle-like handles which terminate in stylized animal heads (Fig. 110). Again the heads gracing the arching 'neck' resemble the heads of swans, although they are usually described as stylized horse heads.[213] This just might be a faulty designation, since the horse did not figure prominently in any other orna-mental motifs. The opposing spirals in which the fibulae had ended had also been affected by the departure from the spiral-motif. Instead the fibulae ended in large plain flat discs at best decorated by one single spiral sweeping from the rim into the centre. The elongated socket axe had become the dominant type, while just as in the south the plate or tang grip sword had replaced the full grip sword.

The innovation of a bronze pill-box-shaped belt attachment during the preceding period had come to assume a certain prominence among the inventories, not without first having undergone a significant change in style; it had become more than twice as large, basin-shaped and conical with two flat loops (Fig. 111). Originally provided with a lid, it is suggested that these were still worn attached to the belt, serving as 'handbags'. During the next phase these 'hanging basins' were to become quite cumbersome.[214] A most significant find belonging to this period is the sun-disc vehicle and horse, found in the moors near Trundholm, the key evidence in support of a northern sun-cult.[215] To this period also belongs the rock-face art of southern Scandinavia and northern

109. Spiral fibula with clappers, *c.* 1200 B.C., dredged from the river Main near Frankfurt.

110. Embossed bowl from Borgbjerg, Denmark, *c.* 900 B.C., southern import, the sweeping neck having been added in the north.

111. Bronze hanging basin from Brook near Lübz in Mecklenburg, *c.* 900 B.C., the late Northern Bronze Age.

163

Germany representing a whole range of motifs such as little hollows, hands, foot prints, circumscribed crosses, ships with looping prow and stern both manned and unmanned, individual representations of anthropomorphic forms captured in cultic gestures and dances of groups of people in processions, as well as 'gods'. That all of these represent religious activities is not disputed.[216]

Phase V, c. 900–c. 700 B.C., represents another peak of the Northern Bronze Age, as though in response to a compelling inherent law which forces the culture to break into a last bloom, a splendid flourish before its final extinction. The emphasis rested on body ornaments which all displayed greater size, weight and splendor at the expense of comfort (Fig. 112).[217] The 'hanging basins' had become still larger, more voluminous and elliptical. The plates of the fibulae assumed a still larger and vaulted kidney shape with characteristic C-shapes and small concentric sets of circles engraved on them. Neck and arm rings had become very showy. From the late period of this phase come a number of exquisite neck rings which by means of a torsive technique were worked in such a fashion that the winding spiral thread reverses itself several times before thinning into interlocking clasps. If the rings were not of bronze one might imagine the ridges and grooves to have been squeezed out of a cake-decorator. Equally elegant are screw-pins, c. 20 cm long, which ascend in a very finely worked thread up the slim stem, curve gracefully at the top before swooping down to be caught in a triple coil, the shape of the whole pin nearly resembling that of the treble clef.[218] Here too the show of bronze exceeds the actual amount of bronze used. The rich decoration of these ornaments acquired a 'baroque' quality as linear and pointilinear patterns of cresting waves, bands of interlocking ʃ-curves, zigzags, endless mushroom stem and cap patterns covered the bronzes, both inside and out, tendrils ending in birds' heads, thereby animating the patterns. The earlier static forms had exploded with an organic dynamism.[219] Even the sword-pommels evolved from a simple cross-bar until they culminated in two antenna-spirals coiling towards one another in opposite directions. The lurer reached the peak of their technical development. In Denmark the great predominance of women's ornaments among the votive offerings in the moors has led to the conclusion that people revered, and appealed to a feminine divinity, perhaps a goddess of fertility.[220]

Phase VI, c. 700–c. 500 B.C., shows full regression. The southern influences became ever more dominant. Having switched to the new material—iron—these influences were carried north with new vitality. Iron swords based on southern models—mainly Hallstatt types—replaced the bronze swords. In general the north succumbed to a cultural impoverishment. A contributing cause for this regression was the emergence and expansion of the Celts across central Europe, who cut the northern cultures off from their southern connections.[221] It was to be many centuries before these northerners bestirred themselves anew and entered history as the Teutonic branch of the Indo-European peoples.

Remarkable is the pronounced sense of a particular identity which gave to the Northern Bronze Age its characteristic individuality. In spite of the wide area in which the northern bronzes are found, the effect is always one of a unity of style, though there are of course a few variations limited to certain locations.[222] The evidence does not allow any conclusions about the organization of this culture in political terms. The stylistic cohesion cannot be taken as an indication of the existence of a socio-political unit centered in Jutland, the Danish Isles and Sweden, which had brought the lands south of the North and Baltic Seas under its control.[223] No doubt, the bronze-amber trade was not a casual exchange of commodities but subject to some organization. It is reasonable

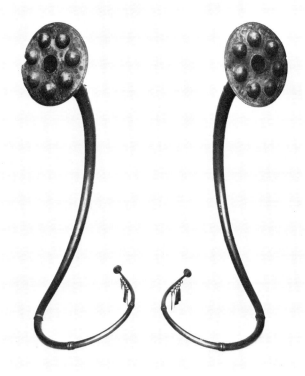

112. Bronze helmets from Viksø, North Sjaelland, *c.* 800–400 B.C., imported from northern Italy. Visible fittings for plumes. Stylized face on each helmet. Shadow of a figurine wearing such a helmet.

113. A pair of lurer from Brudevolte, Denmark, made from *c.* 1200 B.C. onward.

to assume that the searching for, collecting, transporting and exchange of amber brought political organizations into being which mirrored those developed in the south around the mining, distribution and control of metals during the Chalcolithic and the Bronze Age. The fur trade may have played a supporting role.

The society which engaged in this exchange of resources and which provided the motivation for such a sophistication of style must have been wealthy and highly cultured to be receptive to foreign influences, to sponsor the development of a strong sense of identity and clarity and to appreciate the attention paid to minute detail, not to mention the ability to meet the costs of these articles, seeing that all bronze had to be imported. One can sense their pleasure in owning fine weapons and delicate metalwork. On the other hand, it is an amazing fact that the people of the Northern Bronze did not see in amber—northern gold—a material on which to display their own artistic abilities,[224] preferring to export it as a primary resource to be transformed artistically at its point of destination, lending support to the theory that it is the consumer and not the producer who determines taste.

Two conclusions recommend themselves for the Northern as well as for the Central European Bronze Age. It is apparent that the people of the Bronze Age went to great lengths and took great delight in covering bronze surfaces, even of small articles, with ornamentation among which dynamic linears, as opposed to more static geometrics, predominate and in which a certain preference is given to animal representations. A restlessness is to be perceived in the coils, spirals and convolutions. Line bands become wave patterns, interlocking ʃ-curves become cresting waves and cresting waves terminate in tendrils which in turn are transformed into gracefully floating birds. A mere line has become an organism as though deliberately fulfilling a law of its own.[225]

The second conclusion is drawn from the sites on which the bronze finds are usually made. Most of the bronzes do not come from graves, but were found and continue to be found in the moors, in former lakes, ponds and old river beds. Owing to the number of pieces usually found, accidental loss can only be a minor consideration, and it has therefore been concluded that the bronzes were deposited, the deposition being a part of a cultic ritual associated with a belief in spirits and gods.[226] The depositions would indicate that at least the northern bronzes figured prominently in the service of cult, religion and perhaps even magic. The patronage given to the bronze-smiths would consequently assume a religious motivation. Although it cannot be demonstrated it is possible that the personal bronzes, such as arm rings, pointed discs, neck rings, pins, etc., were not used in a person's daily life but reserved for funerary or ceremonial use.

Of special interest are the lurer. They are large, elongated musical instruments, about 2 m long, ancestors of our modern brass instruments, found frequently in the moors, usually in pairs and tuned in the same key (Fig. 113). It has been observed that each pair is curved in opposite directions, as though to form a symmetrical couple.[227] Cast by means of the lost form method each lur consists of about twelve sections of expanding tubing, the ornamented couplings serving to enhance the long S-shaped horns. The mouth-pieces resemble those of modern brass instruments. The 'bell' is a flat disc on which bosses are raised in symmetrical arrangements.[228] Similar to the modern susaphone, the bell faced forward over the player's shoulder, over either his left or right shoulder, depending on the curvature with which the lur had been cast. Carrying chains and clanging metal pendants completed the instrument. Capable of producing up to sixteen tones,[229] their sound resembles that of the lower range of modern French horns and euphoniums. When played in combinations the harmonious effect is quite 'Romantic' in a nineteenth-century sense, as any visitor to the National Museet in Copenhagen can hear for himself. Considering that modern brasses produce a hard, sometimes blaring sound,[230] these cast bronze instruments created a warmer, more mellow tone. In themselves these lurer are an indication of the great skill and sophistication of technique of which the craftsmen of the north were capable. The instruments are unique to the Northern Bronze. The use to which these lurer were put is uncertain. Scandinavian rock-face art represents them being used in what appear to be ritualistic contexts related to the cult of the sun. Like so many of the other bronzes these lurer have been found mainly in the moors, as though they too had been intended for sacrificial deposit. If these lurer had offertory value, then to which divinities were these sacrifices made? Can one deduce a preoccupation with polar opposites from the opposing curvatures of the lurer? Were the northern gods divided into groups of male and female divinities?

114. Engraving of a razor found near Bremen, dated to *c*. 900 B.C. Original has been lost.

115. So-called sun disc, *c.* 1400–1100 B.C., of embossed sheet gold, from Moordorf near Aurich.

They were probably early manifestations of later Germanic cults, since, archeologically at least, no rupture is indicated in the interim.

Two important artistic motifs of the Northern Bronze were aquatic birds, frequently associated with circles or discs, and ships. Not infrequently the two were blended to give the ships ∫-shaped prows and sterns (Fig. 114). On razors, knives, urns and other bronze vessels, together or singly, in total or in parts, these two motifs appeared in the area of the Northern Bronze during Phase IV, gaining special popularity during the Indian Summer of the culture in Phase V. Although there was a tendency to represent ships as symmetrical at bow and stern, the truly symmetrical ship occurred only rarely.[231] On bronzes the ships are usually represented with only one keel line, although ships within ships were a common ornamental design, and the rock-face carvings tend to show ships with double keels. The rock-face representations show a coexistence of (bird-) ships and figures arranged in processions, or men and women dancing with a disc between them. It can not be determined whether the scenes are to be seen in some consecutive order. However, their intimate connection with a sun-cult appears to be indicated. That a solar religion was widespread in Bronze Age Europe has been generally accepted (Fig. 115).[232] It is even held that in the north this religion must have provided a remote ancestry to the Germanic religion of later times, and that it was this sun-cult which during the early Northern Bronze Age interfered with the expansion of a southern cult in which the bird-ship idea played an even more prominent role.

There is abundant evidence of central European influences exerting themselves in the north. The representation of Mycenean dagger forms and of two-wheeled chariots among northern rock-carvings has been found convincing to the point of agreement with an older view that the splendid spirals which ornament articles of Phase III

167

116. Solar chariot from Trundholm on Sjaelland, *c.* 1100 B.C.

117. Detail of the solar disc from Trundholm.

(*c.* 1200–*c.* 1100 B.C.) of the Northern Bronze Age were indebted to Mycenaean influences, transmitted from the Danubian lands.[233] That this contact did exist is indicated by southern-style bronze swords which have been found in the north. In spite of this stream of influences from central Europe,[234] a correspondingly significant change in religion may not have been effected, with the result that the bird-ship motif established itself only on a rather superficial level during this early period.

The key-piece in the evidence favouring the existence of a sun-cult is the famous Sun-Disc Vehicle from the moor at Trundholm on Zealand.[235] A horse mounted on four wheels is represented drawing a disc mounted on two wheels (Fig. 116). A large bronze disc engraved in the style found on the ornamental belt discs of the early period with three sets of linear circles separated by areas of closely adjoining concentric circles was covered with sheets of thinly beaten gold into which absolutely identical designs were engraved (Fig. 117).[236] The explanation usually given sees the horse drawing the sun across the sky during the day.[237] Whether this interpretation comes close to its original conception can of course not be determined. It may, however, point to that same common religious source from which stems the later Greek myth of Helios—the sun—who drove his glowing horse-drawn chariot across the heavenly vault from east to west during the day, while a ship brought them back during the night.[238] Both sun and horse would have been important to the northern Bronze Age farmers, symbolizing vital and mysterious powers of nature. It may be that the Trundholm Sun-Disc Vehicle was a native model of a larger disc drawn about the fields during a harvest ritual.[239]

From Phase IV (*c.* 1100–*c.* 900 B.C.) onward, however, the abundant evidence among the decorated metal work would support the idea of change in the religious beliefs. Circular and spiral representations developed into cresting waves, while straight lines were transformed into undulating and interlocking horizontal bands of ∫-curves, including the representation of aquatic birds, engraved on all sorts of bronze weapons, vessels and implements. These designs seem to reflect a somewhat different view of the world than the beliefs which appear to lie behind the Trundholm Sun-Disc Vehicle. These ideas probably originated to the south of the area dominated by the Urnfield culture.[240] A later Greek myth sees Apollo carried across the sky by swans, as though the swans

168

were the chariot. As was pointed out above, it is possible that the sun-bird iconography of central Europe originated in the eastern Mediterranean and the Aegean, which had already developed the idea of birds associated with deities, such as the winged sun-disc motifs of the Ancient Near East, the swans, eagles and ravens standing in attendance on the deities.[241] Perhaps the bird representations of the Urnfield culture, on the cauldron vehicle of Acholshausen for instance, were swans. As the bird motif moved north it combined iconographically with the older horse motif—the Trundholm horse?—to appear on the prows and sterns of ships. It was the Urnfield culture which proliferated these ideas and transmitted them to the north where the motifs inspired the cultural flourish during Phase V,[242] *c.* 900–*c.* 600 B.C.

An intriguing component of the Northern Bronze is to be found in the representations on the rock-faces of southern Sweden, on the island of Bornholm and on many of the boulder foundlings left scattered about by the retreating ice, in Denmark and northern Germany.[243] Besides being roughly divisible into northern and southern groups, they can probably also be arranged into an early and a later period.[244] For the early period *Schalensteine* appear to be characteristic. These are rocks and boulders into which bowl-like indentations, several centimetres in diameter, have been ground. Some of these bowls can be dated to the late Neolithic where they often appear on the cap stones of megalith tombs, and it has been conjectured that they formed part of the megalithic funerary ritual. Why would they have been applied to the upper surface of cap stones? The suggestion has been put forward that some final rite took place involving these indentations while the last surface of the rock tomb was still visible as the earth mound was being raised. On the other hand it has been suggested that these indentations and other designs, such as the hands and circumscribed cross on the tomb of Bunsoh (Fig. 118), were applied during the early Bronze Age, when the stone surface of the tomb was once again visible as a result of the erosion of the earth mound. There is also some

118. Cap stone with ground out bowls, hands and a circumscribed cross, *c.* 2000 B.C. or later, at Bunsoh in Schleswig-Holstein.

169

119. Rock carving from Engelstrup, Denmark, after *c.* 1400 B.C., showing ships, figures, couple dancing around a 'disc'.

120. 'Deities' stone from Anderlingen, north-east of Bremen.

evidence from Sweden that these indentations continued to be made as late as the eighteenth century of our era, when it was reported that people still smeared butter and honey into the bowls as an offering to the elves and other fabled beings.[245] Whether this was a custom which had been preserved over almost 3000 years can not be determined. It is of course quite possible that a Neolithic tradition might have survived into the Bronze Age, especially if funerary in nature, above all in the north, where the Neolithic population had not been displaced or assimilated totally by the Corded Ware culture. These bowl-shaped indentations are by far the most frequent motifs and are not only restricted to rock tombs. On other surfaces they often appear among other motifs without any recognizable connection. Since rocks and rock art resist methods of precise dating, it can not be established whether the various reliefs came into being simultaneously or sequentially. Perhaps the bowls, sometimes placed at the center of a circle, or linked together by lines and grooves or associated with encircled crosses, formed part of the earlier sun-cult. Perhaps, as in the eighteenth century, evaporable materials were offered to the sun.

Quite different, probably from an early period, i.e. Phase II of the Northern Bronze (*c.* 1500–*c.* 1200 B.C.), and suggestive of new religious ideas, are the figural scenes represented on the rock-faces but also on the interiors of the stone cist graves, already in evidence during the Chalcolithic, such as the ox-drawn cart representation accompanied by pine-twig patterns on the stone cist at Züschen. These rock-face pictures show warriors, players of lurer, dancing figures, plowmen, carts, ships, processions, ceremonies (Fig. 119), 'holy' signs such as 'sun' crosses and 'sun' wheels, circles and sets of concentric circles, hands and footsteps.[246] Scattered among them are the bowl indentations. It can no longer be determined whether some continuing relationship existed among these motifs. The figural representations bear traces of coloring. No doubt the people who carved these reliefs did so within the framework of a cult. Up to the Middle

Ages art was cultically or religiously motivated. Its roots were always to be found outside of the sphere of profane daily life and it never came about for its own sake. It bears repeating that it was funerary pottery which was ornamented, motivated by cultic considerations. With the probable exception of simple ornamental bands, symbolism is basic to all ornamentation.

A link between northern Germany and the heartland of the Northern Bronze on the one hand, and funerary practices and rock-face art on the other, is provided by the so-called *Götterstein*—'deities stone' from Anderlingen, in the Elbe-Weser peninsula.[247] This stone was the sw end stone of a stone cist, 2 m long, 70 cm wide and 1 m high, covered by a tumulus 25 m in diameter and still 2 m high. The chamber was not centered in the tumulus, since other tree coffins had occupied the tumulus. According to the inventory—some small articles, an axe and a violin-bow fibula—the funeral can be dated into Phase II of the Northern Bronze Age, when violin-bow fibulae first appeared. The *Götterstein* bears three schematized human figures (Fig. 120). A natural uneven indentation in the stone separates the figure furthest to the right from the other two. The figure on the right sustained some damage when the villagers struck at it after it had been found. The figures had been carved into the stone. The two on the left are men, one turned to its right, hands raised in the air, the fingers of the left hand spread apart, the other figure is turned to its left, hands raised in front holding an axe by its handle. The third, a rather shallow figure, perhaps a woman, standing apart, looks away to its left extending its arms in front. Before the figures had been carved into the stone, the grave had been set on fire, perhaps in a purification ritual, and then once more after the pictures had been finished, as the smoke-stains would indicate. Comparisons with Swedish rock drawings suggest that the axe- or hammer-swinging figure just might be a representation of a thunder god, while the figure with the spread fingers might represent the radiating sungod, if analogies with similar representations from ancient India are correct.[248] The third figure may have lost its divine attributes. Perhaps the group can be seen as an early trinity. Many other interpretations have been advanced. It has also been surmised that the scene depicts an excerpt from a funeral ritual.[249] Whatever the interpretation, stylistically it belongs to the rock-face art of the Northern Bronze. For Germany this stone is still unique. The Scandinavian rock-face pictures include figures and symbols. Some of these symbols have been identified as swords and spears and when linked to the figures that carry them have been connected with the known northern gods of the last pre-Christian centuries, such as Freyr and Odin. It is possible that the northern rock-face representations have preserved early phases of a northern religion.[250]

Prior to the introduction of cremation and the depositing of the ashes in urnfields, inhumation in stone cists and tree coffins under a tumulus was the standard form of burial. Of the two methods the tree coffin grave has yielded the greater amount of information about textiles and other organic materials, while only stone and metal implements have been preserved in the stone cists.

Tree coffins are characteristic for the early phases of the Northern Bronze. That many of these tree coffins have been preserved depended on a chance combination of circumstances and a unique process. The surviving tree coffins consisted of tree trunks of freshly cut oak, the stems ranging from 0.70 to 1.30 m in diameter. Once the trunk had been split, no mean task in itself, it was hollowed out with adzes, chisels and hammers.[251] Reassembled with the body inside, the coffin would then be placed either in a pit, or on a specially prepared pavement of stones and supported on either side by stones. An earth mound was then raised over it and the grave precinct marked off by a circle of stones. The mound itself could reach a diameter of 20-40 m, rising 5-8 m in height.[252] It has been suggested that the stone circle which enclosed the grave had originally been laid out roughly around the tumulus and had initially not been an actual part of the grave and that only erosion of the tumulus had caused the earth to flow around the stones of the circle and made them appear to be a part of the grave.[253]

If the coffin was placed in a pit, or if it was covered by a hill of sand, then nothing would eventually be left of it, except for a discoloration of the ground, the supporting rocks and the personal bronzes which accompanied the corpse. However, if the tumulus was made of sod, especially heath sod, then under certain conditions the coffin and its contents had a chance of survival. Rain would soak through the sod and release the humus acid from it. The sod base would retain the water and prevent deeper percolation. Under favourable conditions the humus acid would solidify and seal off the edges of the grave mound. Gradually the coffin would be enclosed by acidic water. At a depth of 2 m the accumulation of acid would cause a reduction, along with the formation of a gelatinous layer. If this layer was reinforced by ferrous and calcium particles it would form a hardening crust which would seal off the coffin in its acid bath under an airtight vault. Finally, if conditions were just right, that is, if the rate of deterioration was not faster than the rate of encrustation, then the coffin and its contents survived. Here the tannic acid released by the oak stem assumed a complementary function by preserving such organic matters as cow hide, sheep's wool, human hair and clothing, in some instances contributing to mummification. On occasions skeletons have been found.[254]

Coffins found in Denmark have preserved sufficient pieces of clothing, even whole ensembles for men and women, to provide sufficient information about the dress of the day. Clothing was made of both fine and coarse wool, spun into a thick thread, to produce a tweed-like cloth. Since spindles are not present in the inventories, the thread was probably spun on a hook. Out of this thread was woven for men the cloth for head coverings, cloaks and close-fitting clothing. No trousers have been found. Headwear took the form of a cloche-shaped cap, cloaks were oval and of varying length, while the close-fitting clothing took the shape either of a jerkin (a longer piece of cloth covering the front was fastened at the back by two bronze buttons at the corners, held in place around the middle by a belt of leather or cloth), or a shorter, skirt-like garment fastened around the middle with a piece of string. Tied leather sandals provided the footwear. The mandatory sword was carried in a shoulder hanging. Flint nodules and stones with which to strike sparks were carried in a leather bag. Women's clothing consisted of a knotted woolen cap or an artfully knotted hairnet, a short blouse with three-quarter length sleeves, sometimes with embroidery, a belt which ended in tassels, the knot usually being covered by an ornate pointed disc. Skirts were either short, consisting of ropes, similar to a grass-skirt, and wound around the waist twice, or almost floor-length. Socket-like fittings of bronze sometimes decorated the ropes of the skirts. The mandatory comb of bronze or horn was tucked in the belt. Sticks of rouge have also been found. Leather sandals completed the wardrobe. One female corpse had its feet wrapped in strips of cloth, another wore a jacket. Large pieces of cloth and woollen blankets have also been preserved. Hair was worn either cropped short or long and skillfully arranged, held in place by the hair-net. During the later Northern Bronze Age women wore clothes of a tartan-like or herring-bone weave, cut in one piece into floor length dresses, folded down and gathered at the shoulders. A cape of sheepskin or fur might complete the outfit. No under-garments have been found.

The coffins also preserved such personal possessions as sewing utensil boxes of bark, wooden bowls, shafted axes, bronze daggers hilted with antler or bone, buttons, pins and toggles of wood, horn combs and even a folding chair of ashwood. In the north the transition to cremation might be indicated by a bundle containing the ashes of a child in a woman's coffin. Another coffin contained a cauldron vehicle of central European workmanship. The cauldron contained cremation ashes.[255]

The weakening of the cultural influence exerted by the Northern Bronze may be read from the Bronze Age finds in such fringe areas as north-western Germany in which the vitality of the early and middle periods of the Northern Bronze had stemmed the spread of the Urnfield culture. For the period of the Late Bronze–Early Iron Age the far greater number of finds in the northwest belonging to the Urnfield culture suggests a greater dominance of the southern influence. By comparison, a sharp decline has been observed in the number of finds which could be attributed to relations with the Northern Bronze.[256] This lack of finds of northern origin, however, is not conclusive evidence for a decreasing influence, since the dramatic decrease of bronze implements in the grave inventories may be a reflection of the growing shortage of bronze. The ceramic evidence, for instance, demonstrates that western Hanover continued to be a part of the northern cultural area.[257] On the other hand, throughout the Bronze Age the bronzes from the Lüneburg area, though within the sphere of influence of the Northern Bronze, cannot be accommodated within the Montelius system. Instead they show a distinct variance from the northern groups, pointing to a great deal of regional manufacture characterized by ornamental differences of style, to the point that the area has been designated as the northern extension of the south German Bronze Age cultures. The relative independence of this region could be attributed to its wealth acquired from the transit trade in copper, bronze and amber, and from the growing demand for salt during the late Bronze Age.[258]

The discussion of the European Bronze Age, based on the archeological evidence, has demonstrated once again that any attempt at determining the dynamics of events and the movement of peoples from the evidence, must remain in the realm of probabilities and possibilities, since historical events can be deduced only in a secondary way from the archeological source materials. These can serve as evidence of cultural change, leaving the questions unanswered as to the actual nature of the event.[259] Thus a key concern in central European prehistory, the presence of the Indo-Europeans and their identification with any of the culturally identifiable groups, the reconciliation of possibilities and probabilities, must remain problematic and a source of continuing interest.[260]

Though grave inventories make accessible only a selection of the cultural elements and excerpts of the intellectual attitudes maintained by prehistoric man, it is evident from the manner in which prehistoric man cared for his dead that his burial practices constitute an interlink of cultural oscillations which, however, are a continuum. In funerary practices the most basic attitudes to life and death are echoed and the most conservative forms of cultural expression are documented. It would follow that any radical departure from traditional burial practices would point to a significant change in religious conceptions as they apply to attitudes about life and death. Regrettably funerary practices alone give only marginal information about their cultural context, revealing very little about the priorities assigned to burial rites. What, for instance, was the relative significance which people of the Northern Bronze attached to burials, to rock-face art and to the depositing of bronzes in the moors? What of mores and ethics?

Without some of this information the adoption of cremation does indeed appear to be a radical departure from tradition, representing major changes in religious attitudes. The introduction of cremation has been deemed to be such a change in funerary practice that it just had to reflect an extensive impetus and has consequently been seized upon as a convenient event with which to associate the arrival of a new people—the Indo-Europeans again—were it not for the fact that cremation and the burial of urns was known during the Upper Neolithic, that inhumation and cremation coexisted in the same cemeteries, that cremation graves first imitated inhumation graves and that later many urns were deposited in the slopes of tumuli, and that certain cemeteries demonstrate a seamless transition from inhumation to cremation.

Burial rites show that in spite of innovations the retention of traditional elements emphasizes an archeological continuity in variation, in which the innovations were subjected to a process of filtering and refining by traditions. Thus in central Europe Úněticians, Tumulus and Urnfield cultures alike were tumulus builders.[261] The late Úněticians used low grave hills, 1–1.5 m high, but 10–30 m in diameter. That these were re-used frequently is indicated by the presence of up to twelve additional graves in each mound. The grave at the center was probably the original. These hills are now so low that they are generally unrecognizable, having been plowed over in the course of many centuries. They have been best preserved in forested areas.[262]

Only gradually did cremation become the dominant funerary form. The urnfield cemeteries were less of an innovation, since from *c.* 1800 B.C. on, tumulus graves in some areas occupy extensive gravefields, with secondary urn burials. In fact some central European tumulus gravefields show a very extensive period of use with burials from the Bronze Age into the Early Iron Age (Fig. 121). Tumuli are of many sizes and appear to have been scattered at random. Since these gravefields rarely exceed one hundred graves they point to small settlements in the vicinity. Occasionally stratified and fortified sites have also been located. Such an extended period of occupation of the same cemeteries is evidence of continuous habitation and stable sedentariness of the population. The Úněticians' immediate neighbors to the south and south-east had been cremating their dead throughout the first half of the second millennium B.C. and their rites must have been known to them. The eastern regions of the Úněticians are the first to indicate the appearance of cremation, where cremation as a sacrificial rite may have been practiced.[263] From a later period, *c.* 1000 B.C., come urns with the cremated remains of cattle, sheep and cats, all the more curious since these were not part of the grave inventories, but located under their own tumuli.[264] Why was this special attention paid to animals? Excavations in Thuringia have revealed traces of offerings placed beneath the coffins. Usually bones of young cattle have been found.

As a funerary practice cremation was first adopted by the southern Úněticians located in Moravia, western Slovakia and southern Bohemia. Until cremation became the generally accepted funerary practice, inhumation in supine position, the body placed either in stone cists or tree coffins, was usual though not universal. The 'royal' graves of Leubingen were placed inside funerary houses before being covered by a tumulus.

From northern Germany comes evidence perhaps indicative of the transition. Near Hamburg a tumulus was opened which showed that at least on this occasion a roofed hut, a sort of mortuary house, was erected to contain one large and one smaller tree coffin placed on a stone pavement. At some point in the ceremonies the mortuary house was burned down, and the remains covered with an earth mound.[265] Funeral pyre graves appear to have preceded this practice.

121. Gravefield, *c.* 800-200 B.C., at Pestrup near Wildeshausen, with over 500 preserved tumuli, an indication of settlement continuity.

In the Lüneburg area, the southern fringe of the Northern Bronze, tree coffins under tumuli dominated during Phases I and II, *c.* 1700-1200 B.C. Flat graves are rarely found. During Phase III the coffins decreased in size, probably in response to the influence of the Urnfield culture to the south. By the end of Phase III, *c.* 1100 B.C., cremation had established itself as the dominant form of funerary practice in northern Germany, and in the core area of the Northern Bronze by the end of Phase IV, *c.* 900 B.C.[266]

In the Saar-Mosel area something of the evolution of hill-grave construction has been retraced.[267] During the Tumulus Period of the Middle Bronze, a simple tumulus, *c.* 26 m in diameter, was raised over an excavated body grave. Somewhat later[268] a smaller tumulus, only *c.* 10 m in diameter, came to be raised over grave chambers of stone or wood long enough to contain a body, regardless whether it was a body grave or a fire grave. Stones covered the grave chamber which was positioned either N–S, or SE–NW. The ashes of the remains, separated from the funeral pyre ashes, were spread evenly across the floor of the grave chamber. In the funeral pyres bronze objects survived temperatures of up to 900°C. This temperature had to be achieved if everything was to be burned. The fire would then be extinguished to allow the bones to be collected for burial. It has been surmised that family members may have retained some pieces as mementos. During the late Urnfield Period the ashes were piled in a little heap at one end of the chamber.[269] Directioning of the chamber no longer conformed to any one particular custom. The hill itself received a pavement-like rock-packing, not only in the Saar-Mosel area. Later still in the late Urnfield Period the pyre ashes were no longer separated from the body ashes. All the ashes were spread evenly across the burial chamber.[270] The funerary vessels were placed in the ashes. The tumulus increased again in diameter, and additional burials were placed into its slope. Long barrows, up to 120 m in length, are a unique feature in this area.

Although flat fire graves became the dominant form of burial during the Urnfield Period, the tumulus somehow survived, in Hesse for instance, where there are occasional tumulus fire graves, as well as secondary urn burials in the slopes of the tumuli.[271] The urnfields allow the classification of four types of graves: stone cists (cubic stone boxes in which the urn stood on a stone slab surrounded and covered by stone slabs, placed about 1 m below the surface); urns placed under a stone vault; urns placed under stone slabs, and urns without any stone protection.[272] The urn itself was usually capped by a bowl-like lid. Generally the bronzes had been placed on the ashes and any other gifts were at the very top. Sometimes the gifts had been placed on top or beside the urn. One feature that recurs in Hesse is the presence of the bones of a suckling pig. The presence of rich graves suggests the presence of an aristocracy. The Hessian grave inventories indicate links with the Lusatians in the east, with north-eastern Bavaria, eastern France and south-western Germany.[273] The graves in Saxony and Thuringia have yielded glass beads, remnants of leather, and diverse pendants made for example of river mussels and animal teeth.[274]

While in the burials of the Tumulus culture weapons and tools dominated, the Urnfield culture witnessed an increase in the amount and the variety of pottery which had been placed in the graves, ceramics in fact having shed their subordinate role. This was not for esthetic reasons, of course, but to provide containers for the funerary provisions. Though the presence of food and drink in the vessels is hard to determine, the presence of bones suggests that meat constituted a part of the provisions. In the eastern steppes horse meat was a frequent ingredient, but also the western urnfields have yielded occasional horse bones.[275] Meat was included in the provisions especially in the mountain regions of Switzerland and of the Black Forest, perhaps because of the cattle breeding in those parts. The reasons for the combination of cremation and provisioning are not obvious. The rationalizations must have been subtle indeed. It has been suggested that the pottery and the food were a part of the funerary feast, and, in order not to be re-used, were buried with the deceased. Bavarian urnfields have yielded up to thirty pieces of pottery per burial (Fig. 122).[276]

Socio-economic considerations may have contributed to the adoption of urnfield-type burials. In view of the many man-hours required to move the great amount of earth to raise a mound, and in view of the location of these extensive cemeteries on

122. Pottery, after c. 750 B.C., from the urnfield at Schirndorf/Kallmünz north of Regensburg. All of the pottery on one board came from one grave.

176

123. Megalith grave at Bunsoh, surrounded by one stone circle immediately around the grave and another further down the path.

arable land, an increasing population may have found the old ceremonies too impractical, especially when one considers that the available earth in the vicinity may not have been enough. The effort demanded may have exceeded the resources a small community could muster.

In connection with the cist grave of Anderlingen it has been mentioned that a purification-by-fire ritual was used, perhaps to purge the grave chamber prior to the depositing of the corpse. In Thuringia, the presence of charcoal and hearths found on grave chamber floors points to similar fires, while drops of birch-tar and molten amber can be associated with the probable use of aromatics, perhaps of torches, during the funerary procedings. That the burial ceremonies were extensive is indicated by fly larvae found on the skeletons, which suggests that the corpses were kept in the open for many days before they were sealed in the tombs. The earth mound was then surrounded by one or several stone enclosures.[277]

What may have been the purpose of these stone 'circles'? While the megalith graves of the north had been enclosed in stone settings, the stone enclosures of the Bronze Age do not seem to have been intended as retaining walls. They differ in shape, construction and in height. Some were made of dry wall up to 1 m high and 0.50-1 m wide. They range in shape from circular, to oval, to almost square. Occasionally more than one circle of stones has been found, an inner circle being located under the tumulus, perhaps an enclosure belonging to an earlier, smaller grave. In Westphalia and in the regions of the Lower Rhine the tumulus had been surrounded by a circular or four-cornered ditch, up to 0.50 m deep and 0.20-1 m wide. During the Late Bronze Age this ditch appears to have been made even deeper and wider. In some locales evidence of double or even triple 'palisade' enclosures has been uncovered.[278] The megalith at Bunsoh, in Schleswig-Holstein, its capstone covered with engraved bowls, hands and a crosswheel, was surrounded with two settings of stones (Fig. 123). It would appear that some cultic significance was attached to the practice.

124. Ornamented pommel plates on fullgrip swords of the late Bronze Age.

125. Bronze swords of the Urnfield period from Erlach near Rottal-Inn (l), Königsdorf near Bad-Tölz (m), and München-Theresienstrasse (r).

The weapons finds in the moors and in the graves shed some light on possible inventiveness, fighting strategies, religious attitudes and social organization. The presence of newly invented 'weapons' of questionable usefulness, such as the dagger-shaped, adze-formed, hoe-like, halberd-mounted hacking tool found from Ireland to Hungary, must have had only limited application. Perhaps inspired by obsolete stone tools, this strange implement with its 40 cm long blade, may have enjoyed ceremonial use and/or served as a mark of social distinction. On the other hand it may be a reflection of experiments in weapons technology.[279] It is generally agreed that Bronze Age weapons caused fighting techniques to be essentially hand-to-hand combat. The early full grip sword appears to have been a stabbing sword, held in such a fashion that the thumb pointed up, resting on top of the pommel plate (Fig. 124). Until *c.* 1600 B.C. it was a short sword, i.e. a long dagger. The long swords, the lower third of the blade weighted, belonged to the Urnfield culture.[280] Even in this instance though, it has been argued that since many of these swords did not have a guard at the hilt with which to parry and catch an opponent's blow, leaving the hand unprotected, these long swords were not cleaving swords either. On the other hand some hilts have been cast so as to form a guard (Fig. 125). Considering the value attached to bronze articles, it stands to reason that a warrior would want to keep his metallic weapons in hand and not risk losing them by using them as missiles. Were the battle axes used as throwing axes? Did the warriors throw their spears or use them to form a bristling phalanx? Bows and arrows were in use, and casting forms for arrow tips have been found. Considering that Roman legions went to great lengths to retrieve their iron weapons following a battle, the Bronze Age warrior may have been even more attached to his weapons.

Regional differences in armament seem to have existed. In some areas spears, bows and arrows did not coexist with swords in the graves, implying the existence of higher and lower military ranks—swords for leaders, spear for the common warrior. In others the sword was associated with axes and daggers in the graves, while in Lüneburg bows and arrows alone have been found.[281] It has been suggested that spears and axes may have served as missiles, since they tend not to be found together, but rather appear to complement the sword. In the Lüneburg area the grave inventories reflect two stages of armament. While during the first three phases of the Bronze Age axes, daggers, bows and arrows made up a warrior's equipment, the later phases point to warriors being armed with spears and short swords. In general, however, axes and daggers occur far more frequently than swords and spears or lances. One can only guess at the reasons which led the people of the Bronze Age to equip the deceased mainly with weapons for offense, but not with protective armor, such as helmets, body armor, greaves for arms and legs, and shields. Shields were generally of leather, modern tests having shown that bronze shields offered only little protection.[282] Bronze helmets and shields are known, however, but come mainly from hoard depots or from deposits, which, owing to their unusual locations, could signal a votive intention.

The predominance of daggers over swords in the grave inventories may be related to the circumstance that in some locations and during certain periods swords especially tended not to be included in the graves at all. For these same periods more swords have been retrieved from streams, lakes and ponds than from graves. In one of the Danish tree coffins, for instance, the deceased did wear a sword scabbard but it only contained a dagger. What had prompted this substitution? The robbing of graves, a contemporary activity, may have been a factor. More probable are sacrificial and consecrational considerations which led to the depositing of these precious weapons on sacred sites. Whatever the reason, the sword 'sacrifices' did remove many of them from use, which suggests that these consecrations were of extraordinary importance. Though thousands of these swords are on display in today's museums, many thousands more must be buried in old river beds and in dried-up ponds, to be brought to the surface by modern dredging operations and construction projects.[283]

There is some agreement that the sword was an elitist weapon, representing a status symbol for the leaders, perhaps a warrior caste, during the Urnfield culture. If one takes into consideration the incredible, almost stagnant typological uniformity of the weapon,[284] and associates this technological conservatism with an identifiable social group, then this continuity of style must have been an expression of the cultural continuity of the population and of its social organizations. Although these swords do show regional variations in ornamentation, during a period of almost a thousand years and extending into the Iron Age, and over a distance of more than 1000 km the central European bronze swords differed only in detail. In southern Germany and Austria, areas close to the source of metals, it has been found that only 7.5–8 per cent of graves are sword graves. In fact, in the valley of the river Inn and in the vicinity of Munich large cemeteries of over 100 graves yielded only proportionately few swords. This suggests that not all armsbearing men wore swords, or at least that they were not buried with them. Though most cemeteries contained at least three sword graves, no cemetery had more than ten sword graves. On the other hand small gravefields have a proportionately higher ratio; for instance, in one location out of eight graves three were sword graves. Such ratios also come from other locations.[285] Taking differences between the various Bronze Age cultures into consideration, such as the greater use of swords during the Urnfield Period, it could be concluded that the sword graves reflect a society differentiated by rank.

No doubt, social differentiations which had evolved during the Chalcolithic continued to develop. The division of labor associated with mining, working of the ores and the control of the distribution of copper and bronze ingots, semi-finished and finished articles, and the exchange of goods in return for other commodities such as amber, furs and salt, during the later Bronze Age, contributed to the formation of social groups differentiated by degrees of wealth. Rich grave inventories have been found throughout central Europe. Spectroscopic analysis of the finds has linked them to the copper deposits of central Germany and Bohemia. From the graves something of a social structure has been deduced. In spite of minor regional variations this structure appears to have prevailed for over a thousand years. An upper crust of 'princes' is indicated by chieftains' graves, which by their separate location, elaborate structure and rich inventories (Fig. 126) stand apart from the cemeteries such as the mortuary houses at Leubingen and Helmsdorf. With their wealth of bronze axes, halberds, daggers and chisels, and gold arm rings, pins, hair rings and spirals (Fig. 127), elegant pottery and high quality stone implements, they are readily identified as 'royal' graves.[286] In Lüneburg Heath, for instance, the combined analysis of burial practices, clothing and ornaments shows that the tumuli were re-used by successive generations, while the total number of burials was not very large, indicating that the graves of these necropoli were not used by the population as such.[287] While the reoccupation of graves points to the continuity of one family, it may be conjectured that they also played an important role in the dynastic claims of some families or constituted open assertions of the legitimacy of the succession. The presence within the cemeteries of male graves, rich in gold objects, as well as in copper or bronze weapons and tools, suggests the presence of a nobility. A third type of graves is rich in metal artefacts—weapons, tools and ornaments—but without gold objects or particularly showy articles. The majority of the population though, appears to have been buried in pits or under low earthen mounds, in poor graves either unfurnished or equipped with only a few pots.[288] No doubt it was this group which provided the labor to build the large tumuli. When the tumulus at Helmsdorf was excavated, it took ten men four weeks to remove half of the burial mound. The rocks used in the construction of the Leubingen tomb had been brought from 10–30 km away.[289]

The social organization required to carry out such building projects as the 'royal' graves at Leubingen and Helmsdorf may have been headed by an oligarchy, if the contemporary graves of several chiefs found in fairly close proximity have been correctly interpreted. This governing council, perhaps reflecting a confederation supported by a nobility, may have been an early manifestation of later military democracies found in the ancient world.[290] While weapons point to temporal attitudes, the princely grave of Acholshausen with its cultic implements indicates the possible evolution of a priestly caste, suggesting a yet further social differentiation. Mass graves—pits or stone cists— their skeletons deposited in random fashion showing injuries to the skull, have been interpreted as the probable graves of sacrificed people, perhaps of enemy prisoners.[291] Did this society keep slaves? In the pre-Christian world the execution of prisoners was usually associated with ritual killing as an offering to the gods. The motivation was frequently provided by economic insufficiencies. If sent to the gods as interceding messengers on behalf of the group, one expects and usually finds more ceremonious treatment of the deceased. It is more likely that Bronze Age society lived too close to the subsistence line to make slavery economical.

Not only the grave inventories but also the size of the tumulus served to reflect the status of the deceased. Excavations have confirmed that tumuli over 7 m in height were

126. Gold vessels from Eberswalde near Frankfurt on the Oder, c. 1500 B.C.

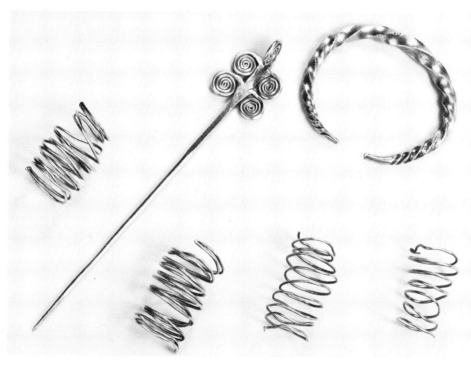

127. Gold pin, arm ring and gold wire coils, c. 900 B.C., from a depot at Trassem near Saarburg.

128. Razor, c. 900 B.C., from the 'royal' grave at Seddin, north-east of Wittenberge.

'princely' graves. From the Úněticians to the Urnfield Period the size of the grave mound and the wealth of the inventory imply a differentiated social structure, even though the Urnfield Period with its seemingly egalitarian manner of burial at least suggests a 'democratic' belief in the after-life which cancelled out the social distinctions of earthly life. In 1899 a grave mound was discovered near Seddin, some 25 km NNE of Wittenberge, dated to the ninth century B.C. i.e. the Late Urnfield Period.[292] Named the 'Royal Grave of Seddin', it measured 126 m in diameter and was still 8 m high. The c. 30,000 m³ had once required 150 man-years to be piled up to a height of 11–12 m. For centuries it had been used as a quarry. The mound contained a grave chamber 1·60 m high and 2 m across, built of overlapping stone slabs to form a false vault. Foundling stones had been used for the walls. The walls and perhaps also the vault had once been smoothed with a coat of clay to which designs in red and white had been applied, perhaps to simulate decorative curtains. On the floor of stamped clay, covered by a bronze lid, stood a large urnlike clay vessel related to late Lusatian ware, which contained a very large bronze vessel (Plate 3b) covered with a bronze lid fastened down with eight loops of bronze wire. Its handles had been broken off so it would fit into the urn. The bronze vessel, its embossed pattern pointing to its southern, probably Italian origin, contained the burned remains of a man, 30–40 years of age. On the ashes lay a curved knife, of the razor type (Fig. 128), ornamented with an engraved cresting wave pattern characteristic for the Northern Bronze, with two rings fastened into the grip, a cup with a ring and a socket axe, all of bronze. Most extraordinary are two iron pins evidently of exeptional value to their owner. These pins are the earliest known examples of iron in Europe. The man was a person of cosmopolitan culture. The urn also contained the toe-joints of a marten, as well as bits of fur, perhaps the remnants of a coat. Near the urn a short sword had been stuck in the ground, its tip pointing upward.

Six smaller vessels accompanied the urn of this Bronze Age noble. Two of the urns contained the cremated remains of two young women. It is to be expected that the two women joined the man in death, who knows whether voluntarily or not, as companions in some other realm. The practice of having nobles accompanied by wives or female servants had already been noted in the Leubingen grave of the Únětician Period, where a young woman had been placed across the man's torso both facing upward, and obviously continued into the Urnfield Period. Elsewhere, during an earlier period a man had been killed with bronze-tipped arrows and placed in a tumulus along with a woman, a youngster and a child, perhaps the man's family.[293] Had he fallen in battle, or had he been executed (one bronze arrow tip was found in his back), or was he ritually sacrificed, or the unfortunate victim of intrigue, the object of revenge, or an executed criminal? What rationale would have prompted the killing of the other three? A blood feud or dynastic rivalry would come most readily to mind. The other cause and effect relationships could stimulate interesting speculations: did the man's family follow him into death once he was no longer there to support existence on the subsistence line; was his cowardice also avenged on the other members of his immediate family; was the whole family a select sacrifice sent to the gods as intermediaries, which was not an extraordinary occurrence? Unfortunately, the questions can only be asked.

Owing to the meticulous recycling of broken bronzes the identification of Bronze Age settlements has been so difficult as to be a rare occurrence. Since the common articles of stone differ so little from their Neolithic predecessors, it has even been assumed that nomadism based on cattle breeding was practised in some areas during the Bronze Age. Settlements have been found which speak for sedentariness and a greater stress on agriculture.[294] Cultic evidence at some sites shows continuity of settlement and considerable density of population since the Neolithic, on high ground, by the shores of lakes, or islands and in riverbends, locations which offered natural protection. From this choice of defendable locations, periods of turmoil used to be deduced. Fortified locations, especially towards the east, suggest the probable existence of administrative centers, of residences of rulers, which perhaps resembled the early cities of the Mediterranean, the effect of an influence which came into east central Europe via the Balkans and Hungary. Villages would quite naturally be located in the vicinity of water, where the softer soil could be worked with Bronze Age implements, such as the scratch-plow, and where the ready availability of ground water would favor the location of wells.

For some parts of Germany only modest information about housing and settlements has come to light. In the south-west houses were small, 4–6 m long, up to 4 m wide, rectangular in design and built of wood with clay finish. Some fortified settlements, with moat and earthworks, have been identified on elevated points. In Schleswig-Holstein evidence of a house has been found, 25 m long and almost 10 m wide; its walls were made of split logs which had been driven into the ground. Divided into three sections, each unit had its own entrance. This outline of the floor plan is the only information available.[295] However, the general settlement picture presented by excavation points to villages consisting of eight to fifteen houses set up irregularly in an enclosure, the houses measuring 6–10 m in length and 3–5 m in width, consisting of rows of posts, with walls of wattle daubed with clay packing. Internal subdivisions are only seldom in evidence, though small additions to the main structure were made frequently. Auxiliary buildings for storage or stables are not indicated. Grain was kept in storage pits. Livestock must have stayed out of doors even in wintertime. From east central Europe comes evidence that the village and the adjoining domain were enclosed by a fragile fence of sticks and branches, probably intended to offer night-time protection for the livestock, but too frail to withstand an attack.[296]

In view of the incomplete information about Bronze Age settlements from central Europe, the finds made on lakeshore settlement sites offer much welcome detail. Articles lost through the floorboards and off the platform could not be retrieved as readily, making identification and dating possible. Good detail comes from a former island settlement at Bad Buchau, on the Federsee, a site which has offered much information about Neolithic lakeshore settlements.[297] During the fourteenth century B.C., the Urnfield Period, the village occupied an island which had been surrounded by several lines of off-shore palisades (Fig. 129). For the outer perimeter 15,000 pine stakes had been cut, 8–9 m long, which had been driven into the lake bottom to a depth of 3 m. The entrances in the NE and SW were reinforced by towers. Several additional defensive towers had been placed along the western palisade—facing the shoreline—and one tower along the eastern palisade. An inner palisade was considered necessary where the outer ring of pilings had to be driven in some 40 m off-shore, owing to the shallowness of the water. An opening in the inner palisade allowed passage to and from the island on that side. The palisade could be reached from the island by means of seven bridges. Dugout canoes and rafts were needed if one wanted to reach the mainland (Fig. 130). Retaining walls of pilings, backed up by pavements of stone or timber, prevented the banks of the island from eroding. Two villages had occupied the island. The first had consisted of thirty-six one-room houses, 4 m × 4 m in size, and one two-room house, which one assumes to have been the house of the chief who presided over the c. 200 inhabitants of the island. While some of the houses had been built of horizontal timbers

183

129. Model of the island settlement at Bad Buchau, *c.* 1400 B.C.

130. Dugout canoe, after *c.* 1200 B.C., from the Federsee moor near Bad Buchau.

in the style of North American log cabins, others were of upright posts and wattle, daubed with clay, the standard Bronze Age style in central Europe. If the pilings have been interpreted correctly as palisades and protective towers, then there can be little doubt that the village had a defensive purpose, and the term *Wasserburg*—water fortress—is justified. It is not clear whether the island village was constantly occupied or whether it served as a place of refuge during times of danger. Neither is it known how this village came to an end.

Some two hundred years later a second, smaller village of U-shaped three-room houses with stables and granaries occupied the island.[298] Nine farms of varying size, the largest 110 m², have been identified (Fig. 131). Built more sturdily, the houses consisted of horizontally placed logs, their inner walls finished with wattle and daub. In two rooms hearths were placed close to the wall. One large house, with six rooms, twice the size of the others, with a porch and open walls, has again been designated as belonging to the chief. Already the Neolithic shoreline settlement on this lake stood out from other Neolithic settlements on account of its large building set apart in the center of the village. An agricultural community, it yielded granaries with storage vessels containing traces of wheat, barley and millet, broad beans and poppy seeds. The settlement kept cattle, sheep, goats, horses, dogs and pigs. People hunted deer, elk, boar, and fished using nets—clay sinkers have been found—and enriched their diet with wild apples, wild strawberries, raspberries, blackberries, hazelnuts, water chestnuts and acorns. Deer antlers were used for hoes and hammers, flax was spun, bronze sickles and arrow heads were cast, pottery was decorated with designs in red and black. Wooden axles and cartwheels (Fig. 132) indicate that carts were used for transport, probably pulled by oxen. Leather horse bridles indicate that horses were ridden. Among the bronze articles were winged axes, chisels, spears, arrow heads, bracelets, pins, and knives with wooden handles, as well as chains of bronze rings, which may have served as currency. This village shows similarities with a fortified Early Iron Age island village of the Lusatians in western Poland.[299] Thanks to the occasional carelessness of its Bronze Age villagers and the preservative nature of water, mud and finally moor, the Federsee village has yielded much useful information not available from elsewhere. The moor even kept a record of its fiery destruction.

Pollen diagrams of the Bronze Age show a retreat of the forests accompanied by an expansion of fields. Wheat pollen increased while barley, coarse oats and rye receded. The keeping of goats and sheep who fed on saplings thinned out the forests. Dental analysis has shown that an increase of caries accompanied the increased consumption of cereals as a staple food. The removal of burial mounds has also shown that fields were plowed twice, once lengthwise and then across, a reflection on the inadequacy of the scratch plow, still only a forked branch, at best reinforced by a polished stone for increased effectiveness. Such shallow plowing would quickly lead to soil exhaustion.[300]

It must also be asked whether during the Bronze Age the lakeshore dwellings had been located off-shore or not. It has been generally accepted that the present off-shore location of the pilings, 40–50 m off-shore in some instances, is the result of a rise in the water level. When a prolonged dry spell during the last century made visible deliberate arrangements of pilings just under the surface, the earlier view of off-shore settlements placed on platforms above the surface of the lake was supported largely by analogy with contemporary practices from other parts of the world. It has since been established that during the Chalcolithic and Bronze Ages, people did settle on 'moist' moor-like ground, and that obviously some advantages for the population derived from these locations.[301] It has been argued that these sites were chosen in order to free all the available arable land for cultivation and not waste it by placing buildings on it.[302] In the case of the mountain lakes with only narrow strips of land along the shore, this line of argument does recommend itself. The Mondsee in the Austrian Alps east of Salzburg has even accommodated researchers with a convenient landslide to account for the rise in the water level.[303] For the Swiss lakes it has been shown that there are sections of shoreline which had been settled during only one phase of either the Neolithic or the Bronze Ages, while others were considered suitable for settlement several times. However, not even the most suitable locations had been settled continuously. Thus no shoreline settlements can be identified for a long phase of the Tumulus Period, even though settlements have been identified in the vicinity. It is probable therefore that this period saw high water levels in the Alpine lakes which discouraged human establishments.[304]

131. Model of the island settlement at Bad Buchau, *c.* 1100 B.C.

132. Disc wheel with hub, after *c.* 1200 B.C., made of three planks, found in the Federsee moor near Bad Buchau.

Aside from graves, depots are the other major source for determining the Bronze Age inventory of styles. The term 'depot' has been applied to deposits and accumulations of articles, usually bronzes, ranging in number from a few pieces to a thousand kilograms of bronze. They have been found in moors, on hilltops, near springs, in running water, in ponds and lakes, along roads, in caves and pits, among tree roots, under rocks, placed in urns, lying about loosely or carefully arranged, their organic containers having rotted away long ago. These depots proved ideally suited for establishing style inventories and as indicators of the contemporaneity of types. In central Europe there are many depots which can be dated to the Early Bronze. Their number decreased during the Tumulus Period, only to increase again in number during the Urnfield Period. The Northern Bronze knew rich depots during all of its periods. The finds range from best quality work, such as artfully ornamented vessels, jewellery, weapons, tools, musical instruments, helmets, shields, down to broken pieces, ingots, partially molten pieces and crude ores. The great multitude and diversity of the finds has led to many theories as to the possible motivation behind these deposits.[305] Discounting accidental loss, it has been suggested that these depots are forgotten caches, reflecting unsettled times, trade goods hidden but not recovered, foundry stockpiles of scraps and ingots, private treasures, funerary inventories and especially votive offerings, which were part of some cultic ritual. Depending on the condition of the find and its location, all of the above could appear to account for the existence of these depots. New ones are constantly being unearthed as a result of new land being brought under cultivation, strip mining, construction projects, peat and rock removal and the dredging of waterways.

The active trade in copper and bronze which supplied Europe from the Atlantic to the Black Sea with valuable artefacts is readily associated with the image of a Bronze Age pedlar offering his wares, exchanging gossip, spreading influences and affecting taste as he criss-crossed central Europe, bringing bronzes north, amber and furs south. Even though a sample case has been found, the image of the busy trafficker is probably too romantic. The spread of goods from central Germany and Bohemia to the Baltic and beyond was most likely not the exclusive work of itinerant traders who hid their wares when in danger. To name just one group, the relative wealth of the Lüneburg area and the cosmopolitan appearance of the finds made in this area[306] would lend support to the theory that influences and merchandise were transmitted inter-tribally, and that the metal products were not the possession of traders but belonged to those same leading oligarchies, and by extension to their communities, who controlled the mining, working and distribution of the ores in the first instance,[307] although this does not exclude the possibility of distributors working on consignment. These considerations have been prompted by the fact that the depot finds are often too large and heavy to have been transported readily, so that the theory has been advanced that the many finished, semi-finished and crude articles, as well as the semi-circular ingots, constituted the tribal or communal assets, hoarded not out of necessity but as economic regulators—a rudimentary banking system.[308] Was a group's wealth measured by its hoard? Did it replace the value attached formerly to the size of herds? Sound shifts in the consonants of the Indo-European languages a thousand years later, known as Grimm's law, support this association.[309] But why were these treasures not retrieved?

With the de-emphasis of the theories that the Bronze Age was characterized by invasions, migrations, turmoil and insecurity, there has also been a de-emphasis of the notion that roadside depots were laid down by traveling salesmen, bronze casters and smiths, who justly feared an ambush which they then did not survive. Invariably their tools were not among the finds.[310] The fact that they were found along the roads has not been linked conclusively with trade. That they were not deposited by communities fearing an attack is at least suggested by the absence of good domestic vessels and implements. Many depots contain intentionally broken or partially melted pieces or even melted lumps.[311] A further complication stems from the fact that the depots tend not to be near recognizable settlements or burial sites. It has been suggested that the depots were funerary gifts not placed in the graves in order to keep them from falling into the hands of grave robbers.

Why then were these deposits made? Recent research prefers to consider these depots as votive offerings, as sacrifices and consecrations.[312] Allowing that some of the afore-mentioned circumstances contain an element of truth, cultic considerations appear to be the most acceptable. The religious connotations recommend themselves especially if the deposits were made in places accessible only with difficulty, such as special locations in the moors, on mountain tops, or in deep caves, or near springs, under isolated megaliths or other unusual natural occurrences[313] which might have suggested to Bronze Age man some reflections about nature as an animated universe. Animism attributes a spirit or soul to inanimate things. What better way to account for the extraordinary, for an isolated bolder in a plain, or an unexpected spring, than to identify it with the presence of a spirit whose benevolence is sought, or gratefully acknowledged, whose supposed anger is to be placated, or whose continuing generosity is to be assured. The deliberate 'design' in which the deposits were placed at a site would point to the depot having a cultic function, rather than being an accidental loss.[314] There is, of course, no concrete information about Bronze Age man's religious expectations or of the principles of his faith. Nevertheless, a nature religion is probable.

With great frequency, finds of swords, daggers, axes, helmets and many other whole or broken implements have been made in association with water, and they continue to be found in rivers, wells, ponds, lakes but also in pits and caves—for the later Iron Age sacrificial pits became an especially predominant characteristic—as though these places rendered a means of contacting subterranean forces, or provided access to some other, perhaps nether-world. A well has been found in Berlin–Lichterfelde, made of a hollow oak trunk.[315] Once the well could no longer be used it had been filled in carefully. Almost a hundred vessels, nearly all little jugs and cups, had been stacked in the well, carefully separated from one another by cushions of grass. Pollen analysis showed them to have contained willow and birch pods, wild vegetables, spices, grains and probably also honey. The whole collection of vessels had then been covered over with twigs and reeds, and had probably been marked with a stake around which additional offerings may well have been placed. From later Germanic times one knows of a ritual in which a vehicle and its attendants were sunk in a lake as part of the cult. For the Bronze Age it has been suggested that animal sacrifice accompanied by a feast may have been followed by submerging the vessels and other remains in order not to desecrate the cultic implements, or to preserve them from malevolent worldly or other-worldly powers.[316]

It is curious that some fairy tales such as The Frog Prince, or the tale of 'Frau Holle' appear to reflect a cultic residue transmitted by means of folklore. In fact, fairy tales and folklore, the depositories of the unconscious memory of a people, preserved mytho-poetic accounts of beliefs, events and circumstances belonging to the Bronze Age. Thus it was told of the tumulus of Seddin that it contained the remains of a king in a threefold coffin of copper, silver and gold, albeit an approximate confirmation. Of

133. Kettle vehicle, *c.* 1200 B.C., from Peckatel,
Mecklenburg. Part of the inventory of a tumulus.

the tumulus near Hamburg which contained the burned-down mortuary house, it was
said that it had a fire burning within. Of another grave mound it was said that it held
a king whom a wily woman had beheaded—archeologists found a skeleton, its head at
its feet. The kettle wagon from Peckatal (Fig. 133) in Mecklenburg was found in the
Ketelberg, a mountain of which it was said that it was inhabited by gnomes who lent
kettles to people who asked for them.[317]

It has already been observed that cultural groups cannot be identified archeologically
until their distinct components have become consolidated. It has thus not been possible
to ascertain archeologically the consolidation during either the Neolithic-Chalcolithic
or the Bronze Age of a culture or of related cultural groups that could be marked with
the label 'Indo-European'. This scenario was developed during the nineteenth century
by comparative philologists, which saw an Indo-European people setting out from the
Eurasian south-east, gradually occupying Europe and parts of Asia Minor; but it could
not be supported by the evidence. It was noted above that the carriers of the Corded
Ware culture had not appeared suddenly in the east and raced across Europe. The
conclusions which had assigned to the carriers of the Corded Ware–Single Grave–Battle
Axe culture the role of 'Indo-Europeans' had been formulated too hastily in order to
accommodate the 'arrival' theory.[318] The weakness in this and similar hypotheses had
been the basic assumption of a recognizable structural unit, represented by language,[319]
culture, society and race.

Even though the Indo-Europeans cannot be linked with any of the distinct prehistoric
groups whose presence in central and eastern Europe is attested to by finds, their
probable origin is now generally accepted to be the area between northern central
Europe and southern Russia, although their exact point of departure cannot (yet?) be
determined.[320] They cannot have burst upon the scene suddenly, since there are no
indications of a marked cultural rupture. The Corded Ware and Bell Beaker cultures

reflect sufficient stylistic coexistence with one another, and continuity of ornamental motifs, of burial practices, of settlement sites and of cultic traditions with later Bronze Age cultures to suggest that the Indo-Europeans are a European synthesis at the end of a cultural continuum.[321]

The geographical congruence of the Bronze Age cultures with earlier cultures, the fact that the various cultural styles were not unrelated to previous styles, that innovations were adopted and adapted, points to the presence of groups in Europe who were characterized by an ability to assimilate and to adjust to regional requirements in the area of their origin as well as in the regions into which they expanded. It follows that the effects of such an expansion bear the marks of regional variations, indicated by those modifications of the cultural elements which resulted in the transformation of the Bronze Age cultures into the various Indo-European crystallizations. Comparative philology has helped to bring some order into an extensive realm of suppositions.[322] Owing to the early evolution of the High Cultures of the Ancient Near East, and because of the extensive archeological investigation of these cultures, a great deal is known about the Indo-European languages of Asia Minor and the eastern Mediterranean from the second millennium B.C. onwards. By contrast very little is known about the languages spoken in central Europe before the time of Caesar. Once languages are known they are a most exploitable element, serving both as a common denominator by which to identify the Indo-Europeans as a group and to differentiate them from one another.[323]

The phonetic particularities of a series of European, Asian and Near Eastern languages show characteristics shared by some 15 language groups. Using as a criterion the word for 'hundred' philologists have divided the Indo-European languages into either 'centum' or 'satem' languages, the Latin and Iranian equivalents. The 'centum' group embraces the following sub-groups of languages: Celtic, Italic, Germanic, Illyrian, Hellenic and, from the borders of China, Tocharian; while the 'satem' groups include Sanskrit, Mitannian, Iranian, Armenian, Phrygian, Scythian, Thracian, Albanian, and the Baltic and Slavic languages. Hittite, identifiable as one of the earliest Indo-European languages, stands somewhat apart from these classifications.[324] The oldest known Indo-European languages are Greek, documented as early as the fifteenth century B.C., Hittite and Mitannian, extant in written form since the fourteenth and thirteenth centuries B.C., and the Indo-Aryan languages, also documented since the fourteenth century B.C. By contrast, the Germanic, Baltic and Slavic languages are late manifestations. In spite of the great spread over time and distance, philological consistencies are in evidence. To indicate just a few of these relationships: Sanskrit *pitā*, Greek *patér*, Latin *pater*, French *père*, English *father*, German *Vater*; or Mitannian *aika* (one), *tera* (three), *satta* (seven), Sanskrit *eka* (one), *tri* (three), *sapta* (seven) = Hittite *sipta* = Greek *hepta* = Latin *septem* = French *sept*, English *seven*, German *sieben*. For central Europe the linguistic interrelationship is in evidence only in relatively 'recent' history.

Another denominator common to the Indo-Europeans is to be found in the religious sphere. Here too, it is assumed that the Indo-Europeans drew upon a common mytho-cultic source, the traces and variations of which are reflected in such concepts as creation, death, immortality, underworld, gods, fates and nature.[325] Thus, for instance, throughout the entire area of their expansion from India to the Atlantic, the presence of sky gods provides a common link. For the Indo-European Hittites in Asia Minor and for the kingdom of Mitanni in the Fertile Crescent—a kingdom of strong Indo-European coloring, where a population of Hurrians was dominated by a ruling caste of Indo-Europeans,[326] as indicated by their names—Indian deities figure prominently in their

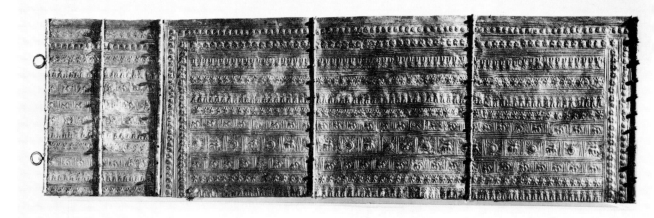

134. Embossed sheet bronze, *c.* 700 B.C., from Kaltbrunn near Konstanz. Mediterranean influence is apparent.

pantheon. Thus the Amarna correspondence of the Eighteenth Dynasty of Egypt[327] and its use of the winged sun disc, referred to above, document sun gods and storm or thunder gods as the chief gods for those two kingdoms. Vedic India has in Agni the god of fire, who in heaven is the sun, Indra, characterized by a thunderbolt, and Varuna, the guardian of the cosmic order, who sits in a palace in heaven. Later Greek mythology weds northern sky gods to Mediterranean earth goddesses. Zeus has a thunderbolt for an attribute, while Helios-Apollo is the sun god and the omniscient bringer of light. The Germanic north, according to later records, has in Wodan-Odin an all knowing god, in Thor a god of thunder and a sun god in Freyr. However, already the rock art of the Northern Bronze suggests the veneration of sun and thunder gods, if the 'Three Deities Stone' of Anderlingen is correctly interpreted. As a northern variant of that same Indo-European religion, the northern rock art is contemporary with the religious ideas of other Indo-European cultures.

During the last centuries of the Bronze Age a cultural change announced itself, hesitatingly at first, the Iron Age. Early iron was more precious than bronze. The 'royal' grave at Seddin had contained two iron pins. Their part in the funerary inventory indicated their value.[328] Occasionally thin iron wire had been imbedded in articles of bronze, such as razors, and sometimes knife blades were made of iron. No doubt the earliest examples had been imported, again probably from the south-east. In the Near East Hittite iron had triumphed over Egyptian bronze.

Again the changeover from bronze to iron was not sudden. For centuries the two coexisted so that bronze was in use far into the Iron Age. It was seen above that Phases II–V of the Urnfield culture coincided with Hallstatt Phases A_1, A_2, B_1, B_2, Hallstatt period being the designation for the Early Iron Age in central Europe. It would appear that the supply of available bronze was diminishing, partly as a result of funerary and cultic practices which removed tons of bronze from circulation. There is an indication that the final phase of the Urnfield culture was marked by extensive unrest which probably interfered with the bronze routes, but which definitely recast central European culture. From here on the Greeks and Etruscans to the south and the proto-Scythians to the east constitute a strong influence on the material cultures of central Europe (Fig. 134). The outcome is the brilliant proto-Celtic Hallstatt culture of the Early Iron Age.[329]

4. Hallstatt:
The Farflung Connections of the Early Iron Age

The town of Hallstatt, some 60 km ESE of Salzburg, in Austria, is the type station where since 1846 the most extensive and comprehensive finds pertaining to the Early Iron Age have been made. So far over 2000 graves have been opened in its prehistoric cemetery.[1] These graves indicate that the cemetery was in continuous use for nearly 700 years, until c. 300 B.C., the middle period of the La Tène. La Tène, a town on Lake Neuchâtel in Switzerland, is the type station where artefacts of the subsequent Celtic Iron Age were first characterized. As with all type stations, neither site may be assumed to have been a production center; they merely document the stages in the cultural development in south central Europe, when iron came into general use.[2]

The advent of the Iron Age witnesses the eventual superimposition of iron over bronze. It is the late Bronze Age, the south German Urnfield culture, stretching from the Tirol to the Rhineland and eastern France, which provides the comparative chronology for the Early Iron Age, in that Urnfield Phases II–V correspond to Hallstatt Phases A_1, A_2, B_1, B_2. This period of transition has been designated 'Hallstatt period' to differentiate it from the 'Hallstatt culture' which comprises Hallstatt Phases C, D, and La Tène A.[3] The consistent occurrence of harp fibulae (Fig. 135) in the grave inventories helps to characterize the period before c. 800 B.C., while monochrome pottery is an aid to the dating of graves for the period c. 800–500 B.C.[4] It has been found that the Halstatt graves which can be assigned to the late Urnfield culture, i.e. Hallstatt Phases A and B, did not produce any red pottery with geometric designs applied with graphite. At the same time southern Bavaria did produce such pottery (Fig. 136). From here it must have spread into Austria at the beginning of the Hallstatt culture, c. 750–720 B.C.[5] It has already been observed that for Bavaria north of the Danube, pottery with white paste encrustation provided the demarcation between Bronze and Iron Ages, datable to the middle of the eighth century B.C.

Before setting out to examine the Iron Age, it will be useful to recall that by the end of the Bronze Age a resourceful people had evolved in Europe, probably identifiable with the Indo-Europeans, who were able to adopt and adapt innovations. They had emerged at the end of a cultural continuum — Únětician, Tumulus and Urnfield cultures — whose styles were related to those of earlier periods, and whose burial practices oscillated between inhumation and cremation, sometimes engaging in the practices simultaneously, sometimes consecutively, neither practice ever totally displacing the other in all regions.(Fig. 137). Thus tumulus cremation graves with secondary urn burials are known, cemeteries in some areas were used for burial throughout the entire age and

Plate 4. Situla fragment from Moritzing, Tirol.

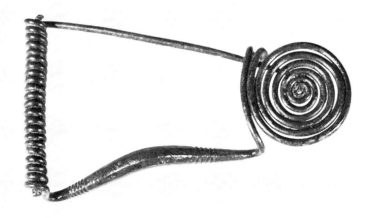

135. Harp-fibula of the early
Hallstatt period, before *c.* 800
B.C., from grave 19, a
cremation grave, at
Statzendorf, Lower Austria.

136. Red bowl with graphite
geometric patterns, *c.* 700
B.C., from southern Germany.

137. Urn with remains, early
Hallstatt period, *c.* 700–600
B.C., from Goldenstedt-Einen,
northern Germany.

193

	Central Europe	Northern and north Central Europe	Relations	Intercultural Sites	Art and Industry	Cultural Features Funerary Practices	Climate
			crystallization of western provinces into a Celtic realm	La Tène			drop in temperature in Scandinavia
					'Baroque' taste		advent of the moist Sub-Atlantic Climate
500 B.C.		La Tène A	possible Scythian raids into central Europe		coexistence of geometric ornamentation in western provinces and of representational Situla Art in eastern provinces	sacrificial funerary rites	
		Hallstatt D		Vettersfelde Hirschlanden Beilngries Frög Strettweg Gemeinlebarn Gross Mugl Býči Skála Großeibstadt Heuneburg		red and black pottery	
	Jastorf				horse motif	cremation	
600 B.C.	house and face urns in northern Germany		Anaximander's world map mentions 'Keltoi' in the European North-west			princely graves dagger graves timbered wagon graves	very dry climatic conditions
						inhumation	
		cultural continuum from the Chalcolithic to the La Tène					
700 B.C.			possible links with eastern nomads		iron utensils bronze ornaments	coexistence of cremation and inhumation	
	Wessenstedt				horse motif	sword graves
	Continuation of Northern Bronze Age	Hallstatt C	invading horsemen		'Hallstatt ducks'	reintroduction of tumuli	
		Late Urnfield Phases II-IV	western provinces linked with Italy and the Mediterranean	Hallstatt	coexistence of bronze and iron	appearance of grave chambers	
800 B.C.		Hallstatt A_1A_2, B_1B_2			monochrome pottery	continuation of Urnfield funerary practices	
			cultures of the eastern Alps linked with Greece and the Black Sea		harp fibula		
					princely societies		
			salt mining and trade		continuation of earlier social structures		
					introduction of iron		

Chart 7. The Hallstatt Culture, c.800 B.C.–c.450 B.C.

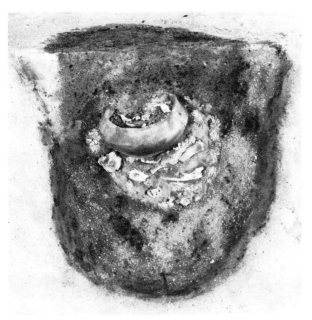

138. Urn and grave shadow, after *c.* 600 B.C., from Emsteck-Gartherfeld, northern Germany.

beyond, and hill forts and lake-shore settlements show continuous occupation, the former likely to have been administrative centers from which control over resources and their distribution or the supervision of trade routes was exercised. These were probably ruled by princes or ruling oligarchies, as is suggested by the size of the graves and their funerary inventories. Especially in the central Alps only a very small percentage of the graves were sword graves, which points to a society differentiated by rank. Hessian grave inventories indicate links with the Lusatians in east central Europe, as does the fortified island settlement in the Federsee during the eleventh century B.C., which shows a similarity with a fortified village of the Early Iron Age in western Poland. That same eleventh-century settlement in the Federsee yielded fragments of leather bridles pointing to the use of horses for riding. Finally, the inventory of the ninth-century 'royal' grave of Seddin with its two iron pins, the earliest examples of iron found in central Europe, signals its princely occupant to have been a man of cosmopolitan culture and a beneficiary of extensive trade relations.

The inventories of the Hallstatt graves show its society to have been a continuation of those earlier copper-mining societies in the area.[6] Mining, with its division of labor, would provide that constant and conservative component which would prolong the life of those institutions which regulated the mining, working, control and distribution of the ores.

This continuation of Urnfield characteristics lends to the early Hallstatt period a great degree of uniformity, such as the working of sheet bronze, for instance, or the negligible variety in clothing and equipment of the deceased, or the continuing rect-angularity of houses, considered to be one of the influences emanating from central Europe and associated with the Urnfield culture, although the history of the style can be traced to the Banded Ware culture of the Neolithic. A most important factor, however, is the retention of Urnfield burial practices. In the area of the Austrian Hallstatt culture traditional burials—cremated remains deposited in urns placed in flat graves—belong to the beginning of the Hallstatt development (Fig. 138). Not until the seventh century B.C. will there be a change in the burial rites.[7]

It might be argued that the isolation enforced by the rugged terrain of the Alps would favor the preservation of obsolete cultural elements particular to the Urnfield culture.[8] Yet the Hallstatt development in the western and eastern Alps was not entirely a derivation of the earlier cultures since they also reflect the adjustment to southern and south-eastern influences respectively. Thus the cultures of the western Alps acted as a link between Italy, the western Mediterranean and the princely societies of south-western Germany, while the hierarchic mining societies of the eastern Alps profited from the stylistic developments originating in the turmoil of Achaian Greece. The inventory of trade goods which came from the south into central Europe is extensively recorded in the graves of the Iron Age cemetery at Hallstatt.

The cultural development from Urnfield to Hallstatt culture loses its linearity towards the end of the seventh century B.C. when the depositing of urns is replaced by a practice which sees the ashes spread over the floor of the grave, now square or rectangular in shape. Furthermore, in some locations the ashes are not gathered in urns; instead a tumulus is raised immediately above the funeral pyre.[9] What would have prompted the return to tumulus burials? Residual cultural elements of the earlier Tumulus culture, perhaps? In some regions these hill graves are characterized by their very large pottery inventories, probably the dishes in which the funerary meal was served rather than the containers for the provisions for the journey. It is significant that the richest graves in the Hallstatt cemetery are the cremation graves. By contrast, the inhumation graves are poor. These become general during Hallstatt D, implying an impoverishment of the culture during its last phase.[10]

Two artistic motifs are very noticeable during this early period: the so-called 'Hallstatt ducks', which, however, support the idea of Bronze Age continuity, and the emphasis on horses for purposes of ornamentation (Fig. 139). It is held that this preoccupation with horses reflects the presence at the end of the Urnfield culture of intruding, iron-equipped horsemen.[11] These however, do not appear to have been accompanied by any other cultural inventory, so that the proof of their presence rests largely on a predilection for the horse motif (Fig. 140), and things associated with the horse, such as bridles and other horse trappings. In some areas under the Hallstatt influence male graves emphasize the connection with horses, especially the wagon graves, where four-wheeled wagons were placed in timbered burial chambers over which a tumulus was subsequently raised.[12] A link has been seen here with the *Kurgan* (Russian for tumulus) peoples of the area north of the Black Sea,[13] an area to be occupied by nomadic Scythians by the end of the seventh century B.C., but which does not account for the presence of bridles in the eleventh-century island settlement in the Federsee. The practice of erecting timbered grave chambers has already been noted in connection with the 'royal' graves of the Únětician period during the Early Bronze Age.

No doubt, the area occupied by the Urnfield culture witnessed periodic outbreaks of hostility. Hallstatt C occupies an area reduced to Austria, Bavaria, Bohemia and Moravia. It is held that this compacting of the cultural area in question had been performed by intruding mounted warriors who settled along the Middle Danube and in the south-eastern Alps, where they became sufficiently sedentary to leave archeological evidence and to be absorbed by the indigenous population. The evidence is provided by the association of native bronze work with bronze bridle bits and other horse gear, including oriental prototypes.[14]

Contrary to the rather slow westward expansion of bronze technology, the spread of iron into Europe took only a few centuries. Known in the Near East since Neolithic times, by the thirteenth century B.C. iron technology appears to have become a Hittite

139. Personal ornaments from Hallstatt. Horse fibulae from cremation grave no. 778, gold platelets from grave no. 679.

140. Horse miniature on the rim of a situla, after *c.* 800 B.C., from Frög near Villach in Carinthia, Austria.

secret.[15] With the disintegration of the Hittite kingdom the knowledge of the working of iron was dispersed quickly, in part by the Thraco-Phrygian invaders, in part by refugees from Hattiland (the land of the Hittites). Its first appearance in central Europe would have been in the form of imported articles, such as the two iron pins found in the ninth-century 'royal' grave of Seddin. Evidently a prized possession and a sign of special status, the pins figured prominently in the grave inventory. These two items, as well as others found elsewhere, show that it was at first introduced as a precious metal, hence its use for jewellery, or as iron inlay in bronze objects. The greater durability of iron over bronze was not readily apparent at first and the more complex conversion of iron ore into hard iron more than outweighed the general availability of the ore in all parts of Europe.[16] The ores were those same ferric oxides—hematite and limonite—of which Paleolithic Man had made such extensive use, and which occur in a soft earthy form as surface ores. The complex processing of iron itself contributed to its esteem as a precious metal. Additional magical qualities must have been attributed to iron, seeing that the earliest iron articles were probably made from meteorite iron. Its explained origin must have lent it considerable cultic significance, especially for the fashioning of charms and amulets.

Though the Hittites knew how to cast iron, European iron workers had to content themselves with wrought iron and ultimately with an early form of steel, mainly because the very high temperatures required—$1535°C.$—for melting iron for purposes of casting could not be obtained in rudimentary furnaces.[17] All that the European Iron Age could do was to reduce iron ores to a pasty wrought iron or impure steel. This iron paste consists of almost pure iron and impurities, called bloom, which make it rather soft and therefore easy to shape. The bloom content facilitated shaping and forge-welding by hammering. However, the resultant tool or weapon was no match for one of good tin-bronze, and though the manufacture of iron was far less demanding than the casting of bronze, it was not until the discovery of carbonizing, a technique which converted wrought iron into an approximation of steel, that iron came to displace bronze. Until then its malleability was also its greatest weakness in that it was too soft, too easily bent and dulled and too brittle to withstand a sudden impact. A hardening process had to be discovered before iron could become an effective substitute for bronze.

An early furnace was no more than a hole in a slope facing the prevailing winds, with an opening at the base to provide the necessary draught (Fig. 141). Charged with surface iron ores and charcoal, the temperatures achieved were adequate to transform

197

the ore into a pasty cake which could then be shaped by hammering. These lumps of iron amounted to only a few pounds at first. After cooling, the iron would be reheated over charcoal and hammered into a dense mass, a process which drove out some of the slag. This forging process allowed the surfaces of the iron to absorb carbon which when hammered produced hard and wear-resistant surfaces. This process was improved further if the desired object was tempered, by subjecting it to a low-temperature treatment alternated with quenching and repeated hammering through which the properties of the iron were improved—its toughness increased, brittleness reduced and its flexibility improved.[18] Depending on the varying nature of the slag residue, the behavior of the finished product was not at all predictable. Much depended on the skill of the smith and on his ability to assess and control the variables. No doubt the spirit world was called upon to assist in the forging process and it is equally probable that far into the Middle Ages it was this spiritual participation in the venture which was considered to have imbued the truly good swords with their nearly mystical qualities. It also follows, however, that consistently superior ores would be in great demand (Fig. 142). The eastern Alps were such a source and those who regulated its exploitation knew how to draw both profit and power from the exercise of such controls.

The initial coexistence of bronze and iron, and the eventual displacement of bronze, involved a transition period of nearly 500 years not only because early iron was no immediate match for the more durable tin-bronzes but also because the threatened bronze technology met the challenge with remarkable resilience. Late graves yielded a wealth of bronze jewellery, bronze vessels and 'kitchen' utensils of sophisticated sheet-metal workmanship. When the final displacement came it seems to have been conditioned by technical necessities, perhaps in the wake of a prehistoric arms race. Most important, however, the acquisition of the new iron technology based on readily

141. Furnace for the smelting of surface iron-ore, surrounded by lumps of residual slag from the bottom of former smelters. From a settlement of the Roman iron age at Scharmbeck near Hamburg.

142. Bars of crude iron, *c.* 700 B.C., from a depot at Aubstatt, near Königshofen, southern Germany.

available surface iron ores must have meant increased independence from the centers of copper and tin mining and bronze production and distribution. A 'democratization' of society may have been effected during the Early Iron Age, but what new aspects came to play a role in the daily life of the ordinary individual is not entirely apparent.

It is the Hallstatt culture which witnesses the spread of iron as a useable metal, while bronze comes to play mainly an ornamental role. Though Hallstatt is one of the earliest iron-working locations, neither Hallstatt, nor La Tène for that matter, can be considered as primary centers of iron production. Instead their value lies rather in being extensive find sites. The archeological evidence reveals the settlement on the Hallstätter See to have been a trading center founded on an independent economic basis, and without rival in Europe during the early first millennium B.C. Its economic basis was the mining and distribution of rock-salt. Salt was the export article. The other finds were imports. In general the imports were finished products, their various places of origin indicated by their respective styles.

While a population of hunters and nomads finds sufficient sodium in wood ash and in meat, generally eaten rare—stories of the Huns placing their meat under the saddle until both sides were seared are probably exaggerated—the need for salt appears to be an accompanying phenomenon to settlement, agriculture and the keeping of livestock, since vegetable food does not contain sufficient salt.[19] During the Iron Age the demand for it appears to be greater. This increased demand can be attributed, in part at least, to the climate, which at the end of the Bronze Age saw the advent of dry conditions. During the period 700–500 B.C. Europe had indeed been subjected to a dry heat wave which lasted for about 200 years. The need for an increased dietary use of salt as a safeguard against dehydration would be the motivation for the salt trade. Lake levels were lower, and it has been estimated that there was only about half as much rainfall as now. The drought was intense enough to encourage the migration of peoples to moister sites. Dry conditions would have made it possible to dry meat in the open air. Moor-geology indicates that by 500 B.C. the dry climate was giving way to the moist sub-Atlantic climate. Henceforth meat would have to be salted for preservation through the winter.[20]

143. Miners' tools, hammer and pick, from the Hallstatt mines, *c.* 800–500 B.C.

To supply the demand for salt required a staggering effort. The salt layers of the Salzkammergut in the Austrian Alps are located between formations of 30–60 m of non-yielding rock. With the tools available to the salt miners of Hallstatt they could advance into the rock at a rate of 1 m in about one month, that is to say that it might take up to five years of toil just to get to the salt formations. It was obviously worth the effort, since in some of the mines the yield was 80 per cent salt.[21]

Salt preserves everything, so that the abandoned salt mines have maintained complete inventories of organic materials such as tools (Fig. 143), torches, textiles, hides, curative herbs and even excrement, a source of information about the miners' staple diet of barley, beans and millet. In baskets of wood and hides, carried by means of a headband the Hallstatt miners brought the salt up from a depth of up to 300 m and 1·5 km inside the mountain, sustaining injuries and perishing in the shifting rock formations. In 1734 one miner was found completely preserved and 'grown' into the salt. At the time one did not look for pre-historic salt miners, and he was buried without arousing much curiosity in the scholarly community.[22] Such a find has not been repeated. It has also been argued that the salt was obtained by hollowing out the rock, filling it with water, then drawing off the super-saturated salt solution, before letting the water evaporate. If the Hallstatt miners knew this process, then the Middle Ages rediscovered it.[23]

The salt trade brought prosperity to the settlement which probably merchandized its own ware rather than waiting for passing traders. Since the settlement had its back to the water the salt probably did not leave the area by means of the lake.[27] Considering the terrain, caravans of porters and pack animals were the likely means of transportation by which the salt would have reached the transcontinental traderoutes in all directions. They would have returned with quantities of amber from the north, weapons and ornaments (Fig. 144) from Bavaria and Württemberg in southern Germany, embossed bronze vessels with narrative friezes—*situlae*—from Italy and the Middle Danube, horse bridles from further east, and glass beads and vessels from the Balkans.[25] Of special significance is an ivory sword grip with amber inlay, its materials brought together from distant points of origin.

From the ninth century B.C. onward the entire area in which the Hallstatt culture evolves presents itself as a supplier of raw materials and as a consumer of influences. The extensive trade links brought foreign imports from Etruscan Italy and the Greek colonies of the western Mediterranean as well as from the Hungarian plain, the Adriatic, the Balkans and Greece and its eastern colonies along the shores of the Black Sea (Plate 4). This acquisition of exotic wares as well as of technological innovations stimulated the cultural areas of the late Urnfield culture to develop those characteristics which identified the Hallstatt cultures from eastern France to the western Carpathians (Fig. 145). Thus the analysis of the bronze hilt of a particular eastern type of dagger was found to be of a composition common to the Moravian area.[26] It could be speculated that eastern visitors commissioned the dagger in a local workshop. The literature on this era is much enamoured with the idea of hostile invaders, superior in their horses, bringing their knowlege of working iron into the area and superimposing their cultural presence upon the established population. The supporting evidence consists of new metal types associated with horse trappings of eastern origin, especially bridle-bits, and the bones of horses.[27] Why the presence of bridle-bits should necessarily point to the first use of riding horses is not clear, since the North American Indian, for instance, rode his horse quite well without forcing a bit between its teeth. The contact with

144. Neck hanging of the early Iron Age, after *c.* 800 B.C., from Lehmden, northern Germany.

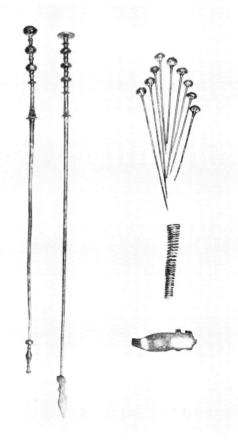

145. Personal ornaments from cremation grave no. 393, Hallstatt. Originally the headed pins were joined together to form a many-headed pin.

sporadic raiding parties, such as those of the Scythians during the sixth century B.C., as a source of influence, rather than contact as a result of prolonged settlement, is at least an acceptable possibility.[28] Cultural influences need not be transmitted in person. In view of the extensive trade connections, the intrusion and settlement of mounted invaders is not necessarily an essential catalytic source of cultural change. The evidence from the various areas of the Hallstatt culture does not point conclusively to specific signs of belligerence or aggressive expansion or to any existing cultural elements which might have transformed the 'hostile horsemen' and induced them to moderate their warlike ways.

By the middle of the sixth century B.C. the exchange of goods and information had made it possible for Greek geographers to link ethnically identifiable peoples with certain cultural areas.[29] Thus the first known world map, drawn by Anaximander of Miletus (c. 610–c. 540 B.C.), places *Keltoi* into western Europe. Though inaccurately placed, the name *Keltoi* points to his knowledge of such a people to the west during Hallstatt Phases C and D. Other people to the north are identified only as 'Hyperboreans'. No doubt, the population of south-central Europe contained Celtic elements, among others, which enjoyed a rich culture based on a flourishing economy founded on iron and salt, in some regions. Thracian and Scythian peoples were to be found on the eastern plains where the latter penetrated into north central Europe, as indicated by

Map 21. Influences upon the Hallstatt cultures, c. 800 B.C.–c. 450 B.C.

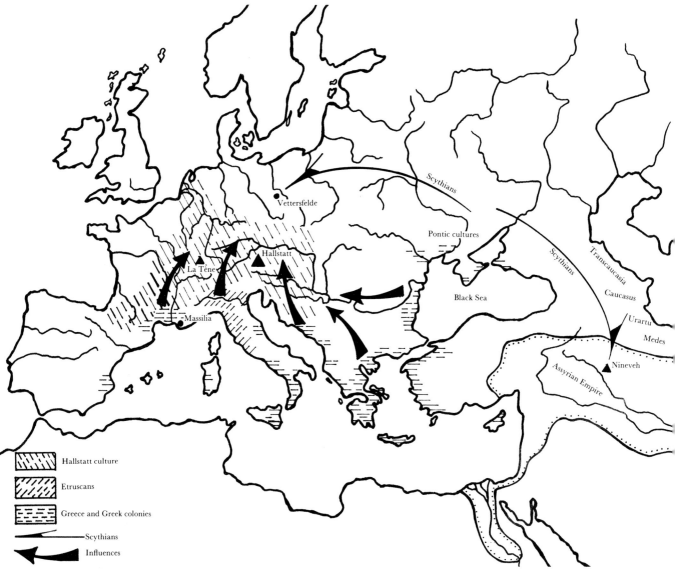

146. Scythian decorative gold ornaments, middle of the fifth century B.C., probably from southern Russia.

Scythian finds (Fig. 146), especially the treasure found at Vettersfelde in Brandenburg, evidence of a possible raid during the late sixth century B.C.

Through the areas of the Hallstatt culture the initiatives made by the peoples along the shores of the Mediterranean saw merchants penetrating far into the interior of Europe. The material and technological imports which they brought up the Rhône, across the Alps or up from the Adriatic into the area of the Hallstatt culture—beak-mouthed wine jugs, tripod cauldrons as well as Greek painted tableware from the Greek colonies, such as Massilia[30]—must have been accompanied by religious and social influences as well (Fig. 148).

As with the Bronze Age cultures, the mining of ores and the distribution of finished and semi-finished products indicate the existence of administrative structures. It is possible of course, that the consideration of economics as a prelude to political organization may be receiving undue emphasis. The mining of salt and iron ores and their distribution throughout Europe by means of an extensive trading network would build on earlier administrative experience, either by descendants of those who controlled the earlier bronze technology, or by those 'horsemen' who superimposed themselves over the native population and assumed nominal control of the industry, allowing those with the necessary administrative skills to wield effective control. Either approach would allow for a large measure of continuity, which in turn would account for the development of cultural elements from the Urnfield culture into the Hallstatt and beyond, effecting only gradual change. Analogies with many similar situations in recorded history would lend support to such a scenario. In short, what is brought by the conqueror may then be modified by the vanquished.

During the Hallstatt, quite conclusive social differentiations become apparent. Already towards the end of the Urnfield period great social contrasts had appeared, as reflected in the funerary equipment, where rich graves suggested an aristocracy, while very poor, regressive graves suggested an impoverished population. Consistent with its transitional nature, the Hallstatt cemetery itself, with its wide range of grave inventories, points to such differentiations, while the hill forts, with vast 'princely' grave mounds in their vicinity, indicate that some members of the communities were the beneficiaries of exceptional treatment in death, and by inference, probably also in life. It is of course difficult to envisage a realistic image of that society in view of the encumbrance of associations and biases which such words as 'fortified place' or 'princely grave' evoke in us.[31] In the absence of definitions historical metaphors are used, which may create entirely the wrong impressions about aristocrats, dynasties, princes, lords, cultural elites, warriors, subjects, miners and craftsmen. Some caution is therefore advisable in formulating an image of these Iron Age societies, since there are no indications as to the nature of any social infra-structures, the systems of mutual dependencies, the hierarchical dispositions, or the concentration of political, economic or spiritual power.

As archeological activity continues, the information about the Hallstatt cemetery is subject to constant modification and re-interpretation, especially when it comes to expressing the finds in statistical terms, so that the funerary evidence excavated so far from this cemetery can really only speak for itself. It is hazardous to deduce a picture of the structure of Iron Age society from the cemetery which is valid even for just the mining settlement, let alone for the surrounding territory. Thus, for instance, only very few of the graves contained the remains of women or children. Where was the home base for this mountain valley settlement, 400 m above the lake? Was the work seasonal? Were the miners natives or 'guest laborers'? How was their work regulated, and by whom?

The grave inventories have been used to construe something of a social picture. The early period during which the cemetery was in use (800-600 B.C.) is characterized by the inclusion of swords in the grave inventories. These sword graves yielded the richest

148 (right). Situla and stand with ornamental ducks and 'sun-bursts' from Hallstatt.

147. Golden dagger from cremation grave no. 696, Hallstatt.

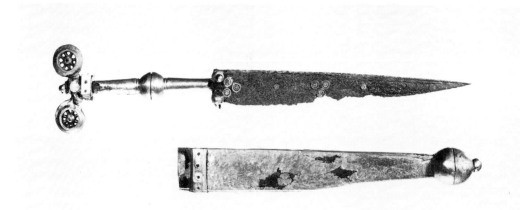

gifts, totalling almost half of the wealth of the entire grave field, although the graves were only few. In view of many other less well-equipped graves, these sword graves point to a small social group, whom one tried to identify as an elite of merchant princes. The years 600–500 B.C. were characterized by the inclusion of daggers (Fig. 148). Though the dagger grave period was only a century long, it yielded twice as many daggers, as the earlier period had yielded swords, suggesting the existence of a dagger-wearing 'aristocracy', that is to say, a turning to ruling 'oligarchies' and an expansion of the power structure. The common element in the cemetery is that all graves are flat graves, of which some 45 per cent are cremation graves, the remainder being inhumation graves. The fire graves contained the rich inventories, and of these the sword graves were the richest in jewellery. Only some 26 per cent of the burials contained weapons, although here the reports are not in agreement, some suggesting an equal split between the two types of burial. Even so, the 'non-military' graves are rich in belthooks, fibulae, arm rings, amber and even glass during the late period. Only a small number of graves was found to contain no equipment, or only pottery. Some were double graves of adults, or of adult and child. Occasionally even four burials were found in one grave. Graves with the remains of women and/or children or of young or old men were rare. Considering the high mortality rate among children a great frequency of children's burials should be expected. Yet of the 75 children's graves unearthed at one point, only 19 graves contained children under five years of age, 28 graves held children between five and ten, and only 5 graves held youngsters between ten and fourteen years of age. A rough calculation suggests that only about 150 people occupied the site at a time during the early period. This population increased to about 300 people in later times.[32] It is apparent that the Hallstatt mining community does not offer a representative cross-section of society, but is largely a society of middle-aged men. It is structured abnormally in that it creates the impression of two groups, one military and the other miners and carpenters. Their interrelationship cannot be determined, although some images come to mind: overseers and slaves, privileged ruling class over exploited workers, or foreign conquerors with a modern technology dominating underdeveloped natives. Because of the presence of horses in the arsenal of motifs, the theory of the dominating horsemen-conquerors finds much favor in the literature. What is certain is that the Hallstatt settlement consisted of a largely male society engaged in mining and in its protection.

Neolithic, Chalcolithic and Bronze Age settlements in the flatlands, on islands and on hilltops were frequently fortified. The suggestion that the growth of the fortified settlements such as the Heuneburg were largely a response to population pressures originating in the east depends on the acceptance of 'invading horsemen'. The Heuneburg is a unique phenomenon north of the Alps.[33] Located on a terrace, it overlooks the upper Danube, 60 m below, providing its occupants with a commanding position over the valley and the natural trade route which it represents (Fig. 149). Excavations of this excellent strategic site have shown that the earliest fortifications can be dated into the Early Bronze Age, the Únětician Period, c. 2000 B.C., when a wide V-shaped ditch and a wall of earth and wood impeded access from the approachable north side. During the Middle Bronze Age, the Tumulus Period c. 1700 B.C., a new system of fortifications replaced the old. For a subsequent period of 400 years the hilltop was unoccupied until c. 1200 B.C., when an Urnfield settlement was established on the site. The sixth century saw representatives of the Hallstatt Culture move onto the plateau to occupy it for c. 200 years. During the La Tène period it and many other such sites in southern Germany and Switzerland were destroyed and not rebuilt. During the first and second centuries A.D. it was again occupied when incorporated into the Roman Empire. The Celtic and Roman periods have not yet been fully assessed. During the sixth century A.D. it was garrisoned by units of Merowingian Franks during their occupation of the Alaman territories. In all, the site indicates at least twenty-four habitation levels (Fig. 150).

The early Hallstatt settlement of the Heuneburg is the most noteworthy (Fig. 151). It is approximately triangular, the tip pointing NNE. On its accessible sides it was protected by a double earth-work and ditch system which contained an organized village. Access through flanking gates was provided by a curving causeway under the south-western wall. The western portion of the wall is an early example of a timber-reinforced stone wall. This style uses a system of squared wooden beams, joined together with wooden pegs, assembled in layers of frames and boxes, anchored into the ground and resting on a stone foundation. The substance of the wall consisted of broken stones and earth, stabilized by the timbered framework. It probably reached a height of 4 m and may have been surmounted by a wooden parapet. This technique of building originated in central Europe. It is held that a proto-Celtic 'family' had made this fort its hereditary seat. In the ensuing years the Heuneburg developed extensive trade relations with the Mediterranean settlements such as Massilia.

Probably as a result of close and perhaps personal contact with the Greek colonies to the south, the N, NW, S and SE portions of the wall were built following Mediterranean models. A massive wall of sun-dried clay bricks was raised to a height of about 4 m, on a base of broken and cut stone, some 500 m long, requiring c. 1000 m³ of stone which had to be brought up from about 6 km away. The NW portion of the wall was further reinforced by eight massive, rectangular bastions set at regular intervals, 10 m apart. Above the double earthwork and ditch system on the W side and on the NE and SE portions of the defenses, a lower wall of wood and stone completed the fortifications.[34]

The brick was made of a mixture of clay and sand into which chopped chaff and straw had been added for bonding. Made in boxes measuring 40 cm × 40 cm × 6–8 cm, the sun-dried bricks were assembled in a checkerboard pattern, held together by clay with only a low sand content and with built-in reinforcing beams. Exterior and top surfaces were finished off with a water-repellent clay slip and were probably white-washed. The visual effect would have been quite striking. Inside the settlement the provision of ditches and drainage ducts was designed to protect the walls against the dissolving effects of moisture.

The settlement appears to have been well planned. Rectangular houses were placed parallel to the wall and quite close to it, separated by narrow passages only about 1 m wide. The middle of the 'town' appears to have been an open space. An extensive drainage system drew the water off and allowed it to seep through the broken rock foundation of the clay wall towards the south-east. There is evidence that the community was divided into quarters along occupational lines, in the Mediterranean fashion, i.e. it showed urban traits quite unknown north of the Alps. At least one such quarter has been excavated. It had contained the local bronze industry. Sufficient evidence has been assembled from remains trodden into the stamped clay floors to identify the functions of the individual houses as furnaces, smelters, casting rooms and workshops. The buildings themselves vary in design from 10–13 m long, 3·6–7·3 m wide houses, to square structures, 4·8–4·9 m in size, resting on oaken sleeper beams. Oak was the preferred building material.[35]

The role which this fortified hilltop settlement played is not entirely clear. No doubt

149. The Heuneburg near Hundersingen overlooking the Danube. Its present appearance owes much to the Middle Ages.

150. The Heuneburg from the Danube plain.

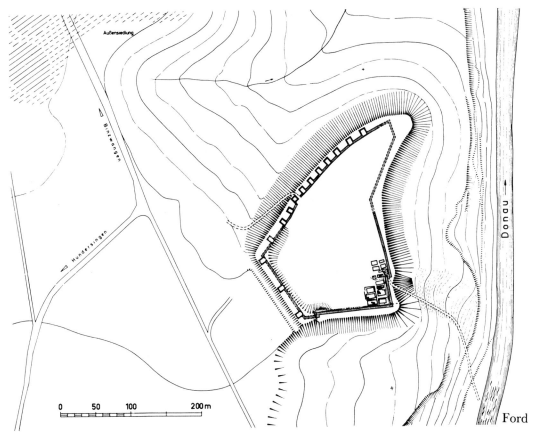

151. Plan of the Heuneburg, period IVb, phase 1, with schematic overview of the buildings located in the SE corner. Shaded area to the NW marks the probable location of the neighboring settlement.

it fulfilled many functions as an administrative, economic, social and religious center. The workshops of the Heuneburg indicate that the fortress was a manufacturing center, a nucleus for trade and the dissemination of influences, a point where indirect contact with some aspects of the southern cultures could be made. Its defensive role is apparent, but it is not known whether the fortification did or could offer refuge to the surrounding population, since the population density of the fortress must have been considerable. Perhaps some of its inhabitants farmed the land nearby, thus making the Heuneburg agriculturally self-sufficient. No doubt the settlement also contained at least one religious shrine. The open area in the middle may have been the necessary space for large assemblies.

It is reasonable to assume that the Heuneburgers were aware of the fragility of their clay walls and that they would offer less resistance to a concentrated assault than did the *murus gallicus*. The value of having such a 'modern' wall may have lain in the prestige it bestowed upon the settlement. As an impressive display of ostentation and power it may, for a while, have accomplished as much as a more effective system of defense. The experiment on the Heuneburg found no imitators among the other Hallstatt settlements. Even at the Heuneburg later fortifications show no links with Mediterranean developments. As a probable seat of power it had obtained its wealth from the flourishing trade with the south. This wealth may have provided the motivation for its destruction.

209

Perhaps a decline had already set in, its prosperity diminished and its defenses decayed, leaving it too weak to withstand an attack. As a fortified settlement it represents the beginning of town life and urban development north of the Alps.

About 2 km from the Heuneburg there is a vast tumulus, 13 m high and 80 m in diameter, after restoration, one of the largest of its type in Europe. In local parlance it is called the 'Hohmichele' (Fig. 152). It has been designated a 'dynastic' burial mound.[36] Owing to its proximity to the Heuneburg one assumes it to be the grave site reserved for the 'princes' of the Heuneburg. Such princely burial mounds are to be found from eastern France to Czechoslovakia.[37] The largest Hallstatt tumulus is located outside the village of Gross Mugl in Lower Austria (Fig. 153). An examination of the Hohmichele revealed it to belong to Hallstatt D, the early sixth century B.C. The older, lower section, about 4 m high, contained inhumations in graves I–VIII, while cremations in the more recent graves IX–XIII had been placed into the next 7 m of earth. The earth layers confirm that the mound was raised over many years.[38]

Of special interest are two of the earliest graves. Both are wagon graves contained in timbered grave chambers. The larger wagon grave contained the remains of a woman, while the smaller chamber contained a man placed on a cowhide, and a woman, both laid out under a funerary wagon, with the harnesses of two horses. Both chambers had been robbed while the tumulus was under construction during subsequent burials. The thieves must have searched for precious jewellery, for the chambers still yielded a whole range of bronze vessels, fibulae, and glass and amber beads. Normally the primary

Map 22. Principal sites of the Hallstatt culture mentioned in the text.

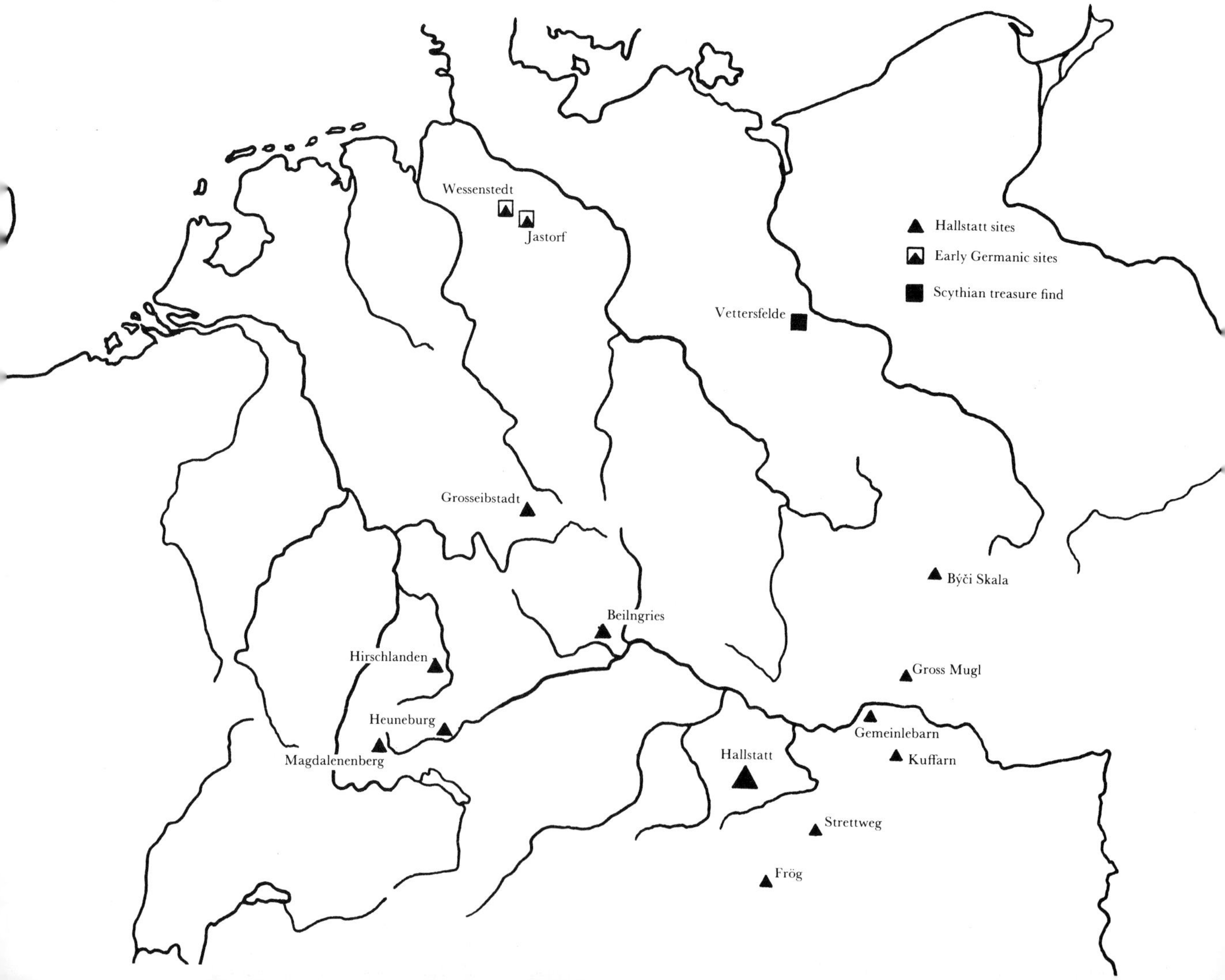

152. The 'Hohmichele', burial mound of the Hallstatt period, near the Heuneburg.

153. Burial mound of the early Hallstatt period at Gross Mugl in Lower Austria.

154. The Magdalenenberg on the outskirts of Villingen in the Black Forest. The timbers of the grave chamber were cut in 551 B.C. Three wooden spades abandoned by grave robbers were dated to 504 B.C.

211

burials in these princely tumuli are male graves. Female burials are secondary burials, placed either into the man's grave chamber, or deposited into the slope. Dendrochronology (tree-ring dating) has made it possible to establish the date when the trees were cut down, and if grave robbers were careless and left one of their wooden spades behind, a date particular to that tool can also be fixed, as has indeed been done in the timbered grave chamber on the Magdalenenberg (Fig. 154), outside Villingen in the Black Forest.[39]

Wagon graves such as these are a key component supporting the argument on behalf of the invading horsemen from the east. However, while the northern Balkans, Bohemia and Moravia know cremation graves associated with horse skeletons and eastern bronze wares during the early sixth century, the western timber-grave tumuli know only the symbolic representations of horses through the inclusion of horse trappings. The custom appears to have been modified into an influence as it entered central Europe. The grave chambers of the Hohmichele contained archery equipment, specifically a quiver with fifty-one iron-tipped arrows pointing upward, a feature which has been identified as Scythian funerary practice, and fittings for two bows.[40] Very surprising is the find of real Chinese silk threads in the textiles used in the wagon graves of the Hohmichele tumulus, where it had been used in clothing and in the draperies with which the wagon and chamber had been furnished. The presence of these items points to the enriching nature of the contact between eastern and western groups, both enjoying the benefits of

Map 23. Princely burial mounds of the Western Hallstatt culture after *c.* 700 B.C.

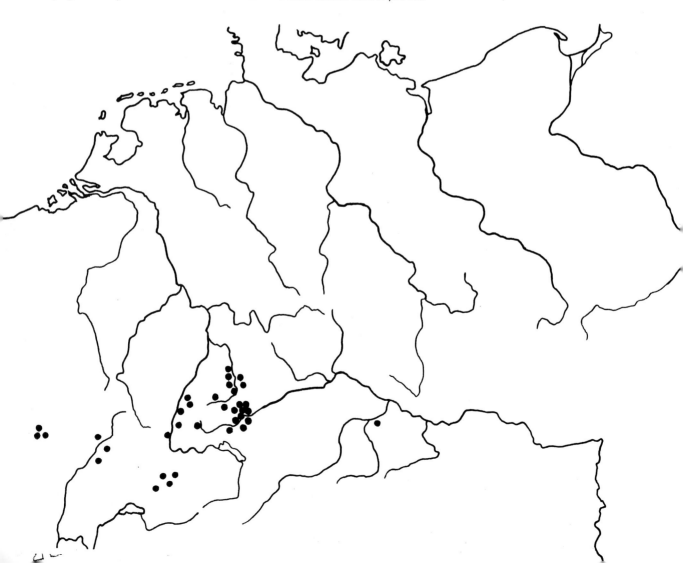

prosperity. The suggestion of a foreign horsemen-nobility imposed on an indigenous population is not born out conclusively by the evidence from the tombs of the Hallstatt Culture. Nor does the Hohmichele reflect anything of the political structure or power of the Heuneburg nearby.[41] Only suppositions remain, since reliable methodological principles allowing sociological evaluation of the grave inventories have not yet been developed. Even for simple societies it is difficult to deduce inner social connections, since it is generally unknown under what circumstances burials took place. Can it be assumed that everyone was interred, or was the burial rite in itself a sign of distinction? Why is there such a shortage of women's and children's graves? Did the inventories reflect an individual's attachment to his personal possessions, or did they reflect the intentions and expectations of those who remained behind? What factors prompted the repeated oscillation between cremation and inhumation? The question must remain open, whether burials and funerary inventories are at all reliable sources on which to base any social, political or ethnic conclusions.[42]

The evidence from the graves shows that at the turn of the eighth to seventh centuries new types of harnessing had come into use, larger bridle bits, for instance, suggesting that a larger breed of horses had come into the area of the central European Hallstatt culture, probably from the Danubian areas to the east. Bridle trimmings even appear among the finds in the north, although later Roman descriptions of Germanic horsemen almost dragging their feet on the ground when mounted indicate that the use of the larger horse did not spread northward. In the area of the Hallstatt culture the evidence consists largely of horse harnesses, vehicle ornaments and fittings. It follows that horses, wagons and chariots would also have acquired a military significance and influenced the nature of warfare.[43] The introduction of iron would in itself have distributed the burden of battle onto the lower ranks. While Bronze Age fighting probably saw opposing 'hero'-leaders challenging one another to fight in full view of their armies, the great availability of iron with the ensuing equalization of weapons at the lower social levels, equal in quality and similar in type, would have contributed to the 'democratization' of war.[44]

Grave chambers—residences for the dead—first appeared in eastern central Europe at the western rim of the Carpathian basin during the earlier phases of Hallstatt C. Only about a third of them, however, are wagon graves, equipped with wagons, horses and harnesses. This custom seems to have been shared more widely since many of the old European cultures placed parts of vehicles into the graves. The Greek, Etruscan and Italic peoples, the inhabitants of western Lombardy and the southern Tirol and even the north-western Urnfield people in the area of the river Maas appear to have practised it. Central Europe itself, though, did not engage in this ritual until Hallstatt C, when it appeared in north-eastern Bavaria and the cultural area just north of the Alps.[45] The influence moved westward.[46] However, while wagon graves were characteristic for Bavaria and Bohemia during the seventh century B.C., by the sixth century they were no longer discernible there as a burial practice, while in Baden-Württemberg, eastern France, Switzerland around the Upper Rhine and Bern they were just then being adopted by the culturally dominant groups.[47]

The eastern origin of burying the deceased accompanied by a vehicle or some vehicle parts is supported by a structural detail of these Hallstatt vehicles. The construction of the wagon wheels in central Europe is so closely related to specific principles of construction used in the Near East that either a direct dependence on the east or a common source is possible.[48] The latter is the more probable. The earliest wagon graves with a

Hallstatt-type inventory—trappings such as yokes, harnesses, signs of personal distinction, and the positioning of weapons, especially daggers—were found in Transcaucasia, datable to *c.* 1000 B.C. Then during the eighth century the cultural area between Urartu–Assyria and Transcaucasia came to be the most important supplier of wheels and horses.[49] This area was the region of principal contact between the high cultures of Mesopotamia and the nomads of eastern Europe from the Danube to the Caspian Sea. Except for the iron hoops, the new Hallstatt construction of spokes, hubs and the bending and splicing of the wheel is most similar to those produced in Assyria–Elam in the time of King Tiglath-Pileser III during the second half of the eighth century B.C. Via the steppes of southern Russia a whole range of articles under strong eastern, perhaps Scythian, influence came west, as shown by wheels, the style of bridling, but also shaft-hole axes, double and single edged swords and daggers.[50]

It is unlikely that the various areas of the Hallstatt culture from the Pyrenees to the Balkans, with their cultural variations, would all have the same reason for building wagon graves. It has been suggested, and it is very acceptable, that a link existed between the means of locomotion in horse-drawn carriages and the spiritual derivation of an idea, of supra-regional acceptability and not tied to any specific group of carriers of such an idea, of the journey to the Beyond.[51] Such concepts would account for the high degree of uniformity in the burial practice. Thus the deceased of Mont Lassois in eastern France, those along the Neckar, of the Heuneburg and of Großeibstatt in Franconia perhaps belonged to a social set related by common religious beliefs as reflected in the burial practices. Probably of eastern origin, the belief of this dominant caste of the Hallstatt culture may well have provided the spiritual basis for the cultural power and pre-eminence of this group.[52] Although horse trappings were the most frequently found inventories, in central Europe it was not customary to slaughter the horses, as was the custom elsewhere. Instead the burial ritual made use of symbolic representations. Thus the presence of horses and wagons was indicated figuratively by the disposition of horse harnesses, especially bridles, and wagon parts, especially wheels—*pars pro toto*—with the deceased placed on the floor between the wheels of the simulated carriage. This figurative placement of horses and vehicles affected the positioning of accompanying vessels as well as the dimensions of the chamber. Apparently however, of the harnesses found at Grosseibstatt, only old, useless, hastily repaired, mismatched equipment was laid out in the grave chambers, just enough of a selection to fulfill the symbolic requirements.[53] If this is a correct analysis, it suggests the superficial adherence to a paling tradition, rather than the mark of the social distinction of the deceased.

In the cemetery at Hallstatt the weapons graves of the earlier Hallstatt period are satisfactory indicators of social differentiation in that they suggest the armsbearing man to have enjoyed a position of rank, especially in view of the circumstances that the majority of graves were found to be without weapons. The Hallstatt gravefield reveals that about 45 per cent of the graves were cremation graves and that these were generally warrior graves,[54] in that up to 70 per cent of the armsbearing population preferred cremation.[55] However, as was stated before, only a small percentage (26 per cent) of the graves actually contained weapons. The practice of cremation is in itself a continuation of earlier Urnfield practices, which would suggest, the representations of horses in their graves not withstanding, that these warriors were descendants of the earlier culture and not invader-horsemen. The cremation sword graves also yielded the richest inventories of fine sheet bronze work (Fig. 155). The inhumation graves are generally without

155. Ornamental sheet bronze belt from a cremation grave, Hallstatt.

weapons, and are therefore largely not warrior graves, though not necessarily poor in their furnishings.[56] By contrast the wagon graves further north, supposedly characteristic for the warrior horsemen, are inhumation graves, such as the Hohmichele, which curiously enough has cremation graves in its upper, later burial zones. In the Hallstatt cemetery the richest graves had been located without a specific plan throughout the cemetery, except that each of these graves formed something of a nucleus for several graves with average or inferior inventories. Several of the weapons graves formed a group, accompanied by at least one very rich grave and several average or poor graves. Each of these groups was composed of graves for older and younger men. The weaponless male graves tended not to differ from those of women, except in their jewellery. The graves of the women of the prominent group would also be among the rich weaponless graves.[57] In the fire graves the ashes were found in little heaps on the floor, having originally probably been placed in containers of organic materials. In all only three cremation urns have been found, two of which were of bronze.[58] In the body graves the deceased lay in a supine position, their arms either alongside, or with one or both arms folded on their chest. W–E positioning was customary, the head facing east. Oval tublike slabs of openfire burned clay have been found, about 10 cm thick and between 37 cm–3·60 m long, on which the corpses had been placed. All the graves had been placed at a depth of 1–1·50 m. The floor had been stamped, and sometimes covered with fine sand. Traces of wood beneath some skeletons suggest that the deceased rested on a wooden bier. Often the grave had a covering of coarse and broken stone.[59]

Problematic is the almost equal coexistence of inhumation and cremation graves.[60] Inhumation had been a rarity even during the late period of the Urnfield culture. Only during the Hallstatt did it become a common practice. S–N positioning was customary,[61] so that W–E arrangements at Hallstatt are exceptional and probably determined by the eastern exit from the valley.[62] What would have prompted the return to the construction of timbered grave chambers and to tumulus burials? Evidently cremation and inhumation imply different ideas about the nature of death, but one can only speculate about the actual relationship between changing ideas about the Beyond and their effect on mortuary procedures. It can be expected that notions about the continued corporeality and capability of the deceased to act must have been basic to the practice of inhumation. Following this view it would seem that man had difficulty envisaging a total separation of physical body and metaphysical soul. Instead he seemed to have accepted the notion of a material soul[63] which remained behind with the body, free to move about the burial chamber and make use of its inventory or to reoccupy the body at will. With such notions the deceased may have been seen to lay continued claim to his terrestrial possessions. These implications when transferred to the practice of cremation make the latter practice appear to be a great deal more subtle and sophisticated. From our vantage point a return to inhumation then suggests a regression to simpler notions about death. Did this age differentiate between the dead and those who have died? At what point did the deceased pass from a state of having died, where he maintained his continuing corporeality and ability to act, into a state of final death, when the grave chamber could be re-entered for possible re-use? Originally even the tumuli of the Hallstatt culture had been intended for single occupancy. What change in concepts allowed the addition of other dead into the burial mound? When was it safe for the grave robbers to intrude? These questions hover in the background to the burial practices of every prehistoric period.

The questions about continued physicality assume a special significance for contemporary multiple burials in one chamber: was the additional corpse a close relation who had died of natural causes; a voluntary suicide; had the person been murdered by stealth, or was his/her death a ritual sacrifice.[64] At the Hohmichele, beside evidence of swine sacrifice, there is evidence of hair sacrifice on the basis of *pars pro toto*. The notion that hair is the seat of life, related to concepts of dignity, identity, strength, honour or shame, is of course not unknown. Its presence in graves would suggest a reduced form, a substitute for human sacrifice. This substitution may have been a sophistication.[65] In a cave at Býči Skála in Moravia, north of Brno, was located a sixth-century wagon burial, complete with wagon parts, harness fittings, personal jewellery, bronze vessels and pottery. This find was accompanied by evidence of grain offerings as well as of animal and human sacrifice. In all the skeletal remains of forty people were found, mostly women (companions?). Some of the skeletons were not complete; heads, hands and feet had been removed. Fragments of a detached skull are reported to have been strewn with grain. Nearby were found the remains of two quartered horses. A cauldron contained a human skull. At another point in the cave, accompanied by pottery, a skull was found that had been made into a drinking cup.[66]

Evidently the idea was to demonstrate some position of eminence which the deceased had enjoyed in life. Particularly lavish burials would make the graves those of the leaders of society. In the instance of those graves which only gave a semblance of social position—old and broken harness pieces, etc.—it is conceivable that there was a desire to create a misleading prosperous image of the deceased in people's memory—the indigent who is buried in his best clothing. Thus the inventory may not be a true reflection of the role which the deceased actually played in daily life. The intentional creation of an illusion of wealth might then be seen as an upward equalization for an existence beyond death, to compensate for any insufficiencies the deceased may have had to endure in life.[67]

It used to be calculated that a tumulus such as the Gross Mugl, the largest Hallstatt burial mound, was erected in one day by about two thousand people. This calculation was the result of a great overestimation of the size of the population. The local prehistoric

156. Biconical urn with incised designs, after 700 B.C., from Buchheim near Freiburg, colored reddish-brown and black.

cemetery of some ninety graves is one of the largest in Lower Austria, but when the time span is calculated during which the settlement was inhabited, only about sixteen people lived there at a time.[68] Regardless of the accuracy of this calculation, the tribute which the small population paid to the deceased, in labor alone, was immense.

As one would expect, the adherence to crematory practices would continue the need for ceramic containers in which the cremated remains could be deposited. This type of funerary ware is not in the least extraordinary. It is different with the vessels deposited in the 'residences for the dead', the timbered grave chambers of the southern Hallstatt. These graves were equipped with a wide variety of hand-made pottery, voluminous storage vessels, bowls, basins, plates and cups, to hold either the provisions for the journey or to serve the funeral party in some festive means (Plate 5a). Even though there are regional variations which must reflect regional differences in taste, some characteristics are constant across the entire area of the Hallstatt culture (Fig. 156). Thus the larger storage vessels show a degree of uniformity in that they rest on a conical

157. Brown urn from Kappel on the Federsee in southern Germany, *c.* 700 B.C.

158. Biconical urn colored black, red and beige, *c.* 700 B.C., from Kappel on the Federsee.

159. Low-waisted urn, beige and red, after *c.* 700 B.C., from Waldwies near Stockach in southern Germany.

218

160. Tiered bowl, after 700 B.C., from southern Germany, colored a dark and lighter brown.

base which flares into a bulbous midriff. From a flattened shoulder the neck may taper gently or steeply and terminate in an everted lip, or in the absence of a neck have a wide opening set right at the shoulder, finished off by a flange (Fig. 157). From west to east the storage vessels adhere to this basic form. Generally the conical base is not ornamented. The decorative motifs begin at the curve of the belly and then occupy midriff and neck. The pottery is characterized by its red and black appearance, though a beige finish is not uncommon (Fig. 158). The red color is obtained by mixing iron oxide into a clay solution. The black is graphite. The 'café au lait' finish is produced when the clay slip is fired. As such the painted black and red pottery is a continuation of Late Urnfield styles as they were found in the Rhenish and Swiss areas.[69] As though it had used the Danube this painted pottery spread from south-western Germany to eastern Austria during Hallstatt C.[70] A characteristic form for the western area is a vessel resting on a cylindrical foot, supporting a low-waisted bulbous belly with pronounced shoulders and a high, tapering neck with only a gently everted lip (Fig. 159).

161. Plaster replica of biconical black and red urns as found at Gemeinlebarn. The reconstruction, including the figurines, does correspond to the archeological finds.

162. Biconical black urn, *c*. 800–500 B.C., from a tumulus of the eastern Hallstatt culture, from the Burgstall near Sopron in western Hungary.

It may be decorated with red lines, which stand out against geometric designs. This style has been termed 'Batik' style—concentric circles, triangles, checkerboard patterns and inset semi-circles have been applied to create a negative effect, as though stenciled.[71] With painted pottery no other types of ornamentation are used to accentuate the designs.

There is also a type of incised pottery, decorated with incised lines, sometimes pine-twig patterns, impressed concentric circles, terraced and recessed ever-decreasing triangles, diamond shapes, chevrons, zigzags, imprinted concentric circles alternating with double lines of stylus-like incisions, and linear patterns of three or six grooves, probably made by drawing moistened fingers over the soft clay. These designs are frequently emphasized through the use of color, usually red, black and beige. The surfaces of the vessels are usually divided into smooth zones, painted but without designs, and areas decorated with incised and/or impressed, and/or painted designs. White paste encrustation may highlight some of the designs. The interior of bowls is generally given a concentric treatment, which when looked at in cross section shows the bowls to have been built up in two or three tiers rising from the base.

Of interest is an apparent emphasis on triangular motifs, frequently arranged in sets of three, thus 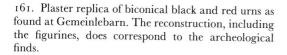 or , although a freehand technique sometimes prevents a successful completion of the symmetry. Groupings of three or multiples of three appear to be popular—three concentric circles, three finger-grooves, three lines, fields of nine concentric circles, fifteen triangles arranged in five groups of three, and so forth.

From Gemeinlebarn in Lower Austria come large biconical vessels in basic red with graphite triangular divisions, linear designs and meanders. These vessels once had figurines placed on the shoulder ridges, such as women carrying bowls and baskets, mounted warriors armed with spear and shield, men and women, and a stag. Little bronze water-birds had been fastened to the everted lip, the so-called 'Hallstatt birds', which had decorated so many objects of the Bronze Age (Fig. 161). From nearby also came the red and black bowls with bovine heads for handles, the Iron Age continuation of a tradition that began in the Chalcolithic. As part of the funerary inventory they may well have played a symbolic (sacrificial?) role in the burial rites. To be found throughout Lower Austria, the eastern Burgenland and Styria to the south, further to the south-east, this pottery probably reached into the Greek sphere of influence.[72]

A more likely reflection of Greek influences, but related to the vessels from Gemein-lebarn, are ornamental motifs on black pottery of basic Hallstatt design, found near Sopron in western Hungary (Fig. 162). The belly of the vessels is divided by linear triangles, drawn freehand and with three fingers. Most of the uneven triangles are filled with concentric circles; others contain a set of three triangles. Most noteworthy are the incised triangular line figures, covered with impressed concentric circles, which are located on the neck. Probably a stylization rather than a record of a particular trend in fashion—tent dresses—these human representations are exceptional for the Hallstatt culture and can probably be attributed to influences radiating from the Greek colonies in the Adriatic.[73]

It is significant to note that during the Hallstatt culture the making of pottery had become a regional manufacture made in production centres which reflect regional tastes (Fig. 163).

An interesting example of foreshadowing is the abstract face with the triangular ears extending over its head which peers out from among the 'Batik style' ornamentation of a high-necked vessel from Marking-Erkenbrechtsweiler near Nürtingen (Plate 5b).[74] Dated to the turn of the seventh to sixth centuries B.C., Hallstatt D, this face suggests a typological link with the head representations of the later Celtic La Tène culture. Additional significance rests in its being a rudimentary example of representational art, all the more noteworthy in that the south-west German Hallstatt generally does not aim to make figural statements; instead the Early Iron Age contents itself with geometric

163. Conical urn with incised ornamentation, colored beige, red and black, after c. 750 B.C., from the district of Straubing-Bogen, Bavaria.

164. Situla lid with repoussé horses and 'sun bursts', c. 700 B.C., Hallstatt C, from cremation grave no. 507, Hallstatt.

designs. Since the Bronze Age, of course, the small ornamental water birds of bronze had enjoyed universal popularity throughout the entire area of the central and northern European Bronze Age. In combinations with sun discs, ship symbols and horses, as *repoussé* work on sheet bronze, or worked in the round as terminals on vehicles, buttons, or handles, these typical water birds, whether ducks or swans, provide a link not only between the area of the Northern Bronze and the Alpine areas to the south and south-east, but also between the mythological symbolism of the Bronze Age and that of the Iron Age, both in its Hallstatt and La Tène versions. That it also suggests a cultic continuity is evident (Fig. 164). The sun disc–swan–horse association carried over from the Bronze Age would certainly contribute a dimension to the interpretation of the horse motif present in so much of the Hallstatt inventory.[75]

The so-called 'Hallstatt ducks' are found not only decorating the rims of pottery but are also mounted on metallic vessels and embossed on smooth surfaces, in association with sun wheels. Southern Austria contributes some unique finds in this context. A large tumulus at Frög, near Rosegg, about 20 km east of Villach in Carinthia, yielded small figurines of lead which had once been stuck to the funerary pottery (Fig. 165). It is probable that they had been affixed to the vessels in the associations shown in the reconstruction—spoked sun wheel, flanked by water birds. Of special interest is the presence of a cruciform anthropomorphic figure, standing with each foot on a disc on which concentric circles are clearly visible.

Except for the occasional clay model, or the pointilinear schematization of horsemen on pottery, figures, especially human figures, are very rare for the south German Hallstatt culture. By contrast the east Alpine Hallstatt makes more frequent use of all types of representations, whether molded in the round or embossed, the latter especially on the *situlae* of the south-eastern regions.

A most intriguing composition is the 'ritual' vehicle from a cremation grave at Strettweg near Judenburg (Fig. 166), some 85 km west of Graz in Styria.[76] Part of the rich inventory of a chieftain's grave, the vehicle was associated with an iron socket axe, a spear head, bridle bits, embossed harness parts and belt plates, painted pottery and a cremation urn of bronze mounted on a stand, quite alien in form and probably a

165. Appliqués of lead—'sun disc'—flanking duck, and an anthropomorphic figure, after *c.* 800 B.C., from Frög near Villach in Carinthia.

166. 'Ritual' vehicle, after *c.* 700 B.C., from Strettweg near Judenburg in Styria.

reflection of 'orientalizing' influences spreading northward from Italy. The functional ancestry for this vehicle probably has to be sought in that common experience which motivated the construction of those Bronze Age kettle vehicles described in the previous chapter. The composition is dominated by a very slim female 'goddess', about 23 cm tall, naked except for earrings and a wide belt indicated by encircling and vertical lines, who holds a very wide and shallow bowl on her head. She stands on an engraved solar wheel. The bowl has additional support from two pairs of intersecting bars. To the left she is preceded by an axe-wielding man, to the right by a woman with earrings. These two are flanked by horsemen on the man's left and on the woman's right side. In conformity with the symmetry the horsemen carry an oval shield on their outside arm while a raised spear in the throwing position is held by the inside arm. Both horsemen wear crested helmets of the Urnfield type, a stylistic import from the south. Immediately in front of the pair, two female figures lead a stag by its antlers. An identical arrangement of figures is set up behind the 'goddess', but facing in the opposite direction. Four heads of bulls or deer terminate the four corners of the chassis. Four eight-spoked wheels complete the composition. The figurines bear a resemblance with the figures mounted on the shoulders of the red and black urns from Gemeinlebarn, described above. The interpretation of this composition is much more problematic. The fact that the two groups move in opposite directions has led to the rejection of the composition as a sacrificial procession. Calling the dominant figure a 'fertility goddess',[77] or terming the group a representation of the Hallstatt pantheon has also been found unacceptable for lack of supporting evidence, though the figure must be central to whatever ritual is being represented here. The bowl may have contained some sacred liquid at the time of its deposition in the grave. It may be the influence of archaic Greek mythology which is represented here in Hallstatt forms.

The Hallstatt cemetery itself has yielded representations of human figures ranging from merely suggested anthropomorphic forms to more carefully articulated representations. Thus from one of the older weaponless cremation graves comes a disc of sheet bronze divided into a central circular area and an outer ring (Fig. 167). Five sets of three embossed grooves divide the central area into pie-shaped sections, each of which may once have been embellished with colored glass, or precious or semi-precious stones. The outer ring is subdivided into five areas marked off with nine, ten or eleven embossed grooves. The fields separating the embossed areas again bear the scars of possible stone settings. Each of the sets of embossed lines radiating from the center is aligned with the assumed stone settings in the outer ring. The edge of the disc had been finished off with a welt of some pliable material. Hanging from thirteen short double link chains are uniform rattle-plates, anthropomorphic in shape as though cut from the sheet bronze with a prehistoric gingerbread-man cookie-cutter. Most of the terminal chain links

167. Bronze disc fibula with anthropomorphic pendants, after *c.* 800 B.C., Hallstatt C, from cremation grave no. 778, Hallstatt.

168. Fibula with 'anchor' pendants, *c.* 800–600 B.C., Hallstatt C, from cremation grave no. 577, Hallstatt.

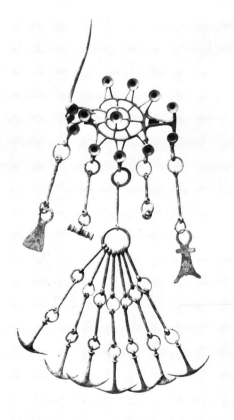

Plate 5a. Funerary vessels of the late Hallstatt period. It is a curiosity that while the fine pottery dates to Hallstatt C, the objects of bronze which formed part of the inventory of this cremation grave belong to Hallstatt D. Found at Orsingen-Nenzingen, this colorful pottery is among the best produced in prehistoric central Europe.

Plate 5b. 'Batik Style' urn with stylized face, after *c.* 600 B.C., Hallstatt D, from Marking-Erkenbrechtsweiler near Nürtingen, south of Stuttgart.

Plate 5c. Golden cloak fastener, *c.* 900–500 B.C., import from the British Isles into the area of the Northern Bronze Culture. Found near Verden in northern Germany.

225

169. Dagger hilt with manikins, after *c*. 600 B.C., Hallstatt D, from an inhumation grave, Hallstatt.

170. Miniature male torso, probably from the rim of a vessel, after *c*. 600 B.C., Hallstatt D, from cremation grave no. 585, Hallstatt.

have two 'ginger-bread men' hanging from them. No doubt when polished to a high gleam and embellished with colorful stone settings, this disc with pendants was very effective.

From a later aristocratic cremation warrior grave comes an exotic creation dominated by a hanging 'anchor' motif (Fig. 168). The upper part suggests a radiating sun wheel. The terminals may have been studded with colorful glass or 'gems' to highlight the radiance. Of interest in this composition are two rattle-plate pendants hanging in the middle section which suggest themselves to be male and female (divine?) anthropomorphs. The 'female' is all A-line skirt terminating in a loop for a head. The 'male', on the other hand, shows a bit more detail—spread legs and stubby arms and the same loop for a head. Elsewhere these 'male' figurines have indeed been accepted as human representations.[78] But more interesting is that on rattle-plates the 'male' figurine has been abstracted even more by narrowing the torso, sweeping the legs outward and rounding out the downward curve between the 'legs', to assume the shape of rudimentary anchors. It is therefore conceivable that the 'anchors' on this hanging are really extreme stylizations of the anthropomorphic form suspended above them. What may have begun as an iconographic abstraction may have undergone the transformation to symbolic form. The people of the Hallstatt culture certainly were not familiar with anchors, certainly not with anchors so modern in appearance. Their pick axes were constructed very differently. The two pieces described above would indicate that

226

171. Axehead with horse mounting, *c.* 700 B.C., Hallstatt C, from cremation grave no. 697, Hallstatt.

172. Axehead with horseman, *c.* 700 B.C., Hallstatt C, from cremation grave no. 641, Hallstatt.

certainly in some quarters pendulous ornaments were favored, which in their free-swinging motion would emphasize the rhythm of the moving body. Their function may have been cultic. An inhumation dagger grave, hence an aristocratic burial, of the sixth century B.C., Hallstatt D, yielded an antenna-dagger which contained within the curvature of its hilt two symmetrical skeletal figures (Fig. 169), while a cremation grave of the same period held a miniature male torso, with an arm ring on each arm (Fig. 170). Both of these pieces have physical details worked out sufficiently to qualify as human figurines.[79]

Particular favorites among the animal representations of the eastern Hallstatt are horses, attached to the rims of vessels, to objects such as axe heads, to the catch plates of fibulae, embossed on sheet bronze, sometimes surmounted by riders or assembled into groups to simulate teams hitched to a wagon. Of interest is a horse cast onto an axe head (Fig. 171) which is said to be the actual depiction of a steppe pony.[80] Archeological evidence from Hungary and the eastern Alps indicates that certain anatomical characteristics are quite different from local breeds, such as its slender elongated neck and hammerhead skull, set-back ears and bristly mane, proportionately short legs and the set of its tail, which suggest familiarity with such a breed of horse, either through contacts with eastern nomads or through the actual presence of such horses in the eastern Alps. The horse itself is not particularly noteworthy for its artistic execution. It was a popular practice to use the horse motif on elaborations of 'safety pins', where the

227

profile of a horse replaced the bow of the pin. On the larger, more elaborate fibulae, especially those with pendant rattle plates, the horses assume an ornamental function, usually facing one another, over a trough perhaps. On sheet bronze the horses may appear in association with solar symbols. An indication of the craftsmen's casting skill is provided by an axe found in a cremation grave dated into Hallstatt C.[81] Here a bronze horseman has been cast onto the axe head (Fig. 172). Especially noticeable, however, is the awkwardness of the composition. Perhaps an afterthought, the lack of sophistication of horse and rider stand in marked contrast to the elegant workmanship one finds in other work of the Hallstatt culture. Probably of local manufacture, this piece, as well as the horse on the axe head mentioned above, would indicate that the technology had been mastered while artistic skill was still lagging behind that of other areas. Even the zigzag ornamentation visible on the blade and the shaft socket is only rudimentary. From Hungary one knows elegant clubs/hammers in the shape of a horse's arched neck and head. These have been designated as 'scepters'.[82] It is very apparent that the two Hallstatt axes had a ceremonial function. Perhaps they too were insignia of rank and distinction. From the tumulus at Frög, a site ravaged by a century of tourists, come representations of horsemen, miniature figurines of cast lead, which had been fixed to the urns (Fig. 173).[83] The casters of these figurines went to some length to emphasize that the horses were stallions. Greater attention was paid to the more detailed depiction of the head and mane of a horse, while for the rest of the body and the rider a superficial treatment had to suffice. A very interesting find at Frög is a miniature wagon and three teams (Fig. 174). Some of the heads appear to be horse heads. Remnants of the structural details of the wagon suggest that the wagon once had a

173. Lead appliqués, horsemen, after *c.* 800 B.C., from Frög near Villach in Carinthia.

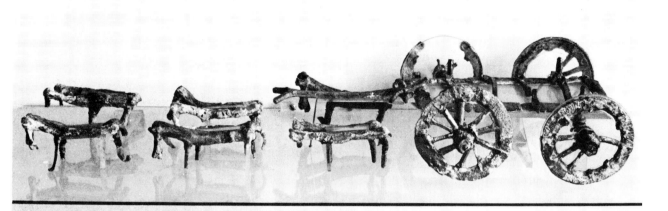

174. Miniature ritual wagon with three teams of horses, lead, after *c.* 800 B.C., from Frög near Villach in Carinthia.

superstructure; perhaps it too had been a model of a vessel vehicle which played a significant part in the funerary ritual. In its toy-like realism this miniature vehicle may be symbolic of the one which bore the deceased to his funeral. It may indeed provide a clue for the processional aspects which were a part of the princely burials.[84]

While the Frög horsemen are definitely riding their mounts, there are stylized representations of horsemen found from southern Germany to Scandinavia which show 'circus riders', the riders apparently standing on the backs of their horses; in one instance on clay vessels from Beilngries in Bavaria, the horsemen appear to have slung the reins around their own heads.[85]

Two other animal representations from Hallstatt are of interest. One is a crude model of a bronze bull, stiff and 'wooden' in execution, on 'saw-horse' legs, its head reduced to a beak-like muzzle, while only the details of its sweeping long horns, its dewlap and genitals are worked out in detail (Fig. 175). The model shows the same lack of stylistic sophistication as do the horses on the axe heads from Hallstatt.[86] The three pieces come from the older warrior graves. Quite a different matter are the two bovine figurines, one large, the other much smaller, which form the handle of a dipping vessel (Fig. 176), found in one the later weaponless cremation graves of Hallstatt D.[87] As might be expected, the figurines, though still stylized, reveal a high degree of accomplishment. The prominent horns on the small animal notwithstanding, the group is frequently referred to as cow and calf. They may indeed be aurochs. The incised geometric ornamentation, consisting of a simple meander, flanked by two bands of alternating squares and a band of sawtooth pattern, disappears under a baseplate on which the small cow and the hind legs of the large cow have been fastened. The large animal protrudes into the vessel, with its forelegs resting on a support which rises from the bottom of the bowl, a clever solution. The figurines and the bowl were not necessarily conceived simultaneously. The curved lines of the bovine figurines show no relation to the geometric ornamentation on the bowl.

This dipping vessel was associated with large pails and small drinking cups. It seems that Hallstatt wine drinking customs required an ensemble of special vessels—ceramic, metallic and even glass—which tend to appear in male graves in various stages of completeness. Smaller ensembles also appear in women's graves. It was customary to thin the wine with water and to flavour it with spices in a large mixing vessel from

229

175. Bronze miniature of a bull, before *c.* 600 B.C., Hallstatt C, from cremation grave no. 507, Hallstatt.

176. Vessel with miniature cows, after *c.* 600 B.C., Hallstatt D, from cremation grave no. 671, Hallstatt.

which the wine was ladled through a sieve into a situla.[88] The bowl with the bovine figurines may have served as such a ladle. These situlae wich were ornamented with human situations, such as funerary and sacrificial processions, but usually showed festive occasions, were taken to the guests who used cups to dip out the wine into drinking bowls. The narrative friezes on the situlae testify to such a procedure.

Up to this time the decorations on objects had been ornamental and non-narrative. This so-called situla art was derived from Mediterranean forms.[89] Pollinated by Mediterranean influences from Greece and the northern Adriatic, the Hallstatt culture of the late sixth and early fifth centuries B.C. came under the influence of the southern narrative style. Articles with such decorations appeared as far north as Lower Austria. However, the influence did not spread further west. By the end of the sixth century B.C., the generally uniform Hallstatt culture had become a common phenomenon throughout the southern portion of central Europe. During the same period the Celts were crystallizing as an historically identifiable group in south central Europe. The dynamic vitality of the developing Celtic ornamental style may well have provided the counterthrust which prevented the narrative style from spreading into central Europe. That would not happen until the early centuries of the Christian era. The situla from Kuffarn in Lower Austria which depicts a banquet like the one alluded to above, as well as a mule-chariot race, is a late example of the art. After 496 B.C., mule-chariot races were permitted at the Olympics,[90] a circumstance which helps date the situla. It was found in a grave associated with articles from the Celtic La Tène culture.

The evidence on behalf of foreign influences, including the presence of foreign craftsmen in the area of the Hallstatt culture, whether of eastern origin—Pontic or Anatolian—or southern origin—Greek or Etruscan—is to be found in the objects dealt with above. In that context the unique statue of a warrior found at the base of the tumulus at Hirschlanden, west of Stuttgart in Baden-Württemberg, is all the more puzzling.[91] It is readily apparent that two quite different attitudes towards artistic expression are reflected in this statue (Fig. 177). While the front of the understated torso

230

177. Warrior stele, after
c. 500 B.C., from
Hirschlanden near
Stuttgart.

has been worked in relief—dagger, belt, hands and arms—the back and the lower portion have very clearly been worked in the round, in the robust and vital archaic-classical style of the Mediterranean, perhaps Etruscan in inspiration. Even the sculptor's technique is identifiably southern. This stylistic difference invites speculation. Was it the work of a native sculptor familiar with Mediterranean techniques which aim for greater realism of representation? If so, why was the upper body carved in such a rigid fashion? Or did the craftsman adhere to and compromise with the stylistic demands of a cultic convention? In any case, one can imagine the heated debate and ensuing frustration before a compromise was reached. The detailed equipment of the statue with its conical helmet, neck ring, antenna-hilted dagger and double belt, indicate that the warrior represented here belonged to that leading caste that occupied such fortresses as the Heuneburg, several of which are to be found in the vicinity of Stuttgart. Their contact with the western Mediterranean would account for the southern influence evident on the statue.

Almost 1·80 m tall, the statue must have been placed on top of the tumulus, which contained sixteen inhumations in all, including two wooden coffin burials, superimposed and centrally located. The upper grave with which the funerary stele may be associated most readily, contained a fragment of a Hallstatt-type fibula, as well as an open-work belt-hook characteristic of the Celtic La Tène. The circumstances surrounding this statue point to a confluence of factors during the fifth century B.C.: the conical helmet derives from the south-eastern Alps; the neck ring with its embossed ornamentation and the dagger are characteristic finds in the princely graves of the Hallstatt; the double belt is also a part of the grave inventory; while the power and virility intimated by the lower part of the body suggests an indebtedness to the Mediterranean. Symbols of potency such as the representation of bulls, stallions and other phallic figures in connection with aspects of the funerary rituals imply some indeterminate link between virility and death.

The fact that this monumental sculpture is the first of its kind north of the Alps is noteworthy of itself.[92] Why have no others been found? Is the warrior from Hirschlanden merely the first one made of stone? Were others made of wood? Scanty evidence indicates that wooden carvings existed, even antedating the demarcation stones, which were decorated with geometric designs, and which encircled the burial mounds of the late Bronze Age. No transitional evidence linking the 'anthropomorphic' menhirs of the Chalcolithic with the Hirschlanden stele has yet been uncovered. Funerary steles are decorated with geometrics. It is, however, probable that the representation of human forms was not within the thematic repertoire of central European craftsmen, and that just as the narrative technique had to assert itself in the eastern region as an influence, so the choice of the human form as an appropriate object for artistic representation had to await the Celtic encounter with the Greeks and Etruscans of the western Mediterranean, when monumental sculpture in central Europe appeared to become the reserve of the dead, or perhaps of the gods.[93]

What characterized the style and taste of the culture-carrying caste during the Hallstatt era? Comparisons with the extensive evidence from other contemporary cultural areas make the total Hallstatt inventory look like a collection of missing links. Though the amount of material datable to this period is extensive, it sheds no light on the fundamental motivation of the time. Did the people of the Hallstatt era see themselves as spectators or participants? The evidence does not allow any conclusions about the extent to which the 'art' is a response to a social, let alone a cosmic environment. Instead, the Hallstatt presents itself very much as a periphery without a center. As yet no mirror is held up to nature providing the yardstick; 'art' itself is the point of departure, confined however, within the limits of only a few motifs. Attempts at reproducing likenesses, whether human or animal, remain experimental. Hallstatt art does not represent reality, or inquire into the laws of nature, but probes, stylizes and interprets reality and reduces it to rigid abstractions.[94] Yet it is apparent that the artistic achievements have passed through the filter of the human personality to give to this art a personal mode of perception and expression.

The elegant simplicity of Bronze Age art, especially that of the North, had suggested a dynamic, imaginative probing and enthusiastic spontaneity, its patterns forever changing, always in flux, somewhat chaotic, unpredictable, uncertain and of sporadic behavior. Such art might reflect the movement of branches, the swaying of reaching tendrils, the drifting of clouds, the effect of the wind on waves, the scurrying of animals, the song of birds, their soaring flight, and their gliding elegance on the water, all those undetermined forms of expression found in nature that cannot be systematized or reduced to rules. A repeatable order is found in these organic patterns which does not require rational sequences of an alphabetical or arithmetical sort to be perceived and understood. These organic patterns suggest a non-rational, probably mythical way of thinking.

The organic dynamism of Bronze Age art gives way to rigid patterns of geometric forms and morphic designs. The Hallstatt centuries are marked by a tendency to tame the unpredictable patterns and to fix them into some kind of rational order and relative stability. It is significant that these indications of rational thinking should be contemporary to the first indications of the advent of organized political units in central Europe, if the circumstances associated with the Heuneburg have been correctly interpreted. It would suggest a gradual shift from the maturity of individualistic cultural activity into organized dependence. It is readily apparent that a transition from a flexible arrangement of open and freely associated elements and influences to more solid, stable and organized systems would have significant implications. It is a truism that a highly organized society is detrimental to creativity, which flourishes in less settled times. Whether this oscillating process has its central European beginning during the Hallstatt centuries is a matter of speculation. It appears to have been a complex period which reflected in its stylistic sense both order and disorder. The coexistence of solid yet moving elements enriched the visual experience by setting outlines in motion and dissolving contours into undulations (Fig. 178). The achieving of an effect appears to have been the governing principle. The Hallstatt attitude to style then is characterized by the separation of function and form and the abstraction of forms not taken from the natural realm but from geometry, subjected to exaggeration. Objects are especially marked by a renunciation of practical purposes to the extent that the ornamental excesses threaten to endanger or obliterate the function which a fibula or urn was originally intended to perform.

The personal taste of the leading Hallstatt caste appears to have favored the grand gesture. The return to tumulus burials, the size of the mound, the erection of a funerary stele, the idea behind the wagon graves, the emphasis on gleam and color, vast inventories of vessels, the presence of silks and other rich, imported fabrics, of shells and coral, of amber, of bronze and gold, of many-headed pins, arm rings, neck rings, necklaces, pendants, of golden daggers, colored beads, glass, and especially the keeping up of appearances through the suggestion of wealth rather than its presence, implies bombast, exaggeration and ostentation, processional pomp and a tone of arrogance that borders

178. Fibula with miniature horses, with chains and rattle plates, after *c.* 800 B.C., from cremation grave no. 505, Hallstatt.

on the baroque.[95] It would be helpful if it could be demonstrated that the tumuli were pyramid analogies and that these tumuli, just as the pyramids, reflected a belief in the origin of the world as the emanation of a hill out of the waters of chaos, to which hill all life returned via the tombs of kings. The extension of the privilege to others would explain the multiple and secondary burials in these tumuli and the pains which were taken to suggest wealth and station.

Ceramics and metals exist in sufficient number. Both are characterized by an emphasis on ornamentation. The presence of pottery is noteworthy since it now resumes a conspicuous place in the grave inventories. At first glance one is surprised by the potter's skill, only to notice that his flourish conceals a small number of basic forms and decorative designs, pointing to an impoverished inventiveness. Without benefit of the potter's wheel the craftsmen produced showy and exaggerated vessels, boldly cavernous in design, precariously placed on a conical base, their thin walls weakened confidently by means of an ornamental technique which included protrusions, incisions, impressions and 'perforations', with an apparent emphasis on the 'dematerializing' effects of negative space. Attempts at giving texture to the bulbous surfaces are complemented by the use of color, mainly black, red and beige, either painted on or created by means of inlays and incrustations. Though the choice of designs is limited and the forms appear to be standardized, the clear enunciation of the geometric decorations imparts to the vessels an air of precise and deliberate definition. As was pointed out above, this earthenware, colorful and textured in the western regions, fades towards Austria, where it is characterized by having been painted with the darkest and shiniest black. Of course, just as the red and graphite black ware spreads towards the west, so geometric western ware is to be found towards the eastern regions of the Hallstatt. The two styles coexist without being dependent on one another. Except for the use of urns with bovine heads typical in the more easterly regions, tectonic rigidity is the overall effect created by Hallstatt pottery.

The artistic attention paid to metals shows the continuity of some of the themes which originated during the Bronze Age. However, the manufacture of sheet bronze and gold, of wires and coils, is not new and does not undergo any technological improvement. Compared to the Bronze Age, style undergoes regression and that exhaustion of the artistic imagination mentioned above. The showy pretension of the gleam of burnished surfaces attempts to compensate for an impoverishment of design, while inventiveness appears to be directed towards the assembling of a multitude of disparate elements, such as the 'anchor' hanging, or the axe heads surmounted by horses and rider, described above. Nevertheless, the optical effect achieved by the accumulation of details on the many-membered fibulae, with their trapezoid and circular rattle-plates, chains and ornamented catch-plates, creates in the end an impressive and harmonious entity. The long pendants, the textured and polished surfaces of the fibulae and hangings, the combination of pendulous motion, in itself an enhancement of the movements of its wearer, and the tinkling sounds produced by the chains and plates, lends them an air of playfulness, suggesting that the emphasis had been placed not on function but on the creation of an effect. The recurrence of the horse motif, already noted on the axes, would point to the ceremonial use of these pendants. One has associated these hangings with shamanistic practices.[96] No doubt, the carefully ornamented gold dagger found at the Hallstatt site was also a part of the ceremonial arsenal of a dignitary. It could hardly have served as an effective weapon without being seriously damaged.

Within the context of its cultural area, Hallstatt ceramic and metal-working techniques are marked by their own particular sophistication. As was indicated above, pottery styles are not distributed evenly throughout the eastern and western provinces of the Hallstatt. Similarly, leading bronze forms found in the eastern provinces are absent in the west, such as the many-headed pins, spiral coil fibulae and the elaborate hangings, but particularly the 'realistic' representations of men, women and animals (Fig. 179).[97] A particular feature of the south-eastern Alps are the relief friezes which decorate the situlae with the largely festive activities of man during the period. Not of Hallstatt origin, they attest to the westward cataract effect of foreign influences. On the other hand the western province is distinguished for its production of the only extant human sculpture in the Man from Hirschlanden described above.

At their greatest expanse the Hallstatt provinces stretched from central and eastern France, western and southern Germany, parts of Switzerland, Danubian and Alpine Austria, into western Hungary and the north-western Balkans. On the periphery the culture influenced Bohemia and Moravia, Silesia, parts of central Germany, the Palatinate, the regions straddling the middle and lower Rhine, with the Pyrenees and the northern Iberian peninsula locked off in severed pockets. Hallstatt taste extended to all of these areas.

The center of the western Hallstatt province crystallized in southern and south-western Germany, from where it spread to France and Switzerland. It is characterized by princely grave mounds and wooden grave chambers large enough to contain wagons and the trappings to simulate a team of horses.[98] In Switzerland[99] north of the Alps, bronze articles with decorative iron inlays were found which belonged to the late phase of the Swiss lake-shore settlements. In the southern Alps articles of iron appear much later than elsewhere. Here there is almost a total lack of really rich graves, the richest inventories comparing to those of a noble warrior in the south-eastern Alps. It is held that this points to only insignificant social differences among the population. There are graves which are rich in ceramics and women's ornaments, but neither precious metals nor imported articles of any importance figure in the grave equipment, which leads to the conclusion that gradations of wealth are not reflected in the inventories and that social station found little echo in the burial rites. In fact something of an inverse relationship appears to have existed, since the most presumptuous tumuli yield the

Map 24. The Hallstatt cultures, *c.* 800 B.C.–450 B.C.

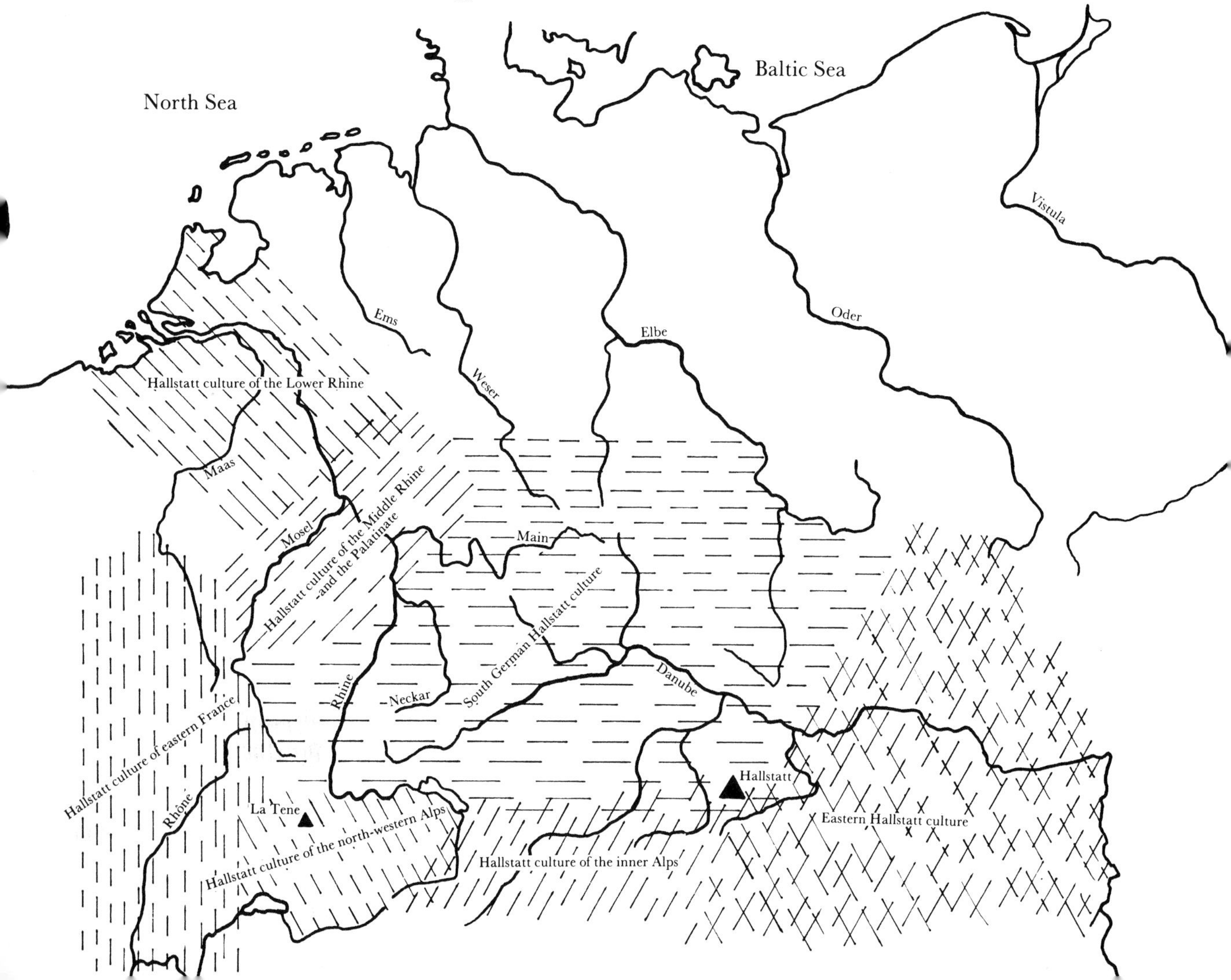

North Sea

Baltic Sea

Vistula

Ems

Elbe

Oder

Weser

Hallstatt culture of the Lower Rhine

Maas

Mosel

Hallstatt culture of the Middle Rhine —and the Palatinate

Main

South German Hallstatt culture

Rhine

Neckar

Danube

Hallstatt culture of eastern France

Rhone

La Tene

Hallstatt culture of the north-western Alps

Hallstatt culture of the inner Alps

Hallstatt

Eastern Hallstatt culture

179. Belt hook of sheet bronze from Vace, Yugoslavia, from an inhumation grave. See Fig. 185 for details of armor.

smallest number of metal objects. Open to outside influences, especially from the south, foreign types do figure in the inventories, but often these are local imitations and adaptations rather than outright adoptions. As is to be expected, the concentration of imports is found along the trade routes crossing the Alps. Without favoring any particular passes, the north–south traffic between the Etruscan cultural area and the emerging Celtic realms to the north is especially important. At first Switzerland is only a transit area. Not until later does it become a customer, and from the end of the Hallstatt onward it participates with its own situlae in the trade which it expands during the early La Tène period. East Alpine influences were introduced either through the immigration of eastern craftsmen or through eastern contacts. Thus pottery shows Venetic influences. The cultural cataract apparent in the Alpine traffic is strictly east to west, which as late as the fifth century B.C. brings many foreign, especially Venetic, influences into the Alpine regions of Switzerland.[100] Etruscan trade with the Celtic north is in evidence as early as the seventh century B.C. It peaks during the sixth and fifth centuries. Towards the end of the fifth century the Celts themselves severed the trade routes to the north. Shortly after the beginning of the fourth century B.C., the great Celtic migrations into Italy broke the power of the Etruscans. In the fourth century Celtic finds also appear in graves associated with indigenous types. The modesty of the finds suggests a population of farmers and craftsmen who participated in the traffic of goods over the passes.

Further north the Hallstatt culture of the Palatinate shows definite links with the preceding Urnfield culture, and later on, with the succeeding La Tène culture. Stylistically the Palatinate Hallstatt is related to the northern fringes of the western Hallstatt along the upper Rhine and Rhenish Hesse, all based on some materials of the very late Urnfield culture. The essential elements, derived from the Urnfield culture, are noticeable everywhere, with regional variations.[101] Here too tumulus and flat grave burials are to be found. In the Rhine valley the use of urns provides the link with the Urnfield culture. Inhumation graves saw up to three pieces of pottery placed at the feet of the deceased. The presence of animal bones and grain points to funerary provisioning. Personal ornaments are the exception. Some graves, however, contained no ceramics but the deceased were decorated with heavy bronze rings.[102] In the more mountainous regions to the west the presence of a new population is indicated by the complete

237

absence of mortuary provisioning, but the presence of an extensive array of bronze neck rings, earrings, whole sets of arm rings, leg rings, fibulae and belt plates. Except for jewellery there was no differentiation between men, women and children in death.[103] Cremation graves—urns and heaps of ash—were also located under tumuli. Though there is little differentiation in the funerary equipment these graves contained almost no bronzes. According to their pottery they were related to the Rhine valley group. The links with the south German Hallstatt are in evidence only through the presence of imports. For the Palatinate inhumation is the dominant custom, without any specific orientation of the corpse, which was laid out mainly supine—arms alongside or laid in the lap, or on the chest, and even some fetal positioning. Graves are characterized through stone circle enclosures, about 1 m high, as well as through encircling ditches. The grave mound may contain up to ten burials or as few as one, but three to four burials per tumulus is the general rule. Without being systematic, pit or surface graves were used for the central burial(s), while additional graves were set into the slope. In the highlands most graves received a protective stone covering. In the Rhine valley stones were not used.[104]

The regions of the lower Rhine were again only a remote province. Whatever contact existed with the south produced no noteworthy benefits. Compared with Hallstatt pottery, ceramics from this area are colorless, and though decorated with geometrics the urns are painted with graphite. The urn and accompanying vessels were covered by a tumulus. The graves contained only very few metal objects. No social stratification of the population is indicated. Without apparent cultural identity of its own, the peasant culture merged easily with the La Tène.[105]

Central Germany serves as intermediary between the regions still further north and the more advanced southern cultural areas of the late Urnfield and Hallstatt cultures. The rivers flowing northwards facilitated the traffic of goods across the central Highlands. Their relative wealth in ores assured the continuing cultural contact. While north-western Germany seems to have been completely isolated between 1000 B.C. and 100–200 A.D., the north-eastern regions appear to have maintained links with the Etruscans in northern Italy until c. 400 B.C., when the import of southern wares was halted. This cessation of trade can be attributed to the disruption caused by the eastward migrations of the Celts. From c. 800 B.C. on, northern Germany had developed house urns and face urns, some even with metal earrings, perhaps inspired by the Villanova culture of northern Italy, or perhaps developed independently.[106] During the Iron Age Lower Saxony around Hanover continued to use the bronzes of phases V and VI (Plate 5c). Even for the La Tène there is no evidence of fibulae, razors, iron belt hooks, nor are there any advances in the manufacture of ceramics. Cremation graves are unequipped. However, heaps of bones in graves begin to replace urn burials, although urnfields, for instance those at Pestrup mentioned in Chapter 3, show continued occupation till 200 B.C. and cremation graves continue into the period contemporary with Imperial Rome.[107]

Some 30 km south of Lüneburg two sites—Wessenstedt (800–600 B.C.) and Jastorf (600–300 B.C.)—have been identified, after which the earliest Germanic cultures were named. Located between the Oder in the east and the Weser to the west, the Jastorf group reached south to encounter the northern fringes of the Hallstatt provinces.[108] To the east it was in contact with the derivatives of the Lusatian culture. These contacts were not only peaceful and commercial, but also expansionist and therefore warlike. In future centuries these descendants of the Northern Bronze Age populations reinforced

180. Sword scabbard of eastern origin, showing orientalizing animal motifs, from the Scythian treasure found at Vettersfelde.

by migrations from Scandinavia and resident north-western Celts, were to push westward across the Rhine without encountering too much resistance. The Celts inhabiting the former Hallstatt lands, on the other hand, were to put up much stiffer resistance.

Evidence from the eastern Hallstatt regions shows that during the late Hallstatt two 'chains' of fortifications, many of them on elevated sites, had come into being in Lower Austria, Burgenland, Hungary and western Slovakia. Rather than assuming a coordinated defensive system, the sites were probably local cultural and political centers, since the social organization most likely did not exceed that of extended families and clans, of tribes at best.[109] However, here too the Hallstatt came to a close by c. 400 B.C., brought about by that same Celtic expansion.

The possibility of a threat may also have loomed in the eastern steppes, where the Scythian realms north of the Black Sea constituted a powerful force. In 612 B.C., contingents of Scythians were involved in the capture of Nineveh, one of the capitals of the Assyrian Empire. The danger of invasion from the east was probably minimal, but almost 300 years of Assyrian expansion, conquest, destruction, displacement of peoples, resettlement, terror and the collapse of the Empire kept the Near East in turmoil.[110] The presence of 'orientalizing' motifs in south-eastern Europe has been attributed to these events. The repercussions of these events had also contributed to the synthesis of an 'animal style' in the Pontic regions, based on Scythian motifs of mythical and big-game animals, executed by Greek artists or artists trained in Greek traditions. Lions, panthers and gryphons are of Near Eastern inspiration. This artistic synthesis captures a strange vitality in the movement of its animal representations and in its stylizations. The predominance given to the animals is almost total, so that there are only a few traces of anthropomorphism.[111] One of the fundamental themes of Scythian steppe art

239

181. Gold appliqué fish, possibly a shield ornament, before *c.* 500 B.C., part of the Scythian treasure from Vettersfelde in eastern Germany.

is the combat between two animals (Fig. 180), which, it has been suggested, symbolize tribal conflicts fought by their respective totem animals. That the west had knowledge of the Scythians was indicated by the quiver with Scythian arrows found in the princely grave chamber of the Hohmichele tumulus. A better idea of Scythian wealth is given by the pieces belonging to the sumptuous hoard found at Vettersfelde near Cottbus.[112] The find was unearthed by a plowman. At the time it was not established whether the

182. Belt hook of sheet bronze from Magdalenska Gora in Yugoslavia, from an inhumation grave.

183. Grindstone, after *c.* 800 B.C., Hallstatt C and D, from Essfeld in southern Germany.

treasure had been part of a grave or connected with a settlement. Probably part of a chief's treasure, it is not known how it had arrived in eastern Germany—perhaps as a gift, or as booty, or perhaps abandoned by a Scythian raiding party (Fig. 181). Small finds which continue to be made indicate that Scythians may very well have penetrated into Lusatian territory. However, Scythian burial mounds or evidence of the type described by Herodotus have been found only in the vicinity of the lower Danube.

As has been pointed out above, by 500 B.C. a moist sub-Atlantic climate had displaced a drier continental climate. This deterioration of climatic conditions had induced people in the Alpine regions to seek out areas low in precipitation, generally warm, with little frost and on black and brown earth soils, up to an elevation of 200 m above sea level, where a growing season of up to 230 days per year could be expected. This fact makes the Hallstatt site all the more exceptional, since in Austria at least the population is essentially agricultural.[113] This characteristic accounts for reduced economic power and cultural influence compared to those other areas of the Hallstatt where manufacturing and the distribution of goods played a larger role in the economic life of the people. As a result these agricultural areas clung to their cultural patterns, thereby obscuring any tendency to develop and change. More conservative, these cultural provinces were vulnerable and susceptible to foreign influences;[114] and from the sixth century B.C. onwards, central Europe engaged in continuous contact with the cultural areas of the Mediterranean to the south and the Balkans to the south-east. The introduction of different motifs for the decoration of metal surfaces (Fig. 182), and the possible apprenticeship of northern craftsmen in Etruria and in the Greek colonies of the western Mediterranean, provided the Celts, the heirs of the Hallstatt, with invention and new stimuli to artistic expression. It appears that the lifestyle enjoyed not only by the inhabitants of the fortified manufacturing centers but also in the agricultural communities was of a level comparable to that of the Middle Ages (Fig. 183).[115]

Around 500 B.C. Denmark registered a 2°C drop in temperature. The Scandinavian glaciers descended some 200 m. The walnut tree lost some 80,000 km of terrain and the northern boundary of the agricultural area shifted from 68° to 60° North. By 300 B.C. inundations along the shores of the North and Baltic Seas and a rise in the ground water level had brought about a reduction of inhabitable land at a time when the area appears to have experienced an increase in the population. The 'Winter of the Giants' referred to in later northern mythology may be an echo of the advent of the great frost.[116]

5. The La Tène Culture: The Celts

In the area of the Hallstatt culture, decisive changes were taking place during the sixth century B.C., as the western Hallstatt province was drawn ever more into the emerging Celtic sphere, while the eastern domains of the Hallstatt established distinct relations with the cultural areas located along the northern Adriatic and the north-western Balkans (Fig. 184). The Hallstatt contribution to the formation of these two cultural areas is significant.

The economic and cultural contacts which existed between the western Hallstatt and the Etruscans and the Greek colonies of the western Mediterranean during the sixth century, and which contributed greatly to the material culture of the region, have already been noted (Fig. 185). It is through the contact with the Greeks that the people of the region enter into the records of the Greek historians, philosophers, geographers and ethnographers, who mention a people which they identify as *Keltoi*.[1] Anaximander of Miletus (*c.* 610–540 B.C.), the first to draw a world map, places the *Keltoi* along the north-western periphery of Europe, and Hyperboreans beyond a northern mountain range. There is no reason to suspect that the term *Keltoi*—the brave and noble ones— was any more specific, apt or accurate a designation of a people to the Greeks than were the Hyperboreans, a people so unknown that the North Wind was seen to be their border.[2] Hecataeus of Miletus (born during the late sixth century), who leans on the map of Anaximander, and Herodotus (born *c.* 485 B.C.) mention specific settlements of these *Keltoi*, especially those of south-eastern Spain. Plato (*c.* 427–347 B.C.) includes them in a list of barbarian peoples who are given to drunkenness, while Aristotle (384– 322 B.C.) has the *Keltoi* attacking the waves.[3] Fourth-century Greeks counted the Celts along with the Scythians and Persians among the most important barbarian peoples.[4] Not until the time of the Roman encounter with the Celts did Greek writers meet the Celts personally. Thus Polybius (*c.* 208–*c.* 126 B.C.) aims to clarify to the Romans the image of the Po Valley Celts in Cisalpine Gaul, while Posidonius of Apameia (*c.* 135– 51 B.C.) studies the Celts in southern and eastern Gaul from his base in Massilia. In most cases the writers of antiquity who wrote about the ethnology and religion of barbarian peoples were content to extract passages from earlier writers, so that only little new knowledge about a people like the *Keltoi* came into circulation.[5] Most frequent are references to Posidonius, whose historical works had been enriched by numerous ethnographic asides. Diodorus knew, for instance, that the Celts were descended from Hercules and a Celtic princess, and that their son Galates had then imposed his name on his subjects.[6]

184. Hallstatt helmet and breast- and backplate, *c.* 700 B.C., from Kleinklein in Styria, Austria.

To the people of the Mediterranean, the Celts were tall, pale-faced and warlike barbarians who swarmed out of the unexplored wilds of the trackless northern forests to terrorize the southern cultures, to seek mercenary service in the Hellenistic kingdoms of Alexander's successors, and even to settle in Asia Minor as Galatians. Initially the term 'Keltic' must have been a convenient label with which to identify that multitude of diverse cultural manifestations which have come to be known as the La Tène culture. Labelled as *Keltoi*, the carriers of the La Tène culture appear on the border between prehistory and recorded history.[7]

Neither the map of Anaximander, which placed the original home of the Keltoi against the north-western ocean, from where they were seen to have asserted their dominance over the rest of central Europe, nor the later writings of antiquity, which perpetuated his view, can be taken at face value. Nor can the cultural transition from Hallstatt to La Tène be attributed to another ethnic infiltration, or to the immigration of a clearly defined and homogeneous people. Migrations in prehistoric Europe were extremely rare.[8] The transition to La Tène was largely material in nature, so that most probably the appearance of the Celts is the result of regional cultural developments in the area straddling the Upper Rhine and in south central Europe north of the Alps,[9] out of a conglomerate of peoples who had evolved there from older populations and who had occupied those parts in the course of the preceding millennia, perhaps the result of internal social conflicts with the merchant aristocrats of the Hallstatt. The evidence demonstrates a cultural continuum from the Chalcolithic to the La Tène.[10] As such the Celts are the direct heirs of Bronze Age Europe and its Neolithic past and the first identifiable northern crystallization of Indo-Europeans. Perhaps the result of yet another 'Inner Colonization', the whole process is not clear. The upper demarcation of the La Tène is lost in the Gallo-Roman culture during the Roman Empire.

As proto-Celts their presence during the Hallstatt pre-dates their crystallization during the La Tène when they emerged in the western Hallstatt provinces with a uniform material culture.[11]

The crucible in which the La Tène culture came into being during the early fifth century B.C. is located in south-western Germany, northern Switzerland and eastern France, an area divided rather than contained by geographical features, an area characterized by those princely wagon graves, the visible testimony of an heroic and aristocratic past. From the fifth century on the adventurous Celts swelled out of the area of their origin in all directions: north to Thuringia; along the Rhine to the Hunsrück–Eifel mountains and to the Lower Rhine; west into Belgium and into France to a line following the rivers Marne and Saône; and east into Bavaria, parts of Bohemia and Austria, most of the territory formerly occupied by the Hallstatt. By 400 B.C. even northern Italy and perhaps even Sardinia and Sicily came to be occupied by Gaulish Celts.[12] They contributed to the decline of the Etruscans and defeat of the Romans. In 387 B.C. they put Rome to the torch and besieged the capitol—unsuccessfully. Groups of central European Celts pushed further east into the Danube Basin. Some even crossedn the Carpathians. In 335 B.C. Alexander the Great met with one of their delegations. Some fifty years later, taking advantage of the political and cultural turmoil

Map 25. Celtic expansion and the core area of the La Tène (after 500 B.C.).

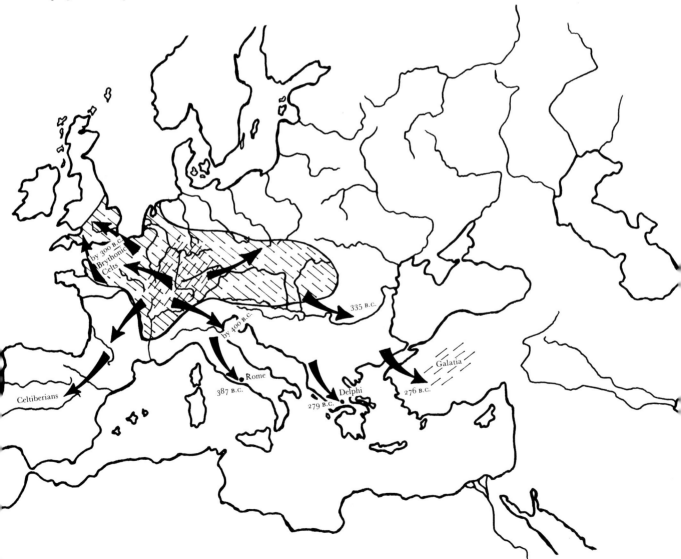

185. Bronze mask from Kleinklein in Styria, Austria. This mask along with two hands was found in the same grave as the helmet and armour shown in illustration 184.

following the disintegration of Alexander's empire, they invaded Greece; Celts occupied Delphi in 279 B.C., only to be decisively defeated. Some tribal fragments were invited to participate in the wars waged by the new Hellenistic kingdoms. Some Celtic mercenaries even reached Asia Minor. After 276 B.C. they formed the Galatian buffer-state in the heart of Asia Minor. In the west, by 300 B.C. Brythonic Celts had established themselves in Britain, Goidelic-speaking Celts having arrived there earlier. By the third century, Celts had pushed into southern France, and had occupied Spain, where they mingled with the native Iberians and became known as Celtiberians. It is these western groups, reinforced by Cisalpine Gauls, who supported Hannibal's attack on Rome during the Second Punic War (218–201 B.C.). At the end of the third century B.C. the Celtic realms extended across Europe from the Atlantic to the Black Sea.[13] It is possible that in a northward direction the Celts had penetrated the Central German Highlands and had begun to dominate the northern tribes. It is claimed that two fortified sites located near Sievern, 8 km north of Bremerhaven, are Celtic fortifications—oppida.[14] Their presence this far north is surprising, since this would place these Celtic posts into territory normally thought to have been occupied by a Germanic population.

Whether the Celts in their dispersion formed a conscious ethnic unit is not clear. However, there can be little thought of political or religious unity among them. Nor can one assume a common language spoken in all the Celtic provinces, though as late as the fourth century A.D., St. Jerome maintained that the Galatians in Asia Minor spoke the same language as the Celtic tribe of the Treveri in the west.[15] Feelings of solidarity among the Celts need not be expected. The presence of Celts in Hannibal's army did not deter Alpine Celts from attacking the Carthaginian army as it crossed the Alps.

By 175 B.C. the Romans had overcome the Cisalpine Celts. The Celts in the Balkans had been driven back into central Europe. Those of the eastern Alps entered into a

245

	Cultural Periods	Historical Summary Central Europe	Central European Cultural Features	Sites	Artistic Style	Climate
Birth of Christ		15 B.C. Tiberius and Drusus make Danube northern frontier of the Roman Empire	rupture of the cultural continuity in central Europe and submersion into the Gallo-Roman culture of the Roman Empire	before 15 B.C. fall of Manching	Romanization of taste	
		58–51 B.C. Caesar's Gallic Wars establish the Rhine as frontier				
100 B.C.		Cimbri, Ambrones and Teutones criss-cross Europe	'oppidum' culture fortifications	Rynkeby Gundestrup Dejbjerg	cauldrons and wagons	
	La Tène D			Manching Basel Otzenhausen	from Manching red and white consumer ware	
		175 B.C. Rome overcomes Cisalpine Gauls Celts are driven from the Balkans	progressing urbanization and industrialization	Bern Passau Třísov	graphite pottery	
200 B.C.			emergence of warlords	Kelheim Altburg Staré Hradisco	'sword style' intricate surface designs	
			transformation of the political structure of Celtic society	Staffelberg Magdalensberg	'plastic style' objects worked in the round mainly from Moravia	
	La Tène C	276 B.C. Celts create Galatian buffer state in Asia Minor	appearance of Celtic coinage			
300 B.C.		279 B.C. Celts attack Delphi by 300 B.C. Brythonic Celts arrive in Britain	return to cremation decline of prosperity	Waldalgesheim	'Waldalgesheim style' non-figurative interlace 'rococo' taste	inundations along northern shores rise in ground-water levels
	La Tène B	335 B.C. Celts meet with Alexander the Great on the lower Danube			free hand symmetry dynamic stylizations non-representative style	
400 B.C.		387 B.C. Celts sack Rome after 400 B.C. Celtic expansion	disappearance of large burial mounds strong influence from Italy princely wagon graves	Hölzelsau Schwarzenbach Waldgalscheid Reinheim Weiskirchen Besseringen Heidelberg Pfalzfeld Holzgerlingen Hochdorf	animated ornamentation organic dynamism openwork portable art monumental stone sculptures 'early style'	
500 B.C.	La Tène A Hallstatt D	crystallization of western provinces into a Celtic realm	'sacred monarchies' introduction of chariots	Grächwil	human faces orientalizing influences	

Chart 8. The Celtic La Tene Culture, after c.450 B.C.

loose association with Rome, to establish the Celtic kingdom of Noricum, the Regnum Noricum, which, as a result of a century of ordered relations with Rome, developed such a cultural affinity with Rome that the kingdom's transformation into a Roman province in 16/15 B.C. proceeded quite peacefully. In 61 B.C. Caesar broke the last Celtic resistance in Spain, while during his *Bellum Gallicum* (58-51 B.C.) he conquered Gaul, making the Rhine the eastern boundary of the new province. In 15 B.C. in a single campaign Tiberius and Drusus, the stepsons of Augustus, extended Rome's northern frontier beyond the Alps to the Danube.[16] By then north central Europe was largely Germanic. Between the millstones of Roman and Germanic expansion, nearly five hundred years of Celtic contribution to European cultural history came to an end.

The first steps towards the Celtic migrations appear to have been taken when the early Celts expanded from the area between Burgundy and the Upper Danube into the central Rhineland, Mosel and Saar regions and the Marne Basin, where princely graves attest to the prosperity and lavish tastes of the Celtic aristocracy. This move was probably motivated by an attempt to take possession of the sources of iron ore of which they knew through deliberate search.[17] This led to an intensive exploitation of the iron ore deposits, not only on the middle Rhine but also further east in Bohemia. The Celts furthered the development of an iron technology not only for the domestic but also for the export market, through the evolution of designs for artistic as well as functional purposes. By means of this technology they gained that superiority of weapons which allowed them to realize their political aspirations. It was here in the centre of western Europe that they assimilated the classical cultural influences from the western Mediterranean. It was here that they evolved those characteristic motifs of the La Tène artistic style. It was in this region that the people became identifiable as an ethnic and cultural group. It is held that as a result of these syntheses the Celts were well on the way to forming the third major European culture during the last centuries B.C.,[18] beside the Greeks and Romans, before this process was halted abruptly by Roman expansion.

No doubt their military predominance, based on their iron technology, facilitated their expansion into the south-west of Europe (Fig. 186). As heirs of the Hallstatt, which probably was proto-Celtic in any case, the Celtic 'expansion' throughout the Hallstatt provinces may not have been perceived as the coming of a new people. Only as they entered new lands, not previously associated with the Hallstatt, were they registered as marauding barbarians and a threat to the existing Hellenistic civilization and the evolution of Rome. It was not appreciated at the time that these wandering Celts were not just raiding war parties of barbarian nomads, but migrating tribes in search of land

186. Celtic sword from Oberschwarza in Styria, Austria.

on which to settle, who probably knew of established 'urbanized' settlements, even though they came from the unknown vastness of the northern forests. Naturally a desire for riches or a spirit of adventure may well have induced warlords or younger chiefs to lead splinter groups away from the hereditary tribal lands, thereby attracting others in their wake. They knew agricultural techniques, they observed diplomatic etiquette, and had a keen sense of military strategy with which they bested the Roman legions on several occasions, though in the end Roman tactics proved superior. Incidentally, the Celtic long-sword, designed as a cleaving sword, was effective only in the terrifying charge. If the enemy units held their ground and retained their closed formation, their counter-attack with the shorter stabbing sword invariably proved successful, since the Celtic sword had an unfortunate tendency to bend—a combination of length and pliability of the blade—which only too often made the Celtic warrior very vulnerable as he bent over to straighten his blade by stepping on it.[19]

It is not known what internal or external pressures caused the Celts to set out on their dispersion. Whether the expansion was stimulated by some inner dynamism, an increased level of cultural expectations promoted by the contact with foreign goods, ideas and techniques, by over-population, by a simple sense of adventure, by the cultural stress on the fighting life of the freeman, by political and social unrest or by the pressure exerted by the movement of peoples in northern Europe, the effect was a disruption of the traditional north–south relations, when a people with an explosive potential burst

Map 26. Tribal groups at the time of Caesar's campaigns in Gaul, 58 B.C.–51 B.C.

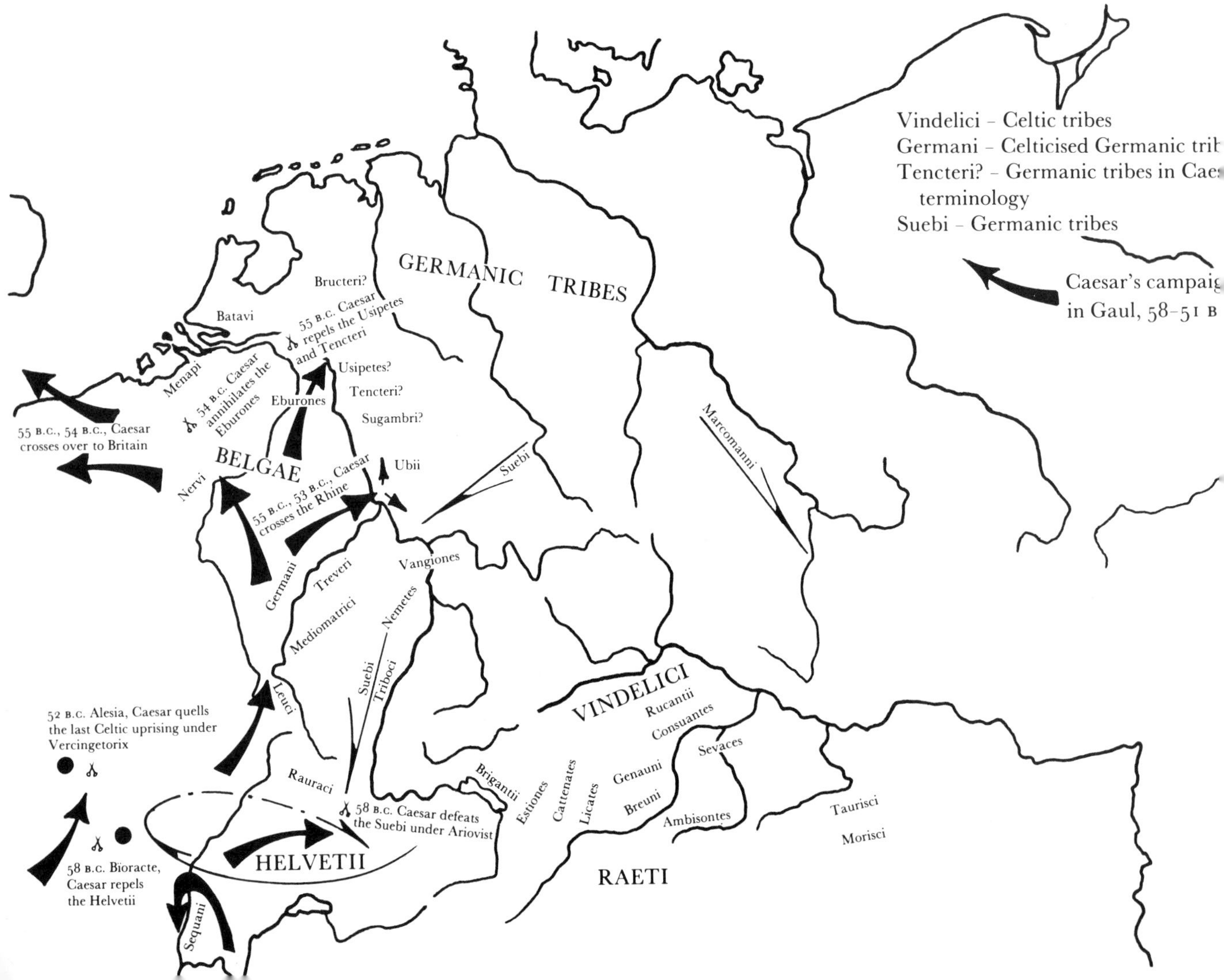

Vindelici – Celtic tribes
Germani – Celticised Germanic trib[
Tencteri? – Germanic tribes in Cae[
   terminology
Suebi – Germanic tribes

Caesar's campaig[
in Gaul, 58–51 B[

Bructeri?

Batavi

55 B.C. Caesar repels the Usipetes and Tencteri

Menapi

54 B.C. Caesar annihilates the Eburones

Usipetes?

Tencteri?

Eburones

Sugambri?

55 B.C., 54 B.C., Caesar crosses over to Britain

BELGAE

Nervi

Ubii

55 B.C., 53 B.C., Caesar crosses the Rhine

Germani

Treveri

Vangiones

Suebi

Mediomatrici

Nemetes

Triboci

Leuci

52 B.C. Alesia, Caesar quells the last Celtic uprising under Vercingetorix

Rauraci

VINDELICI

Rucantii

Consuantes

Sevaces

Brigantii

Estiones

Cattenates

Licates

Genauni

Breuni

Ambisontes

Taurisci

Morisci

58 B.C. Caesar defeats the Suebi under Ariovist

58 B.C. Bioracte, Caesar repels the Helvetii

HELVETII

RAETI

Sequani

GERMANIC TRIBES

Marcomanni

out of the center of western Europe.[20] This area without finite boundaries, in which contraction or expansion were the only available options, released a people whose warlike characteristics allowed only one great fear, 'that the sky might fall on them'— the legendary answer given to Alexander the Great by the Celtic delegation and recorded by his companion Ptolemy.[21] Objects characteristic of the Celtic La Tène have been found as far east as the Volga river and as far north as southern Scandinavia. From these finds, however, it is not possible to conclude, as a general rule, that wherever La Tène material is in evidence one may also expect to find Celts or even Celtic influences. At the same time the central Europeans and eastern nomads, such as the Scythians, probably had more in common than is readily admitted.[22] That there was contact between them has been observed above, and it led to the westward transfer of eastern forms and motifs.

The La Tène is a thoroughly Celtic phenomenon. It begins c. 450 B.C., and comes to an abrupt end with Caesar's campaigns in Gaul (58-51 B.C.), while the last evident elements of the Celts are assimilated in the Gallo-Roman culture of the Roman Empire, though vestiges of Celtic style resurface periodically in the cultural history of Europe.[23] It is regrettable that in his accounts Caesar relies heavily on the available literature, rather than basing his descriptions of the Celts in Gaul on more direct and extensive observations of his own.[24] In one respect he muddies the waters, for his own political reasons evidently, when he reports to the Roman Senate that the Rhine serves to separate Celtic tribes on the west bank from Germanic tribes on the east bank, a people much more fierce and warlike than the Gauls whom he had just conquered, and against whom it would be necessary to wage punitive campaigns, presumably until they too had been pacified.[25] It is agreed that in Caesar's time no clear divisions could be drawn between Celtic and Germanic peoples, and that the tribe of the Germani on the left side of the Rhine was really a Celtic tribe.[26] Their name was to provide the designation for two Roman provinces and for the land east and north of the frontiers of the Roman Empire.

The site at La Tène on Lake Neuchâtel in Switzerland was discovered in 1857, when unsystematic collectors looking for old artefacts from Swiss lake dwellings, as they thought, came across a whole range of items, which speedily found their way into private collections and into museums. Hence the total number of finds is unknown. This find however drew attention to the Celts. In 1872 the Swedish archeologist Hans Hildebrand attached the label 'La Tène' to the Celtic Iron Age. This was largely again a matter of convenience since the site was neither a central place of manufacture, nor do the items found there all date from c. 450 B.C., the beginning of the period identified with the name 'La Tène'. In fact the sloping lake bottom presents a reliable chronology based on stratification. The large number of finds made there also suggests that the site drew on a population settled over a much wider area than that of a community located directly on the lake. It has been proposed that the main site of La Tène was a cult site, where objects were deposited in the water, probably as votive offerings to water spirits.[27] Such cult sites, with similar deposits, are known throughout the Celtic provinces. Most prominent among the finds are weapons and objects for more personal use. However, the whole range of human activities is represented, not only warfare but agriculture, hunting, fishing and life on and near the water, as demonstrated by wheels and parts of vehicles, metal and leather horse trappings, woodwork, basketry, pottery, kitchen utensils, ropes, coins and ingots. The variation in quality suggests that the wealthy as well as the poor brought their votive offerings to this site. Though a social cross-section

249

is indicated, women seem to have played at best only a minor role in this particular cultic activity, since objects known exclusively from the graves of women are almost entirely missing. That those who engaged in the ceremonies here also engaged in human sacrifice is borne out by some of the evidence.

As a cultural domain those parts of Europe characterized as La Tène profit from the synthesis of supportive and contrary influences which at various times extended into Europe: Greek, Etruscan, Persian, Scythian and Balkan, as well as northern and ancient indigenous tendencies, all played their part in shaping the enigmatic Celtic Iron Age.[28] Very apparent is the continuity of the cultural patterns from the Chalcolithic onward. Social differentiations came into being with the mining and distribution of copper: a protective military aristocracy was established, and an estate of artisans evolved; priestly initiates into cultic practices, supported by a population of warriors, merchants, miners and farmers, who over the centuries came to live in concentrations in and near those Celtic fortified settlements known as 'oppida', noteworthy in themselves as illustrations of the progressing 'urbanization' which was taking place, are evidence of the gradual evolution towards a high culture in prehistoric central Europe.[29] Truly unique, however, is the high artistic achievement of the La Tène, the expression of a feeling that did not strive for the representation of things, but sought to give expression to a mysteriously motivated imagination occupied with animated ornamentation, inter-twining patterns and an organic dynamism.

Under the term 'oppidum' a whole range of diverse settlement types has been

Map 27. Some Celtic oppida in central Europe (after *c.* 200 B.C.).

assembled. To Caesar an oppidum was a city-like settlement or a fortified refuge, a center of trade and commerce, of economic and political authority, a tribal focal point of the Celts.[30] He does, however, differentiate between 'oppida' and 'urbs'.[31] Caesar's observations in Gaul may be generally appropriate, though not all the oppida found in Germany necessarily had these functions. Other, non-administrative reasons may have motivated the construction of fortifications on defendable locations characterized by difficult access. It is important to note that no direct connection is evident between such settlements as the Heuneburg of the Hallstatt period and the oppida of the late La Tène period,[32] though the site at Otzenhausen, an oppidum of the first century B.C., yielded pottery of the fifth and fourth centuries B.C.[33] The Heuneburg remains an exception, for few if any oppida predate the second century B.C. It has been suggested that by the end of the early La Tène, fortified settlements came into being in a few peripheral areas of the Celtic domains, and that in Bohemia the middle LaTène witnessed the fortification of some sites.[34] The selection and fortification of defendable sites along the northern fringe of the Celtic core area can be rationalized as a response to southward pressures exerted by non-Celtic peoples. It does not, however, account for the fortification during the middle LaTène of the settlement at Manching in the Danube plain of Lower Bavaria. It is conceivable that for the early period the use of such terms as 'defensive perimeters', 'fortifications' and 'hill forts' burdens these settlements and their systems of walls with a role they may not initially have been intended to fulfil. Nowhere in central Europe did these 'fortifications' develop into 'urban' settlements,[35] though in the early Middle Ages a number of these sites were reoccupied. Another possible fallacy is the view that the ramparts point to the military nature of the settlements where a dominant group of foreigners perhaps established itself over a native population, although in this instance echoes of earlier patterns of economic control, power and resultant prestige and ostentation may indeed be playing a role. Generally the location of the oppida was linked to the presence of raw materials, trade routes on water and land, and river crossings over which these settlements must have exercised control, imposed tolls and collected tributes, at the same time offering a measure of security to the traffic as well as to the neighboring population. The oppida located east of the Rhine and extending to the Weser river and the Central Highlands appear to have been intended to protect mines and metal workshops, thus playing a specific economic support role in the center of Germany.[36] Several open stations located in lowland regions are known, which, like Basel or Berne, were relocated onto hilltops during the late La Tène.[37] Here again the sites at Basel, Manching, Passau and Třísov in Bohemia played an important economic part in the production of pottery, while the Bohemian sites generally straddle the Bohemian river system, the main route for the amber trade. There open lowland stations are not known; instead by the end of the middle La Tène, walled sites were appearing in the mountainous regions.[38] Towards the end of the first century B.C., however, the sites were abandoned, a circumstance attributed to the appearance of the Germanic Marcomanni.[39] In any case, defensive measures seem to be a late feature, rather than a point of departure. It has been suggested that the development of the Celtic oppida as a form of settlement was probably a response to Greek and Roman examples.[40] Following Caesar's Gallic Wars the Celtic oppida in Gaul faded into insignificance. The urban beginnings were not continued by the Romans who established their forts on sites determined by their own sense of strategy,[41] so that the oppida continue as cultic sites, as at Otzenhausen,[42] if at all. The Celtic areas, transformed into Roman provinces, developed a new network of communication and economics, delimited by the northern

187. Staffelberg, site of a Celtic oppidum, near Staffelstein, north of Bamberg, Bavaria.

frontier and the garrisons of the Roman Empire. With the establishment of these frontiers and the effective elimination of the Celts as a culturally identifiable force north of the Danube and the assertion of Germanic tribes, central Europe underwent a rupture in its cultural continuity more marked than during any previous period of transition.

These oppida are the most striking aspects of the Celtic Iron Age. As 'type stations' of the late La Tène they justify the term 'oppidum culture'.[43] To refer to the oppida as 'urban centers' is correct only insofar as these settlements were not exclusively agrarian villages, the proximity to good soil not being a vital factor,[44] so that, terrain permitting, only a small part of the population was engaged in agriculture. As such, an oppidum serves to designate that point in the cultural development of Celtic society when some of its members switched from the pursuit of agriculture to administrative, commercial and manufacturing activities. Such points of transformation have been noted for the Chalcolithic, Bronze Age and Hallstatt periods and appear to be characteristic for the transition towards 'industrialization'. Though a link with the city cultures of the Mediterranean is possible, many of the oppida in Germany did not undergo continuous occupation, which in itself would hinder the evolution of a 'city state' in the sense of the Greek 'polis'. Nor did the oppidum usually enclose an 'acropolis'.[45] The choice of location, usually on promontories, table rocks, hilltops or high plateaus, characterized by precipitous slopes on at least three sides, and perhaps by a bend in a river, would have made most of these places rather inconvenient sites on which to establish permanent habitations (Fig. 187). Their obvious defensibility, requiring only a minimum of fortification, may not have been the primary criterion for their positioning. The ready visibility of these sites provided the various tribal groups with an identifiable point of reference.

Certainly in the core area straddling the middle Rhine, or such production centers as Manching, the oppida dominating a tribal area would have had political, economic, administrative and cultic features. At the center of manufacture and trade, their power and wealth was demonstrated by their ability to mint their own coinage. There is considerable support for the idea that the most important oppida formed the tip of an economic pyramid, from which an agricultural and industral base was administered. Thus the region administered by the oppidum at Manching was probably the tribal territory of the Celtic tribe of the Vindelici.[46]

Certainly during the last century B.C. the organizational authority of the oppidum must have been extensive to make it possible for the outer walls of the Kelheim oppidum to be rebuilt three times and the inner walls to be rebuilt twice within a few years, a total of 11·5 km of wall, all the more impressive considering the vast amount of stone and timber required for the *murus gallicus* type of construction.[47] For the oppidum at Manching the stone had to be quarried at Neuburg on the Danube, some 24 km and one river-crossing away.[48] The ramparts at the oppidum at Třísov in southern Bohemia took up to three years to build.[49] The fortifications at Otzenhausen were erected about 100 B.C. 'Royal' graves nearby and the evidence of earlier fortifications, as well as other archeological traces, indicate that this hilltop had been occupied throughout the preceding centuries. The ramparts raised during the first century B.C. were 4–5 m wide, built in the wood frame and rock style of the *murus gallicus*. The collapsed wall which closed off the promontory to the north is still 10 m high and some 40 m wide at the base (Fig. 188). In other places the steep slopes are surmounted by ridges of rock still 2 m high and 17 m wide at the base. In all some 228,382 m³ of stone was required (Fig. 189). Iron nails of local manufacture are still to be found in the rubble. The source of the iron ore was very close by (and was still mined there during the eighteenth century A.D.). The fort was later allowed to disintegrate. The absence of any trace of fire suggests that the hill fort was quietly abandoned after the establishment of the Roman administration, though the presence of a Roman sanctuary indicates its continued use for cultic purposes.[50]

Compared to the contemporary building programs carried out around the Mediterranean, these northern structures are not impressive, but for an area in which some historians saw only frantic hordes of barbarian warriors, they show cultural unity and a rather considerable degree of administrative organization, so much so that they provided an adequate basis for the administrative demands of the Roman Empire.[51]

Information about the oppidum at Manching is very extensive. Its origin probably has to be placed into the third or second century B.C., thereby helping to establish some continuity with the preceding Hallstatt. On a slight elevation near the Danube, it is a circular lowland settlement, initially without defensive perimeter, and thereby quite different from other oppida, more akin in fact to the circular cities of the Mediterranean. Over the centuries people used the wall as a ready supply of cut stones, as was customary wherever the 'Romans' had left convenient deposits of stone. In 1858 some 1000 gold coins had been found, called 'little rainbow bowls' because of their shape (Fig. 190), but it was not until 1880 that the site was accepted as a Celtic camp—the idea of a permanent Celtic settlement north of the Alps some 200 years before the arrival of the Romans being initially unacceptable. Besides, there was a wave of Germanomania. A gravefield of the middle La Tène nearby, discovered in 1893, was not associated with the

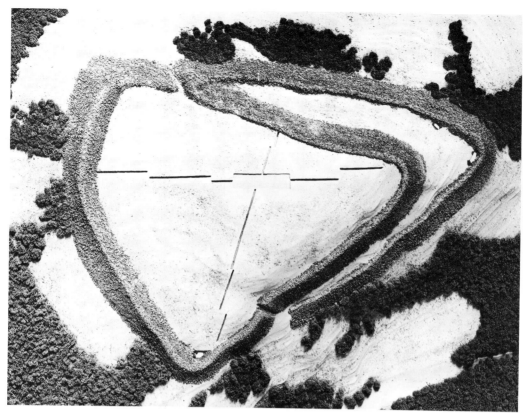

189. Model of the defensive perimeter of the oppidum at Otzenhausen.

188 (left). Remains of the 'murus gallicus', after *c.* 100 B.C., at the oppidum at Otzenhausen in the Palatinate, western Germany.

190. Celtic coins so-called rainbow bowls, *c.* second-first century B.C., from unknown sites.

191. Celtic fairlead with stylized bovine heads, before *c.* 50 B.C., from Manching in Lower Bavaria.

255

oppidum, and it was not till 1938 that the site was accepted as such. But by then a military airfield was being built on a large part of the oppidum and the military priority made a hurried exploration necessary. The systematic excavation took place between 1957 and 1961 (Fig. 191).[52]

With an east-west axis of 2·3 km and a north-south axis of 2·2 km the circular settlement had a circumference of over 7 km, contained by a *murus gallicus*, the most eastern instance of such a construction of timber frames and rocks.[53] In subsequent centuries the Romans had used some of the limestone for the pavement of their fort nearby, while the rest survived in the walls of nearby villages, leaving only the earth-works. In them people dug for the iron nails which had held the timber frames. Two thousand years of farming and erosion wore the 5 m high earthen wall down to 2·4 m. Today it is 20–30 m wide at the base, in all some 400,000 m³ of earth.[54] Considering that today a man can move 3 m³ of earth in a day, it would take some 200 men two years to pile up that much earth. Since there is no evidence of a ditch, the earth had to be transported to the site. The strategic location of the oppidum must have outweighed the inconveniences involved in building the limestone wall with its earth backing. The statistical calculations for the construction of this wall are impressive. The wallface required about 200,000 m³ of cut limestone which, without the broken rock needed to fill the wood frames, amounts to *c.* 538,200 metric tons of stone. It would take a fleet of 100 ten-ton trucks 538 trips each to move the rocks to the site.[55] It took 40 m of timber for every meter of wallface, and the wall was over 7000 m long, in all *c.* 280,000 linear meters of timber. Forty-eight nails were needed for every meter of wallface, for a total of over 336,000 nails, each 20–30 cm long and 1 cm square, for a total of 80 tons of finished iron, or four railway cars.[56] The nails probably came from Kelheim, the limestone came from Neuburg on the Danube, the timber was probably cut up-river and floated down the Danube, while the earth was dug somewhere nearby, all a remarkable undertaking. If one adds into this process the producing of the necessary charcoal and the mining of the great quantities of iron ore required to produce 80 tons of finished iron, not to mention the man-hours needed to make over 300,000 iron nails, it is apparent that an efficient economic infrastructure must have existed which could meet such a demand in what must have been a short period of time, if the enclosure was indeed the response to a potential crisis. The rot to which the timbers were subject after only a few years forced the inhabitants to erect a second wall of vertical timbers in front of the stone wall. Recessed into the wall, and of the pincer type so that attackers would be vulnerable from the side, the gates were shielded by a wicker screen. Under the east gate the skeleton of a six-year-old child was found, no doubt the consecrating sacrifice.[57] The site is all the more extraordinary in that it involved the redirecting of three watercourses. Initially the Manching oppidum must have been located right on the south bank of the Danube, probably on a ford. It is likely that it was a toll station and transfer point on the intersection of north–south and east–west trade routes.[58]

What were these walls designed to protect? Usually the ramparts enclosed an area larger than was actually necessary for habitation. The variety of housing evident at Manching and at other oppida suggests that the population of an oppidum reflected an extensive social and functional range, arranged in specially designated urban quarters, so that it is possible to speak of a degree of urban planning.[59] A wealthy quarter was often located near the center of the settlement; at least, that is where most luxurious articles, as well as the most solid houses, have been located. Other quarters contained the workshops of artisans and craftsmen who had been attracted to these settlements to

192. Celtic bull and ram, bronze, after *c.* 100 B.C., bull from Weltenburg near Kelheim, the ram from Sempt near Ebersberg.

satisfy the needs for luxuries and functional artefacts (Fig. 192). Smithies, foundries, glassworks, pottery kilns and even mints made the major oppida the economic nerve-centers of their respective tribal areas. Manching was most heavily settled at the center, the houses appearing to be one-family dwellings of post and wattle construction, probably gabled and thatched. For climatic reasons the houses tend not to face north. Some six hundred storage pits have been located, usually at the rear of the house. Grain found in them had been slightly smoked, to prevent germination. The area between the wall and the town center was taken up by larger farm-like areas 70 m × 50 m or 60 m × 60 m, dominated by longhouses 35–41 m long and about 6 m wide. These longhouses seem to have been subdivided. The raising of livestock may have been an important activity, judging by the extensive finds of animal bones, such as those of horse, cattle, sheep, goats and pigs. In some instances the craftsmen's quarters were located on the periphery, quite close to the walls of the oppidum. In other instances a wide strip of uninhabited terrain separated the center of the settlement from its fortifications. The Manching wall system had four gates. An east–west road has been established, a north–south road is assumed. Roads tended to have a pebble paving over a stone-packed road-bed.[60] At Třísov in southern Bohemia, the buildings were arranged just inside the protective perimeter, along a central channel with cisterns, which did not interfere with the main road. Třísov oppidum happened to enclose two elevations, with the settlement situated in the depression between the two 'citadels'. The cisterns would guarantee an adequate water supply. For a hilltop oppidum water would always be a key concern.[61] The oppidum at the Altburg near Bundenbach (Fig. 193), some 50 km south-east of Bernkastel-Kues on the Mosel river, is noteworthy for its special precinct separated from the remainder of the oppidum by a palisade. It is assumed that it segregated the

257

193. Model of the Altburg near Bundenbach in the Hunsrück mountains, western Germany, a settlement of the Hunsrück–Eifel culture during the late La Tène, after *c.* 200 B.C.

chief's residence from the rest of the settlement. Over a period of a hundred years, *c.* 150–50 B.C., some two hundred houses had occupied the fortified area, some sites having been rebuilt five times. The buildings were 8–12 m long, rectangular in shape, built in the half-timbered style, with a fine slip covering the exposed timbers for protection against the weather.[62] At Třísov, while one of the two elevations was occupied by craftsmen's quarters, the other northern 'citadel' appears to have been devoted to religious pursuits. A *temenos*—a four-cornered entrenchment for cultic purposes—superimposed on earlier cultic sites, was situated on that northern 'acropolis'.[63]

The importance of these sites must have derived from the combined presence of a religious group and of a military and political nobility supported by industry and commerce (Fig. 194). When associated with the administrative structure, this hierarchy must have contributed to the oppidum's prestige and to its standing as a religious focus. As cultic sites some of these oppida retained their importance for centuries, long after they had been abandoned as commercial or administrative centers. Thus the Celtic sanctuary at Otzenhausen continued to be used as a cult site during Roman times, when a small Roman temple, probably dedicated to Diana, was erected inside the deserted fortress.[64]

194. Votive figures from Gutenberg-Balzers, Liechtenstein.

The development of such organized settlements as the more outstanding oppida seems to point to a transformation of the political structure of Celtic society which was taking place during the last two centuries before the Christian era. Archeological elements—fortifications, self-contained settlements, wealthy town centers, 'princely' and religious precincts—seem to be manifest indications of the presence of political and administrative units which dominated the Celtic tribal realms. These areas reflected early notions of developing statehood. Within such districts it is conceivable that some tributary relationships existed among the various communities and that a hierarchical ordering of these communities guaranteed a smoothly functioning system of supply, manufacture and distribution of raw materials, goods and produce.[65] It has been suggested that the terminal of such a trading network, where exchange and administration came together, developed into an oppidum.[66] It can be accepted that the early Celtic forms of statehood show a marked resemblance to archaic Italian and Greek states.[67] Caesar noted that the Gauls west of the Rhine were administered by senates and magistrates drawn from a political oligarchy composed of rural and urban patricians rather than from a military caste.[68] Thus to Caesar the Ubians, for instance, across the Rhine from modern Cologne, were praiseworthy for being ruled by leaders and a senate,[69] while the Helvetii illustrated a tendency towards legal and administrative centralization. Quite evidently these practices predate Caesar's personal presence in Transalpine Gaul.[70] Similar perhaps to the Celts in Noricum in the eastern Alps, the western Celts too had adjusted to Roman influences until they too moved into what has been called 'the community of sentiment' with Rome.[71] While the Celtic gentry adopted Roman ways, the Romans encouraged the oligarchies and bolstered the tottering ones against unruly warlords who, though they had great wealth and the backing of private

Plate 6a. Celtic vessel from the settlement at Basel–Gasfabrik.

Plate 6b (below left). Gold arm ring showing eastern elements, *c.* 450 B.C., from Reinheim, southeast of Saarbrücken in the Palatinate.

Plate 6c (below right). Gold torc showing eastern elements, *c.* 450 B.C., from Reinheim.

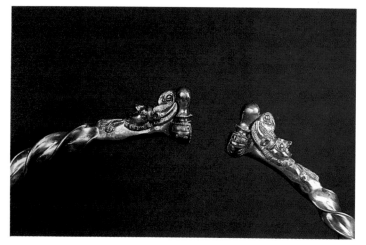

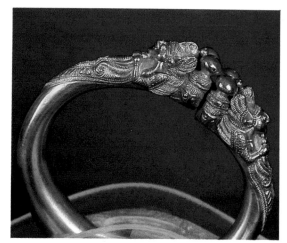

armies, were excluded from wielding effective power. Not wishing to jeopardize their economic basis, the oligarchies in turn tended to support the Romans[72] to the extent of not coming to the assistance of such warrior leaders as Vercingetorix (whose name was Celtic for King-of-very-many-warriors) in their struggle with Caesar. The economic ties proved more tenacious and promising than the cultural ones.

Usually located on a choice site, the local nobility probably had little difficulty in attracting distant trade and exotic goods, as well as the necessary craftsmen who soon gave the more prominent oppida the desired self-sufficiency. Quite evidently the production of luxuries and necessities far exceeded the needs of the resident patricians, so that an extensive trade could flourish in metals, glass, clay, and especially in pottery at Manching and Třísov.

Generally the oppida were situated in the vicinity of natural resources such as iron ore, gold, graphite and clay, near intersections of traditional trade routes, both over land and on the water, or at the head of these trade routes, such as the oppidum of Staré Hradisko in Moravia, which served as clearing point for northern amber over all of the Celtic world.[73] Not content just to distribute the iron ores which they mined or the raw iron they smelted, they also engaged in a trade in finished items, for instance the nails produced at Kelheim for Manching walls. The iron industry is well documented in the oppida, from smelting furnaces to smithies complete with tools, slag and raw iron cakes. Though the production of iron was still limited until the middle of the late La Tène period, thereafter it was characterized by excellence and was in abundant supply. As during the Hallstatt, raw iron was traded in ingots, perhaps as a form of currency, for finishing elsewhere. Among the artisans were included blacksmiths, cartwrights, carpenters and leatherworkers. Special skills were developed in the manufacture of jewellery and other personal ornaments, especially glass objects such as beads and bracelets and little animals in brilliant blue, and above all in enamelling techniques.[74]

Most extensive was the import of Mediterranean wines in amphorae. Following the decline of the extensive relations between the Hallstatt princes and the cultures of the western Mediterranean, a time which had seen a brisk trade in wine, the late La Tène of the second century B.C. enjoyed a renewed influx of southern wines, imported in amphorae and especially in bronze luxury vessels. This trade came up the Rhône river from Massilia in the west.[75] In the eastern regions Roman amphorae have been found at Stradonice in central Bohemia. Metal vessels of Roman provincial origin, as well as local imitations, have been discovered.[76] On the Magdalensberg in Carinthia, Austria, a colony of Italian merchants had scratched into their cellar walls the Italian points of destination of their trade goods, mainly iron objects, jugs, platters, rings and hooks.[77] From this and other evidence it is apparent that enterprising Romans were trading into Transalpine Europe by the first century B.C. The possibility exists that Celtic Europe was criss-crossed by itinerant craftsmen who carried distribution centers into areas not in the immediate vicinity of the established trading centers, as mobile terminals of long-distance trade.

The use of Macedonian, Hellenistic, Greek Colonial and Roman Republican motifs on Celtic coins is evidence of extended contact. By 300 B.C. the Celts had begun to stamp their own coins. At first these were only adaptations of Greek coins, staters of Alexander and his father Philip of Macedon. Minting molds of clay and many coins have been found at Manching.[78] Owing to their concave shape they came to be known as 'little rainbow bowls', presumably associated with the legendary pot of gold. At Manching there was even the practice of counterfeiting and worse, when gilt base metals

195. Celtic gold coins, after *c.* 350 B.C. (l.) coin of the Treveri from an unknown site; (m.) coin of the Treveri from Wahlen, east of Merzig in the Palatinate; (r.) coin of the Treveri from Dudeldorf, east of Bitburg in the Palatinate.

were passed off for genuine.[79] Macedonian coins would have come up the Rhône from Massilia. Roman denars came north by many routes. The most common Greek motifs represented on the obverse of coins are Apollo or Hercules, while horse and rider or chariot and charioteer are represented on the reverse of coins bearing stylized likenesses of Philip II of Macedon and his son Alexander the Great. The minting and use of coins, both of bronze and of gold, points to the transition from barter to money as a form of exchange (Fig. 195). It shows the Celts to be adapting to a money economy.

The effectiveness of the oppida appears to come to an end in the last half of the first century B.C. The northern ones, built in the Celtic manner and located between the Rhine and the Weser rivers, appear to have been deserted in the face of pressure from the Germanic north and east, without being occupied. The Bohemian oppida probably fell to the Germanic Marcomanni.[80] Manching, the capital of one of the tribes of the Vindelici, if not the capital of that entire Celtic nation, may have fallen before 15 B.C., probably in an inner-tribal conflict rather than at the hands of the advancing Romans. Over two hundred skeletons, mainly male, have been found, all of them killed.[81] Numerous depots of valuables and many weapons have been discovered, pointing to the catastrophic end of the oppidum. Roman weapons, however, have not been identified. Charred wood indicates that the oppidum went up in flames. Its Celtic name did not enter into Roman records.

An oppidum offered only little other than its walls as protection against attack. Without flanking towers the defenders could not even threaten the attackers with crossfire. Without in-depth defenses, without long-range weapons and heavy projectiles, an oppidum was no match for the formations of even a single Roman legion and its mobile artillery. In the west, the oppidum at Otzenhausen, though credited with being one of the focal points of Treverian resistance against the Romans, appears not to have borne the brunt of a Roman assault. The significance of the oppida seems to have receded as the populations and possible garrisons relocated to the new centers of the Roman occupation. Rome generally ignored the Celtic centers and established its own network of towns and markets linked by a new system of roads, except if a particularly strategic site made continued occupation and fortification advisable.[82] South of the Danube La Tène sites did not influence the development of Roman urban patterns either, as Roman *castellae*—forts—encouraged the growth of supportive settlements. It was not until the seventh and eighth centuries A.D. that garrisons of the Merovingian and Carolingian kingdoms reoccupied some of the old Celtic sites. It is from these garrisons that some of the hilltop towns of the Middle Ages were to develop.

Owing to the general homogeneity of Celtic designs, inter-Celtic trade is difficult to determine from the archeological evidence. However, a striking feature in the oppida is the presence of fine painted pottery. The quality of the ware is in itself an indication of an elevated lifestyle. The ceramic industry sheds some light on the relations between some of the Celtic realms, in that graphite-enriched clay from southern Bohemia, Lower Austria and the area around Passau came along the Danube to Manching, some 150 km up river.[83] Graphite was much in demand for its use in crucibles, but also for pottery because its presence in clay increases impermeability, conductivity and heat retention (Fig. 196). The trade in lump graphite extended to the Rhine in the west, to Thuringia, northern Bohemia and Silesia in the north, to the Carpathians in the east, and to northern Italy and Yugoslavia in the south.[84] Graphite pottery from Třísov, complete with identifying potters' marks, has been found in the Alps around Salzburg and as far west as Basel, but less in Bohemia,[85] implying that the oppidum at Třísov may have been oriented towards the Danubian region. Graphite ware constitutes about 25 per cent of the pottery found at Manching.[86]

A very characteristic type of pottery has been associated with that oppidum, almost making Manching a ceramic type station. Here a red-white consumer ware was mass-produced and traded west into Switzerland and France, north into the Rhineland and east beyond Bohemia into the Vistula region in Poland and to the river Tisza in Hungary (Fig. 197). Vast amounts of shards have been located at the center of the oppidum. Manching pottery is wheel-thrown. The technique appears to have been acquired by the Celts through their contact with the Greek colonies along the Mediterranean and Black Sea coasts, from where it was passed to the Celtic heartland. Manching pottery stands out in that it has no links with any of the earlier ceramic types prevalent in central Europe, neither in the clay used, nor in the basic shapes, nor in the ornamental designs applied to it. Manching ware rather creates the impression of a Mediterranean manner of manufacture. Most surprising is the uniformity of design and decoration found at many sites throughout the area from western France to Hungary, strongly suggesting series production in large quantities (Fig. 198). Production techniques—type of clay, firing, painting—seem to have been standardized.[87] The jars were first formed by hand, the turning on the wheel being a secondary process by which slender ascending forms of a simple elegance were achieved. The exteriors were finely smoothed, while the color effects were attained during the firing.

Jars or tall urns are the dominant ceramic forms. These exist in two variants of the basic color scheme: a white base with red zones, or a red base with white zones. With the former, the red zones serve to limit and emphasize the area of ornamentation. With the latter scheme the white zones dominate. Many variations of alternating color bands are therefore possible.[88] The ornamental designs are sepia colored. It is assumed that the ornamental bands had primarily a decorative function. In spite of creating the impression of having been stencilled on the jars, the designs are marked by a freehand symmetry, gathered in narrow strips, bundled lines, waves, zigzags, or arranged in wide bands of vertical geometrics alternating with horizontal geometrics (Fig. 199). The decorated area may be covered with a grate pattern, fields of symmetrically arranged dots, or crescents, or checkerboards, as well as with curvilinear vegetable designs and Mediterranean motifs (Plate 6a). The designs succeed in creating an illusory interplay between perforated designs and solid background, between ornamentation and base and between positive and negative space. Great variety of decoration coexists with standardization of forms.[89]

The ceramic evidence from this region shows that there was continuing indigenous settlement of late La Tène populations coexistent with Roman military posts during the early Augustan period. In the Roman province of Raetia, the area south of the Danube,

196 (top). Graphite pot from Manching, after *c.* 200 B.C.

197 (right). Celtic pottery, after *c.* 200 B.C., found in Worms on the middle Rhine.

198 (below). Celtic vessel from Manching, after *c.* 200 B.C.

painted pottery of the Manching type continued to be produced into the period dominated by the reign of Augustus, the beginning of the Christian era.[90]

The center of fifth-century Celtic power and culture, located between the Alps and the middle Rhine, the Mosel and Saar rivers, is distinguished by the richly equipped 'princely' graves which continue to be uncovered in this region. From the upper Danube to the Seine in the west, wooden grave chambers have yielded Etruscan and Greek bronzes and splendid jewellery of bronze and other precious metals, pointing to a social group which in its burial practices was separated from the rest of the population. Located in burial mounds, these rich graves stand out from among the other, simpler inhumation and cremation graves, whether arranged as flat graves or as low grave hills. Although these latter graves also show differences of more modest wealth in their inventories, the rich contents of the large tumuli indicate that their occupants had enjoyed an elevated social position.[91] Our imagination readily grants these dead the title 'prince', 'potentate' and 'ruler', even though their socio-cultural roles may actually have lain in different areas of human activity. Since the Bronze Age, taking the grave at Acholshausen as an example, one may also expect to find representatives of the spiritual estates, and even of those who as theocrats combined in their own persons temporal as well as spiritual functions. The evidence found in the grave mounds suggests that these individuals occupied lofty positions and engaged in high-level cultural activities which brought precious objects into their possession. The location of these objects in the timbered grave chambers makes it clear that articles were spread out with flair to allow the gleam of the metallic ornaments to emphasize the splendor of clothing, wall hangings, draperies and other perishable materials. Fortunately oxidizing bronze has a preservative effect on such sections of cloth as might be covered by the bronze, so that under suitable circumstances bits of fabric have been preserved. Exemplary was the timbered funeral chamber which was uncovered in September 1978, east of Hochdorf, 10 km west of the famous oppidum on the Hohenasperg, the probable residence of the princely occupant of the grave. During the Iron Age the Hohenasperg and its surrounding region had evidently been a seat of power similar to the Heuneburg to the south-east. The burial has been dated to about 530 B.C., during the transition from Ha D_1 to Ha D_2. Though it is a four-wheeled wagon grave, normally a Hallstatt characteristic, it has been designated a Celtic burial and its occupant a Celtic prince, a man of about forty, who with the impressive height of 1·83 m towered over his contemporaries. This grave is unique in that it is the first grave to have been found intact,

199. Celtic pottery, after *c.* 200 B.C., from Groß Gerau (l.) and Bensheim (r.) near Darmstadt.

undisturbed by grave robbers, possibly because of its construction. Located in an excavation two meters below ground level at the center of the tumulus, it measured 11 m × 11 m in size. The wooden grave chamber, 4·7 m × 4·7 m, had been surrounded by a larger wooden chamber, 7·4 m × 7·5 m, with the space between the walls packed with broken stones. Additional cross-beams reinforced the ceiling of the chamber.

The sod and loess construction of the tumulus, 60 m in diameter, provided the rock–timber grave chamber with an air- and water-tight seal. This factor, as well as the poisonous oxides released by the large quantity of metal deposited in the grave, countered the bacterial decomposition of such organic things as wood, leather and the many meters of textiles. The walls and the floor of the chamber had been lined with multi-colored and patterned fabrics. The complete funerary inventory could be recovered. It showed the deceased wearing such personal adornments as the golden torc around his neck—the customary insignia of princely rank—and such unusual gold objects, made expressly for the occasion, as two snake fibulae, an arm ring on his right arm, a wide strip of sheet gold fastened to a leather belt, and a dagger in an ornamented golden sheath, its grip wound with gold. Decorative strips of sheet gold, ornamented with embossed geometric patterns, once outlined his upward-pointing shoes. A large iron razor and a nail cutter made up his personal toilet articles. Three fishing hooks and a quiver of arrows point to his interests out of doors. His garments could no longer be seen, except for a flat conical hat of birch-bark discs, which had been decorated with circular patterns.

Map 28. Celtic princely graves.

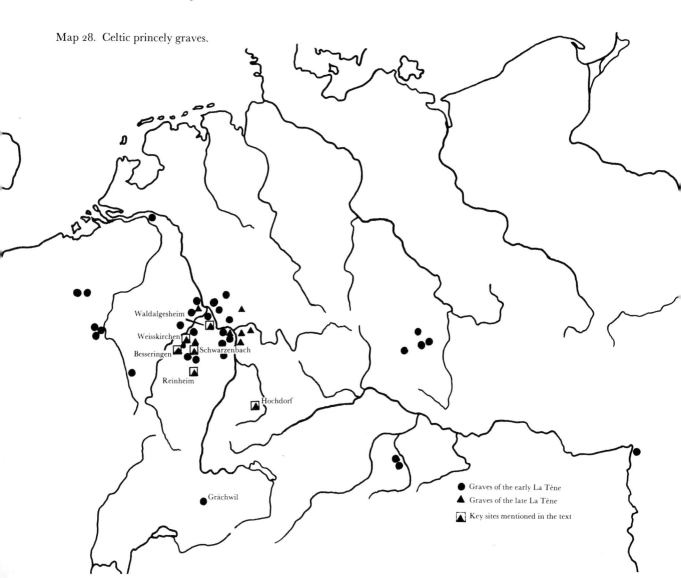

200. Backrest of the funeral couch from Hochdorf, c. 530 B.C., central section.

201. One of two endsections of the funeral couch from Hochdorf, c. 530 B.C.

His retainers placed him on a sofa-shaped bier made of bronze, 3 m long, assembled from six pieces of sheet bronze riveted together. Embossed in the center of the backrest of the funeral couch are three groups of two figures each performing a 'sword dance' (Fig. 200); at each end are represented a team of stylized horses pulling a four-wheeled wagon on which stands a figure holding shield and spear (Fig. 201). This couch is supported on the raised arms of eight female figurines, cast in solid bronze. With each figurine standing on a wheel, the couch could be rolled forward and back. Seat and backrest had been cushioned with furs, leather and fabric. This couch is a unique piece of furniture, suggesting south-eastern influences, though a local origin cannot be excluded.

Characteristic for a wagon grave of the Hallstatt period is the four-wheeled vehicle. On this one the box is narrow and elongated, trimmed with decorative sheet metal fittings. The sturdy wheels are fixed with large hubs. In the box lay the harnesses of two horses, a wooden double yoke richly ornamented with bronze, two bridles with iron bits, the leather parts amply set with bronze discs, and lastly a goad, 1·90 m long, fitted with a bronze tip. Though it is not unusual to find such metal fittings, it is unusual to find the organic matter, such as wood and leather, so well-preserved.

Essential components of this grave are the eating and drinking vessels. Eight drinking horns were hung along the south wall of the chamber. Only the gold ornaments and bronze fittings, as well as bone-beads attached to the ends, survived. A ninth horn, made of iron and nearly 1 m long, fitted with gold bands, survived intact. In the north-west corner stood a huge bronze cauldron of southern origin, decorated with three large bronze lions. Traces of a honey- or mead-like drink were found in the cauldron. Inside the kettle was found a bowl, 15 cm in diameter, of hammered gold, perhaps a drinking or dipping vessel. The box of the wagon also contained nine bronze plates, stacked together with three large bronze platters or bowls. An iron axe with a well-preserved wooden handle, an iron lance tip and a large iron knife (possibly a carving-knife), probably completed the implements.[92]

The wealth of gold, bronze and even iron, as well as the luxurious fabrics contained in this tomb make it only too apparent why prehistoric grave robbers were not intimidated by the threat of penalties in this or the other world.

In eastern Gaul, a large number of women's graves figures among the wealthy graves, rich in decorated neck, arm and ankle rings.[93] One such regal grave, from the fourth century, was discovered by chance near Reinheim, south-east of Saarbrücken in the Saarland.[94] Once covered by a mighty tumulus, circumscribed by a ditch, the oak-timbered grave chamber yielded many articles for daily use, and feminine jewellery of great beauty. Except for a shadow, 60 cm high, the mound and the chamber had completely eroded. The human remains had been absorbed into the ground. Much more luxurious than neighboring male graves, this was the tomb of a lady of high social rank. Positioned north to south, the lady wore a golden torc around the neck and an arm ring of unique design, and reflecting eastern Mediterranean taste (Fig. 202), arm rings of gold, slate and light green glass, the latter probably of Italian origin,[95] and two fibulae, one a golden disc fibula, the other a disc fibula in the shape of a rooster. Both fibulae appear to have been heirlooms. At her side lay a hand mirror, its anthropomorphic handle having a 'Janus' face with typical 'leaf-crown' ornamentations. A small box at her left shoulder contained little bronze chains, 120 amber pearls, some colored glass pearls and rings, and an assortment of personal amulets, a little bronze man for instance, perhaps another heirloom. The inventory included eating and drinking vessels,

202. Torc and arm ring from Reinheim, early La Tène.

such as two bronze plates and two conical gold leaf shells worked in a repoussé and perforated technique (the cups which they had enclosed having perished), as well as a tall bronze decanter surmounted by a bearded centaur on its lid. These pieces had been wrapped in white linen. This was indeed a person with great personal wealth which remained hers even in death.[96]

These two graves are representative for very many such 'princely' graves, the Hochdorf grave representing the transition from Hallstatt to Celtic times, the Reinheim grave representing the early La Tène. With the advent of the middle La Tène the archeological evidence points to a decline of prosperity. The raising of impressive regal grave mounds was discontinued and the inventories show ordinary objects taking the place of gold. The transition to the La Tène is also marked by the displacement of the four-wheeled Hallstatt funerary vehicles by two-wheeled chariots,[97] in itself perhaps a sign of changing battle tactics, though it is possible that the four-wheelers were specially constructed funerary vehicles, while the two-wheelers were actually in use.[98] For some time wagon and chariot burials were to be the prevailing practice from France, Belgium and Holland in the west, to Hungary, Romania and Bulgaria in the east. In this area the archeological materials show that strong links existed between the western and eastern groups. The central group, from the Rhineland to Austria, however, appears to have been affected by strong cultural influences from Italy, as demonstrated by the greater abundance of grave goods.[99] Here too the middle La Tène serves as a line of demarcation, as the practice of chariot burials comes to a halt during the late phases of the early La Tène.[100] As burial by inhumation recedes, cremation comes back into vogue. However, during the late La Tène there is some evidence of a brief revival of inhumation as a

269

funerary practice. In any event, considering the cultural diversity of the Celtic 'Diaspora', uniformity of funerary practices throughout the entire area cannot be expected (Fig. 203).

As was the case in previous periods, the changes in burial practice must have been prompted by social changes and struggles with varying religious ideas. No doubt some shift in the way of viewing the world must have been fundamental. Just as cremation seeks the dissolution of physical nature, inhumation is practiced by those who wish to continue the corporeality of being. Similarly, the demise of the princely graves implies significant socio-political changes.

One attributes to the early Celts submission to 'sacred monarchies', to theocratic rule, as it persisted in Ireland for over another thousand years. Perhaps these 'princely' graves were raised as the last resting place for 'royal' priests, who in their temporal and religious capacity acted as intermediaries between their people and the gods, representing the people to the gods and the gods to the people. As in Egypt, perhaps, the primeval hill of earth represented the world rising out of chaos, so that these earthen tombs were identical with it, not as metaphors but in actual fact. Perhaps every tumulus by virtue of its shape shared in this fundamental sacredness. Hence the funerary rites of passage would see the princely personage acting as emissary to the gods and thereby bringing about the reintegration of the individual into the cosmos. The vast princely tumuli, whether Hallstatt or La Tène, are a visible indication of a hierarchical ordering of Iron Age society. Where the cemetery at Hallstatt reflects a degree of egalitarianism, certainly in the graves of its noble occupants, such huge grave mounds as the Hohmichele, the one at Gross Mugl, the many wagon graves and the chambered burial mounds erected by the Celts during the early La Tène, point to a certain remoteness of the culture-carrying elites—an accessible remoteness however, which allowed for participation by association with those who mattered, with those who determined policy, with the military and with those who commissioned the imaginative ornaments. If the deceased was indeed a royal priest, a sacerdotus, or a priestess such as the noble lady of the Vix or even of the Reinheim burial, then even those who provided the labor for the large earth mound had probably been assured of some spiritual rewards. The possibility that such a sacerdotus existed in the hierarchy was demonstrated for the Bronze Age with the individual buried at Acholshausen. Whether Iron Age society only a few hundred years later continued to maintain such a position cannot be demonstrated, though it is possible for the Hallstatt and the early La Tène.

For the late La Tène the diversity of Celtic social organization is certified by the classical writers.[101] Thus Diodorus, Caesar and Strabo speak of 'druids', very wise men to whom were assigned a multitude of functions including sacrifice, divination, public affairs, justice and education. 'Bards'—poets and singers—who as seers practiced incantations, and 'vates', who engaged in the physical aspects of study to foretell events, completed the membership of the sacerdotal class which dominated the entire field of theological, doctrinal, cultic, functional and administrative activity.[102] Dynasties of elite families probably existed, from among which the royal personage was selected. The life of this individual must have given ample evidence that he was the chosen of the gods, by virtue of which he was elected to the 'kingship'. No doubt the sacerdotal class would interpret the will of the gods to the electorate, just as its superior knowledge of transcendental things, as manifest in its counsels and influence, would help it to exercise control over the king. Nevertheless the principles underlying the ritual installation of the temporal ruler would differ so fundamentally in assumptions and level from the

203. Celtic helmet, *c.* 100 B.C., from Mannheim.

initiation of the religious leaders that an exchange of roles would be tantamount to usurpation.[103] However, the sacerdotal personage—the royal priest—could claim jurisdiction over the spiritual as well as over the temporal, even military realms. Some time during the last millennium B.C., the advent of a temporal kingship delimited the spheres of activity, until the spiritual caste reserved for itself the care and teaching of doctrinal concerns, while the king was charged with its protection. This division of powers was not settled for all time and much of the cultural struggle in the historical development of Europe was to be caused by the polarizations brought about by this partition of functions. The two cannot be equal. Ideally they can be in equilibrium, each pursuing its ends in harmonious cooperation. At all times (and the Investiture Struggle between the Holy Roman Emperors and the medieval Papacy is only one excellent illustration), sacerdotism can exist alone and independent of royalty and of the state, while the king is dependent for his justification and the very legitimacy of his office on the consent of the sacerdotal group.[104] In modern history the doctrine of the Divine Rights of Kings is the last unsuccessful royal attempt to claim direct heavenly installation on the throne as the chosen representative of God on earth. Already in Celtic times it was the priestly caste which motivated and initiated the coronation, consecration and enthroning of the king, an act it could reverse just as easily and depose the king, if he proved unjust, incapable of or resistant to carrying out the tasks entrusted to him. Then the druids could prophesy, if not actually provoke, the catastrophe which would end the king's reign. The expiation could take the form of a ritual sacrifice of the person of the king.[105] There is evidence that among the Celts the deterioration of druidic political power permitted the weakening of institutions and of traditions, especially the decline of the sacred monarchy. It appears that with the decay of the spiritual aristocracy which had imposed and regulated the spiritual uniformity of the culture, the self-aware Celtic upper crust became an exploiter of human resources and a mere consumer of the products of creativity. According to Caesar's accounts, power and money politics allowed people to seize the tribal leadership and hold on to it through a lavish display of material power without bothering to maintain even the illusion of a sacred kingship.[106] Whereas the earlier order saw the king supported by the sacerdotal group and, beneath it, a council of aristocratic elders—the Nervi had six hundred councillors[107]—designed to act as a guarantee against usurpers, the new order of tribal chiefs was supported by the chief's personal following. This following consisted of fellows in arms bound to the chief in friendship to the death, of dependents who may have entered the chief's entourage quite voluntarily, and of clients, who through a process of indebtedness, service and protection had come to be indentured to the leader. Caesar speaks of a chief among the Helvetii—Orgetorix—who, when called before the assembly, appeared with ten thousand followers to protect him.[108] There can be little question that this act was not within the law and not in accordance with the practices of the old sacred kingship. The new social conditions made for instability as aristocratic upstarts began to determine events. Making up in bravado—Vercingetorix, he who has an overabundance of foot soldiers[109]—what they lacked in legitimacy, they sought to dominate by intimidation, as is reflected in their names when compared to less telling names which were also used among the aristocracy. This reach for power alienated and isolated the warlords from the ruling oligarchies and the broad mass of the people—Vercingetorix did not have the unanimous support of the Gauls, only of his dependents and others like himself—and ultimately contributed to the loss of Celtic independence when it facilitated the Roman conquest of Gaul.[110] The Celtic situation appears to have been aggravated by the self-contained tribal structure which favored dissension among the clans rather than the formation of greater political structures.[111] Caesar reports the hostile parting of clans, probably his understanding of the Celtic dependencies, which suggests that the social network did not extend beyond this group. In itself an encapsulating process, it aided the internecine tribal disputes and centrifugal tendencies, which fifty years earlier had permitted the Cimbri and Teutons to roam freely through the Celtic lands and to settle temporarily among the Gauls, and which in the end allowed the Romans to carry out the piecemeal conquest of Gaul.[112] The opposition to Rome was political and military rather than cultural, in any case. Centuries of influences, mercantile interests and economic ties with the south had removed any real reasons for resistance. The oligarchies in Gaul must have seen their opportunities in an inclusion of Gaul in the Roman concert of nations, which at the same time would rid them of the troublesome warlords. Discounting a heroized but politically inept Vercingetorix, who could not rally the Gauls to his cause, no great leader emerged among the Celts who was backed by a popular movement, or by a new power structure, or by common interests, or by a unified realm.

The stylistic problem which is basic to central Europe from prehistoric times to the present is to be found in the unresolved and opposing polarities brought about by the interplay of stylistic influences between the Mediterranean and northern approaches to style. In describing the northern approach to style we have seen, and will continue to see, that terms such as organic, vegetable, animal, open form, ornamental, dynamic, centrifugal, calligraphic, aniconic, decorative, polyphonic and atonal are generally appropriate; in describing the Mediterranean approach to style such terms as tectonic, formal, anthropomorphic, closed form, narrative, static, centripetal, iconographic, functional, melodic and tonal are generally fitting.[113] That the formal sense is an echo of spiritual and ethical elements which pervade a cultural area's view of the world is readily appreciated.

It is the deliberate and consistent selection of a vast array of mutually supportive characteristics which makes that process of choice the expression of a certain temperament.[114] Already the central and northern European Bronze Age had taken great delight in ornamenting even small surfaces with dynamic linears and expressed a certain preference for animal representations. The coils, spirals and convolutions had expressed a certain restlessness, line bands had evolved into wave patterns, interlocking ſ-curves had become cresting waves, which in turn terminated in tendrils, only to be transformed into gracefully floating birds. Mere lines had become organisms. Southern and south-eastern influences could readily be identified, and will continue to be readily identifiable, by the representation of compact units, by a positive and opaque presence of the object, a sculpture in the round—the Hirschlanden figure, for instance, by the depiction of narrative scenes such as on the situlae of the south-eastern Hallstatt, the preoccupation with the human form, in every instance reflecting the results of analysis, close observation and rationalistic interpretations. In the north the fascination is with the movement of lines, with the intricacies of pattern and the suggestiveness of ornamented surfaces. These features have proven to be an obstacle to understanding based on reason. Compared to the obscure intentions of northern forms and their potential for discord, the disciplined depiction of symmetrical structures with harmonious proportions which are basic to the artistic forms produced by the Mediterranean have at all times been more easily grasped.

Since the Renaissance a view tends to assert itself which sees northern artistic efforts through the ages as barbarous with only the occasional spark of greatness for which a southern stimulus then has to be sought and is usually found. It is this persuasion which has been quick to label the artistic endeavors of the La Tène a phenomenon without known ancestry but mature and completed and totally original when it first emerged in the middle of the fifth century B.C., the product of Celtic Europe.[115] At best, one conceded to it a gradual accumulative development under the varying local conditions to which the Celts adjusted in their dispersion across Europe. However, the tenacity with which the ornamental motifs and techniques of Celtic art clung on into the Middle Ages and beyond suggest that the distinct forms of the La Tène were extremely well rooted in indigenous central European traditions,[116] and that the underlying concepts behind these forms of expression are fundamental to the formal sense of the area, not only during the Iron Age but also in twentieth century European culture. It has been demonstrated in previous chapters that cultural indicators can only be grasped at that point when they are fully developed and adequately represented across the cultural area. For Celtic art the middle of the fifth century B.C. is the point at which its development becomes apparent throughout the Celtic realms from the Pyrenees to the Carpathians. In spite of regional variations Celtic art is marked by an inherent aesthetic unity throughout.

The great name behind the early analysis and classification of Celtic art is that of Paul Jacobsthal, who in the 1930s established the groundwork on which the excellent literature on Celtic art continues to draw. In his *Early Celtic Art* he sees in Celtic art a confluence of the Classical art of the Mediterranean transmitted to the Celts by way of Italy and the east, where Italic, Scythian and Persian peoples placed their stamp on it; of eastern art, especially Scythian and even Persian art, marked by its particular animal style; and of European native art, by which Jacobsthal meant the geometric style of the Hallstatt.[117] Jacobsthal was a classical archeologist who quite accidentally encountered the Celts while studying Greek pottery in Stuttgart. Since then many new finds have been made, which, however, do not invalidate his work. Nevertheless, scholarship today attaches a much greater importance to the link between La Tène art and the curvilinear style of non-representational Bronze Age art,[118] especially to that of the north, and the focus on the sequence of influences which Jacobsthal suggested has been sharpened.

To the expansion of the Assyrian Empire in the Near East, especially to its second and third phases (885–763 B.C., 747–612 B.C.) is attributed the spread of orientalizing decorative motifs and skills, when artists and artisans sought refuge in the west, where they influenced the commercial and artistic worlds of the Etruscans and the colonial Greeks.[119] From now on Italy and Magna Graecia produced adaptations of eastern metal vessels which bore such ornamental elements as lions, snakes, birds and winged goddesses—the 'Mistress of Animals'. During the sixth century a large crater with these ornamental motifs was placed in a Celtic princely grave at Grächwil in the Canton of Berne in Switzerland (Fig. 204).[120] An import from the south, it must have reached Switzerland via the wine trade route from Massilia up the Rhône river. Later, following the disruption of that route, Etruscan and Alpine routes bore that traffic. Though it seems that objects of such ostentation were produced expressly for the purpose of satisfying the desire for display of these princely 'barbarians', as patrons these princes of the late Hallstatt did not commission articles decorated with such exotic orientalizing motifs, in itself an illustration of the selective process mentioned above. Nor did they accept naturalistic figures or narrative sequence, while vegetable motifs and ornamental elements were accepted and adapted into twisting vines and spiral convolutions to fill even the smallest spaces with harmonious and curvilinear interlace. Already at this time the area that is now France had entered into such close empathy with the classical Mediterranean cultures that it did not share fully the formal sense of La Tène art.

A second orientalizing stimulus came from the expedition which Darius I, Great King of Persia, led against the Scythians (513–512 B.C.), followed by the incorporation of Thrace and Macedonia as satrapies of the Persian Empire. This location of Persian power in south-eastern Europe may have had an influence on the art of the northern Aegean and the western Black Sea coasts.

A third but related orientalizing stimulus may have entered Europe when Persian treasure lost during the Persian Wars (499–479 B.C.) was traded into the interior.[121] Many items such as helmets, beakers and cups, bearing the imprint of oriental fashion, appear to have been made by the native craftsmen of the area. The Danube would have served as the convenient waterway along which these articles would have reached points still further inland. During the Hallstatt mounted peoples had penetrated into eastern central Europe and the Carpathian Basin, bringing oriental wares and tastes into south-east central Europe.[122]

The sporadic Scythian raids between the sixth and fourth centuries discussed above, did not leave much material evidence, and even less information about the Scythian

204. Bronze hydra from the princely grave at Grächwil, near Berne, Switzerland. After *c.* 600 B.C. it was traded north from the western Mediterranean. It depicts the 'Mistress of Animals'.

influence on Celtic style. Nevertheless, in the animal-dominated iconography found occasionally in Celtic art can be seen an influence of the eastern nomads.[123] Both Celtic and Scythian art is held to be characterized by an identity of inspiration and artistic expression, by a vigorous dynamism full of imagination, and by a predilection for stylization, in that both shunned classical, naturalistic representation. Especially animals turning their heads to the rear, as well as confronting groups of animals, are seen to be an identifiable Scythian component in Celtic art.[124] The use of enamel and coral inlays is held to be yet another example of the Scythian influence.[125] Some seven hundred years later the use of enamel and coral in the art of the Germanic migrations will also be attributed to the contact between Goths and post-Scythian eastern nomads. Though the eastern animal style has access to Europe, it is far less influential than the style from the other areas of influence. It is evident that mythical beings and ferocious beasts met with no response among a people such as the Celts[126] whose attitude towards the universe did not find icons relevant. Instead of prizing sacred representations they chose to take great delight in the organic intertwine of calligraphic lines and the peculiar dynamism of space-filling ornamentation.

It was suggested above that the characteristic forms and motifs of the La Tène were descended from indigenous central European ornamental traditions and that the concepts basic to these motifs reflect the formal sense of the area. Perhaps from the

Paleolithic, but certainly from the Neolithic onward, a heritage of ornamentation reaches up to Celtic times. The extension of the Bronze Age Urnfield culture far into the Hallstatt period, as well as the duration of the Northern Bronze Age up to the beginning of the La Tène, the presence of Celtic oppida in northern central Germany and the north-south flow of exchange goods—in short, the persistence of the preceding cultures into later periods makes the questions of the ancestry of Celtic style and techniques, of direct contacts and possible influences much less a matter of conjecture. The contribution of the restlessness of the living designs of Bronze Age ornamentation to the La Tène style is not at all tenuous. To see the contribution of 'native' art only in terms of the transmission of linear Hallstatt geometrics would appear to be rather limited. More important is the Hallstatt component which contributed the tendency to create the effect of penetration and the actual perforation of the surface, thereby evoking an ambivalence between pattern and background—the creation of negative presence. It was pointed out that Hallstatt style as expressed by the body ornaments with their emphasis on body movement could be termed Baroque. The lighter style of Celtic art invites comparison with the Rococo.

The patrons of this art were the occupants of the princely wagon graves of the Celtic core region between the Danube and the Seine.[127] The lavish tastes of this rather selective ruling caste promoted the influx of goods from north, east and south, thereby providing the cultural climate in which the local craftsmen could develop that synthesis in which the various influences were kept in balance. It was the genius of the La Tène craftsmen which enabled them to adopt and transform these many influences into the characteristic non-representative curvilinear ornamental style, set quite apart from the representative intentions of the classical styles of the Mediterranean.[128] Though commissioned by the leading houses, the execution of the style does not reflect the changing tastes of changing dynasties. As was suggested above, the rapid dispersion of the Celts accompanied by the setting up of regional workshops provided variations on constant themes across a wide area, even within a short time span, so that the style of ornamentation in itself is no aid in the establishing of an absolute chronology.[129]

Reference was made to the possible religious-shamanistic motivation of Hallstatt art. Celtic art may have been similarly motivated. Owing to its abstract and non-communicative, non-narrative character, the spiritual message of prehistoric art is not accessible to us. Even in later Celtic art, in the so-called Insular Style of Celtic Christianity, which produced such masterpieces of calligraphic ornamentation as the Book of Kells, the magnificent non-figurative interlace will be pushed into the frame and ultimately rejected for its inability to convey the Christian message. The motifs of even early Celtic art hint at a mysterious cohesion of the universe based on some intuitive knowledge of hidden forces. Placed on the edge, in a position where man has empirical knowledge of one world and intuitive knowledge of another, he protects himself with magical ornaments and talismans. Perhaps that is the intended function of the sacred torc which a Celt wore around the neck, protection against the spiritual dangers which surround him on all sides and lurk just beyond his reach, ready to pounce upon him at certain times of the year, as is still reflected at Hallowe'en, and in similarly preserved customs in old Celtic areas of the Black Forest and the Alpine valleys. Against such supernatural dangers rituals and ritual art are the only safeguard. Centuries of education in the humanistic traditions of the Christian West interfere with our appreciation of non-figurative, abstract art—even with that of our own time.

It is interesting to note that the high period of Celtic art coincides with the late

276

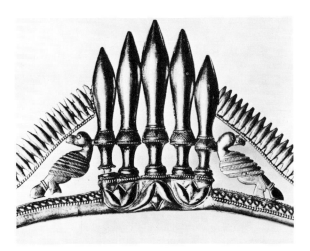

205. Gold torc from Besseringen near Merzig in the Palatinate, c. 500–450 B.C., probably an import from Persia.

206. Belt hook showing orientalizing influence, c. 450 B.C., from Weisskirchen, north-east of Merzig in the Palatinate.

Hallstatt and the early and early middle La Tène, the period of the princely burial mounds, of the wagon-chariot graves whose occupants, it has been argued, were members of the sacred monarchies, the royal priests. As was noted above, with the advent of the middle La Tène the archeological evidence points to a decline of prosperity reflected in an impoverishment of the grave inventories, to a discontinuance of the practice of raising regal burial mounds and preparing chariot graves, to the decline of Celtic art. The period witnesses the rise of the warlords and the onset of the Celtic migrations. By the time of Caesar's conquest of Gaul, Graeco-Roman influences had moved into the gap left in the Celtic core area by the fading Celtic cultural pre-eminence.[130] It needed only the military conquest of the Celts by the Romans to complete a process of acculturation begun several centuries earlier.

Before that happened, however, the Celts created a thoroughly original style of artistic expression of great ornamental beauty. Jacobsthal recognized three main divisions in early Celtic art, which he termed an Early Style, the Waldalgesheim Style for which he admitted a sub-group, the Sword Style, and the Plastic Style. It is possible that these divisions may not survive as the growing evidence raises local styles to new prominence.[131]

The Early Style of Celtic art has been dated to the first half of the fifth century B.C., by means of the association of Greek and Etruscan articles in the grave inventories. It is a less independent style, in that classical Mediterranean and oriental influences played a role in shaping it. Hence it admits to symmetry of composition and to representation. Though foreign inspiration is behind these objects, they are not copies but the experimental interpretive responses of local craftsmen to native and foreign stimuli.[132] It is of interest that even in such an early period of innovation and development we should encounter masterpieces.

The more spectacular pieces bear an oriental stamp, such as the gold torc from Besseringen (Fig. 205), which apparently is not just the product of an orientalizing influence but an authentic oriental import, probably from Achaemenian Persia.[133] On this torc two eagles in confronting positions, their heads turned back, flank five balusters in the middle. The origin of this motif is to be found in the Near East, from where it was introduced into central Europe as early as the Bronze Age, to be used in the sun-disc-flanking-waterbird symbolism. Thereafter the symbol returned to Europe on several occasions from the south and from the east, where Italic, Greek and Scythian peoples

277

were well-acquainted with it. Important to notice on the Besseringen torc is the perforated technique in which it was worked.

This orientalizing tendency is further demonstrated by the confronting disposition of animals on the bronze and coral inlaid belt buckle from Weisskirchen,[134] where confronting pairs of fantastic winged 'lions' flank a human mask, all with their heads turned back (Fig. 206). Even these are part bird, part human in design. Concern for the compactness of the composition has forced awkward positions on two of the griffins. While the two outer griffins sit comfortably on their haunches, the two inner ones are squatting uncomfortably on the coral inlaid pedestal, having to rest their forelegs on the paws of the other two. The mask is surmounted by inclined, spiraled ʃ-curves, while the pedestal bears characteristic Celtic lobes of coral inlay. Again the perforation technique, reminiscent of the Scythian animal style, is as apparent in the openwork as it is implied by the patterning of the coral inlay. Close examination reveals that the composition is not symmetrical. The griffins' wings, for instance, are not identical between the left and right groups.

Most resplendent in their orientalizing are the torc and arm ring from the princely grave at Reinheim.[135] The woman who wore these during the late fifth century evidently shared the ornate taste of the eastern Mediterranean. Through contacts between north and south, eastern stylistic elements had entered the Celtic lands, where they had been subjected to the northern formal sense. The arm ring is a hollow torc of gold, weighing 117·1 g, with the ends terminating in symmetrical compositions (Plate 6b). A human torso, arms held tightly across the chest, is surmounted by a masklike head wearing a bird stylization as a head-dress, a hooked beak and eyes hunched between inverted wings.[136] The composition terminates in droplet knobs over stylized owls' heads. The lower part of the body is intimated through abstract ʃ-curves which end in a triangular decoration. The symmetrical composition of the torc (Plate 6c) is related to that of the arm ring, in that the ends terminate in droplet knobs over owls, surmounting the same helmet-like head-dress shaped like a predatory bird. The head, however, is a carefully articulated, sharply profiled, smiling sphinx-like face, with a beaded cord around the neck which hangs down in three tassel ends. The number three is imbued with mystical powers in the Celtic inventory of symbols. The hollow gold torc is twisted evenly to form a 'thread' and weighs 187·2 g. Though the two rings exude a strong individuality, they are clearly related and the work of the same goldsmith. It is conceivable that the winged 'goddess' of these torcs is related to the 'Mistress of the Animals' on the Grächwil hydra, on whose head an eagle had been placed.[137] Using motifs current in the Celtic realms, the artists combined spirals, human and animal forms into a large number of works of great splendor in which the natural and supernatural worlds are fused (Fig. 207). Their number is far too numerous to be itemized here.

One innovation of the Early Style was the introduction of human faces into the Celtic orientalizations; another was the attachment of miniature figures, both human and animal, as the base of flagon handles, or as lid mounts (Fig. 208).[138] The use of coral for inlay mentioned above was also used for surface decoration, as the two brooches from the Reinheim grave indicate.

The classical heritage, sometimes intricately interwoven with others, is reflected in the presence of palmettes, lotus blossoms, vegetable designs, petals, parts of flowers,

207. Celtic flagon, after *c.* 450 B.C., from the Dürnberg near Hallein, Austria.

208. Celtic flagon, after *c.* 450 B.C., from Schwarzenbach near Otzenhausen in the Palatinate.

foliage, lyres, heads and tendrils, to name just a few. It is this repertoire of forms which was to prove productive for the next decorative period. The most likely source for these motifs is northern Italy and especially Etruria of the fifth century.[139] Bearing some of these motifs are perforated gold bands from the regal grave at Reinheim. Not particularly elegant in execution, the perforations do not contribute to that optical ambivalence which encourages the elusive play between design and background. Here the perforations are meaningless holes. More intricate and explicit are the two ornamental strips of gold foil from Waldgallscheid which show palmettes sprouting from among the feet of the two outward leaning ʃ-shaped lyres (Fig. 209). Here again the perforated intervals are meaningless. Only the gold outlines the pattern.

The most superb piece, however, is the unique bowl from the Celtic grave mound at Schwarzenbach in the Hunsrück (Plate 7a).[140] It has been suggested that the original bowl was probably of red clay, or perhaps of wood. In either case the intervals emphasized by the golden openwork decoration may not have provided as vivid a contrast as the modern mounting of gold on black. The gold work, only partially preserved, consists of four separately worked parts: the plain upper rim folded over a bronze core; a narrow strip ornamented with an arcade of hanging lotus buds; the dominant central panel subdivided into two zones of openwork; and a sheet gold base decorated in repoussé, its rim decorated with an inverted arcade of standing lotus buds.

209. Ornamental gold strips, *c.* 450 B.C., from Waldgallscheid near St. Goar on the middle Rhine.

Between the arcades of hanging and standing lotus buds the openwork comes to life in a magnificent composition of luxuriant lotus blossoms, palmettes, discs, lobes and leaves, their contours emphasized through repoussé, giving a granular effect to the outlines starkly silhouetted against a dark background. Close examination of the sheet gold base shows a most intricate repoussé pattern of two-leaved lotus blossoms and two flanking three-part whirligigs. Whirligig, lotus blossom, whirligig constitute a group formed by a continuous running line with the interval between the whirligigs of the consecutive groups forming inverted lyres. Standing on the lotus bud arcade of the rim the pattern grows in toward the center. The intricacy of the center is such that combinations of gracefully interlinked spiral ʃ-curves form intervals of inverted lyres and lotus blossoms, or of lotus blossoms and lyres, which have intervals of three-part whirligigs, giving that familiar and elusive play between pattern and background, with the difference that in the spiral patterns of the base, whether lyre, lotus or whirligig, the interval is not just a meaningless space, as in the two zones of openwork, but forms a self-sufficient design from the range of Celtic ornamental motifs. The entire composition is an excellent example of the imaginative subtlety and great artistic skill displayed in the Early Style.

Another aspect of ornamental openwork is provided by the Celtic belt hooks, such as the one from Hölzelsau in the Alps.[141] Here a manikin is suspended in a lyre formed by confronting ʃ-curves, of which each terminal is the shape of a horse's head, with very pronounced engraved eyes. The ʃ-curves rest on a closed lyre which again terminates in horseheads. Duck-like birds are attached to the outside of the sweeping curves of the lyre. The composition forms a pyramid in which the manikin is suspended upside down, its hands holding the horses' muzzles. It has been suggested that the animals in these pyramidal compositions of interlinked anthropomorphic, animal and decorative forms are of eastern origin, perhaps an influence of the Scythian Animal Style. The belt hook in question had broken in Celtic times and had been reinforced with a bronze backing. Evidence of Celtic metal workshops extends well into central Germany where the mineral deposits of Thuringia provided the necessary supply of ores.

The period of the Early Style also knows monumental stone sculptures. Wooden ones, which may well have existed, have not survived.[142] More pieces have probably survived than is realized, since many stone heads, for instance, were used in the ornamentation of Christian churches of later periods, especially during the Romanesque period. No doubt the relocation of these sculptures into a consecrated context was prompted by the attempt to render harmless any residual ominous powers. It would appear that the religious connotation was either transmitted through an oral tradition, or sensed. The dating of the few extant examples can only be based on style of workmanship and ornamentation.

It is useful to recall the life-size stone statue of a Hallstatt warrior which once surmounted the burial mound at Hirschlanden. Characterized by naturalistic legs, but by a highly stylized torso, this funerary stele bears some resemblance to a Janus-headed stone sculpture from Holzgerlingen (Fig. 210) in south-west Germany.[143] Attributed to the earliest La Tène, the earliest fifth century B.C., this double-sided stone pillar has been taken to represent some ancient mythical figure. Its anthropomorhic shape is indicated by a very elementary relief of the right arm, once bent over the stomach on the obverse and again on the reverse, and by a very rudimentary Janus-head, whose two faces show no expression and only the simplest facial outlines. One facial side is badly worn. The waist is marked by a wide flat belt without buckle. Below the belt the stele is an unarticulated block of stone terminating in a tenon joint for placement in a solid socket,

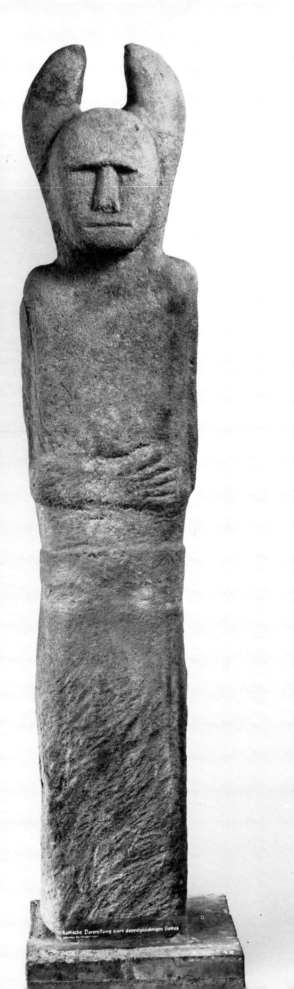

such as a wall. Rising from the shoulders, a 'twin-horned' head-dress, a so-called leaf-crown, extends above the head on both sides. The stele is about 2·25 m tall and four-sided. It is not a sculpture in the round.

Janus heads were a frequent motif among the Celts. The earliest Celtic janiform heads appear to have originated in central Europe, or along the Rhine, and do not seem to have come up the Rhône from the Mediterranean into the Celtic core area.[144] It is consequently hazardous to assume any link between these janiform heads and the Roman god Janus, though the tenon joint on the Holzgerlingen stele could mean that like the Roman Janus, this figure too was a stern deity set up, perhaps over a gable, from which vantage point it could face ahead and behind, who saw past and future, who saw the two worlds between which life unfolded. It is not unduly surprising that these polar opposites should be brought together in the same figure.

A clear link between the ornamental style of the metal workers and those working in stone is the four-sided tapering stele from Pfalzfeld (Fig. 211), west of St. Goar on the Rhine.[145] Again, this is not a sculpture in the round. Today it stands about 1·50 m tall, the top having broken off. Drawings made of it in 1608 and again in 1739 show it to have been taller, but already then the tip was missing. Perhaps it too had terminated in a janiform head and had fallen victim to an attack by idol smashers. As late as 1739 folklore held the obelisk to have had a head. Upon its entrance into history in 1608 it is recorded to have been located just east of the apse of the village church, a site to which it had probably been moved not for safekeeping but as a means of rendering the old magic impotent. It cannot be denied that the stele evokes phallic associations. The early drawings show its bulbous base placed above ground. The four surfaces are not dressed accurately, while a cross-cut shows that the four corners are not uniformly cut at right angles, so that the taper of any one of the sides is askew. This irregularity is echoed in the ornamentation. Though each panel bears the same ornamentation, the designs are asymmetrical and the panels are not congruent. Each trapezoid surface is framed by a rope pattern. On each panel there are linked ʃ-curves and a leaf pattern just inside the frame, and an inverted lyre just beneath the break. The most notable feature on each side is the pear-shaped head with the exaggerated 'ear lobes', the so-called leaf crown rising above it and an inverted 'fleur-de-lis' design extending downward from the chin. The resemblance of this pendant motif to the tassels hanging from the neck ring of the 'sphinx' on the Reinheim torc is striking. It will also be recalled that one of the urns of the Western Hallstatt, discussed above, bore an angular sepia design of a face with two inverted triangles rising above it, quite similar in conception to the curvilinear heads of this stele. The heads are not truly vertical, nor are they on the same level, nor do they have the same facial expression. Each head wears a headband from which rises a trefoil. It is apparent that the four panels are no more than decorated surfaces. Interlinked ʃ-curves surround the tapering base. The Celtic integration of faces into the spirals or tendrils gives rise to that characteristic Celtic ambiguity, the interrelatedness of living things blurring the contours, as specific delineations evolve from one representation into another. In this fashion the Pfalzfeld heads, as well as the Heidelberg fragment, combine organic motifs with human images. Never, however, is nature the actual model.

The head fragment from Heidelberg (Fig. 212) may very well be the type of head

210. Janus-headed stone sculpture from Holzgerlingen, south-west of Stuttgart.

211. Tapering four-sided stele, *c.* 300 B.C., from Pfalzfeld, west of St. Goar on the middle Rhine.

212. Front view of a head fragment, *c.* 400 B.C., from Heidelberg.

213. Rear view of the head fragment from Heidelberg.

which surmounted a stele such as the one described above.[146] It bears some of the same characteristics as do the heads represented on the Pfalzfeld pillar, the leaf crown serving both faces, the trefoil on the brow, the stylized face and the penetrating stare. The back of the head bears another face (Fig. 213), though this one is extremely stylized. Two arched lines—one from the left, the other one from the right—slice the circular face into sections dominated by large oval 'eyes'. While this stylized face is completely rounded, the facial features on the front show only eyebrows, eyes and nose, the mouth and chin area having broken off. Is this a Janus head? Why the difference in stylization? Why does the face on the reverse appear to be complete in contrast to the fragment on the obverse?[147] Are the two faces contemporary? If the janiform steles could see in front and behind, were they a part of the ritual inventory? What of the four heads on the Pfalzfeld stele; do they also play a role in man's dealings with the world of the supernatural? Do these pillars form a component in the arsenal of ritual safeguards? Were they thought to be imbued with magical powers and was their decapitation a form of magic? Is there any significance in the persistent stare with which these heads confront the viewer?

It is conceivable that the small number of stone monuments is to be attributed directly to the iconoclasm of early and medieval Christianity, which saw in these stone figures heathen images and connections with pagan cults. On the other hand many more stone heads of Celtic origin could probably be identified among the head representations in central European churches, especially those of the Romanesque period.[148]

The fascination with heads evident in the *têtes coupées* of the south-western Celtic realms, especially those in Provence, points to the cultic importance of heads in Celtic ritual.[149] Ancient sources had the Celts appear to be head hunters, who attached their enemies' heads to their saddles. A head cult is seen to be the central tenet of a brutal faith among the Celts. From the Rhineland no such evidence is extant. Nevertheless, disembodied heads interwoven with foliage and vines, in association with animals, were to stimulate many of the ornamental motifs of the Insular Style in Celtic Christian Art, and of the decorative friezes of the Romanesque.

The shortage of finds of monumental art has caused art historians to assign to Celtic portable art perhaps an undue significance. The wealth of vegetable motifs can, however, also be found in stone relief from the early fourth century. Celtic art of the fourth century B.C. can be called Classical in that the characteristic ornamental motifs assert

284

themselves with unparalleled uniqueness and elegance. This Classical period is not the result of an evolutionary process in some Darwinian sense which insists on a sequence of generation, maturity and degeneration, for there is evident coexistence of quite individualistic stylistic variations. Nor does it suddenly subordinate its essential linearity to a more representational and naturalist manner of depiction. Instead it maintains its imaginative originality, its fascination for a mysterious unreality of dismemberment, which suggests hostility to the representation of nature. Consistent with earlier practice, humans and animals are not portrayed realistically but are abstracted in conformity with the dematerializing techniques of ornamentation. The falsification, explosion and misappropriation of forms and fragments is its chief characteristic. Treated with a virtuosity not previously encountered, geometrical designs are animated to become living ornaments arranged into intricate space-filling patterns of an extraordinarily delicate elegance and grace. The creative blending of stylizations of human, animal and vegetable patterns gives evidence of a fantastic imagination with a limitless ability to transform the visible into abstractions.[150] When this period enters its decline, the ornamental art just comes to a halt and is not marked by degeneration. Many centuries later, a new stimulus will cause it to flourish into new life.

Within the 'Classic' style there is evidence of a particularly individualistic personality at work, identified by the 'Waldalgesheim Style', attributed to the workshops of one anonymous Master of Waldalgesheim.[151] In 1869 a farmer disturbed a rich Celtic double chariot burial dated into the later fourth century B.C. The grave was found at Waldalgesheim, just west of Bingen on the Rhine. Its contents of personal jewellery and wagon fittings gave insight, for the first time, into the intricate stylistic innovations used by the Celts along the middle Rhine, making it a stylistic type station of the middle La Tène. The grave contained a situla from the Campagna in Italy, dated to the fourth century B.C. and probably brought north by Etruscan traders or agents.[152] The association of the finds with this classical piece allowed an approximate dating of the grave; even the patina on the vessel corresponded to that on the other Celtic articles in the grave. Of special importance to our discussion is the embossed floral ornament under the handles, since this ornamental motif is considered to have provided one of several stimuli for the Waldalgesheim Style. The motif is an inverted pyramid composed of symmetrically arranged leaves and flanked by ʃ-spiraled tendrils to give it the appearance of a broad curved triangle. Of course such curved triangles were not a totally new motif in Celtic art, as demonstrated among the pieces of the Schwarzenbach find.[153]

The grave yielded a severely damaged flagon, evidently an heirloom, since its engraved ornamentation assigns it to the Early Style, a solidly cast bronze bracelet of 'beaded' bronze balls, two ornamented horn-terminals off the chariots, a damaged openwork fair-lead cast as a whole, four looped 'eyes' of bronze with decorative enamel, two sheet bronze mountings with repoussé heads and stylized bodies, interlinked openwork plaques with intertwining perforated figure-eight patterns, an engraved flat ring, an iron linch-pin and, among the most important finds, two torc-shaped arm rings and a torc (Plate 7b).[154] The golden torc, almost 20 cm in diameter, was assembled from independently finished parts—the curved triangle repoussé patterns of the actual hoop, the cushions decorated with friezes of continuous serpentines, the two concave rings which link the cushion with the buffers ornamented with ʃ-spirals, and lastly the ornamented base-plate. The fittings of these different components are disguised through the attachment of gold wire beads. The torc itself is tubular and undecorated. Though the basic structural component of the curved triangle are two ascending pairs of ʃ-spirals, the cohesive elements of the base of the triangle are crossover tendrils which create a figure-eight effect. That same figure-eight crossover is to be found in the same location on the two arm rings, 6·5 cm in diameter, just behind the buffers. Here a broader curved triangle, more squat in shape, completes the figure eight. Unlike the torc, the arm rings are decorated with polymorphous repoussé ornamentation. Arranged in freehand symmetry, the relief works into the center from the tips of curved triangles, to convex cushions of sequential 'Phrygian cap' half-spirals, to the central field consisting of an ornamented encircling crossover band which unites the two halves of the pattern advancing from both sides. At the point where the encircling band intersects, two antithetical mask-like faces peer out of the triangular spaces. The various parts of the ornamentation are delineated by repoussé dots.

Only occasional faces emerge from among the intertwining coils. The two sheet bronze mountings are all the more interesting because they each bear a repoussé head and stylized torso (Fig. 214). Quite disintegrated when first found, they have been restored to show pear-shaped heads, akin to those of the Pfalzfeld obelisk, and surmounted by so-called Egyptian Hathor, or Near Eastern Astarte wigs with upturned lobe-curls,[155] not unlike some modern hairstyles. Even with the upturned curls, the resemblance with the stone head and its leaf-crown from Heidelberg is apparent. Of greater interest though is the space-filling repoussé ornamentation of the chest, shoulders and arms, where the intertwining flexibility of the crossover motif demonstrates how easily it could be adapted to the ornamentation of any surface, to the inclusion of any variation of linear or curvilinear themes.

It might be expected that such openwork techniques continued into the period of the Waldalgesheim Style. The apparent Celtic fascination for the ambivalent optical abstracting play with positive and negative space, with positive and negative presence, so familiar to the northern artists, is also in evidence in this chariot grave. In this particular instance, however, and quite unlike contemporary pieces found elsewhere, on the Waldalgesheim objects the negative spaces play an entirely subordinated role in that they do not constitute an independently interlinked design but serve only to silhouette the positive pattern. Such is the case with the bronze fair-lead as well as with the figure-eight plaques. Nevertheless the translucence of the design does not submit to the opaqueness of the form.

These, and many similar articles from other sites,[156] delight in the beautification of even discouragingly small surfaces of any shape with curving, pliable and adaptable triangles composed of tendrils or tentacles writhing across the surface with coiled alertness and reptilian grace. This lends to the economic surface treatment an uncoiling restlessness, made all the more interesting not because of an innate careless spontaneity but because of its studied imprecision. In spite of their freehand symmetry, the harmony which these compositions achieve make one's preoccupation with them a satisfying exercise. On the other hand, the centrifugal tensions guarantee to the design the endurance of its inherent dynamism. After the end of the fourth century B.C. the style of the continental Celts displayed the necessary strength to confront successfully further foreign influences.

A related variation of the Waldalgesheim style is to be found on sword scabbards and lance blades where organic patterns have been stamped on the surfaces, very much from that same inventory of patterns already discussed, though particularly fascinating for their originality in positioning the ornamental designs (Fig. 215).[157] While the Waldalgesheim workmen practised modeling in the round, this Sword Style knows

214. Sheet bronze mountings from Waldalgesheim.

surface ornamentation only. While one Hallstatt sword scabbard had been ornamented with designs as well as with narrative strips, the La Tène swords and lances of the second century B.C., depict only the patterning of surface designs. Pleasantly surprising is the ingenuity and nonconformity with which the armorer decorated his weapons. The quality of Swiss swords made them a desirable article of trade. Their tendency to be found in lakes, ponds and rivers, as well as in moors and swamps, suggests that the sacrificial rites already followed during the Bronze Age and even earlier were still being practised during the second century B.C. and even later (Fig. 216).[158] It also suggests that such ornamental weapons played a particular cultic role and that the ornamentation, not only on the swords, had a magic function *vis-à-vis* the unknown forces which dwelt beyond the frontiers of personal experience, beyond the grave and death.

Prior to this Sword Style variation, another three-dimensional style had asserted itself during the third century B.C., to which Jacobsthal had given the name Plastic Style and which had provided the Celts with objects worked in the round.[159] Because of their alien appearance, one sees in them a Celtic response to influences absorbed in the south-east during the Celtic migrations.[160] The greatest number of such objects comes from Moravia, near the eastern edge of central Europe.[161] This Plastic Style concerns itself with the representation of opaque forms rather than with the suggestion of evasive designs, and an expression of the mysteries of the Celtic imagination can be found in it, but not the Celtic sense of style. Human, semi-human and animal forms found admission into the inventory of forms (Fig. 217). It is a characteristic of this style that the artists disposed rather freely of their subject matter. The Celtic artists dismembered and reassembled their forms into rather fanciful creatures, whose disparate features were held together in such curvilinear arrangements as became characteristic for the illuminated gospels of the Celto-Christian Insular Style. The characteristics just described

215. Engraved space-filling ornamental designs, the 'Sword Style', after *c.* 200 B.C. (after Jacobsthal, *Early Celtic Art*, Plate 73, No. 129).

216. Engraved ornamental designs, the 'Sword Style', after *c.* 200 B.C. (after Jacobsthal, *Early Celtic Art*, Plate 279, No. 472).

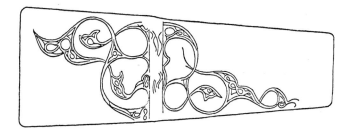

217. Hubnails, after *c.* 100 B.C., from the Celtic oppidum at Manching.

218. Celtic flagon from the Dürnberg near Hallein, Austria.

predominate in eccentric combinations of animal, vegetable and human masses and fragments[162] intertwined with curvilinear interlace blended into grotesque and mythical formations to form bows and catchplates of fibulae, or handles on flagons and other receptacles. The human features never predominate (Fig. 218). In spite of that, their relationship to the object remains ornamental, especially if one takes into account the coral and enamel settings in eyes and nostrils with which such objects had been studded. As such these Celtic three-dimensional forms are the conscious expression of a baroque formal sense characteristic for central Europe.[163] Three-dimensional they may be, but they are still not representational art. At most they suggest a growing preparedness to accept living forms as a third alternative to vegetable and geometric designs.

The Celtic inclination towards the heavily ornamental is also reflected in body ornaments, especially in heavy bronze bracelets, or possibly anklets, worked in a very pronounced plasticity.[164] Conceivably a more elaborate articulation developed from earlier arm rings; the bracelets worked in this Plastic Style have acquired such globular features as balls of different sizes, piggy-back groupings, knobs decorated as though with coral clusters, blisters, bosses, horizontally placed ∫-spirals, and polyhedrons arranged in hills and valleys. The knobs on some rings are exaggerated to resemble vertically bisected halves of eggshells (Fig. 219). Some protrusions are 3·7 cm high.[165] The knobs of which the bangles have been assembled are generally hemispheric or

288

219. 'Eggshell' rings, from Scharditz in Moravia.

220. Celtic ankle rings, from Klettham near Erding in Bavaria, third or second century B.C.

hollow. Their surfaces are worked as contorted and interlocking spirals, interlacing contoured triangular whirligigs, lyres and facial features with slanting eyes, the whole ring assembly appearing to have been encrusted with barnacles (Fig. 220). The inner perimeter may be round or polygonal. What impresses most about these body ornaments is their rugged and powerful workmanship. Though some rings come from Switzerland, here too Bohemia, south-eastern Germany, Austria and Hungary have yielded the bulk of the finds, suggesting south-east central Europe to be the production center of such bracelets.

In conclusion it can be said that in spite of the great extent of our later preoccupation with the Celts the origins of their art cannot yet be specified beyond saying that Classical, Eastern and Bronze Age and hence also Hallstatt elements were involved in the synthesis. This confluence produced essentially linear, especially curvilinear, two-dimensional, decorative designs in a deliberately non-anthropomorphic mode, generally satisfied with surface ornamentation. Even its zoomorphic designs avoid an overt representation of living things. Nature appears only in stylized forms, in geometrics and floral decorations, with only the occasional concession to stylizations of the human head. The indifference to imitation and realistic representations appears to be total. Instead the explosion of forms, their dismemberment and deformation appear to be the aim. One senses the effects of mythology lurking behind the designs. That Celtic art is an integral part of its religious context can be assumed quite readily even if it is not narrative and not expressed in iconic terms. Even the Plastic Style plays with forms (Fig. 221). The term 'Baroque' is frequently applied to the conception and execution of Iron Age art. Within that classification the Waldalgesheim Style represents something of a refinement, excelled in fragile elegance only by the 'Rococo' traceries of the Sword Style. The Plastic Style continues earlier formal intentions. It is quite evident that for Celtic art the term 'Baroque' does not characterize an end-stage, a stage of culture fatigue and decline. Where would its generation and maturity have to be sought? The art of the Celts does not know this orderly textbook sequence. As has been observed with the other cultural aspects discussed above, never are all regions in the same phase, resolving the same concerns, or even linked with one another pursuing a common formulation. The Celtic realms were not a uniformly organized commonwealth. Instead it may be suggested that far from yearning for noble classical simplicity and quiet

289

221. Silver torc from Trichtingen. The torc has an iron core. It weighs 6.744 kg, and may have been made in the Balkans.

grandeur, Celtic art is Romantic art,[166] one which prefers the unresolved tensions, the erratic to the rational, asymmetry to symmetry, imbalance to balance, abstraction to representation, open to closed form, translucence to opaqueness, the organic to the tectonic, and the amorphous to the morphous.[167] Because it does not objectify, the meaning of Celtic art is less accessible, a circumstance which encounters a lack of humanistic understanding engendered by centuries of schooling in the Humanistic traditions of the Mediterranean, and which always considered being, especially man, as the measure of all things rather than as their echo.

The submersion of the Celts in the Gallo-Roman culture of the Roman Empire did not transform completely the cultural climate which had produced early Celtic art. Already earlier the geographic dislocation of some Celtic tribal groups towards the European north-west had rescued aspects of Celtic art, from where it was to reassert itself during the early Christian centuries north of the Alps. But even here the non-narrative, space-filling ornamentations of such works as the Book of Kells, the First Cover of the Lindau Gospel, or the Tassilo Chalice, to name just three,[168] had to yield their ornamental pre-eminence to representations of effigies, until they had again been displaced from the surface of illuminated pages, gospel covers and holy vessels. Once again however, by way of Mediterranean floral patterns a synthesis of northern motifs will find its way smoothed for entry into the medieval ornamental inventory of the cloister arts and of church architecture. This is not an instance of stylistic tenacity, but more probably a fundamental response to a view of the universe, a consistent expression of a trans-alpine psychology, which will henceforth not be absorbed by outside influences but which will transform them.

222. Assembled wagon fragments, after *c.* 100 B.C., from Dejbjerg on Jylland, Denmark.

223. Repoussé mask and metal cut-outs from the Dejbjerg wagon.

224. Cauldron fragment, *c.* 100 B.C., from Rynkeby near Kerteminde on Funen.

Two objects of related interest were found in Denmark. These are the fragments of a bronze cauldron found in a bog at Rynkeby on Funen, and most of the component pieces of a unique silver cauldron found in 1891 at Gundestrup on Jutland. A third piece, of cultic rather than of artistic interest, is the reconstructed four-wheeled wagon from the bog at Dejbjerg on Jutland (Fig. 222).[169] The pieces were found in 1881 and in 1883, scattered about the moor. They belonged to two different wagons which had been taken apart and deposited as offerings. It is argued that these items originated in central Europe.[170] It is also agreed that the Rynkeby vessel and the pieces of the ceremonial wagon are of Celtic origin. Described as ritual wagons and commonly associated with the cult around the Germanic goddess Nerthus mentioned by Tacitus, the Celtic evidence consists of four repoussé human masks and the rather stereotyped patterns of late La Tène ornamental metal cut-outs fastened to the wagon (Fig. 223). The Nerthus cult will be discussed in a later chapter. The Celtic origin of the Rynkeby fragment is indicated by the head of a woman worked in relief, complete with 'Hathor' wig and lobe curls (Fig. 224), reminiscent of the two heads on the mountings of sheet bronze found at Waldalgesheim, and the massive torc with buffer terminals. The head is flanked by two bull torsos with raised forelegs.[171] The cauldron was made of thinly hammered plates of sheet-bronze riveted together. The inside surface of very accomplished repoussé workmanship depicts a boar and a wolf-like creature. It is estimated that this cauldron was made by southern central European craftsmen during the first century before our era.

Much more enigmatic is the silver cauldron from the bog at Gundestrup. Initially it was too readily identified as Celtic in origin. The analysis of its workmanship, of its themes, its scenes and the apparent influences upon it which has been carried out over

292

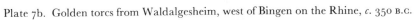

Plate 7a. Openwork gold leaf bowl fittings, *c.* 450 B.C., from Schwarzenbach near Otzenhausen in the Palatinate.

Plate 7b. Golden torcs from Waldalgesheim, west of Bingen on the Rhine, *c.* 350 B.C.

225. Repoussé plate from the so-called cauldron from Gundestrup, in western Himmerland on Jylland, Denmark, *c.* 100 B.C.

the last few decades suggests that the pieces came into being in a region which witnessed the convergence of contributing influences, such as in the Carpathian Basin. From there a short portage over intervening mountain ranges would have brought the vessel into the long established north–south trade pattern which followed the routes down the Elbe, Oder or Vistula rivers to the sources of the amber, fur and perhaps even of the slave trade. In addition, the common source of silver was Spain and the Carpathians. Gaul to the west of the Rhine, let alone Spain, is held to be an unlikely origin for the vessel, since such a route would be contrary to the established, almost natural trade patterns once the vessel had crossed the Rhine. Coming from the west it would have had to buck the current created by the enforced retromigration of the Celts and the westward relocation of their cultural centers. Motifs found in Thrace, Bulgaria and southern Czechoslovakia worked in Persian, Scythian and Thracian techniques have been shown to have an intrinsic affinity with some of the motifs present on the Gundestrup cauldron. Some of the evidence makes the silver cauldron an eastern piece with orientalizing elements. Some other elements appear to be Celtic in theme. Differences

226. Outer plate from the Gundestrup cauldron.

in workmanship and in sophistication allow the conclusion that various craftsmen created the bowl and panels out of which the cauldron came to be fashioned.[173] It is conceivable that the component repoussé panels and bowl-shaped base had not originally been intended to form a bowl but some other shape and that its function as a bowl had been a secondary utilization. That it was used as a bowl, even with an inner panel missing, is indicated by the slit-sleeve fitting set on the vertical panels to form a rim. The cauldron had been taken apart—the panels were found lying in the base—at the time of its deposition in the moor, perhaps to defuse its alien magical powers and to make it a fitting votive offering to the spirits who inhabited the locale, in conformity with practices already observed during the Bronze Age. The debris which had collected in the bowl indicates that it stood exposed for a long time before it settled. It can be assumed that the exotic animals and strange events depicted on the cauldron were something of a mystery to its last owners. Heirs of the Northern Bronze, they had become a proto-Germanic group of peoples, who, by the time of the La Tène, can be identified in central Germany by their pottery—the Jastorf, Ripdorf and Seedorf ceramic cultures. The two cauldrons and the ritual wagon are conclusive evidence, however, that Celtic and Germanic peoples engaged in the exchange of goods of great cultural and material value. That the cauldron was a precious object, and hence a worthy offering, may have been the prime consideration in its acquisition. It may of course have come north as tribute or as booty. Occasional resident or itinerant Celtic artists among the Germanic tribes may have had a hand in some Celtic pieces found in Schleswig and in Denmark, such as the Dejbjerg wagons. For the Gundestrup cauldron this is most unlikely.

The cauldron was reassembled to form a vessel 42 cm high and 69 cm in diameter.[174] One of the inner plates is missing. The cauldron weighs 9 kg. Whatever its quality as a receptacle may have been, it is impressive for its workmanship—the embossing, chasing and finishing—even though it is ambivalent in its meaning (Fig. 225). One must once again attribute to it an obscure cultic function. In that sense the figures, animals, plants and other objects can be seen to represent gods and their attributes, while the events represented become ritualistic exercises. Attempts to interpret each detail of the various panels have on occasion risen to rhapsodic heights, making of its several artists spokesmen of a higher awareness of the formative processes of the soul in search of harmony and balance, guardians of the secrets of a supra-sensual form of being, who knew of the secrets of transfiguration.[175]

Because the artwork is representational and in some instances even narrative, these silver panels stand out as not being typical Celtic work. Neither are such exotic and ferocious creatures as lions, dragons, dogs with a head at both ends, griffins, elephants, 'spotted' wolves, ram-headed snakes and 'Minoan' bulls to be found on works normally associated with the Celts.[176] And if one also considers that the techniques used to indicate variations in surface texture are eastern—different types of punches to achieve different effects—then it is apparent that the cauldron is not the product of a purely Celtic imagination. That an unretrievable mythology lurks behind the scenes represented can be safely assumed. The base plate which shows a bull about to rise, its body worked in relief and its head sculpted in the round, indicates a decidedly oriental technique. In general it can be said that the Gundestrup cauldron lacks the gentle elegance associated so far with the organic interlacing patterns of the western Celtic ornamental tradition. All the more reason to seek the origin of the cauldron in the transition areas of the former eastern Hallstatt culture, an area long familiar with realistic narrative techniques, the situla art for instance, and with anthropomorphic representations.

The outer plates of the cauldron do not show events.[177] They bear static representations of four male and three female torsos, the heads usually flanked by other figures both human and animal, fantastic in appearance. All figures are placed in some relationship with one another, dancing, wrestling, holding one another. While the torsos are only roughed in, the upraised hands of the dominant figure, and especially the heads, are expressed in great detail. In representing the hair, and especially the beards, the artists at work on this collective effort paid careful attention to detail (Fig. 226). On one panel a subsidiary 'servant' figure is busy braiding the hair of the 'goddess', twisting four strands of hair into three. Almost all of the torsos are wearing torcs. Attempts have been made to interpret these groups of figures as cultic units and symbolizations of the affairs of gods and mortals. If these torsos are gods and goddesses arranged in polar opposites of trinities, then they reflect the influences of the eastern Mediterranean, the Aegean and Pontic regions. Among the western Celts it is not appropriate to speak of a

227. Inner plate of the Gundestrup cauldron, *c.* 100 B.C., showing the 'bull sacrifice'.

228. Inner plate of the Gundestrup cauldron, showing the 'circular parade'.

'Pantheon' in pre-Roman times,[178] since that suggests ideas about gods in anthropomorphic shape, and the gods of the pre-Roman western Celts were represented in animal form, as stags, bulls, horses, boars and birds of prey and were probably treated as totems, as ancestral animals. It is worth considering that animals had been associated with divinities as early as the Paleolithic and that zoomorphic gods may have been the indigenous divinities of central Europe.

While the outer panels impress with their symbolic stability, the inner plates suggest movement and the narration of events,[179] though thematically two panels—a female torso flanked by two elephants, two griffins, two wheels, and a wolf beneath the torso, the other a male torso holding half a wheel held by a figure wearing a horned helmet, flanked by two spotted wolves and surmounting three griffins and a ram-headed snake— actually belong with the outer panels. The panels do not fit completely. Three inner panels are quite unlike all the others, although cross-references of detail indicate a relationship between them. On one panel three very powerful bulls worked in relief are about to be stabbed in the chest by three men poised below and in front of them (Fig. 227). Beneath every bull and at the level of the men a voracious dog-like leaping animal is situated, while above them a spotted feline is tensely crouched. The tail of each bull resembles an ear of grain. Foliage surrounds the bulls. No doubt the scene with its depiction of tension and vitality records a purging sacrifice. Details of the clothing are consistent with that worn by the subsidiary figures on the outer panels. A very Celtic scene is represented on a panel which shows a 'circular' parade (Fig. 228). The incidence of Celtic details is significant in that the warriors carry Celtic shields, some wear animal-crested helmets, and three blow war trumpets—carnyx—with boar-headed bells such as the Galatians are reported to have used in order to demoralize their enemies.[180] Skeletal analysis made at Manching even identified the skeletal type of the horses represented on this panel as being a breed actually used by the Celts.[181] The scene is divided horizontally by a flowering 'tree'. The scene is dominated by a tall figure which raises the body of a man upside down in order to immerse him in a cauldron. Approaching the cauldron from beneath the horizontal tree is a squad of six men armed with shields, spears and round helmets, followed by a man with only a 'sword' over his shoulder, but wearing a boar-crested helmet, followed by three carnyx blowers. In the section above the horizontal tree four spurred horsemen appear to be galloping away from the immersion, one of each pair with lances at the ready. Their

229. Miniature animals, probably mountings, from Gutenberg-Balzers in Liechtenstein.

230. Inner plate from the Gundestrup cauldron, showing a horned figure seated among animals.

helmets are crested with an arc, horns, a boar and a bird respectively (Fig. 229). Whether the snake which precedes them at eye level is meant to be in their van, or merely above the carnyx is not certain. In front of the advancing spearmen and directly beneath the cauldron a canine animal rises on its hind legs, its paws held out in front as though to hold back the troop. It is tempting to see circular movement in this scene as the spearmen advance up to the cauldron in order to be immersed and then to ride away on horseback. That would suggest a death–rebirth cycle, which would make the scene the artistic projection of an initiation–transfiguration ritual. The circular arrangement of the scene could lead us to believe that. It is possible that what looks like a cauldron is really the opening of one of those deep Celtic pits in which some hapless victim is being sacrificed by a larger than life 'sacerdot', the royal priest, with the armed menfolk in attendance, an event so rare that it was found worthy of being represented. It should be remembered that the Gundestrup cauldron is not a document on which is recorded a certain aspect of the religious life. It can only appear to us as an artistic expression in a visionary mode.

Compared to the order which reigns in these two panels, the last one is chaotic and full of unrest (Fig. 230). The scene is crowded with animals: two bulls, eastern in origin, two confronting and pawing lions, a dog which resembles the lions in the sweep of its tail and its scale-like mane, a spotted wolf and, most curiously, a man on a dolphin, a Mediterranean motif. Much of the space is filled with leaves, mostly arranged in groups of three. The panel is dominated, however, by a figure seated Buddha-fashion, not unlike some early Celtic stone sculpture from south-eastern France, wearing the same striped and belted knee-length suit as all the other figures, including the 'royal priest' from the panel to the left. This figure holds a horned snake in its left hand and a torc in its right. It also wears a torc around the neck. The face is beardless. The man wears a helmet crested with a stag's antlers. This antler-crested figure has stimulated much debate. It has been seen as a shaman who can assume guises and change shapes,[182] or the Horned God, the Lord of the Animals, or an initiate attaining a mystical level, but most often and by means of retroactive attribution one sees in it the Celtic Stag God Cernunnos. The basis for this view is a unique but defective inscription and quite similar representation on a Celtic altar dedicated to the god Esus located under Notre Dame in Paris.[183] Most monuments come from central and south-eastern Gaul and date from the first century A.D. The link between antler-crested divinities and the god Cernunnos need not be compelling, since their age may well predate Celtic and even Indo-European times. Besides, antler-crested helmets were not uncommon. The tradition which sees great religious significance in the stag as a symbol of demonic vitality and virility has a great past. As an influential force it caused the conversion of St. Hubert when he encountered the legendary stag with a cross located between its antlers. The meaning of the composition on the cauldron remains a riddle, an unintelligible juxtaposition of mysterious cultic relationships.

As has been mentioned above, the technique of the base plate with the reclining bull worked in relief and only its head worked in the round, is of oriental origin (Fig. 231).[184] Like the torsos on the outer panels, this plate had been covered with thin gold foil. The bull is a very virile specimen. Just as on the other bulls so here too the tail terminates in an ear of grain. At its feet crouches a scaly 'wolf' with bulging eyes. Behind the bull's neck a dog is seen running, while a figure with raised sword and dressed in the same style as the other male figures of the cauldron is poised above its back. Again, leaves and crawling vines fill the empty spaces. Some similarities then exist here with the scene depicting the triple bull-sacrifice. Considering the eastern origin of the technique it has been thought conceivable that an early stage of an eastern mystery religion might be reflected in this scene.[185]

While the outside panels are more categorical and abstract in composition, the inner panels appear to us to be more communicative in that they offer insight into some aspects of Celtic religious practices. The cultic events and narrative elements represented on the cauldron are not to be seen elsewhere, and may very well be a record of activities no longer practised even when the Gundestrup cauldron changed owners. Without the underlying mythology to elucidate the panels, their symbolic meaning must remain obscure. It would be hazardous to draw inferences about Celtic religion from the scenes represented on the cauldron. This leaves us with the impression that Celtic religion of the pre-Roman period is obscure for lack of information. Because Celtic religion is first recorded in the historical accounts of ancient writers of the last century B.C. who filter Celtic beliefs and practices as well as names through their own religious understanding and associations, and because Celtic religion in general is handed down in a Celto- or Gallo-Roman end stage, it appears appropriate to postpone the discussion. To reverse the process and to try to separate the fundamental Celtic characteristics from the conceptual modifications and adaptations to which they were subjected during the Roman centuries, and to try to clarify the ambivalence of identities which had accrued to them, would lead to inaccuracies and distortions.

Suffice it to refer here only to archeological evidence of cultic practices. But even here

231. Inner base plate of the Gundestrup cauldron, showing a reclining bull.

not all the evidence found in the Celtic realms is universally distributed. Anthropomorphic statuettes of male (Fig. 232) and female (Fig. 233) deities are known from the
Regnum Noricum, originally a Celtic kingdom in which, from the second century B.C.
on, acculturation with Italy made such progress that in 16/15 B.C. the area was incorporated into the Roman Empire as the province Noricum without opposition. Human
statuettes probably of religious significance are also known from Manching. On the
other hand, contrary to evidence from France, east of the Rhine, skull sanctuaries set in
arches seem to have been unknown, nor is the practice of a skull-cult among the Gauls,
first mentioned by Posidonius of Apamea,[186] indicated among the Celts north of the
Alps. However, between the middle Loire and the river Salzach and the river Main
and the Alps, four-cornered precincts called *temené* (Fig. 234) have been located. Such
a *temenos—Viereckschanze* in German, literally a four-cornered earth-work—was a cult
site. The German term, though an apt description, is not acceptable to all, as it suggests

301

232. Celtic male gods, after *c*. 200 B.C., from the Regnum Noricum.

too much of a defensive function for the site. The ditch and piled up wall of earth were no more than an emphatic line of demarcation, within which was contained the sacred precinct, shielded from view of those on the outside. It is conceivable that there also existed precincts surrounded merely by a fence, but since such evidence cannot have survived, such a supposition cannot be substantiated. These square-shaped earthworks are so frequent throughout the area in question, that it is safe to assume that in every instance they were erected as an expression of a common purpose. These sites, of which so far 70 have been identified in Baden-Württemberg alone, probably served a multitude of functions attended by large numbers of people. No site has yet been completely examined. Preliminary finds suggest that these precincts originated during the middle Hallstatt period and ended during the early Roman period. It has been observed recently that these precincts can often be found in the vicinity of burial mounds.

One gate allowed controlled access to the precinct. Most of its inner area was free of buildings, making large assemblies possible. In one of its corners a building may have been erected, in which case it must have played an as yet unspecified role in the cultic exercises taking place. An important feature of the precincts is the presence of one or several shored-up shafts, up to 35 m deep. Their contents accumulated with time and tend to show reduction stages of fat, blood and meat and other organic substances, all probably sacrificial in origin (Fig. 235). Traces of fire at the base of the shaft or around its mouth point to occasional use of votive fires, for burnt offerings perhaps or for some other priestly activity. On two occasions a wooden pole was found leaning against one

233. Celtic goddess, after *c.* 200 B.C., showing Etruscan influence, from the Regnum Noricum.

234. Boatman, before *c.* 176 B.C., pre-Roman terracotta from the sacred precinct on the peak of the Magdalenenberg, north-east of Klagenfurt in Carinthia.

235. Fragment of a stag representation carved of oak, perhaps part of the frieze of a wooden 'temple', found in the shaft of the precinct at Fellbach-Schmiden, north-east of Tauberbischofsheim.

of the shaft walls, made secure at its base with stone wedges.[187] Their depth is surprising, since there is no evidence on which one could base the notion of an underworld or of subterranean forces. To what powers were these votive offerings made? There is reason to believe that human sacrifices were the exception and that substitutions were possible. It is reported that sacrificial victims were selected from among criminals and prisoners of war, whose execution was sometimes delayed for as many as five years until an appropriate occasion had arrived.[188] It is also generally accepted that the Celts practised a nature religion and venerated such natural phenomena as unexpected sources of water or protrusions of rock; thus springs or menhirs fulfilled a mysterious function (Fig. 236). Trees must have symbolized a life force, especially evergreens, but also beech and oak. It is of interest that the Synod of Liptinae of 743 A.D. chastised the recently Christianized western Saxons for engaging in superstitious practices which henceforth were to be punished severely, among them the veneration of sacred groves called *nimidae*.[189] It has been argued that since other Germanic dialects don't seem to have this word in their vocabularies, the word and the concept to which it applied must have been a cultural transfer from the Celts in whose vocabulary an analogous word *nemeton* exists and which was productive in the formation of place names such as Augustone-meton in Gaul, Tasinemeton in Noricum and Medionemeton in Britanny. In Galatia a site of justice was called the Drunemeton—the Oak Grove. Latin knows the word *nemus* for holy grove and in Greek it is *nemos*.[190] These words suggest that both word and concept are of early, Indo-European origin, reflecting an ancient familiarity with word and concept and the adherence to prehistoric customs, right up to the edge of recorded history. The western Saxons may very well have adopted the word, if not necessarily the practice, as part of a cultural exchange.

In the old Celtic core area west of the Rhine the last phases of the pre-Roman Iron Age and the advent of Roman Provincial culture represent a transformation of the Celtic character of the late La Tène. As we have seen Caesar writes of great aristocrats accompanied by large entourages of dependents, priests, officials and courtiers, of warlords, of assemblies and of parades of military might and splendor. The grave inventories, however, reflect very little of this, rather an equalized mass of people among whose graves only those of women show slightly richer funerary gifts. Among a few grave mounds and flat cremation graves the prevalent form of burial is inhumation in flat graves. That is the characteristic of a regional late La Tène ceramic culture centered in the area of the Hunsrück–Eifel mountains. Though cremation is rare, the cremation graves do contain representative inventories of good pottery of uniform character, but only a few simple metal ornaments and implements.[191] Before it melded with the Roman Provincial culture, the final stages of this late La Tène group showed little marked difference from the Roman Provincial culture. The cemeteries contain distinct La Tène graves, whose inventories contain imports from the Gallo-Roman area or from the area of the Belgae, as well as graves with nothing but imports.[192]

Around Trier the tribe of the Treveri had reputedly provided Caesar with his best cavalry which he deployed so effectively against the Gauls. One had concluded that the Treveri therefore must have been at least a mixture of Celtic and Germanic elements, the latter having moved in from the Germanic groups located to the north and north-east. However, no trace of any Germanic pottery has been identified. Instead it has been found that at least according to ceramic evidence the origin of this late stage of the La Tène can be attributed to cultural impulses radiating from the south-western quadrant around Trier, that is to say, from central Gaul.[193] Shortly after Caesar's successful campaigns in Gaul the Treveri were forcefully integrated into the Roman Empire, thereby losing not only their political independence but their cultural identity as well, as they came under the leveling influence of Roman culture. The archeological evidence underscores this clear break with the late La Tène in that the old grave fields are abandoned and inhumation is replaced by cremation, though flat graves are maintained. In no cemetery has continuity of burial from the La Tène to Roman Provincial times been observed.[194] Even later the romanized Celtic population made only infrequent use of the La Tène cemeteries. The beginning of this break coincides with the government of Augustus,[195] though the process does not unfold evenly throughout the Palatinate area. In the valleys of the Saar and Mosel it came earlier. Only a few finds can be placed in his reign and that of his successor Tiberius. Only for the reigns of Claudius and Vespasian does the number of finds increase. The prelude to the decline

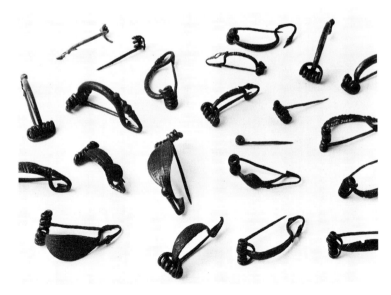

236. Fibulae, votive offerings found in a spring, *c.* 370–300 B.C.

of the La Tène in the western Palatinate was much more advanced. In the Rhine valley it does not merge with the Roman Provincial culture until the Tiberian period, while in the mountains the indigenous elements clung on with even greater tenacity.[196]

The relatively short transition may have been linked with two circumstances: the invasion of the Germanic Suebi and the collapse of Celtic leadership. The establishment of a Suebian dependency among the left-Rhenish tribes from the Palatinate to Alsace and their ultimate defeat by Julius Caesar in 58 B.C. must have seriously disturbed both fiber and fabric of the Celto-Germanic populations in the area. No doubt, some of the population had joined Ariovist's Suebians and had been much reduced in the defeat, allowing such new tribes as the Nemetes, Vangiones and Triboci to settle in the area. The second shock to the culture was probably provided by the loss of the cultural elites, of whom Caesar writes that they died in battle, or in uprisings, that they were removed either as prisoners of war or as hostages, or that they had entered Roman service, or had elected exile in Britain or among their neighbors east of the Rhine. Following the failure of the uprising of 54/53 B.C. the leading families of the Treveri are reported to have crossed the Rhine, to settle among the Germanic tribes.[197] The ceramic evidence to the contrary, some tribal links may have existed after all.

Thereafter the Romanization of taste and of the culture in general is indicated by the adoption and imitation of things Roman, and by a change in mental attitude. Richly decorated jewellery gives way to richly decorated pottery of high quality, characterized by its finer clay, thinner walls, more uniform color and surface finish, probably fired at higher temperatures in superior kilns. Weapons and equipment appear only rarely in the graves. Instead glasswares such as drinking vessels, urns and ointment flasks take their place. Inscribed gravestones now marked the cemeteries. Stone construction appeared. The Celtic world was gradually absorbed in the Roman Empire until indigenous features were no longer readily apparent.[198]

An historical curiosity is the area around modern-day Cologne. It was not a part of the Celtic realm, and its population was neither Celtic nor Germanic, but the remnant of a third but unknown group of Indo-Europeans who had come under Celtic sway.[199] To Caesar they were Celts. The Eburones and Ubians may have been members of this group. Caesar's categorical division of the peoples along the Rhine allowed for only two groups. A third group does not seem to have fitted his political purposes. In any case, in 53 B.C. when the Eburones assumed an ambiguous attitude towards him he annihilated them.[200] The Ubians, subjected to pressures from the Germanic Suebi to the east, requested to be given land on the left bank of the Rhine. They were assigned the land of the exterminated Eburones. In 38 B.C. Marcus V. Agrippa settled the Ubians on plots of land, giving them a measure of self-rule in return for taxes and military service. Their oppidum Ubiorum, the center of their tribal area, was to become a mercantile center. The *ara Ubiorum*—the altar of the Ubians—made it an important religious center. In 50 A.D. the prosperous city received the name Colonia Claudia Ara Agrippinensium, after Agrippina, the daughter of Germanicus.[201] The modern city Cologne-Köln—derives its name from this Roman designation.

It is likely that the Celtic populations which occupied central Europe were not entirely displaced in the troubled centuries which followed. A Celto-Germanic population must have existed in the central regions in the last few centuries before our era. Some others, no doubt, were caught in the wake of migrating tribes. Still others, on the other hand, especially those within the Roman frontiers, were affected only marginally by the movement of peoples. Some areas were not touched at all by the Germanic migrations. In the search for ethnic homogeneity and historical evidence for national-istic ideologies and national pride of descent, Celtomania in France and a new 'Furor Teutonicus' in Germany classified neatly and boldly where caution should have pre-vailed. Attempts to extend national histories based on ethnic assumptions into the most distant past, led to claims that the German people of the Wilhelminian Empire in Germany already existed as potential proto-Germans among the Battle Axe 'People'. Even north of the Alps one misconstrued what should have been apparent, namely that the Germanic element carries less weight in southern Germany than might be assumed, while the Celtic components probably deserve more credit than they are given. The Celts were 'overlayered'.[202] The names of many German rivers—Rhine (Renus), Neckar (Nicer), Main (Maenus), Dubra (Tauber), Ruhr (Raura), as well as the Aller, Brenz, Elbe, Enz, Iller, Isar, Lahn, Lippe, Weser—are reputedly of Celtic origin, though their etymology is not totally certain. A similar list of mountains could be compiled, thus the Rhön in central Germany is reputedly derived from the Celtic 'roino' meaning hill, way or limit and reflected in the German word 'Rain', while the Tauern range in the southern Alps commemorates the Celtic tribal name of the Taurisci. These names point to a continuing oral tradition. Throughout the centuries the Celtic popu-lation substratum provided a resonant presence for the periodic revival of Celtic themes introduced by the Hiberno-Scottish missions of the sixth century, by the Insular Style of the seventh and eighth, by the Arthurian legends which enlivened literature from the Middle Ages to the time of the Emperor Maximilian I, and by the Ossianic enthusiasm of the eighteenth century.[203] With other northern elements on the one hand and positioned antithetically towards the Mediterranean influences on the other, the Celtic element contributes to the particular central European ambivalence, to that optical play between mysterious obscurity and rational clarity, between negative space and positive pattern, between diffuse integration and distinct individuation, now favoring one, then the other, but most inclined to the enriching manipulation of both.

Map 29. The Germanic north, *c.* 600 B.C. to the Roman period.

6. Northern Genesis

It was mentioned in the previous chapter that type stations point to the emergence of cultural groups in Germany towards the middle of the last millennium B.C., north of the Central Highlands and some 30 km south of Lüneburg. An earlier group, identified by the type station at Wessenstedt and extending from *c.* 800–600 B.C., was followed by the Jastorf group which dominated a larger area from *c.* 600–300 B.C. Two later groups, at Ripdorf from *c.* 300–150 B.C., and at Seedorf from *c.* 150 B.C. onward, complete the Pre-Roman period. The earliest 'Germanic' cultures have been associated with the Wessenstedt and Jastorf groups. Located between the Weser river to the west and the Oder river to the east, the Jastorf culture extended south to the fringes of the northern Hallstatt provinces, while towards the north a general congruence with the late phases of the Northern Bronze Age can be noted. These circumstances invite questions concerning the extent to which the Northern Bronze, though quite impoverished by now, continued to exert a cultural influence and to what extent the magnitude of the northward thrust of the Hallstatt culture into the same area was instrumental in effecting the crystallization of the Jastorf group in north-central Germany during the transition from Hallstatt to La Tène. Here too extensive migrations have been discounted.[1]

The support for the continuity of an indigenous culture-carrying population can again be derived from the archeological evidence. Gravefields in Schleswig-Holstein, Mecklenburg, western Pomerania, in Brandenburg and in Lower Saxony show continuity of occupation from the Bronze Age far into the Jastorf period and beyond. Late Bronze Age and Hallstatt ceramics find echoes in Jastorf pottery. In fact, a certain homogeneity in ceramics and in metal wares has been documented from the Weser in the west to western Pomerania in the east. As for metal wares the area of the Jastorf culture, especially along the middle Elbe, appears to benefit from the Hallstatt influence. The 'royal' grave of Seddin has already suggested that an indigenous population gradually became acquainted with the use of iron, at first in the form of imported articles, until the craftsmen working in metals came to be converted to the use of iron. Early Jastorf metal objects such as belt hooks, or sheet-bronze belts, have been found to be clearly indebted to Hallstatt forms. The desire to share in the iron technology must have provided the motivation for the northerners to seek contact with the Hallstatt provinces to the south. The discovery and ready availability of swamp and surface ores allowed the northerners to engage in the development of an independent iron industry which contributed to a certain independence from imports. That these resources were insufficient in the end is indicated by the increasing presence of a Celtic influence on the material culture of the later Jastorf group. La Tène metal objects were adopted towards the beginning of the third century B.C. and by the mid-century wheel-turned pottery began to make its appearance in the contact areas.[2] These same regions must have witnessed the meeting of Celtic and proto-Germanic peoples. The specific contributions from the various quarters to the genesis of these northern peoples during the early period cannot be assessed, given the present state of knowledge. By the end of the second century B.C. central Germany was oriented towards the La Tène culture. The presence of oppida in the area indicates that this remained so into the middle of the last pre-Roman century. It was during this period that wagons and such cauldrons as the Gundestrup basin were traded northward.

It has been found that the northern imitations and adaptations of Celtic pieces often bear a degree of ornamentation quite beyond the usefulness for which they were intended.[3] Although this decorative adaptation to conform to northern conceptions of style may have been prompted by an aesthetic sense, the stylistic embellishments may have been cultic in motivation, as though to imbue a weapon, for instance, with magical effectiveness. A peasant culture, the Jastorf group probably did not provide a social structure such as could support artists and craftsmen,[4] so that it is likely that the more exemplary pieces were either imported or the work of itinerant Celtic craftsmen. However, the interaction between Celtic and northern peoples broke off when the region appears to have found a focus located further north. This break coincided with the fading of the cultural vitality of the continental Celts, their retro-migration into central Europe, and their ultimate inclusion in the Roman Empire.

These factors contributed to the coming together of cultural affinities, their encapsulation against other neighboring groups and the ethnic definition of the group in north central Germany. At the same time this Jastorf group would have developed as a linguistic unit as well. The transition area between northern and Celtic populations is the likely crucible in which the melting process took place, rather than in the core area of the Northern Bronze. It has of course been shown in previous chapters that archeological cultures need not be identified with ethnic cultures. Earlier notions which held that proto-Germanic peoples emigrated from Denmark during Stage VI of the Northern Bronze Age have been abandoned by archeologists in view of the absence of any marked decrease in the funerary evidence in this area, though historians of the German language continue to echo related theories.

The genesis of proto-Germanic ethnic groups is to be sought around or after 500 B.C. in a setting which archeology alone cannot unravel. The separation out of proto-Germanic groups from their Indo-European context has largely been accomplished by means of comparative linguistic analysis and the isolation of linguistic units which conform consistently to their own inherent phonetic and structural laws. The interrelationship of the Indo-European languages was outlined briefly at the end of chapter 3, where it was pointed out that the Germanic languages are the result of a late process of differentiation. This process must be understood to have been a protracted one extending over very many centuries. From a practical point of view the question concerning the process of differentiation which separated proto-Germanic from the other Indo-European languages is still burdened with nineteenth-century theories of biological naturalism which see the evolution of languages along family-tree lines,[5] thereby presupposing an Indo-European proto- or root language from which others branch out according to organic laws of development. This view would also postulate the emergence of a uniform proto-Germanic language, from which the Germanic languages would evolve. In view of the significant links between Germanic, Celtic and Italic languages on the one hand and Baltic and Slavic languages on the other, the question arises[6] whether Germanic branched out from the Indo-European stem in conjunction with these other languages or whether Germanic branches came in contact with branches of those other languages, or if perhaps the agreement among Germanic, Italic and Celtic languages, as reflected in the names given to lakes and rivers,[7] does not suggest a common proto-European language as a transitional stage between proto-Indo-European and the individual European languages. Quite evidently this is an area for specialists, who have yet to formulate an acceptable answer.

It is part of the problem that studies of German etymology—that branch of linguistic science which is preoccupied with the origin of words—have developed an extensive and complex body of literature. Convincing histories of the German language, almost all of which develop the Indo-European context, have established an intricate philological system quite independent of the archeological evidence. Complications derive from the cultural contexts with which the etymological analyses have been provided and the chronologies which have been developed.[8] In general, neither cultural contexts nor chronologies can be reconciled with the archeological evidence. Repeated references to aspects of this problem have been made in chapters 3 and 4.

The problem in itself is fascinating because the etymological discoveries have been embedded in ethnological contexts, by means of which an attempt has been made to reconstruct the historical development of words in the light of cultural backgrounds and chronologies that cannot be substantiated.[9] For the historians of language, who were anxious to find a glorious setting for the crystallization of the Germanic peoples, the brilliant culture of the Northern Bronze was ideal. Having obtained agreement that the Germanic peoples originated in Scandinavia they continue to see them established in Jutland, Schleswig, Holstein and over varying expanses of the North German Plain between the Weser and Oder rivers, as early as *c.* 1000 B.C. and as descendants of the legendary 'Battle Axe – Corded Ware' people. This approximate date is difficult to accept in view of the uninterrupted cultural development of the Northern Bronze Age.

Convincing use of the available etymological evidence is made in the specialized literature which demonstrates by means of the names of rivers and places, of terminology related to the political community and of a vast assortment of other words that prior to their migration to their historical locales, groups speaking Italic, Illyrian or Venetic or even Baltic or Slavic languages must have been neighbors of the Germanic-speaking groups.[10] The migration in question is known to have taken place during the Urnfield period, towards the end of the second millennium B.C. This comparative etymological evidence would therefore suggest that proto-Germanic was spoken in the territories adjoining the northern provinces of the Urnfield culture. That would necessitate on the one hand the admission of a Germanic link with the Lusatian cultures, deemed to be proto-Slavic, and on the other hand of a westward migration of the Germanic-speaking groups, if we are to find them in Denmark and across the North German Plain by *c.* 1000 B.C. The cultural ruptures which such a relocation would have entailed are not in evidence. In attempting to flesh out the linguistic skeleton, etymology was burdened with selected cultural evidence which in the meantime has proven to be inconsistent with the archeological findings. Making use of very scanty etymological evidence, historians of the German language have even been led to draw maps which show that by *c.* 750 B.C. the populations inhabiting the North German Plain could be divided into

West Germanic groups established between Rhine and Oder, and East Germanic groups settled between the Oder and the Vistula and areas further east.[11] Though this seems to be true for much later times, such distributions appear to be premature. It appears futile to try to establish even an approximately absolute chronology, considering that for this early period archeological, historical and linguistic aspects beg to be compared which lend themselves, however, only to very restricted comparisons. Not until the linguistic hypotheses have been brought into some accord with other evidence can maps showing such patterns of distribution and expansion be accepted as valid.

What has been established is the occurrence of a sound-shift *c*. 500 B.C. which differentiated Germanic from the other Indo-European languages. This First Sound-shift, or Grimm's Law because it is usually associated with Jacob Grimm, one of the Brothers Grimm, categorizes a consistent transformation of specific consonants in Indo-European into corresponding consonants in Germanic.[12]

Simplified, the Indo-European consonants *p*, *t*, *k* shift to *f*, *þ*, *χ* in Germanic, as for instance *p* in sanskrit *pita*, Greek *pater*, Latin *pater* corresponds to *f* in Gothic *fodar*, German *Vater*, English *father*, or Latin *tres* into Gothic *threis*, German *drei*, English *three*, or Latin *cornu* into Gothic *haurun*, German *Horn*, English *horn*. Though other Indo-European languages may be chosen for illustration, Latin is the preferred language for making the comparisons because of its close correspondence with German—for instance, Latin *pesces*—English *fish*, or Latin *pecunia* (money)—German *Vieh* (cattle)—English *fee*. At the same time as *p*, *t*, *k* shifted to *f*, *þ*, *χ*, the consonants *b*, *d*, *g* shifted to *p*, *t*, *k*. Had this not happened simultaneously, then the Germanic languages would not now have the consonants *p*, *t*, *k*. Thus Latin *turba* (common crowd)—Low German *dorp*—German *Dorf*—English *thorp* (village), or Latin *duo*—Gothic *twa*—English *two*—German *zwei*; or Latin *genu*—Gothic *kniu*—German *knie*—English *knee*. The differentiation of Germanic from Indo-European was of course not restricted just to these consonants. Also involved were the fixing of stresses on root syllables, syntactic changes, declensions and grammatical cases, but this is too extensive an area to be discussed here.[13] The inner-Germanic differentiations which distinguish between German, Dutch and English are the result of a Second Soundshift which took place before the sixth century A.D., a result of the migrations of the Germanic peoples and their geographic dispersion and regional localization. Only after about a thousand years did proto-Germanic evolve into German.

Even the First Soundshift presupposes a lengthy process of socio-cultural and economic coexistence and assimilation in a relatively compact area before a crystallization along linguistic lines would take place. Only after a long period of transition could an encapsulation and isolation from its neighbors produce an ethno-linguistic identity. In central Europe such an encapsulation would never come about entirely by itself. To argue in favor of a Germanic consolidation in the area occupied by the Jastorf group prior to the First Soundshift would not be very convincing. It is argued, however, that the First Soundshift preceded the large-scale introduction of iron into the proto-Germanic area, in that the Germanic word for 'iron' was most probably imported from the Celtic realms along with the raw material, but did not submit to the changes imposed by the laws of differentiation. Proceeding along etymological lines, the reconstructed Celtic word for iron *isarno* is reflected in the reconstructed Germanic word *isarna*. This word is therefore considered to be a Celtic loanword which came into use after Germanic had developed its linguistic identity.[14] As was shown above, it was in the area of the Jastorf culture that the transition to an iron-using culture took place.

The adoption of only one word would be weak evidence indeed on which to base the conclusion that this area witnessed the formation of the Germanic peoples, were it not for a more extensive list of correspondences between Celtic and Germanic words from many areas of activity, pointing not so much to an ancestral relationship as to secondary borrowings as a result of occasional cultural influences. One used to argue on behalf of a Celto-Germanic root-language to account for certain similarities. This idea has been abandoned in favor of attributing common elements to the exchange between adjoining areas of settlement.[15] Since many of the corresponding words have political connotations it was also held that the Celts had conquered and dominated Germanic groups thereby leaving a linguistic imprint upon them. This notion has also been discarded in favor of close political and cultural ties between Celtic and Germanic groups in pre-Roman as well as in Roman times. Thus the Germanic word for 'ruler', reconstructed as *rikaz, presented in Gothic as reiks, is considered to have been borrowed from Celtic rig, prior to the First Soundshift. The Celtic rig is probably derived from Indo-European *reg, as preserved in Latin rex, regis. Indo-European e consistently shifts to Celtic i. Had the word come directly from Indo-European into Germanic, then e would initially have remained e, and later changed to a, according to established laws of vowel shift between Indo-European and Germanic.[16] Some other illustrations of the Celto-Germanic exchange of words are the Gallic word ambactus—servant, client, vassal, known from a Latin source, which is present in Gothic as andbahts, in Old High German as ambahti, the related noun in Gothic being andbahti—service, corresponding to Old High German ambahti, Middle High German ambet and New High German Amt meaning office.[17] Originally the connotation emphasized the High Office as in the religious service. Celtic dunum, the familiar suffix, recurs as Germanic tuna—enclosure, fortified settlement, English town, New High German Zaun—fence.[18] The list of correspondences is extensive. The exchange, however, was not only one way,[19] thus Germanic *brokez—English breeches—Old Norse brok—Old High German bruch—New High German bruch, appears as Gallic braca and is present in Latin during the second century B.C. as braces, braca, to mention only one example. The correspondence between Celtic and Germanic personal names is extensive,[20] where Celtic Catumaros corresponds to Germanic Hadumar, Dagomarus to Dagmar, Gallic Segomarus to Germanic Sigimerus—Old High German Sigimar—New High German Sigmar, or Gallic Teutorix to Old High German Dietrih—New High German Dietrich. The Celtic rig suffix in personal names is particularly productive as illustrated in modern names ending in -reich or -rich, such as Heinrich. Names of rivers and places, especially in the Rhineland, ending in -ich, -ach are later Germanizations of Celtic names,[21] for instance Tolbiacum—Zülpich, Mogontiacum—Mainz, Brisiacum—Breisach. Celtic settlements with their Romanized names continue into the present. Thus we find Noviomagus—Nijmegen, Rigomagus—Remagen, Borbetomagus—Worms, and Cambodunum—Kempten.

In the general system of Indo-European relationships, terms applying to family relationships, animals and plant life would demostrate the greatest resistance to change. This Indo-European heritage is reflected in common Celtic, Italic, Germanic, Baltic and Slavic terminologies dealing with such areas as livestock, agriculture and associated activities, produce, tools, game, fish, predators, insects, weather, buildings, clothing, parts of the body, basic emotions, numerals, figures of speech such as questions and demands, colours and geographic designations of the landscape.[22] Needless to say, to attempt to deal with this extensive range of topics would take more space than is appropriate here. It is apparent from the preceding discussion that Germanic was no more than an Indo-European dialect prior to the First Soundshift. Only as a result of this linguistic phenomenon which occurred around the middle of the last millenium B.C. did Germanic consolidate its individualizing characteristics largely in accordance with the causality inherent in its own linguistic laws. This emergence of a language does not, however, offer any conclusive evidence concerning the racial homogeneity of the people speaking the language. It is a curious fact of German history though, that notions of 'being German' are generally expressed along linguistic lines rather than in terms of nation or race.

In the face of the overwhelming body of philological evidence which sees the proto-Germanic tribal groups in very distant ages, the evidence concerning the ethnogenesis of the Germanic people in the area of the Jastorf culture advanced by more recent archeology appears scanty indeed. However, while the etymological approach to determining the origin of the Germanic tribal groups leads into hypotheses, archeology offers tangible evidence concerning the crystallization of a group, identifiable in terms of its material culture. Though a specific contribution of the Jastorf group to the ethnic genesis of the Germanic-speaking northerners is hard to determine, its general participation cannot be denied in view of the continuity of settlement of the area. In need of revision are maps which show West and East Germanic populations distributed across the North German Plain from the Rhine to the Vistula as early as c. 750 B.C.

The Jastorf culture was characterized by its use of cremation burials in extensive urnfields.[23] In that regard the link exists with the practices of the Northern Bronze Age.[24] During the last four centuries B.C., cremation and urn burials in extensive fields took place on Jutland and across the North German Plain. On Jutland the urn was covered by a low tumulus or it was placed into older tumuli as a secondary burial. Funerary gifts still accompanied the remains but they were fewer in number, more modest—clothing ornaments, iron pins, fibulae, iron shears and crescent-shaped razors, belt hooks and buckles—and they accompanied the deceased onto the pyre, rather than being added to his ashes.[25] In the light of the preceding discussion it is important to note that most of the graves have been found on Jutland rather than on the Danish islands. Towards the end of the era the funerary gifts are again richer and more varied. Cremation remains customary, as does the depositing of the remains in urns, with or without tumuli. Celtic stylistic influences are in evidence.[26] Silver appears for the first time, although bronze as the metal for ornaments maintains its role until Roman times.

Archeological assessments made in Schleswig-Holstein suggest that originally some 6500 urnfields were located there. Of these only about 1 per cent had been excavated; enough, however, to form representative opinions about the nature of the finds.[27] The cemeteries show that between c. 1100 B.C. and the end of the first millennium of our era, cremation was the dominant funerary practice here as well. This span of time allows conclusions about stability or fluctuations in population densities, mortality rates and even population dislocations. Thus the almost complete cessation of urnfield burials during the fifth century A.D. is seen to reflect the emigration of the Angles and Saxons to England.[28] Occasionally the urnfields have been found in the vicinity of extensive fields of Bronze Age tumuli, suggesting not only a cultural affinity but also population continuity in the region between c. 1100 B.C. and c. 500 A.D. One of the larger urnfields has been excavated at Schwissel, just south of Bad Segeberg in Holstein. On an area of 1·25 hectares, just over 3 acres, about 3000 urn burials have been located, of which 2500 urns have been unearthed. They had been deposited there between c. 500 B.C. and c. 50 B.C.[29] The cemetery had grown from south to north, thereby indicating a chronology. During the second century A.D., urn burial was resumed but the direction in which the urns were deposited was now different, suggesting a break in the continuity of the culture if not in that of the population. It has been possible to calculate an average mortality rate of seven adult deaths per year. Such a mortality rate represents a fairly large population. In the absence of an identifiable settlement which could be associated with the cemetery, it remains an open question whether the urnfield accommodated a larger region or only one settlement. Children under six do not appear to have been cremated and their burials are not in evidence in the cemetery.

The question of the relative constancy of the population density in this region in the decades just prior to 100 B.C. is of some importance. It is commonly held, though with some degree of scepticism, that some time around 150 B.C. three 'Germanic' tribes—the Cimbri, Teutones and Ambrones emigrated from Jutland and Schleswig-Holstein to appear in great numbers in south central Europe towards c. 120 B.C. where in subsequent years they contributed greatly to the unrest in the northern spheres of influence of the Roman Republic, until they were annihilated in 102 and 101 B.C. by Marius, who incidentally did not refer to them as 'Germanic'. The basis for this belief rests on two circumstances: in 5 A.D. Tiberius launched a naval expedition to explore the shores of the North Sea. It reached the northern tip of Jutland and returned with some information about tribal dispositions along the coast of the peninsula.[30] Pliny then refers to this northern tip as the *Cimbrorum promunturium*, the Cimbrian promontory. Tacitus however, gives only vague details about the location of the Cimbri,[31] while on Ptolemy's map they are located on the most northerly extreme of the peninsula. Ptolemy places Teutonoari and the neighboring Teutones between the Elbe river and the Baltic Sea, into present-day Mecklenburg.[32] Strabo, who indicates that on the other side of the Elbe all things are unknown, places the Cimbri to the west of the river. Strabo and after him Tacitus only know that the Cimbri inhabited a peninsula.[33] Furthermore, Tacitus does not relate them to any other tribal group. On the other hand, on the Jutish peninsula names have been preserved such as Himmerland and Thy in the north, and the island of Amrum among the North Frisian Islands which are held to be derivatives of the old tribal names, suggesting that at least some numbers of these tribes did not join the exodus. The emigrating groups must, however, have been large enough to have been able to preserve their original names even when their ranks were swelled by others through whose territories they passed. The archeological funerary evidence does, however, not seem to support the notion of a large-scale emigration from the region. The dispute concerning the origins of these tribes has not yet been resolved. The very Celtic names of their leaders help to complicate the questions even more. Their exploits against Rome will be dealt with below.

To return to the urnfields of Schleswig-Holstein: without exception the adult dead were cremated on pyres and their remains deposited in urns covered either by a lid or a flat stone. While the urns of earlier cultural levels represented specially made funerary ware, the urns of this period had once served as household articles, as is evident from their obvious appearance of having been in use—broken handles, chipped rims and other signs of wear. Even shards of large vessels were used again for burial.[34] The pit in which the vessel was deposited was only slightly larger than the urn itself. During the earlier phases the urn had been protected by a fitting of stones but during the second and first centuries B.C. this custom of stone protection was abandoned in favor of a stone base or a stone cover, until even that was given up and the urns were allowed to stand freely. As on Jutland, metallic funerary articles which accompanied the deceased pertained to his clothing or were worn as 'jewellery'. Only towards the end of the period were the articles placed on top of the ashes in the urn. Traces of wear show that these articles had been used during the person's lifetime.[35] Belt hooks, pins, needles and fibulae are the most common articles in the inventories. Since weapons and tools are not part of these inventories, male or female burials cannot be distinguished without anthropological analysis. In this cemetery social differentiation cannot be deduced from the very uniform grave equipment—the graves contain no precious metals nor particularly generous inventories.[36] Imports from far away are not reflected in the inventories either. Evidently precious objects were passed on to the surviving heirs. An urnfield at Husby, just east of Flensburg in Schleswig on the other hand does allow conclusions about the social rank of the deceased, and towards the end of the era the graves contain such weapons as swords, lance tips, shield fittings and spurs, other rich gifts, and even tools.[37] Further south, at Hamfelde, east of Hamburg, urnfields used from *c*. 100 B.C. to 200 A.D. show segregated burials where the remains of men and women were not deposited in the same cemeteries while a social elite, indicated by rich inventories, was buried in a special area of the cemetery.[38] It is quite evident from the above that the population of this region was not entirely unanimous in some of its cultural expression.

In the more immediate area of the Jastorf group, at Putensen, some 20 km wsw of Lüneburg two urnfields have been uncovered. One urnfield yielded over 700 urns of the Jastorf (600–300 B.C.), Ripdorf (300–150 B.C.) and Seedorf (150 B.C.—0) groups.[39] The urns of the Jastorf period had generally been set into the ground surrounded by protective stone slabs. It is noteworthy that the urns are located in stone perimeters, up to 3 m in diameter, the boulders weighing up to 75 kg. Burials of ashes in organic containers, long since decayed, have also been observed. Set at ground level these stone perimeters were then filled in with a 'pavement' of closely fitted rocks so that a slightly vaulted protective covering had originally marked the location of the grave. Urns not protected by the paved vaults had been marked by upright steles. Drifting sand had eventually covered the site. A wall of boulders surrounded the cemetery. This wall too had been covered by sand. This cemetery did not yield any weapons. In the vicinity another cemetery had come to be laid out from north to south during the period *c*. 100 B.C. to after 200 A.D.[40] It yielded almost a thousand burials in urns or in long-decayed organic containers, many of them richly furnished with grave gifts. These graves yielded weapons. The inventories also indicate social differentiation. One found 9 swords, 210 lance tips, 32 spears, 5 axes, 23 knives, the fittings of 77 shields and 18 spurs, as well as razors, shears, awls, curved blades, fibulae of iron, bronze and silver, belt hooks, ornamental fittings off drinking horns, and many other small articles.[41] A family of elevated station is indicated by burials in imported bronze vessels. The location of their graves and their equipment suggest that five generations of this family were buried here. To the first century A.D. belonged a richly furnished grave in which the bronze vessel yielded not only the usual ornaments but also a silver pin, three pairs of silver fibulae, one bronze and one iron fibula, three sets of spurs, a belt hook, fittings from drinking horns and two Roman casseroles of bronze, as well as remnants of linen and woolen cloth. A cemetery at Deutsch-Evern, just south of Lüneburg, showed continuity of occupation from *c*. 1200 to *c*. 300 B.C.[42] Only from the fourth century A.D. onward is there a departure from the customary cremation burial indicated, when inhumation graves begin to appear beside cremation burials. This is demonstrated in a cemetery at Liebenau, near Nienburg about 50 km NW of Hanover.[42] In a previous chapter reference has already been made to the gravefield at Pestrup, in the Oldenburg region, which showed continuity of burial from the eighth to the second century B.C. In the Oldenburg area it has been found that the urn and the cremation site had been covered by sand, but in order to prevent the heaps of sand from drifting away, layers of heath or moor sods had been used to cover the tumulus. Urns were not used towards the end of the period, only containers of perishable materials. The almost total absence of grave goods makes a chronological arrangement difficult.[44]

The development of a settlement has been observed at Gristede, 12 km NW of Oldenburg, where a hamlet came into being towards the beginning of the Roman Imperial period.[45] Over the next few hundred years this hamlet first shifted gradually onto higher ground. Until the end of the fifth century A.D. a total of twenty-five different farms could be identified. Most of them contained dug wells shored up with hollowed logs, baking ovens, storage barns and fences. During some periods one common fence surrounded whole groups of farm houses. At the turn of the sixth century this settlement was abandoned. Not until the ninth did a population reoccupy the site. No link between the two phases could be established. Similar observations have been made in the whole region. Either a complete exodus or at least a very pronounced thinning out of the population must be held responsible for such a rupture. Although there may be diverse reasons for this, the emigration of the Saxons to Britain would have constituted a major cause for the break in continuity. By analogy one might expect a similar rupture to be indicated in Jutland and Schleswig-Holstein with the departure of the Cimbri, Teutones and Ambrones from their homelands.

Along the North Sea coast from southern Denmark to the estuary of the Rhine in Holland the coastal elevations as well as the natural levées along the coastal rivers are dotted with settlements located on artificially raised hills formed out of the piling up of settlement debris up to a height of 6 m, covering several hectares of usable land. Until the dikes were built these 'Wurten', also called 'Terpen' (-*þorp*, *Dorf*), protected the inhabitants against the frightening storm floods of the North Sea. Excavations of such sites have shown that during the first century A.D. these settlements were still located on level ground, but with the steady rise of the flood-water levels over the centuries the respective levels of occupation kept pace, gradually rising to ever higher elevations. A trench cut into such a 'Wurt' reveals the village horizons of many centuries, the accumulated mixture of clay, manure and other settlement debris serving as an airtight sealant against decay. As a result the wooden outlines of houses, of fabrics, skins, leather, bones of wild and domestic animals, of seeds and pollen of wild and cultivated plants and all sorts of other organic materials and artefacts have been preserved in good condition. Using mechanized equipment it was possible between 1955 and 1963 to uncover and examine such a 'Wurt'—the 'Feddersen Wierde'—in the region of Wursten, just west of Sievern, some 20 km north of Bremerhaven and about 2·5 km inland.[46] The excavation has since been returned to agricultural use at ground level and is of no interest to the visitor. The 'Wurt' had a diameter of *c.* 200 m and covered an area of about 4 hectares (about 10 acres). It rose to about 4 m above mean sea level (MSL). The earliest settlement horizon was located at a depth between −0·3 to +0·3 MSL. It was established during the first century B.C. By 500 A.D. it had been abandoned. Only with the arrival of the Frisians in the eighth century A.D. was it reoccupied.

Such a 'Wurt' offers a unique opportunity to study not only superimposed village structures, in this instance seven preserved horizons of settlement, but also daily economic forms. Walls of wattle as well as interior and exterior posts were preserved to a height of 40–50 cm, making it possible to determine the form of the village within each

317

237. Outline of a longhouse of the 'Wurt' Feddersen Wierde, third century A.D., formerly located north of Bremerhaven.

settlement level (Fig. 237). The houses were of the type already found during Banded Ware and Rössen Ware times—three-naved longhouses divided by a wattle wall into living area and stables. The living area had a floor of stamped clay. A hearth of shards and smoothed clay was located on the floor. Doors leading outside had been placed along the wattle walls which separated living and stable areas. Larger houses also allowed access to the stables on the gable side. In the stables wattle walls subdivided the side aisles into stalls. The central aisle had been 'paved' with sod, the edges faced with beams to facilitate drainage. The livestock, mainly cattle, faced the outside walls. These were finished with smoothed clay packing. The roof was finished with reed. The various settlement horizons showed variations in the size of houses, longhouses 29 m × 29 m × 6·5 m, or others only 10–14 m × 5·6 m.[47] Store houses of similar construction were located close to the side entrances. Consisting of nine posts arranged in three rows they supported a platform, the actual storage area. Storage pits faced with wattle have also been found. House, stable and storehouse constituted an economic unit. During the earliest phase, c. 50 B.C.—c. 100 A.D., the buildings had been set on level ground, arranged in rows in an east–west direction. Four settlement phases could be assessed during which this layout was in effect. Only with the first century A.D. did the raising of mounds become necessary. With it came a change in layout which saw the establishment of a radial pattern around an open 'village square'. This arrangement remained in effect until the fourth or fifth century when the settlement was abandoned. At first one erected the farming units on barrow-like mounds about one meter high. During the first and second centuries only about fourteen establishments made up the settlement.[48] The horizon representing the third to fourth centuries indicated that the settlement had increased to twenty-four farming units arranged in inner and outer rings. By the third century the settlement horizon had been leveled out. The 'Wurt' had taken on an oval shape. Fences and ditches surrounded each farming unit. In some instances the enclosures contained one large and one or more smaller units, suggesting the existence of larger economic units, headed by the larger establishment. The finds of semi-finished articles of wood and bone indicate that crafts complemented the agricultural activities. Mills, weaving shops, smithies for bronze and iron, and workshops for the making of pottery, baskets, wooden and leather articles have been identified.

While smaller units tended to occupy the north-western part of the settlement, from the beginning of the second century on, the south-east was dominated by a large establishment, a longhouse, 20 m × 6 m, which, instead of stables, contained a large hall.[49] Even later horizons show the continued existence of this hallhouse. The stables were housed in a nearby building. Storehouses and workshops of varying sizes completed the unit. During the third century an oaken palisade and ditch surrounded this unit. Its singular character suggests that it enjoyed a particular function; perhaps it was the residence of the village 'chieftain'. The finds allow no conclusions about the social status of the people inhabiting this 'manor'. That it must have constituted a social center is indicated by the presence of an 'assembly-hall' on the site, first in evidence in settlement horizon 4 of the second century. The building, 25 m × 6·5 m in size, contained no stables, nor were any storage facilities located nearby. Under the entrance to this community hall the remains of a dog were found, and under its hearth those of a pig, evidently ritual sacrifices. To the east of the palisade a human skeleton was found, also probably a ritual burial since cremation was customary. More than twice as many Roman terra-sigillata shards, pearls, glass, Roman coins and fibulae were found on this site than in the rest of the 'Wurt'. Especially around the 'manor' did these finds of imported articles appear in some concentration. Trade and manufacture must have been focused at this site. The family must have enjoyed an hereditary preferential status within the village community based on land ownership and trade.

While horizon 4 showed a preoccupation with the raising of livestock and the pursuit of agriculture, complemented by manufacture, horizon 5 points to the existence of specialist craftsmen and perhaps even of seafarers who could not at the same time supply their own provisions and therefore found themselves in some sort of dependent relationship with the 'manor'. About 240 hectares of pasture but only about 50 hectares of arable land were at the disposal of the farming units. By counting the stalls it can be determined that about 176 cattle belonged to the village during the first and second centuries of our era. During the third century the livestock had increased to about 440 cattle.[50] Examination of the bone finds reveals that in autumn the herd was thinned out, evidently because of insufficient fodder for the winter. Bone analysis showed that among the domesticated animals cattle represented 49·3 per cent, sheep 23·7 per cent, horses 12·7 per cent, pigs 11·1 per cent and dogs 4·2 per cent. The animals were smaller than today; thus cattle measured 1·10 m and horses an average of only 1·30 m in height. Since the upgrading of the livestock was still not practical at this time, the stock gradually degenerated, as is substantiated by the ever-decreasing size of the stalls in the stables. Only higher ground could be cultivated, which indicates that arable land was

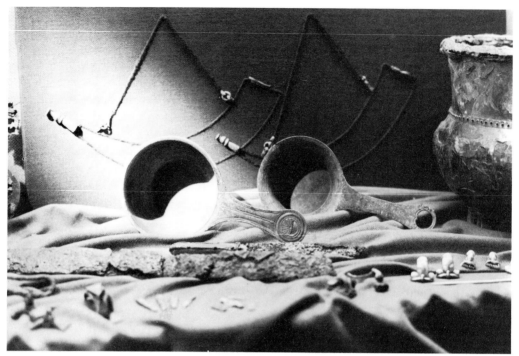
238. Princely grave inventory, including two Roman casseroles, early first century A.D.

at a premium. The ground was tilled with the turning plow. The fields were cultivated only in summer. The yield from the land constituted roughly 50 per cent barley and oats, 25 per cent field beans (*Vicia fava*) and some 25 per cent linseed and rapeseed as a source of oil. Other bones indicate that deer and elk, domestic and wild fowl and fish (even sturgeon) complemented the diet of these coastal dwellers.

Ceramic and metallic evidence indicates that already at the earliest settlement horizon the village engaged in trade with the inhabitants of Frisia and with the Romans on the lower Rhine (Fig. 238). These trade links were developed during the second century A.D. and reached their greatest volume during the third, when coins, terra-sigillata pottery, pearls and glass came to the 'Wurt'. Even grindstones of basalt-lava from Mayen in the Eifel mountains, west of Koblenz, made their way to the Weser estuary.[51] In exchange the coast dwellers traded animal fats, hides, dairy products perhaps and cloth. For the people of the rather treeless shorelines, lumber for construction, as well as charcoal for the smithies, would have had to be imported, no doubt in exchange for livestock. A small harbor with docks was available during the first century. Later the small bay had filled in, so that the area came to be included in the 'Wurt'. The port had probably been relocated further west.

It appears then that at the time of the earliest settlement a free peasant society enjoyed a balanced egalitarian social structure, reflected in the equality of property ownership. From the first century on, however, a social imbalance seems to manifest itself with the emergence of hereditary privilege, which saw peasants and craftsmen enter a dependent relationship with the 'manor'. Nothing can be deduced from the evidence about the 'Wurt' and its role towards the hinterland, nor about its seafaring populations. Classical sources identified them as Chauci.

By the fifth century the incursions of the North Sea caused the settlement to be abandoned. The increased salinity of the low-lying areas deprived the villagers of their drinking water, turned the meadows into salt marshes and in the end forced the inhabitants to give up their way of life. With their impoverishment the houses became smaller and the farming units deteriorated to a point where the population could no longer support itself. It left in search of greater security. Some 18 km further inland a settlement with very similar house construction, similar hall-houses and similar history has been identified. A small gravefield nearby of the fourth and early fifth century showed urn burials in assocation with early Saxon pottery. Of special interest is the presence of rye among the cereal grains found here.

From the third century B.C., wheat, barley, flax, lentils and peas were generally cultivated throughout central Europe. From the second century onward oats, millet, beans, poppy and carrots were common, with rye appearing as an accompanying weed. Probably since the first century B.C. and as a response to a deterioration of the climate, rye became a standard crop, a hardier grain less susceptible to the inconstancies of the weather. Archeologically rye is not really in evidence until the fourth century of our era.

The deterioration of the climate at the beginning of the Iron Age, already referred to in the previous chapter, made it more necessary to shelter the livestock during the winter months. The actual stabling of animals was introduced during the first century B.C. The accumulated manure made possible the fertilization of the fields, which in turn alleviated the problems associated with soil exhaustion, which again freed farming communities from the pressures of relocation every few years. Though habitation sites are still relatively unidentified, those that have been located in Jutland, in Thy and in Himmerland, for instance, show thick layers of accumulated debris and many superimposed housing sites such as only prolonged periods of occupation can leave behind.[52]

Originally the peasant populations lived on individual scattered farms. Only gradually did groups of farms, small hamlets and eventually small villages come into being. Though the 'Wurt' Feddersen Wierde is located quite far to the north, in many respects it can serve as a representative example for the development of village life across the North German Plain. In general the raising of livestock appears to have been the primary activity, with agriculture a vital means by which to supplement the food supply. Initially the soil-surface was broken with a scratch plow, that same inefficient method used since Neolithic times, which exhausted a field in three to five years, whereupon the field had to be allowed to revert to its wild state. After ten to fifteen years it had regained its limited fertility. Even with the stabling of animals and the improved fertilization of fields the problem did not vanish since it forced on the farmer a limit to the size of the field which he could take under cultivation.[53] The amount of organic fertilizer available was limited in that the farmer was not interested in the straw, since the ears were merely sickled off and the straw burned on the fields. Though the ashes returned some minerals to the soil, it was not sufficient. Only with the invention of the scythe were the stalks cut off as well. The search for arable land would remain a problem. Pliny speaks of a turning plow with wheels being in use in Raetia during the first century B.C. The Germanic peoples have been credited with the invention of a heavy plow drawn by eight oxen and equipped with mould-board and coulter to turn the soil instead of just scratching it, as did the Celtic and Mediterranean plows, suitable to till the heavy clay lands of the north European forests.[54] Perhaps this is too generous an attribution. Whatever the case may be, deeper plowing and turning of the soil would have increased the yield and indirectly contributed to overpopulation.

It has been calculated that one hectare could feed two people.[55] It would require eight or nine days to work one hectare with a scratch plow. Considering the accompanying work and the planting period, two or three field workers could take three hectares under cultivation annually. Using a sickle it would take one person ten days of backbreaking work to harvest one hectare of cereal grain. The stalks of cereal grains were short. These circumstances alone point to the important role which the raising of all sorts of livestock and gathering would play in the economy. Only about 3 per cent of the bones found in some villages represent game. The prevailing method of plowing was to lay out long and narrow fields.[56] It was necessary to avoid turning team and plow around as much as possible. It is likely that land was communal property, redistributed annually. Both Caesar[57] and Tacitus[58] refer to this practice. However, this distribution meant one thing if every spring new land first had to be cleared—probably by means of a slash-and-burn method—before being taken under cultivation, and it meant another if an established settlement realloted the communal land to its farmers. In the first instance clearing, plowing, exploiting and exhausting the soil is not likely to allow the evolution of a privileged group of landowners.[59] In the second instance a policy of annual redistribution would intentionally prevent the rise of such a group of landowners. Assuming such a policy existed in the 'Germania' described by Tacitus, then by the second century this policy had broken down, as illustrated by the 'Wurt' at Feddersen Wierde. One can only wonder how such a policy of redistribution could be applied to livestock.

It is apparent that the economic base was rather precarious. Any disruption of a normal planting and harvesting cycle, such as crop failures brought on by drought, hail or excessive rainfall, let alone enemy raids, would have had a calamitous effect on a population living so close to the subsistence line. Mere harassment at crucial times in the year would have made life in a disputed location quite untenable.[60] Without a sizeable accumulated surplus, hunger must have been a familiar occurrence. As it was, the food value of the agricultural produce consumed was desperately low.

Though he was probably not entirely vegetarian, the Tollund man, one of the bog people found in Himmerland, Denmark, had a stomach and intestine content that consisted mainly of weeds.[61] Along with some barley his last meal contained knotweed, linseed, goose foot, spurrey, 'heart's ease', 'gold of pleasure'—*Camelina sativa*, flax, blue and green bristle-grass, camomile, hemp and nettle, all ground into a meal and served as gruel. Analysis of the remains in the alimentary canal showed that he lived for another twelve to twenty-four hours before he was killed. After eating this mess, the poor man should have been spared any further indignities. It is safe to assume that such was a usual diet during the last century B.C. Since livestock was kept for dairy purposes, meat cannot have been a dietary staple. The last meal of the Grauballe man, who died in Himmerland in *c.* 300 A.D. contained sixty-three varieties of grain, plus eleven types of weeds over and above those found in the Tollund man.[62] Since the analyses do not reveal any evidence of greens or fruit, it has been surmised that these executions had taken place in winter or early spring, perhaps as a ritual sacrifice to carry messages to the gods to hasten the arrival of spring. Using a hand-held stone it requires almost an hour to grind 1 kg of wheat grain into a usable flour.[63] The 'flour' contained particles of the grindstone which accounts for the excessive wear of the teeth. Grains of stone can be found in stomach contents.

The depositing of offerings in the moors, already practised in previous ages, continued into the fifth century of our era. Bronze ornaments, weapons, musical instruments, ritual wagons, cauldrons, food and all sorts of domesticated animals had been sacrificed in the moors. Even today popular beliefs see in moors and peat bogs, with their luminous vapors, sites of terror, dwelling places of gods and demons, of restless and vengeful ghosts and of spectres, who with illusory lights lure their victims off the marked and laid-out paths to certain death. Such poor wretches are found frequently.

The extraordinary treatment which was meted out to some select individuals after 200 B.C. and which stands so much apart from the common funerary practices of the age, suggests that the well-preserved corpses found in the north European bogs are also a form of sacrificial offering to the gods. However, because this 'sacrificial ritual' is by no means uniform, it is not possible to state that the motivation behind all of the human depositions is the same. Nevertheless they do seem to fall into two categories—one sacrifical, supplicatory and intercessional, the other expiatory and punitive. About seven hundred 'bog people' have been found in the last two hundred years alone and more continue to be found as the removal of peat enters new areas and reaches greater depths. Finds have been documented in Norway, Sweden, Denmark—the greatest number of finds has been recorded here—the British Isles, Holland, Schleswig-Holstein, Western and Central Germany and in Lower Saxony—the area with the second greatest frequency of finds.[64] In some instances only parts of the body have been found, especially heads, as for instance the decapitated head of a fifty- to sixty-year-old man, fractured on its left side, displaying an intricate figure-eight knot on its right side, found in a bog at Osterby, wrapped in a sewn cape of deer skin (Plate 8a).

As can be imagined this practice invites a great deal of speculation. Tacitus gives a fairly detailed account of the fertility ritual surrounding the goddess Nerthus whose cultic area includes large sections of Denmark and Schleswig-Holstein.[65] This cult included the sacrifice of those who had witnessed the mysteries of the cult and had touched the goddess in ministering to her. This circumstance has been linked to the bog-people whose possible participation in such a ritual may have led to their death. Perhaps they were prisoners kept expressly for such a purpose. Whereas strangulation was a common form of execution in these instances, and as many of the dead still have the twisted rope around their necks, and as a bronze figurine of a 'goddess' appears to wear a double neck ring, it has been suggested[66] that the noose is indeed a replica of the sacred torcs, also incidentally very much in evidence on the male and female representations on the Gundestrup and Rynkeby cauldrons. This would suggest that the victims were consecrated choices of the cult around the goddess. That they were special is supported by the repeated observation that their hands are finely formed with well-groomed fingernails, indicating that they had not performed any heavy manual labor. One recorded instance from Sweden tells of a king who was hanged by his people as a sacrifice to the corn goddess to secure a good harvest.[67] Such sacrifices would be supplicatory and intercessional. It has been thought possible that after a ritual marriage the bog-men had for a little while played the part of god and husband to the goddess, especially during the spring festivals and the prescribed processions through the fields, before being subjected to the demands of the cult, the consecrated sacrifice. There followed the deposition in a hallowed part of the moor. In some instances other sacrifical items, especially wheels and other cart fragments, have been found in the sacrifical moors. Even in Germanic times there was sacrifice to water spirits and those inhabiting the moors, usually combined with other offerings to the gods, involving animals and cultic meals. On the other hand religious law may have played a role in the enforcement of the death penalty. Certain crimes may have been conceived to have roused the anger of the gods, in which case the deaths were expiatory executions motivated by the hope of appeasing the offended divinities, in the hope that their wrath might be averted from the community. Such executions were not accompanied by gifts. Shameful deeds invited severe punishments which ranged from expulsion from the community and the custody of its laws, making the culprit an outlaw, to his actual execution. A close link must have existed in people's minds between the sacrifice and the death penalty. According to Tacitus,[68] among the Germani traitors and renegades were hung from trees; cowards, poor fighters and war dodgers and those who engaged in unnatural acts were plunged into the moors and covered with brush, with the guiding principle that the punishment should be in accord with the crime, that public crimes should be punished publicly as visible deterrents, while the memory of abominable acts should be hidden in darkness. Female adultery led to the woman having her hair shorn in the presence of her relatives, followed by her expulsion from the village, a degradation still known in modern times. Here too death in the bog must have been a harsh interpretation of the law. It is illustrated by the girl found in the bog at Windeby, south of Eckernförde in Schleswig.[69] Except for her disintegrated chest, she was extremely well preserved (Plate 8b). Bone analysis showed her to be fourteen years old. Her hair had been shaved off on the left side of her head, on the right side it was up to 5 cm long. Her body bore no signs of maltreatment. Though she had been blindfolded, the leash-like collar around her neck had not been used to strangle her. This suggests that she had been led from the village blindfolded, dressed only in a short furry cape, and drowned in the bog. Some large stones found beside her must have weighed her down. The bones had retained their shape, the skin, where present, and her brain had been preserved in the acid enriched water. She too had grown up with quite inadequate winter diets. Pollen analysis indicates that she lived during the first century A.D. Two staves had been broken over her, probably an indication of the finality of the verdict, a practice preserved idiomatically even in modern German. Of interest is the gesture expressed by her raised right hand—the tip of the thumb protruding between index and middle finger, the 'fig'. It is a well known European expression of obscene defiance, probably directed against her executioners.

Common features encountered in the circumstances surrounding the moor-corpses are decapitations, crushing blows to the head, throat slitting and strangulation after torture, breaking of bones, mutilation and dismemberment. No doubt the oozing out of life into the earth associated with the cutting of the throat must have had ritual significance. The placement and deliberate arrangement of sticks over the corpse, the sticks being held in place by stakes, forked sticks and other pegs, as though to suggest that the body was actually caged, separates those who drowned accidentally from those executed. The victims tended to be at least partially unclothed, covered with no more than a leather cap and/or short or long capes. Generally ropes or twisted thongs around the neck suggest hanging or strangulation. One such corpse, among many, was found in the moor at Dätgen in the district of Rendsburg–Eckernförde.[70] The humic acid had preserved the headless body from total decomposition. The body was anchored by arm-thick birch stakes. About 3 m away was located the head, also held down with pointed sticks rammed into the ground. The man was about thirty years old, 1·70 m tall, with well-groomed finger- and toenails and an intricately formed hair-knot, a Suebian knot according to Tacitus, itself a sign that the man was a member of an elevated social group. He had been stabbed numerous times in the chest, one wound through the heart no doubt being the fatal blow. He had also received a severe beating as shown by the many fractures all over his body. His genitals were missing. The unsuccessful attempt to sever his head by cutting through his throat led to a decapitating blow from behind. His stomach contents yielded such cereals as millet, wheat and other weeds, but also cervine hair, demonstrating that his last meal contained meat of deer. Carbon-14 analysis dates his death to 170 ± 35 years B.C. Rather than looking at this brutality as an expression of outright cruelty, there appears to be behind it a superstitious fear of magical powers which would allow the deceased to return. The torture preceding his death deprived him of his harmful powers. Perhaps here lie the reasons for this man's emasculation. The greater his power in life, the greater the threat to others after his death, so that the mutilations were protective measures, especially in the case of adulterers, sorcerers, desecrators and murderers.

Separate and distinct deposits of clothing have been found submerged in the moors (Fig. 239). Except for their discoloration these were very well preserved by the acids of the bog water. Complete wardrobes of women's clothing, made of a fine tartan patterned weave, have been brought to the surface. In general they show continuity with styles already found during the late Bronze Age, and discussed earlier. As has already been shown for earlier periods, the image of fur-clad savages is fanciful. The relief on a Roman sarcophagus at the Museo Capitolino in Rome, depicting the defeat of the Cimbri shows that some of the northerners emphasize the nudity-in-battle aspect. Curiously enough the naked warriors carry Celtic shields.[71] Later representations on the columns of Trajan (98–117 A.D.) and Marcus Aurelius (161–180 A.D.) show the Trans-Danubian warriors—non-Germanic Dacians and Germanic Marcomans, but also Trajan's Germanic bodyguard, wearing trousers but with bare torsos, short capes, or loose-fitting short- or long-sleeved and thigh-length tunics covered by a short cape held together at the right shoulder by a round fibula. Some tunics extend below the knee. Trousers, tunics, capes, and cloaks have been recovered from the moors (Fig. 240). The trousers in themselves are not particularly Germanic, but rather appear to be a function of horsemanship. Ankle-length trousers or knee-length breeches recommend themselves for the man on horseback. They appear as a logical item of clothing to come from the eastern plains into the Celtic realms. Very short capes have been recovered with 'executed' bog-men. Double skins have also been found—capes of inner and outer fur, leather caps, woven cloth mantles with fringes, large enough to serve as blankets, (Fig. 241) scarves, belts and leather shoes (Fig. 242). Thus the Tollund man had a belt around his middle, but what was it that it had been intended to hold? A linen tunic? Linen does not survive in the bogs. Its manufacture was known in the Bronze Age. In general men's clothing does not show continuity from earlier periods. In view of the deteriorating climate, the rather skimpy clothing for men, documented also by Tacitus, is indeed puzzling (Fig. 243). When compared to the high fashions and rich fabrics worn by the Celts to the south, the impression created by northern garments is one of widespread poverty. The evidence may not be representative in view of the practice of cremation.

Moor-geology takes advantage of the fact that moors grow upward,[72] allowing the identification of strata, so helpful in the fixing of dates. Analysis of the pollen preserved in the moors allows the observation of changes in vegetation including types and extent of forests. It is consequently possible to reconstruct the physical world in which man lived well before historical records begin.

The area between the rivers Ems and Elbe is especially characterized by moors. In earlier periods these seemingly endless, soggy, bottomless, treacherous wastes appeared

239. Woollen cloak, worn and patched, perhaps a sacrificial deposition, early centuries A.D., from a bog at Dätgen near Rensdorf.

240. Cloak and trousers of a corpse found in a bog at Damendorf near Eckernförde, early centuries A.D.

hostile to man. To Romans such as Tacitus, Germania appeared to be no more than trackless forests and impenetrable swamps. As such the moors acted as natural barriers to cultural influences, as obstacles to the movement of peoples, promoting isolation. They forced the Romans to try to reach the estuary of the Elbe by sea. As inhospitable and treacherous as the moors and marshes were to foreigners, to the wanderer in the dusk, and to the unwary, the fens were not entirely impassable for the initiates and their vehicles. As early as the Neolithic, the inhabitants had learned to lay out roadways of logs and sticks by means of which they could cross over the more reliable sections. Of course the natives knew how to vault from solid tuft to solid tuft, where to hunt and gather or dig peat for fuel. In their vastness the moors must have represented the unknown, the unfathomable, the realm of hostile spirits, of subterranean gods, perhaps of the nether world, where men vanished without leaving a trace. No wonder man

326

241. Fragments of a woollen cloak with tassels and a skirt, found in a bog, first century A.D.

242. Leather shoes and human skin preserved by peat acid, belonging to the corpse found in the bog at Damendorf.

327

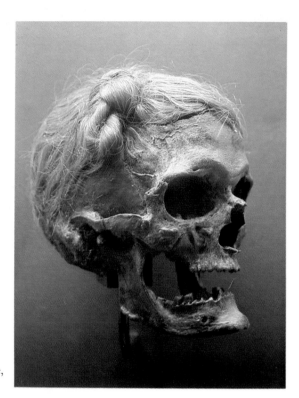

Plate 8a. Man's head found wrapped in a cape, from a bog at Osterby near Eckernförde, early centuries A.D.

Plate 8b. Girl's corpse from a bog at Windeby near Eckernförde, early centuries A.D.

243. Column base, showing Germanic captives wearing short capes, relief from the so-called Praetorium in Mainz.

deposited such a vast assortment of offerings there. The properties of the moors are such that organic materials are preserved. Hardwood may be entirely waterlogged and as soft as butter, but any objects made of such wood do not lose their shape. This is not the case with softwood.

No doubt the Mesolithic hunters had marked out paths as they followed the game. Some time before the sixth century B.C., the inhabitants of the northern moors had developed techniques of building roadways ideally suited to the terrain. On a leveled 'railbed', for instance, on two spaced 'rails' running in the desired direction, split beams were placed, providing a level, almost gapless road surface. At the ends of each beam holes had been chiseled through which stakes had been driven to fasten each beam in place (Fig. 244). Much smoother than a washboard road, one such road of beams had crossed the Wittemoor from Hude to the former tributary of the river Hunte, some 20 km east of Oldenburg.[73] During the third century B.C. the road, c. 3·5 km long, had been staked out and then two crews worked toward one another from opposite ends. Its northern section had been constructed of straight unsplit stems of alder, while the approaching southern section had been made of cleanly split oak timbers, 2·7–3 m long, each staked in place, a remarkable effort if one considers the required man-hours. The wooden surface had been covered with sod to protect the wood. Sealed off against the air, these logs have survived. The significance of this particular road was that it connected the sod-ore deposits around Hude—over 50 smelters have been found—with a former tributary of the river Hunte, a navigable river which flowed into the Weser, a transportation system which connected a point inland with the open sea.[74] A limited network of such roads crisscrossed the various moors in the north. They offer some idea about settlements and communications between sedentary populations. Migrant populations do not build roads. In one instance pine trees had sprouted beside the road.

329

Dendrochronology showed that they grew to be eighteen years old, which gives an approximate indication of the life expectancy of such a road.

Ideally suited for crossing soggy terrain, the method of construction offered only a precarious crossing over moving water, or over terrain affected by varying water levels, where the beams could not be secured against hooves, wheels and currents. It has been found that such danger spots were protected by 'gods'. On this road near the crossing over a brook, cult sites had been established on either side of the road, each site having been placed under the protection of a divinity, on one side of a goddess, on the other of a god. The divine pair had been carved with an axe from oaken planks, simplified in outline but quite stylized in execution.[75] Between the gods, and spanning the roadway, a gate of squared beams and a transverse board terminating in 'horns' had been erected. Further north, four additional wooden figures have been located along the road, each near a short decayed section where some peril existed for those using the road. These four figures had been knocked over so that the broken tips were still stuck in the ground, indicating their original positions. All six had been removed, placed beside the road and deliberately covered with peat. This had probably been done when the road was abandoned. No longer needed, the protective spirits had been returned to their realm. Of interest is the abstract appearance of these 'divinities'. A basic anthropomorphic shape characterizes them all. While the male representation (Fig. 245) has a clearly defined head and squared neck, the body is treated more symbolically and perhaps magically, having four 'ribs' carved beneath the 'shoulder' on its left side and six 'ribs' beneath the 'shoulder' on its right side. It had only one centered and squared-off leg. The overall impression is rectangular. The female representation (Fig. 246) on the other

244 (facing page). Log road No. VI, *c.* 50 B.C., from the Great Moor north of Diepholz in Lower Saxony.

245 & 246. Male and female 'divinities' from the moors south of Oldenburg, found near a split-log road. The two formed a cultic pair. After 400 B.C.

331

hand is more curvaceous. Still very stylized, the head, torso and hips, although cut in a zigzag, flow more continuously into pointed legs, reminiscent of Paleolithic 'Venus' figures. The genital area is clearly indicated on the female form, but not apparent on the male. Of the other four images one was a board with a figure roughed in with a few blows of an axe, two others were no more than poles provided with facial features, and the fourth had the shape of a hammer. In front of the female figure sharpened stakes had been driven into the ground on which to place offerings.[76] Neither fur nor bones have been found, however.

Many such sacred sites have been discovered between Scandinavia and the Central German Highlands. In a bog in Jutland, for instance, a heap of stones had covered a 3 m tall 'goddess', a forked oak-branch of generally anthropomorphic form, slender, with identifiable 'hips' and an unambiguous incision where the fork begins.[77] No other identifiable parts were added. Among items of obscure purpose, the presence of a number of Iron Age pots identifies the spot as a sacrificial site, probably dedicated to fertility and/or harvest rituals. The bog was her abode to which she retired between festivities, unless the goddess was herself a sacrifice in the end. Other such deities have been uncovered throughout the area (Fig. 247). Using pieces of wood whose natural shapes often suggested anthropomorphic forms with sexual connotations to their beholders, the northern populations set up divinities, probably conceived in pairs. Ceramic deposits are invariably associated with these sites. Without wanting to suggest that these people saw latent sexual representations every time they looked at a tree, it is apparent that their cults centered around a nature religion which paid specific attention to fertility, growth and reproductive cycles, characterized by an emphasis of generative and especially vegetative and organic processes (Fig. 248). The notion of sacred trees is of course not restricted to northern Europe; however, this apparent link between the

247. Cultic post terminating in the shape of a 'head', from Werlte near Achendorf, early centuries A.D.

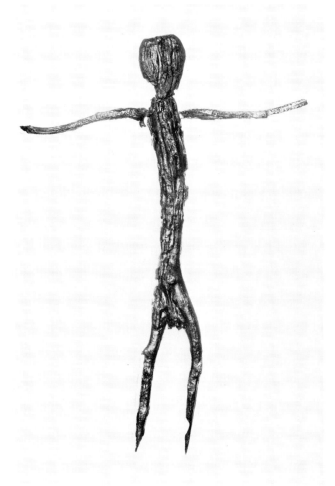

248. Cultic figure from the island of Fehmarn, early centuries A.D.

249. 'Divine pair' found near a sacrificial site, cultic figures from Braak near Eutin, after 500 B.C.

organic elements and abstract principles will continue to be a productive northern characteristic. The choice of wood recommended itself since few workable raw materials were available to them. As in earlier times the northerners were still not carving their own amber. In spite of their sophisticated tools and skill as craftsmen, the awkward crudeness of all these figures is striking and must have been deliberate.

Most explicit is a pair of 'tree gods' found in a moor at Braak near Eutin in eastern Holstein, some 35 km north of Lübeck (Fig. 249). Associated pottery fragments have been dated to the bronze to iron transition phase, 500–400 B.C. Carbon-14 analysis of the figures has corroborated this date.[78] Made of two forks of knotty oak, both male (2·80 m) and female (2·3 m) figures had specially attached tenon-arms set in mortises. Up to the shoulders the wood of the 'tree gods' had been subjected only to minor modifications; the necks however, had been worked roughly without regard to realism. Yet the female received much more attention in the finishing. The facial features of both were worked out with the same technique, but while the male head bears no other distinguishing marks, the female goddess wears a bun on the top of her head (Fig. 250). The two figures are distinguished by additional 'naturalistic' detail, in that the male figure once had a distinct remnant of a branch protruding in the area of the groin, just below the fork. The torso of the goddess had two small simulated breasts inserted in

333

mortises. As was the case with Paleolithic 'Venus' figures, so here too the emphasis on sexual and reproductive organs is generally seen to point to the deities' function in terms of fertility. They had been found near a pad of peat moss about 12 m in diameter which had been 'paved' with a layer of stone 60–70 cm thick,[79] which was mixed with layers of ashes and pottery shards, a possible altar on which pottery had been placed, or perhaps smashed in offertory fashion as a wish for fertility and abundance. To this day a German village custom is to celebrate the 'Polterabend' on the eve of a wedding, when well-wishers come and break crockery as an expression of hope that the union will be fruitful. Viking tradition designates some gods with such terms as *trégud* (literally treegod) or *hulgud* (German *Holzgott*, wooden god), pointing to the tenacity of such notions over more than a thousand years, especially when reinforced by later mythology. Thus the northern creation myth has an ash tree transformed into the first man, Askr, and an elm tree into the first woman, Embla. For certain occasions these deities may have worn clothing. These festive garments were probably deposited in the moors afterwards, being too sacred to be worn by humans. Desecration meant certain death. Our scare-crows may be late echoes of such practices, rather than having originally being intended to keep away birds and other creatures, seeing that animals adjust very quickly to stationary novelties. It is conceivable that the ready notion of fertility obscures much weightier ideas about principles of cosmic power. Thus the god from Braak had its genitals hacked off some time before the pair was deposited in the moor nearby. This emasculation must symbolically have deprived the god of all his powers, surely not only of his fertility, for his powers must have transcended such limits. In this emasculation as well, the mutilation must have been a precaution, not only to neutralize the god's great powers over life and death while 'active' on earth, but to remove the threat he consti-tuted even after his deposition. His capacity to be benevolent must have been balanced by his capacity for malevolence. Hence the emasculation. This deliberate act, however, is not consistent with notions about the animal death and rebirth of vegetation gods, for then one would have expected the goddess to have been abused as well, unless there is some unknown significance behind the missing arms. In any case, throughout the area the emphasis put on the presence, absence or treatment of the phallic principle is not at all uniform.

Repeated reference has been made to the Nerthus cult practised in the regions and islands of the western Baltic Sea. Especially on Jutland, Tacitus identified such tribes as the Anglii, Varini and Aviones,[80] who formed a cultic community which participated in rituals dedicated to Nerthus. It is unlikely that the divinity travelled from one tribal area to another, as the arrival here or there could not possibly have coincided with any seasonal processes and accompanying rituals; it must therefore be assumed that tribal delegates assembled in one location,[81] at the deity's sanctuary, to participate in the festivities. The word *Nerthus* has been linked with the Celtic word *nerto*—strength, power.[82] Old Norse has the word *njard*—strong, so that the deity's name Nerthus may very well represent personified vitality and the compulsive drives of nature. Further-more the name Nerthus corresponds to that of the Norse god Njordr, the father of the later god Freyr and his divine sister Freya. Freyr is also known as Ingvifreyr. Ingvi, or in Anglo-Saxon Ing, is the chief deity and ancestral god of the Ingaevones who, according to Tacitus, along with the Istaevones and Herminones form the three ances-tral tribal groups of the Germanic peoples. Thus while the Nerthus tribes belong to the Ingaevones, Nerthus belongs to that line of gods belonging to Ing, the Vanir, the oldest race of gods according to Norse mythology. This etymological and mythological

250. Details of the male and female cultic figures from Braak.

approach provides an ancient name which can actually be linked with archeological evidence. Tacitus refers to the deity as *terra mater*—Earth Mother—which identifies Nerthus as a goddess. Since Tacitus was quite familiar with the concept of the Phrygian *magna mater* but chose instead to apply to Nerthus the term *terra mater* he must have appreciated the difference.[83]

It is probable that the occasion of the cultic festival also provided the opportunity to convene the assembly of tribal councils, the *Thing*,[84] in what may very well have been an interlinked sequence of consecrated events under the auspices of religious ceremonies which included sacrifices. Already the sacrificial practices discussed above suggest that

335

the offerings were made in the presence of extensive congregations. At these gatherings weapons were tabu since the peace of the festival prevailed. Tacitus indicates that the sanctuary was located '*in insula Oceani*'.[85] This led to an unsuccessful search for a possible island location. The festival focussed on a procession in which the goddess was driven about in a vehicle drawn by sacred cows, a traditional aspect when dealing with a goddess linked with fertility and harvest rituals. In what must have been intended to represent a sacred marriage, a priest, the 'husband of Nerthus',[86] accompanied the vehicle and the goddess or her human stand-in shrouded in mystery during this bridal procession through the land. Corpus Christi processions in Bavaria and Austria, in which statues of the Virgin Mary are carried through the fields to bless them, may be a late echo. The vehicles found in the moor at Dejbjerg, illustrated in the previous chapter, may have served such a processional purpose. Following its tour through the world of mortals the holy vehicle and the divine image returned to the sacred precinct where, hidden from the view of the profane, vehicle and goddess underwent a ritual ablution in a small lake,[87] whereupon the slaves who while ministering to them had touched and thereby profaned the image were put to death in the Lake.

In a marsh at Rappendam on Sjaeland in a former lake, parts of twenty-eight wheels, hubs and other parts of wagons and a plough-share had been deposited in distinct groups over many years.[88] Near one group the skeleton of a man was found, as well as the skeletons of at least five sheep and bones of cattle, horses and wild pigs. The close association of vehicles, draught animals and human sacrifice—the three key elements we met in the account given by Tacitus—makes it attractive to consider a site such as this one at Rappendam the location of a sacred precinct, dedicated to Nerthus. Tacitus himself does not mention the sacrifice of vehicles and animals.

It has been suggested that the cart and oxen found chiseled onto a stone slab from the interior of the stone cist at Züschen (*c.* 2000–1800 B.C.), illustrated in chapter 2, are an early representation of the Nerthus cult.[89] However that may be, the suggestion does raise the question about the transition from the symbolic representation of natural forces, sun discs for instance, to the representation of anthropomorphic, more personally conceived gods. If one takes the Trundholm solar disc (*c.* 1000 B.C.) to represent the former, and the 'Deities' stone from Anderlingen (after *c.* 1400 B.C.) to represent the latter, one finds that the two are more or less contemporary. Certainly the people of the eastern Hallstatt were familiar with cultic processions during which a goddess was driven about. The proof is the model of a vehicle from Strettweg on which a tall and slender 'goddess' towers over her entourage of horsemen and sacrificial ministrants, illustrated in chapter 4. Direct links between the eastern Hallstatt and the north did not, however, exist.

Sacrificial sites continue to be discovered, dating from prehistoric times in central Europe to Viking times in Scandinavia. One site, one of the most important sanctuaries, which reached the peak of its use during the third century of our era, has been found in a moor near Oberdorla,[90] about 8 km south of Mühlhausen, in the ancestral tribal region of the Thuringians. At the edge of a lake, 'tree gods' were set up and sacrifices made to them of wooden and ceramic vessels with remnants of food, along with animal bones, a boat, horse heads, hooves and human skeletal remains such as those of a fifteen-year-old girl, as well as the skull and the extremities of a thirty-year-old man.

A common feature at the sacrificial sites is evidence of cultic feasts held on the occasion of the offertory rites, the remnants of which then ended up in the bog. Towards the end of the pre-Christian era the sacrificial sites suggest an increase in inter-tribal warfare. This would mean that the offerings were made to a god of war, or that the gods were sufficiently undefined to be able to unfold the warrior aspect of their being to accommodate this new need. The most significant find of this type is the large seagoing boat found in the moor at Hjortspring[91] on the island of Als, a site which had been a traditional depository of offerings since the Bronze Age. The boat had probably been captured during a fight and had then been offered to the god(s) as a victory offering. It contained equipment including 8 iron swords, 138 iron spear heads, 31 spear heads of antler and bone, about 20 iron shirts, and about 100 wooden shields, rectangular in shape with rounded corners. The spear shafts, 2–3 m long, were made of ash, mountain ash, hazel and willow. The boat was made of five planks, one used as a floorboard and two each for the sides. All five planks had been drawn together and upward to form prow and stern. The planks overlapped somewhat, in the clinker style, which increases both buoyancy and stability. The overlap made it possible to 'sew' the seams by threading bark fiber through two rows of holes 7–8 cm apart. The seams were caulked with pith. The planks were reinforced by cross-ribs. Two thwarts accommodated two rowers each. A large steering oar was found in the boat. Having been damaged by peat cutters the boat is not complete. It is estimated to have been about 19 m long stem to stern, 2 m wide and 70 cm high amidships. Linden, oak, ash and hazel had been used in its construction.[92]

It is documented that before a battle the combatants would consecrate the enemy survivors and all their possessions to the gods. Thus Plutarch, Livius and Dio Cassius describe how after the battle of Arausio, 105 B.C., the Ambrones had followed their oath to offer everything to the gods and thrown all the booty into the river, drowning even the horses and hanging the surviving legionaires. Caesar writes of similar practices among the Celts,[93] for whom any violations of this oath, a desecration in fact, entailed a gruesome death for the perpetrator. When Germanicus came upon the battlefield on which the Cheruski had destroyed three Roman legions in 9 A.D., he found that men and horses had been offered to the gods. In spite of intensive search the site has not yet been found.

Tacitus tells how at the assembly it was also permissible to lay accusations and to bring capital charges of treason, desertion, cowardice, and debauchery, for each of which the death penalty could be imposed.[94] As has been observed, the difference between sacrifice and execution is not always apparent. It appears evident though that towards the end of the pagan period in central Europe, ritual sacrifice and the execution of criminal and asocial elements in the population appear to have fused, in that one tended to select desecrators and outlaws for the religious rites. In the end only the death penalty for criminals remained. For centuries executions retained something of the festive for the onlookers, while even today the religious ceremonial continues to play a part of the execution ritual.

It has been demonstrated that towards the end of the Northern Bronze Age a new impetus was making itself felt in the area north of the Central German Highlands, which found expression in a ceramic culture named after the type station of Jastorf. Although the general limits of this culture are known, the Jastorf culture as such would be difficult to pinpoint were it not generally true that pottery is less of a trade object than metal wares, and that therefore the extent of a cultural influence can be assessed. The observation has also been made that cultural areas which can be grasped archeologically do not necessarily coincide with linguistic and ethnic groups, while the chronologies developed by philology have revealed themselves to be much less finely

337

calibrated than those developed by archeology. The Central Highlands proved to be a border as well as a transition zone, in that on the one hand the Celts themselves did not pass to the north of it in culturally significant numbers, and on the other hand it was in this region that the transfer of iron and iron technology took place, allowing for the contact between Celts and northerners which would bring objects worked in the Celtic La Tène style as far north as Denmark. In this contact the cultural flow was essentially northward with the south acting as donor. The question whether these northerners were Germanic, however, requires a decision in the linguistic realm, because any group speaking a language that had not undergone the First Soundshift, which differentiates the Germanic languages from the Indo-European, was only speaking an Indo-European dialect. Linguistically they can not be identified as Germani until this has happened. Although the disparities in material wealth between the proto-Germanic north and the Celtic south is very noticeable, the same cannot be said for the spiritual realm, in which an inherent relation existed between the two cultural areas.

Some time during the third century B.C., perhaps in the currents created by the westward relocation of the central European Celtic realms, it is conceivable that associated tribes located further to the north made use of the opportunity to cross over the Rhine to establish themselves in northern Gaul.[95] Their encounter with established Celts caused these tribes to spread out from the Argonne Forest to the Channel. In its wake the movement of such a mass of people created a vacuum at first and then a turmoil of populations as other peoples from the Northern Plains poured into the vacated land. The pressure exerted by these northern neighbors may very well have provided some of the motivation for the Celtic resettlement. These people have come to be called Belgae, of whom Caesar writes in the second book of his *Gallic Wars* that the majority of them were Germani from the east side of the Rhine, come to settle fertile lands. The Belgae appear to have been the connecting link between Celts and northerners in central Europe, hence it would be quite consistent to see in them a celticized people originating in the transition area of central Germany. Strabo stresses the resemblance between Belgae and Germani, so that it is possible that some imperceptible gradations existed between Celts, Belgae and Germani.[96] Unfortunately the classical ethnographers were content to identify Celts and Scythians to the north. Between them they assumed a zone of undefined Celto-Scythians. Nor did their curiosity induce them to do linguistic comparisons. They were after all barbarians. The departure of the Belgae from central Europe was most likely a gradual emigration of tribal groups, rather than the abrupt exodus of an entire population. Not by any means homogeneous, they detached themselves in shifts, so that it probably took a century before the main body had crossed the Rhine somewhere between present-day Cologne and Nijmegen, following the logical entrance route into western Europe,[97] leaving behind them a surge of new tribes, involved in a sequence of ever-renewed population syntheses, creating a state of continuous turmoil in what was to become a melting-pot that would not simmer down until the fifth century A.D. As it happened, the new settlement area of the Belgae came to form a buffer zone between Gaulish Celts and Germanic northerners. The tribal names of some of the Belgae have continued in their regional centers; thus the Remi are remembered in Reims, the Suessiones in Soissons, the Belovaci in Beauvais, the Ambioni in Amiens, and so forth. By the end of the second century B.C. the Belgae had been able to consolidate their hold on the area to such an extent that when the migrant Cimbri, Teutones, Ambrones and other allies cut easily through the rest of Gaul, they were checked by the Belgae[98] in 110–109 B.C. The Cimbri and most of their allies may have been late to set out on their migration. They moved south-east towards the Balkans. Only after having been rebuffed there did they turn westward. They arrived in Gaul too late. The shifting populations had stabilized, and the power of Rome in the area was increasing. After repeated rejections of their request for land, ten years of futile wandering had sapped them.

The Belgae, incidentally, promptly claimed descent from the Germani. Aware of their own identity, when Caesar appeared, the Belgae formed a league quite apart from the other Celts. Caesar in turn recognized them for their different language, institutions and customs.

Towards the north and along the Rhine an early 'Germanic' tribe had established itself, the Eburones. Their name suggests that the boar, in German *Eber*, was a totem animal to them. It will be remembered how important a role the boar played among the Celts. It is therefore possible that these Eburones were a Celticized Germanic tribal group existing in some relation of sovereignty with the rest of the population of Gaul. Their chief Ambiorix, a Celtic name very similar to the name of the Belgic tribe of the Ambioni, was the first to play the champion of liberty against Caesar, well before Vercingetorix. The Belgae not only took an active part in the defense of Gaul against Rome but proved to be Rome's most redoubtable adversaries. Part of the Gaulish force assembled to relieve Vercingetorix trapped in the oppidum at Alesia consisted of Belgae.[99] In fact, most of Caesar's great strategic maneuvers, the location of his winter quarters and almost all of his punitive campaigns were motivated by the defiance of the Belgae. In the end he resorted to surrounding them with vassal tribes loyal to him. The Belgae constituted the greatest check to his designs, contributing directly to his invasion of Britain.[100]

The problem concerning the geographical origin of the Cimbri and some of their allies has already been touched on. It is not known what set them on their wanderings. Their own tradition spoke of a hostile sea which had forced them to leave their lands. As has already been pointed out, the archeological evidence in Himmerland, their supposed land of origin in northern Jutland, does not support the idea of a large exodus. Whatever their origin, at first their progress must have been slow as they searched for land, cleared it, put in a crop and then harvested it before moving on, gradually shifting towards the south-east, perhaps induced to do so by the Celtic Boii located in Silesia and Bohemia, until they found their way through the ancient passes at the western end of the Carpathians,[101] perhaps causing the Celtic population to occupy their hilltop oppida. The last king of the Cimbri, incidentally, was called Boiorix, perhaps an indication that detachments of Celtic Boii had joined them. Following the Danube they may have wanted to enter the Balkans but must have encountered opposition.[102] All of this is conjecture, except that in 113 B.C. the Cimbri appeared in Noricum on Rome's horizon, and in recorded history. Negotiations with the Roman commander went well, when quite unadvisedly he launched an attack and was defeated disastrously. The site, supposedly near Noreia in Noricum, in itself too imprecise a designation,[103] has not been found. The Cimbrian host turned north-west and vanished in the Celtic lands north of the Alps,[104] to reappear four years later somewhere on the upper Rhine with the Celtic Tigurines, a Helvetic tribe, in their train.[105] It would seem that for a short time at least the Cimbri were guests among the Helvetii. Some of the Cimbri even stayed behind in the Neckar region.[106] The activities of the Cimbri in the Helvetian area south of the river Main are seen to be a cause for the Helvetian shift towards the south-west, into the western Alps.[107] It has also been suggested that it is only now that

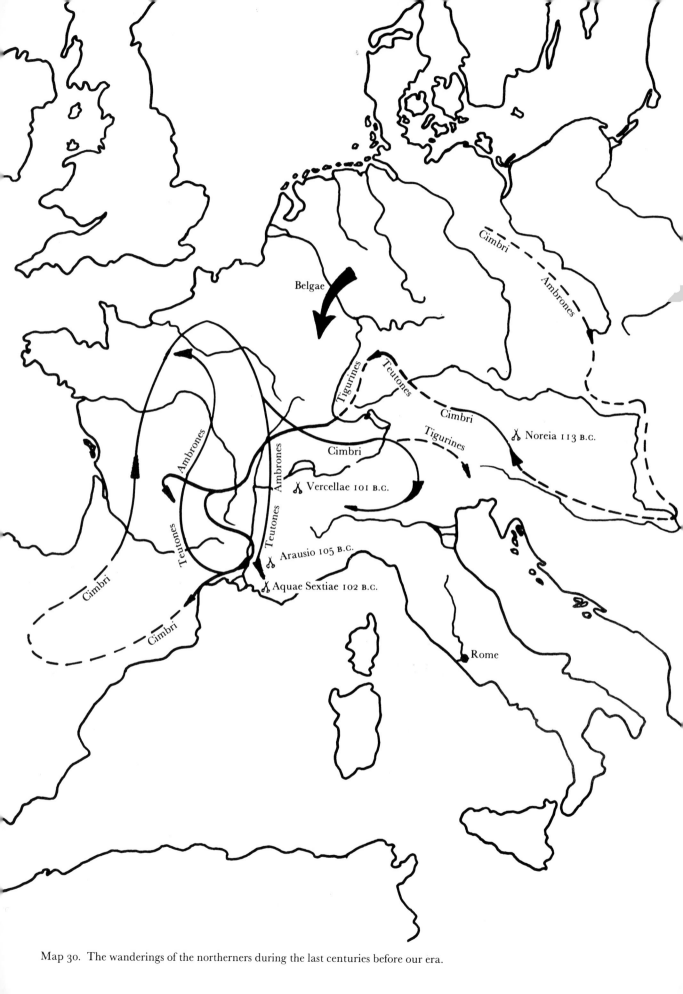

Map 30. The wanderings of the northerners during the last centuries before our era.

the Teutones, either a Celtic tribe settled south of the Main or another of the Helvetic tribes, joined the Cimbri.[108] This tribe is another riddle, which however gains some support from the conclusion that etymologically the word 'Teutones' is of Celtic rather than of Germanic origin,[109] the later maps of Strabo and Ptolemy notwithstanding. Posidonius, the source for many later writers, calls them Celts. Had they not been Celts he might have called them Scythians. The Ambrones may have joined up with them during this time as well. It is a curious sidelight that legionaires in the army of Marius from the Italian region of Umbria thought the Ambrones to be their distant cousins, left behind in their common ancestral lands long ago.[110] From 110-109 B.C. on, the Cimbri and their allies transferred their activities into Gaul, where their initial advance was checked by the Belgae.

The last two decades of the second century B.C. witnessed the final reduction of the Celtic Arvernians in southern Gaul and the transformation of the area into a Roman province. Into the gap left by the Arvernian collapse and the consolidation of the region into a Roman administrative unit, the northern confederation, swollen by tribes and tribal fragments, hoped to thrust itself in order to obtain land.[111] In 109 B.C. the Cimbri destroyed a Roman army and repeated their request for land in return for services and manpower. Their request was denied. The Helvetic fragments and the Cimbri disappeared in southern Gaul. In 107 B.C. a request by the Tigurines for land was rejected and another Roman army was crushed in the resulting battle on the Garonne river. In 105 B.C. the Cimbri reappeared reinforced by the Teutones. The Romans put some 80,000 men into the field against them. The demand for peace and land to cultivate was rejected once again, whereupon the Ambrones inflicted a crushing defeat on the Romans at Arausio, modern Orange, on the Rhône. The bloodbath was completed when the captured booty was hacked to pieces, the horses were drowned in the river and the captives were hanged in one extraordinary offering to the gods.[112] It is also reported that priestesses clad in white robes had led prisoners up to a cauldron, cut their throats over it and interpreted the blood flow. This scene especially has been seen to be a particularly Celtic ritual.[113] Following the battle of Arausio in 105 B.C. the tribes crisscrossed Gaul, ravaging as they went. It is apparent that throughout the early years of this migration the various tribal units acted quite independently of one another, with only loosely formulated 'ideas' about their joint intentions at best. Even if no deliberate strategy was behind these independent expeditions, provisioning the combined tribes off the land in any one location would have been impossible. In the vicinity of Namur they built a fortress Aduatuca to leave their accumulated booty in the care of a garrison of 6,000 men. Fifty years later Caesar encountered these Aduatuci,[114] some 75,000 strong. Having exhausted Gaul the Cimbri swooped into the Iberian peninsula from where they returned in 103 B.C. They met with another rebuff from the Belgae. Following a brief reunification of the various groups on the lower Seine, perhaps to plan the decisive attack on Rome, their repeated successes against Rome's armies must have been a factor in their deliberations, the Teutones struck southward towards Rome around the Maritime Alps. The Cimbri moved eastward to cross the Alps through the northern passes. The Tigurines were to cross the Julian Alps in Noricum.[115] This time the Roman army was prepared for them. Its experienced commander Marius had drilled his troops to the utmost, increased their endurance and prepared them not to take fright at the sight of the northerners' ferocious appearance; but most important, the army reforms which he had introduced gave him a professional army to command.[116] In the autumn of 102 B.C. he met the Teutones and Ambrones at Aquae Sextiae in a

	Type Stations	Migrations	Cultural Adjustments	Economy	Religious Practices	Sites
	Roman Period		Roman influence		Nerthus cult	Gristede Feddersen Wierde
50 B.C.		Caesar's activities in Gaul and along the Rhine	Caesar establishes the name 'Germani'	cattle raising		Gundestrup Rynkeby
	Seedorf	migration and annihilation of the Cimbri, Teutones, Ambrones	'Wurten' settlements along North Sea coast	introduction of the stabling of animals	'bog people'; sacrificial and punitive executions	Grauballe Tollund Osterby Windeby Dätgen
100 B.C.						
150 B.C.	- - - - -				wooden idols	
200 B.C.	Ripdorf		peasant culture	precarious economic base	'tree gods'	Wittemoor Braak Dejbjerg Rappendam Oberdorla Hjortspring
		Westward move of the Belgae from central Europe	washboard roads	scratch plow		
300 B.C.	- - - - -			wheel-thrown pottery	pyre cremation in the north	
				La Tène forms	funerary gifts	
			late phases of the Northern Bronze Age	early iron		
400 B.C.				indebtedness to Hallstatt forms of metal work		
	Jastorf		genesis of proto-Germanic linguistic groups			
			earliest Germanic culture between Weser and Oder rivers	free peasant society	urnfields till c. 500 A.D.	Schwissel Husby Hamfelde Putensen Deutsch-Evern Liebenau Pestrup
500 B.C.						
600 B.C.	- - - - -		continuity of occupation far into Jastorf period			
	Wessenstedt					

Chart 9. Northern Genesis: to the arrival of the Romans.

battle to the death which lasted for four days. For the northerners it was a complete rout. The great number of prisoners taken contributed significantly to the available manpower of Rome's slave-holding society. Late that same year the Cimbri crossed the Alps and promptly defeated a Roman army sent to block their way into the Po valley. The following July (101 B.C.) with the addition of the army of Marius the combined Roman forces inflicted an annihilating defeat on the Cimbri at Vercellae, north of the Po between Milan and Turin. According to Plutarch[117] the July sun and the intense heat of summer did as much to wear down the northerners as did Roman arms. While most of the Cimbrian army was cut to pieces on the field, their front-line fighters linked together with chains, behind the Cimbrian lines another massacre was taking place in their camp. When the Romans reached it they were just in time to witness the mass suicides of the Cimbrian women, who, having first killed their fleeing menfolk and then the weak and their children, proceeded to kill themselves, in order not to fall into slavery.[118] In spite of the carnage the haul in slaves, over 60,000 apparently, equalled the number of Teutones sold into slavery. Sulla, Marius's later rival for power in Rome, defeated the Tigurines in Noricum. The final resolve to gamble everything on one pitched battle indicates the level of frustration and desperation which the wandering northerners must have reached after over twenty years of migration. What could they have hoped to gain by attacking Rome directly?

The significance of these encounters rests on the effect which this experience with the northerners had on all future Roman dealings with the north.[119] Caesar would be able to apply the Cimbrian scare to his rationale for expanding Roman territory in Gaul and for establishing the Rhine as a necessary and permanent boundary behind which civilized regions would be safe from further incursions by these northern savages.[120] The effects on Gaul of the Cimbrian intrusion lay in that it ripped apart the already frayed fabric of Gaulish society, initially weakened by the centrifugal forces of internecine tribal warfare, aggravated by the accompanying tensions in the social structure and by the cultural estrangement brought on by years of Roman influence and the piecemeal reduction of southern Gaul. Considering the tenacity with which the Belgae resisted Caesar,[121] one can only wonder what effect the established presence of these central European tribes in Gaul might have had on Caesar's conquest of Gaul. On the other hand, a Rome which had worn down Hannibal, and now had been able to overcome the loss of four consular armies with such resolute obstinacy, was more than a match for an unstable amalgam of migrant tribes. After each military catastrophe Rome could put ever new armies into the field and emerge still stronger than it had been at the beginning of the conflict (Fig. 251).

The encounter between northerners and Rome advances the definition of the term 'Germani' by one step. Except for such names as Teuto, Teutobochus among the Teutones, and Boiorix, Lugius (Lug is the name of a Celtic god), Claodicus and Caesorix, the language of the Cimbri and Teutones is not known. However, it seems that in Rome the term 'Germani' was first applied to former Cimbrian prisoners after the great slave uprising under Spartacus, 73–71 B.C.,[122] and meant prisoners who came from beyond the Rhine, without there being any implications involved about language or race. The term barbarian was of course all-embracing. Caesar is the first to identify the Cimbri and Teutones as 'Germani'[123] as a part of his division of peaceful Celts and hostile Germani separated by the Rhine.[124] This distinction appears to have been made because of the aggressive war he was waging in Gaul and which he had to justify to the Roman Senate, as Rome prided itself in waging only just wars. To avoid censure and

251. Relief with attacking Roman legionairies, from the Praetorium of the Roman fort in Mogontiacum (Mainz). This relief, as well as the one depicted in Fig. 243 were found in the Roman defensive wall where the blocks found a new use during the troubled times of the later Empire.

possible removal from his command in Gaul, Caesar had to demonstrate to the Senate that the Rhine recommended itself as the logical boundary of Gaul, separating Celts from Germani.[125] For strategic reasons the Rhine would have to be declared the natural limit as a precaution, if Gaul was to remain a secure conquest, and it did not matter to Caesar that ethnologically he was creating clear-cut and convenient differentiations where there were none in the population which he encountered. He came to admit this in the commentaries on his second year of the Gallic war when he recognized the existence of Germani on the left bank of the Rhine.[126] Caesar saw the political need for such a distinction quite clearly, unwittingly providing a self-fulfilling prophecy which gave modern European scholars many years of deliberation on the question around the identity of these 'Germani' and the origin of the word 'German'. Not until the rise of nationalism in the nineteenth century, however, did it become a serious nationalistic problem along ethnological lines between France and Germany. The undeniable effect of Caesar's conquests was the splitting-up of the old world of the La Tène,[127] contributing to the compacting of western Europe into two distinct cultural areas.

The question of definitions is problematic for most of the peoples not only along the

344

Rhine but in central Europe as a whole, right into the middle of the Roman Imperial period. During the last century B.C., populations began to make their presence felt in southern central Europe which, in retrospect, can be termed 'Germanic', but whose presence cannot be determined archeologically. This should not be too surprising if one considers that the abandonment of land in favour of new settlement areas brings with it adjustments to new ways of life. As any observation of immigrants indicates, many customs and practices of the traditional culture are immediately given up; others wither or become a compromise with the new situation. In the short term there will be no distinctive cultural precipitate. In central Europe only gradually, and not until the reign of Augustus, as the result of Roman pressures in the north, did the material culture of the La Tène along the Main, in Thuringia and in Bohemia begin to show affinities with that of the Elbe region to the north. Fifty years earlier, in the times of Caesar, the late La Téne was still very much in evidence there. The oppidum at Manching had not at that time fallen.

It appears, however, that the term 'Germani' was current already before Caesar's arrival in Gaul. It is helpful in the first instance not to see an ethnically identifiable people behind this designation, but a descriptive function, so that the term would not apply to an old tribal name imported into Gaul, but would have been a designation for dangerous invaders, characterized by fierceness in battle, a certain style of fighting, bearing certain arms (Fig. 252) and wearing certain clothing. Thus Pliny in his *Naturalis Historia* speaks of the Celtic Oretani[128] called Germani, who are said to have settled the northern slopes of the Sierra Morena in southern Spain. A group of Gauls are named

252. Northern shield and shield bosses.

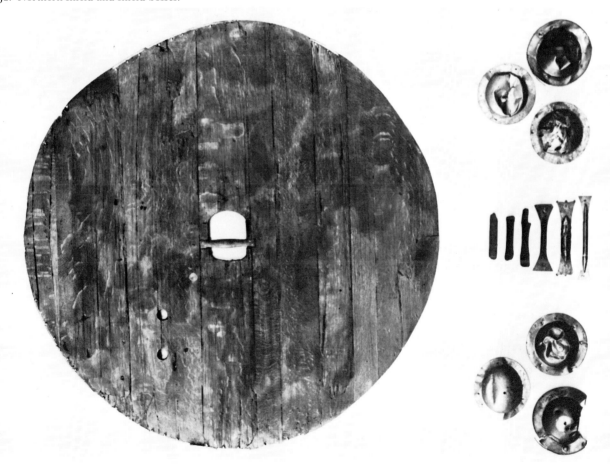

Galli Germani. Conceivably many other groups, perhaps elite social units, bore this term as their surname. Much supposition has given this topic a very extensive coverage in the literature. What is certain is that at the time of Caesar the term 'Germani' can not be an appropriate, unqualified collective designation for the peoples east of the Rhine. They certainly did not know themselves under this name. When the Roman Imperial administration established the new province of Belgica before 14 A.D. it included all the territories west of the Rhine. Only in 85 A.D. were the two provinces 'Germania superior' or 'prima' and 'Germania inferior', or 'secunda' separated from 'Belgica'. Even for Tacitus the concept 'Germania omnis' was intended to exclude these two provinces in an otherwise undefined geographic concept, that knew no eastern limits.[129] It is interesting that some 120 years after Tacitus, the historian Dio Cassius, experienced administrator and governor of Pannonia, still applied the word 'Germania' only to the Roman provinces of Germany, but 'Keltiche' for Germany proper.[130] In this he followed an established tradition among Greek historians. Evidently Caesar's incisive separation of a civilized Celtic Gaul from a wilderness inhabited by hostile barbarians was an oversimplified exaggeration prompted by a contrastive rhetorical method. Had Caesar not identified certain tribes as Germanic, no one would have concluded that they were anything but Celts. The existence of a Germanic ethnic unit derives solely from Roman written sources. Contrary to the practice of the Greek historians who knew only Celts east of the Rhine, the name 'Germani' remained an element in Roman terminology.[131] It was dropped from the official language during the period of the migrations and forgotten, not to be rediscovered till the Renaissance. Prior to the fall of Rome the 'Germanic' tribes coexisted in a pre-ethnic state, marked by hostilities. Not even during the migrations can one speak of anything resembling fraternal relations between the various migrating groups. Co-ordinated operations against a common objective were not characteristic for them. As late as the nineteenth and twentieth centuries the notion of the 'Germanic peoples' became a particularly German problem of mythical proportions. Other 'Germanic' nations, such as the English, Dutch and the Scandinavians, were much less burdened with the idea of a common 'Germanentum'—Teutonism—something the Germans of the 1930s and 1940s could not understand.

The designation 'Germani', however, became standard Roman terminology. As we will see elsewhere, the establishing of the Rhine and Danube frontiers forced upon the center of Europe a political, and especially an institutional development, very much under the guardianship of Rome. Such Celtic elements as had been cut off east of the Rhine and north of the Danube were quickly 'Germanized'. In this process of accultur- ation one might have expected a greater residue of Celtic vocabulary in German. It was these border people, however, who were the first to cross into the Roman Empire and be absorbed there, while those who subsequently took their places had not previously come in direct contact with the Celts. The maps depicting the tribal dispositions during the first few centuries A.D. make it very apparent how quickly displacement, absorption and realignment changed the population patterns among the tribes backed up against the Roman frontiers.

In the overall cultural development the Roman centuries play a two-fold role. On the one hand the Roman presence on the fringes of central Europe forces a cultural consolidation on the population which had hitherto enjoyed the cohesion of a common culture across a variety of geographical regions. Up to this point the rivers had played a role in furthering common cultural expression. With the entrance of Rome into central Europe these rivers became strategic lines of separation which ignored the population patterns established over many centuries. Admittedly the last century B.C. witnessed a transition period; however, the arrival of the Romans in central Europe interrupted the progress of this transition and arrested it before a new synthesis had evolved. Thus the Roman presence effected a rupture in the cultural and especially the stylistic development of central Europe. On the other hand, the coming of the Romans to central Europe replaced what had hitherto only been indirect cultural influences with direct cultural domination. For the next 300 years Gaul, the two German provinces, Raetia, Noricum and Pannonia overflowed with Roman import goods allowing for very little room in which indigenous cultural elements could develop. Especially Gaul and the Rhenish provinces adopted Roman ways and forms to the point that the aesthetic temperament of Gaul-France came to share and propagate the Mediterranean sense of form. The area of central Europe proper did not come under this direct control until much later when Christianity introduced to the area a late phase, a 'Baroque' phase of Roman artistic expression during the Merovingian and Carolingian periods, at a time when the calligraphic Celtic style returned to central Europe, brought by Hiberno-Scottish and Anglo-Saxon missionaries. Coincidentally the Roman 'Baroque' of the fourth and fifth centuries had points of empathy with the Celtic sense for the curvilinear vegetative intertwine and the fascination for the perforated surface. After an interval of about 300–400 years, central Europe would return to its earlier approach to artistic representation, and adhere to it, until the northern kingdoms resumed their direct contact with a largely Christianized Roman heritage in Italy.

Conclusion

In retrospect, our concern has been for the wide connections, for the origin of human activities, attitudes and practices, for the invention of objects and institutions and the development which they underwent. The archeological evidence allows some deductions about the inner structure of some prehistoric societies, as certain aspects of the material culture point to beliefs and customs in life and in the care of the dead. The archeological evidence also helps raise questions about certain traditional assumptions on which a reconstruction of the prehistoric past has hitherto been based. Surveys of socio-political, spiritual and artistic developments appear useful.

During the Paleolithic period, culture developed in Europe in spite of environmental conditions. Man's ingenuity at expanding his inventory of suitable materials from which to fashion and improve his simple tools by means of innovative modifications, his discovery of fire and of the rules of simple mechanics, his organizational talents and his relationship with the world of animals, helped him overcome the vulnerability of his position in an inhospitable environment. Under the improved climatic conditions of the Meso- and Neolithic periods, man came to express a desire for self-sufficiency and a more liberal use of his innovative capabilities. Quite early Neolithic populations spread out from south-eastern Europe to farm the soft-soil regions of central Europe and to raise their herds and flocks. These populations were the aggressive carriers of a food-producing economy. Named for their pottery, these Banded Ware people built their longhouses on choice but isolated sites. It was the succeeding Rössen culture, again identified by its pottery, which assembled in villages on the flat land, on mountains and along lakeshores. Characterized by very long houses, some of the villages yielded evidence of early communal organization. The people using Rössen ware spread onto poorer soils. They represent an expansive phase of early European civilization. They carried the Neolithic northward.

Later regional groups continued Rössen traditions. Making use of trade routes along which stone suitable for the making of tools had been transported, an extensive network of cultural links came into being which probably contributed to the emergence of a dominant ceramic culture in central Europe, the Corded Ware culture. No longer held to have been carried by a 'Corded Ware people' who suddenly appeared from the East and raced across Europe, this culture was a central European synthesis showing strong signs of continuity. In its time it witnessed the transition from lithic to metallic skills. The last of the early metal cultures, the Bell Beaker culture, associated occasionally with Corded Ware, introduced the extensive use of metal articles. The carriers of this culture soon reserved for themselves the exploitation and distribution of the ores, causing the centralization of economic and hence of political power in those fortified centers which controlled the availability of this natural resource. This culture too contributed to the emergence of some of the native cultures of the early European Bronze Age.

Almost imperceptibly the Copper and Bronze Ages evolved out of the Neolithic. Against a backdrop of cultural continuity a prehistoric 'Industrial Age' appears to have extended across these periods, bringing gradual but evident economic and social changes, as the mining, refining and distribution of ores confirmed divisions of labor and hence social differentiations, while cultural and political power accrued to those centers which controlled the industry. Because of the irregular location of the ores, the interdependence of the bronze industry and long-distance trade became axiomatic. Trade in turn contributed to the distinctive wealth of the controlling 'princely' groups. The transition of the great central European Bronze Age cultures sees the 'royal' grave builders of the Úněticians succeeded by the Tumulus culture, the expansionist phase of the Bronze Age, and while the Urnfield culture evolved out of the Tumulus culture, a branch of the latter drifted away toward the south-east, accompanied by much turmoil. Again the arrival of a new people is not evident, since sudden ruptures in the cultural and economic inventories are not apparent, the almost universal adoption of cremation having been a long transition. On the contrary, there is much evidence pointing to the continuity and co-existence of practices, the continuity of habitation and the stable sedentariness of the population. The considerable effort needed to raise the vast funerary monuments reflects continuing social organization. The evidence points to the evolution of the Indo-Europeans in Europe by the end of the Bronze Age at the end of a cultural continuum with common cultural features. The new emphasis on horse motifs has been taken to point to the presence of horsemen, yet no significant ruptures in the other cultural inventories can be demonstrated, just as there is no conclusive evidence of a belligerent expansion.

The late Bronze Age witnessed the gradual imposition of iron over bronze. For nearly five hundred years the two metal industries coexisted. The greater availability of iron ore would account for the relatively rapid spread of the iron technology. It is in this innovation that the cause for the socio-political restructuring of Iron Age society must be sought, as the greater availability of iron ores allowed greater independence from the bronze production and distribution centers. The switch to iron was paralleled by the significance of the salt trade which not only brought prosperity but also new cultural influences to unfold in areas of the Hallstatt culture, helping them to benefit from a flourishing economy. However, the funerary evidence points to extensive poverty as well.

The transition from the early iron Hallstatt culture to the more sophisticated iron-using La Tène culture was largely of a material nature. Early Greek records shed some light on the people who inhabited central Europe. Identified as Celts they appear to be a population synthesis in south central Europe. The first identifiable northern crystallization of Indo-Europeans, they probably did not constitute a conscious ethnic unit. Having seized control of the sources of iron ore, their superior technology also gave them the tactical superiority in weapons and power. During the La Tène social differentiation underwent further development as military aristocracies, estates of craftsmen, intellectual and spiritual castes, a population of merchants, miners and farmers emerged in a social system of intricate dependencies gathered about 'urban' centers, the oppida. Directed by administrative councils, these oppida were located in the vicinity of production and distribution centers, thereby becoming economic, industrial and political tribal focal points capable of sustaining large populations and of attracting long-distance trade. By the time this Celtic world came into prolonged contact with Rome, political power had eroded into the mere display of material power which in turn promoted regional encapsulation, dissension and strife.

The Celtic La Tène culture was developing out of the proto-Celtic Hallstatt cultures by the time the proto-Germanic cultural groups were beginning to crystallize in north central Germany. Archeological evidence in ceramics and metals points to these groups as continuing from the Northern Bronze Age and the central European Bronze and Iron Ages, in an area where early Celtic and proto-Germanic peoples must have met and where foreign craftsmen and trade-borne influences were able to contribute to the development of distinct population groups. The evidence of the early cultural phases points to an egalitarian society. Here too, however, a social imbalance becomes apparent by the time that the northern cultures came into view on the historical horizon. This change is reflected in some settlements of northern Germany which had been built on artificial elevations as protection against an unfavorable environment dominated by a hostile sea. The limits set for agriculture and the ensuing soil exhaustion kept the population very near the subsistence line, without security against misfortune. Forced to leave their lands, the northern peoples engaged in armed conflict with Rome, thereby bringing the prehistoric North in contact with the historic South.

Paleolithic man must have been aware of the vulnerability of his earthly position, and it is probable that he engaged in cultic and religious practices of which no or only little evidence is extant. For Aurignacian man cultic connotations can be deduced from his burial practices and by inference from cultic aspects revolving around the so-called Bear Cult. For Magdalenian man it is evident that he had a culture-creating mental capacity which enabled him to transfer appearances into cultural symbols and to expand and refine his cultural inventory as reflected in burial rites and in funerary gifts. His art may be evidence that he paid homage to life-generating principles, that his natural world was also a spirit world and that his psychological development had reached a point from which he could conceive of a metaphysical order to help him endure his existence with a degree of confidence. It is curious that aside from some sacrificial evidence there is next to no information concerning the spiritual life of Neolithic man. From his funerary practices no conclusions can be drawn, as even the gradual appearance of cremation, to coexist with inhumation, allows no convincing interpretations. Only with the introduction of the megalithic mode of constructing funerary edifices during the Chalcolithic period does it become apparent that the care of the dead assumed a prominent place in cultural activity. No doubt of cultic significance was the setting up of menhirs, both singly and in groups. Without common origin or uniformity of construction the megalith graves were used by several generations and even by successive cultures, as an earlier Funnel Beaker culture was displaced by Corded Ware beakers in the grave inventories. During a period of acculturation, megalith graves coexisted with single graves. From the mid-Chalcolithic period onward these single graves were tumuli raised over tree coffins, located either individually or in clusters, differences in the positioning helping to distinguish the various cultures. During the Corded Ware period it became customary to provision the graves with food. With the Bell Beaker culture, the last of the Chalcolithic cultures, a radical break in funerary practices is evident as the deceased was positioned completely differently and as cremated remains were deposited in urns. The Bronze Age cultures were to continue these practices as a sequence of traditions. Thus while the Úněticians engaged in flat grave inhumation, the later Tumulus culture practiced inhumation in hill-graves, until the succeeding Urnfield culture deposited cremation urns in large cemeteries.

The funerary inventories of the Úněticians displayed a wealth of forms executed with great skill. Regional variety in the bronzes points to the existence of regional cultures. Of special significance are the so called 'royal' tombs. During the Tumulus period bronze was in greater supply. As it was also a time for expansion, the inventories reflect greater variety and new syntheses. With the Urnfield culture, at the end of a long transition, there appears to have taken place an almost universal adoption of cremation for all social groups. The funerary evidence does point to richer inventories, a possible sign that a richer caste was emerging.

It is important to note that most bronze objects were not part of grave inventories, but were found in moors, lakes, ponds and former riverbeds, and were hence part of a cultic ritual. The many large ornamented discs of beaten bronze and gold suggest them to have been part of a religious context, probably a cult dedicated to the sun. Even the large depots of crude, finished and broken bronze objects are now interpreted as having been deposited for religious reasons rather than for security. In this general context the succeeding Hallstatt culture reveals itself to have been a continuation of the earlier Urnfield culture, as cultural characteristics were continued. In the Hallstatt cemetery the richest graves were cremation graves, while the inhumation graves were poor. Elsewhere social differentiation is apparent in graves and their inventories, as well as in the presence of vast fortified places and neighboring burial mounds of vast size often containing a princely wagon burial and many secondary graves. Princely graves, usually chariot graves, are also common for the early Celtic La Tène culture. That their occupants held elevated social positions and engaged in a high level of cultural activity is indicated by the great wealth of their graves. Especially the women's graves were rich in trade-borne jewellery. Heads and faces frequently appear in Celtic art, yet there is no evidence that a head-cult was practised among the central European Celts. Though there is no shortage of information about Celtic religion, this information has been passed down to us in its Gallo-Roman end stage. (Except for a discussion of the religious implications of the Gundestrup cauldron, it seems appropriate to postpone this discussion and to treat the problem in the larger context of Roman Provincial culture in a subsequent volume.) The Jastorf culture of proto-Germanic north central Europe continued with the funerary practices of the Northern Bronze Age. That the cemeteries showed continuity of practice as well as constancy in the numbers of burials, points to the stability of the population, though not to their wealth, for now household pottery and other worn objects were used as funerary equipment. Even jewellery shows signs of wear.

Some tentative conclusions can be drawn about proto-Germanic religion from the votive offerings deposited in the open, the human sacrifices, the tree gods found in the moors and from the writings of Tacitus. Although no uniformity of practice can be deduced from the evidence, the cults seem to have corresponded to tribal divisions, the confirmation in the cult taking place at the annual festivals, marked by trials, executions and perhaps sacrifices. Besides such votive offerings as precious objects, men and women were taken to the moors and bogs as consecrated choices of a cult. It is not clear whether as messengers to the gods their deaths were considered to be intercessional sacrifices, or whether as criminals their death was an expiation. Cut from boards or trees, the proto-Germanic divinities, both male and female, were seen to be anthropomorphic in shape. Set up where the log roads crossed the moors, they protected the traveller against the perils of the journey. As nature religion, the cults emphasized animal fertility and such organic processes as growth and reproduction cycles.

We have said that very early prehistoric man had conceived of a metaphysical order. Magdalenian art is generally seen to provide the evidence for such a statement. The spectacular animal paintings of cave art, but also the portable sculptures as well as the reliefs on cave walls and the carvings on functional objects, appear to express Paleolithic man's compulsion to depict the animals of his world. With keen aesthetic sense he overcame the purely functional and applied ornamental embellishments to the objects he used. It is noteworthy that human forms were not generally a part of his representational repertoire. The brilliance of Magdalenian art was followed by artistic regression and impoverishment, and it was not until the development of ceramic styles and decorative designs that one can speak again of a renewed sense of the aesthetic during the Neolithic period. The rich scale of ornamental motifs makes it apparent that ornamentation was not merely an empty display but an alternative to representation, with its own artistic conventions and possibly its own symbolic code. We had also seen that with the introduction of metals for functional objects, such stone tools as the flint fishtail daggers assumed an extraordinary elegance of design, as though the craftsmen hoped to overcome any material deficiencies by means of an emphasis on style. The progress in bronze metallurgy promoted personal luxury and the enrichment of the inventory of forms, designs and of decorative techniques. Together they contributed to ornateness, elaborate decorative display and a great show of metallic wealth.

Variations in style and technique of ornamentation allow not only the establishment of chronologies but also of points of origin, as southern origins and influences can be traced by means of an embossing technique, while northern craftsmen decorated their sheet bronzes with engravings. These give evidence of great ornamental imagination as static forms ceded to the dynamic flow of restless lines. Bronze Age art combined much individuality with a unity of style. The dynamism of Bronze Age art gave way to static designs as the stylistic imagination of Iron Age artists was inclined to achieve effects through the abstraction of forms derived from geometry, a feature especially evident on pottery. Personal taste favored the grand gesture, exaggeration and ostentation. Also during this period human forms were not basic to the repertoire of forms of the northern craftsmen, though stylized figurines in the form of anthropomorphic pendants or appliqués on vessels do appear in south central Europe, while monumental sculptures have been found in the west. More prominent motifs, continuations from the Bronze Age, are horses and floating water birds. Evidence of southern influences and trade contacts are the large bronze vessels, the *situlae*, with their characteristic narrative friezes usually depicting human activities of a festive and ceremonial nature. Generally, however, art was not a response to a social or cosmic environment, nor did it hold up a mirror to nature. Representational art remained experimental.

Astonishing is the artistic sense of the Celtic La Tène culture. By means of a fantastic imagination, ornamented surfaces reflect a fascination with moving lines and intricate patterns. Derived from the geometrics of the ancestral Hallstatt culture, perhaps also from the dynamic linearity of the Bronze Age traditions, combined with oriental and mediterranean influences, Celtic art developed abstract, non-communicative and non-narrative characteristics as though offering interpretative responses to the challenges of a mysterious universe. Such figural work in stone as exists, though bearing human features, does not illustrate any real desire to represent the human form, nor nature as such, and even when human features do appear on objects, their function remains ornamental and subsidiary. Using a freehand symmetry the artistic aim was a spacefilling curvilinear ornamentation of evasive designs, the animation of geometrics, the deformation and explosion of forms by means of dismemberment. The proto-Germanic North does not appear to have had any stylistic concerns, aside from the few anthropomorphic 'divinities'.

It is held that the non-anthropomorphic mode and the dematerializing techniques used by northern artists are not merely examples of stylistic tenacity, but rather the area's fundamental response to a particular view of the world. The consistent adherence to certain distinctive characteristics suggests that artists, craftsmen and patrons made deliberate and conspicuous stylistic choices. From the material evidence surveyed, culture appears to be a collective attempt at providing answers to the questions posed by man about his position in this life and the next. As long as a distinct set of answers was satisfactory, the distinctive aspects of a culture remained constant and offered that degree of continuity which made for stability. One can conclude that as long as the needs of a given cultural group are met and existing forms serve their intended aims there is no need for change, since cultural forms and institutions which work are not likely to be replaced by experiments. It appears on the other hand, that experiment, innovation and change are a response to inadequacy or outright failure in some sector of a culture's general view of the world.

Illustration Acknowledgements

Dr. K. D. Adam, with his special permission from *Der Mensch im Eiszeitalter*, Stuttgarter Beiträge zur Naturkunde, Serie C, Nr. 15 (Stuttgart 1982), Figs. 1, 2, 12, 16, 17, 18, 19, 20, 21, 24, 25, 27. Augsburg, Römisches Museum, Figs. 98, 103. Bad Buchau, Federsee Museum, Figs. 129, 130, 131, 132, 157, 158. Bamberg, Historisches Museum, Figs. 35, 36. Basel, Historisches Museum, Plate 6a. Berlin, Bildarchiv, Preussischer Kulturbesitz, Plates 1d, 7a; Figs. 44, 82, 92, 96, 97, 108, 126, 128, 136, 146, 160, 180, 181, 209, 236. Bern, Historisches Museum, Fig. 204. Bonn, Rheinisches Landesmuseum, Plate 7b; Figs. 5, 6, 42, 80, 211, 214. Bremen, Landesmuseum für Kunst und Kulturgeschichte, Plate 2b, 5c; Figs. 31, 34, 114. Copenhagen, Nationalmuseet, Figs. 14, 28, 29, 30, 41, 45, 65, 73, 75, 101, 105, 107, 110, 112, 113, 116, 117, 119, 222, 223, 224, 225, 226, 227, 228, 230, 231. Darmstadt, Hessisches Landesmuseum, Figs. 52, 199. Frankfurt a.M., Museum für Vor- und Frühgeschichte, Figs. 47, 76, 109. Freiburg, Landesdenkmalamt Baden-Württemberg, Plate 1a; Fig. 11, 88, 89. Graz, Landesmuseum Joanneum, Figs. 7, 8, 93, 166, 184, 185, 186. Halle (Saale), Landesmuseum für Vorgeschichte, Plate 2a; Fig. 81. Hamburg-Harburg, Helms Museum, Figs. 141, 238. Hannover, Niedersächsisches Landesmuseum, Plate 1c; Figs. 61, 62, 115, 120, 247. Innsbruck, Tiroler Landesmuseum Ferdinandeum, Plate 4. P. Jacobsthal, *Early Celtic Art* (Oxford University Press 1969), by special permission of Oxford University Press, Figs. 215, 216. Karlsruhe, Badisches Landesmuseum, Figs 134, 156, 159, 203, 212, 213. Kassel, Staatliche Kunstsammlungen, Figs. 50, 63, 64. Prof. W. Kimmig, with his special permission from K. Bittel *et al.*, *Die Kelten in Baden-Württemberg* (Stuttgart 1981), Figs. 149, 151. Klagenfurt, Landesmuseum Kärnten, Figs. 140, 165, 173, 174, 232, 233, 234. Köln, Institut für Ur- und Frühgeschichte der Universität Köln, Figs. 22, 26. Mainz, Mittelrheinisches Landesmuseum, Figs. 243, 251. Mainz, Römisch-Germanisches Zentralmuseum, Fig. 83, as reconstructed by Prof. Dr. H.-J. Hundt, Mainz. H. Müller-Karpe, *Handbuch der Vorgeschichte*, I, Plate 271, with the special permission of the author and C. H. Beck'sche Verlagsbuchhandlung. Fig. 3. München, Prähistorische Staatssammlung, Plates 1b, 3a; Figs. 9, 10, 13, 38, 39, 48, 67, 68, 69, 70, 72, 77, 78, 84, 94, 95, 122, 124, 125, 163, 191, 192, 196, 198, 217, 220. Münster, Westfälisches Museum für Archäologie, Plate 3b; Fig. 43. Nürnberg, Germanisches Nationalmuseum, Fig. 91. Oldenburg, Staatliches Museum für Naturkunde und Vorgeschichte, Figs. 54, 137, 138, 144, 244, 245, 246. Saarbrücken, Landesmuseum für Vor- und Frühgeschichte, Plates 6b, 6c; Figs. 40, 202. Salzburg, Salzburger Museum Carolino-Augusteum, Figs. 207, 218. Schleswig, Schleswig-Holsteinisches Landesmuseum für Vor- und Frühgeschichte, Schloß Gottorf, Plates 8a, 8b; Figs. 15, 66, 74, 102, 104, 106, 239, 240, 241, 242, 248, 249, 250, 252. Schwerin, Museum für Ur- und Frühgeschichte, Figs. 111, 133, both photos provided courtesy Römisch-Germanisches Zentralmuseum, Mainz. Singen, Hegau Museum, Plate 5a. Speyer, Historisches Museum der Pfalz, Figs. 46, 86, 90, 100. Straubing, Gäubodenmuseum, Fig. 32, courtesy Dr. H. P. Uenze, Prähistorische Staatssammlung, München. Stuttgart, Landesdenkmalamt Baden-Württemberg, Figs. 200, 201, 235. Stuttgart, Württembergisches Landesmuseum, Plate 5b; Figs. 177, 210, 221. Trier, Rheinisches Landesmuseum, Figs. 99, 127, 189, 193, 195, 205, 206, 208. Vaduz, Liechtensteinisches Landesmuseum, Figs. 194, 229. Wien, Naturhistorisches Museum, Figs. 23, 33, 71, 85, 87, 135, 139, 143, 145, 147, 148, 155, 161, 162, 164, 167, 168, 169, 170, 171, 172, 175, 176, 178, 179, 182, 219. Wiesbaden, Museum, Fig. 190. Wilhelmshafen, Niedersächsisches Landesmuseum für Marschen und Wurtenforschung, Fig. 237. Worms, Museum der Stadt Worms, Figs. 37, 197. Würzburg, Mainfränkisches Museum, Plate 2c; Figs. 79, 142, 183.

Author's photos, Plates 1b, 1c, 3a, 5a, 6b, 6c; Figs. 4, 9, 10, 11, 13, 38, 39, 40, 49, 51, 52, 53, 55, 56, 57, 58, 59, 60, 61, 62, 67, 68, 69, 70, 72, 77, 78, 84, 88, 94, 95, 118, 121, 122, 123, 124, 129, 150, 152, 153, 154, 163, 187, 188, 191, 196, 198, 199, 202, 217, 238, 247.

Notes

1. The Paleolithic: Of Ice, Men, Stones and Things

1 M. Schwarzbach, *Climates of the Past, An Introduction to Paleoclimatology*, transl. from the German, ed. by R. O. Muir (London 1963), p. 192; also K. W. Butzer, *Environment and Archaeology, An Ecological Approach to Prehistory*, 2nd ed. (Chicago and New York 1971), pp. 217, 275.

2 Schwarzbach, p. 182; also Butzer, pp. 285f., for a discussion of glacial moisture conditions.

3 Schwarzbach, p. 183; also Butzer, p. 278. Butzer uses consistently smaller areal estimates.

4 Schwarzbach, p. 190.

5 Schwarzbach, p. 193; see also B. Frenzel, *Die Klimaschwankungen des Eiszeitalters* (Braunschweig 1967), p. 51.

6 See table 36, 'Divisions of the Quarternary', in Schwarzbach, p. 194; also F. C. Hibben, *Prehistoric Man in Europe* (Univ. of Oklahoma Press, 4th printing 1968), pp. 12f., for the names of glacial ages and for northern and southern comparisons.

7 W. Meier-Arendt, 'Die Eiszeit', in G. Biegel, ed., *Kölner Römer Illustrierte* (Historische Museen der Stadt Köln 1975), II, p. 22, hereafter abbreviated to *KRI*.

8 D. Collins, *The Human Revolution from Ape to Artist* (Oxford 1976), p. 50.

9 P. Honoré, *Das Buch der Altsteinzeit, oder Der Streit um die Verfahren* (Düsseldorf and Vienna 1967), p. 100.

10 Schwarzbach, p. 184.

11 A. Rust, *Rentierjäger der Eiszeit in Schleswig-Holstein* (Neumünster in Holstein 1954), p. 7.

12 Honoré, p. 95.

13 Honoré, p. 94.

14 Meier-Arendt, *KRI*, II, p. 22.

15 Honoré, p. 99; see especially Schwarzbach, p. 198, for the levels cited here; also R. Solecki, 'The Old World Paleolithic', in R. Stigler, ed., *The Old World, Early Man to the Development of Agriculture* (New York 1974), p. 48, concerning the relationship between the varying degrees of glaciation and the fluctuations in the sea levels; see also Butzer, p. 24,

for a chart showing variance in shoreline levels with respect to the modern sea levels; also pp. 215–26. Butzer, p. 217, suggests estimates of glacial sea levels during the Würm ranging from 90 m to 159 m. See also Hibben, p. 19.

16 R. Drößler, *Die Venus der Eiszeit, Entdeckung und Erforschung altsteinzeitlicher Kunst* (Leipzig 1967), p. 10; also Butzer, pp. 280f. for details concerning the glaciation in the lower mountain ranges of central Europe.

17 Honoré, p. 100; also Butzer, p. 281, who indicates main Würm midsummer temperature depressions between 7–9°C.

18 Schwarzbach, pp. 184f.; see also Drößler, p. 10; according to Butzer, p. 279, in France the permafrost may have extended south of latitude 46°; Drößler suggests that it was the more favourable climatic conditions which permitted the development of culture. For a general discussion of Ice Age temperatures see also D. Collins, pp. 54–61.

19 Schwarzbach, p. 187; Butzer, p. 278, gives variations of snowline elevation to a high of 1500–2000 m and snowline depressions to about 1000–1200 m. He suggests, p. 110, a snowline depression during the Würm varied between 600 and 1400 m, depending on latitude and location.

20 Rust, p. 20.

21 Butzer, p. 278, has calculated that under modern conditions a drop of the mean annual temperature by 5°C would reduce the mean temperature for November to April to below 0°C, which would increase the number of days with snow from 44 to 218 days per year out of a total 281 days of precipitation, leaving an insufficient length of time to melt the ice and snow accumulated during the winter months.

22 Honoré, p. 95.

23 Butzer, p. 280, indicates, with illustrations, the presence of ice wedges filling fissures in the ground even in the non-glacial regions of central Europe.

24 Hibben, pp. 15f.; also Butzer, pp. 198ff., who describes loess as an unstratified silty sand, typically consisting of quartz (60–70%), carbonates (10–30%) and clay minerals (10–20%); also H. Thieme,

'Die altsteinzeitlichen Funde der letzten und vor-
letzten Eiszeit aus Rheindahlen', *KRI*, II, p. 23; see
also H. Müller-Karpe, *Handbuch der Vorgeschichte*, I
(Munich 1966), pp. 116f.

25 W. Meier-Arendt, 'Die Alt- und Mittelstein-
zeit: Die Zeit der Jäger und Sammler', in Ellershoff,
ed., *KRI*, I (Historische Museen der Stadt Köln
1974), p. 18. See also Hibben, p. 19, for a description
of a general appearance of Europe. See C. F. C.
Hawkes, *The Prehistoric Foundations of Europe to the
Mycenean Age*, reprint of the 1940 edition (London
and New York 1973), p. 8, on 'fluvio-glacial' terrace
formation during the glacial periods; also Hibben,
pp. 14f., for river terrace formations and the river
gravel deposits as a mark of the various glacial
periods. See M. Quennell, *Everyday Life in Prehistoric
Times* (London and New York 1959, 4th printing
1966) for illustration and discussion of glacial river
terraces. See also Collins, p. 47, for a discussion of
terraces as a means to dating, and especially Butzer,
pp. 178ff.: glacial meltwaters leave datable deposits
ahead of the ice front, both during the advance and
the standstill of a glacier. Any tools or fossils found
in the deposits then come from older deposits pushed
along by the ice.

26 Müller-Karpe, pp. 129f.; see Collins, pp. 54–61,
for the relationship between climate, flora and
fauna; see also Butzer, pp. 143f. and pp. 258–62, for
an identification of Pleistocene animals.

27 From a very extensive literature on this subject,
see Hibben, pp. 25–39, for a discussion of early fossil
evidence of Pithecines and anthropoids. For a summary of African hominid finds see Butzer, pp. 413–
35; see especially M. D. Leaky, *Olduvai Gorge* (Cambridge 1971); also Solecki in Stigler, p. 47, concerning finds from the Olduvai Gorge (c. 1·9 million
years) and the Omo Valley in Ethiopia (3–4 million
years); also Holloway, 'Fossil Man in the Old
World', in Stigler, pp. 18–29, concerning the discussion of pre- and early hominids, especially the
finds in the Olduvai Gorge; also M. H. Day, *Guide
to Fossil Man, A Handbook of Human Paleontology* (London 1965), pp. 119–43, concerning the Olduvai
remains; also Collins, pp. 85f, for the Potassium–
Argon dating of the remains at 1·75 million years
and at 1·9 million years, as well as the identification
of Olduvan tools of over 2·6 million years, also a
good discussion of the earliest hominids. See also G.
Clark, *World Prehistory, A New Outline being the Second
Edition of World Prehistory* (Cambridge 1969), pp. 5–
11. See also I. Lissner, *Man, God and Magic*, transl.
from the German by J. M. Brownjohn, (London
1961), pp. 26–38, for a discussion of early fossil
hominids and accounts of their discovery.

28 Müller-Karpe, p. 25.

29 E. A. Hoebel, *Anthropology: The Study of Man*,
4th ed. (New York 1972), p. 145; see also Hibben,
pp. 29f. on *Sinanthropus pekinensis*, and especially Day,
pp. 250–61 on the Zhoukoutien remains.

30 Honoré, pp. 160, 164f.; also Hoebel, p. 148; see
also W. W. Howells, *Mankind in the Making*, rev. ed.
(Garden City, N.Y. 1967), pp. 177–80; also Collins,
pp. 75f.

31 Day, pp. 65–9, points out that no artefacts were
associated with the find, but that a fossil fauna
points to the First Interglacial (Günz-Mindel) or an
interstadial of the Second Glaciation (Mindel). C.
Hawkes, p. 14, points out that the sand in which the
mandible was found succeeds directly to a Günz horizon.

32 Müller-Karpe, p. 65.

33 H. Wingert-Uhde, *Schätze und Scherben, Neue Entdeckungen der Archäologie in Deutschland, Österreich und der
Schweiz* (Oldenburg, Hamburg 1977), p. 14; Collins,
p. 79, believes that Bilzingsleben Man may have
been a *Homo erectus*, hence datable to before 300,000
B.C.

34 Vertesszöllös is located west of Budapest. See
Hoebel, p. 149; also Müller-Karpe, pp. 65, 320, for a
description of the site; Clark, p. 36 and Butzer, p.
441, for the inventory of various stone tool industries. Howells, p. 180, indicates that Vertesszöllös
yields the first pebble tools in Europe. Collins, pp.
75–9, indicates the site to be datable to 300,000
years ago.

35 See Hoebel, pp. 163f.; also Butzer, p. 446, who
describes the Acheulian settlement at Terra Amata
near Nice, dated to the Mindel-Riss Interglacial,
c. 300,000 years ago. Butzer points to the imprints
of stakes to form shelters, surrounded by bones as
though to brace the shelter. Postholes suggest a
central axis for hut-like structures 8–15 m long and
4–6 m wide. See especially H. de Lumley, 'A Paleolithic Camp at Nice', in *Old World Archaeology: Foundations of Civilization, Readings from Scientific American*
(San Francisco 1972), pp. 33–41.

36 Wingert-Uhde, p. 14.

37 See note 173 below, also Butzer, p. 445.

38 The Steinheim fossil may have been a woman.
Hoebel, pp. 157f. See also Collins, p. 79, who dates
the early *Homo sapiens* fossil by means of a uranium
series to be about 300,000 years old; Holloway, in
Stigler, p. 33, suggests that the find could be ancestral to both Neanderthal and modern *sapiens*. In the
same layer was found a hand-axe classified as
Acheulian III. Day, pp. 70–5, supports the similarity with Neanderthaloid features and its possible
relationship to other fossil men. He places it, p. 71,
into the Third Interglacial (Riss–Würm, c. 180,000–
110,000 B.C. according to Butzer, p. 440). Howells,
pp. 219f. also sees the fossil placed between Neanderthal and *Homo sapiens*. J. Hawkes, *Atlas of Ancient
Archaeology* (London 1974), p. 59, identifies it as
proto-Neanderthaloid, of the Mindel-Riss Interglacial. See K. D. Adam, *Der Mensch im Eiszeitalter*,
Stuttgarter Beiträge zur Naturkunde, Serie C, Nr. 15
(Staatliches Museum für Naturkunde in Stuttgart,
1982), p. 5, who assigns Steinheim Man to early
Homo sapiens because of the vertical side walls of his
skull, the pronounced hollows of his cheeks, the

deeply rooted nose and the small size of his wisdom teeth, compared to his molars

39 Holloway, in Stigler, p. 33, suggests the Swanscombe skull may be 400,000 years old; Collins dated it by means of a uranium series to be 200,000 years old. J. E. Pfeiffer, *The Emergence of Man* (New York, Evanston and London 1969), p. 153, suggests a date of *c.* 250,000 years ago, during a period of comfortable climatic conditions. Howells, pp. 219f. supposes that she lived 400,000 years ago. See M. Day, pp. 31–5, for a detailed description of the skull fragment.

40 Hoebel, p. 158.

41 Rust, p. 9.

42 Day, p. 6, suggests that the conception of a use of an implement is the point at which the human level commences. Clark, pp. 24, 30, argues that tool-making is a criterion of man pointing to biological, cultural and intellectual adjustments.

43 Lissner, p. 45, refers to the site of the Giebelstein near Krölpa in Thuringia where finds of charcoal and ash associated with animal bones indicate human activity. The surprising absence of tools leads him to argue on behalf of the early use of wood. It is reasonable to assume that implements of some organic matter were man's first tools. See also Hibben, pp. 40f., who suggests that the selection of stone is an indication of that reasoning power which produces culture.

44 See Hibben, pp. 42–5, for an analysis of the properties of flint. Hibben sees in the appreciation of the advantages of flint over other materials the crossing of the human threshold.

45 Müller-Karpe, p. 320.

46 For outline summaries of the lithic industrial cultures, see Day, p. 7, also R. J. Braidwood, *Prehistoric Man*, 8th ed. (Glenwood, Ill. etc. 1975), pp. 42–62, and C. Hawkes, pp. 12–35. Hibben's cautioning remark, p. 44, that the cultural progression suggested by the lithic cultures is more of a convention into which some aspects of the sequence do not fit all that readily is worth noting. See Collins, pp. 40–54, for the individuals who contributed to methods of classifying the lithic cultures.

47 Hibben, p. 51, suggests Abbevillian to have been an African interlude in western Europe which withdrew again to Africa.

48 Butzer, p. 454, sees Acheulian prominent in Europe in cold and open environments during the glacial stages, in terrain with open vegetation, with an inclination on the part of its carriers to hunt big game. According to Butzer, p. 440, Acheulian is first recorded in Mindel (Elster) age deposits. It lasted through to Riss-Würm (Eem) interglacial times, from 430,000 to 75,000 B.C. See Butzer, pp. 436–61, for an extensive treatment of the Acheulian culture.

49 See Hoebel, p. 150; also Clark, pp. 39–42, who points out that the Abbevillian and Acheulian hand-axe industries extended much beyond the earlier area of pebble-tool chopper industries. With expansion also came variation, thus Hibben, pp.

52–4, identifies seven stages of Acheulian hand-axe development. Hibben, p. 57, is supported by Butzer (see note 48) when he claims the continuation of Acheulian techniques into Mousterian times.

50 See note 38 above. Holloway, in Stigler, p. 33, only mentions that skull and axe were found in the same layer. J. Hawkes, p. 59, claims that the skull was found in association with the Acheulian handaxe. See also Hoebel, p. 149.

51 J. Hawkes, p. 59.

52 Müller-Karpe, pp. 37, 64, 135, suggests that tool finds in larger quantities come from riverbeds which must have been preferred sites.

53 H. Thieme, in *KRI*, II, p. 24.

54 Pfeiffer, p. 134, suggests that a prehistoric hunting band of some 25 members would roam a territory of 500 to 1500 square miles. Butzer, p. 467, argues that seasonal migration was probably not a general phenomenon, possibly confined to the marginal populations at the edge of the tundra, while others were more settled as they depended on more stable animal populations. Butzer, p. 479, concludes the existence of semi-permanent habitation for at least part of the human population.

55 Thieme, in *KRI*, II, p. 24.

56 Müller-Karpe, pp. 293f.

57 See Butzer, p. 205. The entrances and front areas of the caves are affected to varying degree by external weathering agents. Under the overhang (abris) or in the entrance vegetation is possible, contributing to soil formation, while debris falling off the cliff-face accumulates in layers. Inside the entrance and further inside, rock falling off the ceiling and walls accumulates on the cave floor. Some additional debris may be washed or blown in from the entrance.

58 For discussions on the use of fire see Lissner, p. 39, who links fire users with a primeval sense of magical associations; see also Collins, p. 106, and Clark, p. 38. See Butzer, p. 445, for the use of fire at Vertesszöllös, and especially Müller-Karpe, pp. 162–66.

59 Müller-Karpe, p. 67.

60 Müller-Karpe, pp. 293–312, provides a register in which most sites are named, arranged and provided with detailed summaries.

61 See Müller-Karpe, pp. 41–4; also Solecki in Stigler, p. 58. Hibben, pp. 54f., identifies seven stages of Levalloisian and points to the association of Acheulian and Levalloisian.

62 The sequence of prepared core and flake industries—Clactonian-Levalloisian—marks the transition from core hand-axes to flake blades which extends into Mousterian of the Middle Paleolithic. See Clark, pp. 42–7, and Day, p. 90.

63 See Butzer, pp. 462–71, for an account of the Mousterians.

64 See Clark, p. 31, who holds the Neanderthaloid phase of development responsible for the prepared core tradition. E. Trinkaus and W. W. Howells,

'The Neanderthals', in *The Scientific American* (Dec. 1979), p. 118, disagree with the view that all Mousterian toolmakers were Neanderthals.

65 England has many sites with Mousterian tool inventories, but no Neanderthal skeletal evidence.

66 Butzer, p. 463, supports the idea that the forest-tundra and cold loess steppes of Europe are the centre of accelerated cultural innovation during the last glacial period, rather than the warmer Mediterranean areas.

67 Hoebel, pp. 164f.

68 Müller-Karpe, pp. 44–7.

69 From among the extensive literature see Pfeiffer, p. 160f., concerning the find of the Neanderthal fossil in 1856; also Holloway, in Stigler, pp. 9–44, for Neanderthal and other hominids of the Late Pleistocene; also Hibben, pp. 30–4; see also Collins, p. 111, concerning the events surrounding the various finds. See also Howells, pp. 190–204; Hoebel, pp. 165–69; also R. von Urslar, *Eiszeitmenschen am Rhein* (Cologne and Graz 1957), pp. 15–23. Lissner, pp. 178–83, gives a brief discussion concerning Neanderthal man and other finds in France. See also H. Wendt, *In Search of Adam*, transl. from the German by J. Cleugh (New York 1963), pp. 249–58. For a description of the fossil see M. Day, pp. 61–4.

70 See Day, pp. 62f. for early assessments.

71 See Hibben, pp. 31–4, for an argument proposing an Heidelberg-Ehringsdorf-Steinheim sequence of the Neanderthaloid 'family tree', in which Ehringsdorf and Steinheim fossils are considered to be intermediate forms.

72 Holloway, in Stigler, p. 30, argues that Neanderthal fossils should be considered as *Homo sapiens*, since they show only racial distinction from modern man.

73 Müller-Karpe, p. 26.

74 See Holloway, in Stigler, p. 30, for a discussion of the 'classic' and 'progressive' features of Neanderthals. Holloway suggests that the 'progressives' of eastern and central Europe and parts east antedate the 'classics'. See Hoebel, pp. 165–7; also Howells, pp. 190–216.

75 See Butzer, p. 465, concerning the 'classic' Neanderthals of early Würm-age Europe; also Müller-Karpe, p. 177.

76 See Day, pp. 37–41, for a description of the skeleton from La Chapelle-aux-Saints. According to Pfeiffer, p. 163, the La Chapelle skeleton was not typical, in that it was that of an 'old' man of 40–50 years of age, suffering from arthritis of the jaws, spine and perhaps of the lower limbs. Pfeiffer, p. 165, also suggests that Neanderthal man had been caught in an 'ice trap' of prolonged wintery conditions. Clark, p. 12, supports the view that the 'classic' types are a genetic variation developed in territories marginal to or isolated by the ice.

77 P. Lieberman, *On the Origins of Language, An Introduction to the Evolution of Human Speech* (New York

and London 1975), pp. 129f.

78 Day, p. 40, argues that many of the features recognized as being characteristically Neanderthal do fall within the range of modern skeletal variation, which Boule misinterpreted. For a rejection of the early descriptions of aberrant forms of Neanderthal as represented by types found at La Chapelle-aux-Saints and at La Ferrasie, see Clark, p. 12; on the other hand see Lieberman, p. 124f., who disagrees with the claim that Neanderthal fossils do not differ substantially from modern man.

79 Wendt, pp. 564f.; see also A. Leroi-Gourhan, *Les Religions de la Préhistoire (Paléolithique)* (Paris 1964), pp. 48–51, who allows for the probability of cannibalism, which, however, cannot be demonstrated on the basis of evidence. Cutting marks alone do not prove cannibalism.

80 Lieberman, pp. 172–80; see also Hoebel, p. 165.

81 K. J. Narr, 'Cultural Achievements of Early Man', in G. Altner, ed., *The Human Creature* (New York 1974), transl. from the German (1969) p. 120.

82 Lieberman, pp. 126f. argues on the basis of laryngeal evidence that there is significant differentiation in the racial types. Hibben, p. 33, differentiates between 'warm-interglacial' and 'cold-glacial' Neanderthal types.

83 See Hibben, p. 38, for a discussion of the coexistence of Neanderthal and modern types in the Near East; also Lissner, pp. 200f. and Pfeiffer, p. 197, for the Neanderthal types from Mount Carmel in Palestine. See Collins, p. 121, who terms the Tabun skeletons transition skeletons, akin to the Předmost type of an intermediate type, 30,000–20,000 B.C. Holloway, in Stigler, pp. 30f. designates the remains from the Skhul cave at Mount Carmel to have features intermediate between Neanderthal and modern man, while the Shanidar cave in Iraq, *c.* 45,000 B.C., yielded remains apparently 'classic'. He suggests that in all probability the eastern groups are ancestral to modern man. See Day, pp. 83–8, for details concerning the Tabun remains, and pp. 89–95, for the Skhul remains. Collins, p. 121, terms the Tabun skeletons transition skeletons. See also Trinkaus and Howells, in *Scientific American*, p. 129.

84 Trinkaus and Howells, *Scientific American*, p. 122, support the practice of classifying the Neanderthals as a subspecies—*Homo sapiens neanderthalensis*—within our species *Homo sapiens sapiens*.

85 Trinkaus and Howells, *Scientific American*, p. 125, argue that Neanderthals can be differentiated consistently from contemporary populations of *Homo sapiens sapiens*. To them the 'classic' Neanderthals are the only Neanderthals. See also Clark, p. 13, who doubts the emergence of *sapiens* stock from the aberrant forms from La Chapelle.

86 While Holloway, in Stigler, p. 32, maintains that transitional morphological patterns between 'classic' Neanderthal and modern man have not been discerned as yet in western Europe, Hibben,

p. 39, holds the opinion that morphologically modern humans may have appeared in Europe even before the more primitive Neanderthals. See also Trinkaus and Howells, *Scientific American*, p. 131, who, using fossil analysis, demonstrate that anatomically modern man did not derive from a population of Neanderthals, since anatomically modern man were in existence elsewhere when Neanderthals still inhabited Europe. Trinkaus and Howells, p. 132, conclude that these 'moderns' undoubtedly spread, absorbed and replaced various local Neanderthal populations across the Near East and Europe.

87   See Müller-Karpe, pp. 308f., for a detailed description of the site, where from 1914 onward skull fragments have been recovered from 7 locations, all in the same horizon. Aside from human skull fragments no other skeletal parts have been found. There are of course many animal bones, but never associated with hominid bones.

88   Müller-Karpe, p. 26; see also Howells, p. 193.

89   Müller-Karpe, p. 142.

90   The site at Rheindahlen is one of the best known, see note 55.

91   T. Capelle and K. J. Narr, 'Die archäologische Erforschung Norddeutschlands', in *KRI*, II, p. 17. For numerous details of this Mousterian site located in a sheltered valley bottom, see Butzer, pp. 468–71. 72% of the animal bones are of reindeer, 14% are of mammoth, the remainder consisting of bison, horses, woolly rhino and other small animals, fish and fowl. The stone inventory contains about 10% well worked hand-axes of late Acheulian type, the remainder are Mousterian flakes. Reindeer antlers, mammoth ribs and barbed bone points complement the tool inventory.

92   In conversation with Professor A. W. F. Banfield, author of *A Revision of the Reindeer and Caribou, Genus Rangifer*, National Museum of Canada, Bulletin No. 177, Biological Series, No. 66 (Ottawa 1961).

93   Müller-Karpe, pp. 135–41.

94   Müller-Karpe, pp. 141–3.

95   Butzer, p. 479, suggests that early man probably set deliberately to the improvement of overhang shelters. Only gradually did he appreciate the advantages of cave dwelling, especially the relative temperature constancy inside and in front of the caves, Collins, pp. 103–5. Butzer, p. 207, indicates temperatures of cave interiors ranging between 5° and 15°C. in the mid-latitudes. Collins, p. 103, distinguishes between true cave habitation and temporary shelters. Butzer, p. 479, concludes that at least a part of the population used overhangs as semi-permanent habitation.

96   Müller-Karpe, pp. 307f.

97   Müller-Karpe, pp. 293f.

98   From two caves in France comes evidence supporting such suppositions. See Pfeiffer, pp. 178f. and Butzer, p. 468, for details concerning the possible shelters at Combe Grenal in the Les Eyzies region, where there is evidence of posts sunk at the entrance to the cave to support a windscreen of skins or of branches. Perhaps they belonged to a rack used for drying meat. Less ambiguous is the evidence from the cave at Arcy-sur-Cure, Pfeiffer, pp. 205f., where there is evidence of tentpoles set in a semicircle inside the cave entrance which appear to have been set around several hearths.

99   Müller-Karpe, pp. 165f.

100   Leroi-Gourhan, p. 23.

101   Müller-Karpe, p. 143.

102   P. Lieberman and E. S. Crelin, 'On the speech of Neanderthal Man', *Linguistic Inquiry*, 2, pp. 203–22; see also P. Lieberman, *On the Origins of Language, An Introduction to the Evolution of Speech* (New York and London 1975), p. 142.

103   Collins, p. 96, cites Charles Hockett, who proposes the emergence of true language to have coincided with a major behavioral change, one which took place well before the time of Neanderthal man, in the time of the first tool making. Lieberman, pp. 165–70, suggests that while the earliest core tool making techniques could be transmitted by means of a phrase structure grammar, the Levalloisian technique required the ability to use a transformational grammar.

104   Müller-Karpe, pp. 161–71.

105   For a more complete discussion of burial practices during the Middle Paleolithic see Clark, pp. 45ff.; see also Müller-Karpe, pp. 231–4.

106   Though the skulls still showed Neanderthaloid characteristics, this pair dates to about 15,000–10,000 B.C. The funerary implements are Magdalenian, see Urslar, p. 27; also Müller-Karpe, pp. 168, 235ff., 302.

107   This deposition refers to the burial at La Ferrasie, Müller-Karpe, p. 231.

108   Müller-Karpe, p. 168, see note 106.

109   Braidwood, p. 81, discusses this question. See also Lissner, p. 196, who associates fire and ochre with death and the afterlife.

110   Leroi-Gourhan is particularly critical of these ideas.

111   See P. K. Berlin, *Basic Colour Terms, Their Universality and Evolution* (Berkeley 1969). I am indebted for this reference to Professor J. Adams-Webber, Dept. of Psychology, Brock University. See also Floyd Ratliff, 'On the Psychophysiological Bases of Universal Colour Terms', *Proceedings of the American Philosophical Society*, vol. 120, No. 5, October 1976.

112   Leroi-Gourhan, pp. 40ff., suggests that skulls have a better chance for survival than other bones.

113   Hibben, p. 34, in discussing fossil evidence from Krapina in Yugoslavia still shares this view; see also Wendt and others, note 79 above. For details see Day, pp. 76–81.

114   Leroi-Gourhan, p. 30.

115   Leroi-Gourhan, p. 23.

359

116 Müller-Karpe, pp. 303f.

117 Leroi-Gourhan, p. 36.

118 See Lissner, pp. 183–94, for details of this cave, also called 'Drachenloch', and other caves.

119 See Müller-Karpe, pp. 309f. for details of this cave.

120 Müller-Karpe, p. 310, for details concerning both caves.

121 Müller-Karpe, pp. 306f.

122 Müller-Karpe, p. 304.

123 Wendt, p. 558.

124 See Wendt, p. 560, but especially Lissner, pp. 154–77 for details about Siberian and Manchurian attitudes towards bears, their skeletons and the sacrifice of skulls and legbones. Lissner, p. 169, draws the link between bear skull and human skull sacrifice.

125 Lissner, p. 194, expresses the belief that just as the Siberians sacrificed bears to 'an invisible being who is the sky and light and universe—God', so Stone Age Man's mysterious doings in the caves 'were directed toward God and his worship alone', that Paleolithic Man 'believed in a supreme being', 'one god as the creator and sustainer of the world'.

126 Wendt, p. 561.

127 Leroi-Gourhan, p. 36.

128 Leroi-Gourhan, pp. 95–103; also Leroi-Gourhan, 'The Evolution of Paleolithic Art', in *Old World Archaeology: Foundations of Civilization, Readings from Scientific American* (San Francisco 1972), pp. 13ff. See Pfeiffer, p. 237, concerning Leroi-Gourhan's classification; also Collins, p. 132, for a comment on Leroi-Gourhan's analysis of the caves. A most complete treatment of cave art can be found in A. Laming-Emperaire, *La Classification de l'Art rupestre paléolithique* (Paris 1962), especially ch. XIII, pp. 259–87.

129 Müller-Karpe, p. 309.

130 Müller-Karpe, p. 67; Collins, p. 187, dates the transition to the Upper Paleolithic, to 40,000–30,000 B.C. See also Butzer, pp. 472–84.

131 See notes 74–86 above; see also Collins, pp. 116ff. and Pfeiffer, p. 197, for arguments accounting for the disappearance of Neanderthal man.

132 The early conclusion can no longer be sustained that the advanced Paleolithic cultures originated in France. With the identification of similar cultures in North Africa and from Italy to Afghanistan, western Europe appears to have been very much on the periphery, see Clark, pp. 50f.

133 Basing his argument on the development of blade industries, Butzer, p. 473, suggests the Upper Paleolithic cultures to have originated in the near east, from where they were spread by migration and infiltration of food gatherers. Basing his conclusion on skeletal and cultural evidence, Solecki, in Stigler, p. 63, suggests that the first tangible evidence of the Upper Paleolithic comes from the near east, dated to about 35,000 B.C.

134 For Hibben, p. 70, there is little doubt that *Homo sapiens* of the earliest Upper Paleolithic was already a mixture, probably containing most of the elements which later produced the typical European races of modern times. Collins, p. 124, speaks of the self-evident possibility that Cro-Magnon man evolved from Neanderthal predecessors. Müller-Karpe, p. 71, indicates that extreme Neanderthals, such as those of the French Mousterian, have not occurred in central Europe. Müller-Karpe, p. 27; see also Collins, p. 121, who identifies the Předmost skeleton as a transitional skeleton, dated to about 30,000–20,000 B.C. See also Müller-Karpe, p. 50.

135 C. F. C. Hawkes, p. 28, had suggested that Aurignacian had originated in western Asia. See also Hibben, pp. 68f. who refers to Russian work in the Crimea and the Ukraine which is gradually shedding light on the emergence of Aurignacian from Asiatic sources.

136 Müller-Karpe, pp. 49–56, arrives at these conclusions by drawing on evidence present in western Europe. For central Europe the evidence is less plentiful.

137 See Butzer, p. 394, for climatic phases of the European Upper Pleistocene; also Müller-Karpe, p. 305, for details of fossil fauna.

138 Honoré, p. 97.

139 Müller-Karpe, pp. 66f.

140 F. Bordes, *Le Paléolithique dans le Monde* (Paris 1968), p. 173.

141 Leroi-Gourhan, p. 83.

142 We had seen of course, that Clactonian and Levalloisian had used flint more efficiently and had already qualified as 'blade cultures'. See Butzer, pp. 474f., for an itemization and the suggested use of tools.

143 Müller-Karpe, p. 50.

144 Müller-Karpe, p. 120, indicates that the question is not at all undisputed.

145 Müller-Karpe, p. 73; Hibben, p. 69, sees an eastern Gravettian stretching from southern Russia and the Near East into central Europe. This has been disputed by Butzer, p. 477, who deems the term 'eastern Gravettian' to be no more than a catch-all for many distinct traditions.

146 While spears had been the principal hunting weapon, bow and arrow assumed this role during the Gravettian, see Müller-Karpe, pp. 54, 156f.

147 The female statuettes will be discussed more fully below, when dealing with representational art. C. F. C. Hawkes, p. 39, considered Gravettian figurines to be further evidence for the eastern origin of the Gravettian, which on p. 35 he deems persistent enough to bring forth the much later Hamburgian of northern Germany.

148 C. F. C. Hawkes, p. 27, suggests a proto-Solutrean to have originated in northern Hungary. Lissner, p. 213, maintains that Solutrean is in evidence in Spain, south-western and central France and Hungary, while Clark, p. 53, indicates that the Solutrean in France was an indigenous develop-

ment. Müller-Karpe, p. 74, asserts that central and southern Germany has no strata between Gravettian and Magdalenian, representing a west European Solutrean.

149 Collins, p. 187, argues that a reasonably typical Cro-Magnon population was in existence in Czechoslovakia by 25,000 B.C.

150 For details concerning the remains see Pfeiffer, p. 201, and Day, pp. 48–51; also Howells, pp. 207f.

151 Müller-Karpe, p. 75.

152 Müller-Karpe, p. 60.

153 Müller-Karpe, p. 187.

154 Müller-Karpe, pp. 135–41.

155 Müller-Karpe, p. 157; Butzer, p. 480, suggests that the tents of the Hamburgians at Borneck served as shelters all year round. Such a permanent settlement would be probable only if the reindeer herds of that region did not migrate too great a distance between seasons. Butzer, p. 476, however, rejects the idea of reindeer semi-domestication or even of a reindeer nomadism.

156 K. J. Narr, in Günther, p. 121.

157 G. Bosinski, 'Behausungsgrundrisse des späteiszeitlichen Fundplatzes Gönnersdorf' in *KRI*, II, pp. 25–7.

158 The French term 'bâton de commandement' is the term most generally applied to these instruments. There is no agreement on what these objects actually were. Just to sample a few definitions: Solecki, in Stigler, p. 52, agrees with Hibben, p. 79, that these implements served to rack or straighten arrows or spear shafts, while Braidwood, p. 76, sees them as thong-stroppers or arrow straighteners. For Lissner, p. 211, they could be 'wands', symbols of power and majesty, or tent pegs, or ritual drum sticks, or even part of the harness for domesticated reindeer. Lissner, pp. 284f. is much taken by the idea that the batons are shamanistic drum sticks, their decorations singling them out as articles of importance. Honoré, p. 278, suggests them to be the insignia of priests, while Leroi-Gourhan, pp. 127f., gives them a phallic connotation. See also W. Torbrügge, *Prehistoric European Art*, transl. from the German by N. Guterman (Baden-Baden and New York 1968), p. 20, terms them 'pierced staffs' of uncertain use, perhaps symbols of chieftaincy. Laming-Emperaire, p. 23, reports a conversation with Leroi-Gourhan in which he suggests the diameters of the holes provide the 'calibre' of the intended missile.

159 Müller-Karpe, p. 75.

160 See Pfeiffer, p. 239, who suggests that the Magdalenians were too well adjusted to their environment, and that when it changed even for the better, the culture declined as its economic base literally wandered off to a more suitable habitat.

161 Müller-Karpe, pp. 230f; see also K. D. Adam, *Der Mensch im Eiszeitalter*, Stuttgarter Beiträge zur Naturkunde, Serie C, Nr. 15 (Stuttgart, 1982), p. 5, who indicates that the death of the Steinheim woman was caused by serious injuries to the head. The head had been severed and the spinal base forcibly enlarged, perhaps to remove the brain.

162 See note 110 above.

163 See Bosinski, in *KRI*, II, p. 25.

164 This appears to have been the case at La Ferrasie, Müller-Karpe, p. 231.

165 Müller-Karpe, p. 231.

166 One of the more complete skull fragments at Ehringsdorf shows traces of heavy blows to the forehead, Müller-Karpe, pp. 231, 233f.

167 Hoebel, p. 147.

168 Müller-Karpe, p. 238.

169 Müller-Karpe, p. 238.

170 Honoré, p. 323.

171 E. O. James, *Prehistoric Religion* (London 1957), pp. 141–3, 'The Mystery of Birth'.

172 Müller-Karpe, p. 239, gives the extensive detail which follows below.

173 Müller-Karpe, p. 147; see also Collins, p. 99. Clark, p. 41, and Lissner, p. 42, date this hunt into the Riss–Würm interglacial, about 130,000 years ago. In connection with the yew spear found in the Lehringen elephant, Butzer, p. 445 raises the probability of a much more extensive use of wood in these early times than the available evidence generally suggests.

174 Müller-Karpe, p. 148.

175 Müller-Karpe, pp. 152–9.

176 Butzer, pp. 455, 482f., explains the widespread charcoal horizons by suggesting that man deliberately burned extensive tracts of forests as he played his role as the major predator. In his ignorance he contributed to the extinction of many species of fauna. These regenerating areas would be recolonized by new species of flora and fauna, man's tendency to overkill thereby affecting a change in the environment, limited though it may have been.

177 G. Weber-Haupt, *Die Bedeutung des Rentiers im Paläolithikum nach Aussage der Darstellungen*, Phil. Diss. (Mainz 1957).

178 Müller-Karpe, p. 160, suggests that the designs represent snaring nets rather than corrals.

179 Rust, p. 14.

180 Urslar, p. 58, rejects the theory of a 'reindeer era', since vast deposits of reindeer bones have been found in earlier Neanderthal open air stations.

181 See note 147 above.

182 Rust, p. 31; C[14] dating suggests early dates from the Stellmoor at about 13,000 B.C.; see Müller-Karpe, p. 133.

183 K. Bokelmann, 'Die ältere und mittlere Steinzeit in Schleswig-Holstein', in *KRI*, II, p. 33, suggests that the return to glacial conditions began about 11,600 B.C. and lasted for about 3600 years.

184 Bokelmann, in *KRI*, II, p. 33, indicates mean July temperatures of 10°C, with the edge of the ice only some 200 km away from the temporary campsites.

185 Rust, p. 15.

186 See note 147 above; it will be recalled that Hawkes, p. 35, had drawn a link between the 'eastern Gravettian' and the Hamburgians.

187 Honoré, pp. 418f.

188 K. J. Narr, *Studien zur älteren und mittleren Steinzeit der Niederen Lande* (Bonn 1968), p. 234.

189 Honoré, p. 425.

190 For a detailed account of the Meiendorf-Ahrensburg find see Lissner, pp. 291–6; Honoré, p. 420, gives dates of 13,500 B.C. for Meiendorf, 13,000 B.C. for Poggenwisch. See note 181 above.

191 Rust, p. 24; Bokelmann, in *KRI*, II, p. 36, sees no specific use for the Lyngby axe as yet.

192 Rust, p. 37.

193 Bokelmann, in *KRI*, II, p. 36.

194 Rust, p. 14.

195 See Leroi-Gourhan, pp. 1–3, for an impatient reaction to the deceptive mystical superficiality in which observable representations can be shrouded.

196 Leroi-Gourhan, p. 89.

197 Leroi-Gourhan, p. 28.

198 Leroi-Gourhan, p. 29.

199 Müller-Karpe, p. 225.

200 Rust, pp. 2of.

201 Rust, p. 35; also Bordes, pp. 168f. and Honoré, pp. 421–32.

202 Leroi-Gourhan, p. 14, questions the validity of the 'reindeer cult' at Stellmoor. See also Weber-Haupt, p. 27.

203 Müller-Karpe, pp. 224f., 300, 306; see also J. Hawkes, *Atlas of Ancient Archaeology* (London 1974), p. 62, who only mentions a mammoth skull.

204 See Clark, p. 44, who even excludes personal ornaments. Pfeiffer, p. 220, suggests that early man's stone tools are often more aesthetically pleasing than necessary, though that might be more an expression of personal pride than an expression of aesthetics. See also Urslar, pp. 35–45.

205 Müller-Karpe, p. 50; see also note 143 above.

206 C. Hawkes, p. 38, suggests that primitive man knows but one all-embracing world: sense and imagination are for him on the same plane of reality. In all things he will see bodies endowed with forces answering to his own, able to outdo his own, but also perhaps to assist him in his needs and desires.

207 Butzer, p. 482, favors notions of sympathetic magic as a primary motive behind artistic expression. Müller-Karpe, p. 192, envisages a new intensity of subject–object relations. Lissner, p. 206, speaks of the accidental discovery of art in natural forms.

208 Pfeiffer, p. 234, suggests that the use of hunting magic increased with the depletion of the herds which man hunted. It is important to keep in mind Collins's admonition, p. 149, that it is a naive idea to see one single factor as an explanation of all Paleolithic art. See also Drössler, p. 61.

209 See for instance Lissner, p. 215, who, however, sees only religious purposes behind early art.

210 Lissner, p. 246, deduces a magical connotation in cave art from the absence of a base line.

Collins, p. 140, also notes the absence of a base line, the lack of commitment to the horizontal axis, without, however, deducing any mysterious implications from this fact. Laming-Emperaire, p. 135, rejects the magic 'killing' of the prey, as 80–90% of the animals shown are not 'wounded', or even associated with arrows.

211 Lissner, pp. 266, 278, sees reflections of shamanism in the ambiguous figures of cave art. Based on his observations of Siberian practices he describes shamanism as involving neither religious beliefs nor rites and no god, concentrating on the maintenance of communication with souls and spirits. To Lissner, p. 266, shamanism facilitates 'self-severance from mundane existence, a state of heightened sensibility and spiritual awareness, loss of outward consciousness in a state of ecstasy and inspired rapture, where he sees dreamlike apparitions, hears voices and receives visions of truth, during which his soul can leave the body'.

212 See Leroi-Gourhan, pp. 85–91.

213 Leroi-Gourhan, pp. 9of.

214 See Collins, p. 139, on the choice of subject matter in cave art.

215 This Magdalenian representation was found engraved on a piece of eagle bone in the cave of Teyjat in the Dordogne in France, see Müller-Karpe, p. 285, and plate 135,A3.

216 Hibben, p. 81, restricts magic to cave art. For him ornamental art on portable objects does not have this connotation.

217 Honoré, p. 310, draws our attention to the artists' concern for the depiction of the animals' form and movement. See note 215 above.

218 See also Leroi-Gourhan, pp. 79f., 151f.

219 According to Pfeiffer, p. 232, it was the artist's responsibility to transmit traditions, which suggests that art carried an especially heavy cultural burden.

220 Narr, in Günther, p. 125, argues that because the animal character participates in other spheres of existence, man's association with it gives him access to these dimensions. See also Müller-Karpe, pp. 242f.

221 See Honoré, p. 392; see also K. D. Adam, R. Kurz, *Eiszeitkunst im süddeutschen Raum* (Stuttgart, 1980), pp. 57, 71, note 32, for whom the representation belongs to the Middle Ages.

222 Drößler, p. 60; also Müller-Karpe, p. 219.

223 See Collins, p. 153; Drößler, p. 60; Bordes, p. 168; Honoré, pp. 316f; see especially Müller-Karpe, pp. 307f, for details, also plate 202C. See Müller-Karpe, p. 72, for the placement of the figurines in the sediment strata of the cave, cf. especially Adam and Kurz, *Eiszeitkunst*, pp. 81ff.

224 Drößler, p. 43, suggests that once the 'magic' function had been addressed and the purpose been fulfilled, the figurines were broken.

225 See Müller-Karpe, plate 209; also Honoré, pp. 323f.

226 Hibben, p. 81, states that Magdalenian art is inspired by hunting ceremonial.

227 Drößler, pp. 42f.

228 Lissner, p. 244, is of the opinion that fear lay behind the reluctance to portray the human form in effigy. He suggests that this fear of the human image grew up in hunting cultures which had transferred the idea of the danger of pictorial representations. However, see also W. G. Haensch, *Die paläolitischen Menschendarstellungen aus der Sicht der somatischen Anthropologie, Menschenbildnisse auf Gravierungen, Reliefs und Malereien in Südwestfrankreich und Nordostspanien* (Bonn 1968), pp. 128f. who has prepared a classification of 90 human representations, of which only 3 are paintings.

229 Honoré, pp. 342–4.

230 See Lissner, pp. 207–11, for a summary of these 'Venus' figures. He associates shamanistic practices with these figurines; see also Leroi-Gourhan, p. 124, and Torbrügge, p. 15, who states that the female figure predominates in small sculpture.

231 Müller-Karpe, p. 216.

232 Drößler, p. 45. According to Müller-Karpe, pp. 311f. the statuette was found in Gravettian strata, in level 9, for which Müller-Karpe, p. 133, gives a C^{14} date of about 21,000 B.C. Clark, p. 58, agrees that the figurine is Gravettian; Collins, p. 153 dates her to about 27,000 B.C., close to the end of the Aurignacian, and insists that she is the earliest 'Venus'.

233 Torbrügge, pp. 15ff.

234 See Adam and Kurz, pp. 64f., 109.

235 Drößler, pp. 84f.

236 G. Bosinski, 'Weitere Funde aus Gönnersdorf', in *KRI*, II, pp. 29f.

237 Drößler, pp. 83f.

238 Wingert-Uhde, pp. 33f.; see also Adam and Kurz, pp. 55, 67f., 79.

2. The Ceramic Age: Immigration from Within

1 M. Schwarzbach, *Climates of the Past*, An Introduction to Paleoclimatology, transl. from the German, ed. by R. O. Muir (London 1963), p. 201.

2 K. Bokelmann, 'Die ältere und mittlere Steinzeit in Schleswig-Holstein', in *Kölner Römer Illustrierte*, ed. by Gerd Biegel (Historische Museen der Stadt Köln. 1975), II, p. 13, hereafter abbreviated to *KRI*.

3 Bokelmann, *KRI*, II, p. 36.

4 See F. C. Hibben, *Prehistoric Man in Europe*, (Univ. of Oklahoma Press, 4th printing 1968), p. 96, who indicated that the separation of Britain from the European continent occurred during the Boreal Period. J. G. Evans, 'Notes on the Environment of early Farming Communities in Britain', in D. D. A. Simpson, ed. *Economy and Settlement in Neolithic and Early Bronze Age Britain and Europe*, Papers delivered at a Conference held in the University of Leicester, December 1969 (Leicester Univ. Press 1971), p. 11, states that the main post-glacial rise of

the sea-level terminated *c.* 4500 B.C. See also C. F. C. Hawkes, *The prehistoric Foundations of Europe to the Mycenean Age* (London and New York 1973), pp. 56, 66.

5 Bokelmann, *KRI*, II, p. 36; see also H. Müller-Karpe, *Handbuch der Vorgeschichte, Jungsteinzeit* (Munich 1968), II, pp. 154f., who suggests this process to have taken place between the 8th and 4th millennium B.C. Hereafter cited as Müller-Karpe, II. Hawkes, p. 57, dates the advent of the Atlantic Climate and mixed-oak forest to after 5000 B.C. Using a geochronology, J. G. D. Clark, *The Mesolithic Settlement of Europe, A Study of the Food-Gathering Peoples of Northern Europe during the Early Post-Glacial Period*, Reprint of the 1936 edition (New York 1977), pp. 46, 53, demonstrated that during his Mesolithic II (6800–5000 B.C.), charcoal evidence indicated that oak had come to dominate the earlier birch, pine, willow forests, to be succeeded (5000–2500 B.C.) by an alder and/or mixed-oak forest in which elm, oak and lime were the dominant species. See also K. W. Butzer, *Environment and Archaeology, An Ecological Approach to Prehistory* (Chicago and New York, 2nd edition, 1971), p. 572.

6 K. J. Narr, *Studien zur älteren und mittleren Steinzeit der Niederen Lande* (Bonn 1968), p. 23.

7 See Clark, p. 153.

8 S. Piggott, *Ancient Europe from the Beginning of Agriculture to Classical Antiquity* (Chicago 1965), p. 31, points out that with the change in vegetation, red-deer populations had established themselves by 8000 B.C. See also Hibben, p. 87.

9 Hibben, p. 88, deems microliths to be the distinguishing feature of the Mesolithic. See also D. Clark, 'Mesolithic Europe: the economic basis', in G. de G. Sieveking, I. H. Longworth and K. E. Wilson, eds., *Problems in Economic and Social Archaeology* (London 1976), p. 457, who emphasizes the efficiency of microliths, as they made it possible to repair a tool or weapon by replacing parts, rather than having to prepare a new stone tool.

10 E. Stocker, *Die große Zeit der Buchauer Ausgrabungen* (Bad Buchau 1976), pp. 12–18. Already J. G. D. Clark, pp. 199f., singled out the Mesolithic Tannstock settlement on the Federsee in south-west Germany, consisting of 38 oval huts, perhaps representing two periods of settlement. See also Piggott, p. 33.

11 The visitor to the prehistoric secction of the Nationalmuseet at København is subjected to this sound.

12 J. G. D. Clark, pp. 162–77, details techniques, some 24 motifs consisting of geometrics, linears and biomorphic forms, both anthropo- and zoomorphic stylizations.

13 Hibben, p. 102, suggests that a human society of larger groups, such as we know it, evolved during the Mesolithic.

14 Piggott, p. 26, also note 4, p. 64, suggests that recently the status of pottery as a criterion has been

seriously eroded, in that Neolithic societies existed without pottery, at Jericho for instance.

15 Piggott, p. 35, states that north European domestic dogs are the earliest known.

16 Two cultures stand out, the Maglemose culture, centered in the great peat bog area at Mullerup in Sjaelland, see Hibben, pp. 91–3, for greater detail, or Hawkes, pp. 58ff.; but especially J. G. D. Clark, pp. 51–124, for detailed consideration of settlement, sustenance and details of the material culture; the later Ertebølle culture, J. G. D. Clark, pp. 138–53. A large piece of charcoal from Mullerup has yielded an uncorrected C[14] date of 6710 ± 140 b.c., i.e. *c.* 7600 B.C. See *Radiocarbon*, publ. by *The American Journal of Science*, ed. by R. F. Flint, J. G. Ogden, J. Rouse, M. Stuiver (Yale University, New Haven, Connecticut), XV, 1, 1973, p. 88. To correct all C[14] dates appearing in this chapter, use will be made of the conversion table published by R. Malcolm Clark, 'A calibration curve for radiocarbon dates', in *Antiquity*, XLIX, pp. 264f. (Cambridge 1975). Shells from Ertebølle yielded an uncorrected C[14] date of 3180 ± 100 b.c., i.e. *c.* 3950 B.C. An earlier date from the Draved Mose in Denmark was derived from a piece of charcoal of pine, 7440 ± 120 b.c. *Radiocarbon*, XV, 1, p. 87. Owing to the limits of calibration and to the inaccuracies in C[14] dating, at least another 900 years should be added to this date to arrive at a more realistic date. For summaries of Radiocarbon dating principles, see Butzer, pp. 24–37f., who also treats other dating methods; D. Collins, *The Human Revolution from Ape to Artist* (Oxford 1976), pp. 50–3; S. Piggott, p. 12; R. J. Braidwood, *Prehistoric Men* (Glenview Illinois, etc., 8th edition, 1975), p. 4. For details and discussion of the C[14] controversy see C. Renfrew, *Before Civilization* (London 1975), pp. 48–68, 255–68. The inaccuracies of the C[14] method of dating can now be corrected within limits, through the calibration with the annual growth rings, especially of the California bristle cone pine. The technique of dating by means of tree rings is known as dendrochronology, see Butzer, pp. 251f. for a short treatment of the subject. See also Renfrew, pp. 69–83.

In brief, C[14] dates earlier than 1200 B.C. were found to be not early enough, so that a C[14] date of 3000 ± 120 b.c. had to be corrected by adding another 800 years, to about 3800 B.C. A convention was introduced which now indicates an uncorrected C[14] date as 3000 ± 120 b.c. for instance, assigning the capital spelling of B.C. to the corrected, i.e. calibrated date to read 3800 B.C. At a lecture on 'Ultrasensitive Mass Spectronomy with a Tandem van der Graaf Accelerator' by Prof. H. E. Gove of the Nuclear Structure Research Laboratory, University of Rochester, U.S.A., given 12 May 1981 as part of the H. L. Welsh Lectures in Physics 1981, at the University of Toronto, a calibration chart was used on which a C[14] date of 3000 b.c. corresponded to a

calibrated date of 3650 B.C. For details see H. E. Gove, et al., 'Radiocarbon Dating with Tandem Electromatic Accelerators', *Radiocarbon*, XXII, 3, 1980, pp. 785–93.

17 At Ugstein in the Palatinate a piece of wood has been recovered which one supposes to have been part of a boat. It was dated to 23,260 ± 440 b.c., *Radiocarbon*, XII, 2, 1971, p. 211.

18 Bokelmann, *KRI*, II, p. 36.

19 In Jylland these heaps, the so-called 'kitchen middens', consist of such edible shell-fish as cockles, oysters and mussels, but also of other remains of fish, as well as the bones of wild animals, see C. F. C. Hawkes, p. 60; also J. G. D. Clark, p. 140.

20 See D. Clark, in Sieveking, pp. 451–60, who argues that the finds of hunting and fishing implements distort our view of prehistoric man's diet, that in latitudes 35°–55° N, gathered vegetable foods would have provided 60–80% of the diet by weight, and that the hunt was much less efficient in effort and yield when compared to gathering. Our hunting bias sees a straight stick as a spear rather than taking it for a digging stick. The European temperate forests of the Mesolithic, *c.* 7000–4000 B.C., were sources of food very high in edible protein.

21 Display in the prehistoric section of the Nationalmuseet in København. See also T. Ramskou, *Dänische Vorzeit* (København 1972), p. 8.

22 The term 'Fertile Crescent' used to have a more restrictive application. Owing to growing dissatisfaction with this term derived from additional evidence found in the adjoining regions to the east and north, the term is now applied more generally to this area, see R. Stigler, 'The later Neolithic in the Near East and the Rise of Civilization', in R. Stigler, ed., *The Old World, Early Man to the Development of Agriculture* (New York 1974), pp. 98–126.

23 See D. Perkins and P. Daly, 'The Beginning of Food Production in the Near East', in Stigler, pp. 71f., for a summary of the geography of the Near East; also Butzer, pp. 149–66, for a summary of Near Eastern civilizations; Braidwood, pp. 102–40, for a summary of Near Eastern developments into the Neolithic. For an extensive treatment of the area see J. Mellaart, *The Neolithic of the Near East* (New York and London 1975).

24 See Butzer, pp. 541–65, for a discussion of agricultural origins in the Near East, such as the domestication of cereals and animals, as well as the development of tools of wood, bone and flint; see also Perkins and Daly, in Stigler, pp. 71–97; also Piggott, pp. 39f. for the cultivation of noble grasses, legumes and such agricultural techniques as the rotation of crops. Various sources indicate evidence of the domestication of cattle as early as 9000–7000 B.C. Perkins and Daly suggest that the domestication of cattle may even have been introduced from Europe, Stigler, p. 82.

25 Müller-Karpe, II, p. 251.

26 Butzer, p. 553, suggests agriculture to have

been practised as early as *c.* 9500 B.C.

27 Perkins and Daly, in Stigler, p. 72, argue that to define the Neolithic in terms of pottery, polished stone tools and agriculture is to apply criteria derived from northern Europe, which are not entirely applicable to the Near East.

28 Piggott, p. 39.

29 Perkins and Daly, in Stigler, pp. 73-7, indicate that by 9000 B.C. there is at least partial reliance on food production.

30 D. Clark, in Sieveking, p. 460, argues that food production, storage and resource management suggest responses to deteriorating conditions.

31 Jericho has yielded uncorrected C¹⁴ dates of 6250±200 b.c. and 5850±200 b.c., to be corrected by about 1000 years, Renfrew, p. 55.

32 In the wake of V. Gordon Childe's publications, the theory of diffusion of Near Eastern cultural influences over the rest of Europe dominated the literature, to the point that most, if not all cultural accomplishments of European prehistory came to be seen as direct but later derivatives of the cultural areas of the Near East and the eastern Mediterranean. For a summary of Diffusionism, see Renfrew, pp. 20-47. The application of C¹⁴ dating methods did not create any real surprises in dating the Near Eastern and eastern Mediterranean cultural regions, but it did stimulate disbelief when dates from central, western and north-western Europe did not support the diffusionist theory. The application of calibrated C¹⁴ dates left the European diffusionist chronology in a shambles, as the new dates revealed central and western European accomplishments to predate the 'ancestral' achievements of the Aegean, the eastern Mediterranean and the Near East. The theories which saw large migrating groups of dynamic, adventurous cultural benefactors can no longer be supported. See P. J. Fowler, 'Early Prehistoric Agriculture in Western Europe: some archaeological evidence', in Simpson, pp. 153-82, who suggests independent inventions in the north and questions the usual assumption of innovations moving in from the east, p. 159.

33 Renfrew, pp. 17f., favors developments in Europe largely independent of eastern precedents.

34 In spite of anti-diffusionism, there is agreement concerning the spread of the Neolithic agricultural economies from western Asia, Piggott, p. 25; that the basic cereal plants were brought from the Near East, Renfrew, p. 142. The evidence, clothed in the new chronology, makes it apparent that Near Eastern influences were assimilated by dynamic European societies, to appear as characteristically European cultures, Renfrew, pp. 118f. Already C. F. C. Hawkes, p. 80, had indicated that once in Europe oriental features became blurred as they assimilated native elements. Filtering as well as impoverishment were associated results.

35 H. L. Thomas, *Near Eastern, Mediterranean and European Chronology, The Historical, Archaeological,* *Radiocarbon, Pollenanalytical and Geochronological Evidence, Studies in Mediterranean Archaeology,* XVII (Lund 1967), Chart I: 13b, lists an uncorrected C¹⁴ date for the Proto-Bükk culture at Korlat in northeastern Hungary of 4683±100 b.c., or *c.* 5500 B.C. From Eitzum near Wolfenbüttel in central Germany wood-charcoal associated with Banded Ware shards yielded a date of 6310±200 b.p. (uncorrected Before Present), i.e. *c.* 5215 B.C. *Radiocarbon,* VI, 1964, p. 310.

36 Schwarzbach, pp. 202f., indicates that a climatic optimum set in about 5000 B.C. lasting for about 2000 years. See also Thomas, pp. 54f. Butzer, p. 571, dates the beginning of the moist Atlantic phase to *c.* 6200 B.C. lasting to *c.* 3300 B.C. He fits the cultural dispersal into this period.

37 See Braidwood, pp. 141-8; also Hibben, pp. 117-25; see Piggott, p. 27.

38 Renfrew, pp. 104f., compares the effect of the new dates to a fault line. To give just two examples: in Bulgaria the lowest level of the Karonovo tell yielded a date of 5423±150 b.c. (Thomas, Ch. I: 10), i.e. before 6000 B.C.; Gyálarét in south-eastern Hungary was dated at 5353±100 b.c. (Thomas, Ch. I: 13b), i.e. before 6000 B.C. Mellaart's dates for Karonovo I are more recent, *c.* 5000-4329± 120 b.c., 5190 B.C. (Mellaart, p. 254).

39 H. Quitta, 'The C¹⁴ Chronology of the Central and SE European Neolithic', in *Antiquity,* XLI, 1967, p. 47.

40 Renfrew, p. 97; also Mellaart, p. 257, who suggests dates of *c.* 5400-4300 b.c., i.e. *c.* 5170 B.C.

41 Clark, *Antiquity,* XXXIX, 1967, p. 47.

42 Thomas, Ch. I: 12a.

43 Renfrew, pp. 96f., 107.

44 See Butzer, p. 574; also Hawkes, p. 122; Hibben, pp. 116-25; for southern Starčevo see especially Mellaart, pp. 254-69.

45 C. F. C. Hawkes, p. 113.

46 C. F. C. Hawkes, p. 95. C. F. C. Hawkes, p. 105, sees in these spiral patterns an echo of the Paleolithic, the so-called East-Gravettian, of which the site at Mézine, east of the Dniepr, yielded such meander patterns carved into pieces of mammoth ivory. See Müller-Karpe, I, plate 245, for illustrations. A survey of the inventory recorded by Müller-Karpe showed no other similar ornamental pattern anywhere.

47 Fowler, in Simpson, p. 160.

48 C. F. C. Hawkes, p. 123.

49 Renfrew, p. 178.

50 See Renfrew, p. 144, who suggests that the Danube region attracted the first farmers to such areas as were not in demand by the original Mesolithic populations, still sustaining themselves by hunting and gathering.

51 D. Clark, in Sieveking, p. 479.

52 Renfrew, pp. 167-82.

53 Renfrew, p. 174.

54 Renfrew, p. 168, figure 37.

55   H. Müller-Karpe, *Das vorgeschichtliche Europa, Kunst der Welt* (Baden-Baden 1979, reprint of 1968 ed.), pp. 52–75; see also W. Torbrügge, *Prehistoric European Art, Panorama of World Art*, transl. from the German by N. Guterman (Baden-Baden, New York 1968), pp. 58–69.

56   Renfrew, pp. 176ff.

57   Renfrew, p. 181.

58   See Thomas, p. 55. Basing his argument on uncorrected C¹⁴ dates he states that the Banded Ware culture appeared in the Netherlands, central and northern Germany before the middle of the fifth millennium, i.e. as early as *c.* 4500 b.c. or *c.* 5350 B.C. See also Müller-Karpe, II, p. 271; also Butzer, pp. 575ff.

59   For Denmark there are Proto-Neolithic dates (pottery, grain imprints, domesticated animals) from the Ertebølle culture at Christianslund, 3509±100 b.c., i.e. *c.* 4375 B.C.; 3581±100 b.c., i.e. *c.* 4430 B.C.; and from an early Funnel Beaker settlement at Elinelund in Sweden, 3530±210 b.c., i.e. *c.* 4400 B.C. (Thomas, p. 57f. and Ch. I: 20). For a table of dates for the Danish Mesolithic and Neolithic see H. Tauber, 'Radiocarbon chronology of the Danish Mesolithic and Neolithic', in *Antiquity*, XLVI, 1972, p. 107. British dates were most controversial in view of Piggott's late dating of the British Neolithic, reflected in J. G. Evans (see note 4 above), who suggests that the first group of farmers may possibly have reached Britain by means of a land bridge, or possibly over a marshland link across the southern North Sea during the third millennium B.C. and after the rise of the sea level which terminated *c.* 4500 b.c., i.e. *c.* 5350 B.C. Thomas, pp. 52f., gives C¹⁴ dates of about 3500 b.c., i.e. *c.* 4375 B.C., 3303±150 from Hembury, a Windmill Hill culture site, i.e. *c.* 4095 B.C. and 3313±110 from Monamore, Western Neolithic, i.e. *c.* 4100 B.C. (Thomas, Ch. I: 18). From Ireland, Ballynagylly, County Tyrone, come dates averaging 3700 b.c., or about 4520 B.C. See also J. G. D. Clark, 'Radiocarbon Dating and the Spread of Farming Economy', in *Antiquity*, XXXIX, 1965, pp. 46f., who lists C¹⁴ dates for Britain of the late fourth millennium. See Renfrew, p. 107, for a comparative chart. The first farmers in Britain are placed between 4000 B.C.; their clearing of forests, however, is not indicated by C¹⁴ dating until *c.* 3200 B.C., Renfrew, p. 64.

60   The Ertebølle-Ellerbeck culture of Jylland and Schleswig-Holstein would be such an example. See previous note. Ellerbeck yielded a date of 4292±200, or 5170 B.C. D. Brothwell, 'Diet, Economy and Biosocial Change in late Prehistoric Europe', in Simpson, pp. 75–87, indicates, p. 80, that the analysis of food bone from Swiss sites of the third millennium B.C. shows that from 1/2 to 1/3 of the animals used for food were wild.

61   Butzer, pp. 568f., raises the possibility of soil exhaustion near settlements as a motive for dispersal, in any event an appealing solution for dynamic groups living near the margins of 'densely' settled agricultural lands. With a secure economic base a settlement would have to contain its growth or be forced to send out colonists. Renfrew, p. 115, refers to the work of A. Forge, who suggested that 400–500 persons may be the upper limit for a Neolithic egalitarian society. Beyond that population increases may be dealt with by sending out splinter groups to form new colonies.

62   Numerous sites from regions of the Middle Danube to the Rhine and northern central Germany reflect the presence of quite similar cultural elements, the Banded Ware culture, with corrected C¹⁴ dates hovering about 5200 B.C.: Vinča, Yugoslavia, 4426±60 b.c., or *c.* 5280 B.C. (Thomas, Ch. I: 12a); Zseliz Zalavar, Transdanubia, 4415±100 b.c., or 5270 B.C. (Thomas, Ch. I: 13a); Winden am See, Burgenland, Austria, 4168±100 b.c., or 4935 B.C. (Thomas, Ch. I: 15); Wittislingen, Swabia, 4261±110 b.c., or 5215 B.C. (Thomas, Ch. I: 16); Friedberg, Middle Rhine, 4353±100 b.c., or 5215 B.C. (Thomas, Ch. I: 16); these last two sites are also dated at 4070 b.c., or 4940 B.C. and 4170 b.c. or 5050 B.C. respectively (Clark, *Antiquity*, XXXIX, 1965, p. 47). Eitzum near Wolfenbüttel in northern Germany, 6310±200 b.p., or *c.* 5220 B.C., *Radiocarbon*, VI, 1964, p. 310, also Clark, *Antiquity*, XXXIX, 1965, p. 47. The b.p. designation refers to an uncorrected 'before present' date. 1950 has been accepted as the conventional date to represent the 'present'. The B.P. designation refers to a calibrated 'before present' date.

63   Butzer, pp. 574–9, argues that the Danubian culture sought out loess areas, in which the soil could be worked easily, that in fact the pioneer farmers headed for soils and conditions most like those of the lands of their origin. See also Müller-Karpe, II, p. 269.

64   Müller-Karpe, II, pp. 246f., maintains that the cultivation of cereals was spread to Europe by colonization.

65   Müller-Karpe, II, p. 248.

66   Wedge-shaped polished stones, also known as shoe-last celts, associated with shards of linear and curvilinear pottery, were part of the inventory found at Starčevo in Yugoslavia (Müller-Karpe, II, p. 461), and dated between 6000 and 5200 B.C. (Renfrew, p. 97). Shoe-last celts were also found in the Banded Ware settlement at Zwenkau, near Leipzig in central Germany, from which dates were obtained of 4395±70 b.c., or 5250 B.C. (Thomas, Ch. I: 19a); 6160±70 b.p., or 5085 B.C. (*Radiocarbon*, V, 1963, p. 184); 5890±100 b.p. (Berlin), i.e. *c.* 4750 B.C., or 6160±70 b.p. (Groningen) (*Radiocarbon*, XII, 2, 1970, p. 401), calibrated to read *c.* 5085 B.C.; also 4050 b.c. or *c.* 4920 B.C., Clark, *Antiquity*, XXXIX, 1965, p. 47, all calendar dates ranging between *c.* 5200 B.C. and *c.* 4700 B.C.

67   Müller-Karpe, II, p. 269.

68 Müller-Karpe, II, pp. 348, 367. See especially O. Kunkel, *Die Jungfernhöhle bei Tiefenellern, Eine neolithische Kultstätte auf dem Fränkischen Jura bei Bamberg* (Munich 1955), pp. 68ff.

69 See Müller-Karpe, II, p. 252.

70 See H. H. Müller, *Die Haustiere der Mitteldeutschen Bandkeramiker*, Deutsche Akademie für Vor- und Frühgeschichte (Berlin 1964), pp. 15–51. See also H. Müller-Karpe, *Die geschichtliche Bedeutung des Neolithikums*, Sitzungsberichte der Wissenschaftlichen Gesellschaft der J. W. v. Goethe Universität, Frankfurt am Main, (Wiesbaden 1970), IX, p. 67. Also R. Wyss, *Wirtschaft und Gesellschaft in der Jungsteinzeit*, Monographien zur Schweizer Geschichte (Bern 1973), p. 34.

71 Müller-Karpe, II, p. 252.

72 Müller-Karpe, *Neolithikum*, p. 66.

73 Müller-Karpe, *Neolithikum*, pp. 66f.

74 See Wyss, pp. 34f. This was especially the case in the Swiss and south-west German lakeshore villages. See also additional treatment below.

75 Müller-Karpe, *Neolithikum*, p. 66.

76 E. Sprockhoff, *Die Nordische Megalithkultur* (Berlin, Leipzig 1938, unless stated otherwise, all references to Sprockhoff refer to this title); also Piggott, p. 50; see H. H. Müller, p. 8.

77 Piggott, p. 51.

78 Müller-Karpe, II, pp. 346, 369. On p. 147 he points out that the shoe-last celts of western Europe are always imported rock materials.

79 Sprockhoff, *Megalithkultur*.

80 See M. S. F. Hood, 'The Tartaria Tablets', in *Old World Archaeology*: Foundations of Civilization, *Readings from Scientific American*, May 1968, (San Francisco 1972), pp. 210–17. Hood doubts the accuracy of the dates and sees them to be of Mesopotamian origin, transmitted by Syrian traders. Müller-Karpe, II, pp. 276 note 1, 307, 346, is non-committal concerning the signs. He tends to see them as pictograms used in a cultic ritual. A diffusionist by inclination, he allows them to point to possible relations with Mesopotamia, though he stresses fundamental differences between them, such as frontal and profile views, but can not accept them as a form of 'proto-writing'. Renfrew, p. 67, rejects the link on chronological grounds and though he favours the possibility that the markings might be 'proto-writing', pp. 176f., in the end, p. 186, the pictograms of different regions will have fundamental similarities without proving dependence. Regardless of the outcome of the controversy over these inscriptions, the description of the cultural cataract effect which follows in the text, diffusionist though it may be, is valid.

81 Müller-Karpe, II, pp. 123f., 266f., 369, also in *Neolithikum*, p. 17, does place considerable emphasis on this aspect.

82 Such fortifications have been located in Hungary, Czechoslovakia and Germany, Köln-Lindenthal, for instance—see discussion below.

83 Müller-Karpe, II, pp. 26of., suggests that the image of peaceful Banded Ware farmers is badly in need of revision.

84 See H. and H. A. Frankfort, 'Myth and Reality' in H. Frankfort, H. A. Frankfort, J. A. Wilson and T. Jacobsen, *Before Philosophy* (Harmondsworth 1954), pp. 11–36.

85 C. F. C. Hawkes, pp. 74–80, suggests that pottery derives from accidentally burning a clay-lined basket.

86 See note 30 above. See also W. Meier-Arendt, 'Die Zeit der Bauern und Viehzüchter', in *KRI*, I, p. 20, who argues that the new cultivated foods required cooking to release their food value. This need demanded a solution—pottery.

87 See K. H. Brandt, *Studien über steinerne Äxte und Beile der Jüngeren Stein-und Kupferzeit Norddeutschlands*, Münsterische Beiträge zur Vorgeschichtsforschung, II (Hildesheim 1967), p. 1.

88 To give just a few dates identified as Banded Ware by associated finds and arranged chronologically:

Westeregeln, central Germany (Thomas, Ch. I: 19a), 4436 ± 200 b.c. or *c.* 5285 B.C.

Eitzum near Wolfenbüttel (*Radiocarbon*, VI, 1964, p. 310), 6310 ± 200 b.p. or *c.* 5225 B.C.

Friedberg, middle Rhine (Thomas, Ch. I: 16), 4353 ± 100 b.c. or *c.* 5215 B.C.

Wittislingen, Swabia (Thomas, Ch. I: 16), 4261 ± 100 b.c. or *c.* 5140 B.C.

Zwenkau near Leipzig (Thomas, Ch. I: 19a), 4395 ± 70 b.c. or *c.* 5250 B.C. (*Radiocarbon*, V, 1963, p. 184), 6160 ± 70 b.c. or *c.* 5090 B.C.

Clark, *Antiquity*, XXXIX, 1965, p. 47, 4050 b.c. or *c.* 4920 B.C.

Winden am See, Austria (Thomas, Ch. I: 15), 4168 ± 100 b.c. or *c.* 5050 B.C. (*Radiocarbon*, VI, 1964, p. 314), 5940 ± 100 b.p. or *c.* 4840 B.C.

Hallertau, Bavaria (*Radiocarbon*, XVIII, 3, 1976, p. 285), 5990 ± 90 b.p. or *c.* 4910 B.C.

Zwenkau (*Radiocarbon*, XII, 1970, p. 401), 5890 ± 100 b.p. or *c.* 4750 B.C.

Rosdorf (*Radiocarbon*, XIV, 1, 1972, p. 64), 5685 ± 75 b.p. or *c.* 4540 B.C.

Frankenau, Austria (*Radiocarbon*, XIV, 2, 1974, p. 503), 5660 ± 100 b.p. or *c.* 4530 B.C.

89 Rössen date from Zwenkau (Thomas, Ch. I: 19a), 4065 ± 120 b.c. or *c.* 4935 B.C.; from Inden-Lamersdorf (*Radiocarbon*, X, 1, 1968, p. 23), 4800 ± 80 b.p. or *c.* 3635 B.C. H. Quitta, 'Chronology of the Central and SE European Neolithic', *Antiquity*, XLI, 1967, Chart p. 265, indicates Rössen dates to extend from *c.* 5750 b.p. to *c.* 5100 b.p., or *c.* 4590 B.C. to *c.* 3935 B.C.

90 Müller-Karpe, II, pp. 116f., see especially II, 2, plates 196–212, 216–28.

91 Müller-Karpe, II, p. 118.

92 Meier-Arendt, *KRI*, II, p. 21.

93 J. Hawkes, *Atlas of Ancient Archaeology* (London

1974), p. 59; see also Piggott, p. 51; also Hibben, p. 142.

94 See notes 81, 83 above. Müller-Karpe, II, p. 369. It is of course conceivable that designating the implements as weapons distorts the use to which the culture put them.

95 Müller-Karpe, II, pp. 122f.

96 The polished wedge-shaped tools usually go by the name 'shoe-last celts', other names, such as axes, hoes, plow-shares, burden these implements with conjectured functions.

97 Müller-Karpe, II, p. 124.

98 Müller-Karpe, II, p. 396.

99 Müller-Karpe, II, pp. 364ff.

100 See G. Asmus, 'Die menschlicen Skelettreste aus der Jungfernhöhle', in O. Kunkel, pp. 68–77. See note 68 above.

101 Kunkel, pp. 111ff.

102 See Chapter I, note 172.

103 Müller-Karpe, II, pp. 218ff., 261. Also W. Meier-Arendt, 'Linienbandkeramische Siedlungs-gebiete', *KRI*, pp. 38–43.

104 Müller-Karpe, II, pp. 223ff. See Piggott, p. 52, who, however, suggests villages of about 400 inhabitants cultivating about 600 acres/240 hectares per year.

105 See Hibben, p. 126, for details of the Köln-Lindenthal site; also Piggott, p. 50; also R. Kuper and J. Lüning, 'Archäologische Forschungen im Rheinischen Braunkohlerevier: Ergebnisse und Aufgaben', in *KRI*, II, pp. 19ff.; also H. Wingert-Uhde, *Schätze und Scherben* (Oldenburg, Hamburg 1977), p. 50; see also C. Hawkes, pp. 117f.

106 J. P. Farrugia, R. Kuper, J. Lüning, P. Stehli, *Der Bandkeramische Siedlungsplatz Langweiler 2, Gemeinde Aldenhoven, Kreis Düren*, Serie: Beiträge zur Neolithischen Besiedlung der Aldenhovener Platte (Bonn 1973), pp. 1ff. In all, seven settlements were located on the plateau. See Kuper and Lüning, in *KRI*, II, p. 19.

107 Farrugia *et al*. p. 171.

108 Farrugia *et al*., p. 45.

109 Farrugia *et al*., p. 50.

110 Farrugia *et al*., pp. 57–83; P. Stehli, pp. 85–100, offers an analysis of the ceramic finds.

111 Farrugia *et al*., pp. 106–33.

112 Farrugia *et al*., p. 148.

113 Farrugia *et al*., pp. 148f. For the cultivation of cereals in Europe see Brothwell in Simpson, p. 79.

114 Farrugia *et al*., pp. 152–6.

115 Müller-Karpe, II, pp. 227f; also Kuper and Lüning, in *KRI*, II, p. 20. The collective effort required suggests the cooperation of larger groups. Piggott, p. 97, supports the view that the Neolithic farming culture was disrupted by more nomadic pastoral populations. The growing insecurity would lead to the erecting of defenses.

116 W. Meier-Arendt, 'Die befestigte linienband-keramische Siedlung von Köln-Lindenthal', in *KRI*, II, p. 41.

117 Ibid.; also Hibben, p. 127, suggests that the Banded Ware farmers were reacting to the threats posed by the Rössen people to the east, envious of their agricultural lands.

118 Meier-Arendt, 'Linienbandkeramische Sied-lingsgebiete', in *KRI*, II, p. 38, suggests a joint effort by new and established populations; T. Capelle and K. J. Narr, 'Die archäologische Erforschung Nord-deutschlands', in *KRI*, II, p. 17, maintain that the indigenous population was not involved. Müller-Karpe, II, p. 272, excludes the possibility of an indigenous influence on the formation of the Banded Ware culture.

119 T. Capelle and K. J. Narr, in *KRI*, II, p. 17.

120 See R. Kuper, 'Die Rössener Kultur', in *KRI*, II, p. 44.

121 Müller-Karpe, II, p. 133, summarizes this point and indicates that archeological analysis cannot support this contention.

122 See Müller-Karpe, II, p. 273, for a discussion of these relationships. He rejects the notion that the Rössen culture marks the cultural assertion of the Mesolithic population of hunters and gatherers, who, now fully converted to the Neolithic way of life, assumed the domination of the area. See also Piggott, p. 62. C. Hawkes, p. 118, considers Rössen to be a synthesis of Danubian and native elements.

123 See Piggott, p. 47, for a description of dwellings of the Großgartach culture.

124 Müller-Karpe, II, p. 229. The attribution of the Goldberg settlement to the Rössen culture may be an error, see P. Schröter, 'Goldburghausen, Ost-albkreis, Baden-Württemberg: „Goldberg", Häuser der Mittleren Jungsteinzeit', in *KRI*, II, p. 48. See C. Hawkes for details of the Goldberg settlement.

125 Müller-Karpe, II, p. 130.

126 See U. Boelicke, 'Das Erdwerk Urmitz im Kreis Koblenz-Mayen', in *KRI*, II, p. 49. Boelicke points out that such earthworks in the Rhineland date back to the time of the Banded Ware culture.

127 See E. Stocker, *Die Große Zeit der Buchauer Ausgrabungen* (Bad Buchau 1976).

128 See R. Wyss, pp. 13–27, for settlements in Switzerland. See also Müller-Karpe, II, p. 509.

129 Decorated walls were a characteristic of the earlier Großgartach culture. See Piggott, p. 47.

130 Müller-Karpe, II, pp. 228f.

131 Müller-Karpe, II, p. 229; see also Schröter, in *KRI*, II, p. 48.

132 C. F. C. Hawkes, p. 119, sees the Aichbühl settlement to be derived from the Danubians.

133 See notes 127, 128.

134 Stocker, pp. 9ff.; see also Müller-Karpe, II, pp. 230ff. At Egolzwil the outlines of 50 houses were located.

135 Stocker, p. 10; C. Hawkes, p. 136, applies to them the term 'log raft'.

136 Müller-Karpe, II, p. 230.

137 Piggott, p. 89, sees in these houses with porches a style also present in Bulgaria.

138 Hibben, pp. 151–5, still echoes these notions concerning lake-shore dwellings. See also W. E. Stöckli, "Das Pfahlbauproblem heute", in S. Martin-Kilcher, *125 Jahre Pfahlbauforschung*, Sondernummer: Archäologie der Schweiz (Basel 1979), pp. 50–6. Also Ch. Strahm, "Die Ausgrabungen am Neuenburgersee und das Pfahlbauproblem", in S. Martin-Kilcher, pp. 61–4.

139 Müller-Karpe, II, p. 255.

140 H. Müller-Karpe, *Handbuch der Vorgeschichte, Kupferzeit*, III, part 2, p. 933. See also H. Zürn, 'Das jungsteinzeitliche Dorf Ehrenstein, Alb-Donau Kreis, Baden-Württemberg', in *KRI*, II, p. 51, who gives a date of about 3200 b.c., or 3950 B.C. See *Radiocarbon*, VIII, 1966, p. 244, for a date of 5210 ± 120 b.p., or *c.* 6000 B.C. or earlier.

141 Zürn, in *KRI*, II, p. 50; see especially O. Paret, *Das Steinzeitdorf Ehrenstein bei Ulm/Donau* (Stuttgart 1955), p. 19.

142 Paret, p. 13.

143 Paret, p. 20.

144 Zürn, in *KRI*, II, p. 51.

145 Paret, pp. 14–16.

146 Paret, p. 32.

147 Paret, p. 23.

148 Paret, p. 21.

149 Piggott, p. 58, makes this comparison in connection with Swiss lake dwellings.

150 Paret, p. 51.

151 See below for details.

152 Müller-Karpe, II, p. 232.

153 Müller-Karpe, II, p. 289.

154 Müller-Karpe, II, p. 128.

155 Müller, Karpe, II, pp. 134f.

156 See Müller-Karpe, II, pp. 128f., but especially, II, 2, plates 228–237.

157 R. Kuper, *KRI*, II, p. 44, who suggests that the Rössen culture contributed to the formation of the Funnel Beaker culture of the North.

158 Müller-Karpe, II, pp. 362f.

159 Müller-Karpe, II, pp. 366f.

160 Müller-Karpe, II, p. 368.

161 Burials in megalithic stone chambers will be dealt with below.

162 Müller-Karpe, II, pp. 368–70.

163 Müller-Karpe, II, p. 346.

164 Müller-Karpe, II, pp. 347f.

165 Müller-Karpe, II, p. 295; however, the new dating techniques are casting great doubt on the likelihood of such Near Eastern derivations of figural art.

166 See Renfrew, pp. 171–5; the sites are Cayönü in northern Syria (Mellaart, pp. 52, 54), which precedes the uses of hammered and later of smelted copper at Çatal Hüyük by *c.* 1000 years. The first copper beads come from Ali Kosh (Mellaart, p. 82). Concerning the first evidence of gold at Tepe Gawra in northern Mesopotamia, see G. Mahr, 'Anfänge der Metallgewinnung I', in the publications of the Museum für Vor- und Frühgeschichte, Staatliche

Museen, Preußischer Kulturbesitz (Berlin 1973), no. 1142a.

167 The mine was located in the area of Tepe Siyalk, on the north Iran Plateau (Mellaart, p. 189).

168 Renfrew, p. 173f., refers to the documented finds of copper beads at Cernica in Rumania, contemporary with the earlier Vinča culture.

169 See E. Sprockhoff, *Die Nordische Megalithkultur* (Berlin, Leipzig 1938).

170 See Asmut, in Kunkel, p. 74.

171 See Renfrew, pp. 143f. who gives dates as early as 5500 B.C. for Spain and *c.* 4600 B.C. for Britain. See also G. Daniel, *Megaliths in History* (London 1972), p. 8.

172 Renfrew, pp. 85–91, rejects earlier notions that Aegean colonists brought cultural influences to Iberia from where they stimulated the western and northern cultures, and that from there the Iberian passage graves spread up the Atlantic coast. In Britanny and Ireland such graves were being built well before 3300 B.C., while there is no such evidence in the Aegean before 3000 B.C. The megalithic chamber tombs of western Europe predate the pyramids (Renfrew, p. 16).

173 See Renfrew, p. 69.

174 The tombs are characterized by poor inventories, see Renfrew, p. 22.

175 The Egyptian chronology continues to remain reliable.

176 Renfrew, p. 132, argues in favour of local developments in response to local needs.

177 Renfrew, p. 126, rejects the notion of a 'megalithic province', since there is no unity in the prehistoric cultures of the various regions.

178 The megalith structures and their use as graves will be discussed below.

179 Renfrew, p. 231.

180 H. Quitta, in *Antiquity*, XLI, p. 265, gives a range of Funnel Beaker dates from 5350 b.p. to 4850 b.p., or *c.* 4250 B.C. to 3685 B.C. respectively. Funnel Beaker date from Heidmoor (Thomas, Ch. I: 19b) 3344 ± 115 b.c., or *c.* 4160 B.C. in calendar years. A date from Kmehlen (*Radiocarbon*, VIII, 1966, p. 29), of 5360 ± 160 b.p., or *c.* 4250 B.C. Piggott, p. 69, note 66, gives C14 dates for the north German megaliths and Funnel Beakers ranging between *c.* 3190 b.c. and *c.* 3070 b.c., or *c.* 3980 B.C. and 3850 B.C. respectively. See Tauber, *Antiquity* XLVI, 1972, p. 107 for a range of Danish Funnel Beaker dates and sites.

181 J. Hawkes, p. 60.

182 Müller-Karpe, III, p. 319.

183 It will be noticed that the corrected C14 dates do not allow such a neat sequence of cultures as the stratifications of ceramic styles would suggest.

184 See Thomas, Ch. I: 19a for a Baalberge C14 date from Kmehlen of 3571 ± 160 b.c., or 4440 B.C. in calendar years.

185 Samples from Thaygen-Weier were dated between 3120–2990 b.c. and calibrated with bristle-

cone pine wood to give dates ranging between *c.* 3900 and 3775 B.C., see Quitta, *Antiquity*, XLI, 1967, pp. 267f. A reading reported by Thomas, Ch. I: 16, from Ehrenstein yielded a date of 3447 ± 100 b.c., or *c.* 4350 B.C. in calendar years.

186 Dates from this period:

Salzmünde type, Halle, Dölauer Heide (Thomas, II: 19a), 2973 ± 100 b.c., or *c.* 3750 B.C., also (*Radiocarbon*, VI, 1964, p. 310), 4630 ± 100 b.p., or *c.* 3465 B.C.

Pfyn-Michelsberg, Niederwil Switzerland (*Radiocarbon*, IX, 1967, p. 132), 4990 ± 60 b.p., or *c.* 3825 B.C., also (*Radiocarbon*, IX, 1967, p. 132), 4750 ± 60 b.p., or *c.* 3580 B.C.

Mondsee, average of 4 stations at Scharfling (*Radiocarbon*, XVI, 2, 1974, p. 281), *c.* 4812 b.p., or *c.* 3645 B.C., also from Mooswinkl 2 (*Radiocarbon*, XV, 2, 1973, p. 433), 4560 ± 100 b.p., or *c.* 3370 B.C.

187 There are Corded Ware dates from Halle, Dölauer Heide, 4105 ± 100 b.p., or 2755 B.C. and from Dornburg, near Jena, 4065 ± 80 b.p., or 2680 B.C., both dates in *Radiocarbon*, XII, 2, 1970, pp. 400f. Charcoal from the lowest layer of a Single Grave at Vester Nebel on Jutland was dated at 4150 ± 100 b.p. or 2850 B.C.; charcoal associated with a battle axe from Wildeshausen yielded dates of 4040 ± 80 b.p., or 2660 B.C. (*Radiocarbon*, VI, 1964, pp. 355f.), and another date of 3630 ± 80 b.p., or 2095 B.C. and 3550 ± 90 b.p., or 1975 B.C. in calendar years, both dates in *Radiocarbon*, V, 1963, pp. 187f. Another Corded Ware date is listed by Thomas, Ch. II: 19b, from Wildeshausen 2211 ± 80 b.c., or 2860 B.C. which appears to be out of line with the others. See also Piggott, p. 85, who suggests that the Corded Ware culture arrived in central Europe by *c.* 2500 b.c. or *c.* 3245 B.C.

188 The Heidmoor in northern Germany yields a Bell Beaker date of 2139 ± 170 b.c., or 2745 B.C. in calendar years.

189 See Müller-Karpe, III, pp. 400–19, for complete European details.

190 Müller-Karpe, III, p. 403. For details of Egolzwil and other Swiss settlements see Wyss, pp. 13–27.

191 This was the case at Ehrenstein, see Müller-Karpe, III, p. 417; O. Paret, the excavator, did not specify this practice.

192 C. Schindler, "Geologische Unterlagen zur Beurteilung archäologischer Probleme in den Seeufergebieten", in R. Degen (ed.), Zürcher Seeufersiedlungen, *Von der Pfahlbau-Romantik zur modernen archäologischen Forschung*, Helvetia Archaeologica, 12/1981-45/48 (Basel 1981), pp. 71–88. This article deals especially with variations in the lake water levels of Lake Zürich and their causes. See also J. Speck, "Pfahlbauten: Dichtung oder Wahrheit? Ein Querschnitt durch 125 Jahre Forschungsgeschichte", in R. Degen, pp. 98–138. After a lengthy review of the question Speck concludes that even

after the exclusion of many disputed views, the scientific discussion has not been able to establish certainty in the question.

193 See W. Schrickel, *Westeuropäische Elemente im Neolithikum und in der frühen Bronzezeit Mitteldeutschlands* (Leipzig 1957), p. 11.

194 Schrickel, pp. 13f., 17.

195 It is possible that the Bell Beaker culture originated in central Europe as well as in the southwest of Europe, see R. J. Harrison, 'Origins of the Bell Beaker cultures', *Antiquity*, XLVIII, 1974, pp. 99–108. See also J. Hawkes, p. 61, and Piggott, pp. 100f., who suggests that a secondary dispersion from central Europe may be of significance.

196 W. Tempel, 'Die Großsteingräber des Norddeutschen Flachlandes', in *KRI*, II, p. 55. See also E. Sprockhoff, *Atlas der Megalithgräber Deutschlands, in drei Teilen* (Bonn 1965–75), for locations and descriptions.

197 G. Daniel, *The Megalith Builders of Western Europe* (London 1958 and 1963), pp. 13f. All references to G. Daniel refer to this title.

198 See note 178 above.

199 See Renfrew, p. 126.

200 M. Moreau, *Les Civilisations des Etoiles, Les Liaisons Ciel-Terre par les Megalithes* (Paris 1973), pp. 47, 85.

201 See R. J. Harrison, *Antiquity*, XLVIII, 1974, pp. 101ff., who considers east central Europe and the Rhineland to be logical areas of Bell Beaker origin.

202 See Tempel, *KRI*, II, p. 57.

203 K. H. Brandt, *Studien über steinerne Äxte und Beile der Jüngeren Steinzeit und der Stein- Kupferzeit Nordwestdeutschlands*, Münsterische Beiträge zur Vorgeschichtsforschung, II (Hildesheim 1967). In question is one of the dolmen of Haaßel, near Uelzen. See also H. Schirnig, 'Die Königsgräber von Haaßel, Kr. Uelzen', in H.-G. Peters, *Dokumentation, zur Archäologie Niedersachsens in Denkmalpflege und Forschung* (Hanover 1975), pp. 212ff.

204 See H.-G. Peters, 'Die Karlsteine bei Osnabrück-Haste', in Peters, p. 84.

205 See Sprockhoff, *Megalithkultur*, p. 3; see also Renfrew, pp. 39f., 85f., for a brief review of the diffusionist chronology of megalith tombs; see also Daniel, *Megalith Builders*, p. 39f., for the categories first established by Montelius. See Daniel, *Megalith Builders*, p. 43, for a more recent classification; pp. 52–59 for a summary of the northern graves. Charcoal from a dolmen at Vroue, Jylland, was dated at 4570 ± 100 b.p., *Radiocarbon*, XV, 1, 1973, p. 97, i.e. *c.* 3390 B.C.

206 See Daniel, *Megalith Builders*, pp. 48f, for a brief summary.

207 Tempel, in *KRI*, II, p. 57; Daniel p. 57, suggests that while the dolmen was an indigenous Danish invention, the passage grave builders came by sea from western Europe.

208 Tempel, in *KRI*, II, p. 57.

209 Ibid.

210 Daniel, *Megalith Builders*, p. 57; Renfrew, p. 127, has reservations because of the new dating.

211 Sprockhoff, *Megalithkultur*, pp. 3f.; see also Tempel, in *KRI*, II, p. 56f.

212 Tempel, in *KRI*, II, p. 56.

213 Sprockhoff, *Megalithkultur*, p. 46.

214 Piggott, p. 60; Hibben, p. 189; C. F. C. Hawkes, p. 180, supports the idea of religious motivation for the megalith graves. C. F. C. Hawkes saw them to be the product of the conversion of the natives to the 'megalithic religion', defined as the belief in a disembodied spirit to mean belief in a ghost's potency for good or evil to the living, and magic proclaimed by dark strangers who could sail the whole western sea in winged ships.

215 Tempel, in *KRI*, II, p. 55. They do in fact predate the pyramids by about 1000 years and as such represent man's earliest efforts to build in stone, Renfrew, p. 123.

216 Sprockhoff, *Megalithkultur*, pp. 78f.

217 Sprockhoff, *Megalithkultur*, pp. 65ff.

218 See E. Lomborg, *Die Flintdolche Dänemarks, Studien über Chronologie und Kulturbeziehungen des südskandinavischen Spätneolithikums*, transl. from the Danish (Copenhagen 1973), p. 52.

219 W. Tempel, 'Das Großsteingrab in Osterholz-Scharmbeck, Kr. Osterholz', in *KRI*, II, p. 58. See also Sprockhoff, pp. 140f.

220 Daniel, *Megalith Builders*, p. 58, follows C. F. C. Hawkes in this line of reasoning. See note 214 above.

221 Daniel, *Megalith Builders*, p. 59.

222 Such a date is supported by a C[14] date of 2778 ± 80 b.c. for charcoal from a flat grave found under a megalith mound at Odoorn in Holland, Thomas, p. 137. This would indicate the appearance of passage graves shortly after *c.* 3550 B.C. in calendar years.

223 Corded Ware dates are available from Wildeshausen, see note 187 above. Single Grave dates from Vester Nebel in Denmark show an early date of 4150 ± 100 b.p., or *c.* 2850 B.C. Sprockhoff, *Megalithkultur*, p. 83, had indicated that the transition from dolmen to passage grave was marked by the appearance of wound cord patterns on the pottery, a difference of about 800 years.

224 Sprockhoff, *Megalithkultur*, p. 22; see also Ramskou, p. 14, who points to the difference between smaller passage graves with rounded chambers on Jylland, with older inventories, while on the islands the passage graves are larger with pronounced rectangular chambers and younger inventories.

225 Müller-Karpe, III, p. 332.

226 Sprockhoff, *Megalithkultur*, p. 42.

227 Müller-Karpe, III, p. 711.

228 See H.-G. Steffens, 'Großsteingräber bei Kleinenkneten, Stadt Wildeshausen, Kr. Oldenburg', in Peters, p. 102.

229 Sprockhoff, *Megalithkultur*, p. 38.

230 See J. Deichmüller, 'Die Hünenbetten bei Grundoldendorf, Gemeinde Bliedersdorf, Kr. Stade', in Peters, pp. 157f. The author quotes an uncorrected C[14] date of 2800 b.c. or *c.* 3580 B.C. in calendar years. The inventory yielded Incised Ware.

231 Sprockhoff, *Megalithkultur*, p. 42.

232 Sprockhoff, *Megalithkultur*, p. 73.

233 G. Körner and F. Laux, 'Die Steingräber von Oldendorf an der Luhe, Kr. Lüneburg', in Peters, pp. 206ff. The authors quote an uncalibrated C[14] date of 1900 b.c. Using Clark's calibration curve the date would be *c.* 2385 B.C.

234 Renfrew, pp. 132ff, suggests the possibility that population mobility may have interfered with fixed settlements, so that the tomb was the only element of permanence in a given region. Yet to the north of the Visbeck grave sites a Funnel Beaker settlement has been unearthed at Dummerlohausen with more than 40 timber houses.

235 An early Baalberge date from Kmehlen is recorded by Thomas, Ch. I: 19a, 3571 ± 160 b.c. or *c.* 4430 B.C. A late Baalberge date from Halle, Dölauer Heide, reads 2819 ± 100 b.c., or *c.* 3600 B.C. (Thomas, Ch. II: 19a).

236 A date for the Middle Chalcolithic, Salzmünder phase, comes from Halle, Dölauer Heide, 4630 ± 100 b.p. (*Radiocarbon*, VI, 1964, p. 262), or *c.* 3460 B.C. A late Corded Ware date from Wildeshausen shows 3550 ± 90 b.p., or 1975 B.C. (*Radiocarbon*, V, 1963, p. 187).

237 Müller-Karpe, III, p. 719.

238 Müller-Karpe, III, p. 709.

239 Sprockhoff, *Megalithkultur*, p. 24.

240 Hibben, pp. 173, 176, for instance, who still saw the end of the 'Megalithic' brought on by the Single Grave invasion of a new people who swarmed down the Elbe.

241 Müller-Karpe, III, pp. 336ff.

242 Müller-Karpe, III, pp. 716f.

243 Müller-Karpe, III, pp. 705f.

244 Müller-Karpe, III, pp. 227.

245 Charcoal from the lowest level of an undisturbed circle grave of the Younger Under-Grave Period from Vester Nebel on Jylland was dated to 4150 ± 100 b.p., or *c.* 2850 B.C. (*Radiocarbon*, XV, 1, p. 99).

246 Müller-Karpe, III, p. 717.

247 Müller-Karpe, III, pp. 227, 717.

248 Müller-Karpe, III, p. 337.

249 Middle Chalcolithic dates range from *c.* 3500–*c.* 2000 B.C. Bulbous Amphorae also termed Globular or Globe Amphorae from German 'Kugelamphoren', a ceramic culture extending from eastern Europe.

250 Müller-Karpe, III, pp. 732f.

251 Müller-Karpe, III, pp. 734f.

252 Sprockhoff, *Megalithkultur*, pp. 59f, 64. The Baalberge culture was first identified in a tumulus

containing such a cist, see Müller-Karpe, III, pp. 195f. They are a characteristic of the culture.

253 Sprockhoff, *Megalithkultur*, p. 60. Müller-Karpe, III, p. 196f., does not pick up the theme of the south-western origins of the stone cists and confines his discussion of them to the Baalberge pottery culture extended to central and east central Europe. Wherever found the Baalberge pottery level is invariably the lowest.

254 Sprockhoff, *Megalithkultur*, pp. 59f.; see also F. R. Herrmann, *Die Funde der Urnenfelderkultur in Mittel- und Südhessen* (Berlin 1966), pp. 24ff.

255 The usual English designation is 'port-hole', a less burdened term. It is this feature which is known in Iberia, and in some tombs in France, Britain and Sweden, see Daniel, *Megalith Builders*, pp. 44, 61, 97. See also Müller-Karpe, III, p. 740, for the symbolic function of these port-holes.

256 See Herrmann, p. 26.

257 See E. Lomborg, pp. 28–31, for techniques of production; p. 52, for a discussion of the 'seams' and the influence of metal daggers on the manufacture of flint daggers.

258 Herrmann, p. 26; also Müller-Karpe, III, p. 223.

259 Müller-Karpe, III, p. 714. In dating the Hessian cists Müller-Karpe, III, pp. 223f., assigns these graves to the Middle Chalcolithic, into the immediate post-Michelsberg period, contemporary with the Walternienburg-Bernburg phases further to the north-east, or to the Horgen and Golberg III phases of south-west Germany and Switzerland. A Horgen date from Escalon of 2520±60 b.c. (Thomas Ch. II: 17a), can be calibrated to *c*. 3260 B.C. See also W. Schrickel, *Westeuropäische Elemente im Neolithikum und in der frühen Bronzezeit Mitteleuropas* (Leipzig 1957).

260 The Rössen culture ends after *c*. 3700 B.C. As it colonized the regions to the north, its influence on the development of a ceramic style is to be expected. See note 157 above. Funnel Beaker evidence for Heidmoor in northern Germany was dated as early as 3344±115 b.c., or 4160 B.C. (Thomas, Ch. I: 19b), and from Ringkloster in Denmark as early as 3350 b.c., or *c*. 4160 B.C. (Tauber, *Antiquity*, XLVI, 1972, p. 107).

261 Dates for the Danish Ertebølle culture range from *c*. 4900–4100 B.C., see Tauber, *Antiquity*, XLVI, 1972, p. 107; see also Müller-Karpe, III, p. 324.

262 Müller-Karpe, III, p. 321.

263 See G. Hoika, 'Funde aus Großsteingräbern Schleswig-Holsteins', *KRI*, II, p. 59.

264 A late date for Incised Ware is available from Wildeshausen, 2211±80 b.c., or *c*. 2860 B.C. (Thomas, II: 19a).

265 Müller-Karpe, III, pp. 326f.

266 Müller-Karpe, III, pp. 327f.

267 Müller-Karpe, III, p. 323.

268 Müller-Karpe, III, pp. 322f.

269 See Hoika, in *KRI*, II, p. 60; C. F. C. Hawkes,

p. 215, saw in the double axes an influence from Minoan Crete, carrying north a divine symbolism.

270 Müller-Karpe, III, p. 322.

271 Müller-Karpe, III, pp. 194f.; see also C. F. C. Hawkes, p. 124, who considered Jordansmühl to form part of the Theissz-Tisza culture located in the Carpathian Basin.

272 Müller-Karpe, III, pp. 195f.

273 Rössen dates extend from *c*. 4935 B.C. to *c*. 3635 B.C., see note 89 above.

274 Michelsberg dates extend from about 4300 B.C. or earlier to about 3500 B.C. H. Quitta, in *Antiquity*, XLI, 1967, p. 265 shows an early date for Thayngen-Weier as *c*. 5100 b.p., or *c*. 3935 B.C. and a late date of *c*. 4860 b.p., or *c*. 3690 B.C. Thomas, Ch. I: 16, gives a date from Ehrenstein as 3447±100 b.c., or *c*. 4325 B.C. Oak wood from Ehrenstein was dated at 5240±100 b.c., or *c*. 4085 B.C. (*Radiocarbon*, VI, 1964, pp. 309f.). Niederwil in Switzerland, included in the Pfyn culture which was under Michelsberg influence, yielded dates ranging to 4750±60 b.p., or *c*. 3580 B.C. (*Radiocarbon*, IX, 1967, p. 132).

275 Müller-Karpe, III, pp. 198–205.

276 Müller-Karpe, III, p. 200.

277 See C. Hawkes, pp. 244ff. for a brief review of the Michelsberg and the Swiss, Bavarian and Austrian lake and Alpine cultures.

278 Müller-Karpe, III, p. 208; Thomas, p. 114 suggests a date of 2700/2600 b.c. for the beginning of the Baden culture, which if calibrated would read 3530/3430 B.C., which corresponds with dates elsewhere for the beginning of the Middle Chalcolithic. Attempts to link this culture with levels I–III at Troy now prove to be unrealistic, since these Trojan levels are up to 500 years too recent. For Trojan dates see Thomas, pp. 98, 76f.

279 Müller-Karpe, III, pp. 206f.; also Hibben, p. 149, who sees warrior peoples penetrating into the Hungarian plain and to the Baden culture area of Austria. These peoples introduced the horse as a draft animal and brought copper hammer-axes from the east. In the absence of copper in the new areas of penetration they made stone copies of the original metal weapons. Piggott, pp. 95f. also emphasizes the domestication of horses in the Hungarian reaches of the Baden culture. Piggott gives a date of *c*. 2000 b.c., or *c*. 2520 B.C. and that is late for Baden (*c*. 3530/3430 B.C., see note 278). He insists that bridle bits appear *c*. 1500 b.c. at the earliest, i.e. *c*. 1835 B.C. Although Müller-Karpe, III, pp. 205–9, mentions cattle and clay models of carts, absolutely no mention is made of horses or harnesses. Reference, p. 207, to the presence of an arsenic copper axe, stylistically related to stone axes, supports Hibben.

280 From Halle, Dölauer Heide, come transition dates for Baalberge II-Salzmünde, 2973±100 b.c., or 3750 B.C., and 2819±100 b.c., or *c*. 3600 B.C. (Thomas, Ch. II: 19a). A piece of carbonized wood, part of a palisade from the same site at Halle, yielded

a date of 4630 ± 100 b.p., or *c.* 3460 B.C. which may very well represent the middle period. See also Müller-Karpe, III, pp. 209f., for cultural details.

281 Thomas, p. 114, suggests that C[14] evidence, from the Low Countries and from Scandinavia implies that Walternienburg-Bernburg succeeded Salzmünde, *c.* 2500/2400 b.c., that is *c.* 3300/3100 B.C. Müller-Karpe, III, pp. 211f, indicates that Walternienburg is contemporary with Salzmünde, while Bernburg follows somewhat later, the transition being very smooth, however. A date of 3300/3100 B.C. is therefore in line. By cross-dating with the Rivnáč culture at Homolka in Bohemia, where Bernburg cups have been located and Baden Ware was found in the earliest layers, a date of 2438 ± 70 b.c. was obtained from burnt flooring, signaling the destruction of the Homolka settlement *c.* 3130 B.C., see Thomas, pp. 114f. See Müller-Karpe, III, pp. 211–14.

282 C. F. C. Hawkes, p. 231, saw the various axe cultures as an expression of movements of warrior cultures into central and north central Europe and beyond it to the west and south.

283 C. F. C. Hawkes, pp. 217f., 258, suggested the invasion of the Single Grave 'people'—a warlike people—coming down the Elbe River, responsible for splitting the northern Neolithic area into such groups as the Walternienburg, Bernburg, Baalberge and Funnel Beaker cultures, so that the region between Middle Rhine and Elbe became a cultural patchwork with remnants of the earlier Neolithic cultures, without achieving a synthesis at this time, however. Hibben, p. 157, represents the carriers of the Globe Amphora culture, coming from the east, to be such an invading people.

284 The link here is with the Vučedol culture of Yugoslavia. The Homolka site (see note 281) yielded Vučedol footed bowls, associated with Bernburg cups, Bulbous Amphorae and Baden pottery (Thomas, p. 114). Dates from the Mondsee in Austria fall well into the range of the Middle Chalcolithic: from wooden pilings dates have been obtained: 4910 ± 130 b.p., or *c.* 3730 B.C. (*Radiocarbon*, XII, 1, 1970, p. 314); 4560 ± 100 b.p., or *c.* 3370 B.C. (*Radiocarbon*, XV, 2, 1973, p. 433). See note 186 above.

285 Müller-Karpe, III, pp. 220, 428, indicates that copper was mined in the valley of the Salzach as of the Mondsee cultural level, i.e. after *c.* 3700 B.C. Casting molds for copper axes have been found on the Rainberg in Salzburg. Numerous crucibles have been found at the Mondsee sites.

286 In terms of a relative chronology, in some settlements Horgen supersedes Cortaillod or Pfynen levels. C[14] dates bear this out: Cortaillod dates from the Burgäschisee in Switzerland 3035 ± 100 b.c., and 2674 ± 90 b.c., or *c.* 3820 B.C. and *c.* 3454 B.C. respectively, compare well with a Horgen date from Escalon, 2520 ± 60 b.c., or *c.* 3265 B.C., see Thomas, Ch. II: 17a. For details concerning the Pfynen cul-

ture see J. Winiger, *Das Fundmaterial von Thayngen-Weier im Rahmen der Pfyner Kultur*, Monographien zur Ur- und Frühgeschichte der Schweiz, 18 (Basel 1971). For a very general treatment of Swiss lake settlements see H. Müller-Beck, 'Prehistoric Swiss Lake Dwellers', in *Scientific American*, Dec. 1961, reprinted in *Old World Archaeology: Foundations of Civilization*, Readings from *Scientific American* (San Francisco 1972), pp. 226–32.

287 Müller-Karpe, III, pp. 222ff.

288 Corded Ware dates range from 2618 ± 320 b.c., or *c.* 3385 B.C. from Schaarbergen and 2603 ± 55 b.c., or 3370 B.C. from Anlo, both in Holland, see Thomas, Ch. II: 19a, to 3630 ± 80 b.c. and 3350 ± 90 b.c., or *c.* 2065 B.C. and *c.* 1975 B.C. from Wildeshausen in northern Germany (*Radiocarbon*, V, 1963, p. 187). See Piggott, p. 85.

289 Single Grave dates from Denmark range from 4150 ± 100 b.p., or *c.* 2850 B.C. obtained from charcoal from the lowest layer of an undisturbed circle grave of the Younger Under-Grave Period (*Radiocarbon*, XV, 1, 1973, p. 99), to 1950 b.c., or 2455 B.C. (Tauber, *Antiquity*, XLV, 1972, p. 107). Evidently these two cultural phenomena are not entirely congruent in time.

290 C. F. C. Hawkes, p. 218, pointed out that the Single Grave culture funerary inventories were characterized by the inclusion of a cord decorated beaker, a thick butted flint axe and a stone shaft-hole battle axe.

291 Müller-Karpe, III, p. 225.

292 According to Hibben, p. 147, the 'Battle Axe Cultures' have a broader scope than does the Corded Ware culture itself.

293 This view is reflected in C. Hawkes, pp. 232f., who associated with the Corded Ware culture the Indo-Europeans, representatives of the Aryan group of languages and of the 'Nordic Race', though they were not the only such representatives. In their grave inventories he saw a reflection of the 'heroic life'—glorification of the warrior buried with his weapon and drinking vessel. Piggott, p. 89, echoes this view when he sees in the deceased buried in the weapons graves of the Corded Ware culture representatives of an heroic aristocracy and a warrior caste, who, in his estimation, were speakers of lost Indo-European dialects and who had entered central and northern Europe, *c.* 2000 b.c., that is *c.* 2500 B.C. Hibben, p. 147, suggests that the warrior element is foreign to central Europe and that its origins would have to lie in the eastern steppes. C. F. C. Hawkes, p. 237, points out that the Corded Ware warriors were proven horse breeders. As charioteers they would have in their possession a potent instrument of domination. Hibben, p. 146, C. F. C. Hawkes, p. 203, and Piggott, p. 84, all agree on south Russian origins of the Corded Ware culture, with the characteristic pottery everywhere in evidence. Piggott, pp. 84f., insists that the advent of Corded Ware in central Europe constitutes a com-

plete break in the Danubian tradition. Renfrew, pp. 118f., urges greater caution be used when speaking of 'arrivals', 'influences', 'spread' and 'transmissions', when local developments are at least as likely.

294 Hibben, pp. 146f. suggests that the Corded Ware culture came to be most strongly developed in central and north central Europe, with concentrations in Saxony and Thuringia. In central Europe, the Saale River region is the richest in finds—over 700 finds. In an easterly direction— Lusatia, Silesia, southern Poland, eastern Slovakia —the Corded Ware pottery forms become younger, the cultural practices deviate from the norm, the further south-east the phenomenon moves, see Müller-Karpe, III, pp. 228–31.

295 J. Hawkes, pp. 6of. See also L. Wamser, 'Gräberfelder der schnurkeramischen Kultur aus Tauberbischofsheim', in *KRI*, II, pp. 52f.; see also J. Hoika, 'Die jüngere Steinzeit in Norddeutschland', in *KRI*, II, pp. 53ff.

296 E. O. James, *Religionen der Vorzeit*, transl. from the English *Prehistoric Religion* (London 1957), pp. 95ff.

297 The pottery cultures of the Middle Chalcolithic established in the Elbe-Saale region, such as the Salzmünde, Walternienburg, Bernburg, do constitute a typological tradition with the Corded Ware forms, see Müller-Karpe, III, p. 342.

298 See C. Strahm, *Die Gliederung der schnurkeramischen Kultur in der Schweiz* (Bern 1971); see also E. Sangmeister, K. Gerhardt, *Schnurkeramik und Schnurkeramiker in Südwestdeutschland* (Freiburg, Karlsruhe 1965).

299 Müller-Karpe, III, p. 226, part 3, plates 500–8, 512.

300 Müller-Karpe, III, pp. 227f.

301 Müller-Karpe, III, p. 229, points out that this operation was already being performed during the Walternienburg-Bernburg stage.

302 See E. Lomborg, p. 52, also pp. 10–17, 20–6, for typologies of flint daggers, and pp. 28–31, for techniques of manufacture and surface treatment. In Denmark the dagger relieved the axe at the end of the Single Grave phase, which, see note 289, ended much sooner than the Danish Corded Ware period.

303 Müller-Karpe, III, pp. 234f.

304 See G. Hoika, 'Funde aus Großsteingräbern Schleswig-Holsteins', in *KRI*, II, p. 60.

305 Müller-Karpe, III, pp. 237ff., and part 3, plates 509–11.

306 This practice had also been a feature of the Baden culture.

307 Secondary burial in the graves of previous cultures is so frequent that it is almost a characteristic of Corded Ware funerary customs. As burial is a very sensitive area, there must have been spiritual affinity between cultures, pointing either to cultural continuity or a total disregard of the sensitivities of the 'conquered'.

308 See note 315 below for details.

309 See Müller-Karpe, III, pp. 232–7; also Strahm, pp. 120ff., 136.

310 Strahm uses this circumstance to argue for the continuity of the population in Switzerland.

311 Heidmoor yielded a Bell Beaker date of 2139 ± 170 b.c., or *c.* 2700 B.C. (Thomas, Ch. II: 19b). Charcoal from a Bell Beaker grave at Löbnitz, near Magdeburg, in the Elbe-Saale region, was dated at 2030 ± 125 b.c., or *c.* 2550 B.C. (Harrison, *Antiquity*, XLVIII, 1974, p. 103).

312 Müller-Karpe, III, pp. 341–4.

313 See Lomborg, p. 33. This dagger was found at Wiepenhathen, near Hanover.

314 See note 302 above.

315 See for instance C. Hawkes, pp. 250–7; also Hibben, pp. 186–95; Piggott, p. 100; and more recently W. Meier-Arendt, 'Viehzüchter und Jäger an der Wende zur Metallzeit—Die Glockenbecherkultur', in *KRI*, I, 1974, p. 22; also Müller-Karpe, III, pp. 240, 312.

316 Meier-Arendt, in *KRI*, I, p. 22.

317 The specialist literature has differentiated between Cord Beakers and later All-over-cord decorated Beakers. Bell Beakers too are now seen to comprise 5 distinct typological complexes: Portugal-Brittany, Lower Rhine-Wessex, Saxo-Thuringia-Bohemia, Moravia-Silesia-Austria, and the Catalonia-Languedoc-Rhône Valley. Earlier opinion had seen all these regions to form a coherent cultural area, see R. J. Harrison, 'Origins of the Bell Beaker cultures', *Antiquity*, XLVIII, 1974, pp. 100f. A simplification divides these complexes into western and eastern groups, i.e. into Maritime and Central European Beaker forms. In the Netherlands C[14] dating has shown that All-over-cord Beakers pre-date Maritime Bell Beakers. Harrison points to the likelihood that Bell Beaker origins are to be found in the Rhineland, where there is a close Corded Ware, All-over-cord Beaker, Maritime Beaker sequence, and where All-over-cord Beakers are the earliest Bell Beakers, closely followed by Maritime Beakers (*Antiquity*, XLVIII, 1974, pp. 101f.). All-over-cord Beakers are more common north of the Rhine, while maritime forms predominate to the south and west. A second, eastern development is apparent originating with the Vučedol cultural groups in Hungary, linked to the Bohemian-Moravian beakers, rarely decorated with cord patterns, which stimulated a stylistic sequence extending through the Saxo-Thuringian complex to the Middle Rhine-Wessex forms of the Rhineland, see already C. F. C. Hawkes, p. 256. The resulting forms are as old or older than Rhenish All-over-cord Beakers (Harrison, *Antiquity*, XLVIII, 1974, p. 104). An independent central European origin of the Bell Beakers seems to be indicated. The Bell Beaker culture is credited with the spread of copper technology (Piggott, p. 100). C. Hawkes, pp. 244ff., who pointed to the early westward spread of metal

technology from Hungary, may therefore find support in Harrison's argument.

318 Müller-Karpe, III, pp. 244f.

319 See J. Hoika, in *KRI*, II, p. 54.

320 Piggott, pp. 101f., suggests that the Bell Beaker people of the colonizing phase are recognizable by their physiology: they are round-headed, of strong build, contrasting with the other populations of western, central and northern Europe.

321 Müller-Karpe, III, pp. 241f., 488ff.

322 Müller-Karpe, III, pp. 244, 489. But on p. 490 he refers to the beakers as drinking vessels. Hibben, p. 89, suggests that the bell beakers were used to serve an intoxicating brew—beer.

323 Müller-Karpe, III, pp. 242f.

324 Meier-Arendt, in *KRI*, I, p. 22; see Piggott, pp. 100f., who indicates that Britain obtained its metal technology from the Rhineland and the Netherlands. According to Hibben, pp. 185ff., the Bell Beaker influence contributed most to the formation of the Bronze Age, although he points out that many of the northern cultures did not go through a copper period at all, owing to their distance from the sources and manufacturing centres, hence the stone copies. This point will be dealt with in Chapter 3. Piggott, p. 100, points out that in south-central Europe, between Frankfurt a.M. and Dresden, and Berne and Vienna new copper weapons, tools and ornaments appeared, overlapping Bell Beaker evidence.

325 Müller-Karpe, III, pp. 439–43.

326 Müller-Karpe, III, pp. 440f.

327 Müller-Karpe, III, pp. 439f.

328 The absence of the potter's wheel precludes mass-production of pottery.

329 It is this feature which will make the emergence of the Northern Bronze Age such an extraordinary phenomenon.

330 Müller-Karpe, III, pp. 428f.

331 See note 285 above.

332 Although these considerations appear speculative in this context, they will appear quite self-evident in the context of the Bronze Age.

333 This question refers to the presence of a much larger house in a noticeable setting in the Aichbühl settlement, see note 152 above.

334 See Müller-Karpe, III, pp. 445–8.

335 Müller-Karpe, III, p. 457.

3. The Bronze Age: The Inner Colonization

1 In part the diffusionist theories required the concept of merchants and pedlars penetrating into Europe from the south-east, see N. K. Sandars, *Prehistoric Art in Europe* (Harmondsworth 1968), p. 166. C. Renfrew, *Before Civilization, The Radiocarbon Revolution and Prehistoric Europe* (London, 1975), p. 117, points to the need to reassess the evidence concerning the development of a bronze industry in central and northern Europe and its dependence on a system of redistribution, and to establish a period when a purely commercial trade, without complicated social ties, actually got under way. J. D. Muhly, *Copper and Tin, The Distribution of Mineral Resources and the Nature of the Metals Trade in the Bronze Age* (Hamden, Connecticut 1976), pp. 168f., states that the Bronze Age trade in metals was the first trade of significant economic and political impact. J. M. Coles and A. F. Harding, *The Bronze Age in Europe, An Introduction to the Prehistory of Europe, c. 2000–700 B.C.* (London 1979), p. 66, indicate that long-distance trade is attested in only some commodities and only between certain areas; Muhly, pp. 188ff, finds no evidence pointing to the use of Alpine copper in Greece, for instance; see also J. J. Butler, *Bronze Age Connections across the North Sea, A Study in Prehistoric Trade and Industrial Relations between the British Isles, the Netherlands, North Germany and Scandinavia, c. 1700–700 B.C.* (Groningen 1963), p. 2.

2 Bernisches Historisches Museum, *Die Ur-und Frühgeschichte der Schweiz*, p. 5; see also Coles and Harding, pp. 184–99, for details about the Early Bronze Age in Switzerland.

3 T. Capelle, K. J. Narr, 'Die archäologische Erforschung Norddeutschlands', in *KRI*, II, p. 18; see also H. Ziegert, *Zur Chronologie und Gruppengliederung der westlichen Hügelgräberkultur* (Berlin 1963), pp. 46f.

4 See W. A. Brunn, *Die Hortfunde der frühen Bronzezeit aus Sachsen-Anhalt, Sachsen und Thüringen* (Berlin 1959), p. 18.

5 G. Sudholz, *Die ältere Bronzezeit zwischen Niederrhein und Mittelweser* (Hildesheim 1964), pp. 4ff.

6 See Chapter II, note 288.

7 See Chapter II, notes 311, 317. See also M. Gimbutas, *Bronze Age Cultures in Central and Eastern Europe* (The Hague 1965), p. 29, who cites a C14 date obtained from the Heidmoor, from a piece of wood 5 cm below a Bell Beaker layer, at 2020 ± 170 b.c., or *c.* 2540 B.C., and a C14 date obtained from a piece of carbonized wood from 5 cm above the Bell Beaker layer, at 1770 ± 150 b.c., or *c.* 2180 B.C. in calibrated calendar years. The calibration curve used here appears in *Antiquity*, XLIX, pp. 264f; see Chapter 2, note 16, above.

8 See Coles and Harding, p. 67, who convert the traditional date for the transition from copper to bronze, from *c.* 2000 b.c. to a calibrated C14 date of *c.* 2500 B.C.

9 Ch. Strahm, *Die Gliederung der schnurkeramischen Kultur in der Schweiz* (Berne 1971).

10 J. Hoika, 'Die jüngere Steinzeit in Norddeutschland', in *KRI*, II, p. 55.

11 See Chapter II, note 257, above.

12 See S. Piggott, *Ancient Europe from the Beginnings of Agriculture to Classical Antiquity* (Chicago 1965), pp. 71f., who stresses that the working technique was the cold working of native copper. See also Muhly, Supplement to *Copper and Tin*, pp. 83ff.

13 Small copper objects dated to before 4700 B.C.

have been found in the Vinča culture, see Renfrew, p. 174. Renfrew, p. 16, concludes that knowledge of the use of copper may have developed independently in Europe. Its use in the Aegean came several centuries later (Renfrew, p. 167).

14   According to Renfrew, p. 167, the earliest evidence of metallurgy in the Near East dates to before 6000 B.C.

15   Renfrew, pp. 173f., indicates that alloying with tin was known in the Balkans and the Aegean by between *c.* 3000 B.C. (*c.* 2400 b.c.) and *c.* 2700 B.C.

16   A. von Müller, 'Bronzezeit 1800-800 v. Chr.', Museum für Vor- und Frühgeschichte, Staatliche Museen, Preußischer Kulturbesitz, Berlin, bulletin no. 1141 (Berlin 1973). Von Müller gives a date of *c.* 1800 b.c. which would calibrate to *c.* 2230 B.C. Such a date is in accord with the calibrated C14 dates suggested for the earlier part of the Early Bronze Age in central Europe, *c.* 2300–2100 B.C., advanced by Coles and Harding, p. 67.

17   Muhly, pp. 83ff.

18   G. Mahr, 'Anfänge der Metallgewinnung 2', Staatliche Museen, bulletin no. 1142b (Berlin 1973). See also F. C. Hibben, *Prehistoric Man in Europe* (Univ. of Oklahoma Press, first edition 1958, fourth printing 1968), p. 179.

19   K. Eckerle, 'Die frühe und mittlere Bronzezeit 1700–1300 v. Chr.', Ur- und Frühgeschichtliche Sammlungen, Badisches Landesmuseum Karlsruhe, (Karlsruhe before 1977).

20   See Coles and Harding, pp. 63f.; also J. Briard, *L'Age du Bronze en Europe Barbare des Mégalithes aux Celtes* (Toulouse 1976), p. 304.

21   See A. Kernd'l, 'Bronzezeitliche Kupfergewinnung', Staatliche Museen, bulletin no. 1143 (Berlin 1972); also K. Goldmann, 'Depotfunde', Staatliche Museen, bulletin no. 1145 (Berlin 1973). Coles and Harding, pp. 64f. indicate that a crew of about 180 was needed to work one mine, to produce an estimated 12·6 tonnes of mined material a day, of which 315 kg would be raw copper, for further processing and refining. One mine would require about 20 m³ of lumber per day.

22   Hibben, pp. 197f., suggests that tin is a natural alloy in the Near East which ultimately led to the discovery of artificial alloys in Mesopotamia and the Near East. Muhly, pp. 169, 246ff., demonstrates that only stream tin, i.e. alluvial or placer tin, was sometimes available in nugget form. Tin only rarely appears as a metal and then only as an oxide. To be useful an oxide smelting technique would first have had to be developed.

23   Staatliche Museen, G. Mahr, no. 1142b. A calibration of these dates would increase the age of these finds to *c.* 2500 B.C. and *c.* 1710 B.C. Muhly, p. 249, states that the majority of early tin objects come from Holland, dated to *c.* 1500 b.c., or *c.* 1835 B.C. in calendar years. The contemporary use of tin nails in Jutland suggests to him a northern source for tin, possibly pointing to a trade in tin between Britain and the Netherlands during the second millennium B.C.

24   Throughout his book Muhly, pp. 182ff., 241, 251–4, 272ff., 279, 336, emphasizes the relative unimportance of the western Mediterranean in the metals trade prior to the Hellenistic Age, pointing out that there was virtually no copper mining in Iberia in pre-Roman times, that the Mycenaeans had no interests there, and that Iberia was not a factor in Greek and Phoenician westward expansion before *c.* 600 B.C., the approximate date for the founding of Massalia. As for Cornish tin, Muhly, pp. 279, 336, rules out any contact between the Mediterranean and Cornwall via the straits of Gibraltar, arguing for trade routes that followed the Rhine, crossing the Alps via the Brenner Pass to the Adriatic Sea, pp. 272–79, 336, 346, but that even the land route was not in use before *c.* 1600 b.c., i.e. *c.* 2000 B.C.

25   Staatliche Museen, G. Mahr, bulletin no. 1142b.

26   Muhly, p. 256, rejects this commonly accepted option, claiming, p. 99, that the Bohemian tin was inaccessible to the prospectors and that the tin deposits of the Erzgebirge in particular are hydrothermal deposits in granite rock and therefore quite inaccessible, but see also p. 346.

27   Muhly, pp. 97–104, for the development of a bronze technology; also Gimbutas, p. 18.

28   See Muhly, pp. 88ff., for the introduction of copper alloys, and pp. 169–72, for the composition and utilization of copper ores and the availability of tin and copper ores. See also Coles and Harding, p. 18, note 20; Sandars points out that the addition of arsenic, though it hardened the bronze metal, also made it brittle but suitable for casting. See Hibben, p. 198, for a discussion of the effects of tin variance on the quality of bronze.

29   Staatliche Museen, G. Mahr, no. 1142b.

30   Staatliche Museen, K. Goldmann, 'Bronzetechnik', no. 1144; see also Renfrew, p. 172; also Coles and Harding, p. 18, note 20. Sandars, p. 158, argues that such high temperatures could not be an accidental discovery, as an ordinary wood fire can only obtain temperatures ranging between 600–700° C.

31   Sandars, p. 158, indicated that potters' kilns easily reached temperatures in excess of 800°C. Renfrew, pp. 174f., subsequently stated that the Vinča culture fired its pottery at c. 700–800°C, while at Gulmenita pottery was fired at 1100°C, and this before *c.* 4500 B.C. Pyrotechnology had made the preliminary advances to allow metallurgy to follow. It had also been discovered that if ores were heated with charcoal in a reducing atmosphere, fairly pure metals could be obtained, see Sandars, p. 158, for more details about the reduction of oxides. See Coles and Harding, pp. 11f., for characteristics of pottery and metalwork.

32   See Sandars, pp. 160f., for a resumé of the tech-

niques and tools used for casting in clay and stone moulds, the lost wax method, forging, hammering and annealing of sheet metal. See also Staatliche Museen, K. Goldmann, no. 1144.

33 Sandars, pp. 157, 164, suggests that the artists of the Bronze Age needed the sinews of the smith, the hand of the engraver and the faith and imagination of the religious, that they had to be sensitive to special religious and mystical relationships between the raw material, themselves and their finished products, a continuity of process in which the object was endowed with magic. Briard, p. 362, insists that metallurgy and the mysterious powers of fire engendered new religious concepts, as green ores were transformed into a flamboyant flux and then cast into swords and ornaments, imbued with magic powers by a smith-sorceror who invoked the power of the sun. Lore would enhance the fabulous conquest of metal. In Celtic and Germanic lore the weapons-smith enjoyed particular esteem.

34 This is the so-called 'Musterkoffer von Koppenow'.

35 K. W. Struwe, 'Die nordische Bronzezeit', in *KRI*, II, pp. 60–3.

36 Gimbutas, p. 20.

37 Staatliche Museen, K. Goldmann, 'Kulturgruppen der frühen und mittleren Bronzezeit, (2000–1300 v. Chr.)', no. 1146.

38 Butler, pp. 11f.

39 See note 26, above.

40 Staatliche Museen, Mahr, no. 1142b.

41 See Gimbutas, p. 245; and also Struwe, *KRI*, II, p. 60, who, however, uses uncalibrated C14 dates, placing the Únětician culture into the 18th, 17th and 16th centuries. Calibration makes the Úněticians a considerably older culture. See below.

42 See Piggott, p. 120; also Coles and Harding, p. 281, who see in this phenomenon perhaps the earliest and finest example of an organized society able to mount a secondary industry based on the import of raw material. The deficiency made the recycling of scrap metal necessary, thereby initially eliminating the evidence of articles imported from other bronze-working areas, see Coles and Harding, p. 310.

43 Butler, pp. 37ff, 193f.

44 H. Wingert-Uhde, *Schätze und Scherben, Neue Entdeckungen der Archäologie in Deutschland, Österreich und der Schweiz* (Oldenburg, Hamburg 1977), p. 86; also Coles and Harding, pp. 290, 499, for the importance of trackways through the moors, and of marine and inland waterways.

45 See H. Kühn, *Bronzezeit und Eisenzeit* (Köln 1966), p. 53. See also Piggott, p. 134, for references to the trade between the northern areas and the Mycenaean south during the centuries around 1500 b.c. See also Renfrew, p. 214, for the appearance of Baltic amber in the Aegean around the time of the Shaft Graves of Mycenae.

46 See Gimbutas, Foreword; also Coles and Harding, Preface; also Piggott, p. 169, who all indicate that central Europe launched many of the developments of the European Bronze Age.

47 Coles and Harding, p. 31, believe the various chronological systems to be inappropriate for a general study of the European Bronze Age. The modified system first developed by Paul Reinecke is the chronology most generally applied to the European Bronze Age, see Coles and Harding, pp. 24, 32. For northern Europe, and restricted to the classification of the Northern Bronze, the Montelius system offers a convenient chronology. It has subsequently shown itself to be overgeneralized in that it assumes a uniformity both of material culture and of chronological evolution over too extensive an area, see Coles and Harding, p. 278.

48 Gimbutas, pp. 20, 245, emphasizes the cultural continuity of this sequence.

49 Gimbutas, p. 245, uses uncalibrated dates placing the expansion into the 12th century. C14 calibration of Urnfield dates would place them into the 15th century b.c. For Coles and Harding, p. 67, a calibrated C14 chronology does not fit well with the traditional historical chronologies derived from cross-dating. Caution may be in order, pending further clarification. A date of *c.* 1300 b.c. for Reinecke Br. D, as the later Bronze Age, the Urnfield period, would be more comfortable.

50 See Coles and Harding, pp. 336, 388, who indicate that European tribes may have been instrumental in the fall of the Mycenaean and Hittite civilizations. Most cities of the Levant suffered at least one major destruction in this general period. For an extensive discussion of this question, see R. A. Crossland and A. Birchall, *Bronze Age Migrations in the Aegean, Archaeological and Linguistic Problems in Greek Prehistory*, Proceedings of the first International Coloquium on Aegean Prehistory, Sheffield (Park Ridge, New Jersey 1974), where A. Bartonek, in 'The place of the Dorians in the Late Helladic world', pp. 305–11, concedes that while 'Doric' peoples from the north during the 13th century and later may not actually have caused the Mycenaean catastrophe, they emerged as the dominant population in the early first millennium. The question is still unresolved.

51 See Piggott, p. 158; also A. Nibbi, 'The identification of the "Sea People"', in Crossland and Birchall, pp. 203f, who suggests that these 'Sea People' were Semitic nomads; see also A. Nibbi, *The Sea Peoples and Egypt* (Park Ridge, New Jersey 1975). See especially N. K. Sandars, *The Sea Peoples, Warriors of the ancient Mediterranean, 1250–1150B.C.* (London 1978).

52 Gimutas, p. 245.

53 For a summary of the Montelius system, see Coles and Harding, pp. 279f., 491.

54 Gimbutas, pp. 31, 245, has developed this sequence in great detail. Subsequent to the publication of her work, the C14 calibration revolution

377

makes necessary a significant downward adjustment of the Bronze Age chronology.

55 See Coles and Harding, pp. 67, 491.

56 Adherence to this practice was not uniformly observed; certainly the princely grave mounds stand out as an exception.

57 We follow the subdivision worked out by Gimbutas, p. 245. The dates, however, have been calibrated.

58 Coles and Harding, p. 67, deal only with an earlier Early Bronze Age, c. 2300–2100 B.C. and a later Early Bronze Age, c. 2100–1700 B.C. This would conform to the modified Reinecke scheme Br. A_1, A_2, (A_3).

59 This calibrated time frame is in accord with the Tumulus Bronze Age, c. 1800–1500 B.C. as used by Coles and Harding, p. 67, and corresponds to Reinecke Br. B_1, B_2/C_1, the Middle Bronze Age, the end of the Tumulus period corresponding to Reinecke Br. C_2/D (Coles and Harding, pp. 31f.).

60 A beginning of the Late Bronze Age, the Urnfield period, as arranged and calibrated here, does conform with a date of c. 1500 B.C. as used by Coles and Harding, p. 67. From Phase III on, however, the dates show significant variance. For Coles and Harding, p. 491, Phase III lasts from 1200–1100 b.c. (or c. 1495–1385 B.C. rather than c. 1500–c. 1250 B.C., Gimbutas), Phase IV lasts from 1100–900 b.c. (or c. 1385–c. 1100 B.C. rather than c. 1250–1030 B.C.) and Phase V lasts from c. 900–600 b.c. (or c. 1100–800 b.c. rather than c. 1030–c. 880 B.C.). See note 49 above. In the Reinecke scheme Br. D terminates the Urnfield period during the 13th century, see Coles and Harding, pp. 373f. An Urnfield date, late Reinecke Br. D, has been obtained from grave charcoal at a Lusatian site at Chodouny in northern Bohemia 3080±60 b.p., or 1130 b.c., i.e. c. 1415 B.C. (*Radiocarbon*, XVII, 2. 1975, p. 196). This corresponds to Phase III as worked out by Gimbutas and calibrated to end c. 1250 B.C., but it does not correspond to the Coles and Harding dates as they appear uncalibrated on p. 491. It should be noted that for Coles and Harding, p. 491, the Late Bronze Age periods are III, IV, V, and that VI represents the transition to the full Iron Age. Beginning with period III, the salt mining site at Hallstatt enters into the chronology of the Late Bronze Age, thereby providing the chronological bridge with the Iron Age. Thus period III includes Br. D (13th century), Hallstatt A_1 (12th century), Ha A_2 (11th century), period IV includes Ha B_1 (10th century) and part of Ha B_2 (early 9th century), while period V includes Ha B_2 (remainder of 9th century) and Ha B_3 (8th century), see Coles and Harding, p. 516. Period VI marks the beginning of the Iron Age. It is classified as Ha C, c. 700 B.C., see Coles and Harding, p. 379. Hereafter the chronological differences between traditional and new methods of prehistoric dating are minor. See Hallstatt chronology in Chapter 4 below.

61 Hibben, p. 198, sees the Hungarian copper and Bohemian tin lodes as having contributed to the evolution of the European Bronze Age. This may be an assumption in view of the relative inaccessibility of the Bohemian tin. Coles and Harding state, p. 46, that metals are rare in Bohemia. Briard, p. 96, bases Únětician prestige, if not on the exploitation, at least on the control of the Alpine and Balkan copper veins and of the tin sites in Bohemia. Early Únětician dates come from Prasklice in Czechoslovakia 1895±80 b.c., or c. 2380 B.C., from Helmsdorf in central Germany 1775±80 b.c., or c. 2185 B.C., from Leki Male in Poland 1655±40 b.c., or c. 2040 B.C., see Renfrew, p. 102; also *Radiocarbon*, XII, 2, 1970, p. 406. An even earlier date is to be found in Coles and Harding, p. 68, for Leki Male 1950±150 b.c., or c. 2455 B.C. These dates fit into the Reinecke Br. A_1, A_2, see Coles and Harding, pp. 24f.

62 See Gimbutas, p. 250; also Coles and Harding, pp. 33, 45, who conclude that in view of the similarity of Corded Ware and Bell Beaker pottery forms with Early Bronze Age pottery, and the continuity of Corded Ware and Bell Beaker grave furnishings into the Bronze Age, a direct development from the Corded Ware–Bell Beaker cultures may have led to the formation of the cultural groups of the Early Bronze Age of west central Europe. Thus Early Únětician groups are seen to follow Corded Ware, while the contemporary Straubing group to the south continues Únětician forms and even transitions from Bell Beaker to Early Bronze Age forms. For an interesting anthropological analysis of the skeletal remains, see H. Ullrich, *Das Aunjetizer Gräberfeld von Großbrembach*, Erster Teil, Anthopologische Untersuchungen zur Frage nach Entstehung und Verwandschaft der thüringischen, böhmischen und mährischen Aunjetitzer (Weimar 1972). Ullrich, p. 129, finds that the Corded Ware people of central Germany conform significantly to the Bohemian carriers of the Únětician culture. By means of complex craniometric and morphological analysis, Ullrich, pp. 140–4, concludes that the Bell Beaker skull types were absorbed, while the Corded Ware skull types continued into the Bronze Age. From his analysis he deduces that the Bohemian Úněticians were an independent development, a melding of the indigenous population with Bell Beaker people from the south and south-east and Corded Ware types who constituted the dominant group. Only after this synthesis had taken place did splinter groups emigrate into central Germany where other Corded Ware, some Bell Beaker and even some Funnel Beaker population remnants were absorbed. In the end the Úněticians of Moravia, Bohemia and Großbrembach in central Germany would constitute genetically related groups. Ullrich, p. 144, hesitates to apply this conclusion to all central German Úněticians. Coles and Harding, p. 38, are hesitant to accept this particular method of establishing relationships. They do, however, p. 39, accept that the

Großbrembach funerary links with Bohemia are reflected in the orientation of the body and in the burial forms, and that the Proto-Úněticians derive from Bell Beaker predecessors, p. 45. See also Briard, p. 100, who sees Bell Beaker influence on the Úněticians as much greater than that of the Corded Ware. He sees Úněticians occupying Bell Beaker cemeteries, while their equipment betrays a Bell Beaker parentage.

63 Renfrew, p. 102, finds arguments favoring Mycenaean influences on the Úněticians to be unconvincing. More conservative is J. Bouzek, 'Östlicher Mittelmeerraum und Mitteleuropa', in W. Coblenz, F. Horst (eds.), *Mitteleuropäische Bronzezeit*, Beiträge zur Archäologie und Geschichte, VIII. Tagung der Fachgruppe Ur-und Frühgeschichte vom 24–26 April 1975 in Dresden (Berlin 1978), pp. 47–56. Bouzek, pp. 48f., argues in favor of 'metal seekers' moving north-west from the Near East and the Balkans, transmitting the necessary stimuli to the Úněticians. Here the cultures of the Carpathian Basin acted as intermediaries between the Mycenaeans and the northern groups.

64 Gimbutas, p. 21. In 'The destruction of Aegean and East Mediterranean urban civilization around 2300 B.C.', in Crossland and Birchall, pp. 129–39, Professor Gimbutas revises the old dates downward and equates the Kurgan people with the Indo-Europeans. 1500 or more years earlier, i.e. *c.* 4600 B.C. in calibrated calendar years, the Kurganization of the Black Sea region is said to have taken place. During the first half of the fourth millennium B.C. Gimbutas sees a massive infiltration by the Kurgan people of eastern central Europe, see Crossland and Birchall, p. 130. A date of *c.* 3500 B.C. would place the Kurgan arrival in east central Europe into close relationship with the Jordansmühl cultural groups of the Lower Chalcolithic, to be followed very shortly by the early Corded Ware-Battle Axe-Single Grave complex, not that these three phenomena are entirely coexistent. Coles and Harding, p. 7, suggest that there is little in Bronze Age Europe which needs external influence. They regret the habit of thought which introduces invaders from the east to account for change in the cultures of Europe.

65 See Gimbutas, pp. 23, 248; see also Piggott, pp. 123ff.; also Hibben, pp. 201–5, for the expansion of the Únětician culture.

66 Gibutas, p. 250.

67 See Coles and Harding, p. 99, who indicate that the presence of the horse is implied through finds of bridle pieces, while horse bones had been in evidence since the Chalcolithic and were especially frequent on Bell Beaker sites. Using the horse for riding became usual during the later Br. A$_1$ and A$_2$, until it was common by *c.* 1600 B.C. Coles and Harding emphasize that most Near Eastern evidence comes from a later period. The evidence from Hungary is among the earliest.

68 Gimbutas, p. 250.

69 H. Müller-Karpe, *Handbuch der Vorgeschichte*, III, *Kupferzeit* (Munich 1974), p. 252; see also Coles and Harding, p. 34. Sites are known from Bohemia and Moravia, see Coles and Harding, pp. 36f. Towards the end of the Únětician period low-lying open sites give way to fortified sites, often on steep and defensible hill-tops, reinforced by ditches and perhaps palisades. See also Briard, p. 101, who suggests that village construction followed rules of urbanization, pointing to a coherent social organization. Coles and Harding, p. 37, emphasize the continuity of settlement. For details of house construction, see Gimbutas, pp. 26of. Únětician houses were semi-subterranean, in that only the roof was above ground level. The Únětician settlement at Gross Mugl in Lower Austria showed that the houses were randomly placed. See Coles and Harding, pp. 284ff., for details of Early Bronze Age settlement in the Netherlands. Piggott, p. 118, points out that the relatively small houses of Bronze Age Europe reflect the change from extended family longhouses to nuclear family units.

70 Renfrew, p. 246, suggests that the extravagant display of wealth may have brought prestige to the wearer. See also Müller-Karpe, p. 245; also Briard, p. 100.

71 See Müller-Karpe, p. 255; also Coles and Harding, p. 27, who also include spirally-folded finger rings, 'droplet' earrings, spiral beads, amber beads and a variety of cups and jars. See also Briard, pp. 95f.

72 Briard, pp. 97, 362, argues that the Únětician was more of an individualist and that Bronze Age man had acquired for himself, regardless of social position, the right of consideration, the affirmation of his personality.

73 Müller-Karpe, op. 256. With the new dating methods the central European dependence on Mycenaean and other influences from the south no longer sits easily.

74 Gimbutas, p. 35, sees Near Eastern exports reaching the Danube lands from where these objects were passed onto the Úněticians. Once calibrated such dates would be placed into the 24th century B.C. The earlier assessment was based on typological comparisons with the ornaments from Byblos, Ras Shamra and Hama, especially from the levels dating from the period between 2100 and 1750 b.c. Since the Near Eastern chronology is relatively unaffected by C14 calibration, the dependency relationships do not seem to hold.

75 It is thought that the Úněticians controlled the amber trade, see Briard, p. 96; also Gimbutas, p. 48.

76 Renfrew, p. 247, cautions that, of a wide range of Bronze Age implements, only shields and perhaps some varieties of swords can be seen to have been of Mediterranean inspiration. This is not surprising if one considers that Greece itself had no significant deposits of copper and that the mineral deposits of Italy played no role in Bronze Age trade; see Muhly, pp. 187, 336. Piggott, p. 169, points out that central

Europe was ahead of the Mediterranean world at this time in working bronze and that what were once thought to be Italian inventions must now be assessed as copies of imported prototypes from the north.

77 See Struwe, KRI, II, p. 61. Struwe gives dates of 1600–1500 b.c., which when calibrated read *c.* 1975 to *c.* 1835 B.C. B.-U. Abels, *Die Randleistenbeile in Baden-Württemberg, dem Elsaß, der Franche-Comté und der Schweiz*, Prähistorische Bronzefunde, Abteilung IX, 4 (Munich 1974), p. 92, indicates that in western central Europe, swords do not enter the funerary inventories until the Middle Bronze Age and that until then flanged celts (socket axes) were associated only with daggers.

78 Müller-Karpe, p. 252.

79 Ibid.; see also Coles and Harding, p. 38. Briard, p. 176, suggests that the contracted position may have been adopted for practical reasons—a smaller pit required less work.

80 Müller-Karpe, p. 253. Briard, p. 103, points out that these cemeteries do not reveal great social differentiation. Ullrich, pp. 20, 23, 31, 138, provides interesting detail about the deceased buried in the cemetery at Großbrembach: child mortality ran at 40%; 45% of the population died before reaching its 20th year; 51% reached adulthood and maturity. These percentages compare well with those from other Chalcolithic groups. The average age was 20·8 years; for men 21·5 and for women 20·7 years. This is low compared to a Walternienburg population, where for men the average age was 26 and for women 22·8, 40/49 adults, i.e. 81·6% of adults had strong indication of periodontal disease. Únětician men at Großbrembach were tall, averaging 171·1 cm, compared to Corded Ware men whose average height was 164·5 cm; Großbrembach women averaged 156·7 cm, compared to Corded Ware women whose average height was 156·3 cm. Almost without exception the heads of male and female Corded Ware people are smaller than those of the Úněticians. Coles and Harding, p. 290, speculate that the vast number of burials points to the ability of the land to sustain a large population.

81 These 'princely' graves have been dated to the 21st century B.C.; for instance, a wood sample from the Helmsdorf barrow was dated to *c.* 3613 ± 160 b.p., or *c.* 2050 B.C. Of these graves Briard, p. 103, claims that they monopolized in the eternal the accumulated profits of the tribe. Ullrich, p. 144, suggests that these graves indicate the degeneration of an aristocratic society into a military democracy.

82 For details of these 'royal' tumuli, see Coles and Harding, pp. 40ff., 291–308; also Briard, pp. 109–12; also Gimbutas, pp. 260–5; see also Müller-Karpe, pp. 254f.

83 The barrow in question is the Leubingen grave. The mound at Helmsdorf had been raised over an earlier group of Corded Ware burials, see Coles and Harding, p. 41.

84 Coles and Harding, p. 43, suggest that such graves were not typical, but rather are signs of social stratification during the later period of the Early Bronze Age. These barrows yield the most complete inventory of bronze equipment from anywhere in Europe. Briard, p. 103, considers the deceased to be descendants of Corded Ware petty princes who quickly understood the value of the new products and how to profit from the demand. The social structure reflected in the cemeteries denotes a society which shows only very little hierarchical stratification (Briard, pp. 96f.), the graves grouped along family lines (Ullrich, p. 39). In time the Úněticians proved good organizers, planners and distributors, as new professions and crafts such as prospectors, miners, smiths, merchants, scrap metal dealers and warriors to guard the trade routes and of course new social classes came into being (Briard, p. 362). H. Wüstemann, 'Zur Sozialentwicklung während der Bronzezeit im Norden der DDR', in Coblenz and Horst, pp. 195–209, argues that with the improvement in farming and ranching leading to surplus production, differences in interests and needs leading to increasing frequency of hostilities allowed military democracies and war to become common in social life, while improved distribution yielded to an unequal sharing in the production and its profits, resulting in a decrease of social equality as the military organization fostered the evolution of hierarchies. Renfrew, p. 157, thinks it possible that it was the impact of a new technology upon a society already to some extent stratified socially and specialized professionally which allowed the developing institution of the chiefdom to draw together the various forces of a tribal society, combining for greater efficiency and productivity, and to an increase in population. Briard, p. 111, sees wealth reflected in the graves to be the result of tyrannical power, fear and greed, of profits made from the sale of arms by magnates sitting on the amber routes. See Piggott, p. 137, who suggests that they may have exacted a toll from the trade. With some satisfaction Briard notes that the petty princes did not found dynasties and remained an isolated phenomenon.

85 Briard, p. 109, prefers to see the girl of 15 as a sacrifice.

86 Gimbutas, p. 250.

87 Gimbutas, p. 251.

88 See Sudholz, p. 75.

89 Sudholz, pp. 5f.

90 Sudholz, pp. 74f.

91 Müller-Karpe, pp. 26of. See also Coles and Harding, p. 53, who point out that this group demonstrated a preference for river valley occupation.

92 Müller-Karpe, p. 262.

93 See Coles and Harding, p. 56, who also see the Bronze Age occupants of Switzerland settling the uplands, though not much before the second millennium; see also Bernisches Historisches Museum, *Die*

Ur- und Frühgeschichte der Schweiz, p. 6.

94 Müller-Karpe, p. 257; see also Coles and Harding, pp. 50–3.

95 Müller-Karpe, p. 259; see also Briard, p. 112, who credits this group with having achieved a quasi-industrial organization and a well-run system of distribution.

96 K. Willvonseder, *Die jungsteinzeitlichen und bronzezeitlichen Pfahlbauten des Attersees in Oberösterreich* (Vienna 1963–8), p. 1.

97 Willvonseder, pp. 181ff.

98 Willvonseder, pp. 240–4.

99 Willvonseder, pp. 241–7.

100 Müller-Karpe, p. 256.

101 H. Ziegert, *Zur Chronologie und Gruppengliederung der westlichen Hügelgräberkultur* (Berlin 1963), p. 47.

102 See Coles and Harding, p. 67.

103 Ziegert, p. 41.

104 Ziegert, p. 41.

105 Briard, p. 170, insists that in spite of its similarity of form with the Únĕtician grave mounds, the Tumulus culture constitutes a new cultural context, northern, Atlantic and Mediterranean zones remaining largely outside the phenomenon. See Piggott, p. 145, who emphasized that we are dealing with a collective term under which is gathered a lossely-knit collection of Middle Bronze cultures. See Gimbutas, p. 284, for regional groupings. Coles and Harding, p. 44, claim that uniform burial customs prevailed throughout all regions. Gimbutas, p. 281, stresses that Únĕticians, Tumulus and Urnfield peoples were all tumulus builders.

106 Gimbutas, p. 275. See also Coles and Harding, pp. 37f., according to whom Tumulus settlement sites are very rare, but do tend to occupy the Early Bronze Age locations.

107 Gimbutas, p. 275. Again the information about the Tumulus culture has to be gathered from the cemeteries rather than from settlement sites. See Hibben, pp. 205f., who sees in the Tumulus people herdsmen and warriors, descendants of earlier warrior groups.

108 See Coles and Harding, p. 57.

109 For instance, see N. K. Sandars, *Bronze Age Cultures in France, The later phases from the thirteenth to the seventh century B.C.* (Cambridge 1957), pp. 78f., who envisaged arrivals from the Balkans spreading through the Alps into Alsace and south-west Germany, bringing new tools and weapons, new pottery techniques, cremation and urn burial from the Balkans, the Aegean and eastern Europe at the end of the Únĕtician and Straubing cultures. Ziegert, p. 47, suggests quite reasonably that people on the move would have left evidence of their origin in their 'base camp'.

110 See below for a more extensive treatment. Gimbutas, p. 275, laments the customary misconception that changes in the cultural framework can only have been brought by the invasion of new peoples. She blames the tendency on work being done along national lines, thereby impeding a more general overview.

111 Gimbutas, p. 275. Briard, p. 108, suggests that the first stage of Únĕtician expansion had been in the form of the export of new types of weapons and tools, especially of the riveted triangular dagger, the Únĕtician trademark.

112 Gimbutas, p. 31.

113 Gimbutas, p. 23; see also Ziegert, p. 48, who suggest that their familiarity with the soil and agriculture argues against their representation of an extensive herding economy.

114 Gimbutas, p. 277; also J. Hawkes, *Atlas of Ancient Archaeology* (London 1974), p. 61.

115 Gimbutas, p. 277.

116 At this time Greece is in the Late Helladic IIIA period, see Gimbutas, p. 82. LH IIIB–C corresponds to the proto-Urnfield period, see A. M. Snodgrass, 'Metalwork as evidence for migration in the Late Bronze Age', in Crossland and Birchall, p. 210. Gimbutas argues in favor of Mycenaean influences on central Europe. Snodgrass, however, demonstrates that in major respects—the violin bow fibula and the flange-hilted cut-and-thrust sword— the influence is rather the reverse. See also A. Snodgrass, 'Mycenae, Northern Europe and Radiocarbon dates', in *Archaeologia Atlantica*, I (1975), pp. 33–48.

117 The revolution in dating brought on by calibration has thrown the question of influences and imitations into significant disarray. The whole matter of Aegean influences on central Europe needs assessment, see Renfrew, pp. 102, 247, and notes 63 and 76 above, respectively. Snodgrass's admonition that dates be used as a cross-check within a cultural area, not between cultures, should be kept in mind.

118 J. Hawkes, p. 61. Charcoal from a beam of a cremation grave chamber from Hilversum was dated to 3240 ± 35 b.p., or *c.* 1585 b.c., see *Radiocarbon*, IX, 1967, p. 133. For other dates from Holland, see Coles and Harding, pp. 322f. J. Hawkes gives dates as *c.* 1400–1200 b.c.

119 Gimbutas, p. 85. For sites and dates, see Coles and Harding, p. 380.

120 See Struwe, *KRI*, II, p. 61; see P. V. Glob, *The Mound People, Danish Bronze Age Man Preserved*, transl. from the Danish by J. Bulman, original edition 1970 (London 1974), p. 131, who suggests that the mounds were monuments to a life lived in greatness meant to be seen from afar. See also Coles and Harding, p. 300.

121 See Struwe, *KRI*, II, p. 61; also Coles and Harding, p. 328, note 68. Glob, p. 131, claims that turf was used to resist erosion. See a more detailed discussion of the grave mounds below.

122 See Coles and Harding, pp. 299–308, for a discussion of northern burial mounds.

123 See Struwe, *KRI*, II, p. 62; see also Abels, pp. 88–93, for an analysis of grave inventories in terms

of weapons.; also Piggott, p. 146. The evidence of material wealth in the graves suggests a stratified society reflected in the occasional 'rich' graves in otherwise 'poor' cemeteries, Coles and Harding, pp. 60, 302ff., which indicates that only a segment of the population could achieve burial mound status. The enormous amount of labor required implies a large class of subjects, see Glob, p. 131, also Coles and Harding, p. 60. K. H. Otto, 'Die historische Bedeutung der mittleren und jüngeren Bronzezeit', in Coblenz and Horst, pp. 57–69, claims the existence of a cult dedicated to tribal chiefs as the reason behind the immense funerary effort, enhanced even more through the adoption of priestly office, dominating a military democracy supported ideologically through the cult, p. 64.

124 Ziegert, p. 40. The exception noted is the area where the river Neckar enters the Rhine.

125 Struwe, *KRI*, II, p. 62.

126 Gimbutas, p. 88.

127 Gimbutas, pp. 277ff.

128 See the contributions to R. A. Crossland and A. Birchall, *Bronze Age Migrations in the Aegean* (Park Ridge, New Jersey 1974) for a many-sided discussion of the complexities involved.

129 Gimbutas, p. 393.

130 See Coles and Harding, p. 388, for an analysis of the Mycenaean decline. They suggest this to have been a gradual waning of power, lasting over several centuries, the most dramatic fall of Mycenaean sites taking place during the 13th century. Snodgrass p. 35, states that these destructions took place within about fifty years.

131 The 'Northern invaders' theory is supported by the appearance of new types of swords, the flange-hilted cut-and-thrust sword, spearheads, body armor, fibulae, interpreted to betray a distinctive 'European' and non-Mycenaean style, see Coles and Harding, p. 388. They do not doubt that people were on the move and that there was discontinuity of settlement, p. 336. Crossland, 'Linguistics and archaeology in Aegean Prehistory', in Crossland and Birchall, p. 13, thinks it possible that a deterioration of the climate, or fear, or insufficient support from a rich hinterland allowed the Mycenaean centers to decline and induce the population to emigrate. Crossland emphasizes that in the case of Mycenaean civilization it was only a matter of the destruction of a few cultural centers. Once their props collapsed their end was near. Although European tribes may have been involved (Coles and Harding, p. 336), the destruction may have been wrought by roving bands from among the native population of Greece. F. J. Tritsch, 'The "Sackers of Cities" and the movement of populations', in Crossland and Birchall, p. 236, argues in favor of comparatively small groups of adventurers roving about, smaller than tribes and too small to be an ethnic influence. Snodgrass, in Crossland and Birchall, pp. 209–13, argues convincingly that no

reasons other than practicality and greater effectiveness need account for the presence of northern objects in Helladic Greece. See Coles and Harding, p. 388, who also suggest the presence of new types of bronzes reflects the spread of technologically and functionally superior objects. It is reasonable to suppose that without Mycenaean cultural counter-influence, such articles could easily be spread on the backs of pack mules rather than by waves of conquerors.

132 Tritsch, in Crossland and Birchall, p. 238, favors the idea of the vacuum effect following the collapse of Mycenae and of the Hittite Empire. Traditionally the invading northern 'Dorians' had been blamed for the destruction. However, no archeological evidence could be found to support the cultural change which such an invasion would have brought. An inner migration, a relocation of populations, especially if only small numbers were involved, would leave no distinctive trace in the archeological record, see Coles and Harding, p. 388.

133 For a discussion of the traditional view, see Gimbutas, pp. 334–39. For different views, see Nibbi, *The Sea Peoples and Egypt*, and Sandars, *The Sea Peoples*.

134 Gimbutas, p. 284.

135 Briard, p. 103, mentions the cremated remains of children in the vicinity of adult skeletons as early as the Unětician period. During the Tumulus period women and children were cremated (Briard, p. 177). Coles and Harding, p. 44, indicate that while some Tumulus regions practised inhumation, others cremated, and that in some areas women received inhumation burials, while men were cremated, though this cannot be proven. See also Coles and Harding, pp. 500–10.

136 See Coles and Harding, p. 296, for the funerary house at Hamburg–Harmsdorf.

137 Coles and Harding, p. 500; see also W. Menghin, Peter Schauer, *Magisches Gold—Kultgeräte der späten Bronzezeit*, Ausstellung des Germanischen Nationalmuseums Nürnberg, in Zusammenarbeit mit dem Römisch-Germanischen Zentralmuseum Mainz, 25.5.–31.7.1977 (Nürnberg 1977), p. 28.

138 For details concerning cremation burials, see Coles and Harding, pp. 359–66; see also Briard, pp. 294f.

139 Gimbutas, p. 298, points out that V. Gordon Childe, *The Bronze Age* (Cambridge 1930), was at fault. See V. G. Childe, *The Bronze Age* (New York 1964), pp. 173f.

140 R. Pittioni, *Über die historische Bedeutung der Urnenfelderkultur Mitteleuropas* (Vienna, Cologne, Graz 1970), p. 292. Coles and Harding, p. 335, agree that the burial rites show a degree of stability.

141 W. Meier-Arendt, 'Die Metallzeit', in *KRI*, I, p. 23.

142 See Menghin and Schauer, p. 28; also Struwe, in *KRI*, II, p. 62; also Meier-Arendt, *KRI*, II, p. 68.

143 Ziegert, p. 48.

144 Struwe, *KRI*, II, p. 62.

145 See Otto, in Coblenz and Horst, p. 63.

146 Briard, p. 319, states that in the west the influence of the Urnfield culture can be perceived in a renewal of the material equipment.

147 Gimbutas, p. 298.

148 Piggott, p. 134, indicates that body armor was developed in central Europe. Briard, p. 302, points out that it was the defensive nature of these articles which was the great novelty introduced at this time.

149 For details concerning techniques of working bronze, see Sandars, pp. 162f. Of very special interest are the golden cones which along with the bowls and discs are evidence of Bronze Age ideas about religion. Technically such works as the cone from Ezelsdorf or the so-called 'hat' from Schifferstadt are superb examples of the goldsmith's art. The Ezelsdorf cone is 90 cm high and weighs 310 grams, made of sheet gold, 1 mm thick and embossed with 25 different stamps. The Schifferstadt cone is modest by comparison, only 29·6 cm high and weighing only 350·5 grams. Since the sheet gold is so delicate these cones cannot have been used as vessels, but only as shells over a solid core. The circular motifs may provide a link with the sun cult, and may have to be seen in relation to the curious golden bowls and cups which bear some of the same motifs, see Menghin and Schauer, pp. 9-18. See also Briard, pp. 182f. Also Sandars, *Bronze Age Cultures*, p. 115, who indicates that the Schifferstadt cone contained traces of 'incense' gums, balsam and mallow—plant residue, possibly medicinal.

150 R. Christlein, 'Vollgriffschwerter und Lanzen der Bronzezeit', in *KRI*, II, p. 64; see also Abels, pp. 88-93; see also Piggott, p. 146. It was the appearance of these swords in Greece which prompted speculation about northern invaders.

151 The socket axes are also referred to as 'celts'. Abels, pp. 91f., sees them to have been used both as weapon and as ritual implement, as evident on rock art and in deposits at particular sites. During the Early and Middle Bronze Age, the celts were normally associated with daggers, to be joined by swords during the Middle Bronze. During the Late Bronze the celt disappeared as the spear-head gained in prominence, so that sword and lance made up the typical armament.

152 See note 60 above.

153 Gimbutas, p. 310.

154 Pittioni, p. 291.

155 Pittioni, p. 292.

156 Struwe, in *KRI*, II, p. 62. See also A. Kolling, *Späte Bronzezeit an Saar und Mosel* (Bonn 1968), p. 139, who suggests that this was also done with pieces of armor.

157 Gimbutas, p. 310.

158 See Coles and Harding, p. 339, who point out that in spite of various regional groups the Urnfield culture reflects an overall homogeneity in such things as biconical funerary urns, post-framed houses and particular types of bronze objects. See also Wüstemann, in Coblenz and Horst, p. 201, who stresses a social levelling out of the funerary rites during the later Bronze Age.

159 Gimbutas, p. 339. Briard, p. 362, sees in the evidence an appreciation of the spirit of enterprise, the result of the increase in voyages and contacts, necessary to the unfolding of such an industrial society. Coles and Harding, p. 376, argue that while there was a decrease in long distance trade, there was an increase in the local exchange of goods and ideas throughout central Europe facilitated by the community of material culture.

160 See Pittioni, pp. 283ff.; for chronology see also Gimbutas, p. 113; Coles and Harding, pp. 32, 373f., 491, 516. These chronologies are modifications of the Reinecke scheme, where Urnfield VI corresponds to Hallstatt C, the transition to the full Iron Age, *c.* 700 B.C.

161 Struwe, in *KRI*, II, pp. 62f.

162 These trackways, especially those of the Ipweger Moor, have yielded good $C14$ dates: path VII 3650 ± 75 b.p., or *c.* 2095 B.C., *Radiocarbon*, V, 1963, p. 187; 3110 ± 65 b.p., or *c.* 1450 B.C., *Radiocarbon*, XIV, 1, 1972, p. 76; path XXXVI, 3050 ± 55 b.p. or *c.* 1385 B.C., *Radiocarbon*, IX, 1967, p. 133. For additional readings see Coles and Harding, pp. 323, 524.

163 Capelle/Narr, in *KRI*, II, p. 18.

164 Ibid. These northern settlements will be discussed in Chapter 6.

165 See H. Aschemeyer, *Die Gräber der jüngeren Bronzezeit im westlichen Westfalen* (Münster 1966), p. 45, who suggests that Westphalia was not necessarily settled by Urnfield people.

166 Aschemeyer, p. 45; see also Meier-Arendt, in *KRI*, I, p. 23.

167 Aschemeyer, p. 37.

168 See Kolling, p. 24.

169 Kolling, pp. 27f.

170 Kolling, p. 139.

171 Meier-Arendt, in *KRI*, I, p. 23.

172 See note 160 above. Also Meier-Arendt, in *KRI*, II, p. 68.

173 See Gimbutas, pp. 321-4; see also Staatliche Museen, Kernd'l, no. 1148, (Berlin 1973).

174 Although this 'Illyrian theory', has long since been abandoned (see Crossland and Birchall, p. 255), Birchall, p. 329), following N. G. L. Hammond, 'Grave circles in Albania and Macedonia' in Crossland and Birchall, pp. 189-97, concedes that the 'Lausitz' invasion may now be seen as more important than had hitherto been realized. Traditionally the equation was developed by means of philological considerations, using the comparison of the names of sites and of lakes, rivers and streams, see Gimbutas, pp. 336, 339. See Bibliography to Chapter 6, for histories of the German language,

where the Lusatian–Illyrian link is most often dealt with. See also Hibben, pp. 210–15.

175 Biskupin, near Gniesno—German Gnesen—in Poland, is the Lusatian settlement in question. For details see Coles and Harding, pp. 287, 351, 356f., 377ff. Bad Buchau will be dealt with below. See Coles and Harding, p. 380, for Biskupin dates ranging from *c.* 900 B.C.–*c.* 750 B.C.

176 Gimbutas, p. 113.

177 See Chr. Pescheck 'Acholshausen, Ldkr. Würzburg, Fürstengrab der Urnenfelderzeit, um 1000 v. Chr.' in *KRI*, II, pp. 69f. See also Coles and Harding, p. 366.

178 Coles and Harding, p. 514, suggest that the idea behind wheeled cauldrons originated in northern Europe rather than elsewhere.

179 Gimbutas, pp. 316, 341; see also Piggott, p. 142, for a discussion of the wheel motif. Coles and Harding, p. 318, feel that the emphasis on a sun-cult is excessive if the entire evidence is considered.

180 The German term for one of the motifs—circle flanked by curved birds' necks facing away from one another—is 'Vogelbarke', inferring an association with a boat. Using this concept Coles and Harding, pp. 368ff,. see the bird and sun symbols, if joined with boat motifs, perhaps not so illogical if they pertained to the death-cult. Their placement in graves then does make sense. See also G. Kossack, *Studien zum Symbolgut der Urnenfelder—und Hallstattzeit Mitteleuropas* (Berlin 1954), pp. 45–50.

181 See Sandars, *Prehistoric Art*, p. 180, who links the four-spoked 'sun' wheel, flanked heraldically by birds, serpents or volutes, with the kingdoms of the Mitanni and of the Hittites—horse-driving Indo-Europeans.

182 Menghin and Schauer, p. 44, suggest a possible link between the sun disc and the sun-cult of Akhenaton of the 18th Dynasty of Egypt. I recall the association of the Hurrian-Mitannian-Egyptian representations first being made in an undergraduate course in Near Eastern History with Prof. Lambert, at the University of Toronto.

183 Gimbutas, p. 342.

184 See Pescheck, in *KRI*, II, pp. 69f.

185 Coles and Harding, pp. 368ff, see in the bird–sun–boat association a possible link with conditions of rain and drought. See also P. Gelling, H. E. Davidson, *The Chariot of the Sun* (London 1969), p. 21.

186 See Pescheck, in *KRI*, II, p. 70. If these discs are phalerae, then they have had a role as horse trappings or wagon fittings, perhaps associated with priestly functions.

187 Pescheck, in *KRI*, II, p. 70.

188 Kolling, p. 139.

189 Gimbutas, pp. 569–77; see also Meier-Arendt, in *KRI*, II, p. 68.

190 Kolling, pp. 31, 132.

191 For the Northern Bronze the chronology was established by Montelius. This chronology, how-ever, made assumptions about the uniformity of the material culture and its chronological evolution over too large an area. Coles and Harding, pp. 278ff, provide useful summaries of the chronology. See also pp. 32, 342, for comparative chronological sequences, which, however, do not form a seamless continuity.

192 See note 42 above.

193 Gelling and Davidson, p. 3; see also Coles and Harding, p. 282.

194 F. Behn, *Die Bronzezeit in Nordeuropa, Bildnis einer prähistorischen Hochkultur* (Stuttgart, Berlin, Cologne, Mainz 1967), p. 26.

195 To Coles and Harding, p. 313, the Northern Bronze is a Nordic phenomenon in spite of stylistic links with the industries in the area of the Middle Danube. See also K. Tackenberg, *Die jüngere Bronzezeit in Nordwestdeutschland* (Hildesheim 1971), p. 231.

196 Coles and Harding, p. 279, perceive three zones into which the Northern Bronze is to be divided: northern Jutland, the Danish Isles, and southern Sweden; southern Jutland, Schleswig-Holstein and Lower Saxony; Mecklenburg, Brandenburg and Pomerania. See also T. Capelle, *Kunst und Kunsthandwerk im Bronzezeitlichen Nordeuropa* (Neumünster 1974), p. 100.

197 For the extent of this period see Coles and Harding, pp. 280, 342. The beginning of Phase I is not entirely clear, but appears to be contemporary with the end of Reinecke Br. A2, *c.* 1700 B.C., see Coles and Harding, pp. 32, 67. See note 58 above.

198 See Behn, p. 26; also Coles and Harding, p. 342.

199 Period I of the Montelius chronology comes closest to being a 'Chalcolithic' period, when copper was used very sparingly, Coles and Harding, p. 279.

200 Struwe, in *KRI*, II, p. 61; see especially Coles and Harding, pp. 491–532, for whom the uniqueness of the Northern Bronze lay in the talent to transform every foreign influence into a masterpiece, p. 515.

201 See T. Ramskou, *Dänische Vorzeit* (Copenhagen 1972), p. 21; see also Behn, pp. 10, 25.

202 Behn, pp. 12ff.

203 Behn, p. 21.

204 Behn, p. 13.

205 Behn, p. 13.

206 Sandars, p. 196f, sees in the shaving and cutting of hair a ritual solemnity. The switch from tweezers to razors might then have cultic implications, especially when one considers that these razors were decorated with sacred images and activities.

207 Behn, p. 15.

208 Behn, p. 15.

209 See note 178 above.

210 See Briard, p. 360, who considers the creation of the lurer to be the single most astonishing artistic accomplishment of the Bronze Age.

211 Behn, p. 17.

212 Behn, p. 17.

213 Ramskou, p. 25; also W. Torbrügge, *Prehistoric European Art* (Baden-Baden, New York 1968), p. 95.
214 See Briard, p. 210, who is struck by the art of the northern bronze smiths and their skill at turning the most modest toilet articles into masterpieces. Probably derived from wooden prototypes, they were cast by the lost-wax method and decorated with a complex play of engraved spirals and other curvilinear designs. For manufacturing techniques, see Sandars, pp. 160f., who also suggests, p. 182, that the spirals were drawn freehand with a tracer.
215 A more detailed discussion follows below.
216 See below for details.
217 Behn, p. 18; the helmets of Viksø are a case in point, see Coles and Harding, p. 518; Sandars, p. 205, suggests the helmets were worn by protagonists in a ritual drama, rather than in battle.
218 These two items are illustrated in W. Torbrügge, pp. 94ff.).
219 See Sandars, p. 181, for a discussion of ornamental styles.
220 Ramskou, p. 36.
221 Behn, p. 19. Coles and Harding, p. 493 suggest that a drastic deterioration of the climate and a deterioration of the land, accompanied by an increase in population caused culturally disruptive relocations to higher ground.
222 Capelle, p. 100.
223 Coles and Harding, p. 277, do argue that the sudden increase in the amount of metal used was accompanied by a change in the social configuration of the population. See also Gelling and Davidson, p. 3.
224 Capelle, p. 86.
225 See Sandars p. 181, for similarities with central and east European styles and the related emphasis on an asymmetric, organic, non-representational curvilinear ornamental style.
226 These deposits are not restricted to any one area, nor are they a Bronze Age invention. According to Coles and Harding, p. 2, in central Europe stone tool hoards continue up to the Bronze Age. Of two theories proposed, the preferred view today sees the depositions to be votive offerings, rather than emergency burial in times of catastrophe (Coles and Harding, pp. 367f.). F. Stein, *Bronzezeitliche Hortfunde in Süddeutschland*, Beiträge zur Interpretation einer Quellengattung, Saarbrücker Beiträge zur Altertumskunde, 23 (Bonn 1976), p. 118, argues that caches would reflect a random accumulation of new and/or old and possibly broken pieces of all sorts. Votive offerings on the other hand are characterized by typological consistency—only tools, or necklaces, or weapons, always new or in usable condition. Stein does not see that these depots reflect 'turmoil horizons'. Briard, p. 332, refers to money-socket celts in Normandy and Brittany found in hoards, with the socket cast deep into the blade and containing 30–60% lead, and hence too fragile for real use. Sandars, p. 183, links the water sacrifice to metallic

objects with the Ahrensburg ritual (cf. Ch. I) performed at a sacred site. Coles and Harding, p. 368, see water sacrifices as a supplicatory offering to water gods in times of drought, suggesting that deposits in water are of finer quality, p. 374. Briard, pp. 171, 320, offers a military consideration: since rivers and other bodies of water often serve as territorial limits, they would be traditional sites of combat, where the possession of fords might have to be contested. Perhaps to force a victory the warriors sacrificed some of their most splendid weapons to the river god.
227 Wingert-Uhde, p. 85.
228 For Briard, p. 216, the 'bell' is merely a decorative detail, not capable of enhancing the sound. Coles and Harding, p. 518, state that the emphasis in the design was on appearance rather than on tone, that it was an instrument of ceremonial display.
229 See Ramskou, p. 36; also Wingert-Uhde, p. 85. Speaking from experience Briard, p. 218, claims that an accomplished blower can produce 22 tones over a range of four octaves, but that a range of three octaves is more usual.
230 The 'metallic' sound is attributed to the metal having been rolled rather than cast.
231 For an extensive discussion of this motif, see Gelling and Davidson, pp. 43–67. See also Coles and Harding, pp. 317f., for details of ship designs. Sandars, p. 198, attributes to these ships value as archetypal symbols, with the scenes depicting the great acts of gods and heroes. Briard, p. 254, takes the ship engravings on rocks and on objects to point to the importance of the navigation theme, whether in the temporal or spiritual realms.
232 Coles and Harding, p. 318, caution against an overemphasis of the sun-cult, claiming the evidence for such a cult to be selective and not so dominant as is generally suggested. According to Menghin and Schauer, p. 23, sun discs are always isolated finds and seldom present in the funerary inventories.
233 See Gelling and Davidson, p. 21.
234 Sandars, p. 194, thinks it possible that south German craftsmen were active in the north, or, p. 185, that central European influence was exerted on the craftsmen, that curvilinear motifs originated in the Carpathian ring and to a lesser degree, in northern Italy and in Austria, and that in the Danubian province the spirals were used organically rather than geometrically (p. 178). See Sandars, p. 182, for a discussion of north–south relations. Piggott, p. 137, suggests that the Únĕticians as middlemen controlled the amber trade; see also E. Lomborg, *Die Flintdolche Dänemarks* (Copenhagen 1973), pp. 138–48; also Coles and Harding, p. 311. In spite of typological links with the middle Danubian industries in the shape and design of objects, the Northern Bronze was an authentic phenomenon, p. 313.
235 For details, see Sandars, pp. 183f.; Glob, pp. 99–103; Coles and Harding, p. 134; Briard, pp.

214f., and especially Gelling and Davidson, pp. 9–26.

236 The sun disc consists of a gold side (day), and a duller bronze side (night), see Glob, pp. 101ff.; also Sandars, p. 184.

237 The Trundholm horse is a rarity, as it was hollow cast (Sandars, p. 183). Glob, p. 103, is led to claim this technique to be a particularly Indo-European skill. Sandars, p. 184, considers the horse to have symbolic significance because of the intricate ornamental patterns that decorate its head and neck. Gelling, p. 16, suggests that there may have been even two horses originally.

238 Briard, p. 215, sees here origins of later classical mythology, for instance, the Apollo-Phoebus myths.

239 See Glob, p. 103; also Briard, p. 214. To Briard, pp. 306, 315, these symbols reflect religious mores, where fire, the sun, the horse, the wheel are worshipped by a metal-working people, where masculine attributes were displacing older mother-goddesses as a patriarchal society of petty-chiefs evolved, powerful by virtue of its weapons and wealth, obtained through expanding commercial ties.

240 Gelling and Davidson, p. 117.

241 Pescheck, in *KRI*, II, p. 70; also Gelling and Davidson, pp. 119ff.

242 Gelling and Davidson, p. 117.

243 Gelling, in Gelling and Davidson, gives a most complete treatment of the motifs depicted.

244 Capelle, p. 16.

245 J. Hoika, 'Schalensteine in Schleswig-Holstein', in *KRI*, II, p. 65.

246 See Sandars, pp. 199–203, for a brief analysis of the Scandinavian petroglyphs; also Coles and Harding, p. 521; Briard, p. 252, notes that the figurative art of the rock carving contrasts strangely with the abstract and symbolic style which characterizes most Bronze Age art.

247 Capelle, pp. 36ff.; also W. Tempel, 'Bronzezeutliches Steinkistengrab mit Bildstein aus Anderlingen, Kr. Bremervörde', in *KRI*, II, pp. 64f.

248 Tempel, in *KRI*, II, p. 65.

249 Capelle, p. 37.

250 Gelling and Davidson, pp. 34–9.

251 See Sudholz, p. 7; also K. Schlabow, *Gewebe und Gewand zur Bronzezeit* (Neumünster 1962), p. 9.

252 Coles and Harding, p. 328, note 68, estimate that a normal grave mound requires the turf from 1–2 hectares of land.

253 Sudholz, p. 8.

254 Behn, p. 37; also Schlabow, pp. 10ff. See Coles and Harding, pp. 304–8, for conditions favoring the preservation of coffins in the mounds and of the deceased.

255 See Glob, pp. 17–98, for detailed accounts of various tree-coffins and their contents (Gimbutas, pp. 257f.). See also Piggott, p. 156; also Briard, pp. 204ff., for a description of girls' costumes. See Ramskou, pp. 27f. For details concerning the wearing of costume bronzes during the Tumulus and Urnfield periods such as fibulae, arm rings, wheel and head pins, their different types and forms, of discs, rolls, amber, spiralled neck rings, leg rings and pendants, and their placement on the body, see U. Wels-Weyrauch, *Die Anhänger und Halsringe in Südwestdeutschland und Nordbayern*, Serie Prähistorische Bronzefunde, IX, 1 (Munich 1978), pp. 166–85.

256 Tackenberg, p. 237.

257 Tackenberg, p. 239, for a detailed discussion of weapons, tools and ornaments.

258 See F. Laux, *Die Bronzezeit in der Lüneburger Heide* (Hildesheim 1971), pp. 30f., 153–7, who stresses that the prehistoric mining of salt is not indicated.

259 See Ziegert, p. 46.

260 The Indo-Europeans will be dealt with more extensively below and in subsequent chapters. In this connection see R. A. Crossland, 'Linguistics and archaeology in Aegean prehistory', in Crossland and Birchall, pp. 5–15, who suggest that the 'Indo-European theory' is now questioned under the present tendency in prehistoric studies to minimize the importance of movement and mixture of populations in explaining cultural change. See C. Renfrew, 'Problems in the general correlation of archaeological and linguistic strata in prehistoric Greece, the model of autochthonous origin', in Crossland and Birchall, pp. 263–76, followed by discussion. In view of the almost general rejection of migrationist and diffusionist models, Renfrew, in Crossland and Birchall, p. 269, refers to the archeologists in recent years turning to a consideration of culture process, of the way in which cultures change through the operation of local factors.

261 Gimbutas, p. 281.

262 Gimbutas, pp. 274f. This circumstance has also created the false impression that the graves were flat graves.

263 Gimbutas, p. 274.

264 Staatliche Museen, A. von Müller, 'Bestattungen in der Bronzezeit', bulletin, no. 1147 (Berlin 1972).

265 Ibid. The tumulus in question was located at Grünhof-Tesperhude, 40 km up the Elbe from Hamburg. For details, see G. Jacob-Friesen, 'Totenhäuser der älteren Bronzezeit aus dem Niederelbegebiet', in *KRI*, II, pp. 66f. Jacob-Friesen points out that such mortuary houses are exceptional, as they are located in the midst of the tumuli tree-coffin cemeteries. He dates them from the end of Period I to Periods I–III, *c.* 1550–1100 B.C. of the Montelius scheme.

266 Laux, pp. 20f.

267 Kolling, p. 99.

268 'Later' refers to Reinecke Br.D$_2$.

269 Dated as Ha A$_2$, Kolling, p. 99. See also C. Eibner, *Beigaben- und Bestattungssitten der Frühen Urnenfelderkultur in Süddeutschland und Österreich* (Vienna 1966), pp. 50f.

270 Dated as Ha A$_3$, by Ha B$_3$/C stone domes can be noticed (Kolling, p. 103).

271 See F.-R. Herrmann, *Die Funde der Urnenfelderkultur in Mittel- und Südhessen* (Berlin 1966), pp. 18ff.

272 Herrmann, pp. 24ff.

273 Herrmann, p. 46.

274 Von Brunn, p. 18.

275 Kolling, p. 103.

276 Kolling, p. 103, assigns these practices to Reinecke Br. D, when the use of pottery was still infrequent. Its use did not increase till Ha A.

277 Gimbutas, p. 274.

278 Sudholz, p. 8.

279 W. Meier-Arendt, 'Experimente mit Metal: Stabdolch', in *KRI*, I, p. 23.

280 See Christlein, in *KRI*, II, p. 84.

281 See Abels, pp. 88–93; also Laux, p. 135, and Eibner, p. 57.

282 Wingert-Uhde, p. 85.

283 Christlein, in *KRI*, II, p. 84.

284 Ibid.

285 See Eibner, pp. 52f.

286 Gimbutas, pp. 260–5.

287 Laux, p. 157.

288 Gimbutas, pp. 265ff.

289 Gimbutas, p. 267.

290 See note 84 above.

291 Gimbutas, p. 267.

292 Staatliche Museen, A. Kernd'l, 'Das Grab von Seddin', bulletin no. 1156 (Berlin 1973).

293 Gimbutas, p. 285. The burial took place in a tumulus cemetery near Bad Salzungen, Thüringen.

294 Herrmann, p. 6, for greater detail.

295 For more information, see K. Bokelmann, 'Ein bronzezeitliches Haus bei Handewitt im Kreis Schleswig-Flensburg', in *KRI*, II, p. 67. C14 dating produced a date of *c.* 3100 b.p., or *c.* 1440 B.C. The evidence has been protected by a grave and tumulus which had been raised over the remains of a burned house.

296 See Gimbutas, pp. 260f., for Unětician village and house; p. 275, for details of a Tumulus settlement; p. 301, for a few words about Urnfield settlements. See also Coles and Harding, pp. 340f., 494–9. See p. 353, for Urnfield house types.

297 See E. Stocker, *Die große Zeit der Buchauer Ausgrabungen* (Bad Buchau 1976), pp. 26–36; also Gimbutas, pp. 301ff. See also Piggott, p. 147; also Coles and Harding, pp. 354f.

298 Stocker, pp. 30–6; also Gimbutas, pp. 303ff.; see also Coles and Harding, p. 377, for a list of crops and domestic animals. Briard, p. 280, claims that grape seeds have been found in lakeshore settlements.

299 The site referred to is Biskupin.

300 Wingert-Uhde, pp. 90f. The evidence for the crossing furrows comes from the tumuli raised on plowed fields. For instance, the house at Handewitt had been built on such a ploughed field. The preservation of this method of tillage has led to the idea that burial was preceded by a ritual disturbing of the soil, Coles and Harding, p. 328, note 69;

Briard, p. 202, sees in the furrows under the tumuli a fertility symbol, so that the deceased might germinate to a new life beyond.

301 This matter was taken up at length in Chapter 2 above. See also Willvonseder, pp. 281, 284ff.

302 Willvonseder, p. 289.

303 Willvonseder, p. 293.

304 Willvonseder, p. 293; see also Coles and Harding, p. 432, who suggest that the Swiss lakeside settlements were abandoned during the 8th century B.C., probably because of some climatic catastrophe which forced the river system feeding Lake Neuchâtel, for instance, to back up.

305 See note 226 above, in which various possibilities are raised.

306 Laux, p. 157.

307 Gimbutas, p. 268.

308 Gimbutas, pp. 269f.

309 'Grimm's Law' is a complex system in which the consonant shifts which have taken place in the Indo-European languages have been recorded. One of its most rudimentary aspects is pertinent here. For instance, when the Indo-European consonants shifted into Germanic, the I.E. consonants shifted consistently, thus I.E. p, t, k were transformed into Germanic f, þ (th), χ (chi = a sounded h). Taking Latin as a convenient representative of Indo-European, the change into Germanic will be as follows:

Lat. pisces—Gothic *f*isks, Engl. fish, Germ. Fisch.

Lat. tres —Gothic þreis, Engl. three, Germ. drei.

Lat. cornu—Gothic *h*aúrn, Engl. horn, Germ. Horn.

Other soundshifts complete the picture. Relevant to the point made here is the well-known example which demonstrates the relationship between Lat. 'pecunia'—money, and Lat. 'pecu'—cattle. The derivatives here are interesting as Lat. 'pecu' shifts to German 'Vieh' (v = f), Engl. 'cattle', still reflected in the Engl. 'fee'—payment, where the pronunciation of Engl. 'fee' is identical to Germ. 'Vieh'. For an extensive discussion of the entire question, see E. Benveniste, 'Les valeurs économiques dans le vocabulaire indo-européen', in G. Cardona, H. M. Hoenigswald and A. Senn (eds.), *Indo-European and Indo-Europeans*, Papers presented at the Third Indo-European Conference at the University of Pennsylvania (1966) (Philadelphia 1970), pp. 307–20. Benveniste, p. 311, takes the relationship between 'pecu' and 'pecunia' to be assured. He defines 'pecunia' as a collective abstract, designating an economic value signifying movable possessions, p. 312. According to Benveniste, p. 314, Old High German is the only Germanic language where hypothetical Indo-European *peku—, represented by 'feho', 'fehu', 'fihu', has the sense 'cattle'. In Gothic the neuter noun 'faihu' means money, fortune, without relation to animals, but refers exclusively to money and wealth. But see also *Wright's Grammar of the Gothic Language* (Oxford 1966), p. 315, where 'faihu' is given to mean cattle, property, poss-essions, money. Benveniste continues indicating that in Old Norse 'fé' is traditionally translated as 'Vieh' = 'cattle, possessions, money, specifically movable wealth'. Old English 'feo' occurs in the sense of 'cattle, herd' not as frequently as 'money, wealth' (p. 317). *The Middle English Dictionary* by Kurath-Kuhn defines 'fe' as 'movable property, possessions in livestock, goods or money, riches, treasure, wealth' and as 'money as a medium of exchange or as used for taxes, tribute, ransom, bribes, etc.'. English 'fee' relates to French 'fief' which is of significance for the evolution of the feudal concepts, with the emphasis on 'movable property'. Benveniste, p. 318, concludes that I.E. *peku refers to the wider sense of 'movable personal property', of which cattle are a component.

310 Kolling, p. 111.

311 Kolling, p. 111.

312 Staatliche Museen, K. Goldmann, 'Depot-funde der Bronzezeit', bulletin no. 1145 (Berlin 1973).

313 Sudholz, p. 10.

314 Sudholz, p. 11, mentions axes laid out in a straight line; Briard, p. 332, refers to celts arranged in a radiating circle.

315 See Staatliche Museen, A. Kernd'l, 'Opfer-funde der Bronzezeit', bulletin no. 1153 (Berlin 1973); see also Coles and Harding, pp. 354f. For other sites, see H. Geisler, 'Die Opferschächte von Franfurt/Oder-Lossow', in Coblenz and Horst, pp. 307–13. These pits contained mainly the remains of cattle, but also of horses, sheep, goats, pig, stag and beaver. Geisler emphasizes that these were not refuse pits.

316 See Kernd'l, note 315 above.

317 Wingert-Uhde, p. 93.

318 For an attempt to substantiate this theory even with C14 dates (uncalibrated), see H. L. Thomas, 'New Evidence for Dating the Indo-Euro-pean Dispersal in Europe', in Cardona, *et al.*, pp. 199–215.

319 W. P. Lehmann, 'Linguistic Structure as Dia-critic Evidence on Proto-Culture', in Cardona, *et al.*, p. 2, argues that language be used only as a diacritic, not as a primary source for reconstruction of early culture, and that deductions from language must be examined as commentaries on texts and archeological data, but not as primary sources. Crossland, in Crossland and Birchall, p. 7, states that language is not an important cultural trait, relative to others, since communities give it up more readily than other social habits. Any observation of immigrants to North America demonstrates this very clearly.

320 See Piggott, p. 80; also P. Friedrich, 'Proto-Indo-European Trees', in Cardona, *et al.*, p. 11. But see also W. H. Goodenough, 'The Evolution of pas-toralism and Indo-European Origins', in Cardona, *et al.* pp. 253–65, especially p. 262, note 1.

321 For Crossland, in Crossland and Birchall, p. 11, a continuous process over most of south-east Europe from the 4th millennium onwards is one possible hypothesis, the other being a later process, *c.* 3000 B.C., occurring on the steppes of western Asia. Renfrew, in Crossland and Birchall, p. 272, is not too taken with the idea that the origin of the Indo-Europeans is to be sought in the region east of the Carpathians, in what he calls the 'Pripet marshes'.

322 The paper by P. Friedrich referred to in note 320 can serve as an example. Friedrich itemizes 18 tree units with 27 names for trees which can be traced in the Indo-European daughter languages: these are birch, Scotch pine, junipers and cedars, aspens and poplars, willows, maples, alder, hazel, elm, ash, oak, hornbeam, beech, cherry and yew, see Cardona, *et al.*, pp. 11–34. See also Piggott, p. 80.

323 See note 309 above as an illustration.

324 W. F. Albright and T. O. Lambdin, 'The Evidence of Language', Chapter iv, *The Cambridge Ancient History*, Vol. I, Pt. 1, Prolegomena and Pre-history (Cambridge 1970), pp. 140ff., indicate that Proto-Hittite was evident in Cappadocia as early as the 24th century B.C., but that Hittite was sharply defined and quite different from Indo-European by the 16th century B.C., perhaps considerably earlier, as the official language of the Old Hittite Empire.

325 Albright and Lambdin, *CAH*, I, 1, p. 144, point out that the Indo-Europeans worshipped Vedic gods and employed specific Indic forms of the numerals. See also C. Watkins, 'Studies in Indo-European Legal Language, Institutions and Mythology', in Cardona, *et al.*, pp. 321–54; also C. S. Littleton, 'Is the "Kingship in Heaven" Theme Indo-European?', in Cardona, *et al.*, pp. 383–404; and D. J. Ward, 'An Indo-European Mythological Theme in Germanic Tradition', in Cardona, *et al.*, pp. 405–20.

326 See Albright and Lambdin, *CAH*, I, 1, p. 153, who suggest that the Hurrians, of Armenoid physi-cal type, accompanied the Indo-Aryans in their advance west- and southward.

327 Albright and Lambdin, *CAH*, I, 1, p. 128, state that the continued presence of the Indo-Euro-peans is well documented in the Amarna Letters of the 14th century B.C. where they actually make up a majority of the non-Semitic rulers mentioned.

328 See Coles and Harding, p. 534, who mention an iron awl found on a trackway in Holland, and dated to *c.* 1170 b.c., or *c.* 1340 B.C.

329 Of late the idea enjoys some popularity that the Urnfield Culture represents a proto-Celtic people, see Briard, p. 286. However, if the notion of a cultural Bronze Age continuum is acceptable, then the Tumulus and even the Únětician cultural periods may be regarded as periods in which the proto-Celts underwent the earliest processes of emergence. In fact, Briard, p. 96, sees in the 'koine' Úněticians a

proto-Celtic phenomenon. On the other hand, p. 287, Briard seems to wonder whether the change in burial practice—from inhumation to cremation—might not mark such a point of emergence, especially if seen in conjunction with technical innovations and the occupation of fortifiable sites, a sign of unrest and insecurity brought at least by the infiltration, if not the invasion of peoples. In response Briard repeatedly, pp. 172f., 287, rejects the idea on the grounds of extensive regional variety and particularism and casts the 'epic theory into the realm of romantic reveries'. Coles and Harding, p. 337, suggest that there is some consensus that a proto-Celtic, if not a full Celtic society is in place during the late Urnfield. However, p. 367, they present the case that there is little which is specifically 'Celtic' in Urnfield Europe, the process being too gradual, and that no single culture or era should be sought as the immediate source of Celtic origins, as nothing is known of a Celtic language till historical times.

To press the case too vigorously that Celtic origins are to be sought in the Bronze Age cultures of central Europe implies that Germanic origins are also to be sought in the brilliant cultures of the Northern Bronze Age. The search for a beginning in a spectacular past may be atttactive for a variety of reasons, but little of real value is to be gained by it. In Chapter 5 we will hold the view that the Celts emerged out of the brilliant Hallstatt culture. In Chapter 6 it will be argued that the Germanic cultures evolved out of the rather humble Wessenstedt and Jastorf groups in Lower Saxony on the southern fringe of the faded culture of the Northern Bronze Age in an area where proto-Germanic and proto-Celtic cultural domains met.

4. Hallstatt: The Farflung Connections of the Early Iron Age

1 See J. Finlay, *Celtic Art, An Introduction* (Park Ridge, New Jersey 1973), pp. 27ff.; see also S. Piggott, *Ancient Europe from the Beginnings of Agriculture to Classical Antiquity* (Chicago 1965), p. 187.
2 A. Ross, *Everyday Life of the Pagan Celts* (London, New York 1970), pp. 18–25. See also J. X. W. P. Corcoran, 'The Origins of the Celts: The Archaeological Evidence', Chapter 1, in N. Chadwick, *The Celts* (Harmondsworth 1971), p. 31.
3 Refer to K. Kromer, *Von frühem Eisen und reichen Salzherren, Die Hallstattkultur in Österreich* (Vienna 1964), p. 25; also M. Gimbutas, *Bronze Age Cultures in Central and Eastern Europe* (The Hague 1965), p. 113; however, Gimbutas, p. 131, argues that the application of the term 'Hallstatt' to the central European Late Bronze phases dating back to Reinecke's time is a misunderstanding. 'Hallstatt' properly belongs to the Early Iron Age, the period of the Hallstatt cemetery. But see also J. M. Coles and A. F. Harding, *The Bronze Age in Europe, An*

Introduction to the Prehistory of Europe, c. 2000–700 B.C. (London 1979), p. 516.
4 K. Kaus, *Chronologie und Bestattungssitten der Hallstattkultur in Niederösterreich und in Nordburgenland* (Vienna 1973), p. 345.
5 Kaus, p. 360.
6 J. Briard, *L'Age de Bronze en Europe Barbare des Mégalithes aux Celtes* (Toulouse 1976), p. 362, represents the situation as one where Bronze Age warrior princes ceded their position to Iron Age merchant princes, though in turn this group assumed the appearance of a warrior caste, whose superior weaponry helped it to dominate a part of Europe, p. 341.
7 Kaus, p. 335.
8 Kromer, *Salzherren*, p. 161.
9 Kaus, pp. 271ff. For Piggott, p. 174, it is more important to note the continuity of culture during the first millennium B.C. than a division between cultures based on a change in technology. See also Coles and Harding, p. 523, for whom continuity is indicated in such areas as subsistence strategies, metal and ceramic industries, burial sites and practices. It was noticed in the previous chapter that the spreading of ashes or the raising of a tumulus over the cremation site had been practiced earlier. New now are the square or rectangular graves.
10 K. Kromer, *Hallstatt, Die Salzmetropole des ersten Jahrtausends vor Christus in den Alpen, Katalog zur Ausstellung* (Vienna 1963), pp. 20ff.
11 See Piggott, pp. 175ff., for Cimmerian and Scythian expansion. Piggott, p. 177, takes metallic bridle-bits as evidence of Cimmerian raiding parties penetrating far into western Europe. Also H. Müller-Karpe, *Das vorgeschichtliche Europa*, Serie: Kunst der Welt (Baden-Baden 1979), p. 128. See also Coles and Harding, pp. 403f., concerning Proto-Scythians and Cimmerians, including 'Thraco-Cimmerians'. See N. K. Sandars, *Prehistoric Art in Europe* (Harmondsworth 1968), pp. 210f. Also Briard, p. 341, who questions the eastern influences and considers the invasion of 'Thraco-Cimmerians' as something yet to be proven.
12 See Piggott, pp. 179f.; see also T. G. E. Powell, 'From Urartu to Gundestrup', in J. Boardman, M. A. Brown and T. G. E. Powell, *The European Community in Later Prehistory, Studies in honour of C. F. C. Hawkes* (Totowa, New Jersey 1971), p. 186. Powell suggests that these tumuli may point to enriching interchanges taking place during periods of prosperity. See also Kaus, p. 273.
13 See the various writings of Gimbutas, especially *Bronze Age Cultures*; see also Piggott, pp. 81f.
14 For a short review of this question, see Powell, in Boardman, *et al.*, p. 185, who does not appear to accept unequivocally the eastern invaders theory.
15 See Piggott, p. 185; also F. C. Hibben, *Prehistoric Man in Europe* (University of Oklahoma Press 1968), p. 238. See also Sandars, p. 209.

16 Sandars, p. 209; see also Hibben, p. 239, on the availability of iron ore in central Europe.

17 Hibben, p. 237, indicates that the reduction of iron ore to its metallic state involves a series of discoveries rather than a single invention.

18 See Sandars, p. 209; also Piggott, p. 185.

19 Kromer, *Salzherren*.

20 Kaus, p. 264; Piggott, p. 171, points out that the salt trade would also make possible the trade in food products.

21 Kromer, *Hallstatt*, pp. 26–9.

22 H. Wingert-Uhde, *Schätze und Scherben, Neue Entdeckungen der Archäologie in Deutschland, Österreich und der Schweiz* (Oldenburg and Hamburg 1977), p. 113.

23 Kromer, *Hallstatt*, p. 26, argues that this method was not developed till the Middle Ages. Opinions differ: see Briard, pp. 330f. for techniques of salt manufacture; see also Coles and Harding, pp. 61, 63, who support the idea that salt was obtained by the evaporation of brine already during the Early Bronze Age. See also E. Penninger, *Der Dürrnberg bei Hallein*, I, Katalog der Grabfunde aus der Hallstatt- und Latènezeit (Munich 1972), pp. 18ff.

24 Kromer, *Hallstatt*, p. 24.

25 See J. V. S. Megaw, *Art of the European Iron Age, A Study of the elusive image* (Bath 1970), pp. 14ff.

26 Powell, in Boardman *et al.*, p. 186.

27 Megaw, p. 13.

28 Megaw, pp. 13f.

29 Powell, in Boardman *et al.*, p. 187.

30 Megaw, p. 15; see also Piggott, p. 195.

31 See G. Kossack, *Gräberfelder der Hallstattzeit an Main und Fränkischer Saale* (Kallmünz 1970).

32 Kromer, *Hallstatt*, pp. 21–4; also Kaus, p. 263. See especially K. Kromer, *Das Gräberfeld von Hallstatt* (Florence 1959), and Kromer, *Salzherren*, pp. 55f.

33 See Briard, p. 341; also Piggott, pp. 204f.; also Sandars, p. 227. See especially E. Gersbach, 'Die Heuneburg', in *Kölner Römer Illustrierte*, II (Historische Museen der Stadt Köln 1975), p. 71.

34 H.-E. Nellisen, 'Eine Lehmziegelmauer von der Heuneburg', in *KRI*, II, pp. 71f. Piggott, pp. 204f., suggests that the crowding of the bastions along the north-west wall indicates no real understanding of their function, but shows merely a desire to imitate southern fortifications, the style having been brought back by mercenaries returning from service south of the Alps. Nellisen thinks it possible that the brick wall was erected for display purposes. Sandars, p. 227, points out that the wall faced a friendly settlement, rather than protecting the vulnerable western approaches, where one relied on the familiar timber and stone packing.

35 See E. Gersbach, 'Heuneburg, Hausgrundrisse', in *KRI*, II, pp. 72f. For details of house construction in general, refer to M. Funder, 'Die Häuser der Hallstattkultur', dissertation under K. Kromer, (Innsbruck 1977).

36 See G. Riek, H. J. Hundt, *Der Hohmichele, Ein Fürstengrabhügel der späten Hallstattzeit bei der Heuneburg*

(Berlin 1962); Megaw, p. 45, speaks of a trader-chieftain dynasty.

37 Megaw, p. 14.

38 See Riek and Hundt; see also Megaw, p. 45.

39 Riek and Hundt.

40 Megaw, p. 45; see also Piggott, pp. 183f., 205ff., who suggests that the grave may have been that of a captain of bowmen. He sees in the arrows the probable method of defending a fortification such as the Heuneburg. But see also Powell, in Boardman *et al.*, p. 189, who allows that the flat hammered arrowheads find parallels in the north Pontic region, though they are not distinctively Scythian.

41 Riek and Hundt, p. 109.

42 See Kossack, *Gräberfelder*, pp. 155f.

43 G. Kossack, 'The construction of the felloe in Iron Age spoked wheels', in Boardman *et al.*, p. 159. See also Kossack, *Gräberfelder*, p. 124, concerning the introduction of a larger breed of horses.

44 Kromer, *Salzherren*, pp. 95f.

45 Kossack, *Gräberfelder*, pp. 124f.

46 Hibben, p. 246, argues that the Hallstatt culture spread as a result of military expansion and domination.

47 See L. Pauli, 'Das Gräberfeld Großeibstadt', in *KRI*, II, p. 100.

48 Powell, in Boardman *et al.*, p. 186, thinks a common Median source to be a possibility.

49 Kossack, *Gräberfelder*, pp. 129f.; also Kossack, in Boardman *et al.*, pp. 143–63, especially p. 159.

50 Kossack, *Gräberfelder*, p. 130; also Powell, in Boardman *et al.*, p. 186.

51 Kossack, *Gräberfelder*, pp. 125, 168.

52 Kossack, *Gräberfelder*, pp. 155ff. Piggott, p. 184, appears to favor the influx of new ideas rather than of new populations, as the early graves contained no eastern imports.

53 Kossack, *Gräberfelder*, pp. 40ff.; also Pauli, in *KRI*, II, p. 100. Piggott, p. 179, sees similarities in the symbolic horse burials with Cimmerian practices, and analogies with the burials of chieftains of the eastern steppes.

54 Kromer, *Hallstatt*, p. 21.

55 Kaus, p. 260.

56 See Megaw, p. 49.

57 Kaus, p. 260, points out that the graves of men and women were about equal in number, and that the proportion of children's graves was however very low.

58 Kromer, *Salzherren*, p. 55.

59 Kromer, *Hallstatt*, p. 21; Kromer, *Salzherren*, p. 55, stresses that the manner of burial was not uniform, nor representative of a general population, as the graves account only for those who died on the mining site, and not for those who died while away on trips.

60 Megaw, p. 49.

61 Kossack, *Gräberfelder*, p. 39.

62 Kromer, *Hallstatt*, p. 21; also Kaus, p. 276, who indicates that pieces of meat accompanied the de-

ceased into the grave, predominantly parts of pig, but also of sheep and cattle.

63 Riek and Hundt, p. 119.

64 Riek and Hundt, pp. 119, 130f.

65 Riek and Hundt, pp. 123-31.

66 Megaw, p. 58; see also Sandars, p. 215.

67 Kossack, *Gräberfelder*, p. 123. It is possible that as in other societies, the afterlife was the reserve of the privileged and high born.

68 Kaus, p. 333.

69 Kaus, pp. 271ff., contrasts ceramic continuity with the introduction of changes witnessed during the transition from Urnfield to Hallstatt times.

70 Kaus, p. 360.

71 Megaw, p. 46, sees here a degree of southern influence.

72 See Sandars, pp. 212ff., 216.

73 See Megaw, p. 46; Sandars, p. 212, suggests that this ware had no local ancestry, the use of graphite pointing to a return to the south-eastern Gumelnita tradition. See also Piggott, pp. 169-99.

74 Megaw, pp. 46f.

75 Megaw, pp. 23, 50f. See also T. G. E. Powell, *Prehistoric Art* (London 1966), pp. 170ff.

76 See Megaw, p. 54; also Sandars, p. 214, and Piggott, p. 181.

77 See W. Torbrügge, *Prehistoric European Art* (New York and Baden-Baden 1968), pp. 147f. Sandars, pp. 214f., thinks it doubtful that the group represents a sacrificial procession. Sandars suggests that either a Greek craftsman was working under Hallstatt direction, or that a Hallstatt artist had been apprenticed in a Greek workshop.

78 See Magaw, p. 51, note to illustration 20.

79 Megaw, p. 50, suggests that the little man may be carrying a drinking vessel in his left hand. He was probably attached to the lip of a vessel, as though raising himself over its edge.

80 Megaw, pp. 49f.; also Powell, p. 174.

81 Megaw, p. 49; see also Torbrügge, p. 179.

82 Torbrügge, pp. 178f. See also E. F. Meyer, *Die Äxte und Beile in Österreich*, Serie: Prähistorische Bronzefunde, IX, 9 (Munich 1977), p. 28, who considers them to be lordly insignia, in the nomadic tradition.

83 See Kromer, *Salzherren*, p. 158; also Torbrügge, pp. 116f.

84 Torbrügge, p. 122; also Kromer, *Salzherren*, p. 158.

85 See Torbrügge, p. 180, for illustrations.

86 Powell, pp. 174f.; also Torbrügge, pp. 109f.

87 Torbrügge, pp. 105, 107; see also Powell, p. 175; Megaw, p. 58; see also Kromer, *Salzherren*, p. 58.

88 Kromer, *Salzherren*, pp. 57f.

89 See especially J. Boardman, 'A southern view of Situla Art', in Boardman *et al.*, pp. 123-40; see also Torbrügge, pp. 142f, and Megaw, p. 52. Piggott, p. 171, suggests that situlae were of central European origin, the animal ornamentation showing indebtedness to Greek 'orientalizing' tendencies. See

Sandars, pp. 223f.

90 Kromer, *Salzherren*, pp. 58f.

91 See Megaw, p. 47; also Torbrügge, p. 135; for details see also H. Zürn, *Hallstattforschungen in Nordwürttemberg, Die Grabhügel von Asperg, Hirschlanden und Mühlacker, Veröffentlichungen des staatlichen Amtes für Denkmalpflege Stuttgart* (Stuttgart 1970), pp. 53-7, for an analysis of the tumulus; pp. 67-71 for the stele. For a brief account, see H. Zürn, 'Die hallstatt-zeitliche Kriegerstele von Hirschlanden', in *KRI*, II, p. 78. Sandars, p. 248, suggests the statue to be a monument to the divinized or heroic dead.

92 See Powell, p. 205, who cautions against seeing in such a sculpture a representative example of the art, considering that as heathen objects they had little hope of surviving the Middle Ages.

93 See A. Beck, 'Die Grabstele von Tübingen-Kilchberg, Baden-Württemberg', in *KRI*, II, p. 79.

94 See Megaw, p. 23; also Sandars, pp. 211-14.

95 See G. von Merhart, *Hallstatt und Italien, Gesammelte Aufsätze zur frühen Eisenzeit in Italien und Mitteleuropa, Bearbeitet und herausgegeben von Georg Kossack* (Mainz 1969), pp. 2f.

96 Torbrügge, p. 111. For a detailed analysis of rattles and rattle-plates, amulets and other objects of exotic origin, see L. Pauli, *Keltischer Volksglaube, Amulette und Sonderbestattungen am Dürrnberg bei Hallein und im Eisenzeitlichen Mitteleuropa* (Munich 1975), pp. 116-36.

97 Merhart, p. 3. An accompanying type of article is the sheet bronze belthook. For a detailed discussion, see I. Kilian-Dirlmeier, *Die hallstattzeitlichen Gürtelbleche und Blechgürtel Mitteleuropas*, Serie: Prähistorische Bronzefunde, XII, 1 (Munich 1972).

98 Kromer, *Salzherren*, p. 145.

99 See M. Primas, *Die südschweizerischen Grabfunde der älteren Eisenzeit und ihre Chronologie* (Basel 1970), pp. 99-103.

100 Primas, p. 102.

101 See H.-J. Engels, *Die Hallstatt- und Latènekultur in der Pfalz* (Speyer 1967), pp. 32-6.

102 Engels, p. 18.

103 Engels, p. 18.

104 Engels, pp. 16ff.

105 W. Meier-Arendt, 'Frühe Eisenzeit im Kölner Raum', in *KRI*, I, p. 25.

106 K. Simon, *Die Hallstattzeit in Ostthüringen* (Berlin 1972), pp. 7ff.

107 D. Bohnsack, *Die Urnengräber der frühen Eisenzeit aus Garbsen, Kreis Neustadt am Rübenberge, und aus dem Stadtkreis Hannover* (Hildesheim 1973).

108 Sandars, p. 232. This culture will be discussed more fully in Chapter 6, below.

109 Kaus, pp. 310ff. Kaus presents arguments against the notion of Hallstatt lines of fortifications in the sense of a 'Limes'.

110 See Sandars, pp. 209ff.

111 P. Lambrechts, *L'Exaltation de la Tête dans la Pensée et dans l'Art des Celtes* (Bruges 1954), p. 13; see also the many references to Scythian art in Sandars;

also Megaw, p. 69.

112 E. Weski, 'Skythisches Gold', Staatliche Museen Preußischer Kulturbesitz, Berlin, Antikenmuseum (Berlin 1976); see also Piggott, p. 176, for Scythian expansion and influences.

113 Kaus, pp. 340ff.

114 Kaus, p. 343.

115 Powell, pp. 182f.

116 E. Demongeot, *La Formation de l'Europe et Les Invasions Barbares. Des origines germaniques à l'avènement de Dioclétien* (Paris 1969).

5. The La Tène Culture: The Celts

1 See W. Dinan, *Monumenta Historica Celtica*, I (London 1911), for notices of the Celts in Greek authors. See also T. G. E. Powell, *The Celts* (London 1963), pp. 15f.; also A. Ross, *Everyday Life of the Pagan Celts* (London and New York 1970), pp. 28f.; also M. Dillon and N. K. Chadwick, *The Celtic Realms* (London 1967), p. 1, for brief treatments of this topic.

2 See Dillon and Chadwick, p. 2, where the name 'Celtic' is linked with Gothic *hildja*—to fight; see also M. Dillon, *Celts and Aryans, Survivals of Indo-European Speech and Society* (Simla 1975), p. 22, where he suggests that the name 'Celt' is probably akin to the Old Norse *hildr*—battle and cognate Germanic words, to mean 'warrior'. According to Powell, p. 17, the term was generally used in a comprehensive way, including tribes with different names.

3 Dillon and Chadwick, p. 3; see also Dinan, pp. 9, 37, 39.

4 Powell, pp. 16f.

5 See S. Piggott, *Ancient Europe from the Beginnings of Agriculture to Classical Antiquity* (Chicago 1965), p. 227.

6 See *Diodorus Siculus* in Twelve Volumes, with an English translation by C. H. Oldfather, Loeb Classical Library (Cambridge, Mass. and London 1961), Bk. V, Ch. 24, pp. 161f. Timaeus suggests the country is named Galatia after Galatos, the son of the Cyclops and Galatia, see Dinan, p. 145.

7 See H. J. Eggers, E. Will, R. Joffroy, W. Holmquist, *Kelten und Germanen in heidnischer Zeit*, Serie: Kunst der Welt, ihre geschichtlichen, soziologischen und religiösen Grundlagen (Baden-Baden 1964), p. 125. Concerning the Celtic presence in Anatolia, Hieronimus of Cardia wrote that no eastern king carried on a war without Gallic mercenaries, and that the princes believed that without the aid of the Gauls they could neither maintain their power, nor, if lost, recover it. Summoned by the king of Bithynia, they brought him victory and stayed to form a Graeco-Gallic state, see Dinan.

8 This point has been made several times in the preceding chapters. Here see J. Finlay, *Celtic Art, An Introduction* (Park Ridge, N.J.), p. 28, who is supporting an opinion offered by Neustupny.

9 See Miles and Chadwick, p. 1; also Piggott, p.

215; see also J. Harmand, *Les Celtes au Second Age du Fer* (Paris 1970), pp. 10f. See also H. Noelle, *Die Kelten und ihre Stadt Manching* (Pfaffenhofen/Ilm 1974), p. 16; and J. V. S. Megaw, *Art of the European Iron Age, A study of the elusive image* (Bath 1970), p. 16.

10 Arguments in favor of continuity of culture imply a continuity of populations as well. Since language is one of the key criteria for establishing ethnicity, an attempt to do so in the absence of the linguistic criterion can not be convincing. Material evidence may be distributed by trade and hence say nothing at all about user ethnicity. Since nothing is known about the language(s) spoken by the carriers of the Urnfield cultures, nor about the language of the Hallstatt culture, it may be prudent not to insist too much on the term 'Proto-Celts' during these earlier periods, even in the face of the continuity of the material culture. For Dillon, in *Celts and Aryans*, pp. 12f, and in *Celtic Realms*, p. 2, the identification of the prehistoric inhabitants of Bohemia, Bavaria, the Rhineland and Gaul as Celts, must rest on linguistic foundations. See also Powell, pp. 18f. and 28ff.; and Harmand, pp. 9f. In any case, many ethnic groups will have played a role in the territories occupied by the people collectively called 'Celts'.

11 Powell, p. 52, advances the tentative hypothesis that does not appear to have effected much of an echo in the literature, that the name '*Keltoi*' belonged to the 'royal tribe', which had subsequently become the name adopted by the peoples of the Hallstatt provinces. See Harmand, p. 10, who cannot accept this hypothesis. For Powell, the Hallstatt is a typically Celtic culture, pp. 49f.

12 See Megaw, pp. 18f.

13 See Dillon and Chadwick, pp. 3–6; an extensive literature exists on this subject.

14 The site has been excavated by W. Haarnagel. Reference in K. Hauk, *Goldbrakteaten aus Sievern* (1974).

15 See Powell, p. 23.

16 Caesar's campaigns will be treated more fully in a subsequent volume, along with accounts of the activities of Drusus and Tiberius.

17 J. de Vries, *Kelten und Germanen* (Berne and Munich 1960), pp. 32f.

18 W. Meier-Arendt, 'Mitteleuropa während der späten Eisenzeit', in *Kölner Römer Illustrierte*, II, p. 80.

19 Polibius recorded this observation in *The Histories* in Six Volumes, with an English translation by W. R. Paton, Loeb Classical Library, (Cambridge, Mass., London 1960), I, Bk. II, Ch. 27–31, pp. 307–19, his account of the Battle of Telamon.

20 See N. K. Sandars, *Prehistoric Art in Europe* (Harmondsworth 1968), p. 232, who points out that it was a peculiarity of the Celtic tribes for them to split into segments before setting out in different directions. As a result the same tribal name appears in several parts of Europe. This 'diaspora' would

also account for the rapid spread of a typical stylistic treatment of objects over large areas in Europe.

21 See Ptolemy, Son of Lagus, in Dinan, p. 89, as recorded by Strabo, VII, 3, 8.

22 See Sandars, p. 229; also de Vries, *Keltische Religion* (Stuttgart 1961), p. 6; see also Powell, pp. 166ff.

23 The British Isles will generate the so-called Insular Style during the 7th and 8th centuries A.D.; the literature of the Middle Ages will bring Celtic themes into vogue; the Emperor Maximilian I will be much taken by Celtic subject matter, while in later centuries the preoccupation with intertwining decorative patterns may be seen to have been stimulated by that same attitude to ornamental forms that characterized Celtic art. To put it more boldly: where in the cultural history of central Europe the classical forms of Mediterranean art, for instance, encounter opposition in the north, during the Romantic Period, for example, the opposition appears to draw on residual components rooted in the prehistoric past.

24 See Julius Caesar, *The Conquest of Gaul*, translated by S. A. Handford (Harmondsworth 1965). See also Piggott, p. 227.

25 This question will be entered into more fully in a subsequent volume. See Piggott, pp. 223f.; also Sandars, p. 232.

26 Powell, pp. 164f.

27 Refer to J. M. de Navarro, *The Finds from the Site of La Tène* (London 1972).

28 See Sandars, pp. 227–32.

29 Megaw, p. 18.

30 Julius Caesar, *The Gallic War and other Writings of Julius Caesar*, translated with an Introduction by Moses Hadas (New York 1957), pp. 18, 183f., 192. These references concern Bibracte and Alesia. All references to Caesar will quote pages from this edition. See also Ross, p. 85; also Piggott, pp. 216–20. See especially the papers in B. Cunliffe and T. Rowley (eds.), *Oppida in Barbarian Europe*, British Archaeological Reports, Supplementary Series II (Oxford 1976), p. 82. See also Harmand, pp. 77–80.

31 These terms are usually translated as 'strong-holds' and 'towns', see Caesar, p. 7.

32 See J. Collis, 'Town and Market in Iron Age Europe', in Cunliffe and Rowley, p. 5, who suggests that the La Tène settlements had more in common with Roman and even medieval sites.

33 See S. Gollub, 'Der Ringwall von Otzenhausen', in *KRI*, II, p. 86.

34 J. Collis, in Cunliffe and Rowley, pp. 5f.

35 Collis, in Cunliffe and Rowley, p. 5.

36 W. Meier-Arendt, 'Die späte Eisenzeit: Köln in der Randzone der keltischen Latène-Kultur', in *KRI*, I, p. 26.

37 Collis, in Cunliffe and Rowley, pp. 7f.

38 Collis, in Cunliffe and Rowley, p. 5.

39 Collis, in Cunliffe and Rowley, p. 8.

40 Meier-Arendt, in *KRI*, I, p. 26.

41 Collis, in Cunliffe and Rowley, p. 8.

42 Gollub, in *KRI*, II, p. 86.

43 Collis, in Cunliffe and Rowley, p. 5.

44 Collis, in Cunliffe and Rowley, p. 10.

45 See H. Noelle, *Die Kelten und ihre Stadt Manching*.

46 Piggott, pp. 216f.

47 See Caesar, p. 165, for a description of the *murus gallicus*. See also F.-R. Herrmann, 'Kelheim, Stadt-mauer des keltischen Oppidum', in *KRI*, II, p. 84.

48 Noelle, p. 113.

49 See J. Břeň, 'Earliest Settlements with Urban Character in Central Europe', in Cunliffe and Rowley, p. 93.

50 Gollub, in *KRI*, II, pp. 85f.

51 D. Nash, 'The Growth of Urban Society in France', in Cunliffe and Rowley, p. 107. In this paper Nash deals with central and eastern Gaul.

52 See Noelle, pp. 102–45; also Piggott, pp. 216ff. See also H.-E. Nellissen, 'Das keltische Oppidum Manching', in *KRI*, II, pp. 84f.

53 Noelle, pp. 102, 112; see also Břeň, in Cunliffe and Rowley, p. 91.

54 Noelle, p. 102.

55 Noelle, pp. 114ff.

56 Noelle, pp. 112f.

57 Noelle, p. 121.

58 Noelle, pp. 104f.

59 See Collis, in Cunliffe and Rowley, p. 5.

60 See Noelle, pp. 127–45.

61 Břeň, in Cunliffe and Rowley, p. 92; also J. Břeň, *Třisov, A Celtic Oppidum in South Bohemia* (Prague 1966), for details of the early excavations of the oppidum.

62 R. Schindler, 'Die Altburg bei Bundenbach, Kr. Birkenfeld', in *KRI*, II, p. 92.

63 Břeň, in Cunliffe and Rowley, p. 92; also Břeň, *Třisov*, pp. 30ff. See also pp. 434ff. below.

64 Gollub, in *KRI*, II, p. 86.

65 See Nash, in Cunliffe and Rowley, p. 104.

66 Nash, in Cunliffe and Rowley, p. 106.

67 Nash, in Cunliffe and Rowley, p. 128.

68 Nash, in Cunliffe and Rowley, p. 128; see also Caesar, pp. 7, 14.

69 See J. Bracker, 'Herkunft und Umsiedlung der Ubier', in *KRI*, I, p. 30. Caesar, p. 75, speaks of state or nation. Only indirectly, p. 78, does he make mention of leaders and of a senate. In general, tribes with which Caesar enters into alliances are credited with being ruled by a senate, the Remi, for instance, p. 42. Alliances can be negotiated only with equals.

70 Nash, in Cunliffe and Rowley, p. 128.

71 See G. Alföldy, *Noricum*, translated by A. Birley (London and Boston 1974), p. 47, for the Roman occupation of Noricum.

72 Nash, in Cunliffe and Rowley, p. 129.

73 Břeň, in Cunliffe and Rowley, p. 88.

74 Collis, in Cunliffe and Rowley, p. 10.

75 Collis, in Cunliffe and Rowley, p. 13.

76 Břeň, in Cunliffe and Rowley, p. 93.

77 Collis, in Cunliffe and Rowley, p. 13; see also

Alfõldy, pp. 44ff.

78 See Noelle, p. 232; also Megaw, pp. 31f. Both sources suggest that the coins were introduced by way of the Lower Danube.

79 Noelle, p. 233.

80 Collis, in Cunliffe and Rowley, p. 8.

81 See Nellissen, in *KRI*, II, p. 85.

82 See Collis, in Cunliffe and Rowley, p. 8.

83 Collis, in Cunliffe and Rowley, p. 16.

84 See I. Kappel, *Die Graphittonkeramik von Manching, Die Ausgrabungen von Manching, herausgegeben von Werner Krämer* (Wiesbaden 1969), pp. 24, 58.

85 Břeň, in Cunliffe and Rowley, p. 88.

86 Kappel, p. vi.

87 See F. Maier, *Die bemalte Spätlatène-Keramik von Manching, Die Ausgrabungen von Manching, herausgegeben von Werner Krämer* (Wiesbaden 1970), pp. 5–15.

88 Maier, pp. 15–20.

89 Maier, pp. 42–70.

90 Ibid.

91 See J. Keller, *Das keltische Fürstengrab von Reinheim* (Mainz 1965), p. 1.

92 See J. Biel, 'Fürstengrabhügel. Eberdingen-Hochdorf', in Bittel, Kimmig, Schiek, *et al.*, *Die Kelten in Baden-Württemberg* (Stuttgart 1981), pp. 395–8.

93 See Megaw, p. 17.

94 See note 91 above; also H.-E. Nellisen, 'Das Grab einer keltischen "Fürstin" von Reinheim, Kr. St. Ingbert, Saarland', in *KRI*, II, p. 91; see also Megaw, pp. 73f., 79f.

95 Nellissen, in *KRI*, II, p. 91.

96 See also Finlay, pp. 48f, who detects a hint of Etruscan feeling in the human masks, especially when viewed in profile. See Powell, in *Celts*, pp. 84f., 261f.; also T. G. E. Powell, *Prehistoric Art* (London 1966), p. 192, who sees clear evidence of Persian inspiration in the torc and bracelets.

97 See P. Harbison, 'The Chariots of Celtic Funerary Tradition', in O.-H. Frey (ed.), *Marburger Beiträge zur Archäologie der Kelten Festschrift für W. Dehn zum 60. Geburtstag am 6. Juli 1969* (Bonn 1969), p. 34. Powell, in *Celts*, p. 47, links the use of two-wheeled funerary chariots with direct trade with the Etruscans, also pp. 104f.; Piggott, p. 238, suggests following a review of the evidence that the Celts learned little of value from the Etruscans concerning chariot construction. Piggott prefers east European and west Asiatic origins.

98 Harbison, in Frey, p. 41.

99 Harbison, in Frey, p. 40, supports the central European link with Etruria.

100 Harbison, in Frey, p. 44.

101 See F. LeRoux, *Introduction générale à l'étude de la tradition celtique*, I (Rennes 1967), pp. 43–6.

102 LeRoux, p. 52. These groups will be dealt with in greater detail in a subsequent volume.

103 LeRoux, p. 38.

104 LeRoux, pp. 35, 39, argues that this division of powers is a characteristic Indo-European parti-

tion of functions.

105 LeRoux, p. 38.

106 Caesar, p. 15. The example is Dumnorix and his retinue. On p. 40, Caesar makes it sound as though the usurpation of authority were a common event. See also p. 97.

107 Caesar, p. 54.

108 Caesar, pp. 7, 137, 153f.

109 See H. Birkhan, *Germanen und Kelten bis zum Ausgang der Römerzeit. Der Aussagewert von Wörtern und Sachen für die frühesten keltisch-germanischen Kulturbezeichnungen* (Vienna, Cologne and Graz 1970), p. 64.

110 See Caesar, p. 154, for the recruiting methods employed by Vercingetorix. Caesar may have colored his report.

111 Noelle, pp. 73ff.

112 Caesar, pp. 134, 170f., 188ff.

113 See R. Hinks, *Carolingian Art—A Study of Early Medieval Painting and Sculpture in Western Europe* (Reprint, University of Michigan Press 1966), pp. 72–93. See also Finlay, pp. 17ff.

114 Heinrich Wölfflin, *Principles of Art History; the Problems of the Development of Style in Later Art* (London 1938), p. 10. The work first appeared in 1915 as *Kunstgeschichtliche Grundbegriffe*. See also Megaw, p. 11, who has traced a Wölfflin echo in Sir Herbert Read, *Meaning of Art* (1956), pp. 65f.

115 See Dillon and Chadwick, pp. 287ff.

116 Sandars, p. 226; also Finlay, pp. 17, 21; see also Megaw, p. 17, for whom La Tène art is a unique amalgam.

117 P. Jacobsthal, *Early Celtic Art* (Reprint, Oxford University Press 1969), pp. 155–60. These classifications have been adopted by Sandars, pp. 227–231; also Powell, *Prehistoric Art*, p. 187; Megaw, p. 17. It should be noted that although these terms continue in use, there is general dissatisfaction with the terms.

118 See Sandars, p. 227.

119 Jacobsthal does not specify the Assyrian expansion as a cause for the spread of orientalizing tendencies of style. Sandars, pp. 229ff, sees the impetus originating with the expansion of Achaemenid Persia, see below. Megaw, p. 19, follows Sandar's argument with reservations. The Assyrian theory is advanced by T. G. E. Powell, 'From Urartu to Gundestrup: the agency of Thracian metal-work', in Boardman *et al.*, p. 183. Powell, p. 189, supports the Achaemenian theory advanced by Sandars.

120 See Sandars, pp. 234, 273, 278, who suggests such craters to have been exotic rarities, which did, however, have an effect on Celtic artists as they selected the mysterious figures represented on the craters as models for their own mysterious creations. See also Powell, in Boardman *et al.*, p. 183, who point out that the northern princes did not adopt the exotic forms into their own preferred inventory of forms.

121 See note 119, above. Especially Powell, in

Boardman *et al.*, p. 189.

122 The effects of Scythian incursions are mentioned by Megaw, p. 17; also Sandars, p. 229; Powell, *Prehistoric Art*, p. 187; and Finlay, p. 44. See also Piggott, p. 241.

123 Megaw, p. 17, points out that this strain is the most difficult to follow to its origins.

124 See P. Lambrechts, *L'Exaltation de la Tête dans la Pensée et dans l'Art des Celtes* (Bruges 1954), p. 16.

125 Jacobsthal, p. 159, sees it as a Caucasian influence on Celtic art.

126 See note 120.

127 Finlay, p. 50, suggests that those warrior chiefs were not only moved to military adventure, but were sophisticates who enjoyed the arts.

128 See Sandars, p. 226.

129 Sandars, p. 232; see also Megaw, p. 39.

130 See Sandars, pp. 233, 274f. See also Piggott, p. 243.

131 Megaw, p. 38; see also note 117 above; also Sandars, p. 233.

132 See Megaw, p. 17; also Sandars, pp. 233, 234. See also Dillon and Chadwick, p. 289; and Powell, *Prehistoric Art*, pp. 186ff. See especially F. Schwappach, 'L'art ornamental du "Premier style" celtique', in P. M. Duval and C. Hawkes (eds.), *Celtic Art in Ancient Europe, Five Protohistoric Centuries* (London, New York and San Francisco 1976), pp. 61–109, who points to the distinction between eastern and western stylistic provinces of the 'Early Style'. Jacobsthal had not had personal access to the evidence from eastern regions of central Europe and had consequently developed his 'Early Style' on evidence obtained in the areas of the more westerly La Tène, the Rhine–Marne region. While the west utilized such curvilinear floral motifs as palmettes, leaves, lotus blossoms and lyres, the more easterly regions preferred geometric ornaments, based mainly on such abstract forms as arches, circles and intersecting circles, and ʃ-curves. In Bavaria, Thuringia, Bohemia and Austria these geometric decorations were typical, probably derived from ancestral Hallstatt roots.

133 See Jacobsthal, pp. 169f.; also Megaw, p. 25, especially p. 67. See also Joffroy, in Eggers *et al.*, p. 140.

134 Jacobsthal, p. 197; also Megaw, pp. 69f.; and Sandars, p. 235, who is reminded of Persian lions and of Luristan mythology.

135 See Megaw, pp. 79f.; see also Nellissen, in *KRI*, II, p. 91; and especially Keller, pp. 31ff.; also Joffroy, in Eggers *et al.*, p. 140.

136 See Sandars, p. 281, who points to this transition from water fowl to birds of prey.

137 Torbrügge, p. 208.

138 Megaw, pp. 28f; see also Sandars, pp. 235f.

139 Jacobsthal, p. 155, suggests that the Celtic finds in Italy are generally not of the Early Style and do not betray any artistic initiative. See O.-H. Frey, 'Du Premier Style au Style de Waldalgesheim,

Remarque sur l'évolution de l'art celtique ancien', in Duval and Hawkes, pp. 143f.

140 See Jacobsthal, p. 167; also Megaw, pp. 59f.

141 Refer to Torbrügge, pp. 191f, for an illustration. Torbrügge assigns it to the middle La Tène. Also Jacobsthal, p. 198; Megaw, p. 84, assigns it to the late La Tène, see Plate 95, for an illustration. See also Powell, *Prehistoric Art*, pp. 188f.

142 Wooden figures are known from southern and eastern Gaul, see Dillon and Chadwick, pp. 297ff. See also Finlay, p. 52.

143 See Jacobsthal, p. 166, who points to its tenon-joint as evidence that it must once have been mounted on a wall, which in turn would support the idea that the Celts did know 'architecture', see Dillon and Chadwick, p. 294. See also Sandars, pp. 247f.; also Powell, *The Celts*, pp. 137f.; and Megaw, p. 48; also Powell, *Prehistoric Art*, pp. 206ff.

144 See Sandars, p. 249.

145 Powell, *The Celts*, pp. 134f.; also Powell, *Prehistoric Art*, p. 208; Dillon and Chadwick, p. 294, suggest a derivation from fifth-century Etruscan jewellery designs. See Megaw, p. 77, and especially Jacobsthal, pp. 165f.

146 For such a completion see Powell, *The Celts*, p. 133; see also Finlay, p. 53. Powell, in *Prehistoric Art*, p. 209, takes issue with Jacobsthal's designation, p. 9, that this head is a Janus. Megaw, p. 64, also calls it a Janus head.

147 Sandars, p. 247, pays special attention to the trefoil sign on the forehead.

148 K. Willvonseder, *Keltische Kunst in Salzburg* (Salzburg 1960), indicates that Celtic stone heads are known to have been used in church walls in Carinthia, for instance.

149 This topic can not be treated as fully in a central European context, as the evidence occurs mainly in southern Gaul. For a full discussion see P. Lambrechts, see note 124 above. See also Dillon and Chadwick, pp. 294ff.

150 See Dillon and Chadwick, p. 287.

151 See E. M. Jope, 'The Waldalgesheim Master', in Boardman *et al.*, pp. 165–80. Jope attributes the term 'Classic Celtic Style' to C. F. C. Hawkes, see p. 178 in Boardman *et al.* The Waldalgesheim Style has been seen as a direct outgrowth of the Early Style. Frey, in Duval and Hawkes, p. 148, restricts the Early Style to only one region, that of the princely graves, and observes that only in the Marne region does this relationship really exist. To Frey, pp. 152f, it is clear that the Early Style and the Waldalgesheim Style are two distinct phenomena. See also discussion of Frey's paper in Duval and Hawkes, pp. 160f., where Frey suggests more than one master at work in different workshops.

152 See Jope, in Boardman *et al.*, p. 168; but also Frey, in Duval and Hawkes, p. 149. Also Jacobsthal, p. 184.

153 Frey, in Duval and Hawkes, p. 149, argues that the work of the Waldalgesheim 'Master' is not

an isolated case, as demonstrated by the ornamentation of a lance found in Hungary. See illustrations 11 i, j, k, in Frey, in Duval and Hawkes, p. 150.

154 Jacobsthal, pp. 183f. Also Megaw, pp. 78f., especially pp. 95f. See especially Jope, in Boardman *et al.*, pp. 165–80.

155 See Megaw, pp. 93f.; Sandars, p. 238, indicates that such wigs were foreign to Greek and Etruscan representations.

156 A distribution map of finds in the Waldalgesheim Style shows this style spread from Switzerland to Bohemia and Austria, but not through the area of the Early Style, see Frey, in Duval and Hawkes, p. 152.

157 See Jacobsthal, pp. 95ff.; also Megaw, pp. 34f., who prefers the term 'advanced Waldalgesheim Style'. See also Sandars, pp. 244f.

158 See Sandars, p. 245. It is possible that these highly ornamented swords were never intended for combat, but for sacrificial use as votive offerings.

159 See Jacobsthal, pp. 97–103; see also Finlay, p. 56. See the discussion in Duval and Hawkes, p. 181–4, for meanings of the term 'plastic'. Jacobsthal uses French and German meanings of the word.

160 Finlay, p. 56; also Sandars, p. 244; but also Frey, in Duval and Hawkes, Discussion, p. 162, who argues that the Plastic Style may embody some Early Style traditions as well as some of the Waldalgesheim Style. See also Sandars, pp. 240ff.

161 See Megaw, p. 30; also V. Kruta, in Duval and Hawkes, p. 181.

162 Megaw, p. 23.

163 Megaw, p. 30. Jacobsthal, p. 103, suggests that certain 'baroque' tendencies are anticipated in the metalwork of archaic Italy.

164 'Plasticity' is here taken to mean three-dimensionality.

165 See Jacobsthal, pp. 99ff., 191, also Plates 259–79.

166 Finlay, p. 17.

167 See Sandars, pp. 275–84, 293; see also Megaw, p. 38.

168 These three examples belong to the 8th century A.D. See Hinks, *Carolingian Art*, cf. note 113 above.

169 Megaw, p. 129; See P. V. Glob, *The Bog People, Iron Age Man Preserved*, translated from the Danish by R. Bruce-Mitford (Ithaca, N.Y. 1969), pp. 168ff. See also Piggott, pp. 244f.; Powell, *The Celts*, p. 167.

170 See Powell, in Boardman *et al.*, p. 198.

171 Powell, *Prehistoric Art*, p. 225, claims that faces and bulls are not of a Celtic but of an eastern tradition. Finlay, p. 57, shares this opinion. Sandars, p. 252, states that pairs of confronting animals on the surviving inner panel are very much a La Tène motif. Megaw, p. 138, sees the faces to have an affinity with work originating in Gaul.

172 See Sandars, pp. 253–7; also Megaw, pp. 131ff., for details of individual plates. See especially Powell, in Boardman *et al.*, pp. 197–205.

173 Megaw, p. 131, suggests that three craftsmen were involved in making the cauldron. See also O. Klindt-Jensen, 'L'Est, le Nord et l'Ouest dans l'art de la fin du IIème et du Ier siècles avant J.C.', in Duval and Hawkes, pp. 233–45.

174 Sandars, p. 253.

175 For an interpretation of the cauldron in the spirit of Rudolf Steiner, see R. Grosse, *Der Silberkessel von Gundestrup—ein Rätsel keltischer Kunst, Ein Zeugnis des Läuterungs- und Einweihungsweges bei den Kelten* (Dornach, Schweiz 1963).

176 Ram-headed snakes are a Near Eastern motif, see Sandars, p. 255. Powell, in Boardman *et al.*, p. 183, suggests a Celtic preference for the representation of gentler creatures, rather than of ferocious beasts.

177 See Powell, in Boardman *et al.*, pp. 200f.

178 Questions concerning Celtic religion will be treated extensively in a subsequent volume. Because Celtic religion has been recorded largely in its later Gallo-Roman guise, I have thought it best to treat it as an aspect of Roman Provincial culture.

179 See Powell, in Boardman *et al.*, pp. 201f.

180 Sandars, p. 253.

181 Powell, in Boardman *et al.*, p. 202.

182 See Sandars, pp. 278, 282.

183 See Powell, in Boardman *et al.*, p. 202, who believes that too much has been made of this representation and its identification as Cernunnos. He prefers the view that the divinity is represented in shamanistic guise surrounded by shapes which it may assume.

184 Powell, in Boardman *et al.*, p. 203, joins Sandars, pp. 256, 324, note 86, in attributing an oriental origin to the base plate, perhaps a former phalera. According to O. Klindt-Jensen, in Duval and Hawkes, p. 236, it would be impossible to deny the relationship between Gundestrup and phalera art.

185 See Sandars, p. 231, where the reference is made to Mithraism; see also Powell, in Boardman *et al.*, p. 195.

186 See Posidonius of Apamea, in W. Dinan, pp. 317f.

187 Noelle, p. 194f.; also Powell, *The Celts*, pp. 138–45. See also J. Filip, *Celtic Civilization and its Heritage* (Prague 1962), p. 168; see Ross, p. 136–40; and de Vries, Keltische Religion, pp. 191f. See also Piggott, pp. 230–5. See also Bittel, Kimmig, Schiek *et al.*, pp. 104–13.

188 See Filip, pp. 169ff.; also Powell, *The Celts*, pp. 152ff.; for details see Caesar, pp. 135ff. LeRoux, pp. 59–70, argues that Celtic human sacrifice was a religious necessity which appears in relation with the conception of the sacred and cosmic equilibrium, not to be judged morally, but rather metaphysically.

189 De Vries, Keltische Religion, pp. 183–9.

190 De Vries, *Kelten und Germanen*, pp. 8of. See also Bittel, Kimmig, Schiek, *et al.*, pp. 104–17.

191 G. Mahr, *Die jüngere Latènekultur des Trierer Landes, Eine stilkundliche und chronologische Untersuchung auf Grund der Keramik und des Bestattungswesens* (Berlin 1967), p. 2.

192 Mahr, pp. 4f., 203.

193 Mahr, pp. 1–7, 206, emphasizes that the Treveri belonged to the Hunsrück-Eifel culture and not to the late La Tène.

194 H.-J. Engels, *Die Hallstatt- und Latènekultur in der Pfalz* (Speyer 1967), p. 76.

195 Mahr, p. 11, points out that the ceramic evidence in particular shows continuous development from Urnfield to Roman times.

196 Engels, p. 76.

197 Caesar, p. 132.

198 Mahr, pp. 59f.

199 W. Meier-Arendt, in *KRI*, I, p. 26.

200 Caesar, pp. 150f.

201 J. Bracker, 'Die Stadt der Ubier', in *KRI*, I, pp. 31, 33.

202 Noelle, pp. 7f. See also Bittel, Kimmig, Schiek *et al.*, pp. 19, 75.

203 Birkhan, p. 38.

6. Northern Genesis

1 H. Seyer, 'Ethnogenese der Germanen in der Jastorfzeit', in B. Gramsch, ed., *Germanen—Slaven—Deutsche, Forschungen zu ihrer Ethnogenese* (Berlin 1968) pp. 43ff.; see also H. Keiling, 'Jastorfkultur' in B. Krüger, *Die Germanen, Geschichte und Kultur der germanischen Stämme in Mitteleuropa* (Berlin 1978), pp. 87–96; H. Birkhan, *Germanen und Kelten bis zum Ausgang der Römerzeit, Der Aussagewert von Wörtern und Sachen für die frühesten Keltisch-Germanischen Kulturbeziehungen* (Vienna, Cologne and Graz 1970), p. 103, who suggests that the Jastorf culture is difficult to pinpoint as to beginning and location. H. Krüger, *Die Jastorfkultur in den Kreisen Lüchow-Dannenberg, Lüneburg, Uelzen und Soltau, Göttinger Schriften zur Vor- und Frühgeschichte*, ed. Herbert Jankuhn (Neumünster 1961), suggests a chronology in which in the north Jastorf a (*c.* 600–500 B.C.) corresponds to Hallstatt D in the south, Jastorf b (500–400) to La Tène A, Jastorf c (400–350) to La Tène B, Ripdorf (350–120) to La Tène C and Seedorf 120–0) to La Tène D, with a revision in which Jastorf c-Ripdorf corresponds to La Tène B–C and Jastorf d–Seedorf to La Tène D. Using the association of bronze finds, K. Nuglisch and E. Schröter, *Hausurnen und Jastorfkultur an der mittleren Elbe, Die Gräberfelder von Latdorf und Aken, Wissenschaftliche Beiträge der Martin-Luther-Universität Halle-Wittenberg* (Halle 1968), pp. 36–45, see the early phases of Jastorf as contemporary with Latène A–C or even Hallstatt D₂, as suggested by other sources, especially Schwantes, the ceramic evidence pointing to influences of the earlier Urnfield Culture, the bronze finds pointing to Hallstatt D.

2 Birkhan, p. 16; cf. Keiling in B. Krüger, pp. 91ff.; and Nuglisch and Schröter, p. 54.

3 R. Joffroy in H. J. Eggers, E. Will, R. Joffroy, W. Holmquist, *Kelten und Germanen in heidnischer Zeit* (Baden-Baden 1964), p. 9.

4 Ibid., p. 7; cf. also Keiling in B. Krüger, p. 97.

5 C. J. Hutterer, *Die Germanischen Sprachen, Ihre Geschichte in Grundzügen* (Budapest 1975), p. 14.

6 R. Ris, E. Seebold, 'Deutsche Gesamtsprache und germanische Sprachen', in H. P. Althaus, H. Henne, H. E. Wiegand, *Lexikon der Germanistischen Linguistik* (Tübingen 1973), p. 400.

7 H. Krahe, *Germanische Sprachwissenschaft* (Berlin 1966), 6th ed., I, p. 14.

8 For instance H. Krahe, P. v. Polenz, *Geschichte der Deutschen Sprache* (Berlin 1970), 7th ed.; F. Tschirch, *Geschichte der Deutschen Sprache*, I, *Die Entfaltung der deutschen Sprachgestalt in der Vor- und Frühzeit* (Berlin 1966); H. Moser, *Deutsche Sprachgeschichte* (Tübingen 1965), also available in English; L. Mackensen, *Deutsche Etymologie, Ein Leitfaden durch die Geschichte des Deutschen Wortes* (Bremen 1966); or W. W. Chambers and J. R. Wilkie, *A Short History of the German Language* (London 1970); J. T. Waterman, *A History of the German Language* (Seattle and London 1966).

9 Hutterer, p. 17.

10 Polenz, p. 12.

11 T. Frings, *Grundlegung einer Geschichte der Deutschen Sprache* (Halle 1957), p. 145.

12 Polenz, p. 16.

13 Polenz, pp. 17f.

14 Krahe, p. 23; also Birkhan, pp. 120–34, for other metals including silver and gold; also Hutterer, p. 147.

15 Polenz, p. 15.

16 A. Bach, *Geschichte der deutschen Sprache* (orig. publ. 1938, 8th expanded edition Heidelberg 1965), p. 50.

17 Bach, p. 50; also Hutterer, p. 47.

18 Polenz, p. 15.

19 Krahe, p. 23.

20 Tschirch, p. 57.

21 Tschirch, p. 56.

22 Mackensen, pp. 20–48.

23 Seyer, in Gramsch, p. 45; also H. Krüger, pp. 12f.

24 T. Ramskou, *Dänische Vorzeit* (Copenhagen 1972), p. 45; also Keiling in B. Krüger, p. 91.

25 Keiling, in B. Krüger, p. 13; also Ramskou, p. 45.

26 Ramskou, p. 46.

27 J. Hoika, 'Urnenfelder in Schleswig-Holstein', in *Kölner Römer Illustrierte*, ed. G. Biegel (Historisches Museum der Stadt Köln 1975), II, p. 97, hereafter abbreviated to *KRI*. See also H. Jankuhn, *Einführung in die Siedlungsarchäologie* (Berlin and New York 1977), pp. 85f.

28 K. Raddatz, 'Das eisenzeitliche Brandgräberfeld von Husby in Schleswig', *KRI*, II, p. 97.

29 R. H. Behrends, 'Das Urnengräberfeld von Schwissel, Kr. Segeberg', *KRI*, II, p. 98; Keiling in

B. Krüger, pp. 100f., indicates that there was no sudden desertion of pockets of settlements or influx into the Jastorf area, but rather a continuity marked by concentration of population. Cf. H. Krüger, p. 16, who emphasizes the continuity of funerary practices into the late La Tène, with a stable population remaining in place.

30 Velleius Paterculus, *Compendium of Roman History*, transl. by F. W. Shipley, Loeb Classical Library (London 1961), CV, CVI, 269ff. Hereafter references to the Loeb Classical Library will appear as LCL. Also R. Much, *Die Germania des Tacitus, dritte, beträchtlich erweiterte Auflage unter Mitarbeit von Herbert Jankuhn* (Heidelberg 1967), p. 39.

31 Tacitus, *Germania*, transl. by M. Hutton, LCL, pp. 187f; also Much, p. 418. All references to Tacitus will list the LCL edition *Germania*.

32 Much, Map no. 2.

33 Strabo, *Geography*, transl. by H. L. Jones, LCL, III, 7.1.3, p. 159; also Tacitus, *Germania*, pp. 187f.; and Much, p. 148.

34 Behrens, *KRI*, 1975, II, p. 98; H. Krüger, p. 17, suggests ritual damaging of urns: one handle deliberately broken off, holes, bottoms broken out.

35 Ibid., pp. 23–40.

36 Ibid.

37 Raddatz, in *KRI*, II, p. 96.

38 Hoika, in *KRI*, II, 98; H. Krüger, p. 17, indicates that in the immediate Jastorf area the poverty of inventories prevents the distinguishing of male from female graves.

39 W. Wegewitz, 'Gräberfelder der Vorrömischen Eisenzeit und Römischen Kaiserzeit in Putensen, Kr. Harburg', in H. G. Peters, ed., *Dokumentation zur Archäologie Niedersachsens in Denkmalpflege und Forschung*, p. 239.

40 Wegewitz, in Peters, p. 242; H. Krüger, p. 19, suggests a decrease of princely power and a state of dormancy of an aristocratic social order, not to be revived till the encounter with the Roman world recommended it.

41 Wegewitz; see also Keiling, in B. Krüger, pp. 91ff. concerning the lack of uniform characteristics.

42 G. Körner and F. Laux, 'Das Gräberfeld von Deutsch-Evern, Kr. Lüneburg', in Peters, p. 228.

43 A. Genrich, 'Der altsächsische Friedhof bei Liebenau, Kr. Nienburg/Weser', in Peters, p. 76.

44 H.-G. Steffens, 'Grabhügel der Vorrömischen Eisenzeit', in Peters, p. 110.

45 D. Zoller, 'Die kaiser- bis völkerwanderungszeitliche Siedlung auf dem Gristeder Esch, Gristede, Kr. Ammerland', in Peters, p. 112f.

46 W. Haarnagel, 'Die Grabung auf der Wurt Feddersen Wierde und ihr Ergebnis', in Peters, pp. 176–88; also F. Millar *et al.*, *The Roman Empire and its Neighbours* (Engl. ed. London 1967), pp. 309ff., for general discussion.

47 Haarnagel, in Peters, p. 182.

48 Haarnagel, in Peters, p. 184.

49 Haarnagel, 'Feddersen Wierde/Ostfriesland, ein Dorf im freien Germanien', in *KRI*, II, p. 198.

50 Haarnagel, in Peters, p. 186.

51 Haarnagel, in Peters, p. 188.

52 Ramskou, p. 50.

53 F. Schlette, *Germanen zwischen Thorsberg und Ravenna* (Leipzig, Jena and Berlin 1972), p. 53.

54 V. G. Childe, *What happened in History* (Harmondsworth 1957), p. 242.

55 Schlette, pp. 53f.

56 Ramskou, p. 50; also Schlette, pp. 50–4.

57 Julius Caesar, *The Gallic War and other Writings*, transl. by Moses Hadas (New York 1957), p. 74, p. 139. All future references will be made to this edition and cited as *Gallic War*.

58 *Germania*, p. 169; also Much, pp. 335ff.

59 *Gallic War*, p. 139.

60 E. A. Thompson, *The early Germans* (Oxford 1965), p. 27.

61 P. V. Glob, *The Bog People, Iron-Age Man Preserved*, transl. from the Danish by R. Bruce-Mitford (Ithaca, N.Y. 1969), p. 33.

62 Glob, p. 56.

63 Schlette, p. 55.

64 Glob, p. 101.

65 H. Jankuhn, in Much, p. 449; also F. Millar, pp. 316f. for discussion of northern cults, divinities and sacrificial practices.

66 Birkhan, pp. 554–61; also Glob, p. 156.

67 Glob, p. 166.

68 *Germania*, pp. 149f.; also Much, pp. 212ff.

69 Glob, pp. 110–14.

70 K. W. Struwe, 'Die Ausgrabung einer Moorleiche und ihre Deutung', in *KRI*, II, 93f.

71 *Germania*, p. 157; also *Gallic War*, p. 74; Much, pp. 260ff.; see also P. G. Hamberg, *Studies in Roman Imperial Art*, with Special Reference to the State Reliefs of the Second Century (Rome 1968), plate 38, 'Battle of Greeks and Gauls', the so-called Sarcophagus Ammendola, Rome, Museo Capitolino.

72 H. Hayen, 'Moorarchäologie im nördlichen Niedersachsen', in Peters, pp. 128–40.

73 Hayen, in Peters, p. 133.

74 Hayen, in Peters, p. 134.

75 Hayen, in Peters, p. 136.

76 Helga Wingert-Uhde, *Schätze und Scherben, Neue Entdeckungen der Archäologie in Deutschland, Österreich und der Schweiz* (Oldenburg and Hamburg 1977), p. 98.

77 Glob, p. 180.

78 Struwe, 'Die Götterfiguren von Braak-Eutin', *KRI*, II, p. 88.

79 Struwe, in *KRI*, II, p. 88.

80 *Germania*, p. 197; also Much, pp. 441ff.

81 Much, p. 451.

82 Much, p. 450.

83 *Germania*, p. 197, note 2; also Much, p. 450.

84 Much, p. 451.

85 *Germania*, p. 196; Much, p. 452.

86 Much, p. 455.

87 *Germania*, p. 197; also Much, pp. 457f., and R. Hachmann, *Die Germanen* (Munich, Geneva and

Paris 1971).

88 Glob, pp. 167f.

89 Jankuhn in Much, p. 459, refers to H. Kirchner, 'Eine steinzeitliche "Nerthus"—Darstellung'.

90 Struwe, 'Götterfiguren', cf. no. 78 above, *KRI*, II, p. 89; also Hachmann.

91 Glob, p. 185.

92 Ramskou, p. 48; R. T. M. Wheeler, *Rome beyond the Imperial Frontiers* (London 1954), p. 59 suggests the chainmail shirts to have been of Asiatic origin.

93 *Gallic War*, p. 137.

94 *Germania*, p. 149; also Much, p. 213.

95 A. Grenier, *Les Gaulois*, Avant-propos de Louis Harmand (Paris 1970), p. 82.

96 *Gallic War*, p. 41; see also J. de Vries, *Kelten und Germanen* (Berne and Munich 1960), p. 51; and Strabo, III, 7.1.2, p. 153.

97 Grenier, p. 82.

98 *Gallic War*, p. 41.

99 *Gallic War*, p. 196.

100 *Gallic War*, p. 100.

101 E. Kornemann, *Römische Geschichte*, 6. Auflage bearbeitet von Hermann Bengtson (Stuttgart 1970), I, p. 418.

102 Géza Alföldy, *Noricum*, transl. by A. Birley, (London and Boston 1974), p. 35.

103 Alföldy, p. 47.

104 Alföldy, p. 37.

105 *Livy*, transl. by B. O. Foster, LCL, XIV, 79, calls the Tigurines Gauls; Much, p. 422; also Kornemann, I, p. 418; de Vries, p. 59, and Max Cary, *A History of Rome, Down to the Reign of Constantine* (London 1957), p. 306.

106 Much, p. 353 and 417.

107 Kornemann, I, p. 419.

108 Ibid.

109 Grenier, p. 86; Dio Cassius in *Dio's Roman History*, transl. by E. Cary, LCL, IV, p. 383, suggests that the Cimbri and Ambrones were Celts.

110 Grenier, p. 87; also H. Hirst, *Geschichte der deutschen Sprache*, reprint of the 1925 edition, (Munich 1968), p. 45.

111 Cary, pp. 306f.; also Grenier, p. 87.

112 *Livy*, LCL, XIV, p. 79; also Dio Cassius, XXVII, 91, 1–4, for details of the situation preceding the battle.

113 de Vries, p. 96.

114 *Gallic War*, p. 54.

115 Alföldy, p. 37.

116 Kornemann, I, p. 423; also G. Webster, *The Roman Imperial Army to Caracalla* (London 1969), pp. 37–9, on Marius and the army reforms.

117 Plutarch, *The Parallel Lives: The Life of Marius*, transl. by B. Perrin, for the battle of Aquae Sextiae, pp. 503–21, for Vercellae pp. 529–39.

118 Plutarch, *Life of Marius*. Plutarch gives similar accounts of the women at Aquae Sexteia, pp. 51ff. and at Vercellae, p. 537. *Livy*, LCL, XIV, pp. 81f., reports that at Aquae Sextiae 90,000 prisoners were taken and at Vercellae 60,000.

119 Kornemann, I, p. 427.

120 *Gallic War*, pp. 25, 29.

121 *Gallic War*, p. 41.

122 Birkhan, pp. 492–510 for names among the Cimbri and Teutones; see Grenier, p. 86 for the reference to the Spartacus uprising.

123 *Gallic War*, p. 29.

124 G. Walser, *Caesar und die Germanen, Studien zur politischen Tendenz Römischer Feldzugsberichte* (Wiesbaden 1956), pp. 86f.

125 C. M. Wells, *The German Policy of Augustus, An Examination of the Archaeological Evidence* (Oxford 1972), pp. 14f.; also M. E. Wightman, *Roman Trier and the Treveri* (New York and Washington 1971), p. 19, who suggests that Caesar needed an excuse for his difficulties on the Rhine.

126 *Gallic War*, pp. 41f.

127 Wells, p. 30.

128 de Vries, pp. 55ff. and also Much, pp. 72f., both of whom express considerable uncertainty about this name, while K. Kraft, *Die Entstehung des Namens 'Germania'*, Sitzungsberichte der Wissenschaftlichen Gesellschaft an der Johann Wolfgang von Goethe Universität Frankfurt/Main, Band 9 Jahrgang 1970 Nr. 2 (Wiesbaden 1970), pp. 46f. note 2, rejects the Germani Oretani notion completely.

129 *Germania*, p. 129; also Much, p. 29.

130 Dio Cassius, LCL, LVI, pp. 38ff. E. Cary's note.

131 Strabo, LCL, II, 4.4.2. p. 239, to whom the Celti and Germani were kinsmen; also LCL, III, 7.1.2. p. 153, where he sees very little difference between Celti and Germani, holding 'that it was for this reason that the Romans assigned to them the name "Germani", as though they wished to indicate thereby that they were "genuine" Galatae, for in the language of the Romans "germani" means "genuine".'

Bibliography

1. The Paleolithic: Of Ice, Men, Stones and Things

Karl Dietrich Adam, Renate Kurz, *Eiszeitkunst im süddeutschen Raum* (Stuttgart, 1980).

Karl Dietrich Adam, *Der Mensch im Eiszeitalter*, Stuttgarter Beiträge zur Naturkunde, Serie C— Nr. 15 (Stuttgart, 1982).

Günther Altner, ed., *The Human Creature* (Garden City, N.Y. 1974).

Badisches Landesmuseum, *Veröffentlichungen*, (Karlsruhe 1977).

A. W. F. Banfield, *A Revision of the Reindeer and Caribou, Genus Rangifer*, National Museum of Canada, Bulletin No. 177, Biological Series No. 66 (Ottawa 1961).

P. K. Berlin, *Basic Colour Terms, Their Universality and Evolution* (Berkeley 1969).

François Bordes, *Le Paléolithique dans le Monde* (Paris 1968).

Robert J. Braidwood, *Prehistoric Man*, 8th ed. (Glenview Ill.; Dallas, Texas; Palo Alto, Cal.; Tucker, Ga.; Brighton, Engl., 1975).

Karl W. Butzer, *Environment and Archaeology, An ecological approach to Prehistory*, 2nd ed. (Chicago and New York 1971).

Grahame Clark, *World Prehistory*, A new outline being the second edition of *World Prehistory* (Cambridge 1969).

Desmond Collins, *The Human Revolution from Ape to Artist* (Oxford 1976).

Michael H. Day, *Guide to Fossil Man, A Handbook of Human Paleontology* (London 1965).

Rudolf Drößler, *Die Venus der Eiszeit*, Entdeckung und Erforschung altsteinzeitlicher Kunst (Leipzig 1967).

Burkhard Frenzel, *Die Klimaschwankungen des Eiszeitalters* (Braunschweig 1967).

Burkhard Frenzel, *Climatic Fluctuations of the Ice Age*, transl. by A. E. M. Nairn (Cleveland and London 1973).

Wolf Günther Haensch, *Die Paläolitischen Menschendarstellungen aus der Sicht der Somatischen Anthropologie, Menschenbildnisse auf Gravierungen, Reliefs und Malereien in Südwestfrankreich und Nordostspanien* (Bonn 1968).

Christopher F. C. Hawkes, *The Prehistoric Foundations of Europe to the Mycenean Age*. Reprint of the 1940 ed. (London and New York 1973).

Jacquetta Hawkes, *Atlas of Ancient Archaeology* (London 1974).

Jacquetta Hawkes, asst. by David Trump, *The Atlas of Early Man* (London and New York 1976).

Frank. C. Hibben, *Prehistoric Man in Europe*, 1st ed. 1958, 4th printing (Univ. of Oklahoma Press 1968).

Pierre Honoré, *Das Buch der Altsteinzeit, oder Der Streit um die Vorfahren* (Düsseldorf and Vienna 1967).

William W. Howells, *Mankind in the Making*, 1st ed. 1959. Revised ed. (Garden City, N.Y. 1967).

E. O. James, *Prehistoric Religion* (London 1957).

Kölner Römer Illustrierte, I, ed. Maria Wellershoff (Historische Museen der Stadt Köln 1974).

Kölner Römer Illustrierte, II, ed. Gerd Biegel (Historische Museen der Stadt Köln 1975).

A. Laming-Emperaire, *La Signification de l'Art rupestre paléolithique* (Paris 1962).

M. D. Leakey, *Olduvai Gorge*, vol. 3. 'Excavations in Beds I and II, 1960-63' (Cambridge 1971).

A. Leroi-Gourhan, *Les Religions de la Préhistoire (Paléolithique)* (Paris 1964).

P. Liebermann, *On the Origins of Language, An Introduction to the Evolution of Speech* (New York and London 1975).

Ivar Lissner, *Man, God and Magic*, transl. from the German *Aber Gott war da* (1958, 1960), by J. Maxwell Brownjohn (London 1961).

Hermann Müller-Karpe, *Handbuch der Vorgeschichte, I* (Munich 1966).

Karl J Narr, *Studien zur älteren und mittleren Steinzeit der Niederen Lande* (Bonn 1968).

Old World Archaeology: Foundations of Civilizations, Readings from *Scientific American* (San Francisco 1972).

John E. Pfeiffer, *The Emergence of Man* (New York, Evanston and London 1969).

Marjorie Quennell, *Everyday Life in Prehistoric Times*, 1st ed. 1959, 4th Printing (London and New York 1966).

Alfred Rust, *Rentierjäger der Eiszeit in Schleswig-Holstein* (Neumünster in Holstein 1954).

Martin Schwarzbach, *Climates of the Past, An Introduction to Paleoclimatology*, transl. from the German, *Das Klima der Vorzeit*, ed. by R. O. Muir (London 1963).

Robert Stigler, ed., *The Old World, Early Man to the Development of Agriculture* (New York 1974).

E. Trinkaus and W. W. Howells, 'The Neanderthals', in *Scientific American*, December 1979).

Rafael von Urslar, *Eiszeitmenschen am Rhein* (Cologne and Graz 1957).

Gisela Weber-Haupt, *Die Bedeutung des Rentiers im Paläolithikum nach Aussage der Darstellungen*, Phil. Diss. (Mainz 1957).

Herbert Wendt, *In Search of Adam* (New York 1963).

Helga Wingert-Uhde, *Schätze und Scherben, Neue Entdeckungen der Archäologie in Deutschland, Österreich und der Schweiz* (Oldenburg, Hamburg 1977).

Lothar F. Zotz, *Das Paläolithikum in den Weinberghöhlen bei Mauern* (Bonn 1955).

2. The Ceramic Age: Immigration from Within

Antiquity, A Periodical Review of Archaeology, ed. G. Daniel (Cambridge).

A. Billamboz, H. Schlichterle, *Pfahlbauten, Urgeschichtliche Ufer- und Moorsiedlungen*, Neue Forschungen in Südwest-deutschland (Stuttgart 1981).

R. J. Braidwood, *Prehistoric Men*, 8th ed. (Glenview, Illinois; Dallas, Texas; Palo Alto, California; Tucker, Georgia; Brighton, England 1975).

K. H. Brandt, *Studien über steinerne Äxte und Beile der Jüngeren Steinzeit und der Stein-Kupferzeit Nordwestdeutschlands*, Münsterische Beiträge zur Vorgeschichtsforschung, Band 2 (Hildesheim 1967).

K. W. Butzer, *Environment and Archaeology, An Ecological Approach to Prehistory*, 2nd ed. (Chicago and New York 1971).

J. G. D. Clark, *The Mesolithic Settlement of Northern Europe, A study of the Food-Gathering Peoples of Northern Europe during the Early Post-Glacial Period*, reprint of the 1936 ed. (New York 1977).

S. Cole, *The Neolithic Revolution* (London 1959).

D. Collins, *The Human Revolution from Ape to Artist* (Oxford 1976).

G. Daniel, *The Megalith Builders of Western Europe* (London 1963).

G. Daniel, *Megaliths in History*, Fourth of the Walter Neurath Lectures (London 1972).

R. Degen (ed.), *Zürcher Seeufersiedlungen. Von der Pfahlbau-Romantik zur modernen archäologischen Forschung*, in Helvetia Archaeologica, 12, 45/48 (Basel 1981).

H. Frankfort, *et al.*, *Before Philosophy, The Intellectual Adventure of Ancient Man*, first published Chicago 1946 (Harmondsworth 1954).

J.-P. Farrugia, *et al.*, *Der Bandkeramische Siedlungsplatz Langweiler 2 Gemeinde Aldenhoven, Kreis Düren*, Serie: Beiträge zur Neolithischen Besiedlung der Aldenhovener Platte (Bonn 1973).

H. C. Fritts, *Tree Rings and Climate* (London, New York and San Francisco 1976).

C. F. C. Hawkes, *The Prehistoric Foundations of Europe to the Mycenean Age*, reprint of the 1940 edition (London and New York 1973).

J. Hawkes, *Atlas of Ancient Archaeology* (London 1974).

F.-R. Herrmann, *Die Funde der Urnenfelderkultur in Mittel- und Südhessen* (Berlin 1966).

F. C. Hibben, *Prehistoric Man in Europe*, first ed. 1958, 4th printing (University of Oklahoma Press 1968).

E. O. James, *Prehistoric Religion* (London 1957).

Kölner Römer Illustrierte, I, M. Wellershoff, ed. (Historische Museen der Stadt Köln 1974).

Kölner Römer Illustrierte, II, G. Biegel, ed. (Historische Museen der Stadt Köln 1975).

O. Kunkel, *Die Jungfernhöhle bei Tiefenellern, Eine Neolithische Kultstätte auf dem Fränkischen Jura bei Bamberg* (Munich 1955).

E. Lomborg, 'Die Flintdolche Dänemarks, Studien über Chronologie und Kulturbeziehungen des südskandinavischen Spätneolithikums', Phil. Diss., translated from the Danish (Copenhagen 1973).

S. Martin-Kilcher, *125 Jahre Pfahlbauforschung*, Sondernummer: Archäologie der Schweiz, Mitteilungsblatt der Schweizerischen Gesellschaft für Ur- und Frühgeschichte, 2, 1 (Basel 1979).

J. Mellaart, *The Neolithic of the Near East*, with 164 illustrations (New York and London 1975).

H. H. Müller, *Die Haustiere der Mitteldeutschen Bandkeramiker*, Deutsche Akademie der Wissenschaften zu Berlin, Schriften der Sektion für Vor- und Frühgeschichte (Berlin 1964).

H. Müller-Karpe, *Das Vorgeschichtliche Europa*, Serie: *Kunst der Welt, ihre geschichtlichen, soziologischen und religiösen Grundlagen* (Baden-Baden 1968).

H. Müller-Karpe, *Die geschichtliche Bedeutung des Neolithikums*, Sitzungsberichte der Wissenschaftlichen Gesellschaft an der Johann Wolfgang Goethe-Universität Frankfurt/Main, Band 9, Jahrgang 1970, Nr. 1 (Wiesbaden 1970).

H. Müller-Karpe, *Handbuch der Vorgeschichte, II, Jungsteinzeit*, in 3 Teilen (Munich 1969).

H. Müller-Karpe, *Handbuch der Vorgeschichte, III, Kupferzeit*, in 3 Teilen (Munich 1974).

M. Moreau, *Les Civilisations des Etoiles, Les liaisons Ciel-Terre par les Mégalithes* (Paris 1973).

K. J. Narr, *Studien zur älteren und mittleren Steinzeit der Niederen Lande* (Bonn 1968).

Old World Archaeology: Foundations of Civilization, Readings from *Scientific American* (San Francisco 1972).

O. Paret, *Das Steinzeitdorf Ehrenstein bei Ulm/Donau* (Stuttgart 1955).

H.-G. Peters, editor, *Dokumentation zur Archäologie Niedersachsens in Denkmalpflege und Forschung*, Herausgegeben im Auftrage des Niedersächsischen Ministers für Wissenschaft und Kunst (Hanover 1975).

S. Piggott, *Ancient Europe from the Beginnings of Agriculture to Classical Antiquity* (Chicago 1965).

Radiocarbon, ed. R. F. Flint, *et al.*, published by *The American Journal of Science* (New Haven, Connecticut).

T. Ramskou, *Dänische Vorzeit* (Copenhagen 1972).

C. Renfrew, *Before Civilisation, The Radiocarbon Revolution and Prehistoric Europe* (London 1975).

E. Sangmeister, K. Gerhardt, *Schnurkeramik und Schnurkeramiker in Südwestdeutschland* (Freiburg i. Br. and Karlsruhe 1965).

W. Schrickel, *Westeuropäische Elemente im Neolithikum und in der frühen Bronzezeit Mitteldeutschlands* (Leipzig 1957).

M. Schwarzbach, *Climates of the Past, An Introduction to Paleoclimatology*, translated from the German, *Das Klima der Vorzeit*, ed. by R. O. Muir, London 1963.

G. de G. Sieveking, J. H. Longworth, K. E. Wilson, ed., *Problems in Economic and Social Archaeology* (London 1976).

D. D. A. Simpson, ed. *Economy and Settlement in Neolithic and Early Bronze Age Britain and Europe*, Papers delivered at a Conference held in the University of Leicester, December 1969 (Leicester 1971).

E. Sprockhoff, *Die Nordische Megalithkultur* (Berlin, Leipzig 1938).

E. Sprockhoff, *Atlas der Megalithgräber Deutschlands*, in 3 Teilen, (Bonn 1965–75).

P. V. D. Stern, *Prehistoric Europe, From Stone Age Man to the Early Greeks* (London 1970).

R. Stigler, ed., *The Old World, Early Man to the Development of Agriculture* (New York 1974).

E. Stocker, *Die große Zeit der Buchauer Ausgrabungen* (Bad Buchau 1976).

C. Strahm, *Die Gliederung der Schnurkeramischen Kultur in der Schweiz* (Berne 1971).

H. L. Thomas, *Near Eastern, Mediterranean and European Chronology, The Historical, Archaeological, Radiocarbon, Pollenanalytical and Geochronological Evidence*, Studies in Mediterranean Archaeology, XVII, 1, Text and 2 Charts (Lund 1967).

W. Torbrügge, *Prehistoric European Art* (Baden-Baden and New York 1968).

J. D. Van der Waals, ed., *Neolithic Studies in Atlantic Europe*, Proceedings of the Second Atlantic Colloquium, Groningen, 6–11 April, 1964, Presented to Albert Egges van Giffen, Groningen 1966 (1967).

H. Wingert-Uhde, *Schätze und Scherben, Neue Entdeckungen der Archäologie in Deutschland, Österreich und der Schweiz* (Oldenburg and Hamburg 1977).

J. Winiger, *Das Fundmaterial von Thayngen-Weier im Rahmen der Pfyner Kultur*, Monographien zur Ur- und Frühgeschichte der Schweiz, 18 (Basel 1971).

P. Wolff, 'Die Jagd- und Haustierfauna der spätneolithischen Pfahlbauten des Mondsee', Phil. Diss. (Vienna 1975).

R. Wyss, *Wirtschaft und Gesellschaft in der Jungsteinzeit*, Monographien zur Schweizer Geschichte (Berne 1973).

3. The Bronze Age: The Inner Colonization

B.-U. Abels, *Die Randleistenbeile in Baden-Württemberg, dem Elsaß, der Franche-Comté und der Schweiz*, Prähistorische Bronzefunde, Abteilung IX, Band 4 (Munich 1972).

H. Aschemeyer, *Die Gräber der jüngeren Bronzezeit im westlichen Westfalen* (Münster 1966).

F. Behn, *Die Bronzezeit in Nordeuropa, Bildnis einer prähistorischen Hochkultur* (Stuttgart, Berlin, Cologne, Mainz 1967).

Bernisches Historisches Museum, Abteilung für Ur- und Frühgeschichte, *Die Ur- und Frühgeschichte der Schweiz* (Berne, no date).

J. Briard, *L'Age du Bronze en Europe Barbare des Mégalithes aux Celtes* (Toulouse 1976).

W. A. von Brunn, *Die Hortfunde der frühen Bronzezeit aus Sachsen-Anhalt, Sachsen und Thüringen* (Berlin 1959).

J. J. Butler, *Bronze Age Connections across the North Sea, A Story in Prehistoric Trade and Industrial Relations between the British Isles, the Netherlands, North Germany and Scandinavia, c. 1700–700 B.C.* (Groningen 1963).

The Cambridge Ancient History, Vol. I, Pt. 1, *Prolegomena and Prehistory*, ed. by I. E. S. Edwards, C. J. Gadd, N. G. L. Hammond (Cambridge 1970).

T. Capelle, *Kunst und Kunsthandwerk im bronzezeitlichen Nordeuropa* (Neumünster 1974).

H. Cardona, H. M. Hoenigswald and A. Senn (eds.), *Indo-European and Indo-Europeans*, Papers Presented at the Third Indo-European Conference at the University of Pennsylvania (1966) (Philadelphia 1970).

V. G. Childe, *The Bronze Age* (first published 1930, 2nd reprinting, New York 1964).

J. M. Coles, A. F. Harding, *The Bronze Age in Europe, An Introduction to the Prehistory of Europe, c. 2000–700 B.C.* (London 1979).

R. A. Crossland, A. Birchall, *Bronze Age Migrations in the Aegean, Archaeological and Linguistic Problems in Greek Prehistory*, Proceedings of the First International Colloquium on Aegean Prehistory, Sheffield (Park Ridge, New Jersey 1974).

W. Coblenz, F. Horst (eds.), *Mitteleuropäische Bronzezeit*, Beiträge zur Archäologie und Geschichte, VIII Tagung der Fachgruppe Ur- und Frühgeschichte vom 24–26 April 1975 in Dresden (Berlin 1978).

C. Eibner, *Beigaben- und Bestattungssitten der Frühen Urnenfelderkultur in Süddeutschland und Österreich* (Vienna 1966).

P. Gelling, H. E. Davidson, *The Chariot of the Sun* (London 1969).

M. Gimbutas, *Bronze Age Cultures in Central and Eastern Europe* (The Hague 1965).

P. V. Glob, *The Mound People, Danish Bronze-Age Man Preserved* (1970), translated from the Danish by J. Bulman (London 1974).

C. F. C. Hawkes, *The Prehistoric Foundations of Europe to the Mycenaean Age*, reprint of the 1940 edition (London and New York 1973).

J. Hawkes, *Atlas of Ancient Archaeology* (London 1974).

F.-R. Herrmann, *Die Funde der Urnenfelderkultur in Mittel- und Südhessen* (Berlin 1966).

F. C. Hibben, *Prehistoric Man in Europe*, first edition 1958, 4th printing (University of Oklahoma Press, 1968).

Kölner Römer Illustrierte, I, M. Wellershoff ed. (Historische Museen der Stadt Köln 1974).

Kölner Römer Illustrierte, II, G. Biegel ed. (Historische Museen der Stadt Köln 1975).

A. Kolling, *Späte Bronzezeit an Saar und Mosel* (Bonn 1968).

G. Kossack, *Studien zum Symbolgut der Urnenfelder- und Hallstattzeit Mitteleuropas* (Berlin 1954).

H. Kühn, *Bronzezeit und Eisenzeit* (Cologne 1966).

F. Laux, *Die Bronzezeit in der Lüneburger Heide* (Hildesheim 1971).

E. F. Mayer, *Die Äxte und Beile in Österreich*, Serie: Prähistorische Bronzefunde, IX, 9 (Munich 1977).

W. Menghin, P. Schauer, *Magisches Gold—Kultgeräte der späten Bronzezeit*, Ausstellung des Germanischen Nationalmuseums Nürnberg in Zusammenarbeit mit dem Römisch-Germanischen Zentralmuseum Mainz, 26.5.–31.7.1977 (Nuremberg 1977).

J. D. Muhly, *Copper and Tin, The Distribution of Mineral Resources and the Nature of the Metals Trade in the Bronze Age*, Reprinted without alteration from the Transactions of The Connecticut Academy of Arts and Sciences, New Haven, Connecticut, Vol. 43, Pages 155–535, March 1973, with a supplement published May 1976 as Vol 46, pages 77–136 (Hamden, Connecticut 1976).

H. Müller-Karpe, *Handbuch der Vorgeschichte*, III, Kupferzeit (Munich 1974).

A. Nibbi, *The Sea Peoples and Egypt* (Park Ridge, New Jersey 1975).

H.-G. Peters (ed.), *Dokumentation zur Archäologie Niedersachsens in Denkmalpflege und Forschung* (Hanover 1975).

S. Piggott, *Ancient Europe from the Beginnings of Agriculture to Classical Antiquity* (Chicago 1965).

R. Pittioni, *Über die Historische Bedeutung der Urnenfelderkultur Mitteleuropas* (Vienna, Cologne, Graz 1970).

T. Ramskou, *Dänische Vorzeit* (Copenhagen 1972).

P. Reinecke, *Mainzer Aufsätze zur Chronologie der Bronze- und Eisenzeit*, Nachdrucke aus: Altertümer unserer heidnischen Vorzeit, 5, 1911; und Festschrift des Römisch-Germanischen Zentralmuseums 1902 (Bonn 1965).

C. Renfrew, *Before Civilization, The Radiocarbon Revolution and Prehistoric Europe* (London 1975).

I. Richter, *Der Arm- und Beinschmuck der Bronze- und Urnenfelderzeit in Hessen und Rheinhessen* (Munich 1970).

N. K. Sandars, *Bronze Age Cultures in France, The later phases from the thirteenth to the seventh century B.C.* (Cambridge 1957).

N. K. Sandars, *Prehistoric Art in Europe* (Harmondsworth 1968).

N. K. Sandars, *The Sea Peoples, Warriors of the ancient Mediterranean, 1250–1150 B.C.* (London 1978).

P. Schauer, *Die Schwerter in Süddeutschland, Österreich und der Schweiz I, Griffplatten-, Griffangel-, Griffzungenschwerter* (Munich 1971).

K. Schlabow, *Gewebe und Gewand zur Bronzezeit* (Neumünster 1962).

A. Snodgrass, 'Mycenae, Northern Europe and Radiocarbon dates', *Archaeologica Atlantica*, I (1975), pp. 33–48.

Staatliche Museen Preußischer Kulturbesitz, *Veröffentlichungen des Museums für Vor- und Frühgeschichte* (Berlin 1972, 1973).

F. Stein, *Bronzezeitliche Hortfunde in Süddeutschland*, Beiträge zur Interpretation einer Quellengattung, Saarbrücker Beiträge zur Altertumskunde, Band 23 (Bonn 1976).

E. Stocker, *Die große Zeit der Buchauer Ausgrabungen* (Bad Buchau 1976).

G. Sudholz, *Die ältere Bronzezeit zwischen Niederrhein und Mittelweser* (Hildesheim 1964).

K. Tackenberg, *Die jüngere Bronzezeit in Nordwestdeutschland* (Hildesheim 1971).

H. Ullrich, *Das Aunjetitzer Gräberfeld von Großbrembach*, Erster Teil, Anthropologische Untersuchungen zur Frage nach Entstehung und Verwandschaft der thüringischen, böhmischen und mährischen Aunjetitzer, mit einem Beitrag von G. Hensel, 'Stonatologische Untersuchungen' (Weimar 1972).

U. Wels-Weyrauch, *Die Anhänger und Halsringe in Südwestdeutschland und Nordbayern*, Serie Prähistorische Bronzefunde, XI, 1 (Munich 1978).

K. Willvonseder, *Die jungsteinzeitlichen und bronzezeitlichen Pfahlbauten des Attersees in Oberösterreich* (Vienna 1963-1968).

H. Wingert-Uhde, *Schätze und Scherben, Neue Entdekkungen der Archäologie in Deutschland, Österreich und der Schweiz* (Oldenburg, Hamburg 1977).

H. Ziegert, *Zur Chronologie und Gruppengliederung der westlichen Hügelgräberkultur* (Berlin 1963).

4. Hallstatt: The Farflung Connections of the Early Iron Age

K. Bittel, W. Kimmig, S. Schiek, et al., *Die Kelten in Baden-Württemberg* (Stuttgart 1981).

J. Boardman, M. A. Brown, T. G. E. Powell, eds. *The European Community in Later Prehistory, Studies in honour of C. F. C. Hawkes* (Totowa, New Jersey 1971).

D. Bohnsack, *Die Urnengräber der frühen Eisenzeit aus Garbsen, Kreis Neustadt am Rübenberg, und aus dem Stadtkreis Hannover* (Hildesheim 1973).

E. Demongeot, *La Formation de l'Europe et Les Invasions Barbares, Des origines germaniques à l'avènement de Dioclétien* (Paris 1969).

H.-J. Engels, *Die Hallstatt- und Latènekultur in der Pfalz* (Speyer 1967).

I. Finlay, *Celtic Art, An Introduction* (Park Ridge, New Jersey 1973).

M. Funder, 'Die Häuser in der Hallstattkultur', Dissertation (Innsbruck 1977).

M. Gimbutas, *Bronze Age Cultures in Central and Eastern Europe* (The Hague 1965).

F. C. Hibben, *Prehistoric Man in Europe* (University of Oklahoma Press, 1968).

K. Kaus, *Chronologie und Bestattungssitten der Hallstattkultur in Niederösterreich und im Nordburgenland* (Vienna 1973).

I. Kilian-Dirlmeir, *Die hallstattzeitlichen Gürtelbleche und Blechgürtel Mitteleuropas*, Serie: Prähistorische Bronzefunde, XII, 1 (Munich 1972).

Kölner Römer Illustrierte, I, M. Wellershoff, ed. (Historische Museen der Stadt Köln 1974).

Kölner Römer Illustrierte, II, G. Biegel, ed. (Historische Museen der Stadt Köln 1975).

G. Kossack, *Gräberfelder der Hallstattzeit an Main und Fränkischer Saale* (Kallmünz/Oberpfalz 1970).

G. Kossack, *Studien zum Symbolgut der Urnenfelder- und Hallstattzeit Mitteleuropas* (Berlin 1954).

K. Kromer, *Das Gräberfeld von Hallstatt* (Florence 1959).

K. Kromer, *Hallstatt, Die Salzhandelsmetropole des ersten Jahrtausends vor Christus in den Alpen*, Katalog zur Ausstellung (Vienna 1963).

K. Kromer, *Von frühem Eisen und reichen Salzherren, Die Hallstattkultur in Österreich* (Vienna 1964).

P. Lambrechts, *L'Exaltation de la Tête dans la Pensée et dans l'Art des Celtes* (Bruges 1954).

J. V. S. Megaw, *Art of the European Iron Age, A study of the elusive image* (Bath 1970).

G. von Merhart, *Hallstatt und Italien, Gesammelte Aufsätze zur frühen Eisenzeit in Italien und Mitteleuropa, Bearbeitet und herausgegeben von Georg Kossack* (Mainz 1969).

E. F. Meyer, *Die Äxte und Beile in Österreich*, Serie: Prähistorische Bronzefunde, IX, 9 (Munich 1977).

L. Pauli, *Keltischer Volksglaube, Amulette und Sonderbestattungen am Dürrnberg bei Hallein und im Eisenzeitlichen Mitteleuropa* (Munich 1975).

E. Penninger, *Der Dürrnberg bei Hallein*, I, *Katalog der Grabfunde aus der Hallstatt- und Latènezeit* (Munich 1972).

S. Piggott, *Ancient Europe from the Beginnings of Agriculture to Classical Antiquity* (Chicago 1965).

T. G. E. Powell, *Prehistoric Art* (London 1966).

M. Primas, *Die südschweizerischen Grabfunde der älteren Eisenzeit und ihre Chronologie* (Basel 1970).

G. Riek, H. J. Hundt, *Der Hohmichele, Ein Fürstengrabhügel der späten Hallstattzeit bei der Heuneburg* (Berlin 1962).

A. Ross, *Everyday Life of the Pagan Celts* (London and New York 1970).

N. K. Sandars, *Prehistoric Art in Europe*, Penguin History of Art (Harmondsworth 1968).

K. Simon, *Die Hallstattzeit in Ostthüringen* (Berlin 1972).

W. Torbrügge, *Prehistoric European Art* (New York and Baden-Baden 1968).

H. Wingert-Uhde, *Schätze und Scherben, Neue Entdekkungen der Archäologie in Deutschland, Österreich und der Schweiz* (Oldenburg and Hamburg 1977).

H. Zürn, *Hallstattforschungen in Nordwürttemberg, Die Grabhügel von Asperg, Hirschlanden und Mühlacker, Veröffentlichungen des staatlichen Amtes für Denkmalpflege Stuttgart* (Stuttgart 1970).

5. The La Tène Culture: The Celts

K. Bittel, W. Kimmig, S. Schiek, et al., *Die Kelten in Baden-Württemberg* (Stuttgart 1981).

H. Birkhan, *Germanen und Kelten bis zum Ausgang der Römerzeit. Der Aussagewert von Wörtern und Sachen für die frühesten Keltisch-Germanischen Kulturbezeichnungen* (Vienna, Cologne and Graz 1970).

B. Boardman, M. A. Brown, T. G. E. Powell, *The European Community in Later Prehistory* (Totowa, N.J. 1971).

J. Břeň, *Třisov, A Celtic oppidum in South Bohemia*, translated by B. Vančura (Prague 1966).

Julius Caesar, *The Conquest of Gaul*, translated by S. A. Handford (Harmondsworth 1965).

Julius Caesar, *The Gallic War and other Writings*, translated by M. Hadas (New York 1957).

N. K. Chadwick, *The Celts* (Harmondsworth 1971).

B. Cunliffe and T. Rowley, *Oppida: the Beginnings of Urbanization in Barbarian Europe*, Papers presented to a Conference at Oxford, October 1975, British Archaeological Reports, Supplementary Series 11, 1976.

M. Dillon and N. Chadwick, *The Celtic Realms* (London 1976).

M. Dillon, *Celts and Aryans, Survivals of Indo-European Speech and Society*, Indian Institute of Advanced Study, Simla (Simla 1975).

W. Dinan, *Monumenta Historica Celtica, Notices of the Celts in the Writings of the Greek and Latin Authors from the tenth century B.C., to the fifth century A.D., arranged chronologically, with translations, commentary, indices and a glossary of the Celtic names and words occuring in these authors, in three volumes*, Volume I (London 1911).

Diodorus Siculus in Twelve Volumes, with an English translation by C. H. Oldfather, Loeb Classical Library (Cambridge, Mass. and London 1961).

P.-M. Duval, *La Vie quotidienne en Gaule pendant la Paix Romaine* (Paris 1967).

P.-M. Duval and C. Hawkes, *Celtic Art in Ancient Europe, Five Protohistoric Centuries*, Proceedings of the Colloquy held in 1972 at the Oxford Maison Française, (London, New York and San Francisco 1976).

H. J. Eggers, E. Will, R. Joffroy, W. Holmquist, *Kelten und Germanen in heidnischer Zeit*, Serie: Kunst der Welt, ihre geschichtlichen, soziologischen und religiösen Grundlagen (Baden-Baden 1964).

H.-J. Engels, *Die Hallstatt- und Latènekultur in der Pfalz* (Speyer 1967).

J. Filip, *Celtic Civilization and its Heritage* (1960), English translation by R. Finlayson Samsour (Prague 1962).

I. Finlay, *Celtic Art, An Introduction* (London 1973).

O.-H. Frey (ed.), *Marburger Beiträge zur Archäologie der Kelten, Festschrift für Wolfgang Dehn, zum 60. Geburtstag am 6. Juli 1969* (Bonn 1969).

P. V. Glob, *The Bog People, Iron Age Man Preserved*, translated from the Danish by R. Bruce-Mitford (Ithaca, N.Y. 1969).

R. Grosse, *Der Silberkessel von Gundestrup—ein Rätsel keltischer Kunst, Ein Zeugnis des Läuterungs- und Einweihungsweges bei den Kelten* (Dornach, Schweiz 1963).

I. Harmand, *Les Celtes au Second Age du Fer* (Paris 1970).

C. and S. Hawkes, *Greeks, Celts and Romans, Studies in Venture and Persistence*, Archaeology into History I (London 1973).

W. Heiligendorff, *Das latènezeitliche Gräberfeld von Berlin-Blankenfelde* (Berlin 1965).

P. Jacobsthal, *Early Celtic Art* (Reprinted, Oxford University Press 1969).

I. Kappel, *Die Graphittonkeramik von Manching, Die Ausgrabungen von Manching, herausgegeben von W. Krämer* (Wiesbaden 1969).

J. Keller, *Das keltische Fürstengrab von Reinheim* (Mainz 1965).

Kölner Römer Illustrierte, I, M. Wellershoff, ed. (Historische Museen der Stadt Köln 1974).

Kölner Römer Illustrierte, II, G. Biegel, ed. (Historische Museen der Stadt Köln 1975).

P. Lambrechts, *L'Exaltation de la Tête dans la Pensée et dans l'Art des Celtes* (Bruges 1954).

F. LeRoux, *Introduction générale à l'étude de la tradition celtique I* (Rennes 1967).

G. Mahr, *Die jüngere Latènekultur des Trierer Landes, Eine stilkundliche Untersuchung auf Grund der Keramik und des Bestattungswesens* (Berlin 1967).

F. Maier, *Die bemalte Spätlatène-Keramik von Manching, Die Ausgrabungen von Manching, herausgegeben von W. Krämer* (Wiesbaden 1970).

J. V. S. Megaw, *Art of the European Iron Age, A Study of the elusive Image* (Bath 1970).

J. M. de Navarro, *The Finds from the site of La Tène* (London 1972).

H. Noelle, *Die Kelten und ihre Stadt Manching* (Pfaffenhofen/Ilm 1974).

S. Piggott, *Ancient Europe from the Beginnings of Agriculture to Classical Antiquity* (Chicago 1965).

Polibius, *The Histories in Six Volumes*, with an English translation by W. R. Paton, Loeb Classical Library (Cambridge, Mass. and London 1960).

T. G. E. Powell, *The Celts* (London 1963).

T. G. E. Powell, *Prehistoric Art* (London 1966).

405

A. Ross, *Everyday Life of the Pagan Celts* (London and New York 1970).

N. K. Sandars, *Prehistoric Art in Europe*, The Pelican History of Art (Harmondsworth 1968).

F. Schlette, *Kelten zwischen Alesia und Pergamon, Eine Kulturgeschichte der Kelten* (Leipzig, Jena and Berlin 1979).

W. Torbrügge, *Prehistoric European Art* (New York and Baden-Baden 1968).

J. de Vries, *Kelten und Germanen* (Berne and Munich 1960).

J. de Vries, *Keltische Religion* (Stuttgart 1961).

A. Weitnauer, *Keltisches Erbe in Schwaben und Baiern* (Kempten/Allgäu 1961).

K. Willvonseder, *Keltische Kunst in Salzburg*, Schriftenreihe des Salzburger Museums Carolino Augusteum, 2 (Salzburg 1960).

6. Northern Genesis

Géza Alföldy, *Noricum*, transl. by A. Birley (London and Boston 1974).

Hans Peter Althaus, Helmut Henne, Herbert Ernst Wiegand, *Lexikon der Germanistischen Linguistik* (Tübingen 1973).

Adolf Bach, *Geschichte der deutschen Sprache*, 8th expanded edition, originally published in 1938 (Heidelberg 1965).

Helmut Birkhan, *Germanen und Kelten bis zum Ausgang der Römerzeit* (Vienna, Cologne and Graz 1970).

Max Cary, *A History of Rome, Down to the Reign of Constantine* (London 1957).

W. Walker Chambers and John R. Wilkie, *A Short History of the German Language* (London 1970).

Gordon V. Childe, *What happened in History* (Harmondsworth 1957).

Jan de Vries, *Kelten und Germanen* (Berne and Munich 1960).

Dio's Roman History in Nine Volumes, with an English translation by Ernest Cary, Loeb Classical Library (Cambridge, Mass. and London 1961).

Hans Jürgen Eggers, Ernest Will, René Joffroy, Wilhelm Holquist, *Kelten und Germanen in heidnischer Zeit* (Baden-Baden 1964).

Theodor Frings, *Grundlegung einer Geschichte der deutschen Sprache, dritte erweiterte Auflage* (Halle 1957).

P. V. Glob, *The Bog People, Iron Age Man Preserved*, transl. from the Danish by Rupert Bruce-Mitford (Ithaca and New York 1969).

Bernhard Gramsch, ed., *Germanen-Slawen-Deutsche, Forschungen zu ihrer Ethnogenese, Proceedings* (Berlin 1968).

Albert Grenier, *Les Gaulois*, Avant-propos de Louis Harmand (Paris 1970).

Jacob Grimm, *Deutsche Altertumskunde*, bearbeitet und herausgegeben von Else Ebel, Arbeiten aus der Niedersächsischen Staats- und Universitätsbibliothek Göttingen (Göttingen 1974).

Rolf Hachmann, *Die Germanen* (Munich, Geneva and Paris 1971).

Herman Hirt, *Geschichte der deutschen Sprache*, reprint of the 1925 edition (Munich 1968).

Claus Jürgen Hutterer, *Die Germanischen Sprachen, Ihre Geschichte in Grundzügen* (Budapest 1975).

Herbert Jankuhn, *Einführung in die Siedlungsgeschichte* (Berlin and New York 1977).

Julius Caesar, *The Gallic War and other Writings*, translated with an introduction by Moses Hadas (New York 1957).

Ernst Kornemann, *Römische Geschichte*, in zwei Bänden, 6. Auflage, bearbeitet von Hermann Bengtson (Stuttgart 1970).

Kölner Römer Illustrierte, I, ed. M. Wellershoff (Historische Museen der Stadt Köln 1974).

Kölner Römer Illustrierte, II, ed. G. Biegel (Historische Museen der Stadt Köln 1975).

Konrad Kraft, *Zur Entstehung des Namens 'Germania'*, Sitzungsberichte der Wissenschaftlichen Gesellschaft an der Johann Wolfgang Goethe Universität Frankfurt/Main, Band 9, Jahrgang 1970, Nr. 2 (Wiesbaden 1970).

Hans Krahe, *Germanische Sprachwissenschaft*, I, Sammlung Göschen, Band 238, 6. Auflage (Berlin 1966).

Bruno Krüger, *Die Germanen, Geschichte und Kultur der germanischen Stämme in Mitteleuropa* (Berlin 1978).

Heinrich Krüger, *Die Jastorfkultur in den Kreisen Lüchow-Dannenberg, Lüneburg, Uelzen und Soltau, Göttinger Schriften zur Vor- und Frühgeschichte*, ed. Herbert Jankuhn (Neumünster 1961).

Livy, translated by B. O. Foster, Loeb Classical Library (Cambridge, Mass. and London).

Lutz Mackensen, *Deutsche Etymologie, Ein Leitfaden durch die Geschichte des Deutschen Wortes* (Bremen 1966).

Fergus Millar, *et al.*, *The Roman Empire and its Neighbours*, English edition (London 1967).

Hugo Moser, *Deutsche Sprachgeschichte* (Tübingen 1965).

Rudolf Much, *Die Germania des Tacitus*, Dritte, beträchtlich erweiterte Auflage unter Mitarbeit von Herbert Jankuhn, herausgegeben von Wolfgang Lange (Heidelberg 1967).

K. Nuglisch, E. Schröter, *Hausurnen und Jastorfkultur an der mittleren Elbe, Die Gräberfelder von Latdorf und Aken*, Wissenschaftliche Beiträge der Martin-Luther-Universität Halle/Wittenberg (Halle 1968).

Hans-Günther Peters, ed., *Dokumentation zur Archäologie Niedersachsens in Denkmalpflege und Forschung* (Hanover 1975).

Plutarch, *The Parallel Lives*, transl. by B. Perrin, Loeb Classical Library (Cambridge, Mass., and London).

Peter von Polenz, *Geschichte der deutschen Sprache*, Sammlung Göschen, Band 915/915a, 7. Auflage (Berlin 1970).

Thorkild Ramskou, *Dänische Vorzeit* (Copenhagen 1972).

Friedrich Schlette, *Germanen zwischen Thorsberg und Ravenna* (Leipzig, Jena and Berlin 1972).

Hans Sperber, *Geschichte der deutschen Sprache*, neu bearbeitet von Peter von Polenz, Sammlung Göschen, Band 915, 6. Auflage (Berlin 1968).

Strabo, *Geography*, translated by H. L. Jones, Loeb Classical Library, (Cambridge, Mass., and London).

Tacitus, *Germania*, translated by M. Hutton, Loeb Classical Library, (Cambridge, Mass., and London 1970).

E. A. Thompson, *The Early Germans* (Oxford 1965).

Fritz Tschirch, *Geschichte der deutschen Sprache*, I, *Die Entfaltung der deutschen Sprachgestalt in der Vor- und Frühzeit* (Berlin 1966).

Velleius Paterculus, *Compendium of Roman History*, transl. by Frederick W. Shipley, Loeb Classical Library (Cambridge, Mass., and London 1961).

Gerold Walser, *Caesar und die Germanen, Studien zur politischen Tendenz römischer Feldzugsberichte* (Wiesbaden 1956).

John T. Waterman, *A History of the German Language* (Seattle and London 1966).

Graham Webster, *The Roman Imperial Army to Caracalla* (London 1969).

C. M. Wells, *The German Policy of Augustus, An Examination of the Archaeological Evidence* (Oxford 1972).

Robert Eric Mortimer Wheeler, *Rome beyond the Imperial Frontiers* (London 1954).

Helga Wingert-Uhde, *Schätze und Scherben, Neue Entdeckungen der Archäologie in Deutschland, Österreich und der Schweiz* (Oldenburg and Hamburg 1977).

Index

420